RAMA BHIMA SOMA

RAMA BHIMA SOMA

CULTURAL INVESTIGATIONS INTO MODERN KARNATAKA

SRIKAR RAGHAVAN

cntxt

cntxt

Published by Context, an imprint of Westland Books, a division of Nasadiya Technologies Private Limited, in 2025

No. 269/2B, First Floor, 'Irai Arul', Vimalraj Street, Nethaji Nagar, Alapakkam Main Road, Maduravoyal, Chennai 600095

ISBN: 9789360456870

10 9 8 7 6 5 4 3 2 1

Typeset by Jojy Philip

Printed at Manipal Technologies Limited, Manipal

For all those who believe pluralism to be the only philosophical lodestar

If you quote the maxim 'one may not take what belongs to another', let me ask you, where from does this notion arise if one has not already a notion of possession?

—Raghunatha Shiromani, *Demonstration of the True Nature of Things to Which Words Refer*, a transformative text in the Navya Nyaya (New Reason) school of thought, c. 1500 CE

Contents

Prologue

> I enjoy the juxtaposition of ideas. I play. The end, I have been taught, is not a question of success or defeat, but the abolition of contradiction, of duality—and of the peace it should bring to one. I play the game knowing I am the game. That is the meaning of India.
>
> —Raja Rao

I

If you were ever a young schoolboy growing up in Karnataka, I'd wager that you have played Rama Bhima Soma. Or you might have encountered some variant of it. It requires only a ball, no fixed number of players, no teams, no designated boundary and no premeditation. Someone throws the ball up into the sky, you wait until it pitches thrice—counted off as Rama, Bhima, Soma—and then the game begins. Whoever is nearest to the ball grabs it and begins hurling it at their choicest target, preferably one close by, at whom a good shot can be had. The others try to dodge the ball, and whoever happens to catch it next repeats the process. The game knows no end, and the ball keeps travelling in an infinite loop across the group, creating an endless web of relationships, until such time as collective exhaustion sets in, or ... the bell rings for class. I have only the fondest memories of playing Rambhimsoma, as we would brusquely shorten it; someone or the other would have a tennis or rubber ball at hand, and excitement was always just three pitches away.

It is known by various names across different regions of the state—Pilchendu, Appa-Ippa, Lagge, Tooro Chendu, Biraball and so on. In and around Mysore, which is where I grew up, it is most popular as Rambhimsoma. But the overarching feeling the game is meant to evoke is the same. There is no sense of victory or defeat—the very nature of the game allows everyone a chance to attack and evade attack. If you manage to physically touch whoever is holding the ball, you cannot be targeted. Any number of players may participate, the more the merrier. This spirit of democracy is what lends the game such charm. If we reconcile ourselves to the fact that there can never be a political system that rises above the vested interests of power—the one holding the ball—then the ideal to strive for remains the ball-sharing system, where everybody gets to wield power at some point or the other. Every player flits between brief periods of intense individualism and subsequent identification with the larger mass. It forces one to alternate between the self and the other, between power and powerlessness, and in the long run, generates the feeling of a unified whole, where nobody wins unless everybody wins. It exemplifies what the anarchist thinker Mikhail Bakunin once called the 'continual exchange of mutual, temporary, and above all, voluntary authority'.

It is a demanding game, certainly. You can't go easy on your opponents. If you chuck the ball too casually, the other fellow can catch it and quickly turn the tables on you. You must throw speedily enough to merit a dodge. You must also be crafty enough to stay away from the strongest throwers. Without passion, all is lost, and the game becomes meaningless. When passion turns to hate, though, things might go sour, and friendships could turn into enmities back in the classroom.

The difference between finite and infinite games[1] is that the latter have no notion of an end—the journey is all that matters. The thrill of the moment, the sweat dripping till the end. Finite games have clear victors and goals one can aspire to. In infinite games such as Rambhimsoma, the act of play is paramount, which is what imbues it with such an egalitarian spirit. It is akin to a rite of passage ritual that has been passed down through generations, with no preacher or scribe ever involved in its dissemination. Even the PT teacher did not have to teach us the game. Somehow, everyone just happened to know it. We passed the rite with flying colours—the dirt stains that the ball left on our white shirts were marks of pride too.

During my years of formal schooling, I had much time for games, but little for political education. It baffled me to think that there was any difference between words like 'Marxism' and 'Communism' and 'Socialism', and I found it odd that people should go on professing all these ideologies with such incredible passion. I preferred reading fantasy novels, detective fiction and R.K. Narayan. I could name a few chief ministers, certainly the prime minister and identify Abdul Kalam just from the back of his head. We did have a subject called Civics, but it was terribly boring, and I was quite glad that one could memorise bullet points for answers and get away with it.

Because I studied at a Kendriya Vidyalaya, which is (literally) a Central institution, I never learnt to read and write Kannada at school. I spoke Tamil at home, Kannada at school (and home), and had a smattering of Telugu because we had lived in Hyderabad until I was eight. In retrospect, I'm grateful for the excellent Hindi I picked up at school. It would come in handy on all my future trips to the Himalayas and the extended North. A good chunk of the subcontinent was within reasonable comprehension.

So, it was a wholesome education, by and large, with sports and languages given suitable attention. However, the inability to fluently read Kannada began to bother me as I slowly began to realise that my taste in books had been rather restricted. I had learnt the Kannada alphabet, thanks to a stint in a State Board school during the first standard, and could decipher the headline of a newspaper with some effort. But literary pleasure was still miles away. When I began to discover English literature beyond Harry Potter and Sherlock Holmes, I also stumbled upon a genre completely unknown to me—non-fiction. Now, there were way too many exciting books to read, and I could not be bothered to learn to read in another language from scratch. Yet, the rich potential of the Kannada language (whose humour and evocative delights had firmly dictated our bawdy schoolboy banter), and its undiscovered literature, gnawed at the back of my head. In my years of hot-headed adolescence, I became familiar with every incendiary statement ever made by the journalist and polemicist Christopher Hitchens, but knew nothing about a man named Lankesh, who had lived a similarly controversial, combative and colourful life. I had grown jealous when a friend got Lankesh right in a college quiz—*how and where had he heard about him?*

After finishing engineering (another rite of passage, it would seem), I jumped to do an MA in English, where I knew I would feel at home. At Manipal Centre for Humanities, which is where I landed up through a series of accidents, Shakespeare and Dickens were not nearly as much in vogue as were U.R. Ananthamurthy and Ismat Chughtai. Sanskrit was encouraged as a potential avenue of philosophical and literary inquiry. We were stirred up to read in the language of whatever region we came from, but equally, to learn how to write and argue better in English. All the subjects offered—history, sociology, philosophy, literature—could be vastly enriched by an engagement with literatures in our mother tongues. And so it was that I bought myself a Kannada-Kannada-English dictionary and cracked my knuckles. The first Kannada book I ever read was Shivaram Karanth's novel *Chomana Dudi*.

By then, I had also begun grappling with my political self. My formative years, ever since I turned eighteen, have witnessed the rise of the majoritarian Hindu Right. Through these years, some simple questions have pricked me, and will continue to do so. What are the ramifications of sticking to one's political convictions come what may? Can't everyone just come to a reasonable agreement that inequality and oppression and authoritarianism are undesirable things, and collectively formulate a common humanist doctrine? How do ideologies begin controlling people's minds? Where do artists fit into this societal churn, and what moral stakes do they carry? Most importantly, if someone is clever enough, could they get away with saying anything, just for the sake of unbridled power or glory? I began to feel that the political terminologies we use are mere pawns in a large global chess match that has zugzwanged us all. Everyone uses these terms in their own way, and everyone reacts to them in their own peculiar fashions. What appears to really matter to most people are immediate social realities and everything else that makes life worth living—community, care, understanding, dignity, respect and art. The wavelengths that compete within the refractory space of the prism of *isms* can become quite disorienting indeed.

During the second year of my MA, a friend excavated for me the legend of Saketh Rajan, a Maoist revolutionary from Mysore who was shot dead in 2005 in the Western Ghats. He had lived underground for twenty years, and had authored two volumes of a Marxist history of Karnataka while being incognito. What's more, he and I were from similar social backgrounds; like me, he had learnt to play the mandolin when young; we even shared the same initials—a constellation of delicious coincidences. It was a timely find for a final year student desperately in search of a thesis topic. I became obsessed by his shadowy life but eventually ended up vehemently rejecting his politics and history-making. In the process though, I discovered a remarkable period in the history of modern Karnataka, one where Saketh Rajan was a blinking dot amidst a galaxy of artists, writers, activists and political personages. It is through these initial curiosity quests that the idea of this book began to grow.

Why bring up Rama Bhima Soma? Just another low-hanging fruit grasped for the sake of an exotic book title? I'd say there are at least three distinct interpretations of the title that might be read into everything that this book is concerned with. Most essentially, the idea of a book about the various competing ideologies, ideologues and ideals of the Kannada sociopolitical sphere arose from the intuitive feeling that they could only be spoken about *through* their relationships with each other. Just like that game of my boyhood, this is a world where opposites coincide and where contradictions are balanced precariously. To view any one element in isolation would lead you to miss the larger picture and the richness of the relationships that are being continuously generated by the players. Such at least would be the idealistic vision for this book.

I had forgotten about the game until I stumbled upon a lovely book of Kannada essays[2] (with a compelling abstract painting on its cover) written by scholar B.M. Puttaiah, also a union leader of cycle rickshaw drivers in Bellary district. Tucked in amidst meditations on politics, the dalit movement and the education system was an essay about an endless game with no rules. Days later, when I dug into it, I found myself swirling in memories of Rama Bhima Soma, travelling into the sunlight of a blissful childhood. The essay seemed to go on for ages and ages, just like the game, and I was drawn to the infinite potential of its layered meanings. Puttaiah's essay had studied the game with the distance of anthropological abstraction, but I wondered what it would really look like if real, in-the-flesh players were to be substituted into the fray. It is essentially eureka moments like these that have dictated my play of curiosities. I have marvelled at the wondrous ecosystem of Kannada books—a humbling avalanche that kept prodding me into a dialogue and that set my own little project going. I have followed no particular methodology or school of thought in writing this book, and have endeavoured to read as widely as I could, interview as many people as I could reach, and follow my instincts in chasing the stories that I felt were most poignant, illuminating and interesting. I fell down YouTube rabbit holes, browsed obscure podcasts, and raided libraries and personal collections for old Kannada books. What follows is only *a* history, a personal micro-history, of a vibrant geographical and linguistic space, all of whose nooks and corners I can never hope to reach. Through the act of writing a book, I have tried to bite into and experience a juicy slice of history.

At the heart of this work that blends literary history, journalistic reportage and social history are small biographical sketches of individuals whom I have met or only glimpsed through the work they have left behind. Behind all the names that feature here lie hundreds of equally significant others who could not be included. Each of these chapters could really be expanded into a book in their own right, and it is only because there exists precious little writing on these subjects in English that I have had to bank on thematic diversity rather than comprehensive detail. Yet, I believe that these chapters are at least illustrative of the most important and relevant themes that my research unearthed, and that they might press readers to excavate more stories for themselves. I also hope that my subjective self is sublimated within the larger arena of a history of competing ideas, and that those who care little for my opinions might yet find the narrative web immersive enough to formulate their own.

As I began reflecting on the material I'd collected over the years, certain themes stood out. One unintended thread was the omniscience of Mahatma Gandhi—he features in every chapter, sometimes as a flawed idealist, but oftentimes as a ray of hope in a morally desolate landscape. Similarly, there appear instances at almost every juncture of how the all-important goal of women's empowerment has been repeatedly stumped by patriarchal structures. At several points, the narrative zooms into instances that illustrate how the Left and Right binary of political conceptions in India have stunted our discourse, leading unimaginative, narrow positions to feed on the legitimacy each is granted by the other. This is because politics is always confrontational, but also because simplistic narratives can garner easy takers in the short run. Fundamentalists can thrive on either side of the spectrum.

Indeed, the most interesting characters, the ones I admired the most, could not be slotted easily into an ideological pinhole. And yet, when one puts pen to paper, the difference between the self and the other, that primal binary, is never avoidable—and in that moment, one must take a side, or at least try to discern whose side one isn't on. As my own positions began to emerge from the fog, I felt I was part of a gigantic version of that ball game, leaning towards an idea in some context, challenging it in some other, hoping that none of my own salvos turn out to be low blows. Everything, in the end, boils down to a battle of words, and certain important words have to be rescued from those who deploy them left, right and centre, without stopping to consider what they really mean to convey.

So it was that while I was grappling with the turbulence of my adolescent understanding of the world, I was also trying to understand what the slain Naxal leader Saketh Rajan might have encountered in his formative years. How much of his life was driven by his own will, and how much of it was willed by the world around him? Why do some individuals have politics and confrontation written into their very DNA, while others believe that life really lies elsewhere? How does one separate a certain responsibility owed to society from the hubris of deeming oneself to be capable of speaking for someone else? How does one meaningfully approach religion and spirituality, while avoiding the trappings of crusaders and conmen? During the 1970s, like in so many places around the world, a unique moment of social upheaval was shaping up in Karnataka, where questions like these were being tested through fire for the first time in its history as a modern state.

It was the age of chaluvalis.*

II

> What's gonna happen, sooner or later, all the wretched of the earth, in one way or another, next Tuesday or next Wednesday, will destroy the cobblestones on which London and Paris and Rome are built. The world will change because it has to change … The party is over. That is what is going to happen.
>
> —James Baldwin

There is a reassuringly cyclical quality to the word itself—the chaluvali goes on, incessantly. It stands for constant struggle, and also somehow approaches what we might mean when we say revolution. It is both the struggle and the fruit of the struggle at once. It is pursuit and attainment melded together, like yin and yang. Chaluvali naditaane iratte, alva? *The struggle is ever ongoing,*

---

* *chaluvali. noun.* movement, struggle, agitation.

no?—an activist might say even today. There is a whiff of optimism to the word, a sense of inevitability.

There is a more ferocious cousin to this word too, one that packs more of a punch. 'Bandaya' comes from the Kannada root 'bandu'. It used to carry connotations of inferiority, uncleanness and filth, but grew to mean fight, brawl or struggle—this was before the seventies. Soon, the word would come to be associated with a literary movement that sought to overturn all established conventions in Kannada literature. Bandaya has now evolved to mean democratic political dissent, and is therefore a novelty item forged in the steely crucible of the post-Emergency years.

In Karnataka, the last three decades of the twentieth century were a kaleidoscopic jumble of social movements born out of the churning of a society at once rebellious and responsible. There raged long environmental campaigns, massive farmers' mobilisations, hard-fought labour struggles, subversive street theatre, feminist affirmations, literary battles, student movements, as well as a strong dalit resurgence. It was the best of times, the worst of times, the age of wisdom, the age of foolishness—a grand era of chaluvalis, all in all. The eighties, in particular, was a decade when all of these movements were active, and fed off each other's energies in one way or another.

There was certainly a great deal of romance associated with this world of burgeoning social movements. The poet and playwright Chandrashekhar Patil, an ardent follower of the socialist thinker Ram Manohar Lohia, once invoked Wordsworth (*Bliss it was, in that dawn, to be alive*) to describe the atmosphere of socialism that reigned over Kannada society during the early seventies. It was a socialism that meant different things to different people and for some, it was an ideal that had never really made its way into Indian politics. But agency and urgency came together in the seventies to produce an unprecedented burst of social consciousness, when the quest for an egalitarian society was palpably in the air. Fortuitously, the political regime of the time, under the strongarm leadership of Chief Minister Devaraj Urs, was one that could be called a form of populist socialism. Major land reforms were put into motion, reservation bills were passed and a new coalition of backward communities began staking its claim to power.

A vibrant cultural backdrop had also emerged, wherein artists and writers and journalists and filmmakers were socially conscious like never before (and never since). In his autobiography, *Gandhi Classu*, the Kannada novelist Kum Veerabhadrappa remembers a literary pilgrimage he made to Dharwad in the early seventies, when he was on the cusp of becoming a serious writer:

> Repeatedly fondling the five rupees in my pocket that my father had given me, I realised that I had arrived near the premises of the Karnataka Vidyavardhaka Sangha. Those were the heydays of people's movements in the state. Back then, I couldn't really understand what they were all about. I believed the maxim that a random stone thrown [in Dharwad] would land on a poet or an artist, but I had nothing resembling a stone in my hand. The mannerisms of the people ambling around there were weird. Loose pajamas, jubba, scraggly beard, cigarettes, beedis, a very peculiar and distinct kind of intellectual conversation, some book or another in everybody's hand, random exclamations and mentions of writers and activists ... Because of this, the crowd looked like Gandhari's descendants in their thousands. Even when I was in their midst, I felt unconnected to them. How could I possibly get to know them, and with whose help would I do it?

This passage describes, quite accurately, my own state of mind as I was encountering the same world half a century later. The renaissance that KumVee subtly points us towards was facilitated by educational institutions such as the Vidyavardhaka Sangha and the values that they upheld. Teachers and professors were the 'influencers' of the era, with the capacity to inspire and motivate the effervescent younger generations. What also strikes me about the excerpt is the aspiration and yearning that KumVee couches within his observations. The mannerisms of this group might have been strange, but they are appealing precisely because of it. He is in awe of the intellectual environment he witnesses, and earnestly desires to be a part of it. The odd reference to Gandhari creates a mythical landscape out of the scene, where roamed an entire generation seemingly spawned by a common revolutionary seed.

Indeed, one notices that the various left-leaning chaluvalis that would come to take the stage were, in fact, one large tree with common roots. However, while social networks might have been quite porous, these many movements failed to embrace each other politically, and were often at odds with each other's professed goals. After a grand period of upheaval, romantic dreams of revolution were harshly interrupted by the cold touch of disillusionment. Social steam endures but briefly; political victory is what is needed to keep the engine going. Several attempts were made in the eighties to reconcile various left-inspired organisations and form a third front to challenge the Congress and the Janata Party, but were unsuccessful, largely because of personal animosities and ideological disaffections. During the nineties, the rise of the Hindu Right created a new wave of public mobilisation that rose taller than the ebbs of the rippling Left and began carving out fresh battlelines in the slush. In the meantime, what had once been a vibrant literary ocean within the Kannada public sphere had subsided into a few small ponds where swam a few big fish.

This book is a reconstruction of these enormously interesting times. It documents the transition of a society animated by a quest for equality and justice, down to the seemingly sated neoliberal climate that we have presently arrived at. As much as this is a book of history, I have also wished for it to be a document of the present, of how we are unwittingly still connected to the past in strange and counter-intuitive ways. As much as this is social history, I have also endeavoured to showcase biographical sketches of certain extraordinary individuals from whom we may learn something about the perils of the revolutionary life, about the art of charting creative and fulfilling paths, as well as the artifice that inevitably envelops positions of responsibility. I hope that it gives us a chance to review our worldviews, often rigidly held, through widening our imagination by just a few decades, across which entire value systems seem to have undergone a massive shift.

Of course, no period of time (not even a few decades) can be seen in isolation; they require the context of their own past and future. I submit that the shifty power struggles in the political corridors of twentieth-century Karnataka have constituted one long and complicated game of Rambhimsoma that continues to rage on. Throughout the course of the century, the education and upliftment of the state's citizens have followed a caste pattern—from the brahmins of the early twentieth century, who held almost all the key administrative positions, the baton was passed to the lingayats and vokkaligas, who dominated politics for decades, before finally, in the 1970s, the dalit movement ensured that backward castes were able to reach for their deserved share. Throughout all this, strong anti-incumbency sentiments have always dictated electoral behaviours, and the interplay of caste politics has seen power shifting from one community to another constantly. It has not been a fair game, for it is a human game, and there are still many sections of society that have yet to even glimpse the ball. Time is irrelevant in this game. The ball may go back to anybody. Ideas that are a century old may suddenly come back into currency with great force. That is the beauty—of the game, at least. Likewise, Kannada literary movements of the previous century have battled it out in a similarly charged arena, with each successive generation being, at once, an enemy and a friend to their predecessor.

This book is not a political history that studies the lives of those in power. In fact, it is mostly the opposite—an ethnography of those who challenge prevailing social mores, shape politics from the margins of power, and of why they do so in very peculiar ways. The latent power of civil society is, in fact, the keystone of what political theorists call anarchism (no, not the character-assassinated distortion of the word you might hear peddled on prime-time news channels when farmers seek permission to protest in Delhi). The concept assumes particular relevance today as a non-violent, Gandhian conception of activism seeks to establish ground-up direct democracy, and challenge the State by occupying public spaces and mobilising citizenly consensus regarding pressing concerns. The Shaheen Bagh demonstrations of 2020—protests against the imposition of the Bharatiya Janata Party's controversial amendments to citizenship laws—would be a prime example.

Among other things, this book tries to show how the massive powers grabbed by India Inc over the last few decades have rendered it an elephant in the room that cannot be budged. These pages are also an attempt to set the foundation for a fresh political imagination wherein every citizen can participate, with self-conscious agency, in the creation of a democratic and equitable society. A new argument by no means—it just so happens that this kind of civic idealism has largely been usurped by umpteen new distractions, which has helped the establishment consolidate its supremacy. Like Jambavan encouraging Hanuman to leap across the sea, it seems that civil society too must be reminded from time to time of its latent agency and purpose in order to be fully awakened.

The thematic organisation of this book evolved through an elusive survival-of-the-fittest process during four years of writing. It was also the result of a definite will on my part to avoid simplistic categorisations and chronological history-making, and to strive for layered meanings that straddle multiple ecosystems. For instance, the first chapter (also the largest chapter of the book) revolves around the marga–desi binary, which is a fertile theme that pervades the entirety of the book. The third chapter is situated entirely in South Canara, but other dimensions of the region surface in other chapters in fuller detail. In this way, while each chapter may be read on its own, I trust that the reader will also recognise rhyming strains and enjoy the interplay of ideas across the book. Likewise, writers and activists keep surfacing throughout the book, in different milieus, in different avatars.

Additional miscellany, including translations of Kannada short stories and essays that come up in the narrative, can be found on the website ramabhimasoma.ink. A deeply curious reader who wishes to chase down my references and don the detective's hat may find interesting alleyways in some of my bulkier endnotes that will beget more questions than answers. All translations in this book, unless mentioned otherwise, are my own. For the purpose of readability, diacritics have been avoided. Any and all errors are mine alone.

ONE

Marga, Desi and the Battle of Identities

Heed this request, guru: when I am bored by meditation,
I would like to tell a story in Kannada, with your permission, my lord, placing you at the very beginning.

—Ratnakaravarni (circa sixteenth century)

I

How can he stop telling stories?
Has the man lost his mind?
Times have changed for the worse.
The rains won't arrive properly this time.
Poor fellow has grown senile.
Perhaps it is time to retreat to the forests.

Such are the anxious thoughts of some villagers in Kum Veerabhadrappa's short story 'Kathe Helo Kariajja' (Kariajja the Storyteller) when Kariajja suddenly stops telling stories. He had arrived during an outbreak of the plague, with stories featuring Plague-amma on his lips, which had instilled courage in the villagers' minds. They offered him a hut on the fringes of the village, where he wove story upon story, becoming a living legend. Villagers would consult him on all manner of contingencies, and 'his stories had more power than any hraam hreem mantra'.

> Kariajja would delight at the way his tales took root in others and then grew out in unanticipated ways. He was large-hearted enough to never let any story become bound to the mortars of the intellect. As soon as a story occurred to him, he would release it to the wind by telling it to someone, and then he would watch as it roamed the streets, free and uninhibited. Sometimes, a story would come back to him completely transformed and unrecognisable, with more sub-characters and sub-plots than he imagined were even possible.

Kariajja marries a woman who becomes enamoured with his narrative gifts, and the two of them live in poverty, in a platonic relationship, content with the stories they have. He remains a phenomenon of the masses, and the village elites maintain their mandated distance until, one day, the daughter of the village headman (gowda) is gripped by a mental affliction, and the headman decides to beg Kariajja for help. After the miracle man succeeds (how could he not?), Kariajja moves into the gowda's own home because the headman has promised to now take care of the storyteller like a son. But Kariajja's material upliftment is not without consequence.

> It was now considered disrespectful to narrate, or listen, to any story without offering remuneration, and to save the stories from becoming angry, the gowda began stipulating appropriate fees for different kinds of stories. For physical ailments, astrological concerns, ghost-hauntings and other common problems, people began adopting a standard fee structure, and would pay the gowda before consulting Kariajja. How long could this go on for? Questions began to crop up about how much of the earnings were actually reaching the storyteller. Even as he was wondering how the gowda had come to acquire all the stories in his head and how he was forbidden to enchant his audience until their hearts became full with stories, Kariajja's one decent leg began to totter, and history tells us that this is when Kariajja really became old, and began mirroring history itself.

The story takes a fantastical turn from here, and we jump into Kariajja's body, where all the stories he has not been able to put out freely are fighting amongst themselves, stampeding each other to death, violently charting a political revolution. Kariajja embodies the historical process by which folklore is patronised by political powers, as a result losing the raw freedom of its artistic gifts. Where once it was no less than life itself, it now becomes an instrument of material gain, and the stories suffer for lack of vitality. It is ultimately thanks to the suffocation of his patronage that Kariajja becomes mute and incapacitated. When the gowda comes and pleads lovingly with the defeated Kariajja to come back home, bribing him with a five-acre farm, his wife retorts, *Of what use is a farm to us who have no past/future, eh?*, prompting the mute Kariajja to feebly smile. There is a sense of timelessness to his art—it is incomplete, free and can be taken up by anyone who can then add their own wings to it and make it their own. Its conscience is not individual, but collective; the figure of the author is merely incidental. It is, in the purest sense, art for art's sake.

In a nutshell, this captures what has come to be known in studies of pre-modern culture as the marga–desi binary, where the former denotes an *institutionalised path* laid out by the wealthy elite, and the latter signifies an untutorable *local genius* that thrives in the freedom of being away from all such restrictions. The binary finds explicit mention across centuries, but their relationship has been both collaborative and combative down the ages.

When does Kannada writing begin anyway? While the fifth-century Halmidi inscription from Hassan is usually touted as the first stone inscription in Kannada, there are copper plates bearing older Kannada from earlier years of Ganga rule, which also contain details of who inscribed them—the first recorded scribes go by the names Vishwakarmacharya and Kammara Konguniyaachaari.[1] The proudly professed clan names—vishwakarma and kammara—are indicative of historical times where literacy was the showboat of non-brahmin communities, since the priestly elite were well ensconced in oral traditions.

The ninth-century magnum opus *Kavirajamarga* is the first text in the Kannada language that attempted to grapple with grammar, rhetoric and poetics to create a standardised template of

Map for representational purposes only; not to scale

Amoghavarsha I ruled from Manyakheta till 878, having been regnant for more than six decades. Arts, sciences and trade flourished under his rule, and the Arab traveller Sulaiman at-Tajir deemed him to be one of the 'four great kings of the world'. In the middle of the century, around the time Amoghavarsha was commissioning the Kavirajamarga, Vijayalaya Chola was busy laying the foundations of the Chola Empire, having captured Thanjavur after capitalising on a feud between the Pandyas and the Pallavas.

Kannada. The kavi and the raja—poetics and politics, personified by the poet Sri Vijaya and the Rashtrakuta monarch Amoghavarsha Nrupatunga—are inextricably associated, and one may translate it as 'The Highway of the Poet-King'. It is in this text that the first definition of the Kannada language is offered: *Kannada is the language spoken from the Kaveri up to the Godavari.* This unique literary experiment tries to use Kannada to unify and fortify a geographical region. It seeks to take the desi mother tongue, Kannada, and fuse it with the cosmopolitan paradigms of the Sanskritic universe, the marga.

It is the first text—certainly in South Asia, but also perhaps in the world—that theorises this process of vernacularisation self-consciously.[2] Though this was a fusion project, it would necessarily have to restrict entry and create a language suitable for the court; the division between classical/folk is plainly evident. The writer of the *Kavirajamarga* is acutely conscious of what is desi, and what *should* be marga. While trying to articulate the best way to carry out the mixing of Sanskrit, Prakrit and Kannada (the three languages jostling for attention in pre-modern Karnataka), the *Kavirajamarga* stipulates that certain Sanskrit indeclinables, such as 'itastatam' (this way and that way) or 'punah punah' (again and again), are not to be used with Kannada words.

'If these [Sanskrit and Prakrit] words are mixed with Kannada poetic composition, the effect is not pleasing but harsh, like the splashing sounds of karade and maddale.' (The karade and maddale are instruments associated with the folk arts.)

Certain other words, however, make for perfect bedfellows:

'If these Sanskrit words, however, are used in conformity with Kannada words, the effect will bring happiness, like the pleasing sound of the mrdangam.' (The mrdangam is an instrument associated with classical music.)

We thus have a curious demarcation of literary aesthetics that is revealing of the work's *social* underpinnings. Sri Vijaya's codification of literary aesthetics began to swiftly sweep across the royal courts seeking to establish their glory through literature. The tenth-century Kannada master Adikavi Pampa, who was patronised by the Chalukya king Arikesari II, fused Kannada with Sanskritic prestige in a way that heralded the arrival of a whole new genre of poetic literature. He called his language 'thirulugannada', or the Kannada-marrow—its essence was extracted by the poet-genius and grafted into the cosmopolitan landscape, blurring the boundaries forever.[3]

The zeitgeist of the period between the ninth and twelfth centuries seems to have been one of uninhibited warfare. Death on the battlefield was valorised, heroic ballads were composed, successful cattle raids were seen as markers of glory, and numerous veeragallu, *hero stones*, from this period also highlight the extent to which internecine warfare dominated the land. The Rashtrakutas, Kalachuris, Gangas, Cholas and Pandyas battled for supremacy over the southern peninsula, drenching it in bloody tales. The reign of the heroic courtly imagination was uncontested until the twelfth century, when the emergence of the Sharana rebellion and the vachana, *that which is spoken*, literature shattered its security. In the fiery eyes of the Sharana rebels, 'the temple, the king, and the Rajaguru [the king's priestly guide] formed an evil triumvirate, and any literary culture that needed them was equally evil and degenerate'.[4] This cultural revolution attempted to do away with the hierarchical domination of caste, orthodoxy and divine kingship by creating a heterodox, all-admitting philosophy of life centered around the worship of Shiva. This movement, led by the philosopher and poet Basavanna, was responding to suffering and bloodshed compounded over centuries, rebelling against the cult of the king that had facilitated it. Together, they ushered in the protest, or 'protestant', movement known as Lingayatism or Veerashaivism—the two words are often used synonymously, but remain hotly contested thanks to complex genealogical differences.[5]

Until the twelfth and thirteenth centuries, Kannada literature was dominated by a form known as champu, which was a prose-poetry mixture, consisting of 'grand Sanskrit-derived verses interspersed with often very convoluted art-prose'. It was an art form greatly distanced from the everyday speech of the common man. Poets were obliged to pay homage to their patrons, the kings, and glorify their lives through religio-mythological associations. Adikavi Pampa compared his king Arikesari to Arjuna, and in Ranna's work, the king became Bhima. The key metaphorical contribution of the Sharana rebellion was to feed the 'corpse of the king' into prevailing literary imaginations. After the twelfth century, no great champu eulogising a patron-king by coupling him with a mythological hero would appear in Kannada ever again.

In the course of these centuries, literature had become inextricably linked to religious and spiritual quests. Basavanna's peers had sought to transfer spiritual power into the figure of the solitary ascetic—one whose body-mind had all the resources to carry out this quest. The tension between the ascetic and courtly traditions (both reverential in their own ways) is broken only by the sixteenth-century Jain poet Ratnakaravarni, who is the first Kannada writer to confess that religious meditation bores him—the radical statement with which this chapter began. It is amusing to note that Ratnakaravarni would later come to be better known as an erotic poet and an authority on the science of sex. The critical reactions to Ratnakaravarni's self-inspired writings during his own time also show us the presence of an elite readership, who had substantial influence in both courts and monasteries, who held dogmatic opinions on what constituted literary expression, and were 'sources of dismay' to upcoming poets.

After Ratnakaravarni, the figure of the Kannada poet who wants to simply tell stories, who draws on an inner social conscience and begins to reflect on the place of the individual within a starkly stratified society, becomes more noticeable. By the time the sixteenth-century poet Sarvajna appears, full of wit, satire and humanism, the monopoly of courtly virtues has come to a definitive end. Sarvajna was born into a deeply chaotic society that was attempting to recover from the collapse of the Vijayanagara empire, a period that saw the emergence of what is now known as the Nayaka period in South India.[6] Close to him in time are the famous bards Purandara Dasa and Kanaka Dasa, who laid the foundations of what we now recognise as Carnatic classical music, which arose organically from folk life. Around them, scores of poets, mystics and singers lived and died dreaming of a better world—some of whose names are preserved in hallowed traditions, others lost to the anonymity of history.

The misery of the laity reeling under war is certainly a recurrent theme across centuries. M.M. Kalburgi—the veteran rationalist and scholar who was shot dead (as police investigations have been confirming) by the radical right-wing group Sanatan Sanstha[7] in 2015—succinctly captures the centuries-long sweep of this terror, and its religious flavour, thus:

> In medieval Karnataka, the local Buddhist, Shaiva, Vaishnava, Jain and Sri Vaishnava believers continuously kept destroying one another's shrines. From here onwards, the arrival of Muslim invaders from the north created a new kind of tragedy for all their temples. The ruling elite, who had erstwhile never personally bothered with temple destruction and mass conversion, now became centrally involved in them. A new situation was created, whereby it came to mean that political warfare was also religious warfare. No matter which Hindu idol was destroyed by whom, or even if it had deteriorated naturally, the word on the street was that *Kodali Mohammad Destroyed It*. We must note that Kannada Kaalajnaani[8] literature has captured these terrifying times very well.[9]

Indeed, Muslim hagiographers often capitalised on these terror motifs and employed them exaggeratedly to boost their rulers' aura.[10] The corridors of power in pre-modern India always led straight to religious establishments, and this also meant that economic crises became linked with religious retribution as well. When the Mysore king Chikka Devaraja Wodeyar (r. 1673–1704) radically reorganised his revenue system, the peasants in the countryside (an overwhelming majority) were adversely affected, and they rebelled. On their lips were radical songs that decried the power of the king, such as this one:

> Basavanna the Bull tills the forest land; Devendra Indra gives the rains;
> Why should we, the ones who grow crops through hard labour, pay taxes to the king?

Determined to put down the rebellion, Chikka Devaraja and his advisers decided that the roots of the unrest were the veerashaiva monasteries and their religious professionals. Most of these monasteries traced their origins to the Vijayanagara Empire, a sectarian time when diverse cultures had flourished simultaneously, and owed their heft to the efforts of theologians and intellectuals who compiled digests and commentaries on vachana literature.[11] Centuries later, they were only growing more influential, and Chikka Devaraja hatched a gory plot to assert his own power: 'A grand feast for the jangamas [ascetics] was arranged at Nanjanagudu, the famous Shaiva centre and home to the Nanjundeshvara temple. After the meal, the jangamas were given gifts and money. They had to exit the hall one by one through a narrow lane. The professional wrestlers of the court murdered each one of them, putting four hundred jangamas to death.' Later, 700 monasteries were said to be destroyed, although these numbers could well have been exaggerated.[12]

Even as he was ensuring a pliant citizenry for his kingdom and securing its coffers, official Kannada literature thrived under Chikka Devaraja Wodeyar's patronage, and he himself is said to have composed several kavyas and operas. He also had many ornate Vaishnavite temples constructed, ushering in the Wodeyars' embrace of Sri Vaishnavism, which is a Vedantic faith that travelled from Tamil country to erstwhile Mysore with the great Vaishnavite saint Ramanuja around the twelfth century.

The fall of the Vijayanagara kingdom had seen many lower-caste chieftains converting to Veerashaivism for legitimacy, and many powerful kingdoms led by Beda-Veerashaivas (Scheduled Tribe Shaivas, in present-day terms) emerged, who tried to create the cultural aura essential for sustaining kingship.[13] Yet, for reasons still unclear, the best intellectuals and writers of the times stayed out of these courts, and preferred to be affiliated to the veerashaiva mathas (monasteries), which commanded more symbolic power and authority than most contemporary courts. These mathas continued to remain institutions of great significance, played an important role in the articulation of the Karnataka statehood movement at the onset of the twentieth century, and birthed numerous community-run institutions (education and health, say) that pervade the state today.

In 1700, Chikka Devaraja received a special package from the Mughal emperor Aurangzeb (who was in Ahmadnagar) bearing a signet ring that proclaimed the Wodeyar to be 'Jug Deo Raj' (Lord and King of the World)—in effect acknowledging the maharaja's territories while also ensuring a formal subordination that would involve annual tribute from Mysore. Chikka Devaraja died in 1704, leaving behind a strong state that his successors would prove ill-equipped to handle. By 1761, an illiterate but mathematically gifted military leader named Hyder Ali had risen through the ranks to emerge as king of Mysore, checking corruption in the official ranks and leading his men in numerous battles alongside allies as diverse as the raja of Palakkad, the French Governor General Joseph Dupleix and the Nawab of Tanjore. Soon, he would see the cannonballs of the British army come crashing into Mysore's walls.

The greatest adversary of the British, though, would be Hyder Ali's son Tipu Sultan, who spent the last decade of his life (also the last decade of the eighteenth century) developing a complex theology of warfare, and doing everything he could to consolidate his territory. Today, his legacy lives on as a Janus-faced strawman spawned by political posturing—a malevolent persecutor of Hindus on the one hand, and on the other, a pluralist freedom fighter who embraced all the religions of his land. In reality, he seems to have been something of both. 'At times, both perspectives seem valid, as the ruler enacted many strict Islamic reforms, talked often about *jihad* against the infidels, and destroyed Hindu temples; yet even within the same year, he issued decrees granting land rights and revenues to Hindu temples and *mathas* and made political alliances with Hindu kings throughout South India.'[14] Above all, Tipu recognised the mortal peril his kingdom was in, and went to extraordinary lengths to find allies and crush enemies. He'd even made contact with Napoleon, who was in the process of invading

Egypt and trying to bring French civilisation to African shores. Tipu didn't mind allying with the French even as they were invading prime Muslim lands, and defended his actions to the Afghan court (another ally) by arguing that Mysore was more important in the hierarchy of divine importance. Tipu's eventual defeat would secure the British uncontested entrenchment in the South, and they would soon turn the Wodeyars into a puppet regime.

However, no religious purge, by any ruler of any stripe, could erase the ideas of egalitarianism and syncretism that had thrived in many pockets of the state. The Avadhoota tradition, for instance, had fused Sufism with the Dattatreya cult, creating the syncretic shrine at Baba Budan Giri in the Western Ghats, as well as numerous inclusive shrines in North Karnataka. In the nineteenth century, we see the birth of the mystic poet Shishunala Sharifa (who has now firmly entered the popular imagination through the rock songs of Raghu Dixit), whose father is said to have aspired to unify the best of Hinduism and Islam. The Ramayana, Mahabharata, the verses of Allama Prabhu and Sufi poetry were all equally inspirational in Shishunala Sharifa's upbringing. Deemed a kafir by the Muslim orthodoxy and a mlechha by the Hindu orthodoxy, Shishunala Sharifa apprenticed under his guru Govinda Bhatta (who had also been deemed an outcaste) for many years, and went on to combine his influences into an original body of work that continues to enthral.

This can only be a truncated, inexhaustive summary of the marga–desi binary over centuries of dynamic influences. The most immediately relevant manifestation of the idea has to do with the arrival of colonialism, the impact of which continues to shape our collective identity. The British, who were courted and negotiated with by various maharajas, would establish deep roots by the nineteenth century and create new paradigms with shattering and long-lasting consequences. The arrival of English education would produce entirely unprecedented predicaments, and the agony and ecstasy of its allure would go on to create trauma and exhilaration in equal measure.

II

> Because it is the fate of every educated Indian, whether or not he admits it, never to be completely Eastern, but to be something of a psychological and intellectual masala, with some Western ingredients mixed up. In fact, we are all of us irrevocably mixed-up, as mixed up as a shrouded Hindu corpse in Benares being driven to the Ganga—to its immortal moksha or dissolution in the holy river—on top of a scooter rickshaw: moksha powered by an internal combustion engine, no less!
>
> —Richard Crasta, *The Revised Kamasutra*

Here's a translation of a 1944 pamphlet written by the playwright and humourist T.P. Kailasam:

> *Who's the audience?* You.
>
> *Who's playing?* Who else, but us.
>
> *What exactly is happening?*
>
> Before the elders, lords and emperors can even get a whiff of it, we bring this play to you. Having curried no favour with either K.L. Saigal of Vangarajya, or Pune's Shanta Apte, or Chennai's Subbulakshmi, we look to keep our debt to you on 13-02-1944, Sunday evening, 7.30 to 10 p.m.
>
> You are unlikely to have seen a play like this before. If our expenses don't square up, you won't again, either.
>
> ***Conditions***
>
> If the play isn't up to your standards, the money comes back to you. So, please don't bring counterfeits.
>
> You may smoke cigarettes bountifully. However, please stub your cigarette out when the butt is still decently long, because it might be useful for someone else.
>
> If you request an actor for an encore, they might actually take you up on it. Beware.

Should you bring weeping babies into the theatre, chloroform expenses shall be on you.

Children, come, come, this is free only for y'all.

As a kid, I frequently heard my grandfather and grand-uncle rave about Kailasam. At family gatherings, his evergreen folk song 'Kolike Ranga', which Kailasam had intended as a desi rendition of Harry Carlton's popular English song 'Constantinople', was always the stuff of encores. The words are those of a villager named Kolike Ranga, who packs up his humble belongings and decamps to Mysore city in search of a new living. A representative of the ordinary Indian, bearing a bag of simple dreams, he encounters the grandeur of the city and its power for the first time. The highlight of the song is the part where Ranga has unpacked his frugal meal, sitting near the famous Clock Tower in Mysore, in front of a large bazaar, when he is accosted by an imperial official astride a horse:

He twirled his moustache,
Haranguing me,
Threatening me,
Who are you? Explain yourself!
I said—I am Ko, Ko, Kolike Ranga…

This song would be followed by a delightful narration of assorted jokes and wisecracks that Kailasam had set loose upon the world. Almost all of these involved punning and riffing on English words, which the inimitable Kailasam blended into his Kannada, and which requires a true multilingualism to properly appreciate. Indeed, when Kailasam first appeared on the Kannada literary scene, purists thought his language to be a bastardised creation. When a tribute short film titled *Simply Kailawesome* came out a few years ago, the title was wholly in keeping with his legacy, although the content itself lacked his punch. Amongst his vast surviving repertoire, my favourite one goes as follows. Once, after Gandhi had witnessed a magical performance by the violin maestro T. Chowdiah in Bangalore, he turned to Kailasam sitting right next to him, and asked him who this great man was. Kailasam replied, *Oh Bapuji, you are a great non-violinist, but this Chowdiah is a pukka violinist!*

Born in 1884, in Bangalore, T.P. Kailasam hailed from an elite family of administrators and scholars. His father, T. Paramashiva Iyer, was a judge in the Mysore High Court. Showing all-round promise from a young age, Kailasam graduated from Presidency College, Madras, and gained a scholarship to head to England and specialise in Geology. There, he made a mark as a keen sportsman, excelling at tennis, chess and billiards, and is said to have been an exceptional football goalkeeper. A terrific actor and singer, he was a master at mimicry and at modulating his voice to suit dynamic roles. When he heard the English war song 'It's a long way to Tipperary', he immediately wrote a Kannada song, 'Thipparahalli Balu Doora', set to the same tune, evoking for himself a nostalgic sensation of Old Mysore out there in Old Blighty.

The onset of the First World War forced him back to India, where he took up the position of a government geologist on probation, and continued in this job till the end of the decade. Never imagining that he would end up becoming the enfant terrible of Kannada theatre, he famously quit his job and withdrew from his family, arousing his father's stern displeasure. Cut off from his domestic duties, Kailasam proceeded to a lonely man-cave where he began living a bohemian, solitary lifestyle, like a Diogenes finally set free. He did not write much. Most of his plays were narrated and jotted down by his circle of doting friends. Kailasam's life itself seems like an endless parade of witticisms that were unerringly remembered by those around him and then spread like wildfire, just like 'Kolike Ranga'. Today, the song is fertile ground for endless improvisation, and myriad versions have sprung up across the state—Mysore could well become Raichur.

Celebrated as the great-grandfather of Kannada farce, Kailasam transformed the flavour of Kannada theatre with his entry into the genre. While he was serving as a probationer in the Geological Department in Shimoga, he became a member of the Amateur Dramatic Association, which enacted modern Telugu plays, and even welcomed Rabindranath Tagore as a guest at one of its events. While the dominant works staged back then were highly Sanskritised renditions of episodes from the epics and kavyas, Kailasam's very first play *Tollu Gatti* (Hollow-Solid), written in 1918, brought the pressing social predicaments of the subcontinent to the proscenium with satirical subtlety. The play is a strong critique of the Western schooling system that creates a dehumanised class of employees and paper-pushers. Kailasam himself quit his lucrative technical career, which he felt would merely lead to a distant future with a 'cheap car, a neat home and a compound wall around it'. He had loftier goals, but alas, he was far too ahead of his time to be received as the genius he really was.

Tollu Gatti essentially revolves around the brothers Puttu and Madhoo and their ailing mother. Puttu represents narrow ambition; he wants to 'pass' his exams, land a plush job and find a ladder to climb. He dresses up his ambition by saying it will bring their home prosperity. Madhoo is a more wholesome lad—sensitive and courageous. The mother may be read as a counterfoil to celebratory nationalistic images of Bharat Mata—she is sick, bedridden, and depends on her sons to take care of her. She carries the weight of a deeply patriarchal system that has made her who she is. A grandmother character hovers in the background, bemoaning the arrival of modernity (like a bar of soap or women's freedoms) into their home. Puttu is clever at cracking exams, and does so, while Madhoo fails to secure gainful employment. One fine day, a fire breaks out at home. Puttu chickens out of their home to save his own skin, while Madhoo braves the flames and rescues his mother, even rushing into a burning house to look for an absent Puttu. Later, he faints and collapses, and has to be pulled out. The gathered crowd commends Madhoo's courage, and someone concludes, *You see the difference? Who cares about 'passing exams'? Tollu is tollu, gatti is gatti.*

Kailasam's plays introduced characters never seen before in traditional Kannada drama—a tonsured brahmin widow, a Muslim, or flawed men and women navigating society just like anybody else. He went on to pen a couple of mythological plays in English too.

One of them is *Purpose*, exploring the story of Ekalavya—a short, striking play, where the pathos of the young archer forced to give up his thumb is explored with a profound sense of irony. Here, Drona does not ask Ekalavya to sever his thumb, as the tale normally goes. He commends him, telling him mournfully that Arjuna has sought only fame, and that such narrow-minded goals could never come close to the noble 'purpose' with which Ekalavya had pursued his art. Therefore, Drona concludes with confidence that there is no chance that there could be anybody greater than Ekalavya. Then, Ekalavya realises that he has negated the truthfulness of his guru, who had promised that he would make Arjuna the greatest. In a fit of dutifulness, Ekalavya cuts off his own thumb. Everybody is horrified, not least Ekalavya himself. Then, and this is the most poignant bit, unable to express his anger and terror at losing his most precious gift, he goes back to the statue of Drona he had made to serve as his guru, and starts banging his head against it. Over the years, a small depression has been created on this statue, as Ekalavya bangs his head against it whenever he faces obstacles to his learning. Now, however, no progress in learning, no level up is forthcoming. The ending is a devastating critique of the cult of the guru, of idolising and idealising one who is but human. Its richly layered philosophical inquiry makes the play arresting at every point. Does a branch falling in a forest make a noise if nobody has heard it? Is Ekalavya still the greatest archer if nobody knows about him?

It is telling that Kailasam's subversiveness was not recognised by most of his commentators. Introducing the play in 1928, a senior bureaucrat missed the point by a country mile, and ended up airing some rather hackneyed views: 'The power of tapas as a factor in self-development is the most resounding of our ancient truths, and, in emphasising the potentiality of concentration and single-minded effort, Mr Kailasam is inculcating a lesson which may with advantage be learnt and practised by the Indian people, who drift about apparently with no settled purpose and are to a tragic extent creatures of circumstance.'

More interesting is the 'Foreword' and 'Impetus' written by the classical musician and social reformer Pandit Taranath Rao, who understands the subversion, but cloaks it in other dimensions that Kailasam himself might have hardly implied. Consider these two indicative snippets:

> India after the Vedic age lost the power to present its mighty philosophy *attractively and universally* and the result is hair-splitting, tall-talk dogmatism and inaction. Philosophy has become an intellectual pastime and religion a senseless show of superstitions and fashionable follies. Life and its ways are mostly without meaning and how can such a nation muster strength enough to face dangers threatening from within and outside? More dogma, and that of an abstruse nature, cannot breathe life into the blood of a nation. [...]
>
> Any religion which teaches that this life is all bad and detestable but *fails to give a glimpse of that beyond* is bound to make its votaries poor and cheerless, dull and miserable which in turn must carry with them their active and positive counterparts of jealousy, eccentricity, distrust, fanaticism—and what not—enough to crush any nation. Such is the state of Hinduism now and signs of degradation are not wanting in spite of frothy conferences. In a word, 'convenience' makes all our present religion. This can take us nowhere. The Musalman and Christian has the impetus to work in his desire to proselytise, to expand and to govern himself. Turkey is a living example of it, but we have none of these.[15]

The apprehension couched within these words was a sign of the times. Much like Kemal Ataturk's secular nationalism in 1920s Turkey, Hindu revivalists in Karnataka like Taranath too believed that the rejuvenation of a stagnant, dogmatic religious order would have to come from an engagement with science and modernity. Taranath was a spirited social reformer (also a doctor trained in both Western and Indian medicine) who staunchly critiqued untouchability and caste prejudice, not unlike his contemporary Hindu ideologue Vinayak Damodar Savarkar. He tried to rejuvenate Hinduism by reviving ideas from Tantrism and Shaktism, which he felt could also emancipate Hindu women from child marriages and corrosive patriarchy. However, unlike Savarkar, Taranath was a devoted follower of Gandhi, supported the Khilafat movement and helped collect funds for it, and though religious prejudice is sometimes present in his writings, it was held in check by his Gandhism. He is remembered for his strong opposition towards the Nizam's rule in the Hyderabad-Karnataka region, but also for setting up a school in Raichur called Madrasa-e-Hamdard, which aimed at uniting Hindus and Muslims in the freedom struggle.[16] He continues to be remembered as a great educator and institution builder in the Raichur doab to this day. His son Rajeev Taranath, who passed away in 2024, was a celebrated sarod exponent who had apprenticed under the maestro Ali Akbar Khan.

Pandit Taranath's broader cosmopolitanism helped him look at the past with sobriety. The same cannot be said about the 'high-priest' of Kannada statehood—writer and freedom-fighter Alur Venkat Rao—who had once been Savarkar's classmate at Fergusson College, and had translated Bal Gangadhar Tilak's *Gita Rahasya* into Kannada. In a collection of articles called *Karnatakada Gatavaibhava* (The Grandeur of Karnataka's Past), Alur Venkat Rao presents an exclamatory history, where all kings were paradigms of religious tolerance and co-existed in harmony until the fall of Vijayanagara. Ironically, the Vijayanagara kingdom (which patronised Telugu, not Kannada) was seen as the apogee of Karnataka's cultural past, and Alur Venkat Rao asserts with great confidence that 'the ancient kings of Marathi and Bengali lands did not speak those respective languages, but we can slap our chests and boast with pride that all our kings spoke only Kannada'. Yet, even in this book, I could find no demonisation of Muslim kings—the fall of the Vijayanagara kingdom is attributed to weak kingship following Krishnadeva Raya, and Alur Venkat Rao is satisfied with one line describing the massacre at the Battle of Rakkasa-Tangadi. It just seems to be the case that kings who patronised Urdu could not be assimilated into the Kannada state project, and washed over in blissful ignorance, Alur Venkat Rao simply ignores them.

Kailasam himself never spelt out his purpose in explicitly religious or nationalist terms. He saw himself as a modest Hindu, and never enthusiastically aligned with a political cause. More than anything, he saw himself as an artist, and remained immersed in his work as a kind of solitary penance—explicit political posturing could never penetrate that zone defence. He put it best himself, in characteristically jaunty words:

A poet's guerdon is not gold
Not Parian bust, not trappings brave!
A tear, a titter from young and old
Is all the meed I meekly crave!

Yet, the rising nationalist tenor of the discourse all around was impossible to avoid. The feeling of Hindu emasculation was everywhere, and Kailasam's soon-to-be patron Pandit Taranath had written, way back in 1915, sitting in America and musing over Vivekananda's legacy: 'These people [Westerners] go past our temples and curse the people saying they are idol worshippers who deserve to be in hell. But they can't act this way in front of Indian Muslims. Because then, swords will fall upon them. Hindus are so demure when it comes to such things. They will say, *oh let those fools say what they want*, and move on. That is their nature.'[17] He would go on to pen many essays on the importance of physical exercise and the cultivation of a martial spirit.

Another of Kailasam's close friends was a man named K.V. Iyer, who is one of the most fascinating personalities of early twentieth-century Karnataka. In his first avatar, Iyer was a bodybuilder par excellence, who fused Hatha Yoga with European-style gym culture, and founded Hercules Gym in Bangalore. A personal physical assistant to none less than the Maharaja of Mysore, he was arguably the first bodybuilding superstar of modern India, and enjoyed a doting community of mail-order students who sought to learn the new method he had perfected. There exist unverifiable stories of him even meeting Hitler in Germany, who had marvelled at this dark-skinned South Indian with a body that someone had likened to that of a 'bronze temple god that had somehow come to life'.[18] It is also interesting to note that in the nineteenth century, 'the Hatha yogin was the common pariah of colonial India',[19] despised by orthodox Hindus because they were casteless wanderers, and feared and reviled by the British because of their militant, maverick asceticism.

In the twentieth century, it was upper-caste revivalists like T. Krishnamacharya who rescued Hatha Yoga from ignominy, imbuing it with religious sanction. K.V. Iyer would create his own brand of yoga though, one inspired by European bodybuilders like Eugen Sandow. He was acutely aware of the theatricality of bodybuilding, and desired to give it a deeper meaning: 'Nowadays, except in the imagination of the small boy, the Strong Man is not much of a figure. We go once, perhaps, to see the "Strong Man" lifting heavy weights … What useful purpose will this Strong Man serve in this age of mechanical perfection, except perhaps as a piece of curiosity?'[20]

Iyer sought to fuse the physical cultures of the East and the West, creating a dynamic exercise system in which movements to resist opposing forces are coupled with movements that surrender to opposing forces. He saw limitations in both systems. The Western physical culturist worked only instrumentally on his body, without filling it with real healthfulness and immunity to disease. On the other hand, yoga was inadequate for young men to adequately develop their muscles and stature. The balance was to be found in 'a system of training which can give full expression to all dormant growth', and could be achieved through a sensible combination of the two. There is no doubt that Iyer meant his efforts to be a part of the Hindu renaissance—indeed, this is what distinguishes his endeavour from materialist excesses. Every Saturday evening at his Vyayamshala in Bangalore, 'Iyer would conduct a puja in front of two enormous images of Ram and Hanuman'.[21]

The story goes that Kailasam and Iyer were shooting the breeze one time when Iyer betrayed the fact that he had never read Oscar Wilde. Kailasam mocked and teased his friend, saying he is all brawn and no brain. Iyer appeared to have taken this personally.

After Kailasam's early death in 1944, he immersed himself in deep studies, and went on to pen many novels, including a fictionalised biography of Michelangelo. His most famous novel, *Shantala*, was inspired by the dancing figure of a medieval queen he witnessed in Belur, which he channelled into a medieval-era historical novel set in the region. The book has seen almost twenty editions, and was a standard prescription in college syllabi. It is a celebratory novel written in pompous high-Kannada, like you might expect to hear in a mythological movie starring the revered film icon Dr Rajkumar.

Iyer was a devout Hindu who was married but chose chastity for the bulk of his life, dedicating his life to 'greater' purposes—bodybuilding, literature and a life of austerity. Kailasam too retreated from his marriage mid-life, and spent the rest of his short life wedded to theatre and literature. One wonders how their wives responded to these developments, as they certainly would not have had the luxury of uprooting themselves at will.

Another big literary name in my childhood, also courtesy of my grandfather's vast bookshelf, was of course R.K. Narayan, the only writer of his generation to create a spanking new *mythology* around a quaint little town named Malgudi. As a young boy who grew up reading only English books, it was a breath of fresh air to read of happenings along the river Sarayu, and not the Thames or the Mississippi. I read and reread *Swami and Friends*, comparing all those schoolboys to my own circle of cricket buddies. If Kailasam's meandering journey led him back to Kannada and the richness of its rib-tickling potential for absorbing new words, Narayan was able to hone his subtle humour in simple, evocative English—his first and last home.

In his early books (like *Swami and Friends*), Narayan's prose is raw, vulnerable and slowly realising the potential of a language utterly foreign. His ambivalent response to nationalism and the freedom movement was partly an extension of his family's, who had found in the system pockets to thrive. Yet, there is a strident critique of the education system in his works, beginning with the trauma of primary schooling in *Swami and Friends*, where the English teacher's Christian preaching irks Swami no end. The young boy instinctively rebels against the military regimen imposed on students and runs away in protest. It is a world where cricket and friendship and outdoor adventures are infinitely more appealing than maths and science and geography. Underneath the humour and the bonhomie lies a silent undercurrent of tense violence too. The boys fight amongst themselves, of course, but Swami has other enemies to look out for, like the lower-caste coachman's son, who in one scene brandishes a penknife with a grin, sending Swami into his father's coattails. In Narayan's second novel, *The Bachelor of Arts*, the protagonist rails at how the system has made them 'strangers to our own culture, and camp-followers to another culture, feeding on leavings and garbage'. In *The Financial Expert*, Banker Margayya harbours great hopes for his young son, who proceeds to flunk his exams three years in a row. 'Every little fool has passed his SSLC exam. Are you such a complete fool,' Margayya rages. Later, the boy rips apart his SSLC register, 'which symbolized for him all the wrongs he had suffered in his life', dumps it into a gutter, deciding for himself that no further schooling would be in order, and runs away from home to Madras.

If Sanskrit was the road to marga cosmopolitanism at the end of the first millennium, its position was slowly, but wholly, usurped by English education at the end of the second. The twentieth century saw a new generation of English-bred Indians gingerly befriending an alien culture, tasting its peculiar delights, and making it dance to their own tune. B.M. Srikantaiah's famous devotional song 'Karunaalu Baa Belake' was a direct translation of the Christian hymn 'Lead Kindly Light', and Masti Venkatesha Iyengar's anthology of poems, *Navaratri*, was loosely inspired by Chaucer's *Canterbury Tales.* Throughout this traumatic encounter, they held on to their desi-ness, to whatever degree they could manage, preferring always to keep their windows open to the breeze.

In Narayan's world, we see the hesitation and indeterminacy of lives shattered by a foreign-fangled modernity that they can make only little sense of. By the second half of the century, it is hard to escape the truly irreconcilable contradictions. This is captured best in A.K. Ramanujan's poem about his father:

Sky-man in a manhole
with astronomy for dream,
astrology for nightmare;

Meanwhile, in Kannada, newer forms of desi poetry emerged too. The educationist, activist and poet Dinakar Desai popularised a quatrain style called 'chaupadi', which he says was inspired by his readings of Sarvajna's tripadis (three-liners) as well as William Blake's quatrain stanzas. Here is one of his poems, which might be more appreciable in light of all the history that has been spelt out so far:

Let no poet ever find root or source.
Such things would destroy his force.
The poet should ever be in a state of flight.
And wherever you are, let the mind fight.[22]

And fight he did. Joining the Servants of India Society, founded by Gopala Krishna Gokhale, Dinakar Desai led a life of simplicity and devoted himself to fighting for the rights of the common people. During the thirties and forties, he organised maritime labourers working in the ports of Bombay, and worked to empower the landless dalits and adivasis of North Canara, which was his home. He wrote numerous songs to rouse the peasants, which one may still hear sung with joyous enthusiasm in the region. More than a decade before the 1951 satyagraha at Kagodu (of which you will read in the next chapter), the peasant labourers of Ankola in North Canara had already carried out a similar struggle. Ganapathiyappa, one of the leaders at Kagodu, has written of the inspiration he found in Dinakar Desai's political life. He had even taken Desai to Kagodu to deliver speeches and speak to the beleaguered tenants.

Desai embodied the figure of the artist-activist who dived head first into the social movements that were taking shape in an impoverished landscape. Unlike R.K. Narayan, whose biggest political gesture was a tenuous involvement in the non-brahmin movement in Madras,[23] Desai was a spirited man, certain of his purpose. The aristocratic, colonial apparatus was beginning to crumble, and a new class of educated Indians had to emerge as the conduit between ordinary citizens and the still nascent institutions of democracy. Side by side, the Kannada language would also have to be enriched, its base broadened, its appeal strengthened.

Yet, the popularisation of Kannada amongst the populace of the newly founded state of Karnataka did not owe all its thanks to literature alone. The days of the grand courtly imagination were definitely over, and the much-revered poet of the Kannada renaissance, Kuvempu, was the last of the pantheon of writers who believed in the grandeur of their elaborate style and metrics. It was, in fact, the arrival of cinema and its pervasive appeal that would spread the seeds of modern Kannada in fullest measure. As the writer U.R. Ananthamurthy once said: 'In literature, there is always a tendency to make one language prevail over the other. From Bijapur, Gulbarga, to Mysore, if there is one Kannada that unites us, it is not thanks to a poet, but Rajkumar, that great actor. He spoke "artificially"—it was a bookish kind of a Kannada. But he never made it seem artificial. Sri Vijaya's great dream of having one Kannada was fulfilled when Rajkumar spoke in Kannada.'

The most celebrated exponent of the language, Dr Rajkumar demonstrated how Kannada could be spoken with panache and finesse. Surveying his staggeringly vast filmography, his fans even contend that he taught an entire state how to love and conduct oneself in all manner of domestic situations. Rajkumar vowed that he would never perform in any language apart from Kannada, and he never did, except for one remake of a Kannada original. The humble ideals with which he lived his own life elevated him even further in the eyes of his fans, to whom he was no less than a god. Monarchy may have been replaced by a democratic polity, all manner of revolutionary ideals through the centuries may have decried the image of the god-king, but it would seem that people need a legend, an icon, to look up to and emulate. Yet, unlike his counterparts in Tamil cinema, MGR and NTR, as they were known, Rajkumar actively stayed away from politics, and never attempted to capitalise on his popularity. Shy of ambition, he ruled from the big screen alone. He decried efforts made in his name by fans to imbue Kannada-language politics with violent streaks. The Kannada film industry revolved around this singular figure for a long time, and other actors merely coalesced around him, like 'an emperor and his recalcitrant palegars [feudatories] with their own monarchic ambitions'.[24] In this manner, a new marga had been created for Kannada as an artistic language.

All margas are, however, meant to be challenged. Thus, we arrive at the 1999 cult movie *Upendra*, written and directed by Upendra. The on-screen imagination of the protagonist (whose name is 'Naanu', meaning myself, played by Upendra himself) is an interesting product of the anxieties of those swiftly globalising years. One peculiar quirk of this Naanu is that he smokes a desi beedi couched in a half-cigarette. He once makes a distinction between 'pure Kannada preeti' and base 'English romance', even while openly living a life of epicurean excess and praising Gandhi in the same breath, as though reminding the audience that he is perfectly aware of his scandalous hypocrisy. The character itself is entirely over the top, spiralling into vulgar outbursts often, representing an anarchic, out-of-control brute who goes hunting for the truth sword-in-hand. The egotistic Naanu seeks to seduce three women simultaneously—each representing familial responsibility, pleasure and ambition. The whole story employs a desi Vikram-Vetaal motif, and is supposed to encapsulate the predicament of any individual in modern society. There are violent and crass scenes throughout, many make you cringe, and it is really the one minute of sublime peace at the end of the movie, where the ego has been quelled, that salvages all of it. When the Vetaal asks Vikram what the appropriate ending to the man's hopeless quest to acquire the three women should be, he answers, *he must die, and then he must be reborn again.* Indeed, upon further reflection, one realises that the three women somewhat resemble the holy trinity of Hindu goddesses—as immortalised in the Puranic text Devi Mahatmya—who target the demon known as 'ego' and work to dispel illusions of power and arrogance. The sublime brutality of the movie draws on this culturally omnipresent motif.

M.M. Kalburgi wrote numerous essays delving into the marga–desi binary. In the second of his eight volumes (all titled *Marga*) of collected papers, he spells out a loose theorisation of what this divide broadly entailed. Firstly, it signified an alienation from nature caused by the move from villages to cities. Art also began to *pretend* more. When tangled up in highly restrictive technicalities, relief and inspiration were to be found by drawing on the authenticity of desi land, where art is woven into daily life itself. The best (or the luckiest?) of the desi survives precisely because somebody deemed it to be too invaluable to perish, and held the power to secure for it continual remembrance in the classical path—the marga. Somewhat like Graham Greene championing R.K. Narayan's work and securing for it an entry into the English world of letters. I would like to suggest that the incorporation of a crazy, rebellious movie like *Upendra* into a canon of cult classics, which finds only unadulterated praise on YouTube and Twitter, is also an example of the absorption of unfettered, uncensored desi expression. As one ecstatic YouTube comment proclaims, *this is not cinema, this is life.*

On the cosmopolitan front, though Sanskrit had unseated Persian in the nineteenth century in the exalted eyes of Orientalist scholars, it was irretrievably fossilised in medieval times and could do little to challenge English hegemony. The aristocrat and ex-dewan of Mysore, Sir Mirza Ismail, dubbed one of the cleverest men in India by a fellow administrator, had once been required to tackle the modern predicaments of the famous Sanskrit College in Mysore. When the non-brahmin movement sought to open the doors of the college to everyone, Mirza Ismail, who 'felt that this would destroy the peculiar orthodox atmosphere of this institution and convert it into an ordinary Sanskrit college', suggested that the Mysore college be left as it was, and that only the college in Bangalore be thrown open to everyone. Reflecting on this, he writes in his memoirs of his love for Sanskrit, and the possible contingency where the divorce of Sanskrit from everyday life would mean that 'a light would have gone from the life of the people, and the distinctive features of Hindu civilisation and culture which would have won for it an honoured place in world thought would soon be effaced from the life of the community, to the great disadvantage of India and the world'.[25]

Mirza Ismail was reflecting a long tradition of elites safeguarding Sanskrit's 'peculiar orthodox atmosphere', and implicit in his statement is the absurd fear that a language might die if it is made available to more people. The exclusionary underpinnings of this whole episode remind us yet again that Sanskrit once connected centres of the cosmopolitan world of the Indian subcontinent to each other, but it was never the language of the masses. It survives by virtue of the deep influences it had over various other regional languages—a sobering thought that tells us that languages are dynamic entities, changing shape at every juncture. English, it would seem, is here to stay, for better or for worse. But Kannada too can evolve as a dynamic entity, as indeed it is presently doing. Perhaps we can learn from T.P. Kailasam something of the art of laughing away the task of putting one word in front of another, choosing only those that resonate with us the deepest. What else is there to be done? As Salman Rushdie ends his novel *Victory City*, 'words are the only victors'.

III

> 'If these are all letters for printing, are there two sets of letters for writing as well?' he asked. I said yes, and asked him to memorise the lower case of letters. However great a [Sanskrit] scholar he might be, he was confused by a different set of letters for the same sounds. He got the capital 'F' just fine, but when it came to the lower case 'f' he was lost.
>
> —Viswanadha Satyanarayana, *Vishnu Sharma Learns English*
> (translated by Velcheru Narayan Rao)

The dynamic interplay of marga and desi has been woven into one of the most fascinating artforms still being practised in South India—Avadhaana. The word means 'concentration', and the performance is an incredible display of memory, parallel thinking, impromptu verse creation and numerous other skills. The avadhaani takes centre stage, and is surrounded by either eight prichhakas (ashtaavadhaana) or a hundred ones (shataavadhaana), who pose questions and riddles to the avadhaani, who might be simultaneously playing a game of chess and counting the number of times a bell goes off and constructing a small poem all at the same time; picture a web browser operating a hundred tabs at the same time. Its origins are believed to be in the Telugu language, though it later became popular in medieval Indian courts across the country—Akbar is said to have been a big fan.[26] Today, it is mostly restricted to South India, and in Karnataka, the most famous proponent of the form is a mechanical-engineer-turned-avadhaani, named Shatavadhani R. Ganesh.

In a Ted Talk, R. Ganesh introduces the art form as a 'unique, indigenous, classical Indian art'. The juxtaposition of the indigenous and the classical begs some questions. Is this a desi (indigenous) art form that has attained the status of marga (classical) after centuries of evolution? R. Ganesh is one of few practitioners who are capable of performing in Sanskrit as well, but he must inevitably employ Kannada to reach wider audiences. Avadhaana also carries with it a spontaneity and sense of improvisation that brings it closer to the conception of art for art's sake. However, Ganesh himself emphasises that it is marga, a classical 'fine art'. This seems to come from the fact that the performer requires a deep familiarity with the classical canon of literary works (whether in Sanskrit or regional languages), the Puranas, the mythological epics and the intricacies of the 'classical nature of the language'. In other words, he is a repository of the classical marga, a keeper of memories. 'In the modern age of Kali, how many want to pursue fine arts, classical arts, like Avadhaana? No more takers,' he mourns. The whiff of artistic prestige—'entertainment of a higher order'—is unmissable. Contrast this with the angst of the twelfth-century lingayat poet

'Chowdaiah, of Many Guises', who hailed from the bahuroopi caste of nomadic performers that donned different guises to entertain the rural folk, and had expressed his exasperation with dull audiences, thus: *my kinsmen do not know the beauty of guises.*

It is also interesting to see Avadhaana as a game, and as we know, games dovetailed with the kingly idea of leisure. They were a demonstration of mental acuity, of sharpness, of being able to think on one's feet. To take one instance, closest in time and geography, consider the many games devised by the nineteenth-century Wodeyar king Krishnaraja III, each of which was rooted in either devotion or militarism. Solving his puzzles required an understanding of religious numerology or some other arcane knowledge, such as a relevant poetic text found in one of the royal manuscripts, which would contain a reference to the cipher that held the solution. The games and puzzles carried an esoteric religious significance that was inextricable from the king's royal prestige.[27]

What I am trying to demonstrate is that marga and desi are amorphous labels, or tools, that can shed light on a certain historical phenomenon, within a certain historical context. In the kingly contexts of the nineteenth century, the Avadhaana would have carried a completely different meaning as compared to what it stands for today. Once a private, courtly affair, it has now expanded into the public sphere, into a dialogue with the world at large.

Kalburgi understands the marga–desi distinction through its *content*, an alienation from nature, art becoming more pretentious as it moves away from the lives of ordinary people. D.R. Nagaraj, on the other hand, was a literary critic more than a historian, and therefore a more accomplished cultural theorist capable of approaching the cognitive phenomenon which goes into the *formation* of the desi rebellions. Such an understanding moves away from the biases of individuals and texts, and captures the overall zeitgeist that created it. Consider the following conclusions he once drew:[28]

> There are some dangers to desivaada. It has two delusions. It assumes that its desiness is a pure, unalloyed monolith, within which

everything can be found. It is characterised by cultural naivete and ahistorical optimism. It is always haunted by essentialist concerns. Because it perceives that it is in a pure state, it assumes that all other forces are out to destroy it. Therefore, it assumes, by default, a confrontational and militant defence vis-à-vis the cosmopolitan, universalist paradigm.

It believes that a people's genius can only become creative when it arises out of a timeless cultural resource. It believes that all exterior forces are detrimental to its expression, or at the very least, pose unhealthy challenges to it. It looks at 'others' with only suspicion.

Desi is always the radical fight of a few. Exclusivism and insularity often creep into this endeavour, making it militant.

Desivaada is a simple, attractive answer to the anxiety of the postcolonial condition. Unfortunately, the anxiety only ends up diminishing the strength of local powers.

Desivaada is not an argument involving rhetoric, but an argument involving anxiety.

As one who sees the art and the artist as two sides of the same coin, I'd argue that R. Ganesh can be best understood as an intriguing (though questionable) exemplification of the desi crusader. He sees the Vedas as the unalloyed origin of his value system and of Avadhaana, a word that finds its first mention in those texts. He believes that Western scholarship cannot hope to understand Indian culture, and that only pure desi scholars like himself are privy to its real treasures. He harks back time and again to scriptures, epics and literary classics to elucidate his points—he finds it imperative to do so because Sanskrit comes to be associated with all things of greatness, and even contemporary Kannada becomes weak in his eyes. I had heard from Yakshagana guru Sanjeev Suvarna that Ganesh had arrived in Udupi a couple of decades ago wondering what the fuss about Yakshagana was all about: 'He thought there was nothing of worth in Yakshagana. He had never seen the guru–shishya tradition of Yakshagana closely. But once he came here, he realised that the tenets of Bharata's Natyashastra are being carried on only in Yakshagana today.'

The most illuminating evidence, though, comes in the form of one of Ganesh's books, *Kshattra: The Tradition of Valour in India*, which was translated into English in 2023.

The book seemingly revolves around the two concepts of brahma and kshattra, *wisdom* and *valour*, whose harmony/disharmony across Indian history R. Ganesh wishes to trace. However, this premise is barely addressed, and what could have been a fascinating book transforms into an ideological tract that seeks to demonstrate how all Hindu kings were courageous and valorous and righteous defenders of their faith, while all their Muslim counterparts were barbarians who deserve to be called all sorts of names. It must be emphasised here that Ganesh is no historian, which he admits in the preface, and he does not cite any of his sources. However, his *gesture* through the book tells us something. It is an argument of radical anxiety, driven by the assumption that a culture is in danger, and that it needs apoplectically militant protectors. Many of the present proponents of Hindutva in popular media see themselves as kshatriyas at war, and the word 'kshattra' has caught on like wildfire within this ecosystem.

The drive to classify the collective pool of human resourcefulness into wisdom and action is a not a new one—indeed, it is as old as philosophy itself. We see it in Plato's ideal of the philosopher-king, and in Tamil Sangam poetry, say, which is divided into akam and puram: the first being intimate inquiries into the self, while the latter involves war, politics and heroism. Similar parallels may be found in Greek mythology. Neitzsche had explicated, at length, a somewhat similar binary through his recognition of the Appolonian and the Dionysian—the first a symbol of art, music, poetry, rational thinking and order, while the latter stands for passion, emotions and pure instinct.

To bring this into conversation with the science of the mind, all these binaries tie in uncannily with the neuroscientist Iain McGilchrist's hemisphere hypothesis. Through extensive studies of stroke patients with damaged hemispheres, informed by cutting-edge neuroscience, matched equally by his lyrical connoisseurship of the humanities, McGilchrist's magnum opus *The Matter with Things* argues for a rebalancing of the mind, suggesting that the last 300 years or so of the modern age have forced us to become more and more fixated on ways of thinking typically carried out by the left hemisphere. McGilchrist rails passionately against the moral relativism of postmodern thinkers, while at the same time questioning the excesses of the Enlightenment. He tries to reclaim science from the condescension of postmodernism, *and* from the rigidity of *scientism*. Here's the crux of his presentation: there is a natural asymmetry in our brains—the right hemisphere is larger than the left. The left hemisphere is instrumental in its take on the world, thinks obsessively about its goal and is trained to go for the kill—it is indispensable if we are to survive in this world. But when left to itself, it believes that it knows everything, and will brook no contestation, even in the face of clinching evidence. The right hemisphere is better at capturing the whole, the gestalt. The left hemisphere approaches the world as a problem to be solved, and tears at it in an instrumental fashion, preferring efficiency over grace. The right hemisphere is more accommodative, wiser, appreciative of the arts and in general more *understanding* than the left. It allows for self-reflection and criticism, and is more open to doubt. Of course, this is hardly as simple as demarcating the two halves like pop philosophy tends to do—both hemispheres are complexly involved in all activities, but the quality of *attention*[29] they pay to tasks offers a sharp study in contrast. McGilchrist's descriptions of the left hemisphere mode of thinking are uncannily similar to the dangers of desivaada which D.R. Nagaraj had arrived at. The corroborations pushed me to dig deeper.

McGilchrist's conclusion is that the ideal state of affairs, as dictated by the unique relationship they share, is that the left hemisphere must always be in service of the right—it is a good emissary, but a bad master. He argues that we are presently fostering an incorrigible obsession with problem-solving, with mechanically working our way out of whatever currently ails us, making the left hemisphere more dominating, which is debilitating in the long run. It is a most interesting and readable hypothesis, and I can scarcely get into all the nuances of the book's thousand-odd pages here. The bottom line is that harmony between these two sides can be achieved only by acknowledging the brain's natural *asymmetry*.

However, to expound this complex tale of binaries, as R. Ganesh tries to do, following on Savarkar's prejudiced heels (a more detailed engagement with these ideological strains follows in chapter six), turning history into an exercise of targeted hate, is to miss the point completely. By the middle of the book (if you manage to get through all the inane Nehru-bashing), his bigotry has arrived in naked display: 'Muslims knew only warfare, bloodshed, and constant battle; they knew nothing about emotionally rich aspects of life like art and craft or any aspect related to aesthetics. Because Hindus were excellent traders and businessmen, Muslims would squeeze every last penny from them; and the Hindus would give it to them.' At this point, my patience collapsed, and I was astonished that this book had even been published in translation, and carrying an exclamatory preface even. It is ironic that the art of Avadhaana is itself premised on a harmony of the two modes of being that is the purported subject of Ganesh's book. He calls it 'poorana' and 'dhaarana'—intense focus on a problem, followed by calm introspection which reveals the answer. In other words, shifting between the goal-driven focus of the left hemisphere and the calm introspection of the right. Had this harmony made its way into his writings, they would have acquired some merit. I mused that if one desired to attempt a monograph on brahma and kshattra harmony, there might be no better place to begin than the life and times of the bodybuilder-novelist K.V. Iyer.

An insular approach to history creeps into all political ideologies in different measures. In the case of R. Ganesh, it leads him into a naïve endorsement of Savarkarite Hindutva, driven by dogmatism rather than rigorous history, in stark contrast to the broad-minded early-twentieth-century Hindu conservative literati in Karnataka, who were all Gandhians by and large. When he says something like 'there was always a feeling of one-ness of Bharata and a need to have a great emperor of the land who was above everyone else', Ganesh's conception of history clubs too many political zones (and historical eras) under one homogeneous monolith, while also disregarding all the rebellions denouncing the dominance of the king. Contrast this with the historiography of the mechanical Marxist who sees *only* the decadence of the royal court and the folk heroes fighting feudal oppression across centuries, as though that were history's singular theme.

When this naïve celebration of kingship spills over into present-day culture and politics, the result can only be infantilism. In his TED talk, Ganesh had also brought up his close friend, the painter B.K.S. Verma, whom I remember watching on TV many times when I was young as he improvised exquisite paintings of gods, goddesses and natural landscapes with all manner of paintbrush substitutes. When I Googled Verma, I saw that he had passed away in early 2023, and his Twitter profile held many posts showcasing his environmentalism-themed sketches. There was also a 2019 sketch showing Bharat Mata being anointed with a crown held by Modi and Shah on either side. I wonder if he had believed them to be representations of brahma and kshattra. This might look deceivingly benign, but it is worth remembering that these terminologies are also the preferred defence of the Sanatan Sanstha, the organisation accused of murdering Narendra Dabholkar, Govind Pansare, Gauri Lankesh and M.M. Kalburgi. Their psychiatrist-hypnotherapist founder, Jayant Athawale, has written a tract titled *Kshattra Dharma*, which advocates the cold-blooded elimination of all those who oppose it. Amongst other things, a huge cache of weapons and psychotropic substances have been seized from the Sanstha's premises.[30]

D.R. Nagaraj, of course, was in the process of charting his own desi rebellion, gauging the dangers with great sensitivity. He was harshly interrupted by an untimely death when he was still in his early forties. Even in that brief interim, he'd established a wide reputation for being a prolific and original thinker who, to quote his good friend Ramachandra Guha, 'had accomplished a lifetime's work by the time he reached forty'.[31] In the last decade of Nagaraj's life, he began making a case for how the postcolonial condition created an amnesia that had wiped out an awareness of the diverse spiritual and intellectual traditions that had historically contested Vedic traditions. He sought to rescue and rehabilitate them. In his scholarly writings, he meditated on the complex historical interplay between the Vedic and non-Vedic modes of thought, and how the influence of the latter tended to infuse notions of equality and tolerance into the former.[32] In an interview given to *Lankesh Patrike* in the nineties, he was asked if his philosophy was not rather similar to the Sangh Parivar's, to which he responded:

> When we are talking about any philosophical matters, these complications arise naturally. Just because it is swadeshi thought does not mean it should be restricted to the Sangh. I am talking the language of Gandhi, Ambedkar and Lohia. A culture really blooms only when it reignites the multifaceted strains within itself. This is, in fact, a means to stop the dangerous cultural nationalism of the Sangh Parivar. Shudras, ati-shudras and avaidikas have always seen religion and history in a way that is different from how these people are looking at it. The deathly blow to the Sangh Parivar will only come from these kinds of darshanas [faiths]. Cultural memory is a great asset of desi socialists. If we give that up to the Sangh too, then we will be weaponless, that's all.

Consider also what the bilingual scholar and novelist Shankar Mokashi Punekar wrote in a 1979 introduction to an English translation of the *Avadhoota Gita*:

> Politicising of Hindu revival cannot meet with success. The process itself will alter the nature of the Hindu social organization (based on ritual and practice, not institutionalisation); and convert Hindu stratal order into so many warring classes, each bargaining for economic advantages. On the other hand, all past revivals of Hinduism were accomplished in the name of God and personal salvation, from the days of the Buddha and Shankara, through the Bhagawat movement, till Vivekananda's Vedantic activism and Gandhiji's syncretic Hinduism. India is singularly lacking in political revolutions. Bewildered by this feature, the militant Hindu revivalists try to represent Ramadasa's Mahantas

> as organisers of secret societies, etc. This is simply not true. To represent Yogis and Nathas, Bhaktas and Sharanas, Mahantas and Puratanas, as members of secret societies and commando groups carrying hidden knives in the hollow of their maces is a favourite device of some Indian novelists writing under the influence of Sir Walter Scott and Alexandre Dumas. Hindu revivalism in the past has always been a renewal of worship, not political revolution brought about by secret societies and commando groups.

In his talks, Iain McGilchrist loves bringing up an ancient Native American Iruquois creation myth involving two brothers—one is brash, thinks he knows everything, while the other is more wholesome and wise—that demonstrates how things fall out of balance whenever the brash brother begins to wield more power. *A good emissary, but a bad master.* He argues that cultures and peoples around the world have always intuited that there seem to be two personalities raging within us, and that these have been reflected endlessly in folk imaginations. I felt I saw a similar metaphor in Kailasam's *Tollu Gatti* brothers, but the truly striking corroboration came in the form of the eminent folklorist and novelist Chandrashekhar Kambar's 2015 novel *Shivana Dangura* (Shiva's Drum). After a while, I was seeing the two brothers everywhere—Yakshagana performances in Udupi, professional theatre in North Karnataka, and so on.

The secret of folklore is that you don't learn words at the outset. You grasp the melody first. And then you fit the words into it, Kambar once said in an interview. I read *Shivana Dangura* in the original, and was struck by the sing-songy nature of his prose, and the effortless narrative that propels the tale. Kambar has been rightfully compared to Gabriel Garcia Marquez in his championing of the desi imagination—the non-brahmin mythology of the Belagavi region. Reading his novels, one feels that just a sentence here, or just a word there, is all that it takes to convey the weight of a hundred stories, the gait of a seasoned storyteller, the laconic talent of acknowledging politics and history (even literary history) with subtle nods.

Kambar's mythological imagination is centred around Shivapura, a village that has always witnessed infusions—some welcome, others unwelcome. At the onset of his literary life, in his 1964 poem 'Helathena Kela' (Let me tell you), the arrival of the British, portrayed as a rakshasa (demon), imperils the town and plunges it into a series of traumatic encounters. The rakshasa fathers a son with the erstwhile headman's wife, and this half-English, half-Indian man becomes the central character in his subsequent play, *Rishyashringa*, where he is unable to gain the confidence of the villagers who begin to believe that famine is upon them because of the sullying influence of foreign blood.

In *Shivana Dangura*, Kambar's canvas is still the sweep of the twentieth century, but couched now in a magical realism that blurs time and reflects multiple historical eras. Here, we meet Chenbasava, a landlord's son who is nevertheless treated as an untouchable child because he was weaned on the breasts of the landlord's dalit mistress Tungavva. Chenbasava falls in love with the beautiful Shaari, but the marriage cannot be solemnised because Shaari has been inducted into the devadasi system at a young age, and the god-fearing Tungavva (herself a devadasi) cannot bear the idea of Chenbasava breaking Shaari's divine vow and incurring the wrath of the Devi. Chenbasava makes a compromise by taking Shaari as his mistress, but when Tungavva tries planning a 'proper' wedding for Chenbasava, he erupts into anger:

> You'll scare me by speaking of Devi in every breath? Will your Devi say—*don't marry my daughter, keep her as a prostitute?* Would *any* Devi say that? First, get your thoughts straight … Are you any kind of mother? You're a rakshasi! Mend your mind!

Chenbasava stands for progressive modernism in the novel. He welcomes the land reforms, the arrival of the rationalist dalit movement, participating in the march of history eagerly. The motif of the two brothers is woven into the tale through the character

Kuntirapa (Kunta + Irapa equals Lame Irapa), a cunning Iago-like figure, just like Langda Tyagi in Vishal Bharadwaj's film *Omkara*. With a left leg as crooked as his mind, he becomes Chenbasava's arch rival. Kuntirapa arrives from a neighbouring village, bearing ambitious hopes of land and power. He cleverly befriends Chenbasava's landlord-father, marries Chenbasava's sister, and schemes and connives with the landlord and his gang of drunken thugs. As Kuntirapa rises to power and wins the local election, terrible things happen to the village—farmers are in distress and decamping, crops are wilting under chemical fertilisers, deceit is in the air. After some thugs connive with the police and rape Shaari (Kuntirapa had personally tried it once and failed), Chenbasava erupts into anger, kills the thugs and police who are responsible for the act, and lands up in jail.

Kuntirapa is shown to be fascinated with bones, and his wife is shocked to find bones and elaborate pictures of bones hidden away in her husband's corner, making her wonder if he is a practitioner of dark magic. The bones are directly connected with Kuntirapa's rise to power. This particular imagery, which keeps turning up throughout the novel in numerous ways—and its dark implications—cannot be grasped fully without delving into the history of the school of thought known broadly as 'tantrism'. To this day, the words 'tantra' and 'kutantra' carry only sinister connotations in the Kannada language. As it turns out, Kambar's maternal uncle—a childless man named Ramappa—lived on the edge of the dalit street in their village in Belagavi. For him, 'alcohol and Tantric sadhana was very dear, and he would go to cemeteries at night for sadhana. The young Chandrashekhar Kambar would go with him, and even when he was a child, he had witnessed Tantric rituals from close quarters.'[33] It has clearly influenced Kambar's mythology in intriguing ways.

Tantra (a phenomenon that appears to have originated around the middle of the first millennium) as a whole traced its origins to pre-Aryan fertility and magic cults (its primordial ore), and its influence pervades Buddhism, Shaivism, Shaktism and Sri Vaishnavism.[34] Most importantly, 'tantrism was an attempt to resacralise life in India at a time of religious lethargy'. In the words of the historian of religion Mercia Eliade, it was: 'a "dark age" in which the spirit is deeply veiled under the flesh. The doctors of Hindu tantrism regarded the Vedas and brahminic tradition as inadequate for modern times. Man, they held, no longer possessed the spiritual spontaneity and vigour that he enjoyed at the beginning of the cycle; he was incapable of direct access to truth; he must then "stem the current", and, to do so, he must set out from the basic and typical experiences of his fallen condition—that is, from the very sources of his life.'[35]

A curious classification in tantra (a word that literally means 'instrument') is between the right-hand path (dakshinaachaara), which interprets the five Ms, or panchamaakaara—madya (alcohol), mamsa (meat), matsya (fish), mudra (grain) and maithuna (sexual intercourse)—symbolically, and the left-hand path (vaamaachaara) which interprets them literally. Thus, the left-hand path became the way of niche underground cults, where practices involving sex, magic and intoxicants were taken to be literal prescriptions for life and worship. We can safely say that at least a small minority of religious practitioners[36] believed that indulging in these practices and rebelling against the establishment through the act of becoming its exact antithesis, would lead to liberation of its own accord. A similarly deviant left-hand path also shows up in European cultural history; indeed, the word 'sinister' itself was originally Latin for left, as 'dexter' was for right. This is exactly how the two hemispheres function, according to McGilchrist—the right hemisphere attends to the world in a holistic fashion, while the left attends to it in a piecemeal way. One can treat things metaphorically, while the other treats everything literally, often exhibiting schizophrenia. There is a similarly interesting, though inverted, bifurcation that comes up within the history of caste in South India as well.[37]

In Kambar's novel, we may read a modern avatar of this reformist, stem-the-current strain in Chenbasava's preceptor—an ascetic named Namahshivaaya—who does not believe in caste or religious superstitions, is humanist above all else, blesses Chenbasava's marriage and acts as the spiritual bridge between the educated Chenbasava and the illiterate dalit community they seek to uplift. They contrast sharply with Kuntirapa and his exploitative, epicurean gang of thugs, who are clearly the deviant bunch—they know only desire.

It is interesting that tantrism was also a kind of unexplored novelty that became a mode of serious self-discovery for the mid-twentieth-century Kannada writer Anantakrishna Shahapur (pen name, Satyakaama), who travelled around North India with youthful journalistic spirit more than a decade before Allen Ginsberg and the Beat Generation and the Beatles would go on to undertake similar quests for gurus and spiritual guidance. In the preface to his novelistic expression of these experiences—a book titled *Pancha 'Ma' Gala Naduve* (Between the Five 'M's)—Satyakaama writes:

> Between 1944 and 1956, during a period of tapas, I spent time with many shaktas. While some of them were gatti, others were extremely tollu. This is also the space where the highest number of cheaters have gathered in our country. In spite of them, a truthful universe has emerged amidst them. Within the gatti group, I found many who had a lot of shakti, but had very little scientific knowledge about growing this power and disseminating it. In other words, it was accidental achievement. I have met and interviewed tens of such accomplished individuals. I have seen several displays of their prowess. Yet, they did not possess the full consciousness required for real tantra practice.

Predictably, the first thing the narrator encounters in the novel is a woman of breathtaking beauty who relieves him of his virginity and expands his worldview. He finds himself in prison, gets initiated into the pleasures of smoking marijuana from a chillum-spouting sage, rescues a girl from the clutches of charlatan-rapists, and goes on delirious adventures that would have made Hunter S. Thompson grin with approval. This did not feel like an altogether new world to me. During my own travels in the Himalayas, I have encountered a trishul-bearing baba boast about how he once molested a Kashmiri woman (she was so beautiful he could not 'help himself'), an entire coterie of 'train-babas' who adopt saffron attires to travel across the Indian Railways free of cost, chillum-holding swamis eager to debate the veracity of the epics, and so on. A disturbing and sometimes colourful underbelly, perhaps, but hardly a home for aspirational ideals. In fact, a phenomenon dubbed as India Syndrome has officially been documented, which happens when Western travellers come to India bearing imaginations of a land of exotic mystical experiences, but instead become disenchanted and depressed when confronted with a wasteland of drug excesses and mystical charlatanism.

When I was growing up, I would catch glimpses on television every morning of the Sanskrit scholar Mattur Krishnamurthy, who would interpret verses from the Kumaravyasa Bharata (Kumaravyasa's fifteenth-century Kannada rendition of the Mahabharata) in a calm, meditative tenor. Being a staunch Gandhian, Mattur Krishnamurthy (who also headed Bharatiya Vidya Bhavan in London for a few years in the eighties and nineties) lived a simple life, and sought to rescue a universal humanism from the repositories of ancient Hindu thought. Today, Karnataka's biggest export—within the spiritual trade realm—is Jaggi Vasudev (better known as Sadhguru), a biking enthusiast from Mysore who has fashioned for himself a personality much like Osho's, just as cosmopolitan and filled with English-verve. By his own admission, Vasudev never bothered learning Sanskrit, for he did not want to be 'cluttered by any tradition, any scripture, any teaching'.[38] This does not, however, seem to be preventing him from pontificating on Paninian grammar, the Vedas, etymologies of Sanskrit terms, complex theological histories, or indeed, the cultural significance of the Bharatiya Janata Party. These days, what passes for spirituality and what passes for television journalism have conveniently collapsed into the same order of veracity. The sense of the sacred has been usurped by aspirations to power and pleasure—a notion further exemplified by Sadhguru astride his BMW motorcycle. But of course, Sadhguru the epicure is also a symbolic reflection of the aspirational world that raised him, and of the philosophical void at its heart.

The war of narratives these days is being waged from the pulpits of cyberspace. Keyboard warriors and machinating political cells and mercenary freelancers shoot salvos from whatever armpit of the universe they occupy. These are battles of false promises and bad faith—in other words, not very different from much of human history. Yet, their sheer ubiquity, transported effortlessly into the pockets of unsuspecting users, onto screens hosting debates clearly demarcated into *us* and *them*, has created an unprecedented phenomenon: a totalising arena where truth goes to die a gladiatorial death. A blatant peddling of fake news has been taken up by those who enjoy the sanctuary and fillip provided by the ruling establishment. The hope that marga and desi could hope to harness each other's strengths has suffered in the course of this polarisation. R. Ganesh's half-hearted dream of harmonising brahma and kshattra also perishes in the same process. The Roman emperor Commodus once fought as a gladiator while ensuring that all his opponents were supplied with blunt swords, hoping to gain popularity amongst his people through grotesque chicanery. We must not be fooled by his modern-day counterparts who participate in this slugfest bearing neither shame nor honour.

IV

> Inside every thinking Indian, there is a Gandhian and a Marxist struggling for supremacy.
>
> —Ramachandra Guha

As I walk into Heggodu Prasanna's home in Mysore, I am struck by how spartan it is. A few books, a wooden bench that doubles as a conversational see-saw for two and a cot with no mattress. On further reflection, I am only mildly surprised. For someone whose popular persona in Kannada circles is that of a Marxist-turned-Gandhian, few luxuries would have been lost in the transformation.

Prasanna emerged on stage as a director during the seventies, as a pioneer of the Samudaya theatre movement in Karnataka.

Later, he would involve himself full-time with Charaka—his decades-long pet project—which has created a successful women's handloom cooperative in the village of Heggodu in the Western Ghats. The village is more famous for Ninasam, an arts collective that exemplifies the desi endeavour which channels the best of the cosmopolitan spirit, bearing in mind the perils of provincialism. Here, for decades, a locally bred theatre movement has embraced Shakespeare and the Ramayana with equal fervour, just as its film screenings have equally championed Ingmar Bergman and Satyajit Ray. When I met Prasanna, he was just getting ready to stage his new play, *Ayodhya Kanda*, which had received some pushback from the Left in Karnataka for being politically meek.

Like a principled student of history, I began by probing the origins of Samudaya. Prasanna spoke with the cool detachment of a renunciate:

> P: In the seventies, the science movement became very popular. Two of its strands were gradually developing. One was the Delhi Science Forum, which represented a very 'scientific' science. And then, there was the Sasthra Sahithya Parishad in Kerala, which talked of alternate sciences, sustainable sciences, the Silent Valley Project, and became the harbinger of a new way of looking at science. Similarly, in theatre, in the Marxist theatre of the post-IPTA [Indian People's Theatre Association] generation (after the fifties and sixties), there were two threads. One was the Jana Natya Manch of Delhi, and one was Samudaya from Karnataka. They were as distinctive as the Delhi Science Forum and Sasthra Sahithya Parishad. Jana Natya Manch openly associated with the CPM and committed themselves to doing theatre only for the working class movement. Whereas Samudaya was internally connected to the same Marxist movement, internally committed to the working class, all that is true, but externally we realised that we have to go much beyond the working class, because after all, you have to build a democratic movement. So, what Samudaya did was, we started from culture as it existed there, and went to the more progressive elements in existing Kannada culture, like Shivaram Karanth. We took their works, took their 'renaissance' ideas, if you want to call them that, and moved

beyond that. We also did street theatre, much, much more street theatre than Jana Natya Manch or anybody can imagine.

Me: What about this battle between Marxism and Gandhism that has been raging in your head? How do you personally understand this?

P: If I have to tell you, I have always been an activist and an artist—I keep swinging between these two extremes, trying to manage a middle path. So, this was the swing I took, away from big-city theatre to hopefully a small-town theatre [Heggodu], but eventually it became civil rights activism. That's how Charaka emerged, and so many things happened. That's how my activism had to change. I didn't even realise what was happening to me. The Marxist that I was, that angry person denouncing the whole world! Who will you denounce in the village? The next day you have to live with them, no? You can't denounce and get out. There is no negotiation possible in the formal Marxist way of thinking, because it's me and them, the other, the class enemy. So, the moment you start negotiating, especially negotiating in a rural context, it looks like Gandhism to many people, because Gandhiji was a brilliant negotiator. So, if you are asking about my capability now to negotiate with the reality—yes, I am now a Gandhian. I learnt so much from the women who have made Charaka a reality. It wasn't intended by me. If I say that, I'll be a fool. It happened. My contribution was that I let things happen, and they happened better.

Charaka was started in 1996. It has always been a small cultural niche that tries to remain faithful to the sustainability of rural life. Prasanna speaks of Charaka as the product of a strong urban organisational sensibility that sought to go back to the villages and infuse them with fresh vitality. In keeping with his ideals of minimal dependence, no power looms are used in the manufacturing process. All garments produced at Charaka are coloured with natural dyes like indigo, betelnut and pomegranate. In a 2009 book called *Yantragalanna Kalachona Banni* (Let's Abandon Machines), Prasanna bemoans the arrival of what he dubs yantra naagareekate (machine civilisation), a nebulous abstraction under which he clubs entities and ideas as diverse as: software engineers, chemical fertilisers, crony capitalism, rap music and Batman comics.

In another book titled *Shudraraagona Banni* (Let Us Become Shudras), he had performed a similar juggling act, arguing that we must protest (by becoming shudras and working with our hands) against a machine civilisation that tries to 'turn everyone into a brahmin', which for him means everyone from 'intellectuals, traders, artists, middlemen, entertainers' to 'singers, dancers, priests, and sanyasis'.[39] I did not take to Prasanna's catch-all varna logic. He had fused the Marxist conception of capitalism as a march of productive forces with a rather naïve recycling of varna terminology. In the process, he had abandoned the most vital critique of capitalism—its dependence on cheap outsourced labour—a point that, if acknowledged seriously, would have brought his tenuous argument crashing down. More importantly, the essence of the approach was no different from R. Ganesh's exhortations for building kshattra, taking an esoteric four-fold classification and claiming that it captured some profound aspects of humanity that we could aspire towards. Is our discourse so stunted that the richness of our talent diversity could not be acknowledged without using varna vocabulary? It put me in mind of the rabble-rouser advocate J. Sai Deepak, who spoke of how he had always felt like a kshatriya despite being born a brahmin. Was this a new phenomenon of people 'coming out' as a different caste? A cultural blindspot? Or just the inability to embrace heterogeneity?

In our conversation too, Prasanna could not help but situate his desi initiative (and ideology) against the anxiety of a globalised economy:

> The brahmin is no more a cultural icon. From Kumara Vyasa and Basavanna, it came down to Kuvempu. And from Kuvempu it came down to Rajkumar—the broadest cultural icon that Kannadigas have produced. And he was a great icon—he represents the shudra, he represents Kannada. Why did Rajkumar have to lead the Gokak [Kannada-language] movement [in the early 1980s]? You have to look at it in an integrated way. Rajkumar and the dalit movement, they are not negating English, you see, because they know they can't

> negate English. All the Ananthamurthys and other intellectuals are not negating English. They are looking at it in their backyard, they are putting all the English into their pockets, and then they are trying to tell the rest of the world they should become Kannadigas. This is hypocrisy. Whereas the way the working people do it is different. Of course, now, day by day, their powers are shrinking, their capacity to negotiate is shrinking. Day by day, the capacity of a Kannadiga to negotiate his/her tongue is shrinking. Day by day, the capacity of the working class to develop an alternative market model is shrinking.

I was more taken with Prasanna's views on modern theatre. In a talk delivered in 2013, Prasanna had held forth extensively on 'the contemporary crisis in theatre ecology'. He had railed against the postmodernist conception of the death of the author, and mourned the individualistic turn in theatre—after all, Samudaya literally meant 'community', and the theatre movements he had grown up witnessing had prided themselves on their collective imagination:

> We are in a situation where theatre ecology is seriously damaged. This is not a political or social problem, but something that has gone deep into the body of theatre itself. In the style of acting, in the style of writing plays, what we have seen in the last few decades is that actors have changed. Plays have changed. There is no narrative anymore in theatre. There is no speech in theatre. What you see is mostly experimentation, and in particular, individualistic experimentation. There is no continuity. What theatre of the last few decades is doing, with a great deal of revolutionary zeal, is *upturning.* We don't even know what we are upturning. Texts have become secondary. People don't ask the permission of a playwright anymore before they produce a play, because that relationship doesn't exist. The coming together of the written text and the performative text in a tense relationship—this doesn't exist anymore. If you ask them, they will say, *I have created a new text, and just used yours for inspiration, maybe.*

He had also spoken then of a cyclical process that drives theatre, which reminded me of McGilchrist's assertion that the best art, and our most reliable thoughts, emerge from the churn of an ideation process involving the two hemispheres in a series of mental jumps:

> What is the significance of that oft-repeated saying 'Kavyeshu Natakam Ramyam' [*Drama is the most poetic of all the arts*]? Language goes through a series of processes. From informal, oral speech, the playwright picks up certain words, scenes, and gives it a formal, written outlook. Then, once again, it becomes oral. From orality to written language, and then once again to orality. This amazing cyclic process is what constantly picks up an ordinary word, an ordinary abuse, and gives it an exalted status. When an ordinary word is picked up by Shakespeare, and staged in a formal setting, it suddenly gains a dignity. And that is how languages are shaped. In shaping a language, drama is all-important. Now, we have television, which is a one-sided medium. We just watch it. Everything is performance-based now. But the theatre we grew up doing thrived on *processes*. The rehearsal was part of that process. The performance was just a flower blooming from a plant. Today, we are not worried about the plant, and the flower might very well be a plastic flower, but we still seem to say, *wow, what a lovely flower*.

His solution to the crisis is a retreat into smaller communities, a distancing from power and prestige, from fame and glory, into the quiet authenticity of *little traditions*: 'I used to be against classicalism, I mean, I was a leftist radical who used to say we must go to the masses. But today, I have come full circle, and in this society that has been taken over by the machine, I want to become a classicist in the sense that I just want to work with a small community of actors, and just go on perfecting it. The only way out now is to think small, go to small communities, forego those dreams of featuring in page-three articles in the *Times of India* …'

As Prasanna stood up to prepare some chai, I turned the conversation towards personal territory that I was unlikely to find on YouTube. I drew it back to his youth. *What was young Prasanna like?* Across all my interviews, I found that this clichéd question held the potential for the richest revelations. Prasanna didn't disappoint.

P: When we started bandaya [the rebel literary movement] in Karnataka, all of us were young. Terribly young. I was not even twenty-one. DR [Nagaraj] was there, everybody was so impossibly young. And we had all collected money from the streets, we had hired this hall, a small hall that was falling apart. In Bangalore. And we had invited the greatest revolutionary poet Sri Sri, and we were all sitting there, eyes flashing with enthusiasm, expecting Sri Sri to give us the ultimate truth so that we can go and change the world. And Sri Sri came late, came drunk, and somebody had to actually take him to the stage, and there he just couldn't open his mouth. After a couple of moments, tears started coming into his eyes, and he said 'I am a prostitute!' Because, he had started writing film songs.

But also, I don't want you to connect it in such a simplistic manner. By the seventies, Sri Sri had realised that we were prostituting—we, the revolutionaries. It was the beginning of the end. After that, Hungary collapses, Czechoslovakia collapses, the whole Soviet thing collapses. Around 1989, I was in Delhi directing a play, and at the same time Fritz Bennewitz [German theatre director] was also directing a play in Delhi. Every time he got bored, he would come out and open his heart and we would have long conversations. And especially because we were both very worried about socialism. One day, I saw him looking completely devastated. I asked him what happened? He said Berlin Wall has collapsed, and the entire East Germany has gone West. Even that was not the most poignant statement—he said, I have no country to go back to, I have come out of a country, now I don't have a country to go back to, and that's exactly what happened. The fellow went back and died an unseen, unsung director; they just didn't care for him. You know, according to me, his contribution to Indian theatre is as great as Max Müller's contribution to Indology.

Me: So, a kind of profound disillusionment?

P: Disillusionment of a phenomenal nature. I wouldn't even say disillusionment. Realisation. A realisation of a phenomenal nature.

I realised that we were now entering some uncannily religious territory, and was thrilled to see Prasanna open up candidly. He soon went back to talking about the binary of system/sense that he had brought up in the context of Charaka. Later, I realised that it sounded an awful lot like the hope of harmonising the many divergent binaries that have come up in the course of this chapter.

> Now we have a situation where some of us are saying enough is enough. You can't leave it always to the dumb millions. They have great sense, but they don't have systems and intellectual capacities. You need intellectuals who can understand the sense of the people. Behave like them, but give them a system, like Gandhiji did. What is the greatness of Gandhi? He lived like the poorest man, but he was like a machine, working systematically. Mahadev Desai would be bringing him some letters, he would be talking to journalists, he would be collecting funds, here was a system. You see, systems are a necessary evil. Civilisation is a system. So, we need to deconstruct this horribly complex system—the machine-made world—that we have made into smaller systems, maybe into even smaller machines, I don't know, but it has to be smaller systems. That's all. That's the one ideology, one god, one thought; nothing more, nothing less.

The heart of Gandhi's desiness lay in the fact that he trained his *systemic* eyes on the most essential necessities of ordinary life. He took his political symbolism into the atomistic universals of desi life—a grain of salt, a thread of cotton—and then expanded on them creatively in a way only he could have done. He simplified politics and brought it to the threshold of the village artisan, who had no difficulty in understanding his message. Hearing Prasanna wax eloquent on how Gandhi had filled the Marxism-shaped hole in his adult life, I became a little more convinced that Gandhi might be the most accomplished synthesiser of ideologies that we have seen yet. He held on firmly to the sense of the sacred, and transferred it *tout court* into a philosophy of social activism. He recognised the tragedy of the impetuous Indian youth (having been one himself), and strove to find a meaningful way of harmonising their contemplative and combative parts. He stumbled along the way, of course, but achieved some staggering victories in the process.

Through the symbol of the charkha, art and activism came together in a harmonic chorus that continues to reverberate. Along with it, though, the Gandhian tendency to imbue caste with undying rhetorical meaning survives too.

A few weeks later, I visited a theatre workshop that Prasanna was hosting in Mysore. A small community of actors from across the country had come together in a quaint yoga centre, and as I walked in, everyone had already assembled on the floor in a circle. Sitting in the centre of the circle, Prasanna boomed: *You have to play. Enjoy. Most actors see themselves too seriously. They think they are conquering the world through theatre. In one sense, that might be true. But fundamentally, though, you should treat it as a game. If you don't enjoy the game, you are lost ...*

V

Through one of those serendipitous discoveries that YouTube keeps serving up, I became hooked to a play titled *Kunta Kota Mooka Jaana* (The lame guy is crooked, the dumb guy is wise), live versions of which have been accumulating millions of views online.[40] There exists a genre of professional theatre known as Company Natakas—touring troupes performing at festivals and village fairs for days on end. It was around the 1940s that this genre of secular theatre became really popular. One of its early torchbearers was Gubbi Veeranna's famous troupe, which is also where Rajkumar was first discovered as a talent. A few decades ago, there were more than a hundred such drama companies, but in recent years, only about twenty survive, thanks largely to State subsidies. The Company play *Kunta Kona Mooka Jaana* owes its originality to playwright Jevargi Rajanna, who observed how blind and lame characters pervade rural theatre (and indeed Kannada folk culture at large), and decided to add a mute character to create an entertaining troika. The result is a refreshingly hilarious hotchpotch of one-liners, songs and contemporary urban–rural discourse, largely in North Karnataka dialects of Kannada, involving various scenarios where a blind man and his dissatisfied wife navigate the entry of the 'crooked' brother and his lustful designs. I saw flashes of Kuntirapa in the lame character, but in some other renditions, the trope of the cunning Iago substitute is subsumed under the overarching diversity of the comedy—he can also become an innocent, well-meaning fellow whom the lady genuinely falls for. The comedy's true star is the 'mute' man, who cannot speak cohesively and struggles to convey to the blind man that his wife is having an affair with the lame brother. It is hardly surprising that this veritable comedy of errors has made Jevargi Rajanna a household name in North Karnataka. I felt like I was watching folklore mingling with the postmodern absurdity that has overwhelmed us.

It is perhaps this very realisation (the death of the author, similar to Prasanna's observations) that makes Jevargi Rajanna assess his play in a highly self-critical tenor. Strolling past a board that says 'The rangamandira [theatre hall] is like a temple. Please maintain cleanliness', he says:

> These days, people who have studied up to PUC [pre-university] are coming in to become actors. Back in the day, rangabhoomi theatre was gatti. There was quality. They gave emphasis on tragedy, and comedy was like a side dish. Now, comedy is the primary dish, whereas plot and story have transformed into pickle. Nowadays, the audience is also very smart. They can already say what is going to happen—they are well-informed, they are very intelligent. So, comedy has become gatti, tragedy has become tollu. Earlier, the director would participate deeply in the process. He would explain the literary sensibility, explain the rationale behind words, really work very closely with actors. Now, that is not there.

He argues that professional theatre thrives in Marathi and Bengali because there are many drama halls explicitly dedicated to theatre in these languages, and these venues are made available for the many months of continuous performance that are required for commercial success. In Karnataka, only two dedicated halls for professional theatre existed—in Bijapur and Bangalore—and the former was demolished recently. He calls for more theatres to be built, which would encourage the formation of more troupes.

The performers of these plays are seasoned theatre talents with sensational acting chops. The blind man's character is played by exquisite singers trained under the aegis of the famous Veereshwara Punyashrama in Gadag, which has been training blind, disabled and orphaned children in Hindustani music and other performing arts for almost a century now. The Punyashrama's endeavours were pioneered by the musician, scholar and Padma Bhushan awardee Puttaraj Gawai, and the secular underpinnings of his vision make it a truly exceptional (if oxymoronic) religious institution.

Interestingly, an orphanage becomes a keystone of the final sections of Kambar's *Shivana Dangura*, where Kuntirapa's orphaned daughter (he has left his family and politics has consumed his life) grows up with Shaari, while Chenbasava spends six years in jail. The novel ends on an all-is-well note: Chenbasava and Shaari bring up Kuntirapa's daughter as their own and move back to their village after he is released from prison. The effect is to transcend caste, creed and indeed genetics by presenting a full rebirth made possible through the orphanage's divine capabilities.

The pontiff of Shree Veereshwara Punyashrama, Gadag is revered across the state, not least by Jevargi Rajanna, who says that he is 'the guru who taught the gift of giving to hands that knew only begging'. It reminded me of M.M. Kalburgi's argument that a stream of Veerashaiva philosophy had successfully transferred the idea of divinity from a personified deity into the concept of society itself, thereby making social welfare an act of pure religious devotion. It demonstrates the (rare) power of religion to overcome petty boundaries and assume universal paradigms—it is the same power that Nagaraj and Punekar saw as the undeniable potential of subaltern spiritual movements.

The quest for a guru is something Indian society instils in us instinctively. Finding the right teacher, the inspiring role model, the appropriate guiding philosophy is a personal journey everyone is expected to undertake in their own way. Blind reverence can prove disastrous, as portrayed in Kailasam's rendition of Ekalavya, but the quest can also be enlightened, as all the benefactors of the Gadag school will undoubtedly affirm. To strive for a worldview that is built on harmonious judgement and intellectual humility—that seems to be the perennial challenge.

TWO

Of Attics and Romantics
Literature and Socialism along the Western Ghats

Don't fall for the illusion of communal temper,
Work with the intellect, for the world's welfare
Enough of this sect, that sect, some old sect
Join the cause of humanism
Oh brothers! Come over
to the universal path.

—Kuvempu,
from a song titled 'Emerge out of temples,
churches, mosques'

I

Travelling eastwards from the coastal Canara region, we reach the dense rainforests of the Western Ghats, and the gorgeous slopes of the region known as the Malnad (male + nadu equals rainy land). Cuddled away in the heart of this sublime landscape is Kuppalli, a speck of a village where a giant took his first steps. It was here that Kuvempu, or Kuppalli Venkatappa Puttappa, arguably the most revered writer of the Kannada language, was born in 1904.

If you get a chance to visit Kuppalli, you can waltz through the refurbished homestead where Kuvempu grew up. It is a sprawling establishment, marked by woodworked columns and multiple slants of Mangalore-tile roofs, and is usually crawling with tourists. It is, in equal parts, a museum and a pilgrimage site. Buy a ticket for ten rupees, and you can walk around inspecting all the various artefacts that Kuvempu had breathed around. In a shed outside the main house is a collection of century-old farm implements, including a vintage bullock cart—a nod to the agricultural legacy of the vokkaliga community into which Kuvempu was born. Inside the mansion, treading on cool red-oxide floors, you walk past a traditional stone-floored courtyard that must have witnessed many a downpour, and arrive at a steep staircase leading up to the attic. This, one might say, is the sanctum sanctorum; it is where Kuvempu's entire body of collected works sits proudly, couched in glass cases. It is a significant collection—the man was prolific beyond belief. He composed more than twenty collections of poems, two novels, many plays, one doorstopper of an autobiography, literary criticism, storybooks for children, biographies of Swami Vivekananda and Ramakrishna Paramahamsa, as well as two epic kavyas (epic poems), one of which took him nearly a decade to complete.

There is a curious significance to the fact that Kuvempu's literary legacy has been preserved in the attic, of all places. Consider the following conversation in his 1936 novel *Kanooru Heggadathi* (translated into English as *The House of Kanooru*) that transpires between Chandrayya Gowda (father of protagonist Hoovayya) and the joisa (the brahmin priest):

> 'And that Hoovayya! His head is full of things like Bhagavadgeetha and the Upanishads. He won't even bother about what the workers do around the house. He goes up to the attic and spends all his time reading books!'
>
> 'Why should he bother about such things when there's someone else to toil and keep him going? Listen, give him his share of the property and send him away. Everything will sort itself out then. How can these Shudra children hope to understand things like the Bhagavadgeetha and the Upanishads? Even we find them difficult to understand …'

> The Gowda laughed. '*Come on, I bet you understand them.*' [emphasis mine]
>
> 'It's not that easy, Chandrayya. You don't know how great scholars have struggled to interpret them. There has been no single interpretation they have agreed on … How can these Shudra children hope to make sense of them? Getting to read them will only lead to their ruination. That's all!'
>
> (translated by Ramachandra Sharma and Padma Ramachandra Sharma)

The young man Hoovayya, inspired by Kuvempu's own boyhood and youth, symbolises modernity in the novel. Touched by English education, he has rejected superstitions and religious orthodoxy in favour of a rational and spiritual (as opposed to ritual) outlook. However, being born in a shudra household excluded from the corridors of intellectual pursuits, Hoovayya retreats to the attic in his quest for mental stimulation. The attic becomes a metaphor for a private space away from the prying eyes of traditional restrictions, where solitary reflection and imagination can take flight. I encountered another dimension of this secluded space while listening to the Kannada writer Prema Bhat speak of her first writing attempts when she was a married teenager, sometime in the 1960s.[1] Having moved to Coorg after marriage, she had turned to writing as a way of confronting the loneliness of a large home and a husband absent most of the day. 'I was a little scared of telling him that I was interested in writing, because I did not know how he would respond.' She came from an orthodox, patriarchal family in Udupi. It would turn out, however, that her husband, who had grown up in Mysore and was well entrenched within its literary circles (Kuvempu's cohort), was delighted no end. 'I brought out all the little pages I'd stuffed away in the attic and showed him. I got so much encouragement from him! Since then, I have never stopped writing ever in my life. It became like a tapas for me.'

The word 'tapas' (conventionally translated as 'penance') carries more resonance than apparent. The first books that Kuvempu ever saw were palm-leaf manuscripts hidden away in his grandfather's trunks, and excavated only during festivals and auspicious dates. These were handwritten manuscripts of the Ramayana, Jaimini Bharata, Sahyadri Kanda and so on, painstakingly copied out by some scribe who would have stayed at their house for months on end and pocketed a healthy sum. Yet, they remained objects of mere reverence, and Kuvempu writes in his autobiography *Nenapina Doniyalli*: 'I cannot remember a single instance when grandfather spoke to us about them, told us stories from them or sang from them melodiously.' On rare occasions, an esteemed visitor would sing episodes from the Ramayana, stoking Kuvempu's curiosity. He remembers thinking to himself that should he ever learn to read and write, he would dive into these books and discover those treasures all by himself.

Kuvempu reminisces with gratitude that it was the colonial apparatus which allowed modern education to reach him: 'It is astonishing to think that boys from some corner of Malnad's forest land travelled all the way to Mysore to study. However, it is even more astonishing to think that this impetus and encouragement was provided by Christian missionaries. Till then, the teachers who would come to the landlords' schools were all Kannadigas. Their education levels were so-so. Once they taught the alphabet and basic writing skills, their job was done. Was Kannada enough though? How could we survive without learning English—the language of our overlords?'

In his book *The Beautiful Tree*, the Gandhian historian Dharampal had marshalled colonial administrative records to demonstrate the prevalence of indigenous schooling systems in eighteenth-century India prior to the arrival of the English schools. Riding on Gandhi's refusal to accept a pedagogical vacuum before that arrival, Dharampal excavated an interesting body of colonial missives. He quotes the administrator Thomas Munro as having said that 'there was a school in every village' where traditional education took place. The administrators had also collected data regarding the caste of enrolled students: 'In the largely Kannada-speaking Bellary, the proportion of the twice-born (the Brahmins and the Vysees) went up to 33%, while the Soodras, and the other castes still accounted for some 63%.' We do not know much about how these schools actually functioned, except that this education was dictated by caste, and that one prepared in them for a predetermined social role. In any case, once the British established their missionary schools in the nineteenth century, these indigenous systems were either on the decline or stopped abruptly.

Kuvempu writes that it was the missionaries who assured the villagers that they would release shudras from the intellectual hold of brahmins, help them educate themselves, and send their young boys to Mysore to pursue schooling. He nostalgically remembers a teacher named Moses who had been dispatched to Kuppalli to teach English and preach the gospel. In his household, religious discourse had been limited to rituals; nothing resembling deep conversation around it had ever taken place. Kuvempu grew up in a religious environment which he felt harked back to the Jainism that his family had left behind at some point in history. Thus, Saturday was a pious occasion, and no meat was consumed on that day, a ritual homage to the non-violence of Jainism. When meat was cooked, it was not in the main kitchen of the household, but in a stove located in the backyard. It was practices and observances such as these that made up the bulk of their religious life. Therefore, Moses became the man who first opened up the confines of Kuvempu's mind to religious thought proper. Listening to him preach the gospel of the apostles, Kuvempu felt as if he was getting exposed to something really profound. 'If our forefathers had cared more about the insides of our heads, rather than the kind of hairstyle we should sport on top, we would have been elsewhere altogether,' he muses.

These were years when the non-brahmin movement was beginning to take root in Karnataka. Around the fin de siècle, in the erstwhile state of Mysore, brahmins had found themselves in the most coveted and enviable posts of the administrative system, and a movement soon emerged that sought to unseat them. The battle was characterised by a migration from the sterile countryside towards the corridors of power in the slowly burgeoning cityscape at the onset of the twentieth century. Lingayats, vokkaligas and other castes were 'much slower to leave the land to enter the race for urban advancement', and even when they did, 'they found the brahmin dominance in the urban contest very exasperating'.[2] Lingayats and vokkaligas, who had earlier seen brahmins as people of modest means who deferred to their secular authority in villages, were now stunned by the reversal of roles in cities. The two communities were, in effect, corralled into being by the British censuses. Anybody who bore a personal 'linga' to worship Shiva was deemed a lingayat, and by the 1900s, vokkaliga had 'become a catch-all census grouping which included saltmakers, cowherds, dyers, extractors of iron, Tamil Vellalas, and a Telugu group which followed a "vagrant and wandering life"'. The word vokkaliga essentially means a tiller of the soil, and it has also held on to that sense. In 1961, 'a Vokkaliga association publication asserted that since the ancestors of most Europeans were tillers of the soil, both Khrushchev and Kennedy could be included within the Vokkaliga ranks'.

Both communities grew and prospered during the early twentieth century. Associations were established across the state, and both lingayats and vokkaligas organised themselves to 'plead in the state-level sphere for special provisions for their advancement'. Scholarships were granted and hostels set up for promising students, and these students would go on to dominate politics in the state for decades to come. The organisation of Scheduled Castes and Tribes, however, was much slower to come, though initial steps were already shaping up. Thanks to the policies of Nalwadi Krishnaraja Wodeyar, a distinctly progressive king, hundreds of schools dedicated to the primary education of panchamas (as dalits were then called) had also emerged in Karnataka by the end of the 1920s.[3] These were ably spearheaded by educationists and social reformers like Gopalaswamy Iyer (in Old Mysore) and Kudmul Ranga Rao (in Mangalore), who braved societal scorn to put their ideals into action. Though the percentage of students passing SSLC exams was not great, the ones who did would have grasped English, and could therefore sit for the government service exams—the grandest possible aspiration in those days.

Kuvempu's first attempts at writing were, unsurprisingly, in English. He unapologetically fills his memoirs with page after page of romantic poetry written in English. He might very well have been living in late eighteenth-century England, and putting Wordsworth to shame in the quantity of saccharine verse produced. Any random dip into the book finds some ecstatic description of the natural world.

Life scatters here its richest heaven,
And pleasure floats by madness driven!
And here I linger to admire
This heavenly scene that doth inspire
A heart that least responds to beauty.
(on the Western Ghats)

Sweet poet of the forest,
So cheerful and bright,
Towards heaven thou soarest
Not with half such delight
As thou dost chant thy lays upon bowers nobly delight.
(on the bulbul)

It was thanks to the exhortations of his well-meaning mentor, the Irish-Indian writer James Cousins, that Kuvempu would start writing in modern Kannada, and go on to become its first notable non-brahmin practitioner. Kuvempu's high school teacher had urged the young man to meet Cousins when he was visiting Mysore University in 1924. Cousins's wife, Margaret, would go on to mentor and inspire another big name from Karnataka—the freedom fighter, socialist politician and social reformer, Kamaladevi Chattopadhyay, the first Indian woman to contest an election. Influential enough to convince Gandhi to allow women into public satyagraha, she was also one of the first labour organisers of Mangalore, that port city perennially bustling with industry and commerce. The Cousins certainly had a knack for spotting and nurturing Indian talent.

In 1929, Kuvempu graduated with a degree in Kannada from Maharaja's College in Mysore, and later returned there to serve as principal. In 1956, he would go on to become vice chancellor of Mysore University, where he set up the Institute of Kannada Studies. He combined his love and passion for Kannada with a vision of social equality and communal harmony. Kuvempu actively dissociated himself from organised religion, and often emphasised that he'd stopped going to temples. Instead, he underscored the need to embrace a personalised god, abhorring the monstrosities of fanaticism and religion-mongering in concert with twelfth-century veerashaiva poets like Basavanna and Allama Prabhu. He spoke widely of the need to abolish untouchability, advocated inter-caste marriages and kickstarted a tradition of simple marriages that shunned opulent display.

The anti-caste movement in Karnataka owes an indelible debt to Kuvempu, who rallied for it throughout his life. In his famous speech 'Aatmashreegaagi Nirankushamatigalaagi' (For your own good, let your mind become fetterless), he urged the youth of the country to release themselves from the bonds of sectarian beliefs, and work towards making rural Karnataka more educated, egalitarian and enlightened. Some dalit activists I spoke to remember being filled with an invigorating spirit while listening to Kuvempu. Some had imagined him to be such a mythical figure that when they actually saw Kuvempu in the flesh, delivering speeches in the 1970s, they were astonished to find that this was a living, breathing man and not some long gone legend.

Kuvempu admonished youth for being too enamoured of orthodox institutions, urging them to find solace in the divine qualities of nature, culture and their own selves. He saw the dire need for the birth of a new literature in Kannada that could serve as brain fodder for the emerging generation clamouring for spiritual and moral guidance. At the same time, he would constantly bring up quotations from the Gita and other Sanskrit texts, trying to find a critique from within the very traditions he was attempting to scrutinise—a Gandhian impulse. This led to some dalit scholars of the 1970s (such as Devaiah Harave) to question Kuvempu's acceptance of the supernatural paradigm that characterises these texts—after all, the caste system had emerged out of the imposition of unchanging essences onto a society deemed to be 'naturally' and divinely hierarchical.

As one keeps digging into his memoirs, one is struck by what appears to be a childlike innocence. One must be a little patient to approach Kuvempu on his own terms. In one instance, he starts off a diary entry saying he has been reading Will Durant's *The Lessons of History*, and that this has got him thinking about whether history is the creation of great individuals or merely great forces. Nothing more on the subject is forthcoming as, in the rest of the entry, Kuvempu gets distracted by a moving ant on the book, attempts to kill it by folding the book, and is struck when it survives the attack, calling the whole event an important experience for him.

I realised the importance of this innocence, of the poetic inspiration it births, when I encountered a poem by N.K. Hanumantayya, which put into verse the moral epiphany that Kuvempu had experienced. The feeling was reinforced as videos of Israeli crosshairs training their aim on massing Palestinian refugees began showing up on my timeline, month after month:

On this ant
I put
my hefty foot
and pulled it back
after a while.

The ant is moving again.

Oh, pin-sized being,
I salute your spine
that bears
my weight.

(*Translated by Kamlakar Bhat*)

It is a tendency that is visible across Kuvempu's autobiography. On another occasion, for instance, he notes that he has been reading Trotsky's *History of the Russian Revolution*, and devotes one sentence to its description, adding that it is inspiring and that all politically inclined individuals should read it. In the very next sentence, he changes the subject, becomes overjoyed that a press in Calcutta is all set to publish his book on Ramakrishna Paramahamsa, and ends the entry with the exclamatory *Jai Gurudeva*! Like Will Durant himself, it seems like Kuvempu too subscribed to the view that 'the only real revolution is in the enlightenment of the mind and the improvement of character, the only emancipation is individual, and the only revolutionaries are philosophers and saints'.

He certainly appears to have viewed the cultural sphere as a whole in itself, divorced from the political order, which does not seem to occupy his mind much. In a collection of essays about his father,[4] the writer and polymath Poornachandra Tejaswi recollects a meeting between Ram Manohar Lohia and Kuvempu—a glimpse of Kuvempu's brief brush with socialist thought. Sometime in the early sixties, Lohia had come to visit Kuvempu to try and convince him to lead their Angrezi Hatao Sammelan, which sought to replace English with indigenous languages. Kuvempu declined for logistical reasons, but approvingly told them, 'What you are trying to say in your political discourse is precisely what I am saying within the world of letters as well.' In 1967, the staunch socialist and Lohiaite, J.H. Patel, was elected to the Lok Sabha, and created history by becoming the first person to table his debates in Kannada. Listening to this over the radio, Kuvempu was overcome with elation over his beloved mother tongue finally echoing in Delhi. He was immediately convinced that Patel was a true hero, and that the socialists were to be commended for their initiative. For the rest of his life, he never entertained any critique of J.H. Patel—how could anybody dream of speaking ill of the man who took Kannada to the Parliament, he would argue.

Kuvempu's generation ushered in the classical Navodaya movement—literally meaning 'new dawn', it was the beginning of modern Kannada renaissance—and this was characterised by highly ornate prose and lyrical romanticism. The generations that followed would passionately challenge these modes. During the 1940s, the Pragatisheela (progressives) group drew inspiration from similar movements in Hindi and Urdu literature up north, and resolved to bring a stronger social sensibility to literature. This was followed by the Navya movement which proceeded to investigate the completely neglected subjective self, and finally, the dalit-bandaya movement of the late seventies rejuvenated the socially directed moral conscience of the progressives, and began reclaiming a sense of community from the highly individualised forays that elite Kannada literature had embarked upon. None of these turns was as seamless as this categorisation implies. They were all marked by profound journeys of self-discovery within writers themselves, who tossed and turned over everything they wrote, charting new paths even while questioning them, at once cradling the past and seeding the future. They flew on the winds of political change billowing around the world, and can only be understood in relation to each other, playing out like a thoroughly engrossing four-act play across the wide stage of twentieth-century Kannada literature.

Simultaneously, one must read Kuvempu's preoccupation with classical romanticism and linguistic dexterity with an eye on the history of Karnataka as a region built in the thrall of its mother tongue. At the present moment, when Kannada in the public sphere seems to be fading into the background, one becomes even more conscious of the significance of what Kuvempu and his contemporaries found themselves tasked with in the years after the First World War: creating a whole new world of writing. The first throes of renascent Kannada stemmed from the constructive efforts of the celebrated Geleyara Gumpu (Group of Friends) founded by the poet D.R. Bendre in the 1920s. This was an informal association of numerous like-minded men, almost like a Socratic circle of peers who were attempting to commence a whole new way of intellectual discourse. The Gumpians came from all walks of life, and from diverse corners of the state, and soon expanded out of the small circle of close friends. Similar circles of activity formed elsewhere in the state. They set into motion the revival of Kannada folk songs and ballads, and started regional utsavas (festivals, like Mahanavami Utsava and Pampotsava), all activities that would begin assembling the jigsaw puzzle of Karnataka into coherent feelings and images.

Karnatak College in Dharwad seems to have been the lodestar of literary inspiration during these times, as it continued to be until the second half of the century, when the playwright Girish Karnad would also find his voice in its hallowed premises.[5] The blossoming of the Navodaya literary movement would have been impossible without the institutions that facilitated the Gumpians—besides Karnatak College, these would be, most notably, the Vidyavardhaka Sangha in Dharwad, the Kannada Sahitya Parishat (established by M. Visvesvarayya in Bangalore) and the Yuvaraja's and Maharaja's colleges in Mysore. A literary reading public was created, and Kannada became pedagogically entrenched, thanks to the efforts of these institutions. Emerging from these precincts, poets like Bendre and Kuvempu conjured up the verses that would serve as the anthems of regional pride to glue together an entire state. No mean feat. Often, their verses would travel orally before they were even published. Large audiences would gather to listen to them recite for hours on end, and the most impressive of these lines would become etched in their minds.[6] This is poetry serving its most primal and original motive: of creating, by what philosophers call 'speech acts', an entire community bound together by linguistic bonhomie.

Kuvempu's most revered work is his epic kavya *Sri Ramayana Darshanam*. Running into 877 pages in print, it took him almost nine years of labour to finish the book, and earned Kannada its first Sahitya Akademi award in 1955. It is essentially a retelling of the Ramayana, but deviates from Valmiki's original in some respects. When Sita enters the fire to prove her fidelity after the war is over, Rama also joins her in the flames, and the two come out together, holding hands. Kuvempu also nuances the relationship between Rama and Ravana, who become complementary images of the same powerful force, not starkly antithetic entities. The character of Urmila, Lakshmana's wife who waits for him to return from the exile of fourteen years, is also conceived with great compassion as an eternal symbol of suffering womanhood—recognition that is denied to her in most other versions of the Ramayana.[7] Kuvempu's Ramayana was seen less as a literary work and more as a sacred artefact; in the 1960s, it was even paraded on elephants as a symbol of Kannada divinity. To this day, Kannadigas fervently celebrate and remember Kuvempu, but the secular and egalitarian values he always championed and stood by seem to have dissolved into the backdrop.

During the seventies, when it was becoming clear that dalits were staging a momentous uprising, Kuvempu embraced the task of guiding its path, trying to supply it with a non-violent, self-questioning tone. His speeches were always tailor-made for the audience. In 1974, Kuvempu delivered a speech at a conclave of dalit writers, where he made the following incendiary pronouncement, full with the raw vim appropriate to that historical occasion:

> If you try to attack a tiger with a few stones, it will come and gobble you up after one stone hits its head. To quell the tiger, you must pull back the string of your arrow, and carefully take aim. As you aim at its head, you must realise that it must be felled in one blow. You mustn't leave it with a mere wound. The purohitashahi [priestly domination] tiger is no different. You can't try and combat it with a few stones in your pocket. We must prepare special bullets to defeat it. Let us suppose these bullets are metaphorical. We must use verbal bullets. But in this strange hunt, the first bullet must strike not the tiger, but your own mind! Mind ... Mind ... Mind, first the mind must be cleansed. Personally speaking, I have completely become clear of their influence. I have no truck with them, do you understand? It has been more than fifty years since I ever went to a temple to perform a pooja. I entertain no priests, purohits, or panchaangas ... First, you must cleanse your own mind of its blemishes. This is the sense in which I spoke about—the first bullet in this strange battle must hit your own head.[8]

The style of this metaphoric exercise—of erecting paradoxical metaphors and quickly demolishing them—is highly reminiscent of the twelfth-century philosopher Allama Prabhu, who remains an extraordinary influence on Kannada culture to this day.

Kuvempu's brush with socialist ideals might have been restricted to endeavours such as these, but there was another man from Malnad, another vokkaliga, who would go on to become the face of socialist politics in Karnataka. Like so many politicians belonging to his generation, he was an exceptionally well-read man, who spoke in rich, luminous Kannada, spouting quotations and browbeating philistines. He was arguably the most idealistic politician Karnataka has ever produced, a man famed for his fiery speeches and confrontational energy—Gopala Gowda Shantaveri.

Once, in the early fifties, chief minister Kengal Hanumanthaiah had castigated farmers for not repaying loans by quoting a vachana written by Sarvajna—the sixteenth-century Kannada poet famous for his pithy three-line poems—that went like this:

> Loan incoming—sweet as milk-rice,
> But when creditor arrives,
> A gut-wrenching breakdown, in a trice (says Sarvajna)

As befitting an eminent man of letters, pat had come the repartee from Gopala Gowda Shantaveri, who was then a legislator in the assembly:

> Of what use is a ladder, once the attic is reached.
> Of what concern are people, once the throne is mounted.
> I am the state and you, the people
> Pay up or proceed to the lock-up
> Says the Chief Minister of Mysore.[9]

The ladder and the attic are interesting motifs, which brings to mind a traumatic experience that Gopala Gowda had experienced in 1951, in the aftermath of what is known as the Kagodu Satyagraha, the first peasant uprising in post-1947 Karnataka. Gopala Gowda was one of the leaders spearheading this rebellion. After the police cracked down on the protestors, he avoided arrest and travelled incognito through villages in the Malnad. He lodged as a guest in their homes, spreading awareness on their rights as the tillers of the land, urging them to join the movement. In one such home, he was betrayed. His hosts locked him up and informed the police. In an act of desperation, Gopala Gowda climbed up a ladder and hid in the attic, but when the police arrived, he revealed himself after realising the futility of his act. Covered in soot and dust, he made an inglorious exit from the house, bound by the police, as throngs of people stood watching outside.

The terror of this sense of entrapment would keep returning to him in the years to come.

II

Kagodu. A backward dot on the map, somewhere in the middle of Shimoga district. All Kagodu could boast of when India became independent was one school where the zenith was the fifth standard, one primary health centre where medicines were usually in short supply and one shop where some basic supplies could be bought. There was only one landlord in the village, Guruve Gowda, simply called Kagodu Gowda, and his lands were farmed by sharecroppers who lived under his supreme scrutiny. Their purpose was to toil in the fields and deliver geni (tax) to the landlord. They also laboured away at the gowda's household performing all manner of tasks from caring for cattle to washing clothes. In addition, they would have to perform 'free' labour from time to time. It was exploitation fine-tuned over centuries of practice. The exploited believed they would face divine punishment if they ever transgressed their boundaries. For all practical purposes, the gowda was their lord: it was he who provided them with food and shelter, and it was he who was the final arbiter on all disputes in the village.

Around this time, there lived in Kagodu a man named Kanase Jatya, who was tenanted to the gowda, and belonged to the traditionally lower-caste community of deevas. He was no ordinary deeva, however, but a rebel through and through. His community was obligated to sit on the ground at public events like Yakshagana performances or plays, while the gowda, along with members of other upper castes, coolly took the chairs. But Kanase Jatya was going to have none of this. Somehow, he got a wooden chair made for himself, and would carry it proudly to all these occasions, stunning the crowd.

In the summer of 1951, even as the Nehru administration was moving the controversial First Amendment to the Constitution,[10] a leading cause of which was the government's desire to abolish the zamindari system, the deevas rose up in rebellion against the gowda in Kagodu. Kanase Jatya played an active part in this, spending time in jail as well. It was ostensibly an uprising over the issue of a 'kolaga', a container used to measure rice and other produce grown by farmers. The thrifty landlord would unapologetically use a small kolaga to loan grains to the tenants, but deploy a much larger one when it came to loan repayment. In the aftermath of the protest, when many former sharecroppers decided to rejoin the gowda's services for lack of choice, Kanase Jatya remained aloof. He decided that he would never have anything to do with the gowda, and lived the rest of his life surviving on intermittent coolie labour, preferring to be master of his tiny domain rather than occupying space in a cage. The legend of Kanase Jatya would be remembered by deevas across the region well after his death in the seventies. They marvelled at his singular courage and resilience. Though the agitation itself was unsuccessful, it was a life-changing event for some like Jatya, and signalled the growth of political consciousness amongst the deeva community.[11]

As in the rest of the country, for the greater part of the twentieth century, tenanted croppers in Kagodu lived at the mercy of the landlord—all their necessities would have to be sought from him as gracious gifts since it was a no-cash economy. And then there were the dalit families, who did not even have land to till, and worked as coolies and bonded labourers for the most part. Until the land reforms of the seventies, everyone was simply paid in sacks of rice, or bhatta. If you have lived in Karnataka, you might have heard auto-drivers or labourers ask for their bata. This has nothing to do

with the ubiquitous footwear brand, but is rather a derivative of bhatta, a former norm of basic sustenance. For any event in life, be it a wedding or thread ceremony or even death, the landlord had to be approached for his kind handout.

The satyagraha at Kagodu was led by another extraordinary deeva named Ganapathiyappa, a school teacher who represented an oasis of learning and dignity in an otherwise deprived landscape. To be called Ganapathi itself was an aberration in the community, where men usually went by names like Kariya, Biliya, Neela, Timma and other such tame names. And like his elephant-headed namesake, Ganapathiyappa was a man of letters, who would read the newspapers every day and speak eloquently in rich Kannada. He had taken part in the Quit India movement and courted arrest, and had since kept in touch with Congress leaders. The deevas looked up to this man who would be welcomed and seated with respect even at the headman's house.

Some pan-Indian figures, including Kamaladevi Chattopadhyay, had set up a farmers' organisation in Malnad around 1947, but it was effectively composed of the landed elite. Expectedly, no real reforms were forthcoming from its quarters. Even during Congress debates of the 1930s, Kamaladevi had tried to press for radical land reforms that abolished agricultural rent, but conservative voices had moderated any such amendment.[12] Soon, the Socialist Party separated from the Congress, establishing itself as a strong critic of the parent party. Ganapathiyappa began associating with the socialists, including Gopala Gowda, and plans to foment an uprising against the skewed land ownership began to shape up. The fact that the core members of the organisation were deevas meant that their demands came from lived knowledge. And yet, even this organisation did not care to include castes who were further below in the pecking order. Thus, when the Kagodu rebellion happened, dalit workers remained aloof and even supported the gowda, allowing themselves to be used as his henchmen to put down the uprising.[13] They would later also testify in court in favour of the gowda.

The deevas had asked the gowda to stop using the larger kolaga for loan repayment, but he flat-out refused. This decision had not just been his own—it was a collective one, where all the landlords of the taluk had decided to band together and put their tenants in their place. The gowda ordered the tenants to stop tilling their lands and leave, knowing all too well that they had no place to go. Around March–April 1951, when the tenants started to till their land, which had to be done before the monsoon arrived, the gowda dispatched his henchmen to beat them up, and filed a criminal trespass case against them. Thus began the satyagraha—the farmers would enter their lands with ploughs and carts to till the land, and the police would arrest them en masse along with everything they were carrying. At one point thus, there lay a whole bunch of ploughshares in the local magistrate court. This procedure became so routine that the farmers resorted to symbolically carrying large coconut tree fronds, so that at least their ploughs would be safe at home. This was a centuries-old predicament in a new avatar. Back in the 1680s, peasants protesting against Chikka Devaraja Wodeyar's oppressive taxation are said to have hung up their ploughshares in front of their homes, refusing to till their land.

The upheaval in Kagodu formed a vivid turning point in the life of the writer U.R. Ananthamurthy. His father owned a printing press in Thirthahalli (just fifteen kilometres away from Kuppalli), the de facto den of the newly formed Socialist Party. All of the party's pamphlets and booklets were printed at Maruti Press, which was also where Ananthamurthy befriended Gopala Gowda Shantaveri, whom he would look up to throughout his life. He even wrote the novel *Avasthe* after Gopala Gowda's death in the seventies as a fictionalised tribute to his political guru. On the cusp of adulthood and maturity during the Kagodu years, Ananthamurthy contributed his own writings to the socialist cause, and actively witnessed the rebellion that was being planned right in his backyard. In fact, it was the influence of Ram Manohar Lohia that would make him choose to write exclusively in Kannada.

What did it mean to call oneself a socialist in Gopala Gowda's company? Firstly, it meant a vehement opposition to the pretensions of socialism within the Congress as well as the exhortations for radical atheism coming from the extreme Left. Those like Ananthamurthy and his close friend S. Venkatram (who would go on to become a respected trade union leader in Bangalore) harboured a deep interest in religious thought, and never subscribed to the radical cultural rejections championed by those like Periyar and M.N. Roy. Ananthamurthy was fond of saying that they were seekers who searched for god with passion and only reluctantly emerged with empty hands. Broadly, Lohiaite socialism also meant a more acute realisation that caste was a more appropriate choice of differentiation in rural India than 'class', and it was only by understanding the unique cultural nuances of a regional landscape that one could hope to uplift its people. While the communists chose to organise labourers in cities, Gopala Gowda and his followers had decided to work in villages to uproot feudal oppression. It is testament to the success of Lohia's message of decentralisation that I was able to find numerous translations of Lohia's works in Kannada, where he has thrived, and almost none at all in English.

There was more than a touch of Gandhian idealism tied up with Indian socialism, and it only grew during the 1950s, after Jayaprakash Narayan jumped headfirst into the Sarvodaya Movement. Both the radical Left and the Gandhian socialists came together in their disenchantment with the rigours and duress of democratic politics. The former advocated peasant uprisings, rapid social change and immediate dismantling of feudal structures. The Gandhians—like Vinoba Bhave and J.P. Narayan—decided to appeal to the conscience of the landlords, to plead like Gandhi had pleaded with the Hindus to shed untouchability of their own free will. They implored the landlords to willingly part with their lands and share it with their fellow citizens. This call for moral soul-searching, an attempt at pulling at heartstrings, went on to achieve very little. Which is why those like U.R. Ananthamurthy and Gopala Gowda subscribed to Lohia's hard-nosed brand of democratic socialism. Lohia refused to buy into the Gandhian romance of attempting to spiritually reason with Indian society, and had concluded that 'the greed and desire for power in Indians was unrivalled in the world'. For him, casteism and patriarchy were the two principal problems that needed to be tackled head-on, with a pragmatic grasp of social realities.

In a nostalgic essay recalling those times, Ananthamurthy remembered S. Venkatram as once observing: 'Indian communists are really social democrats, but they see themselves as revolutionaries. Lohia-ites are really anarchists, but they see themselves as social democrats. If only they had behaved with better knowledge of who they were, our politics could have gained much clarity.' The anti-statism of traditional anarchism, which advocates the direct democracy of grassroots action—the belief that society can fundamentally shape itself without the patronising hand of the State—did travel down from Gandhi to Lohia to his followers in some measure. It might have lost its way in the passive activism of Bhave and the misplaced extremism of JP's Total Revolution which preceded the Emergency, but it survived in other avatars.

In Karnataka, the powerful, non-violent activism of the farmers' movement would come to be the most prominent recipient of the anarchist torch.

At Kagodu, the socialists were instrumental to the success of the agitation, but their party did not possess the resources or manpower to spread the movement to other regions, or even force the government to seriously consider its demands. Lohia arrived in Kagodu in mid-June, 1951 and led the protesting marchers for a day, at the end of which he was arrested at Sagara railway station and packed off to Bangalore's Central Jail. The locals of Kagodu, meanwhile, faced increased police oppression and brutality that night. Even Jayaprakash Narayan visited Sagara jail later in September that year, and expressed solidarity with the imprisoned protesters.

A dispassionate assessment would conclude that the socialists themselves were ideologically unclear about the demands to be made. They were unable to map out a blueprint to dismantle feudal oppression, and though they cried the slogan 'land to the tiller', possibly for the first time ever in the Kannada language, they made no serious efforts to bring about a change in land ownership. They did not even address the prevalent issue of bonded labour, completely excluding the most backward sections from their discourse. G. Rajshekar, author of *Kagodu Satyagraha*, concludes that, of all the socialists in the party, only Gopala Gowda seems to have recognised the real changes that needed to be brought about. He would go on to raise all these concerns in the assembly in the years to come.

There were voices within the Congress sympathetic to land reforms, though they were too few and far between. Kadidal Manjappa, who was briefly chief minister of the then Mysore state in the late fifties, was one such voice. He tried to reform the Congress from within, and even wrote a semi-autobiographical novel in 1964, titled *Panjaravalliya Panju* (The Martyr of Panjaravalli), that caused a sensation within the political circles of Old Mysore. The village of Panjaravaralli (which gets its name from a local bhootha, or folk deity, Panjurli) is shown to be a hotbed of superstitions and class domination. Caught between the terror of evil spirits and the fear of the ruling elite, the lives of the villagers are consumed by sorrow and deprivation. The novel also carried a scathing critique of the internal problems plaguing the Congress—gerrymandering elections, corruption and a lack of sympathy for the lives of the downtrodden. It would take the strongarm leadership of Devaraj Urs during the Emergency to finally muscle through land reforms that properly unsettled the feudal order.

Even after the Kagodu satyagraha, no efforts were made by either the Congress or the Socialists to educate the oppressed classes in rural Karnataka or to try and build a base. For all the respect that the deevas felt when Lohia led their protests for a day, they would remain intellectually ignorant of what he really stood for and the ideas he espoused. What emerged from the famous agitation at Kagodu, if anything, then? Disappointment, for the most part. A majority of the farmers re-entered the service of the landlord, who decided to further fortify his controls, and became more stringent in money matters. The deeva community, however, became politically aware of their need to organise themselves. Kagodu Thimmappa, a future legislator, credits the event with creating space for alternative leadership from the backward classes to emerge. A symbolic struggle had planted the seeds of revolution in the minds of the villagers, apprising them of the rights due to them. Just as importantly, it is from the ashes of the Kagodu Satyagraha that Gopala Gowda Shantaveri would emerge onto the political scene in the state, winning the assembly elections from Sagara for the Socialist Party in 1952, riding on the deeva vote bank.

Kagodu went on to inspire more land struggles in Karnataka, although none of them succeeded in truly bequeathing land to the landless tiller, and only managed to augment the land-holding middle class. In 1957, for instance, the socialists in Dharwad district carried out a silent, underreported land struggle in the village of Hebballi.[14] It improved on Kagodu in the sense that dalits were also involved in the struggle. A Gandhian and former freedom fighter named Neelagangayya Pujar (in today's parlance, a true andolanjeevi) was one of its leaders. He loved to do horaata (agitation)—perhaps thanks to this romantic streak, he looked upon the struggle with triumphalism. Critiques have pointed out that he never bothered to visit Hebballi after a quick agreement was reached with the State, and ignored the years of bureaucratic delay that followed. Pujar does not seem to have got along very well with Gopala Gowda, and in an interview to the scholar Rahamath Tarikere, once said: 'Our lifestyles were very different. He had fallen for shoki [extravagance], but I am someone who wants to live a simple life. So, we did not get along too well. He used to say that I am lacking in sophistication.'[15] He also remarked that Gopala Gowda got too caught up in meetings with socialist leaders from other parts of South India, and thus became 'ensconced in pretentions'. Personal differences, sometimes misconceptions, had created many islands of socialist politics within Karnataka at the very outset, which also explains why it never managed to gain a pan-state unity, electorally speaking.

III

Throughout his life, Gopala Gowda maintained an astonishing adherence to his socialist ideals, bordering on the quixotic and romantic. Until the day he died, he did not own a house of his own. When Chief Minister Kengal Hanumanthaiah offered him a site in Bangalore during the fifties, he rejected it vehemently. In 1957, Finance Minister Kadidal Manjappa decided to grant him five or six acres of land, and Gopala Gowda swatted that away too, holding firm to his slogan of *land to the tiller*, and requesting that the land be given away to poor families who needed it more than him. It was only upon the firm insistence of his wife Sonakka that he accepted a site from Chief Minister Veerendra Patil in the sixties, and it was only in the last three years of his life, when his body was wracked by ill health, that he stayed in a relatively comfortable two-bedroom home in Bangalore.

Gopala Gowda also cast a major influence on Kannada culture. He was a well-read man, devouring both Kannada and Western literature. The future chief minister S.R. Bommai had once called

Gopala Gowda the Edmund Burke of Karnataka, acknowledging the impact his fiery speeches in parliament as an opposition leader had created. Burke's political positions—with the exception of his hatred for slavery—bear little similarity to Gopala Gowda's, but their eloquence and dynamic personalities drew admiration from all political quarters. In this sense, no other Karnataka politician can claim to have lived as impactful a life as Gopala Gowda. He was a magnetic personality, attracting into his force field major writers of every Kannada literary movement of the twentieth century and political admirers across the spectrum. Likewise, when the socialist S. Venkatram passed away in the 1980s, Ananthamurthy penned a lovely elegy for him, writing that 'his funeral was attended by poets, workers, journalists, illiterate people, Congressmen, Socialists, dalits, Muslims, men and women across age groups' and presciently observing that 'political figures like Venkatram are only going to become rarer in the days to come'. It is only when red-hot politics is tempered by the calming influence of culture that such phenomena can take place.

Gopala Gowda was an animated and colourful personality, an embodiment of several rasas, often irascible and bubbling with fierce criticism, full of laughter and jokes when in a jolly mood, and capable of biting sarcasm when the situation demanded it. One time, when Ananthamurthy was celebrating his scholarship to study in England a little too fervently, Gopala Gowda had brought him down to earth by pointing out that rats and bandicoots made the trip to England every day on ships, and that the news did not merit excess revelry. He had then unironically followed this up by throwing a last-minute pre-departure party for Ananthamurthy, whose literary and academic growth he always followed with pride.

When he sensed a moral outrage, Gopala Gowda minced no words. In the fifties, some disputes had arisen over the proprietorship of bagair-hukum lands—government-owned tracts that had been cultivated by farmers for years, sometimes decades, without there being any proper documentation to support their ownership. When it came to notice that some plots of bagair-hukum land were reported to be occupied in a village near Shimoga, the following conversation ensued between Sitaram Iyengar, a former member of the Socialist Party who defected to the Congress after Kagodu, and Gopala Gowda.

> SI: So what if they are dalits? They have illegally occupied bagair-hukum land. They must leave. Otherwise, we just set fire—
>
> GG: What did you say?! I dare you to say that once more. You'll set fire to the hutments, will you? Do you know what we'll do? We'll put you in the fire as well! You speak like you're drunk on power, mister, be aware of that.[16]

Recollecting this instance in a tribute piece, Iyengar remembers Gopala Gowda's anger with fond nostalgia as a moment that forced him to reassess his conscience.

One is introduced to this side of the man on the very first page of Ananthamurthy's novel *Avasthe*.[17] We see him as a brash young high-school boy by the name of Krishnappa Gowda, erupting in anger at a petty, vengeful watchmaker: 'Watch out, mister! You talk like that one more time and I'll smash this glass case of yours to pieces.'

From bristling at watchmakers, Krishnappa Gowda graduates to flaring up at the evil of the police and the State, the vengefulness of moneyed and privileged classes, and finally looks wearily at the world itself. While Krishnappa Gowda's private life is completely fictitious, the portrayal stays true to the leader's public life by virtue of its evolving conception of Gopala Gowda's melancholia. He remained effervescent throughout his life, never lacking punch in his speech. His natural compassion towards oppressed castes endeared Gopala Gowda to the dalit leader Basavalingappa in the sixties, and the two became quite close. Basavalingappa would go on to create the famous boosa controversy, which would, in a very profound way, ignite the embers of the dalit movement in the state.

Gopala Gowda served as a legislator for three terms (1952–57; 1962–67; 1967–72), and his assembly speeches make for arresting reading. Even from the fifties, it is quite clear that he prized land redistribution, abolition of bonded labour and the upliftment of the underprivileged above all else. In these flamboyant and hair-raising speeches, Gopala Gowda bristles at the pompousness of bigoted brahmins, mocks the inscription *Government's Work Is God's Work* outside the Vidhana Soudha, holds forth on corrupt officialdom, reiterates his demands for the urgent installation of clean drinking water sources in villages, emphasises the undertaking of small-scale development projects in rural areas, highlights the importance of drought-relief measures and, on one occasion, even castigates Jayachamarajendra Wodeyar for choosing to deliver a speech in English rather than Kannada during an assembly session. He builds strong cases for the improvement of deplorable living conditions in prisons, allocating basic living wages to government employees at all levels, decentralising the state's power structure and for the unification of Karnataka under its rightful name.

One takes away a deep sense of dynamic urgency from these monologues, and it is dismaying that it is only after his death that the major social changes he dreamt of began to actualise under the Devaraj Urs[18] and Ramakrishna Hegde cabinets. It was undeniably the Urs government that created the conditions for backward castes to find a political and social platform in Karnataka. The potable water project for villages was taken up so efficiently and promptly by Hegde's rural development minister, Abdul Nazeersab, in the eighties that he went on to be dubbed 'Neersab' (water-lord). The Ramakrishna Hegde government also went on to significantly deepen democracy in the state through its empowerment of village panchayats, which allowed villages to have a more direct say in their affairs. Gopala Gowda lived long enough to sow his legacy in the state but was never truly able to witness the fruit it bore, and how it transformed the soil.

In *Avasthe*, Krishnappa Gowda often engages in a mental tussle between art and revolution, wondering what his efforts really amount to:

> He dreams of revolution, but is aware that his revolutionary acts so far have been piecemeal ... That he can talk contemptuously of the

> corrupt makes him pleased with himself, but it also worries him that deriving such pleasure has now become a habit with him. When your rage has changed nothing around you, is it any wonder that it becomes a mere habit? For the pain caused by such indignation, for the venting of that passion, Krishnappa tells himself, the poetry of half-crazed men like Kabir and Allama is a much better means than politics. (translated by Narayan Hegde)

Did not Gopala Gowda, like Krishnappa Gowda, also seek refuge in the realm of art and apolitical transcendence? He was certainly a man who found sanctuary in music and literature, and spread his love for them. In an essay titled *The Confusion of Paradoxes*, Poornachandra Tejaswi had once tried to crack open the old chestnut—where does the line between politics and art exist, and how does a writer navigate this ideological minefield? In doing so, Tejaswi takes us on a trip down memory lane, back to his intermediate college days in the fifties, when he had just moved from Mysore to Shimoga. He characterises the writers of Mysore as romantic individuals who stared at the skies and partook of literary rasas, while the prevailing sentiment in Shimoga was one of pragmatic socialism and strong ideological posturing. And yet, paradoxes abounded. If one went to listen to a political speech delivered by Gopala Gowda, one would end up listening to a scholarly lecture on Kannada literature instead. If, as Tejaswi did, one went to Ananthamurthy to learn about literature, one would in turn be introduced to someone like Konandur Lingappa, a firebrand socialist who brooked no delay in his spirited struggles. Reflecting on these times many decades later, Tejaswi concedes that, though he distanced himself from politics to a great extent, much like his father, he did feel that the strange conflation of politics and literature that the Lohiaites of Shimoga taught him was far more vibrant and exciting than anything else. He concludes by writing that the activism of those like Gopala Gowda and Lingappa began to feel like artistic expression in many ways.

In stark contrast, one would be hard-pressed to find a politician today with even respect for writers, let alone one capable of expounding on literature. We must be grateful that, when some lackey had the idea of naming Shimoga airport after B.S. Yeddyurappa, the latter had the sensibility to decline and propose Kuvempu's name instead.

Gopala Gowda, to be sure, was an anomaly in an environment of longstanding illiberalism. His singularity stemmed from a close association with the freethinking literary crowd that coalesced around him. Ananthamurthy had travelled to Mysore for higher education, and his friendship with fellow writers, Gopalakrishna Adiga, Poornachandra Tejaswi, P. Lankesh, amongst numerous others, would go on to produce a breed of artistic and political thinkers who prided themselves on being able to call things out as they saw them. Even as French thinkers in post-war Europe were convening in bohemian salons, Adiga and Ananthamurthy held court in the old-school coffeehouses of Mysore, discussing Eliot and Lawrence, Camus and Sartre. On many occasions, Ananthamurthy emphasised that it was the influence of Lohia and Gandhi that made them treat poetry and literature with singular attention, and as an indispensable part of political discourse.

Adiga, whose verses were on Gopala Gowda's lips during his speeches, penned a trenchant critique of twenty years of state socialism in a 1970 essay titled 'The Lifeblood of Democracy', thus:

> A socialist can also be a democrat, and if he is indeed a champion of individual freedom, he will not espouse the tens of parties that merely chant the mantra of socialism, but rather support the opposition that seeks to uphold individual freedoms. This might seem rather self-evident, but we must note that even while those who call themselves socialists are engaged in bitter internal disputes, they see the parties opposing them—Swatantra Party, Jan Sangh—as traitors to the national cause, as capitalists and casteists, and spare no chance to curse and rail against them, questioning their very

> necessity, treating them as untouchables, while still maintaining that they are upholding individual freedom. This amazes me. This might be a mode of misleading people employed by the communists, but amongst most socialists, this might simply be a product of not thinking about things deeply enough.[19]

The word 'socialism' has traced a sorry trajectory across the political battlefields of the twentieth century. Usurped by tyrants and fascists in the first half of the century, it bore little resemblance to the revolutionary ideas of freedom of expression, workers' and community rights, and the emancipation of women which traditional socialism had envisioned. In the second half, it was used by a totalitarian Soviet state as a linguistic shield to hide the wanton suppression of workers' rights, even as the American propaganda machine employed all its might to vilify the word.[20] In India, socialism became associated with the suffocation of government licensing and political corruption, and so the twin pillars of sensible socialism—education and healthcare for all—were never accorded the importance they deserved. In Karnataka, by the late sixties, a desperate anti-Congress sentiment had successfully replaced socialist ideals to the point that some socialists even protested against Indira Gandhi's abolition of privy purses and the nationalisation of banks. Today, even mentioning the word socialism in the same breath as social equality is likely to raise more eyebrows than draw sympathy.

Democracy, on the other hand, is a word that has largely remained in positive stead, theoretically at least. It is far too important an idea—so much so that a regime that has been branded an 'electoral autocracy' by Freedom House and V-Dem[21] has had to acknowledge its importance, even if it does so by claiming the genesis of democracy in some glorious Indian past. The word 'democracy' itself stands for a pluralism of voices, a multitude of opinions, and cannot easily be appropriated by those with dismissive and polarising agendas.

Having recognised the insularity of the dominant Left, and the potential for fundamentalism on either end of the spectrum, Adiga had also written:

> No system that sees society as a machine, that views individuals as cogs, can bring about happiness, or establish itself well. All efforts that reject the possibility of something that might be out of one's knowledge, exterior to one's personal experiences, different from one's own commitments, will always be in vain … Just like the fundamentalism that says liberation is possible only if you believe in our God, only if you come over to our sect, those who say that only socialism, or nationalisation, can achieve progress, are perpetuating a superstition that is ultimately inimical to the real growth of society.

He did, of course, acknowledge the presence of genuine statesmen:

> I am not saying that there are no gentlemen with genuine concern for the poor within the socialist ranks; however, they are the first to be martyred in the quest for power. In the race of governance, the nice guys never win, and it is always the power hungry and greedy politicians who find victory.

What shines through Gopalakrishna Adiga's essays is his spirited call for democracy in the real sense, and the rejection of what he calls 'pashubala'—beastly shows of strength. He looks upon most politicians and their lackeys as crude brutes who revel in domination and subordination. Adiga bends towards condescension sometimes, seeing himself as somehow above and beyond the petty transactions of the illiterate, 'animalistic' world. However, he does champion universal values of justice and individual liberty above all else, and this tempers his superiority complex with an antidote of meaningful concern.

In the aftermath of the Kannada-language movement of the eighties, Adiga also reflected on the cultural reasons for the proliferation of an apathetic political class. After all, it was the people who were voting them into power. His prognosis was grave:

> We see pretensions as the real thing, and confuse the real thing for pretensions. An actor who has been portraying divine and mythological characters in films seems to people as a god himself. In films, a benevolent character who works for the poor strikes us to be a Mahatma. Even if god himself came down to Earth, we are not in a position to recognise him. We have not just forgotten Mahatma Gandhi; I am sure that even if such a great soul came in front of us again, wearing just a dhoti, we might probably shove ten paise into his hands and tell him to leave us alone. The inability to recognise the actuality of our lives, and the propensity to get excited by pretence, acting and mere deception is a regrettable disease that is plaguing our society.

During the early seventies, he wrote several essays underscoring the need for bettering the education system, which he saw as an understated problem:

> If Independence in our country had really brought unrestricted freedom, philanthropists like Henry Ford might have established new universities that conducted exciting experiments, without any help from the state. However, this did not happen in our country. When the state was incapable of even exercising its basic responsibilities, it set out to do everything outside of its ambit as well. This has erased our independence and made us bend the knee to the ruling classes at every juncture.

It was bearing such hopes of structural change that Adiga contested from the Jan Sangh in the 1971 Lok Sabha elections. Gopala Gowda was dismayed by his decision. Adiga ended up losing to Kengal Hanumanthaiah and never tried to enter politics again.

IV

When the assembly elections in Mysore state (it would be renamed Karnataka only in 1973) were announced in 1972, Gopala Gowda Shantaveri lay ill and bedridden. His home ground—the constituency of Thirthahalli in Shimoga district—lay undefended, and was in need of a strong candidate for the upcoming elections.

Before his untimely illness, the incumbent leader had named Poornachandra Tejaswi as his successor, and the Samyukta Socialist Party had been banking on the writer's popularity, and his heir-apparent status as Kuvempu's son, to win the election for them. However, upon Tejaswi's firm refusal to contest in the elections, the cadres grew desperate.

Kadidal Shamanna, a young and idealistic apparatchik, was asked to accept the ticket in place of Tejaswi, but he too refused. In his autobiography,[22] Shamanna notes that if one had to decide on the basis of personal merit alone, the appropriate candidate was undoubtedly Konandur Lingappa, who had also closely worked under Gopala Gowda and absorbed his vision. However, the party's concern was that Lingappa was not a farmer by profession, and since peasant politics was the dominant strain in Thirthahalli, it was imperative that they find a representative from an agricultural background. Moreover, Lingappa had no property of his own, and no money to support his campaign. To top it all, Lingappa belonged to the bhovi caste, which was considered one of the lowest castes in the region. All of this meant that his chances of winning the election were slim. However, he was the only notable candidate willing to contest. Thus, amidst growing pessimism and resignation within the party, Konandur Lingappa was made to sign the B-Form.

The very next day, Lingappa travelled to Bangalore to visit Gopala Gowda, who was so weak that he could only shed silent tears in response. Lingappa picked up Gopala Gowda's muffler, which was lying by the hospital bed, and proceeded to sport it at every rally in the run-up to the election—it was a metaphorical torch that had been passed on to him by his illustrious predecessor. Needless to say, it evoked strong feelings amongst Gopala Gowda's immense following, and slowly began to transform into a powerful symbol. Riding on the diligent campaigning efforts of the party (Tejaswi, the unwilling candidate, had been an enthusiastic campaigner), Lingappa went on to win the election by over 2,000 votes. When the Karnataka Rajya Raitha Sangha was formed in 1980, the green shawl came to be recognised as a powerful symbol of the movement—a phenomenon for which Kadidal Shamanna claims personal credit. To this day, it remains a common sight on the shoulders of politicians in Karnataka who seek to proclaim brotherhood with the peasant vote bank, and claim to be kin to the soil.

Gopala Gowda's early death can only be attributed to his grinding lifestyle, his excessive drinking and the trauma of abject poverty. He was no stranger to the sorrow of borrowing money for survival, having spent most of his life in dire straits, living off little chunks of money spared by others, sometimes grudgingly. In some of his diary entries, we gain an intimate glimpse of how he must have felt during those penurious years. Gowda had once written of an instance involving a young Konandur Lingappa, who gives him ten rupees upon witnessing his state of squalor, which Gopala Gowda accepts, feeling half-ashamed at having to borrow money from an unemployed student. More or less every socialist in Gopala Gowda's circle seemed to have been awaiting imminent bankruptcy during the fifties and sixties. At one point, the owners filed a case against a party office in Lalbagh because no rent had been forthcoming for a while. All this meant that, by the time Gopala Gowda was in his thirties, his health had been significantly compromised.

After Gopala Gowda's death, there began a cultural and social upheaval the likes of which the state had never witnessed before. The two major urban epicentres of this upheaval are easily discernible: Shimoga and Mysore. Gopala Gowda's Lohiaite politics had transformed Shimoga district into a socialist stronghold. The eminence of Mysore University attracted the brightest of the state, and had transformed the city into a melting pot of thinkers and ideas. The result was a veritable cross-fertilisation of thoughts, a blossoming of literary culture, and the birth of a generation of writers, artists and activists who were determined to reshape society for good.

These years also see the last gasps of a certain species of political idealism playing out against the national backdrop of the Emergency, followed by the protracted collapse of the Congress regime, which had held on to unrivalled power for more than three decades in Karnataka.

Gopalakrishna Adiga's cynicism regarding nice politicians losing out in the race for ambition did not always bear out. One such exception was H.G. Govinde Gowda, also known as the Gandhi of Malnad, whose life serves as a good example of the idealistic trajectory I am referring to, while also highlighting the political compromises that those of his temperament had to contend with.

Govinde Gowda was an ardent follower of Gandhi in his youth, and had participated in the freedom struggle. Under the mentorship of Kadidal Manjappa, he joined the Congress, and became president of the Koppa (a village in Chikmagalur) Municipality Board from 1952 to 1960. Next, he became the president of the Koppa Taluk Development Board for two terms, from 1960 to 1968. During these long tenures, he was able to put his ideals into action, working towards the primary development of the town—electricity, water, schools, roads, bridges and so on. He became disillusioned with the Congress in the 1970s, joined the JP movement, and won the very first assembly elections he contested from Sringeri, in 1983, as a candidate of the Janata Party.

Twice serving as minister for primary education, he is remembered for trying to ensure transparent teacher recruitment (which was, and is, bedevilled by bribery), reserving half the posts for women, recommending the addition of ten 'grace marks' to the exam scores of applicants from rural backgrounds, kickstarting programmes for adult literary, commissioning fine anthologies of children's fiction for classrooms and bringing in Nali-Kali—an innovative model of alternative, holistic education. It bears mention that even Lankesh, known for headlining his magazine with scathing takedowns of politicians he deemed corrupt (almost everyone), had once written benevolently of Govinde Gowda.

Yet, by the tail end of his career, Indian standards had closed in on his legacy. A *Lankesh Patrike* article from November 1998 titled 'Corruption in "Gandhi" Department'[23] pointed towards a sullying of his once-Gandhian ideals, and the dominance of vokkaliga politicians. Even while acknowledging Govinde Gowda's erstwhile virtues, the article argued that he was helpless in the face of the caste politics that had enveloped the government:

> There is a rule that teachers must be appointed purely on the basis of marks scored. Right now, there is a systematic nexus that ensures that high marks are given to candidates from just one caste. The ones holding the authority for evaluating the TCH [Teacher Certificate, Higher] exams are all from the same caste, and close friends of Govinde Gowda—namely, Gangadhara Gowda, Manjappa Gowda and Range Gowda.[24] Their words make the marks, and whoever forks over enough money can become a teacher! What's more, these Gowdas have distributed free TCH seats to institutions they favour!

It would seem that Govinde Gowda, just like Gopala Gowda, was just another lone wolf trying to hold his own in a corrupt pack. If his name survives to this day, it is only because nostalgic historians can see in him a long-lost Gandhian sensibility that is presently nowhere to be found. It is no doubt a similar feeling of warmth that has kept Gopala Gowda's name alive through all these decades too. I grew up a mile away from a private hospital in Mysore set up by his grandchildren in his name. I knew nothing about the man himself, but the hospital was always a dependable landmark in my adolescent head—its emergency services always trusty, its pharmacy open day and night. Streets, circles, localities and statues dedicated to him are scattered across the state. In the early eighties, a newspaper report observed that in a few villages surrounding Thirthahalli, 'there are photos of Gopala Gowda in homes that don't even have one of Gandhi. Some ornament it with garlands and kumkuma and offer pooja.'

The socialists would fall out of the political race in the seventies, surviving merely as ideas and whispers in the afterlives of those who had been martyred in its early flames. Caste politics, always central to how Karnataka has voted, continues to dictate and submerge socialism and other idealisms. Today, social justice politics survive to some degree in Karnataka, thought subsumed under the treasury-driven agendas of our times, and a casual observer may be pardoned for seeing no remnant of its socialist past whatsoever. I'm reminded of *Avasthe*'s ending, where an emaciated Krishnappa Gowda grieves about his helplessness, *All I can do, at the moment, is try to stand up by leaning on this cane.*

Yet, ideas, like phoenixes, can rise out of ashes too, and if history shows us anything, it is that they always do.

THREE

Art As Life
The Aesthetic Universals of South Canara

Napping at midday,
I hear the song of rice planters,
Feel ashamed of myself.

—Kobayashi Issa

Birth of art—
Song of rice planters,
Chorus from nowhere.

—Basho

I

In July 2021, when the monsoon had arrived in its full splendour in South Canara, a friend and I found ourselves ambling around on a large tract of farmland, a few miles east of Udupi. Having braved a few territorial dogs and sheepishly introduced ourselves as researchers, we gained permission from one of the farmers to explore the landscape. There were paddy fields as far as the eye could see, dotted by u-shaped silhouettes labouring on the field—almost all of them women, as is the case with much back-bending labour in the country, and as Shivaram Karanth portrayed so sensitively in his 1942 novel *Marali Mannige* (translated as *Return to Earth*), set in this very region. However, further ahead, we glimpsed a larger group, comprising the whole extended family, including two small girls, pitching in to get the job done. As we trudged towards them, we could hear them singing together in a grand chorus, the strong wind carrying their energetic spirit towards us. The strenuous task of transplanting rice was being performed with great gusto and merriment. This was to be the last day of the season's work, and that feeling of accomplishment lay close at hand. The songs they were singing were catchy, and invoked hearty laughter, mocking aspects of modern culture or the figure of the vote-greedy politician. The eldest son of the family spoke to us later, telling us how the pandemic had brought the whole family together, and how they had all decided to help the women of the household finish the job swiftly. Soon enough, the clouds darkened, and everybody prepared for the incoming shower by putting on raincoats. The two little girls ran joyously around the farm, fetching the planters the protection they needed, glad to be of any help at all. Despite the

heavy downpour, they continued to work, impervious to the wind and the rain.

'Karnataka is proud of its greatest living writer, Kota Shivaram Karanth, but it is also intimidated by him; Kannadigas regard him not just as a writer, but as some kind of a force of nature, like the monsoon,' the civil servant and littérateur H.Y. Sharada Prasad had once reflected on his close friend's pervasive fame. Similarly, the scholar D.R. Nagaraj once called him a lone mountain amidst a landscape of hillocks; the artist (and close friend) K.K. Hebbar paid tribute by sketching a majestic pencil portrait that depicted Karanth with four heads and five hands (one of them pointing heavenwards). Karanth himself wrote an astutely self-aware autobiography titled *Ten Faces of a Crazy Mind*.[1] He was what one might call a sakala kala vallabha, one steeped in every art form. Apart from his life as a novelist, Karanth dabbled in journalism, filmmaking, photography, translation, music composition, carpentry, dance, theatre, Yakshagana, and even produced amateurish drawings. He wrote encyclopaedias and textbooks for children, and went on to spearhead environmental campaigns in the latter part of his very long life. In the end, even the monsoon is only an annual occurrence, but Karanth clearly saw himself as a man for all seasons.

Shivaram Karanth was born in 1902 in the village of Kota, just a few miles north of Udupi, in a reasonably well-off brahmin family—his father was a school teacher who later set himself up in the cloth trade, after his grandfather had lost all his money trying to pursue alchemy. Shivaram was the fourth child in a family of eight brothers and three sisters. The Kota brahmins prided themselves on their puritanism, and young Karanth grew up in an atmosphere of strict orthodoxy.

He did not have many playmates in the neighbourhood, as he had been forbidden from playing with shudra children. This is how Karanth describes the atmosphere of (im)purity he grew up in: 'The children of billavas, toddy-tappers, were not even admitted to school. If we touched them, we needed to have a bath. If any untouchables crossed our path on the way to school, we had to take care that their shadow did not fall on us, which meant that they could come somewhat nearer at noon. We had to remove the "polluted" school clothes at the doorstep of our home. Inside, we moved about in loincloths. This loincloth, made of [cotton] fibre, was considered "clean" however dirty it might otherwise be. My mother and grandmother bathed seven or eight times a day to slough off the pollution of touching their children before they entered the kitchen or the puja chamber.'

Untouchability, in other words, was an all-pervasive phenomenon, holding many layers of purity within its onion-like metaphysics. This is brought out wonderfully in the Kannada writer Vaidehi's early 1980s novel, *Aspryushyaru* (Untouchables).[2] She explores the theme expansively, showing how the phenomenon affects relations between various communities, and *within* the walls of a single household. Vaidehi, the most accomplished writer to emerge from the Kota-Kundapura region after Karanth's generation, knew the Karanths from intimate quarters. She once said, reading out from an essay she had written:

> Every region has a quality, which in turn shares a relationship with the nation, and with the world at large, right? But the *final cause* of your nature is this particular innate quality. The men of the Kota region are rough-hewn, but steadfast—honesty is their first virtue. They are deeply sensitive of being indebted to someone. Even if they carry a sense of proprietorship, their endurance for pain is commendable. Being utterly straightforward, they excel at critiquing and humbling others. They don't easily express love, but carry on with an inward stoicism. They erupt into moments of pride spontaneously. Even if they carry a serious bent of mind, they remain connoisseurs of comedy. They pick fights at the drop of a syllable, and are litigation-lovers. At any moment, they may propose a recourse to law. In their urge to grasp a subject from head-to-toe, they exhibit a most radical curiosity to know the world. They love study and research. They are known to sometimes think too much of themselves, but their masculine selves are tempered by feminine qualities too. They take much pride in their intelligence, but are

also the first to express astonishment at how foolish they can be sometimes. They don't mince words while arguing, but will also express concern that they might have inadvertently hurt someone. They never tolerate ignorance! And they generally ensure that their whims are writ large over every corner of the household! They hold themselves with dignity, and there is always fire in their eyes. All these are traits spread across the men, but they all find their exemplification in just one individual—Shivaram Karanth.

Vaidehi vividly remembers the first time she met Karanth. This was when she was just beginning her literary life, and she had requested an interview with him.

V: What are your thoughts on women's literature in Kannada?

SK: I haven't read much of it, I'm afraid.

V: Why not?!

SK: Whenever something interests me very organically in the course of my studies, I read it. That's it. I have just not happened to come to this yet.

V: Right. What suggestions would you give to young women writers of today?

SK: No suggestions! You please write! That is all. Write first, speak later.

Karanth famously read very little contemporary Kannada writing. Vaidehi did later send him a copy of her novel *Aspryushyaru*, which he admired and commended, though this time he added a suggestion: 'Best if you limit your usage of Kundapura Kannada. It might diminish your readership.'

Vaidehi took this as a challenge, and decided that it was poor advice. There was authenticity in her language that enriched its musical quality.[3] As a Mysore lad who has been living in South Canara for about four years now, the local Kundapura Kannada sounds to me sweeter and more melodious than what I grew up hearing in Mysore, which was mostly school slang, officious newsreader-speak, melodramatic Rajkumar-style pompousness, Tamil and Dakhini infusions—a polyphonic mixed bag. But in Kundapura Kannada, the sounds of the ocean seem awash over the rhythm of the language, creating a certain lilt. One encounters these melodies in Vaidehi's writings, while they are rare in Karanth's works. He had fashioned his own brand of Kannada that was accessible to a broader audience.

In his own way, Karanth championed the emancipation of women through his writings, but as Vaidehi says, 'Karanth doesn't really manage to get into the subjectivities of his woman characters. But that's okay. If he did everything, what would writers like myself have to add? I have picked up from where he left off.' Her own stories, which are largely set in the second half of the twentieth century, invite readers into the intimate predicaments of women engaging with newly found freedoms. The challenges of dealing with patriarchal impositions and the influx of modernity into a deeply orthodox landscape are concerns that pervade her work. In the opening chapter of *Aspryushyaru*, a woman giving birth becomes 'untouchable' during her labours, showcasing the sense of impurity that masculine orthodoxy ascribes to this most primal act. Images of midwives assisting women in labour keep coming up in her stories, and one feels privy to the laborious process in which new societies are birthed, shedding regressive ideas slowly, but surely.

It has become a cliche that men do not understand women, chalking them off as mysterious creatures. On the other hand, women have had no choice *but* to understand men, to place themselves in their shoes sympathetically, to try to inhabit masculine shoes with great sensitivity, as Vaidehi demonstrates in her understanding of Karanth. This seems to be true for other hegemonic binaries founded on skewed power dynamics as well. Lower classes always dream of what affluence might feel like, but the opposite is rarely true. Someone belonging to an oppressed caste seeks the prestige of belonging to an upper social rung, and indeed, the perpetuation of caste in our country is precisely because of the unending hierarchy of caste superiority, where one always has someone else to look down upon and think little of. Shivaram Karanth's greatest legacy is that he broke such social boundaries in ways no Kannada writer had attempted before. He was ever alert to the plight of the underprivileged and the disenfranchised, and much of this sensitivity owes its origins to the deep Gandhian influences of his early youth.

Shivaram Karanth's schooling years in Kundapura (a few miles away from Kota) was engrossing and full of mischief, and he remembers many of his teachers with fondness. Textbooks and school curriculum held little interest for him, and the young boy had deemed cricket, football, swimming, or stealing out at night to watch Yakshagana performances to be more suitable vocations. When famine struck the region in 1918, he helped set up a feeding centre at a private school, where gruel was boiled and served to the needy.

Having sailed through his years of schooling, Shivaram Karanth moved to Mangalore for college, seeking action and excitement. Here too, the sterile classrooms bored him, and he was drawn more to the vigour of the freedom movement. Deeming his teacher's recommendations of Kipling to be uninteresting, he proceeded to read Tagore with enthusiasm. Inspired by the great poet, he was possessed by an ardent desire to visit Santiniketan post-haste, but his father 'vetoed the idea because Bengali brahmins ate fish'. After Gandhi visited Mangalore as part of the Khilafat movement, Karanth could think only of Swaraj and nothing else. By 1922, he had decided to quit college, and to plunge into the freedom struggle full-time. By then, with Gandhi having replaced Tagore as a hero, he began dressing in khadi and learnt how to spin the charkha.

Very early in his life, Karanth had discarded the orthodoxy that his family of proud Kota brahmins was steeped in, which distressed his father. The senior Karanth had also fostered dreams that his son would become a lawyer and settle down in Kundapura, which were quickly defeated by Karanth's dedication to the non-cooperation movement.

This Gandhian idealism lasted for a few years, during which Karanth spoke out against untouchability, campaigned for brahmacharya (sexual restraint) in high schools and rallied for the prohibition of alcohol. He was moved by the trials and tribulations of nautch girls[4] in the region, who faced societal scorn and rejection. When an acquaintance was planning to sell his sisters to rich old men, Karanth persuaded him to wait until suitable grooms could be found. 'For three years, I wandered around trying to find young men from within the community. I searched in North Canara, Bombay and Mysore. I did not succeed. I knew the responsibility I had undertaken. In sheer despair, I wrote to Gandhiji. In reply he said, "Let such girls observe lifelong brahmacharya." This prescription so disappointed me that I shed silent tears. I told myself that Gandhiji does not seem to understand human nature, and thinks that what is possible for him is possible for everyone else.' Much later, in 1970, Karanth wrote one of his finest novels, *Mai Managala Suliyalli* (translated as *The Woman of Basrur*),[5] which revolved around the courtesan traditions of the region, documenting their lives with sympathy.

Karanth read widely and purposefully, educating himself in all the ways his uninspiring formal schooling had not. It was after he encountered the writings of the physician Havelock Ellis and the rationalism of Bertrand Russell that Karanth's callow attraction towards Gandhian puritanism fizzled out. He became disillusioned with Gandhian thought, and decided to devote all his energies to grassroots social action. Spending years in a prison cell did not appeal to the hustling, bustling ball of energy that Karanth was. During the 1920s, he had realised that the new generation needed Kannada reading material, and set about this immense task by himself. He started a journal named *Vasantha*, where he began penning serialised detective fiction. The endeavour was financially doomed from the beginning, and the final nail in the coffin was struck when Karanth realised that many writers were simply translating writings from Marathi or English and passing the pieces off as their own. He was deeply troubled. His own journalism, writing for various magazines across the country, failed to fetch him much reward. These were years of penury, and Karanth fills many pages of his autobiography with descriptions of travel with empty pockets, walking long distances on an empty stomach trying to find subscribers for his journal and the generosity of strangers that helped him carry on.

It is astounding how much energy Karanth displayed during these penurious years. Apart from his journalism, he wrote some twenty plays, a few of which were published and a few performed. He nursed ardent hopes that theatre could be used as a medium for social reform, but the illiteracy and narrow worldviews of many of his actor-peers disheartened him. At the same time, he was beginning to discern the divide between art and activism. As he writes:

> When the playwright's mind is in the grip of an idea, when he conceives a passion for an ideology, he tends to make every one of his characters disgorge the same doctrine. Even if the ideas are honest, even if the situations are appropriate, the characters will not be convincing. There is a good deal of difference between seeing characters through the eyes of other characters and seeing them through the playwright's own eyes. The audience claps when there is reference to causes popular at a given time, like eradication of untouchability, khadi, disapproval of dowry or child marriage and patriotism. But it will only be propaganda, not art. When an artist portrays a situation, he must depict the persons contributing to it in a dispassionate way so that those who see the play come to their own conclusions.

Throughout his work, Karanth seems to be searching for a kind of artistic idealism, exemplified by his own life. In December 2021, when I met Malini Mallya, who was Karanth's companion during his last years and also the inheritor of the rights to his works, I was amused to hear that Karanth only began to substantially read the collected works of Kuvempu quite late in his life, when old age prevented him from any activity apart from reading. Karanth himself writes of his reading habits in his autobiography, saying that he barely read any fiction despite being a novelist, and mostly enjoyed reading non-fiction and enhancing his knowledge of the world. The image of an octogenarian Karanth finally discovering the richness of Kuvempu's works captures the philosophy of srishti-samadhi (creative death) that Karanth poured into his life—he was simply too busy in one mode of creative work or another to have any time to retreat into the works of his greatest living contemporary. He was also never associated with any literary movement, and always remained a singular force.

Karanth's solitary quest for artistic virtues, for a satisfaction divorced from the trappings of name and fame, is compellingly portrayed in his novel *Moga Padeda Mana* (roughly, 'The Mind That Has Matured'), published in 1948. At the dawn of independence, Shivaram Karanth was meditating on the impossible dream of nurturing artistic values in a vastly impoverished and illiterate country. It is the story of a dancer, and it bears mention here that Karanth was an accomplished dancer and taught for many years, too. In fact, Leela Karanth, his wife, first encountered Karanth as her dance teacher while she was in school.

The protagonist of *Moga Padeda Mana* is a dapper young man named Vyasa, who possesses artistic sensibilities, but is forced to study for the bar exam and start supporting his single mother and siblings. Eventually, he abandons his study and ends up joining a dancing troupe that travels and performs across the country. During these escapades, not unlike Karanth himself, Vyasa experiences a disenchantment with the whole business—financial interests invariably trump artistic goals, and the lumpenism of the illiterate audiences dampens Vyasa's hope of ever becoming the kind of dancer that he wants to be *and* be recognised as. It is important to remember that such things as drama and dance troupes were looked upon as hotbeds of vice in the conservative times of the mid-twentieth century, especially in an orthodox temple town like Udupi. The novel makes repeated note of this, and shows how only cosmopolitan city centres like Mangalore or Dharwad or Mumbai housed audiences that were receptive to young men and women performing together. Yet, in these places too, Vyasa bemoans the absence of a truly cultured audience who would see dance as a sophisticated art form and not just as a spectacle of attractive bodies.

Vyasa's call to adventure begins when he leaves his destitute home in South Canara and moves to Dharwad, which was then a flourishing town, a centre of literature and culture, from where the strongest articulations for the unification of the state of Karnataka were emerging. He begins working as an editor at a journal, but is soon taken with a dance troupe that has arrived in town. Vyasa realises that dance alone can be the emancipating force that he has always been searching for, and immerses himself in its practice and study. Possessed by the urge to perform a routine mimicking the dance of a peacock witnessing rain, he travels to a rare corner in north Karnataka where peacocks abound, and spends days waiting to see them dance. At a time when most of dance and theatre involves episodes from the great epics and puranic myths, Vyasa turns to nature for inspiration. After he trains and becomes an accomplished dancer, his most ambitious performance is an enactment of a river meeting with the ocean. The metaphor has aged ironically. Today, the proliferation of dams along the river Sharavathi (which drains into North Canara) has altered its very course, and meanwhile, the sea has been creeping upon the river and the coast, gobbling up portions, spitting them out elsewhere.[6] A modern Vyasa would have to embody a river held back from merging with the ocean and released only in spurts, to which the baffled ocean responds with equally turbulent angst.

It bears mention that Karanth was a pioneering novelist in the Kannada literary renaissance of the early twentieth century. In 1899, a policeman and social reformer from South Canara named Gulvadi Venkata Rao had written *Indirabai*, usually considered the first Kannada novel, which traces the story of a child widow who resists mindless conservatism and fights her way to an educated future. The Navodaya renaissance that followed revolved largely around linguistic extravaganza and reviving Kannada glory. But Karanth rejected this elaborate classicism, and embraced a straightforward prose style that sought inspiration in the realism of everyday life as well as the simple magnificence of nature. Vyasa's metaphorical quest is cut from the same cloth.

Vyasa, a consummate romantic, wishes to start a Temple of Art, where he would be the head priest, separating the wheat from the chaff of aesthetic discourse. During his initial years in Mumbai, he acquires a talented protégé, a young girl named Kirti who becomes his star pupil. Soon, he becomes disenchanted with the plebeian audiences in the city, and moves back to Dharwad to start another school there. In the meantime, his student Kirti is enamoured by the glitz and glamour of the film world, and finds fame and money as an actress known for her seductive, raunchy dance scenes. Vyasa disapproves of this sell-out, a clear violation of the noble designs he had once dreamt for her, and the two become estranged. The story ends when Vyasa receives a message from Kirti in Mumbai, telling him that she is dying, upon which he rushes there to see her. In a saccharine plot twist, she confesses that her present condition owes only to her misguided choices—a botched abortion by a quack doctor is what has sent her to the edge of death. Premarital sex, in other words, becomes the instrument of destruction.

Kirti eventually recovers, and tells Vyasa that she will abandon all her cine-misadventures and follow him to Dharwad to serve as a daasi at his art temple. Such was the novel's hasty and sentimental ending. Critics have bemoaned the fact that Karanth paid little attention to craft, and often wrote novels in quick succession just to make ends meet. He wrote upwards of forty novels, and only a few of them stand out as well-crafted works of art—*Chomana Dudi*, *Marali Mannige*, *Mai Managala Suliyalli*, *Bettada Jeeva* and *Mookajjiya Kanasugalu*, to name the best of them. The novelist A.N. Krishna Rao once compared Karanth's works to diamond ore—it might take us a while to get to the crux of the material, but the endeavour would be well worth the time.

Returning to the novel's denouement, we may yet sympathise with Karanth's valiant attempts at salvaging a certain kind of traditionalism—the relationship between the guru Vyasa and the student Kirti, which is what offers the latter a firm mooring in the end. This relationship remains unsullied precisely because of the artistic idealism that frames it. The search for moral goodness through art is valuable for its own sake, for it can become a life-saving force. This would be the most sympathetic reading of the novel, especially since it would be quite easy from our present-day vantage point to critique the characterisation of a woman as being incapable of taking care of herself without the protection of a competent male. (She even says so in as many words.)

Another highlight of *Moga Padeda Mana* is its keen-eyed portrayal of rural life at the cusp of independence. Towards the close of the novel, Vyasa travels to Rajasthan with friends and family, where he is enchanted by the villagers' life, which is filled with dance and song. He is struck by the way they take solace in art to escape their domestic miseries. 'Their songs were incredibly simple. Still, weren't they powerful enough to capture the joys and trials of their lives?' Vyasa then has the following crucial realisation: 'In all our shastras, dance and music fell for the trap of scholarship, sailing in the ethereal space of miracles, and lost all their power. Our lives are pretentious, and our arts are too.'

In his autobiography, Karanth arrives at a similar conclusion through his travels around the country: 'Our people tend to be carried away by excessive exquisiteness. I have often felt that Belur would have ranked higher in the scale of art if the images had not fallen victim to so much daintiness. You only have to compare the architecture of Belur with the noble simplicity of the seaside temples of Mahabalipuram. Our art, music and architecture have lost the power to move us because of excessive aestheticism. An artist must employ precepts to the extent that it serves his purpose; he is on the path of decline once he begins to show off.' It is this aspiration for simplicity that sets Karanth apart from Kuvempu, across whose works we see a grand, epic aesthetic imagination at play. Karanth preferred a humble realism that would take him closer to the common man, and further away from aesthetic ideals that had already reached an apotheosis.

Moga Padeda Mana succeeds in another sense—in evoking the love for nature that comes so naturally to one who has lived in the South Canara–Malnad region. In this land of lush green forests teeming with wildlife, is it any wonder that Vyasa finds in nature his greatest muse? The present successors to Vyasa's nature-inspired dance style may be seen in the performers of an exhilarating folk art form that continues to enthral the region—Pilivesha, the tiger dance.

II

The entrance to the house signals something grand, ceremonial, majestic, though the house itself is of modest proportions. A tableaux-sized chariot of golden hue, a snarling tiger that has turned black through time, numerous smaller tigers peering at you amidst the detritus of decaying paper and fibre—all these are Ashok Raj Kadbettu's creations assembled in the yard outside. Inside the house: trophies, shields and certificates from a long life of competitive success; numerous masks and busts of feral creatures; a large watercolour painting of a tiger brawling with an elephant. Amidst these, with a grin on his face and a blue tiger-face roaring on his smartwatch, sits their creator, Ashok Raj himself. These artefacts are more scattered than arranged around his home, and there is an anarchic energy to the mess, as though a wild tiger had entered the establishment and swished its tail around every which way. A couple of furry little Shih Tzus scamper around the house, softening the otherwise ferocious ambience.

In May 2023, I found myself in the zigzagging interior streets of Kadbettu village, adjacent to the town of Udupi, in the company of the most famous living exponent of Pilivesha ('pili' means 'tiger' in Tulu), the tiger dance art form that is endemic to the South Canara region. Ashok Raj was in his mid-fifties when I met him. Later that year, he suffered a serious stroke during a performance in Bangalore and lapsed into a coma. His family started a crowdfunding campaign to finance his hospital expenses, and received a heartening response on social media. Ashok Raj passed away in early 2024.

Pilivesha is a rambunctious dance form that is performed on religiously auspicious dates and during festivals like Ganesha Chaturthi, Dasara or Krishna Janmashtami. The dancers paint themselves in tiger stripes and put on a display of wild carnivorous energy, springing and leaping and jigging to steadily quickening drum beats. More daring acts will put on fire-breathing shows, and it was Ashok Raj's troupe that popularised somersaults, back-flips and incredible gymnastic stunts during the eighties, which have now become standard fare. The origins of pilivesha are hazy, and there exist variants across South India, like puliyattam in Kerala for instance. It is a desi motif that has been absorbed into Muharram celebrations as well. In some parts of North Karnataka, Hindus and Muslims both don tiger costumes in syncretic spirit to this day.[7] The tiger itself is a symbol that pervades non-brahmin religious traditions—for instance, Male Mahadeshwara, a deity from South Karnataka, is always depicted riding a tiger. Pilivesha has traditionally been a masculine space, but times are a-changing. Ashok Raj's daughter Sushma is the first female tiger in the tradition, and under her tutelage many other women have been performing as well.

'Ever since third standard, I have been winning art competitions,' he says proudly, throwing a suggestive glance at the paintings all around. Ashok Raj grew up in Udupi during the late seventies. His father had passed away early, and his mother was a traffic constable working in Chikmagalur. The young boy and his siblings had been dispatched to live and study in a school hostel. They would sometimes visit their grandfather: 'He was not a "sound" party, my grandfather. Very unreliable. But during festivals, I would go visit him. Festival, no? That was the first time I saw a Pilivesha, at the temple in Udupi. It was magnificent. I saw the dancers stand up on their hands and pick up coins with their mouth. That was crazy!'

Ashok Raj was nine years old then. Amidst the friendly brawls, banter and horseplay that reigned over the lives of the hostel boys, dance, art, kushti and other feats of physical acuity would keep boredom at bay. In the years to come, Pilivesha would come to be his first love, even as Ashok Raj was winning painting competitions at the district level: 'Back then, Udupi and Mangalore were one district, you know? I would win prizes at the district level.'

When Ashok Raj was in the ninth standard, he was handed the stage at a school function, where he put together a series of thirty different 'pyramids' of varying difficulty—boys climbing on top of each other to form various patterns in quick succession, garnering much applause. A jumble of warm-blooded young fellows capering about and clambering over one another with aplomb. My high-school self would have paid money to watch such a show! That was also the year he first performed at an official Pilivesha event during Dasara in Mangalore. He and his friends had stayed at a local Ganesha temple during the nine days of the festival, eating and sleeping there.

Just like in Karanth's novel, there still remains a stark distinction between the cultural environments in Mangalore and Udupi. In Ashok Raj's long experience of over forty years of Pilivesha, this has been all too apparent.

> In Mangalore, they see it as entertainment, as a festival of jolly enjoyment—gammattu. In Udupi, they don't see it that way. I'm not just talking of Pilivesha. Any other vesha also. They will think, *Oh, they will be coming to our home.* You got it, right? The difference is only this. They don't really enjoy the dance. This is the difference between Udupi and Mangalore. In Mangalore, they offer us great patronage. In Udupi, right here in Kadbettu, our own Kadbettu, nobody does anything of that sort. I mean, if we send across a letter asking for help, they might pool in a few hundred rupees here and there, but we don't do that. Why should we stoop to such levels? We seek out patrons who respect and admire our art.

In and around Mangalore, Pilivesha is an integral part of temple festivities. Ashok Raj describes it with much passion, as an occasion when the entire community comes together to let loose, unwind and pray to the local deity under whose auspices the dance takes place. It is a unifying practice, accessible to everyone, with the potential to dissolve all social boundaries. At the Gokarnanatheshwara temple in Kudroli—built in 1912 by an affluent billava man under the aegis of the social reformer Narayana Guru—devotees from numerous communities and religions gather in syncretic fervour. This is precisely the pomp and joy that Vyasa (and Karanth) once admired in the lives of ordinary people, art as a life-giving force. It must be noted that the billavas were traditionally a lower-caste community, for whom institutional religious access only began in the twentieth century. After the land reforms of the 1970s, which were extremely successful in South Canara, the billavas stood to gain a lot of land from erstwhile land-owning communities like brahmins and jains. However, the acquisition of land did not translate into immediate social upliftment. Mangalore-based journalist Naveen Soorinje argues that the newly landed billavas failed to invest in education and health, and instead tried to secure a religious prestige that had always been denied to them.[8] Today, many billavas are foot soldiers of the Hindutva regime, picking fights on the streets and languishing in jails for extremist vigilante activities, while their socially advantaged puppeteers comfortably enjoy political immunity. In the 2024 general elections, an internal billava rebellion accusing the BJP of denying them real political power after decades of support surfaced to complicate the party's South Canara pitch.

If I have not mentioned Ashok Raj's caste until now, it is because he himself did not care for such terminologies, and only saw himself as an artist—a kalaavida through and through. As far as sectarianism goes, the buck stops with his generation. However, historical and sociological contingencies require me to point out that he was born in a dalit family, and grew up facing challenging odds. The pride and respect with which he carried himself would have certainly moved Karanth, who wrote the first novel in Kannada featuring a dalit protagonist, *Chomana Dudi* (Choma's Drum), all the way back in 1933.

Chomana Dudi is the story of a landless labourer named Choma, whose deepest desire is to have a piece of land to call his own. The story revolves around Choma's desperate, and ultimately unsuccessful, attempts to acquire a plot of land to till. It's a tragic tale. Choma even has to witness the death of his children, and cannot ever do without a bottle at the end of a day. Through all his misery, his sole companion is his dudi. Two decades before Oscar Matzerath started banging away on his tin drum in Gunter Grass's famous novel, Choma was venting his frustration and misery through his dudi. Karanth had understood, without the abstractions and ideological tints of Marxism, that the land question was central to dalit emancipation. The dudi itself has remained a lasting metaphor for the emancipatory power of art. Karanth's metaphor would come alive materially during the seventies, when dalit activists and street theatre artists would emerge onto the streets with a varied assortment of skin instruments sounding their entrance.

Ashok Raj himself would in no way relate to Choma, who would have struck him as a weak character, prone to the bottle, lacking serious dedication to art and practice. As we sit talking in the hall, discussing how Pilivesha is perceived in other parts of the state, a massively built young man walks out from a bedroom, his T-shirt clasping the contours of his trunk-like arms. Sushma Raj's partner, Nishan Kumar, is a bodybuilding champion who has won multiple titles, from Mr Karnataka to Mr India to several other titles at international events across the globe. He also dons the stripes sometimes and takes part in Pilivesha performances around the country. Nishan makes an intriguing comment when talking about the reception of Pilivesha performances in Bengaluru: 'When they start the drum beats here in South Canara, the audience perks up, and the hair on their skin stands up. If the same troupe starts playing in Bengaluru, the people there think it is probably some tamate players, and they ignore what is to come.'

The tamate is a percussion instrument commonly associated with folk traditions, and Nishan's comment makes it out to be a tame artefact, associated with something terribly boring. Ashok Raj smiles at the comment. From the perspective of these larger-than-life characters, I mused, the milder art forms of song and dance associated with the tamate must seem like domesticated avatars of a wild species. There is the pride of warrior ethos in their eyes.

Sushma and Nishan are a famous influencer couple on Instagram, with thousands of admirers keenly following their dance and bodybuilding exploits. Sushma has been working as a model, actor and dancer in Kannada showbiz for more than a decade now. She remarks, 'Earlier, there used to be a unique individual style to each of the Pilivesha dancers' techniques. Now, what I see is that choreography often imposes a regulated style on artists, and there is more conformity than originality, I'm afraid.'

Ashok Raj too bemoans this new phenomenon—the slapping of conformity on what is essentially a wild art. 'There must be diversity in individual expressions. It is not a national anthem, no? Everyone will have their own style. These days, you have choreographed dances, where everyone does the same thing, and then another troupe will come and sing the same jana gana mana ... This kills creative expression.' The metaphor, as I realise later, carries further resonances. The arrival of a majoritarian nationalist ethos in the region (which has been dubbed as the laboratory of the Hindutva Right) has also created restrictions on how Pilivesha should be performed within certain spaces. At Pilivesha events organised by the extended nexus of the local BJP power networks, stunts and gymnastics are prohibited, and more restrictive presentations must be done. 'You can't compare a janapada [folk] art like Pilivesha to shastriya art forms,' Ashok Raj says, pointing out that they are very different ways of relating to the world. 'An attempt is being made to absorb Pilivesha into a classical structure, laying rules and regulations on it. Now, you have troupes that perform specific routines again and again in groups of four. They can't be as gymnastic as the winning troupes, and to stand a chance in these competitions, they have come up with these restrictions. Have you ever seen a tiger move the same way over and over again? It leaps and jumps and rolls every which way while catching prey. The dance must allow anyone to express themselves fully. I fear that the form will be codified and will restrict the free expression of individual personalities.'

A 2023 news article announcing a new Pilivesha contest for the Dasara festivities in Mangalore, to be attended by the likes of Harbhajan Singh, Jonty Rhodes and Rishab Shetty, also mentioned the names of the individual troupes that would be participating in it. At least two of them had a variant of the title 'Gorakshanatha Tigers' (cattle-saving tigers) in their names, which struck me as either intentionally politicised or very unintentionally ironic. It also stipulated that women were not allowed to participate. This lends more substance to Ashok Raj's worry that Pilivesha might become distanced from its wild, anarchic origins, and tamed into a domesticated, straitjacketed art. In its current avatar, there is always something new that a young dancer can hope to do that may be unique to their own personality. There are no teachers of Pilivesha today, but that might change in the future.

This is what Shivaram Karanth had to say in his autobiography, about a similar question:

> Some Bhagavatas [theatre actors], in their infatuation with Hindustani and Carnatic classical music, have killed the beauty of Yakshagana by seeking to fuse the two. Luckily this mania has not spread to North Canara or Malnad. In Kolar and Chitradurga districts, their folk-art—the Bayalata—has also come under the pressure of making it genteel. Reform must come from within and it must retain the basic character of form. The way to go about it is not to impose something from another mode and displace the original impulse. Each form has its own distinctive character and beauty, which must be preserved. Mere love of the novel does not promote creativity either. I am not for total preservation of tradition. Without knowing the impulse behind a tradition, however, it must not be tampered with.

The fact remains that Pilivesha must embrace modernity to survive and thrive. Kannada film songs are usually what makes Pilivesha events click. At an official event in Manipal, marking the inauguration of a new scholarly project documenting local traditions, I saw Ashok Raj and his troupe perform Pilivesha in front of a largely teenybopper college crowd. It was a thoroughly enjoyable performance which soon segued into a medley of Bollywood songs, a big hit with the pan-Indian audience. Some might see this as a bastardisation of local cultures; others might make a pragmatic argument that it is only by picking up new cultural influences that any art form evolves.

Vyasa's idealism and Kirti's sentimental denouement would make little sense to Nishan or Sushma. Ashok Raj says he loved the Kannada movie *Kantara*, especially his favourite part, where the actor-director Rishab Shetty takes on the mantle of the bhootha, or shaman, and shrieks majestically in an ominous, haunting tone. 'I want our Pilivesha moves to become famous and memorable like that scene,' he announces with palpable yearning. It is in aspirations such as these that one sees a collapse of conceptions like janapada, janapriya and pratishthita (folk, popular culture and high culture) that are usually employed in sociological discourse. They might have had a stronger claim a few decades ago, but the democratisation of art, and especially perhaps its accessibility on a portable screen in everybody's hands, has diminished the meaning of such categorical considerations. Perhaps the idealism that Vyasa aspires to may yet be realised in the very medium he rejected: mainstream cinema.

These abstract boundaries have not yet been fully blurred, of course. Bhoothakola is an indigenous religious tradition that has long been associated with subaltern communities, and someone like Karanth would not have been encouraged to go watch it when he was young. It is usually held in temples, nestled away in the interiors of villages, where a man dresses up in the costume of an especial local deity, dancing to frenzied drum beats through the night. The elders and leaders of the village are all present, and there is a kind of orchestrated dialogue that takes place between the bhootha and the village at large. Sometimes, the bhootha can also represent the genuine interests of the masses, and ensure that the landed gentry take ethical political decisions. In the wake of the national success of *Kantara*, attempts to claim the Bhoothakola tradition as a part of 'Hinduism' were met with a critical response by activist Chetan Ahimsa, who argued that Bhoothakola is an indigenous form that is of pagan origins, unrelated to the Vedic traditions that are seen as the fount of Hinduism/Sanatana Dharma. The locals of South Canara seem mostly unburdened by such theoretical concerns—they are simply delighted that films and social media have thrust their art forms into unprecedented limelight. Pilivesha too formed a key motif in another Rishab Shetty film—a gangster story set in Mangalore titled *Garuda Gamana Vrishabha Vahana*.

The fact remains that orthodox-genteel conceptions of art, driven by the intricate and ornate search for the divine, which Karanth had once walked away from, still remains a powerful aesthetic sentiment. Traditions like Pilivesha, Bhoothakola and Yakshagana can be strongly distinguished from that impulse. Both genres signify a tribute to all things considered sacred, but the rasas they evoke are different. In *Moga Padeda Mana*, a musician friend of Vyasa's articulates this difference succinctly after they witness a Yakshagana performance:

> The musical traditions here have very little connection to classical shastras. However, when concerning emotions of sadness, steeliness, or raudra [anger], the music flows most appropriately … The vigorous dance forms that have grown in the region are most conducive to expressing the vira rasa [the heroic sentiment].

To this, Vyasa responds:

> What you say is right. However, since this form is filled with such undulating potential, we can tune it to our desires. It can be made amenable to all rasas. These artists are also traditionalists, and are following old paths.

This might be true for a theatre-based tradition like Yakshagana, which opens up space for experimentation, but those like Pilivesha or Bhoothakola are rooted in the expression of the vira rasa, and it is hard to imagine them shedding their core identity. Yet, as Ashok Raj says over and over, the space for heartfelt individual expression will always remain open as long as the tradition itself remains rule-free.

To learn more about Shivaram Karanth's tryst with Yakshagana, I met with the master of the form, Bannanje Sanjeev Suvarna, who had been Karanth's apprentice for decades. He presently teaches at his home in Udupi, after having distanced himself from creeping bureaucratic forces breathing down his neck at the Yakshagana Kendra, where he had presided as guru for forty years. 'Whatever I am, whatever I am doing today, it is because of Karanth only. Not everyone is as lucky as I was. I believe that it was my destiny to become his student,' he says, pointing out that the plot of land on which he lives had also come to him courtesy of Karanth. And it was Karanth who changed his surname to Suvarna (a river that flows near Udupi).

SS: Karanth was not really a Yakshagana artist. I personally felt that he didn't watch it too seriously, as a study or anything. He was really inspired by Western ballet. He wanted to showcase a local art form to a larger audience, so that language would not become a barrier. He was fascinated by its visual dimensions—the attires, the masks and all that. Yakshagana is originally a bayalata, a play staged in an open field. Karanth wanted to take it to the theatre, to make it a classical form in this way. It was a completely new design—inspired very much by ballet—that he conceived all by himself, and he worked on it for many years. Earlier, certain characters would never become actual characters in the act, like the golden deer or Jatayu. They would just be spoken about by the other characters. But Karanth created new costumes for them and made them come on stage. People became really attracted by this. Music used to be in folk styles earlier, but he made them a bit more classical. The original form had some really loud parts, where the actors would shout. Karanth polished these bits a little to make it suitable for proscenium theatre.

Me: But I remember reading in his autobiography that he did not advocate such a classicalisation of Yakshagana, that it should preserve its traditional roots and so on …

SS: Karanth would say: 'My Yakshagana is a child of my imagination [kalpaneya koosu]. The traditional art must be kept as it is by its traditional practitioners.' He wanted his Yakshagana to be a performance that could touch an illiterate person. It shouldn't matter what language they speak. He really wanted Yakshagana to be felt and enjoyed by the nation and the world at large. He explicitly said that this was not meant for Karnataka at all. He never told anyone else how they should perform, or even suggest that any traditions must be broken. His conception was completely different, you see, just like him …

As it turns out, Yakshagana has taken innumerable new avatars in the course of the past hundred years. It has been used as medium to convey environmentalist concerns, to recreate the life of Jesus Christ, and has also been in service of AIDS campaigns and street theatre. I was intrigued to learn that it has morphed along the lines of caste, which means that different caste communities have been developing their own versions of Yakshagana, dictated by political motivations. I also heard from theatre veteran Shripad Bhat that Yakshagana has become highly communalised in the region over the last two decades, and there is often the trope of a Muslim character whose only function is to berate women. Muslim viewership and participation in traditional Yakshagana has also diminished in this process.

The very first scene in Sanjeev Suvarna's autobiography[9] describes him waiting at Bangalore airport, from where he is to travel alone to London to teach Yakshagana. Bereft of his troupe for the first time, thoughts of his illiteracy, and especially his English deficiencies, make him feel lost and distressed. He movingly describes the angst he has always felt as a result of his truncated primary education. Even when his talent for dance was recognised, his younger self felt incapable of measuring up to the demands of the discipline, and it took the angry determination of his first gurus to pull him back to sustained practice. When Karanth took him on as his protégé, Suvarna's life changed immeasurably.

He narrates how, in London, it initially felt weird performing purely for aesthetic purposes in a contextless land. In a similar vein, he also admitted to me: 'Before my generation, even if you gave an artist a hundred rupees and told him to perform in a way he did not naturally do, he would have rejected it. There was bhakti and aradhane before; now that is not there at all.' However, he is not naïvely ensconced in an older conception of the art—times change, and he embraces the excitement of it. Suvarna's students come from all over the world, and from all walks of life. He has travelled to many countries along with Karanth and his dance troupe. He was even part of the famous director B.V. Karanth's (no relation to Shivaram Karanth) troupe that enacted Shakespeare through Yakshagana, and he recently helped direct a Marathi play that uses the same medium. He draws the line only at the point where the art becomes glitzy and glamorous, falling prey to money-making ambitions. He does not believe in awards and competitions and winners. As a guru, though, he teaches traditional Yakshagana as he learnt it, and only makes pedagogical interventions where necessary.

Sanjeev Suvarna speaks highly about the contribution of the mathas—the priestly orders associated with the great Krishna temple in Udupi—to the growth of Yakshagana. He also credits them with ameliorating caste prejudices in recent times. I sense that, though he is not a deeply religious man, he reveres the matha, and a lot of this has to do with how closely Yakshagana is connected with its history. It was thanks to the efforts of Madhvacharya, the founder of the dualist Vedanta tradition in the thirteenth century, that Yakshagana became wedded to theatre and Vaishnavite devotion, he says. What was heroic content came to be transformed into devotion by blending several folk and classical styles. Bhakti became its central focus. Even today, traditional Yakshagana revolves primarily around episodes from the epics and the puranas, but there is immense space for subversion within the contours of that tradition.

The contrast became evident to me when we were talking about Pilivesha, and he said: *Nobody knows how Pilivesha started, or how it is really culture.* What he meant was that it does not boast centuries of history, of evolution, and in that sense lacks a hallowed past. This said, Suvarna also finds the conceptions of ritualised classical forms mystifying: 'All the classical dances in our country—be it Bharatanatyam, Odissi, Kuchipudi—are performed using hand mudras. They are symbols, but nobody can understand what they are! But Yakshagana can be understood, because there is language, dialogue.' Indeed, Yakshagana is still immensely popular in the region. Although the form continues to draw predominantly from the epics and puranas, its long hours are being shortened to match modern viewers' expectations, and it is also dealing with contemporary themes and predicaments. Today, even Bharatanatyam is creating new mudras, and has incorporated the mundanities of everyday life into its register.

Yakshagana, too, we may conclude, has transcended simplistic labels by diversifying into umpteen styles. Sanjeev Suvarna does not mourn the de-sacralisation of the art as much as he does the dissolution of the guru–shishya tradition. He sees himself as perhaps the last of the traditional practitioners of the art who learnt it while living with his masters, absorbing their legacy, getting to know their kith and kin as his own, and most importantly, passing it on to innumerable others in his turn. Just to take one notable example, the acclaimed Bangalore-based theatre artist Sharanya Ramprakash found in Yakshagana a path to rejuvenate her artistic journey, and in Sanjeev Suvarna a guru welcoming of new paradigms. Women have been entering Yakshagana ever since the seventies, but it is still a male-dominated space. Sharanya Ramprakash ended up staying in Udupi with her guru for two years, learning the ropes of the art form. Later, she created *Akshayambara*, an experimental play that explored what would happen if a woman entered an art form played wholly by men for 800 years. Men had always been playing women, but what would happen if a woman played a man? She decided to take up the *Draupadi Vastrapaharana* episode from the Mahabharata, where she would play the molester Dushasana, while Draupadi would be played by a professional male Yakshagana artist known for performing female roles. This became a celebrated production that brought to life questions of simplistic gender binaries, the collective history of expectations based on those binaries and how one might go about rejecting them. 'We were questioning the tradition with the tradition-makers [gurus] right alongside us! They were so open to questions. They were genuinely, like, yeah, what will happen? The tradition was open to me. That was really when I discovered Yakshagana on my own terms,' she says, with infectious enthusiasm.[10]

Towards the end of 2022, a three-day art exhibition titled *Divyakala* was organised at an art gallery near Udupi. 'Art Inspired by the Divine', it was an exhibition of paintings by American-born artist Drdha Vrata Gorrick, and was inaugurated by the Udupi Admar Matha's junior seer, Sri Eshapriya Tirtha Swamiji, Gorrick's guru.

Gorrick is a talented artist, with a penchant for creating richly detailed sketches of gods, goddesses and intricate temple arches. He also sculpts wooden idols. All his work is carried out with exquisite, mathematical precision. He conducts temple-art workshops, passing on his skills to the next generation of sculptors. It so happens that one of the trustees of the art gallery—which features talented artists from across the region—is Dr Kiran Acharya, an orthopaedic surgeon and professor. He is the son of the late BJP veteran V.S. Acharya, who is credited with the abolition of dalits carrying night soil when he became president of the Udupi municipal council in 1968.[11] It also happens to be that Kiran Acharya and Ashok Raj were students together at the same Kannada-medium school in Udupi. From what I heard, they had always shared a healthy relationship of mutual respect.

Thus, these two broad artistic traditions (the technical intricacy of classical religious art, the raw freedom of Pilivesha) coexist, trying to carve out a space within a new world that has been thrown wide open. Yakshagana possesses the dramatic wherewithal to evolve and diversify beyond its contours, just as Vyasa (and Karanth) had seen it to be capable of. Pilivesha is poised at a crossroads, and change is imminent. The classical visual art traditions, which reached their grandest point many centuries ago, seem to be carved in stone. Its practitioners live on in a past-present-future continuum of pure sacredness, conserving a divine feeling—for themselves, their ancestors and their predecessors all at once.

III

> My works are generated by my intense feeling for my environment. I seek to find myself by following whatever course it leads to.
>
> —K.K. Hebbar

It is often said of the English guitarist and singer Mark Knopfler that he made the guitar sing (a reference to a line from *Sultans of Swing*), and it is with a similarly lyrical gift that K.K. Hebbar made his lines sing. He called them singing-line drawings—evocative, minimalist pencil-line sketches that nonetheless bring out the dynamic elements of his subjects. In fact, he learnt Kathak from a disciple of Birju Maharaj, not to become a performer, but to understand the *rhythm* of the dance, which he would then incorporate into his singing-line drawings. His line drawings of Yakshagana and other local dance forms, for instance, carry a dimension of movement and rhythm. Hebbar also held passionate conversations with his contemporaries, and reflected deeply on his artistic journey. In his own words:

> As I gained proficiency in recording what I wanted in lines, I gradually acquired a style of my own. So far, my aim was to reproduce accurately what I saw or imagined. But once I achieved that skill, I started searching the hidden beauty in the interplay of lines, the evocative quality of straight and curved lines. This quality of rhythmic movement of lines began to engage my attention more and more. I realised that the lines are capable of singing and dancing. These lines are creative rather than imitative.

Oftentimes, he would just lose himself in a certain mood, a certain music, and let his hand run free without keeping his eyes on the paper. Karanth's modus operandi for writing a novel was to lose himself in a frenzy for a few days—as if letting out a torrent of ideas that had been mulled over in his head—and not settling down until the draft was complete. It took him only a month to write more than three hundred pages of *Marali Mannige.* In his line drawings, Hebbar achieved with staggering versatility what Karanth himself had ardently tried, and successfully realised in some works (such as *Chomana Dudi*, a miniature masterpiece, which was reportedly written in a week): to distil the environment, people and culture of South Canara into its most elementary outlines, shunning unnecessary ornamentation, creating a work of art capable of touching one's psyche at a primal level. The white vacuum of Hebbar's singing lines pulls you into completing the story through your own imagination—not merely consuming, but actively creating in your own mind—and effectively drawing you into the little universe it has spawned. It is no surprise that the Hebbar Art Gallery can also double up as a therapeutic sanctuary for troubled souls. There have been attempts to explain this scientifically by neuroscientists with a feeling for art. V.S. Ramachandran, for instance, ties this particular sensibility for minimalism to our evolutionary feeling for perceptual problem-solving, for sniffing out images and movements from the smallest amount of information, that might very well have saved our lives at some moment in evolutionary time. He believes that there are aesthetic universals which an artistic genius can channel into drawings, which then trigger these mental mechanisms in the most 'titillating' fashion. It is for this reason that the novelist Mulk Raj Anand, deeply moved by Hebbar's lines, once wrote:

> Then there are the drawings, in which the worm of line twists and wriggles and writhes along the passing stream of experience, almost like the flower of lightning suddenly illuminating the dark sky. The hungry line now gropes around the curves, circles, sharp thrusts, as though lit by casual flares of perception and begins to breathe its own strange kind of life, with tense dramatic pauses into the inner corners of our dark minds. Already, the line is becoming the shorthand of God, coursing round the spheres, breaking, spilling over on both sides of its two planes.

The book of line drawings[12] that this excerpt has been taken from carries close to thirty sketches—of graceful dance partners, moving images from poverty-stricken households, shy private moments of romance and love, artists in the throes of their passion—but there is one sketch that really stands out. Simply titled 'Plate 8', it is the rawest, most agonisingly evocative sketch of the lot, which brings to mind the bony, jagged figures of the Austrian line artist and expressionist Egon Schiele. Schiele was fascinated by the raw sexuality of the human body, as was Hebbar, who painted numerous nude sketches of individuals, not all of which are available for the general public to view.

'Plate 8' isn't just a study of the human body though, but instead a study of the human condition itself, of being caught up in the march of history. It features a man in motion, struggling to push a bicycle forward, a thick jumble of lines bringing to the viewer's attention the pressure on his hind leg. But the heart of the sketch is the head of the man, which has been dislodged from its place at the top of his neck, where a barebones perimeter is all there is, oddly resembling a bicycle seat. The head, though, has traced a jumble of nerves, sinews and lines to where you might expect the seat, becoming disembodied from the torso and yet connected to it, looking back with a mixture of horror and astonishment towards the path the bicycle has come trundling along. When I showed it to my graphic novelist friend Appupen, he said the man's anatomy reminded him of some of Picasso's sketches.

In this furtive look backwards, the sketch is similar to Paul Klee's painting 'Angelus Novus', made famous by the German philosopher Walter Benjamin, who called it 'The Angel of History', and used it to flesh out his historical theses, wherein the angel is shown to be facing a stark predicament. It sees the wreckage at its feet, and would

Courtesy of the K.K. Hebbar Art Foundation

like to stay and make whole what has been destroyed. 'But a storm is blowing from paradise, it has caught itself up in his wings and is so strong that the Angel can no longer close them,' he writes. It is the storm of progress, and it must be reckoned with. Thinking along this vein, and since 'Plate 8' has remained unnamed, I would like to dub it 'The Common Man of History', a more secular and universal symbol than Klee's angel. Forced to mechanically pedal ahead while his mind looks back with bewilderment towards a past that is ambiguous and incomprehensible, mired in blood and suffering, the man is caught impossibly in a no-man's land between two worlds. As a snapshot of a hopelessly polarised political scenario, it captures the blind attempts of a radical Left to usher in a mechanically imagined future utopia, held back by an equally uncomprehending radical Right that seeks to go back to some imagined glorious past that has long since been left behind, if it ever existed. The hunched, tired posture of the man, his slack arms at the handles, suggests a reluctance to carry on, a desire to call it quits and settle down right here and now. Yet, the activity and energy in the legs—an embodiment of the human doggedness to put one foot in front of the other until the last breath—also suggest the inevitability of struggle, one way or another.

It is only art that is capable of looking at this duality with dispassion, and it is only in that moment of struggle that self-reflective truths may be created. Hebbar was acutely aware of the social realities of his times, and it is ultimately a humanist vision that pervades his mammoth body of work. Born in 1911, he lived through all the horrible wars of the twentieth century, the creation of Bangladesh, as well as the Gulf War in the early 1990s, all of which found passionate expression on his canvas. The characters in so many of his paintings live eternally in deep moments of private agony.

There is another reading of the sketch that we may consider—of the tussle between the West and the East, of the post-colonial condition, of the strange attraction to foreign shores that Gopalakrishna Adiga had once questioned in his famous poem 'Yaava Mohana Murali Kareyitu?' (What enchanting music drew you away?). Hebbar's early paintings were inspired by the landscapes of South Canara, the mythological tales he grew up listening to, as well as local art traditions. Later, he would travel to Bombay, become a part of the modernist art movement there, honing his skills further. And out of this emerged his own unique style—the melancholic crimson backgrounds in his portraits (one of which is doubly reflected in the crimson eyes of a gaunt and grim portrait of Nehru), the dark reflections on war and suffering, and of course, the singing lines he continued to create throughout his life. In a 1984 interview given to *Taranga* magazine, Hebbar was asked precisely this question, what he felt about the clash of the East and the West, as far as art history is concerned. After explaining patiently how history is replete with all manner of influences from both sides, he says:

> It is not surprising for an artist to be inspired by the janapada traditions of his land, or by the samskaaras of his upbringing. But the art becomes great only when this innate, natural conditioning is fused with the heartfelt uniqueness of his creative conscience. Instead of using labels like Western, Eastern, Indian, Non-Indian, it would be better to ask if the painting is good/bad, if it is creative, if it is really novel, and so on.

Indeed, a critic tasked with studying Hebbar had once asked in a moment of mock exasperation, 'Where does one place that creative output which refutes both the national and the regional?' This remarkable talent to assimilate and synthesise anew is certainly thanks to Hebbar's synesthetic brain that embraced all arts with the same feeling. As he says later on in the same interview: 'All that matters to me while creating something are my inner sensations. This is what I meant when I said that I paint so that I can listen to music with my eyes. In this endeavour, studying Western Art traditions has helped me a lot.'

This chapter would be incomplete without mentioning another versatile maverick of South Canara, B.V. Karanth, who set up Mysore's famed theatre institution Rangayana in 1989.

Karanth's first and foremost love was music. He often spoke about how the mystical sounds of the forest creatures, amidst which he grew up, inspired his sense of sound design for the plays he would go on to direct. He was an accomplished vocalist, and his singing talents occupied the first line on his acting resume too. He saw plays as musical compositions first, and as texts later. He preferred to call himself a sound planner rather than a music director.

Inspired by Vinoba Bhave's call to learn Hindi, B.V. Karanth travelled to Varanasi to learn the language and study the literature. Soon, he was reading Kabir in the original, and developed a particular fascination for the various manifestations of poetic rhythm. His initial work in Varanasi revolved around rhythm, and he later moved to Delhi to pursue his PhD. There, his advisor, the eminent writer Hazari Prasad Dwivedi, told Karanth that he would be serving Hindi literature better if he shifted his thesis towards theatre rather than poetry and music. Karanth used traditional instruments with experimental fervour, and always sought to synthesise tradition and modernity in unprecedented ways. When he staged Girish Karnad's philosophical play *Hayavadana*—a retelling of the folktale involving the transposed heads of two men who represent brain and brawn respectively—it drew from traditional theatre and Yakshagana aesthetics, giving the play a Karnataka touch.

When he became director of the National School of Drama in Delhi, taking over from Ebrahim Alkazi, B.V. Karanth infused it with fresh vitality. In the words of director Heggodu Prasanna: 'What B.V. Karanth did was to go beyond just the theory. He started looking at Indian theatre as it was being practised in different parts of the country, and brought them back to Delhi. He made the contemporary actors confront some of these styles, some of these lifestyles, and some of these forms. Thereby, he tried to bring a certain "Indianness" to it all.' It was through such a vision that B.V. Karanth managed to bring Shakespeare alive within the aesthetic contours of Yakshagana.

Having known both from close quarters, Sanjeev Suvarna explained to me that the two Karanths were united in their understanding of Yakshagana and its irreplaceable traditional roots: 'Both B.V. Karanth and Shivaram Karanth believed that the Yakshagana tradition should stay as it is. They saw it as the path laid down by its ancestors that should follow its natural course. Shivaram Karanth used to say that all his experiments would die with him, but that the tradition would keep persevering.' Suvarna also pulled out a fond memory of K.K. Hebbar's appreciation of his performance. 'Eh, our Sanjeeva is really good, huh,' Hebbar had remarked to Shivaram Karanth, who had beamed approvingly. It was Hebbar who sketched and standardised the new costumes and accessories for Karanth's ballet endeavour, which had also required a fresh imagination because women would be playing men's roles. The two often spent time together, creating a porous membrane between them, with ideas streaming through.

One may imagine the heightened atmosphere in a room where Shivaram Karanth and B.V. Karanth and K.K. Hebbar might once have sipped coffee together and exchanged notes on their latest experiments. They were men inspired by the arts and traditions of South Canara, but what set them apart from many of their contemporaries was their urge to articulate an original universalism unbound by tribalistic affiliations to caste, creed, religion or political ideology. By seeking refuge in their humanistic nature, and in the unsullied beauty of the natural environment, they sought to conserve the richest aspects of our collective inheritance, while simultaneously giving birth to new worlds of meaning.

IV

When I interviewed the noted linguist and professor K.P. Rao, credited with developing the first Kannada keyboard and its attendant software, he had some bitter (though I only found it funny) recollections about Shivaram Karanth. Rao too had been part of Karanth's extended circles, because K.K. Hebbar's wife was Rao's aunt-in-law. A teenaged K.P. Rao had once taken a Kannada poem he had written about the heights of the Vijayanagar empire to Karanth, who had summarily dismissed it with some sarcastic remarks. 'If he had something to say, he would say it loudly enough for the whole world to listen. That day, he killed a great poet-in-the-making,' K.P. Rao says, half-laughing, half-serious.

Karanth could be devastating indeed, like the raw force of a natural disaster. We see something of this quality in his depictions of nature too, which is an evolving character in his novels. *Marali Mannige* offers the most sweeping trajectory of how nature has been perceived across the nineteenth and twentieth centuries—narrated through the lives of three generations, from Karanth's grandparents' to his own. For the first generation, nature is a source of misery, inundating their farms, taking lives at will and frightening them into sublime reverence. For those of the next, modern education makes its way into the lives of a privileged few. They leave the villages for towns, sending back money to their villages, but becoming unconcerned about such things as natural environments. The influx of liquid cash causes greed and mischief within the villages, and doesn't really become a force for good. Then comes Karanth's generation, some of whom become disenchanted with the trappings of modernity (like Vyasa in *Moga Padeda Mana*), and beat a retreat back to the soil, back to their roots, finding real inspiration in nature alone.

There is a similar metaphor in *Bettada Jeeva* (The Mountain Soul), where we meet a man who tames the wilderness and makes a home for himself in the wild forested hills of the Western Ghats. Nature becomes the 'nation' for the dwellers of the community he spawns. Then, the freedom movement begins, and the man's young son is attracted to Gandhi, to the bigger nation, and abandons his old parents to their secluded lifestyle. It is safe to say that we are presently in a period where Indians are increasingly forsaking proximity to nature for the more economically attractive life of urban spaces. The exodus from rural India continues unabated. Yet, so many of us still feel the urge to retreat into nature, if only for the aesthetic and spiritual relief it allows us.

Throughout his life, Karanth remained an inveterate traveller, who held an enormous fascination for the natural world. His son, the conservationist Ullas Karanth, says that he probably became captivated by tigers because of all the animal stories that his father would weave for him and his siblings before they went to sleep. This is what Shivaram Karanth had to say of his passionate trips around Karnataka during his youth: 'The panorama that greets the eye from a hillock next to the sea at Bhatkal is unsurpassed. The beach at Karwar could enslave anyone. The crowning glory of Malnad are the Jog Falls. I have not kept count of the number of times I have visited it. The gorge and the precipice are unfailingly alluring. I have sat, soaked, eaten and slept on the banks of the Sharavati river, and have romped on the sand.' He would later go on to travel around the world and pen many a travelogue.

Karanth began to develop a deep dislike towards the nationalistic experiment as it was manifesting in India. Critiques of various species of nationalism pervade his writings, and unlike the ultra-nationalistic Progressive writers of the 1930s and '40s, Karanth was able to capture the swing of a society in *doubt*. Traditionalist writers are able to faithfully capture a society's transition to modernity because they hold enough sympathy for the world they are leaving behind.[13] Karanth had recognised that the powerful sweep of nationalism could wipe away entire communities from its imagination, like the forest dwellers of *Bettada Jeeva*. In his last novel, *Antida Aparanji* (The Nugget Attached), published in 1986, we see a highly sarcastic portrayal of religious posturing and its attendant thirst for land and power. We meet a man who constructs a shrine in South Canara to establish his stature (after having constructed a falsely ancient history for it), and through it pursues his financial greed, a trait which flows down to his progeny in equal measure. At the end of the novel, a discerning citizen delivers his verdict on one of these greedy individuals: 'He creates new schemes at every step, whose goal is singular. He is a gold nugget attached to this town. He is a master at gulping money. He spouts scriptures, but lays down only traps! Still there are people who don't just believe him, but also say that such an attitude is necessary to survive in today's day and age … Whoever desires to become his devotee, follower or friend must bear the exact same mindset.'

Karanth always responded to the political developments of his lifetime with aplomb. In 1952, he contested the Provincial Assembly elections in Puttur constituency as a candidate of the Praja Socialist Party. The caste politics within the Congress dismayed him, as did the malpractices surrounding ballot boxes in those initial years. As he writes, *In the political battlefield, the first casualty is truth.* During the Emergency, Karanth returned his Padma Bhushan in protest, and went on to become the major face of many environmental movements in Karnataka in the years to come. The noted environmentalist S.R. Hiremath told me about an encounter with Karanth at some school function in Kalaburagi during the early 1980s, where Hiremath informed him about the pollution of the Tungabhadra by the rayon fibre factory, Harihara Polyfibres (HPF). Karanth promptly wrote up a well-researched booklet that helped popularise the legal struggle against the industry. The backing of respected writers can enormously benefit environmental movements. The presence of U.R. Ananthamurthy in the movement to save the source of the Tunga from iron ore mining in Kudremukh also provided a great fillip during the early 2000s.

In 1989, inspired by the rise of the Green Party in Germany, Shivaram Karanth (by this time quite an ancient man) decided to stand for elections from Karwar on an anti-nuclear plank. He had been involved in the protests against the nuclear plant in Kaiga (in North Canara), and was planning to use the momentum from these protests. However, it was not as popular a protest as he had imagined, and since he did not bother with political canvassing, ended up losing his deposit by a long margin. In the process, he helped the popular Kannada actor Anant Nag flunk the election as well, having taking away a sizeable chunk of his votes. It must be added that even if the Kaiga movement was unsuccessful in terms of preventing the project and creating an environment-centred political platform, it did inaugurate a scientific temper in the public sphere, holding the government to account and ensuring healthy debate around the safety of the nuclear reactor.

Towards the end of Karanth's life, the kind of myopic politics he had always loathed began to train its eyes on him. In 1995, certain agenda-driven organisations pressured the government to ban Karanth's textbook series, Oduva Aata (The Play of Learning), on petty grounds, which the government considered seriously. One community took offence at a story involving a carpenter, alleging casteism—a troubling reading of the work of a sensitive writer. A Christian group railed against his translation of the Holy Spirit as 'Pavitra Preta' in some chapter, arguing that 'preta' had demonic connotations. Karanth was too old (he was ninety-three) by this time to reckon with this, and Malini Mallya told me with a grin that it was she who had drafted Karanth's official response, writing that the government's succumbing to these lobbies had hurt him deeply.

His textbooks would serve as a good example even today, for those interested in primary pedagogy, of books written with care, verve and simplicity, especially moulded for young minds. Shivaram Karanth was also the first writer to produce books on science in the Kannada language. He would educate himself on the latest developments in the scientific world by procuring English books from abroad and distilling their insights into popular books on science meant for children. He travelled around the country, clicked thousands of photographs, and wrote the first encyclopaedia for children in Kannada in a style that was clear and accessible. He'd translated the American biologist Rachel Carson's classic work *Silent Spring* into Kannada. Even during the 1980s, he was engaged in serious work, and published his Kannada translation of a work of academic psychiatry, *The Great Universe of Kota*.[14] However, his science books never attained great popularity. K.P. Rao remarked to me that they were not received well, and that 'nobody within our own district really used his books'.

Karanth's life—his writings, his activism, his ineluctable influence on succeeding generations—can only be seen in toto, as a vast territory of land upon which his energetic capacity for action delivered a torrential downpour. Yet, one man can do only so much, and it would be foolish to see all his efforts as pioneering ones. It is only his dynamic personality that really calls out to us. In following that age-old maxim of not preaching, but teaching, through sheer dint of personal example, Shivaram Karanth spells out the inspiring tale of a life spent in endless creative pursuit.

FOUR

Saakshi*
Journeys of Self-Discovery

Two friends present their verses,
With wagging tail, he praises
One and barks at the other, this puppy,
Washing away all sense of bonhomie.

His perspective is already firm and set
To this frog, poems must seem like insects
T.S. Eliot is far too bland
And everyone he doesn't understand
Must be deluded.

It's safe to say that for this chump,
All poetry is simply dung falling from mankind's rump.
—H.S. Biligiri, 'Comrade Vimarshaka'

I

In 1953, the budding poet Gopalakrishna Adiga wrote pensively in a letter to his dear friend, the novelist Basavaraj Kattimani:

> I noticed that you have dedicated your book of short stories to Masti Venkatesha Iyengar. I was overjoyed to see that, and I figured it to be a sign of your healthy mindset. Whatever the older literati

* *saakshi*. noun. conscience. evidence. witness.

> might think of us, we must show them our fullest respect, if only to showcase our broad-mindedness. To be honest, I don't think we should really count Bendre, Kuvempu, Masti and others as living writers—we must only reflect upon their works. Whatever human flaws we may perceive in them should not affect us too much. Whatever good resides inside us will keep us alive and propel us further. If our work goes well, we shall see the fruits sooner or later.[1]

Basavaraj Kattimani and others like A.N. Krishna Rao were bearers of the Pragatisheela progressive torch in Kannada literature, rebelling against the ivory towers of the classical Navodaya movement. Just a few years before this exchange with Adiga, a hot-blooded Kattimani had publicly called for a burning of Masti's work of historical fiction, *Chennabasava Nayaka*, because he felt it did a disservice to lingayat history. It appears that he soon realised his folly and tried to make amends through gestures such as this book dedication.

For Kattimani's politically invigorated generation, much influenced by the socialist ideals of the Progressive Writers Movement, literature needed to be involved with the ordinary citizens whose trials and tribulations did not figure much within the Navodaya aesthetic. Gopalakrishna Adiga grew up absorbing these ideals in the 1940s, and his correspondence shows that he looked up fervently to Basavaraj Kattimani, both as friend and mentor. However, as Adiga began developing his own unique lyricism, inspired by the writings of Eliot and Yeats, he emerged from the cocoon of progressivism. In the early 1950s, Adiga wrote numerous letters to Kattimani. During the course of this correspondence, their literary differences surface and become increasingly intense, if always cordial. Adiga argues, in long, passionate letters that literature must plumb the interiors of one's subjective self, and that effecting social change can never be its primary purpose. The atheism of the progressives too failed to touch Adiga, who believed that scoffing at religious beliefs was a cheap act. In a tone that often becomes impatient and exasperated, Adiga stresses to Kattimani that art can never be separated from its aesthetic concerns; one may only strive to combine a social conscience with the practice of art for art's sake. To impose ideological restrictions on creative endeavour is to dampen the very spirit that gives it its mysterious, invaluable force. These views might seem cliched from today's vantage point, but in the mid-twentieth century, the practice of revolutionary literature was yet to find its fiercest critics. Two decades later, in the seventies, these very questions and debates would rear their heads within the Kannada literary sphere once again—history may not repeat itself, but it certainly echoes.

The fifties stood witness to the modernist turn in Kannada literature (Navya, or new), and Gopalakrishna Adiga was to become its prodigious poster boy. This was a fresh literary sensibility, moving away from the ornate romanticism of Navodaya, and rejecting the utilitarian excesses of Pragatisheela, instead attempting to craft a new conscience that could, above all, allow a writer to explore their unique self and individual genius. Towards the middle of the decade, Adiga planned to bring out a new literary magazine—to be called *Sakshi*—that would showcase the best of creative writing and literary criticism, academic ruminations from all manner of disciplines, writings from India as well as translations from the West. Given the financial constraints and the foreknowledge that such a magazine would not enjoy popular appeal or large circulation, the first copy came out only in the early sixties. Around forty issues of *Sakshi* were published sporadically over the next two decades, featuring some of the finest writers of the Kannada language.

I was lucky enough to procure close to thirty of these issues from my grand-uncle's dusty bookshelves at our ancestral home in the village of Talakad. So highly valued were these that he had inscribed most of their front pages with his name as well as the year of purchase. The earliest copy was from 1962, and their survival for more than half a century on a shelf in the attic, prone to attack by termites and assorted vermin, owed much to the pride of their owner. As I gingerly opened each of the magazines, dipping into their contents over the course of many months, the covers featuring ads for HMT watches and Ganesh beedis disintegrated and fell away from the mass, making me feel a little guilty for disturbing their peace.

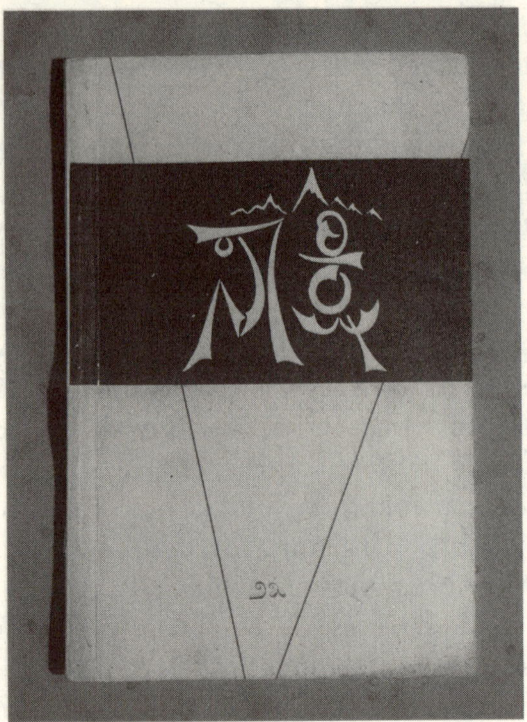

Sakshi, April 1974

Even at first glance, *Sakshi* exhibits a measure of finesse that is missing from the best of Kannada magazines today—alluring typography, the sheer breadth of topics, a difficult-to-place old-school charm, combined with excellent curation and editing. It was ultimately Adiga's editorial vision that made it a landmark in Kannada publishing history. His introduction in the very first issue speaks of the need for a platform where the collective conscience of a literary society may find its voice, rising above the interests of any particular caste or creed. In tone and tenor, it was very different from the progressivism of Kattimani and company, even if it espoused similar concerns of social equality. *Sakshi* embodied a universalist sensibility that embraced the scientific temper of modernity, sought refuge in no particular ideology and only aspired towards a heartfelt humanism driven by calm introspection. As Adiga writes in the introduction:

> Since the core belief behind this endeavour is that truth is the only thing that remains at the end, it does not seek to become the mouthpiece of any individual, group or sect. There will always be space for all manner of subjects and ideologies within its pages. However, all opinions must be submitted with deep deliberation, accountability and honesty. The quest for truth must always be the driving force. All such writings are welcome at *Sakshi*.

The pieces in *Sakshi* ranged widely, from romantic poetry to plays, academic reflections on land reforms, critical reviews of contemporary Kannada novels, insights from archaeology and linguistics, musings on education policies and political debates, and so on. There was one edition entirely devoted to Polish literature. No subject was taboo; the only condition was that the article be well written and well argued. In a 1972 issue, there is a personal account by the linguist and scholar H.S. Biligiri describing his first experience of LSD, which illustrates the magazine's open and adventurous approach, seeking a bold engagement with the counter-cultural trends of its times and plumbing them for an experience of the real.[2] The Navya sensibility was marked strongly by the search for metaphors that could capture the richness of one's inner life, moving away from orthodox notions of timid puritanism, and this seems to have led the writer-seeker into various sensual realms. Friendship (both in personal life and fiction) became an important theme—Shantinath Desai's 1961 novel *Mukti* (Liberation), for instance, is a moving portrait of man's quest for closure after the death of a dear friend—although the Navya writers' exploration of romance largely tended to objectify women as dolls awaiting attention. (Lankesh and Shantinath Desai are notable exceptions in this regard.)

The most common critique of the Navya writers was that they relied far too much on inspiration from the West. This seems a little strange when one considers how the Kannada renaissance of the twentieth century, beginning with Navodaya, had essentially been facilitated by the colonial encounter and the new modes of knowledge that it had bequeathed. Such influence was inescapable. Way back in the thirties, the maverick Kannada poet Pejavara Sadashiva Rao had already introduced a completely fresh imaginary in Kannada poetry that is usually considered as the first sprouting of Navya. His famous poem 'Naatyotsava' is both an aural and visual delight (also the first reference to jazz in Kannada poetry) that captures the emancipation he experienced as a young man studying in Italy:

Lorenzo, El Magnifico![3]
Dedicating a song to you, here you go!
Today is a festival,
a youthful spectacle,
at the altar of adulthood!
Where life forces unite.
As a guru, you stand ineffable,
we have imbibed your lesson!
The jazz sounds come floating,
to induce dance in us!
Oh, there's that grape drink—
to seduce our spirits!
Venetian glass,
And the thrill of Sardinian wine.[4]

Tragically, in 1939, Sadashiva Rao passed away in Italy at the age of twenty-six. He'd been suffering from peritonitis for more than a year and had been hospitalised. In this time, he had already written some exceptional poems, as well as a few essays and short stories. His work gains power through its raw youthful originality, not bogged down by the restrictions of any tradition or lineage—for Sadashiva Rao, the sense of freedom flowing through those jazz nights was a finer guru than any other entity. Just a year before he died, Rao had written, in a letter to V.K. Gokak, who was at Oxford then: 'Until the next deluge comes, it does not seem like our people will gain the strength to break away from traditions that have locked them away in cages for centuries, and move on from clichés like the beauty of the Western Ghats, the charm of sunrises and sunsets, the angst of widows, the chirping of birds, *Vedanta* and so on ... Shouldn't our new poetry also reflect the experiences of those few of us who have travelled abroad?'

Some of his essays, published while in Italy, are absurdly trivial and hilarious, as in one titled 'Feminine Arts', where he tries to dig into the history of fingernail painting:

> Writers of all times and places wonder with surprise why women need to paint themselves. Nobody has ever found a convincing reason. Xenophon of Athens, in his nice book on domestic chores, gently reproaches a young woman for her foolery of painting her cheeks red and white, but he was unable to find another efficacious argument other than the fact that when she would marry, the husband would uncover the trick of her exterior appearance! On the other side, the Indian Kalidasa, perhaps the wiser one, builds highly poetic comments around the heroine who has painted her feet. He knows that nothing could be gained from a discussion [of the need for such embellishment].

As if challenging Sadashiva Rao's perception of feminine ornamentation, we meet the short-story writer Kodagina Gowramma, who stages a fast to ensure that Gandhi visits her home (he visited Kodagu/Coorg in 1933), and then donates all her gold jewellery to Gandhi, urging him to use it for the Harijan cause.[5] Gowramma too perished at a tragically young age—she was twenty-eight when she died in a swimming accident in 1939—and left behind a truncated legacy of twenty-one short stories,[6] which are bold, formally inventive (she employs the epistolary format often) and universal in their concerns. The unique landscape of Coorg does not figure here. The stories might just as well be about any independent woman questioning the pathetic helplessness of men she is surrounded by. Had Pejavara Sadashiva Rao and Kodagina Gowramma lived to attain the full spring of their intellectual adulthood, they might have given the Kannada modernists a run for their money. Instead, the task was left to succeeding generations who would discover a sense of cosmopolitanism while being acutely attached to their linguistic roots in independent India.

In a *Sakshi* issue published in 1973, U.R. Ananthamurthy wrote an essay titled 'Bharateeyate' (Indianness). This has an account of a symposium at which a folk artist clad in jubba-pyjama describes a trip he made to a village in North India. With a camera hanging from his neck, this folk artist reaches a hut, inside which he glimpses a sacred stone dotted with kumkuma. Having asked and received permission from the poor peasant who is the master of the hut, he takes the stone outside to photograph it; later, struck by doubt, he asks the man's forgiveness if he has inadvertently desacralised the stone. The peasant replies that it is not a big deal, he will simply find another stone and apply vermilion to that. Baffled by this response, the artist comes away with the strong conviction that the innocent sincerity of the peasant is at the heart of what it means to be Indian. This story stuns Ananthamurthy and his cohort, who begin to think that all their discussions on Camus, Kafka and Sartre make little sense if they are unable to inhabit the mind-space of that sincere peasant. In a remarkable expression of self-awareness (his strongest suit), Ananthamurthy writes:

> As far as all our literary-cultural discussions go, one thing is becoming clear to me. We are beginning to lose belief in our class. Those of Karanth's generation had faith in their feelings, and possessed a conviction that their thought process could create meaningful values in others. We don't have this self-confidence. We don't see ourselves with a sense of authenticity, and the very bourgeois class that we belong to makes us queasy. To hide this, we dress up in bohemian attires. However, our predecessors believed that their well-being was the well-being of the country at large. We see this all the way from Raja Rammohun Roy, down to the politicians and writers of the 1940s. We are now caught up in a dilemma. I am not saying this is either right or wrong, but that this disbelief has caught up with us, and it is necessary to admit that the material benefits of Nehruvian politics which we have reaped have contributed to this. Hence, the most sensitive of us feel doubtful about our innermost feelings. In this state of mind, we either chase the 'absurd', or feel that the peasant who worships any random stone is the most authentic

Indian. Camus, Kafka or the peasant—all of them become masks adopted by a mind that has no real foundation.

This is also the explanation Ananthamurthy offers as to why the Navya novelists largely eschewed the omniscient narrative voice, and began to explore the mental wobbling of subjective selves. He concludes the piece, thus:

> I suspect that our various modes of approaching the idea of India—the simplicity of the peasant, Vedic orthodoxy, Aurobindo's spirituality, and so on—are also not really useful. Why can't we see the trappings of the innocent peasant with the same obviousness with which we see the failures of our West-inspired lifestyles? To be sure, there were Indians who were capable of this. We err in speaking about all this without referring to the various tussles within our history. What would Tukaram, Kabir, or Basavanna have thought about this peasant? They were able to question the blind faith that this peasant has carried over through tradition. They were able to erupt in anger over the naivety with which this peasant could worship a random stone. Why can't we pick a fight with the peasant as they did? Somewhere in between all these considerations, I feel there exists the possibility of becoming a truly Indian writer.

A few years later, Ananthamurthy wrote a witty short story titled 'A Stallion of the Sun' in which this very idea of the village simpleton is expounded—but he is unable to infuse anything truly original. The story ends with an urban, modernised character named Ananthu becoming fascinated with a village simpleton named Hade Venkata ('Hade' connotes a wastrel), who proclaims that the grasshopper is a 'stallion of the sun', an evocative metaphor that represents the collective lyrical imagination of the 'real' India. The choice between calling a grasshopper a grasshopper and calling it a stallion of the sun becomes the crux of the predicament, the yawning divide between two disparate cultures. A rather pithy summing up of a crucial current concern. Are not the present political slogans demanding something very similar?[7] Practising the linguistic sophistry of changing names, and then deeming it to be more monumental an act than it actually is? At the end of the story, Ananthamurthy is still unable to question the simplicity and naivete that he so clearly wants to—he is held back by a sort of Gandhian appreciation of the spirit of rural India.

There is something to be said here about Ananthamurthy's famous rivalry with another giant of Kannada letters, S.L. Bhyrappa. They have always struck me as two brothers fighting for the attention of the mother, and juxtaposing them gives us a fuller picture of the enormous paradoxes at the heart of literary ideology. Throughout their careers, Ananthamurthy and Bhyrappa were at odds with one another, tongues loose and teeth gritted. Bhyrappa famously disliked the cult of the *Sakshi* magazine, which never really admitted him into its fold. He found linguistic experimentation to be Navya's sole contribution to Kannada literature. It is a historical coincidence that, at the peak of their literary powers, the identities of both these writers were forged through their ideological rivalry over thematically coinciding concerns. Ananthamurthy's *Samskara* and Bhyrappa's *Vamshavriksha* were both published in the mid-sixties; both were meditations on the clash between brahmin orthodoxy and the onset of modernity; both were eventually made into successful films (retaining the names of the novels) with Girish Karnad in the lead role. Their subsequent novels, *Bharatipura* and *Daatu*, revolved around the caste question, again sharing a curiously similar cocktail of idealism and cynicism.

And yet, the two did not garner similar critical responses. No doubt this was because of the vast chasm between their professed political leanings. Ananthamurthy may have been a shaky socialist, but he was an unwavering critic of Hindutva, and Bhyrappa—ever a supporter of the Sangh—now sings paeans to Narendra Modi at every public opportunity. Ananthamurthy grew up pampered and spent the rest of his life scrutinising his privileges; Bhyrappa grew up orphaned (not unlike Savarkar), and spent the rest of his life in search of a motherland.[8] Ananthamurthy's personality is often witty, but humour is wholly absent in Bhyrappa.

When you look purely at their fiction, it almost seems like they each possess something the other desperately craves. Bhyrappa is a hyper-realist who struggles to inhabit the metaphorical, spiritual quotient of his fiction, even when he is retelling the myths. On the other hand, Ananthamurthy suffuses his stories with symbolic allegories that often feel rather distanced from the social realities of his times, which he dwells upon intensely in his essays. Ananthamurthy is certainly a more gifted essayist than Bhyrappa, who wrote very little non-fiction, but Bhyrappa is a far more prolific creative writer, with an exceptional talent for fictional world-building.

Yet, when Bhyrappa's politics begins to enter his work, his novels suffer for lack of vitality, as though what should have been a polemical tract is transforming into a thinly veiled novel. Similarly, Ananthamurthy's deep desire to inhabit a true 'Indian imagination' keeps leading him down thought processes he's already explored in his essays, and he searches in his fiction (especially *Bhava* and *Divya*) for new ways to articulate them. Neither of them endorses the persistence of caste hierarchy, but nor are they able to present a literary vision of how it may be transcended. Neither is able to successfully champion female protagonists engaging with modernity. Bhyrappa can portray a kind of 'feminism' in mythological retellings (Gandhari in *Parva*, Sita in *Uttara Kanda*), but in his novels set in modern times (*Vamshavruksha*, *Kavalu*, *Aavarana*), women who dare to defy orthodoxy and patriarchy are puppeteered into paying a hefty price. Ananthamurthy's female characters are satellites of his male protagonists, enabling their epiphanies, then sidling away. While tragedy pervades Bhyrappa's fiction (his own childhood was filled with terrible poverty, his mother and siblings died in plague epidemics, his father had abandoned them earlier), if there is one quality that unites Ananthamurthy's universe, it is *ambiguity*, a free-floating liberal sensibility forever searching for allegiance, like Bhishma who loved both the Pandavas and the Kauravas—and *that* is tragic in its own right. In many ways, they have together created a body of literature that captures two sides of the same *conscience*: the conscience of failure, of having failed to truly inhabit some timeless essence of a cultural past, and of having ushered in Western modernity far too hastily, of having failed to prevent a war that seems doomed for everyone. For Ananthamurthy, this would lead him towards a strong critique of developmental politics and align him with environmentalists and dalit activists later in his life, while for Bhyrappa, it would create a blinkered political persona that allied him with Hindu supremacists, infiltrated his literature and made him suspicious of everything associated with the liberal Left.

A.K. Ramanujan, born in 1929 in Mysore, was one of the most gifted poets of the Navya generation. He rose to become critically acclaimed for his translations of medieval Kannada and Tamil poetry, his painstaking collection of Indian folktales which were followed by deep scholarship, and his brilliant studies of Indian mythology and culture. Translating the vachanas of the twelfth-century Sharana movement had been part of Ramanujan's way of reckoning with the rigidity of his conservative upbringing. In *Journeys*, a posthumous publication of his diary entries, Ramanajun writes about his reading of the vachanas at the age of sixteen, and how they 'they fitted my own inchoate impulses against caste, the patriarchal oppression of women (especially my mother and sisters), the great division of rich and poor, and even the learned and the illiterate'. His *Soma* poems, reflections on the ancient Rigvedic metaphor of soma—in ritual contexts signifying a drink believed to be a mushroom or plant extract, but in larger essence a search for artistic inspiration and poetic grace—were published recently in an attractive volume.

He was also a stimulating essayist. In his famous 1989 essay 'Is There an Indian Way of Thinking?', Ramanujan produced a comprehensive analysis of this clash of civilisations that continues to dominate our collective imagination. He begins by pointing towards the two non-conflicting sides of his own father, a mathematician and astronomer, who was also a Sanskrit scholar and an expert astrologer. When asked how he could read the Gita religiously, paint his forehead with a namam, and later talk about Bertrand Russell and Ingersoll with passion, Ramanujan's father had responded, 'The Gita is part of one's hygiene. Besides, don't you know the brain has two lobes?'

Additionally, Ramanujan underscores what seems to me the most crucial tenet of the subcontinental social order—its lack of universality. Everything is bound by a very specific context. Consider the following snippets from his essay:

> One has only to read Manu after a bit of Kant to be struck by the former's extraordinary lack of universality. He seems to have no clear notion of a universal *human* nature from which one can deduce ethical decrees like 'man shall not kill' or 'man shall not tell an untruth'.
>
> To be moral, for Manu, is to particularise—to ask who did what, to whom, and when. [Bernard] Shaw's comment, 'Do not do unto others as you would have them do unto you. Their tastes may not be the same' will be close to Manu's view, except he would substitute 'natures of classes' for 'tastes'. Each class (jati) of man has his own laws, his own proper ethic, not to be universalised.

We have little evidence that indicates to what extent Manu's codes (and his gory punishments for breaking them) were actually implemented. What the Manusmriti did was to bequeath an *ideal*—in the same way brahminism would become an ideal dictating status in society—that was commented upon and referenced extensively in Hindu law texts across centuries. It was, as Wendy Doniger puts it, a part of 'the great cosmopolitan scientific literatures of the ancient world'. Similar to the colonialists who would, many centuries later, attempt to grasp the subcontinent's complexity by crudely codifying social behaviours, this too was a megalomaniacal attempt to impose order onto a bafflingly diverse society.[9]

Of course, there do exist universal exceptions in brahminical literature, but *context-sensitivity*, by and large, became an integral part of the science of the land. Referring to numerous representative examples from his studies of ancient texts, Ramanujan demonstrates how everything—from the arts to medicine to sex—became codified within a particular context, a particular season, a particular logic, without which nothing makes sense. Certain historical phenomena, like the democratising idea of bhakti (which Ananthamurthy too recognised in his invocation of Kabir and Tukaram) had challenged this in some measure. The arrival of twentieth-century modernity, of egalitarian thought, of democracy and the Indian Constitution, made the contexts of 'birth, religion, sex, and creed irrelevant, overthrowing Manu, though the battle is joined again and again'. This modernity simply added one more context to the pool, though it has not been easy to accommodate. It is only within a bubble of self-contained references that a certain rule of the land can operate. When the bubble breaks, the contexts change, and new contradictions have to be incorporated and digested by the cultural apparatus. This is often a discombobulating phenomenon. Thus, you can now witness entire franchises of open-to-all restaurants named 'Brahmins' Kitchen' or some such platitude, zealous political cadres fashioning tridents with Star Wars-like flashing lights, or more shockingly, a principal and a few teachers 'sacrificing' a child in a tantric ritual to invite 'prosperity' into their new private school (as happened recently in UP). One lives simultaneously in multiple timelines, where maddeningly confounding contradictions manifest with some rhyme, but no reason. This is India, truly a country of kaleidoscopic reflections and mirages. There is always a context to consider, and particulars always supersede universals. This, then, is the real challenge of the egalitarian project of modern democracy—how to create a new moral conscience that is not derived from the contexts laid down by hierarchical traditions?

Having been forced to acknowledge the existence of grave social inequality, the conservative right at present argues that there existed a utopian moment in history where caste had not sullied social structures, and the logic of multiple classes had fashioned a society that functioned in a symbiotic, mutually reinforcing manner. Its response to the befuddling influence of the West has been, understandably, to point towards a nebulous past unsullied by its influence, and to try and claim this for itself. Before addressing the most pragmatic question of whether this modernity can even be wished away, it would be instructive to interrogate these thoughts, and to see how they have shaped the Kannada literary world.

II

> Who can say if Good Queen Bess
> Was virgin or syphilitic?
> Such trivia once meant little profit,
> Once History dared not make such a query
> Being but sop to national pride.
>
> —Shankar Mokashi Punekar, 'History'

In the late eighties, the eccentric genius of Kannada literature, Shankar Mokashi Punekar, wrote *Avadheshwari*, a novel set in the Ayodhya of Vedic times. An interesting aside to begin with, though: Shankar Mokashi Punekar was apparently an ardent devotee of Sathya Sai Baba, and had announced that whoever spoke against him would perish. When some notable literati debunked the Baba's claim to be a miracle-performing godman, Shankar Mokashi concluded that Sai Baba had himself caused these writers to manifest as evil creatures so that the godman's own divinity would be clearly apparent in contrast. Nevertheless, so lovable was Punekar that the objects of his hearty curse, like the poet Chandrashekhar Patil, accepted it in jolly spirit and continued to consider Punekar a wonderful friend. The blurb on the back cover of *Avadheshwari* carries a note by U.R. Ananthamurthy, excerpted from a personal letter he had written to his friend:

> Dear Mokashi,
> I read your novel *Avadheshwari* in one breath from beginning to end. I feel like I have read a most astounding work of literature. I am indebted to you. The question as to whether your novel is historically accurate is irrelevant to me. Your vision of life is there in it. We have become so influenced by European thought that we did not think that there could be a moral imagination bereft of

> idealism. But you have shown how—vritti dharma, kula dharma, rta[10] [order/truth]—these imaginations can lead to a deep moral conscience and a worldview independent of egotism. Your queen became very dear to me. No one has depicted the niyoga practice as thoroughly and deftly as you have. Could anyone but an Indian have written *Avadheshwari*? Even Yeats would have been jealous of some sections of the novel …

Shankar Mokashi Punekar, whom I discovered appallingly late in my research, stands out as an utterly unique literary personality. I was amazed that nobody had yet written anything significant about him. And quite contrary to Ananthamurthy's perceptions (which were fed by his own disillusionment with Western modernity), I would like to argue that *Avadheshwari* is hardly a paean to the 'deep moral conscience' of ancient social dharmas.

Born in Dharwad in 1928, Punekar lost his mother at a young age, and since his father had left them, was brought up by his grandmother. The precocious young boy grew up to be a much beloved professor of English who would produce a PhD thesis on the tail end of W.B. Yeats's literary career. A genuinely multilingual scholar, the man was as well versed in Gorakhnath and Kalidasa as he was in Yeats. Punekar's early poems were all in English, and he would gain popularity as an English poet. His novels are all in Kannada though, and his first novel, *Gangavva Gangamayi*, captured the domestic environment of an orthodox brahmin family in 1940s Dharwad, full with property squabbles, Marathi-infused tonalities and flashes of Tawaif-Hindustani music, painting a vivid portrait of the cultural milieu that Punekar grew up in. He was also an acclaimed translator, and is famed for his English translation of Kuvempu's mammoth *Ramayana Darshanam*.

His English prose exhibits shades of Wodehouse. Consider this excerpt from a hilarious description of a friend named Deepak Fernandes, 'that marvellous man who has evolved a complete philosophy of life with only two sources to replenish his mind's sap—Swami Ramteerth and Perry Mason':

> I first met Deepak in a third-class railway compartment. His talk was full of analogies from Perry Mason mysteries which made me think that he was a typical Bombay product of the suburban railway reading. On closer scrutiny however, I found in him a deep moral fibre and, strangely enough, most of its twisted strength seemed to have derived from that very exercise. I am myself an admirer of Agatha Christie and have always thought that the ethical inspiration of the present age, after having denied itself all other sources of strength, might turn to detective fiction, so familiar and so profuse a source of moral passion. Of course, there are sissies like Ian Fleming who have muddied the source by diverting the flow into shallow political channels, and totally ignoring the ethical choice.

Between 1965 and 1970, his love for music led him to become the *Times of India*'s writer on the classical music beat, and Punekar went on to pen pieces on Bhimsen Joshi, Pandit Jasraj, Hariprasad Chaurasia, Kumar Gandharva and other artists he loved dearly. Punekar's dreamy side did sometimes lead him into whimsical journeys, as in his study of Indus Valley seals, or in his introduction to *Avadheshwari*, where he completely misunderstands the time scale of continental drift and suggests that various cultures somehow found their way to the Indian subcontinent as their lands drifted along towards it. However, his delightful literary essays,[11] and his studies of medieval and pre-modern India, especially regarding caste in pre-British society, make for insightful and thought-provoking reading. In many ways, he was able to overcome the ideological biases of both the political Right and the Left and produce a worldview that synthesised the best of the marga and the desi. He carried with him, simultaneously, a highly mystical worldview *and* a thoroughly rational mind—something of a rarity in post-Nehruvian India. He came to be known as the foil to the Navya project, and was admired within anti-caste circles as well. When I met the poet Mudnakudu Chinnaswamy, he told me that he had been deeply touched when Punekar agreed to write a preface to his collection of short stories sometime in the nineties, and that getting to see Punekar during his final years had been no less than a 'darshana'.

Punekar's scholarship forms an interesting meditation on the simplistic social justice narratives that we have now become quite familiar with. The word 'brahminism', for instance, seems to connote every social injustice at the same time, and has become something of a political volleyball. What is often missed in these narratives is that brahmins weren't always a homogeneous category, and that brahminism bequeathed an aura of social prestige that inevitably expanded out of the ambit of just one caste. Consider the following observations Punekar makes:[12]

> Lest our perspectives get blurred by the forceful modern reformist trends of social egalitarianism (which is the Dharma of modern India), let us clarify a few issues before proceeding further. What does the Brahminical and Vedic revival mean? Some bright students, suffering from this very egalitarianism, have protested against certain forms of Hindu revival as the revival of Brahminical superiority. This attitude, no doubt, has its merits. However, it must also be noted that Hindu Brahminism was not purely a hieratic order. It wielded little political power until very recently (in the days of the Peshwas). The Brahmin priest was not always a very respected figure; his social influence was limited indeed. All the power and force of Hindu organisation came from the quiet meditators, devotees, givers of alms, the self-disciplined, the truthful; and these belonged to all castes and communities. To respect a Brahmin for being a Brahmin is no more than to respect a cow for being a cow.[13] It is needed on festival days. But found in a sugarcane farm, it gets the treatment any stray animal would get.
>
> The Brahmin, whether a scholar, or a dud, had no *locus standi* without ritual; and the more intelligent he was, the most suspect he would be without the support of a sincerely performed ritual. India has not worshipped intelligence, because it did not develop the values of secular humanism and competitive economy. It will thus be seen that Brahminism as a social ideal was the chief norm-setter for all communities, that what was worthwhile in a Brahmin was his ritual, but he got no special credit for it, the chances of his becoming ridiculous or suspect in a society were more frequent, and to build up a social image a Brahmin needed more ritual than his ordinary

> daily worship—fasts, abstinence, baths, spread over the entire year, extra spending, etc. A Brahmin not performing his Brahminical ritual incurred the ire of all other communities. Brahminism, thus, does not mean the social or economic supremacy of Brahmins or the intellectual superiority of the Brahmin class. What it meant was dependence, expectation, and demand made by the *entire* Hindu community from Brahmin ritual.

When I brought up these excerpts with the historian Manu S. Pillai, he agreed that Punekar had some valid points. We exchanged notes on how there have always been bifurcations within the category of brahmins, of how some—funeral priests, for example—were looked down on, even by non-brahmin groups, because they carried a whiff of inauspiciousness about them. Other brahmins only performed basic household brahminical rituals, and were otherwise engaged in secular professions. In South Canara, a caste known as sthanika brahmins were engaged in cleaning and maintaining temples, and were viewed as lowly by other brahmins. The term itself was historically contested and recent scholarship has argued that even some Buddhists and Jains claimed to be 'true' brahmins around the fifth century.[14] Wendy Doniger once observed about medieval India that 'in actual life, there were Shudra Brahmins, *mleccha* Brahmins, Chandala Brahmins, and Nishada Brahmins (who are said to be thieves and fond of fish and meat.) Some were very close indeed to the folk sources that they incorporated into the Puranas.'[15]

Zooming into Karnataka itself, we see that when the boya tribe was getting absorbed into city-based society around the tenth century, there were 'boya chiefs, boya fighters and also boya brahmanas. From this, it would appear that each section of the boya community identified itself with the corresponding group in the brahminical society, which, by and large, accepted their claims.'[16] Historian S. Settar also problematises the simplistic categories of brahminical/non-brahminical in his study of over two thousand pre-modern Kannada inscriptions, and he sums up this phenomenon thus:

> When the Vedic system had largely fallen flat by the eighth century, the ones who came to fill it were pauranikas [writers of Puranas] and shudras. What this means is that the land grants meant specifically for brahmins between the fourth and eighth centuries had expanded out to non-brahmin communities. Another astonishing fact is that some kingly houses moved away from patronising brahmins and began nurturing other societal groups. It is only natural that this changed environment was not conducive to Sanskritisation.[17]

Punekar's mention of the peshwas too was significant. Pillai pointed out to me that: '... one of the last peshwas went around destroying copies of a section of the *Skanda Purana* because it had unflattering remarks about the origins of the konkanastha brahmins.[18] The peshwas themselves established a rather self-consciously brahminical regime; but this was partly because they came from a community that until the eighteenth century held low status, often lampooned as mere cooks and messengers. That is, they went out of the way to act as conservative brahmins precisely because they were *not* viewed as proper brahmins.'

When one tries to understand how this sense of 'proper' prestige was manufactured, we see that while the hierarchical middle was a contested arena, outcastes have always been viewed by the ruling elite to be in stark opposition to themselves.[19] Kannada literature bears vivid testimony to this. In Raghavanka's 1225 narrative poem *The Life of Harishchandra*, when the sage Vishwamitra sends two holatis (women of the holeya caste) to seduce Harishchandra, the king erupts in anger, 'When you are born *holatis*, who would want to enjoy your youthful exuberance, beautiful figure, or bright mind? Shiva, Shiva ... the very thought is defiling!'[20] He proceeds to whip the two women, 'lacerating their mouths, dragging them by the hair, and beating their bodies to a pulp', following which the two holatis painfully make their way back to Vishwamitra.

This 'culture' of rejection has since permeated into mainstream society. Extending this extreme sense of caste hatred to the present day, Mudnakudu Chinnaswamy argues that the reason behind many of the honour killings we read about in the news—instances of dominant caste families hacking their children to death for marrying dalits—is the fact that caste has become synonymous with religion for shudras, as they have been largely segregated from religious rituals which might otherwise bear the weight of that sense of (im)purity. Dwija (twice-born) dharma is wholly other to shudra dharma, he argues, and only this recognition can enable the search for a new moral order.

For Punekar writing in 1979, the history of caste superiority trumped both social (the Ambedkarite view) and economic (the Marxist view) concerns. In his view, it was mostly a religious and mystical affair, which is again too simplistic. It ignores how the prestige of caste was widely sought out for expressly sociopolitical purposes. He summed up his take as follows:

> In a godless, humanist society, it is better that castes vanish, because castes without their individuating god image can only become pressure groups. But this does not entitle us in modern India to misinterpret our history, tailor our great teachers to our own pigmy size, and visualise the past as one huge chaos in which Brahmins fought Kshatriyas, Vaishyas fought Shudras, Hindus fought Muslims. These are not facts. Because god and salvation were the dominant pre-occupations, they influenced behaviour. Unity was sought at a mystic level. Social customs and manners were not sought to be changed; and gains of the concept of a mystic unity were gradually absorbed, which meant that more humane and enlightened modes of life evolved over centuries.

In another book titled *Harijan Contribution to Medieval Thought* (1991), Punekar comes around to the realisation that economic crises also entailed caste crises, and he accepts Ambedkar's argument that dalits were once kshatriyas, though he differs in situating the event in history. He argues that the greatest contribution to Indian literature came from men of non-brahmin stations—Valmiki, Vyasa, Kalidasa—because brahmins had not prided themselves on their literacy for a long time, and writing and scribing were taken up by others. More interesting is how, drawing on L.T. Kikani's book *Caste in Courts* (published in 1912), Punekar briefly sets out telling instances of caste-related problems in British courts during the nineteenth century. As Manoj Mitta has recently documented in his excellent book *Caste Pride*, the British courts were happy to keep religious, caste-centred issues separate from civil matters. Presenting close to thirty representative cases, Punekar makes a startling argument:

> These court judgements, that seem to be right in front of our nose, can be summarised as below. Within every caste of Hindu society, there tended to exist four varnas—priest, warrior, businessman, and worker. Every sub-caste was made to submit to a specific set of rules, and was made to work co-operatively with every other sub-caste. Because the British courts followed the dictum of religious unobtrusiveness, the charismatic leadership of sub-castes were slowly eroded away. Poor castes lost their leaders, their religious ways of life, and fell into a decline.

Though 'cooperatively' is a utopian stretch, the selective intrusion of the British on certain civil matters (coupled with their partisan relationship with caste elites) did have social ramifications, and it is quite true that the arrival of the modern state made way for the decline of erstwhile religious ways. The rupture is brought out movingly in one of Masti Venkatesha Iyengar's early twentieth century short stories,[21] where a wandering mendicant and folk singer—a jogi named Anjappa—is produced before a court because he has been suspected of stealing a chicken. In reality, a young woman had surreptitiously gifted him the chicken, instead of grain, which was the usual alms given out to those who earned a living through begging. Unable to betray the trust of the woman who has asked Anjappa to stay quiet for her sake, the jogi pleads innocence but does not reveal what transpired. When the judge asks him what evidence he has, Anjappa implores: 'Oh Lord! Who will stand sakshi for me? God alone is my sakshi.' The judge imposes a fine of twenty rupees on him.

S.L. Bhyrappa's mid-1980s novel *Sakshi: The Witness* captured these very courts in a newly independent India, where little seemed to have changed. The novel portrays a rural landscape where courts and lawyers are held in deep suspicion by the villagers, who can only see them as colonial legacies where facts go to die. Caste politics and local power networks have now taken over, and justice remains an elusive entity. In this atmosphere of distrust for the justice system, a well-known thug is pardoned by the society (and by the court, of course) for murdering a coconut thief, and is even celebrated for taking the law into his own hands. It doesn't matter that he is an ill-reputed predator with an eye for teenage girls, as well as a conman known for his violent streak—the unbelief in justice is so deep-rooted that even such a man is allowed leeway.

It is also true that caste has kept fragmenting into further strata, like an infinitely expanding fractal, right up to the present day, quite beside courts or democracy or social reformers. There are mathas (literally thousands of them in Karnataka) for every rung of the social order, and hierarchical organisation continues sharply even today, creating more pressure groups than spiritual liberators. I found Punekar's views thought-provoking, but his utopian emphasis on god alone as the driving force cannot possibly capture the vast breadth of the human condition as it played out across Indian history. In fact, there has been some compelling scholarship that argues exactly the opposite—that because brahminism never had any missionaries to spread its cause, it is more akin to a sociopolitical ideology than a 'religion', and that it was accepted over the centuries because the narratives it created (think of the enormous popularity of the stories contained within the Puranas) were engrossingly palatable and were endorsed generously by kings and other influential sections of society. Of course, it also laid the foundations for a hieratic power structure, but the fact remains that historians are still struggling to meaningfully account for why brahminism became a prevalent historical force, trumping the competing strands of Buddhism, Jainism and tantrism.[22] More detailed histories of a particular geography or region will provide more nuanced and accurate understandings of our messy and chaotic history, where social, religious and economic underpinnings shape history equally, albeit in different ways. Ultimately, it is the stories told, the narratives disseminated (and not how factually historians are able to resurrect the past) that dictate how Indians have related, and continue to relate, to the world.

Returning to *Avadheshwari*—a shining moment in Kannada literature that has received scant attention (compared to Ananthamurthy's *Samskara*, say, which has been commented upon ad nauseum)—we get a rich glimpse of Punekar's social imagination. Set in ancient Ayodhya, and inspired by a few verses from the Rigveda and by images on Harappan seals, *Avadheshwari* constructs a universe of honour-bound rulers, courageous soldiers and flailing orthodoxies, where the characters search for a code of conduct to live by. At its heart is the queen Purukutsani of the Suryavamsha clan; her political shrewdness and strength of character lies at the heart of the novel.

In his brief gloss on *Avadheshwari*, we glimpsed Ananthamurthy's disillusionment with the egotism that arrived with Western modernity, and his hope of finding in the ancient world a better moral compass, where the journey of self-discovery matters more than the blind assumption of a given code. I also suspect that what Ananthamurthy found arresting about the novel is its setting and the timing of its publication. In *Avadheshwari*, the righteous king Trasadasyu feels he has failed as a ruler because he has accidentally injured a child while riding his chariot on the streets of Ayodhya, and an elaborate legal procedure is set in motion to ensure that the child gets justice. The moral imagination of such a landscape stands in stark contrast to what would unfold in Ayodhya less than five years after the publication of the novel. What would have also struck Ananthamurthy is that such an imagination would be coeval with the quest for mystical knowledge and experiences—a journey to the beginnings of history. From the staunch critique of brahminical orthodoxy in *Samskara* to the searching, mystical tone of his final novels *Bhava* and *Divya*, we see a marked evolution in Ananthamurthy's literary imagination, which often led him to being dubbed conservative by the more radical writers of his generation.

Divya begins by presenting two different meanings of the title word—it means a divine experience, and also, an *ordeal.* Only something that has passed the damning ordeal of a personal quest, the rigour of reason, can lead to meaningful spirituality.

Since I began to realise that *Avadheshwari* would end up becoming central to this chapter, I started underlining the word 'sakshi' on every occasion that it popped up in the text, which was quite frequently. Interesting patterns emerged. The most common use of the word was in the context of moral repulsion at sexual misconduct. When the trusted lieutenant Taarkshya finds out that the king Purukutsa has been engaging in intoxicated intercourse with a minor naga girl, he thinks, 'I cannot remain a sakshi for this sin. I must inform the queen.' A similar context emerges when a court official molests a slave woman belonging to the tribal shabara community in a drunken stupor and is summarily fired from his administrative position. He is forced to travel to the forest to seek out an apology, where he encounters a completely different body of laws. He wishes to marry the woman he has assaulted, for he believes it to be the right thing to do—after all, who will marry her after she has been molested by another man? As he soon finds out, the shabaras operate under a different code. They use a model of internal restorative justice and not a retributive one. Each clan is responsible for the fate of their individual members, and the slave woman's tribe makes up for her sexual transgression by feeding ten shabara villages, thereby inducting her back into their tribe. For outsiders and interlopers though, there is a harsh retributive law that applies, and the exiled official only narrowly avoids being castrated.

Another context in which 'sakshi' is used is as *testimony*—to lineage, caste purity and of course in legal proceedings. An esteemed doctor stands sakshi to a young prince's coronation, as proof that he is of royal blood. When a ceremony officiated by adherents of the Atharva Veda (often considered to be full of black magic) asks for the help of a Rigveda brahmin, a four-year-old boy is sent as a sakshi to observe whether the brahmin steps out of the bounds of the Rigveda sect. While showcasing the divisions between brahmins, the trope is also a nod to the proclivity of rulers to seek out brahmins to legitimise their regal stature. For instance, Shivaji went to great pains to anoint himself a Chhatrapati, and priests were summoned from distant lands to act as sakshi. Much later in *Avadheshwari*, we find a Trasadasyu who feels he has failed as a ruler because he has injured a child. And we also find out what actually happened—that his bumbling childhood companion Vrisha Bhatta had begged to hold the reins of the chariot for a while, despite not possessing the skills to ride it well. After Trasadasyu reluctantly handed over the reins, disaster struck, and the wily Vrisha Bhatta blamed everything on the king. The child survived, but the king was determined to ensure justice, and set in motion an independent legal procedure, where his kingly powers were reduced to that of a mere sakshi, a witness in a legal case.

Another important strain in the novel is the existentialism of the king Trasadasyu, who does not know who his real father is. Punekar was fascinated by incest traditions amongst Egyptian royalty, and sees (or imagines) evidence of similar influences in ancient India. The queen Purukutsani, being married to her own brother Purukutsa with whom she never shares a bed, resorts to the niyoga practice—whereby an elaborate ceremony involving an alternative sexual partner is surreptitiously conducted—to birth Trasadasyu. His dharma as a king saves him from purposelessness, the arduous nature of his royal duties distracting him from questions of his birth, but he is unable to find peace throughout the novel. It is interesting to compare this character's ache for self-knowledge with the character of Vrisha Bhatta. After legal proceedings have exiled his family, Vrisha Bhatta leaves Ayodhya with a vow to become a strong warrior and exact revenge. His father Bhima Bhatta (in reality Trasadasyu's biological father too), who does not possess the qualities of a 'proper' brahmin (he drinks, whores and cannot even remember mantras), hopes in the deepest recesses of his heart that his son might redeem his caste heritage, and is aghast when he learns of Vrisha Bhatta's new warrior spirit. Bhima Bhatta later happens upon some of his son's discarded poems, and he proudly exclaims, 'My son is a sage, a poet, a creator of the Vedas!'

Before we chalk off Bhima Bhatta as just a fictional character set in the ancient past, we might want to compare him with the guru Audityanath, head of the Adichunchunagiri Matha for fifty years (until 1915), whose crimes, according to devotees who recorded his misdemeanours, included 'open adultery with loose women, visiting toddy and arrack shops in the neighbourhood of the mutt, his shooting of the Sacred Bull of the temple and the monkeys on the Hill when drunk ...'[23] Indeed, it is now legally mandated that a temple priest can be disqualified for indulging in any of the sapta vyasana, or seven sins—'gambling, consuming intoxicating liquor and drugs, smoking, immoral sexual conduct, [being] involved in heinous crime, stealing and cheating'.[24] The birth-based imposition of high morality on one section of society makes it a pressure cooker that relieves itself with a bang when steam builds up. In Ananthamurthy's 1973 novel *Bharatipura*, the real challenge to the orthodoxy (who are reluctant to accept dalits into a temple) comes not from the West-educated protagonist's revolutionary designs, but from the mental suffocation of the temple priest's son, who goes berserk towards the end of the novel.

The characters in *Avadheshwari* navigate a moral landscape where their birth caste does dictate their lives, but individual traits slowly emerge *in spite of* their lineages. What we are shown is the manner in which caste society restricts the creation of a genuine meritocracy, and why rebellion is not just important, but inevitable. Above all, the novel seeks to emphasise honour, duty and an inward quest for self-discovery, rather than the blind assumption of any given code of ethics. The concern is not with any particular outcome, but with the moral character of the actor *as a whole*. At any moment in life, one is accountable to oneself more than anyone else. The most vital things are left to a personal voyage of self-discovery, that fundamental unit of social freedom which alone can create real democracy, where caste, class and birth are transcended by individual striving towards a brave, new, unknown future.

Avadheshwari is set at a point in history that precedes the totalising rise of brahminism, which rigidified society and subdued individual genius, making rebellion that much more difficult. Power is held to account in the novel, and nobody is above the law of the land, which is always a collective effort. It is the right of a society to hear the voice of a lone sceptic in a crowd of conformists, as much as it is the right of the sceptic to voice his opinion. Like any great novelist worth their salt, Punekar succeeds in removing his authorial presence from the novel, and allows the characters and setting to play out as the story dictates. He champions a powerful woman with a layered personality, upholds humanist virtues, and does it all while spinning a gripping, unputdownable thriller. By no means does the mythological setting make the novel any less contemporary—in fact, he brings it smack into the living, breathing moral predicaments of India of the 1990s, with no ideological baggage. In such creative maturity, and in style, I daresay Punekar surpasses both Ananthamurthy and Bhyrappa.

III

To make words meaningful I
Invoke Siva-Parvati –
Makers of the world
Like word and meaning wed.
—Kalidasa, *Raghuvamsham* (translated by Mani Rao)

You can ask me anything. She wears forthrightness like a badge of honour. Nobody has uttered these magical words in any of my other interviews.

Pratibha Nandakumar arrives apologetic about the delay, but really that's okay, I say, I was just here reading your wonderfully candid autobiography. At her suggestion, we meet in the slightly noisy mid-afternoon canteen at Rangashankara, Bangalore's premier theatre space. The big red bindi on her forehead reminds me immediately of Usha Uthup, but I later realise that she would find the comparison to Uthup's latest Om-imprinted stick-on bindi bothersome. In any case, she finds any comparisons deeply questionable—Pratibha Nandakumar is her own self, and always has been, no questions there, thank you very much. Arriving at the bindi somewhere in the middle of our conversation, she sums up the fissures wrought by modern life very simply and accurately: *Kumkuma is sampradaya (tradition). A plastic sticker is modernity. Torana (leafy festoon) is sampradaya. Plastic torana is modernity*. In that conversation, I expended much energy trying to figure out which side of the fence her allegiances lay, and at each point, like a consummate poet, she stymied my efforts, outgeneralled my list of questions and curveballed me into a conversation with some deliciously mystical undertones.

Now in her late sixties, Pratibha wears her literary persona lightly. Only towards the end of our conversation does she open up about her upbringing. Though filled with financial and personal struggles, her childhood was extremely privileged, and all her siblings were encouraged to pursue what they wished. Her grandfather V.P. Madhava Rao had served as diwan of Mysore and Baroda in the first two decades of the twentieth century. Her grandmothers played tennis and swam in private pools, while her mother was an accomplished horse rider. Pratibha studied at Madras University during the early seventies, and was largely distant from all the cultural developments shaking the firmament in Bangalore. When she came back and published her first collection of poems in 1979, titled *Naavu Hudigiyare Heege* (We girls are like this only), she became an 'overnight star', she says proudly. Her poems have always pushed the envelope, and she doesn't flinch from being provocative. She recollects a recent incident that made me double over chortling:

> Once Subbu Holeyar (a Kannada poet) had asserted at some stage function that 'Pratibha Nandakumar's poems get published easily because she is a brahmin.' And I had erupted—*eh, am I writing with a caste certificate next to me?* And so, after that I wrote a poem that went something like this:

Can one drop one's *brahmin-hood* as easily as one's *bra?*
When I stood at the door, all ready to embark on my journey,
All they saw were the seven generations behind by back.

Then, K. Satchidanandan translated it into Malayalam, and we were at a lit fest in Kerala, where we read out both versions. It split the crowd into two. One group thought it was vulgar, unsophisticated, and they started calling it praakritam,[25] which is the Malayalam word for it. Then, someone came on stage and said, it is not praakritam, it is bra-kritam, haha.

These dialogues around caste had firmly entered the literary discourse in the seventies—a time of boiling anti-brahminism. Ananthamurthy recollects in his autobiography how Lankesh once arrived at his home, telling him to patiently bear with these political developments, arguing that it was a historical necessity that had to find its moment in the sun. During those days, the Kannada literary sphere was a remarkably interconnected group, and writers cared about literature enough to fight about it passionately. When Lankesh published a short story in *Sakshi*[26] that satirised Ananthamurthy through a character called *Ananthu*—an English-educated scholar who is snubbed by institutional corruption and is unable to land the position he wants—the latter wrote to Adiga in deep anguish. Adiga calmly defended his decision to publish the story; it was fiction, after all. When Pratibha joined the ranks of this crowd, she blended in seamlessly.

As far as women poets are concerned, it was just the three of us. Me, Sarvamangala, Sa. Usha from that generation. Before us, Shailaja Udachan had written some beautiful stuff. Those were amazing times. For one thing, it was before the digital era. That had an aura of its own. Everyone was accessible, unlike in the Hindi milieu—where they felt themselves to be exalted and above others, in some sense. We were all intimate friends. When you are young, writing in full confidence about your creative abilities, you don't perceive these things consciously. Only now I am realising what a golden age it was. I felt I never made much use of them—especially Lankesh. It was so casual. Even [Yashwant] Chittal.

Shantinath Desai. Ramanujan and me were soulmates. We wrote a lot of letters to each other.

Indeed, her autobiography contains numerous accounts of flirtatious encounters with unnamed veteran writers, and many have tried to put names to her tales. She finds all this amusing. What lies at the heart of her memoir is a quest for love, a pure kind of love that can never be reached, a quest for her own self above all else. She instinctively protects her personality, feeling that feminist labelling often robs women of their individuality by lumping them together under a larger umbrella:

> Akkamahadevi of twelfth century, Sanchi Honnamma of eighteenth century, Pratibha Nandakumar of twentieth century—everything is supposed to come under women's writing. This is absurd. If you're talking about Adiga, do you start with Basavanna? Then why do that with women? All girls imagine themselves to be Akkamahadevi. In reality, that path is not so easy. The spiritual path is not so easy.

That realisation has come out of the fact that, for the last decade and half, Pratibha herself has been on a spiritual quest that has bamboozled her at every juncture, offering unprecedented realisations on the one hand, while also confirming her conviction that the world is far too mysterious to ever be understood. During our conversation, I read out a few lines I had underlined from Ananthamurthy's introduction to her autobiography:[27] 'A bearer of great emotional and intellectual agility, Pratibha Nandakumar's recent interest in devi upasane reminds me of Yeats. Later in his life, he devoted himself to spiritual pursuits completely. Now Pratibha has found herself resonating with the conception of devi, and she has been writing without a care for what anyone might think. This has been astonishing me.'

> Me: What's Ananthamurthy talking about? I'm very curious.
>
> PN: He is exaggerating a little, okay? See, I grew up in a purely rationalist family. There were zero rituals. Even the Ganesha festival was largely a secular thing—Christian and Muslim friends would

also keep coming over. There was very little by way of spirituality or religion or whatever you want to call it. Apart from the Ramayana and Mahabharata, which I read as texts, I had not really been introduced to much else.

Once, me and a friend had gone to Bellary, where we visited a Durga temple. Oh, that percussion, that blood, those people, so much vibration! It was quite an atmosphere. I felt really strange. After I got back, I got curious about this devi. I had a friend who had read a lot about Kali and all, they said their belief was real, and I thought that is very difficult for me to accept. I took it up as a project—Devi Cult in South India (specifically Chamundi)—and I started talking about it and all. After two-three years, I applied for a research fellowship and got it. I interviewed all these upasakas [traditional practitioners], read everything I could, and I continued for another two-three years.

What I would ask them is this—my rational mind does not allow me complete surrender, and bhakti cannot be taught. I don't know this bhakti. How do I get an entry into this subject? After so many years, if I haven't found entry, how do I do that? Someone told me I should learn [Durga] Saptashati. No matter how much academic study I undertook, I could not hope to understand this tradition. So I went to Shankar Matha, every morning for many days, and learnt Saptashati from a guru. I had to repeat it to him again for another month to prove my grasp. Every line is a mantra. He said, you have only learnt the text. I was sent for mantra deekshe [initiation] to another guru. He told me to come after three months. He told me that, after chanting the mantra 9,000 times, I will *become eligible* for devi upasane. So, I started doing it. In this interim, I had a lot of strange experiences, I met strange people—there was something that I could not connect to my rational mind. I began to feel, yes, *this is real.*

She went on to speak about her fascination with the cult of Chamundi for almost half an hour. When she was learning the mantras, Ananthamurthy would often ask her to tell him all about it, and listen with great interest. She has amassed hundreds of photos that showcase the artistic diversity of the myth of Chamundi and Mahishasura across centuries, and conducted a deep iconographical study. The same way there exist beatific versions of Narasimha, there are peaceful, tranquil postures of Chamundi too. From simple humanoid representations, the devi evolved into multi-armed, multi-weaponed, highly intricate imaginations. Mahisha himself had started out as a bull, but then he began resembling a half-bull, half-man, and now he has entered the crosshairs of political sharpshooters. A few years ago, Mahisha was worshipped as an indigenous warrior-king[28] at an event in New Delhi's Jawaharlal Nehru University. Some Hindu(tva) groups had called it blasphemy, arguing that it infringed on their Durga-consciousness, that it distorted history. Similar things happened in Mysore more recently, when BJP politicians called for a festival dedicated to Mahishasura to be scrapped, citing moralistic concerns that can easily be summed up as—*how can you worship a demon!*

A couple of years ago, Pratibha had delivered a talk on precisely this question.[29] She began by speaking of the emergence of the divine female trinity in the Puranas—Mahakali, Mahalakshmi, Mahasaraswathi—and challenging some feminist scholarship that has tended to read in a negative light the myths involving male gods dispatching goddesses to fight their battles. Chamundi, a regional avatar[30] of the goddess Durga, is sent to kill Mahisha because he has been granted a boon that assures him death only at a woman's hands. Pratibha argues it is 'too simplistic to search for whether women were portrayed as weak/strong—the reality is far more complex'. In her magnum opus *The Hindus*, Wendy Doniger offers a nuanced synthesis of these arguments by pointing out that strong goddesses abounded in regional, desi imaginations, but got stripped of their agency as they travelled upwards through the sieve of Sanskrit elites. Thus, we see the myth of the goddess who is able to vanquish her enemies on her own being transformed into the tale of the same goddess who is only able to do so only after the collective energies of the gods have come to reside in her. Over centuries, powerful folk goddesses tend to become assimilated into Sanskrit retellings where they become no more than sidekicks. A.K. Ramanujan had deftly categorised them as 'breast goddesses' and 'teeth goddesses'—

the former being tame companions to male gods, and the latter embodying unbending strength. On the whole, Doniger concludes bleakly that 'the pious hope of goddess feminists, and others, that the worship of goddesses is Good for Women is dashed by observations of India, where the power recognised in goddesses certainly does not necessarily encourage men to grant to women—or women to take from men—political or economic powers'. For the most part, Pratibha's research too agrees with these conclusions, though she cannot possibly subscribe to Doniger's suggestion that there is a hidden sexual tension underlying the myth of Chamundi riding Mahisha to death.

The sublime force and popularity of the devi myth was also the reason why it necessarily had to be absorbed into the Sanskritic marga. In the Mahabharata, Mohini (Vishnu in disguise) distracts the asuras so that the devas can steal the soma back from them, and the apsara Tilottama conveniently manages to get Sunda and Upasunda to kill each other over her. The first instance of a goddess who actually vanquishes the anti-gods herself surfaces only in the Puranas. Doniger writes:

> Such a goddess, first under the name of Chandrika ('*the Fierce*'), later often called Durga ('*hard to get [to]*'), bursts onto the Sanskrit scene full grown, like Athene from the head of Zeus, in a complex myth that includes a hymn of a thousand names. Many of the names allude to entire mythological episodes that must have grown onto the goddess, like barnacles on a great ship, gradually for centuries. The founding text is 'The Glorification of the Goddess' (Devimahatmya), a long poem probably interpolated into the Markandeya Purana (which also tells a number of other stories about powerful women and goddesses) between the fifth and seventh centuries of the Common Era. It is clear from the complexity of 'The Glorification of the Goddess' that it must be a compilation of many earlier texts about the goddess, either other, lost Sanskrit texts or from lost or never preserved vernacular sources, in Magadhi or Tamil, perhaps.[31]

In her talk, Pratibha had also marshalled some fascinating historical details about how the vernacular (desi) and the Vedic (marga) have still been preserved in the practices of the Chamundi temple in Mysore: 'There was some controversy in the media recently over whether Siddaramaiah had consumed meat before visiting the temple on Chamundi Hill. But Chamundi is a tantric goddess, where Shakti worship used to happen. Mummadi Krishnaraja Wodeyar consciously wanted to convert it into the Vedic stream, and brought a priest named Deshikacharya from Tamil Nadu. Since then, there are two different paddhatis that began to take place in the temple—one that takes place inside the temple, and one outside. One is desi, and the other is Vedic. This happens even today.'

The most important point she makes, as far as I can see, is one of sober pragmatism: 'Now the reason there is no pariharapatya [alternative text] for Devimahatmya is because non-Vedic communities were not given the opportunity to pen their own puranas. So, a new purana that recreates the religious environments of 2,000 years ago has to be created afresh. Thus, if we persist in this endeavour of revising a 2,000-year-old tradition, and a new Mahishamahatmya is written, will it really attain the depth of meaning that the Devimahatmya text—which is a cultural text—has acquired? That is my question.'

The answer to her question is, of course, that it will not. Cultural activism in Karnataka, courtesy of the dalit movement, has in fact tried to show that nothing new need be created at all, and that there are numerous oral traditions that carry centuries of hallowed desi culture within their wombs. (Chapter eight delves into this in more detail.) What I sense in Pratibha is a deep sense of primordialism—though she doesn't agree with the word when I mention it to her—that seeks to travel back to a time of fertility mother goddesses and radical gender equality. She sees Mahisha as originating in the massive cattle-predecessor species known as aurochs, which went extinct a long time ago, and not as a representative of an indigenous people that were antagonistic to Aryans.

Pratibha finds enormous liberation in tales from ancient and medieval India: 'To tell you frankly, if you read the Kathasaritasagara, you will see that they have recorded every single shade of the female psyche. We have not grown one inch further. We are static, really. All this modern sense of liberation—this is nothing. We are stuck. All these things are very relative.' Through this recognition of an indigenous modernity that well preceded colonialism, she is also challenging modern feminist conceptions to grow bolder and widen their ambit.

As we get into the thick of devi conversation, she keeps throwing colourful observations at me, and I admire her sustained interest in the subject, stretching over a decade and more, still capable of filling her with such passion. Her formulations are interesting, always thought-provoking.

> PN: Take the word 'varna'. For a musician, it means notation. For a writer, it is the alphabet. For a painter, it means colour. Blue. Red. Yellow. That itself is Mahakali, Mahalaxmi, Mahasaraswathi. Sometimes devotees just take a stone, and imbue it with these colours. Simple. Primary colours. This symbolism is very profound. I am unable to explain to you properly because of my own shortcomings, but perhaps you see what I am getting at?

I nod earnestly, completely getting her fascination with words and meanings. As a writer, what could be more important?

> Me: So this tradition is very important to you, personally?

> PN: What is 'tradition'?

> Me: Everything you just spoke about …

> PN: No! The way I live—nobody has told me, this is tradition, do it this way, or anything of that sort …

> Me: But you sought out a teacher to learn Saptashati. You sought out instructions to chant the mantras in a certain tone and tenor …

> PN: No, I am not doing it for tradition, for heaven's sake. I am interested in it only for my sake. I am interested in this concept called 'devi'. That's it. My search is still going on. I am still studying.

I throw up my hands (figuratively), and the conversation slowly turns towards literature.

Me: D.R. Nagaraj once asked Ananthamurthy in an interview why there were few prominent women characters in his stories. And Ananthamurthy responded by saying, you shouldn't look for femininity directly, it doesn't have to be embodied in a character, it can be reflected in nature, in the language itself, and so on.

PN: I think Ananthamurthy was just trying to escape from that question, haha. I don't think that is his actual reasoning. I myself presented a critical paper at a seminar, called 'Ananthamurthy's Female Characters', where he was also present. He then came up to me and said, *did you have to really phrase it so strongly?* I responded, *did you really have to write that poorly?* That is how he was made, you know? This male psyche in Indian society is a very complex thing. This applies to women also. You never know when a staunch feminist will reach a point where she says something exactly opposite to what she is supposedly standing for.

I wonder if Ananthamurthy's cultural imagination had subconsciously denied the teeth goddesses entry into his fiction.

PN: My policy is, you should give him his space, but also, don't allow him to occupy yours. I have a very healthy relationship with men. All my male friends know what my thoughts are. I don't try to outdo them, or proclaim myself to be a feminist! I know my position, and I don't feel threatened by anyone. Throughout my life. Even my husband, when we used to fight, was only an irritation, and never a threat.

Me: Yeah, you speak of these fights quite candidly in your autobiography …

PN: We were fighting. We still fight. We are made for each other, but also, we are exact opposites. I don't know why we fight. Sometimes I feel we were very silly. But we fight now also. If you noticed, I have dedicated my autobiography to Nandan. These days, people get divorced over two fights.

I try to use the opportunity to clarify my terminologies.

Me: Right, that's wonderful, so well, that is something I might call a kind of conservative traditionalism …

PN: You cannot put me in that conservative list in any way! If I want to walk out, no force can make me stay back. I am a very strong person, okay? No matter what happens. I have always been. I can never relinquish my 'self' even in love. I cannot dissolve into some other entity. Maybe this is why bhakti doesn't come to me?

There is, however, very little ambiguity when it comes to her positions on contemporary politics. When the infamous Mangalore pub attack happened (extreme-Right activists barging in and attacking women who were lounging there), Pratibha felt that the goons needed to be spoken to in a language they might understand. So she quoted from the Lalitasahasranama, pointing out that amongst the many names attributed to the goddess, there is also 'Madhupriya' (lover of spirits). But it was wishful thinking to be peddling reason with those who were bent upon ignoring it. Paradoxically, the idea that women might have been socially liberated in the past is unpalatable to political groups whose very existence is premised upon a glorious past. She adds:

Now, I don't really understand why it has to be a Ram Lalla temple in Ayodhya. Who told them to immortalise a five-year-old Rama? After the battle, Rama comes back to Ayodhya, gets coronated as king, with Sita by his side. Couldn't that be a better ideal?

I consider what is implicit in this: that the infant idol also represents the infantilising tendencies of the political spokespersons of Hinduism who have got away with whatever hare-brained exercise of emasculated activism they seek to deploy. Recently, the VHP filed a case in West Bengal—the offense was that a lion named Akbar had been allowed to cohabit with a lioness named Sita.

She pauses for a bit. I dig into my meal, left cold and unattended in the heat of our conversation.

PN: The Ramanujan way, that's the best way. He always looked at things beyond what was there at face value.

Me: A new book of his Soma poems came out recently.

PN: He was talking about it to me when he was writing it. Whether it is Telugu courtesan poems, or Bhakti poems, he had an open view. If you want to put me in any 'school of thought', it would have to be this. Now, don't get me wrong. I have been doing devi upasane for sixteen years now. I don't claim I've got it. I don't claim I have understood even one per cent.

I am keen to pick her political mind a little more, and I bring up a headline from early 2024—the Kannada-language protests that happened in Bangalore. English-dominant nameboards were taken down and desecrated and the demand was for a sixty–forty rule, with Kannada letters taking up the majority space.

Me: Now, about what has been called 'Kannada chauvinism'—

PN (pouncing like a hawk spotting a stray rat): No, no, no, don't use such big words. This word chauvinism is used by outsiders—*outsiders*, underline that word! For us, it is an existential question. See, recently there was a release of a book called *Unboxing Bengaluru*. At that event, the Myntra chief was there, some CEO of airports or somebody like that was there, Prakash Belawadi was there. They were talking about the future of the city, but nobody was talking about its past. For them, Bangalore is the world's testing ground. If it succeeds here, it will succeed elsewhere. My thoughts were—what is ours here, really? The kind of lingo they were using told me that these two worlds will forever stay apart.

The village known as Doresanipalya, where local festivals keep happening, is inside of what is called Dollar's Colony (a posh NRI locality)—that is our reality! When I brought up the city deity Annamma to a journalist who has written a book on Bangalore, she didn't know about it only! In all this hubbub of Bangalore as a start-up city, where all sorts of investments are going to be happening, any attempt to reclaim your culture, your language, will be termed 'chauvinistic'. When you ask people to put Kannada nameboards alongside English, you should see the kind of remarks people make. *You* have come to my place, you're finding work and food here, no? If I go to Delhi, don't I have to speak Hindi? So, I don't like words

> like 'fanatic', 'chauvinist', when it comes to the Kannada movement. Yes, what is happening now is for political gain. But I am not a street-fighting-woman, and if someone is actually doing this, I don't condemn them. When you are talking about a movement, can you go by syllabus? Nobody goes by syllabus. As long as there is no rape, murder or other atrocities, it is a valid form of protest—I am not such a puritan in this regard. Because the present condition is really deplorable, and there needs to be a discussion.

If this is the provocative side of her stance, I glimpsed the more accommodating one in an anecdote narrated to me by Ramachandra Guha. In 2017, when Guha received the Karnataka Rajyotsava Award along with the Lohia-ite writer D.S. Nagabhushana, the two had a slightly confrontational email exchange (in English) over their understanding of Gandhi and socialist history, which was later published at length. Nagabhushana had initially chided Guha for living in Karnataka for decades and not knowing Kannada, but he had been won over by Guha's calm responses by the end of their heated exchange. Guha wrote to me that 'this attracted a fair bit of attention, with several proud patriots disparaging me for not knowing the state's language. Pratibha (whom I scarcely knew) spiritedly defended me, and said it was appropriate that Nagabhushana and I were honoured in the same year—it showed the state's open-mindedness. Some years later, after Nagabhushana died, his wife, a well-regarded poet herself, asked me to release the twenty-fifth printing of his Kannada book on Gandhi. It was a fine gesture.' In her piece,[32] Pratibha had defended Guha as a conscientious public intellectual, pointing out that he spoke his mind against any errant government, and that 'he can only be placed next to UR Ananthamurthy in courting controversies'.

Dipping into Pratibha's prose-poetry, I saw how her worldview is always a balancing act, and her treatment of modernity is as ambivalent as it is striking. Her collection *Coffee House* is an exceptional, undercelebrated work of art. Some of the scenes in this volume were staged theatrically at India Coffee House on Church Street many years ago. This was really ahead of its time, she believes, and I'm certain. It has also spawned many imitations. Here's one vignette from the collection:

> Every time Victoria's Secret put up a sale, or Lovable announced a seconds, she would prepare a hot-pack for her husband early in the morning, and head out. Before anybody else, she would pick out the best of the lot by the dozen, haggle over the bill, and then try them all out that very night, awarding them appropriate marks along with her husband. Then, too tired to do anything else, they would conk off.
>
> Now, diagnosed with breast cancer, she sits crying with me in the café.

But my favourite would have to be her poem involving the waiter character Vincent. In Vivek Shanbhag's novel *Ghachar Ghochar*, we meet Vincent, a waiter at a coffee house, whose genesis Shanbhag credits to Pratibha Nandakumar. Vincent made his debut in the following poem, which captures the silent predicaments of the local underdog, and what the shattered dreams of an imagined future can look like:

> A new television had been summoned to the coffee house.
> It was the premiere of a new serial that Vincent had acted in.
> Prem did not like this new development.
> I told him, let it run for a couple of days, what's the harm.
> Vincent had taken leave for a couple of days, to go act.
> When he returned, his style had changed, befitting a hero.
> When she asked for a cigarette, he called upon someone else to go fetch.
> Seetharam's direction needs no further comment—I mused,
> As everybody watched.
> When it ended, at seven in the evening, Vincent's acting drew applause
> *Eh hero*!—they celebrated, and poor Vincent, that day,
> Was unable to serve properly, vacillating between a hero
> And a waiter, not knowing who he was, until finally,
> Someone threw some tips, shouting, *here you go, hero!*
> Vincent fell on the floor trying to catch it,
> And everything was all right after that.

IV

A tree that transforms earth into fruit
Becomes liberated by endless giving.
The songbird that chews bitter neem
Liberates itself by singing,
and more singing.

– H.S. Venkateshamurthy, from the *Muktha Muktha* theme song

I often recall with fond nostalgia how every weekday, when the clock tolled nine-thirty at night, everyone in the house would assemble in front of the television to watch *Muktha Muktha*. The iconic, chilling lines of its title song—*irula viruddha, belakina yuddha, kone illada kaadaata* (against darkness, light wages its war, oh the long, long wait)—would bring everyone at home, from whatever corner we were skulking in, to rapt and eager attention. To watch CSP conduct his iconoclastic cross-examination in court—blowing the lids off the crimes of corrupt politicians, crony middlemen, thugs and a whole assortment of shifty associates—was perhaps the most exciting moment of the day for everyone, age no bar. To a rousing soundtrack, the grins were wiped off the faces of these unsuspecting men and women in the witness box. When the judge (usually played by Baraguru Ramchandrappa or Ravi Belagere) finally delivered the verdict, absolving the innocent, punishing the guilty, a feeling of righteous pride would envelop us, the audience who had diligently watched the hundreds of episodes leading up to this triumph. It did not seem to matter that everyone had known all along who the real criminals were. Nor did it matter that the plot proceedings were oftentimes predictable and repetitive. The sense of victory was worth it for its own sake. All these episodes are now available on YouTube, and the thousands of comments that very nearly erupt into tears stand as testament to the show's storytelling abilities, and to CSP's unshakeable place in the hearts of his fans.

CSP is T.N. Seetharam's (yes, the same Seetharam who appears in the poem on the previous page) television alter ego. Acting as a hotshot people's lawyer in the serials he himself directed, he became something of a cultural icon around the turn of the century. His first hit *Mayamruga* (The Elusive Deer)—a breath of fresh air in an almost non-existent Kannada television landscape—championed independent women boldly embracing modernity, and it struck a chord with women across age groups and cultures. Later, *Muktha* and *Muktha Muktha*, which mostly involved ordinary villagers and farmers waging legal war against corrupt politicians and industrialists, cemented his celebrity status. He still remains a widely beloved figure.

In late 2023, I managed to find a brief chink in his busy schedule to meet him at his home in Bangalore. I was greeted by a massive shelf of English thrillers at the entrance, while his office hosted mostly Kannada books—bifurcated by design, surely. Sitting in his inner sanctum, Seetharam probed my credentials like a cat surveying a suspicious meal. Fearing that I might be yet another nonsense journalist who might record what he is saying and twist it to political (in)convenience, he had already told me the day before that no video recording would be permitted. Seetharam is a big name in the media industry. In fact, he is something like a less nosy version of Karan Thapar in Kannada media, one who allows his guests to speak peacefully, and conducts popular interviews with political leaders, always bearing an interesting bag of questions.

Back in the early seventies, T.N. Seetharam's doting father had desired to make a lawyer out of him, and so the dutiful son studied law. By the time he was practising, he had already become a player on the Bangalore theatre scene, essaying central roles in Kannada adaptations of plays by Sartre and Camus, who were always fussed over by the protagonists of the Navya movement. His father passed away a year into Seetharam's practice, and his sister was soon diagnosed with cancer. The attendant anxieties and travels allowed Seetharam only a sporadic brush with law for close to four years. Afterwards, he plunged full-time into acting and writing. In 1976, he portrayed the character of a rebellious, disillusioned young man in Lankesh's award-winning film *Pallavi*, where a distaste for the corporate sector makes a wastrel of the man, leading him into a life of perennial unemployment.

His years as a lawyer were not wasted upon Seetharam though. They would serve as the inspiration for his greatest, most enduring creation: CSP. Seetharam used to apprentice under a criminal lawyer named Vasudevan. 'He was a very intelligent cross-examiner, and I was also very intelligent,' he asserts, in a rare moment of well-earned boastfulness. Under Vasudevan's aegis, Seetharam picked up a feel for the quick-footed agility that defined the word 'cross-examination' for my teenage-courtroom-drama-buff self who had craved a local alternative to Perry Mason. 'He was so good at trapping people with his questions, and I would also stay up nights, trying to think up how to pose questions. CSP was born in those days. CSP's anger and humour is purely thanks to Vasudevan. Of course, my own character has also come into CSP.'

The distaste for the domination of corporations that once animated his debut breakout character still remains in Seetharam. At multiple times in our conversation, he spoke about something that continues to prick his conscience—the fact that his television shows ran on advertisements and contributed to a deepening of the materialistic market that he cannot ideologically abide by. Sometime in the early 2000s, when *Muktha Muktha* was still being telecast, when Seetharam had already put out thousands of episodes across numerous serials, he was invited to deliver a public talk in Bangalore. He had taken a rather self-deprecating angle in this speech too, asserting that he was really a cheat,[33] and that he had been wasting half an hour of well-meaning citizens' precious time every day. After he said his, a man stood up in the audience—B.N. Gangadhar, then director of NIMHANS, now a Padma Shri awardee—and argued that what Seetharam was really doing was creating a space for relaxation and recreation at the end of long working days, like a cup of coffee, while at the same time explicating a certain progressive worldview, a voice championing the cause of justice for the exploited and the powerless, and that such an endeavour was indeed invaluable.

Me: Did you ever feel that you were creating a kind of chaluvali even as you were acting and directing a TV show?

TNS: What does a chaluvali mean? It always has to take things forward. Chaluvali has to keep happening. If you leave the seed of this chaluvali somewhere, it can grow. Or it may not grow. But the possibility remains. A writer can plant this seed. He might not be able to do much, because there are so many restrictions—bodily, economic, familial, social and so on. Chaluvali is not really running all the time, but to talk about it, to discuss, to showcase it on a screen, that itself becomes important.

My first play was *Asphota* [Explosion], which was set during the Emergency, when we were livid with the Congress. The government that followed did not behave much differently from the erstwhile Congress. You get some kind of disillusionment with every chaluvali, at every point in time. That is my observation. Another play, carrying a similar idea, was *Nammolagobba Naajukayya*. These ran hundreds of shows during the eighties. They were even prescribed as university texts. There is a disillusionment there, but you can't stop at that, or you might resign yourself. There must be some light also, which must inspire something else.

We used to adore Madhu Limaye, the socialist. He became a minister, and then later resigned. So did Madhu Dandavate. But George Fernandes could not do that. Even then, the socialist within him could never be extinguished, and wherever he went, some modicum of it remained. If you are extremely idealistic, you can't do anything at all, because politics will never reach any ideal scenario that you have imagined. So, fragments of chaluvalis remain. Siddaramaiah is also a fragment of the socialist chaluvali. I don't know if D.K. Shivakumar knows anything about the socialist movement—highly unlikely. Mahadevappa, B.R. Patil—they might have known. Like a piece of disintegrating plastic, it survives as fragments somewhere.

Me: A lot of your themes revolved around the farmers' movement—and environmentalism too. Basically, questions of land, no?

TNS: Yes. By the time *Muktha* came up, globalisation had happened. Farmers and globalisation cannot go hand in hand. Gandhi is the only answer for farmers. For other movements, Ambedkar is perhaps the go-to, but for farmers, Gandhi is the best bet. The laws became so diluted that those who were not farmers could also buy land.

Say there is a plot of five thousand acres in some village. Some farmers will be growing flowers, vegetables, rice, or something else. Say the price of land is thirty lakh per acre, someone will come and offer thirty-five lakh, and take up all the five thousand acres. This is what I call globalisation. This is not an Indian concept—it has come from somewhere else. There is a kind of sacred, ethical necessity for the farmer, to grow food for himself and society. For the businessman, this is not so. It is this clash between an ethical necessity and an unethical intrusion that I propounded in *Muktha*, and *Muktha Muktha*. It is no use if you just talk about these things. But if you make a story, people will watch.

My audience when I was making *Muktha*, *Muktha Muktha*, were roughly around thirty years old—a young generation. Now, they are oldsters, thirty years later. What has happened in this interim? Family values have disappeared. This might be true for just upper-caste elites at the moment, but tomorrow, it will reach all sections of society. Then, if you were drawing a salary of ten thousand rupees in Bangalore, it was enough—women wanted to look fashionable, but not earn much money as such. Now, even if you are pocketing fifty grand a month, it is hardly sufficient.

While Seetharam's earlier shows, like *Muktha* and *Muktha Muktha*, were deeply polemical and political shows, with an emphasis on decrying financial and moral corruption, his more recent work (like *Magalu Janaki* [Daughter Janaki], which is about CSP's quest to connect with his daughter from whom he was separated at a young age due to an early divorce) has tended to be more apolitical. The prevailing political atmosphere, where anything can be turned into fodder for outrage on social media, has also led him into this mode of self-censorship.

Me: How did this situation come about? Your work doesn't have the punch it used to.

TNS: You see, Doordarshan belonged to the people back then.

Mayamruga was screened on Doordarshan. When it was owned by the people, I had no restrictions. Then, we moved to ETV, which was owned by Ramoji Rao, who was a good man who understood sensitivities. But then it was sold to the Ambanis. Now, I couldn't say stuff like 'big businessmen cheat the common people'. The channels are now guided by this kind of ideology. They will offer an extra thirty lakh, and ask for portrayals of big, grand weddings, say. I have never shown such weddings—my own wedding was a very simple one. They want us to mesmerise the audience. Now, in addition to advertisements, this is also happening. Moving towards glamour, towards a non-existent world. All this made me do *Magalu Janaki* instead—which is very different from the kind of stories I used to write.

He spoke for a while about how family values have been completely upended in the urban landscape, and he sees children becoming more and more estranged from their parents as they skip continents and settle abroad. It is a theme that keeps cropping up in his recent work. I ask him a question I had asked Pratibha Nandakumar too, and receive a similarly vehement denial.

Me: Would you call yourself a traditionalist?

TNS: No, no, definitely not. Only in this sense of intruding globalisation, you know? Now, if you look at villages, they too are getting shaped in this way. Food—your most basic necessity—can now be ordered through Swiggy. People are separated from their families like never before—there is deep fragmentation. Only in this sense do I long for something of the old order.

Me: Yeah, I came across this theme in the reboot of *Mayamruga* that recently came out. I must admit it felt rather immature—it doesn't seem to have your stamp at all.

TNS (in groaning defence): Yes, that came out in a moment of nostalgic weakness. I have not written it. A few others pressed me into acting, I couldn't deny it ... Please don't ask me about it.

Me: You've dabbled in films also. But you've come back to your sprawling television show format, which I think you are more comfortable with.

TNS: Serials are comfortable because you don't lose money. Films are a gamble, where you are always anxious. You have a captive audience in a theatre hall, whereas your serial watchers are more relaxed at home. They'll go the bathroom, or go make coffee and come sit peacefully. When you have a captive audience, you can't really say what you want to say—it becomes really tricky.

Our conversation ends on a positive note. Of all the progressive strains of social thought that have animated the discourse over the last few decades, Seetharam sees feminism as a lone movement that has kept marching and growing—slow and steady *will* win the race, in his view.

TNS: Feminism is one thing nobody can oppose. At no stage has it been stagnant since so many years. Nobody will mistake me, or black-paint me for my feminism, while they may do so for some other positions no?

Me (half-gushing): I sure hope you're right.

After I finished up my interview with Seetharam, I headed to a relative's place in Bangalore where all my folks had assembled for lunch. A conservative uncle of mine—also a staunch BJP supporter—kicked up a conversational storm regarding present-day communalism, bringing out the dissident in me. Just a few days earlier, a police officer had gone on a rampage through a train in Maharashtra, picking out bearded Muslim men to gun down. A civil war in Manipur was raging, and there was ample evidence to show that it was ethnic violence supported and fostered by the ruling BJP regime. Later, as I was explaining T.N. Seetharam's political journey to my grandmother—a big fan of his work—further interruptions were thrown in by my uncle upon hearing the word 'socialism'. Growing annoyed, my grandma gently retorted, 'See, I don't care about politics and all. I know him from television, and I want to hear more about him, that's all.'

I felt redeemed. And more convinced than ever that T.N. Seetharam has achieved something truly universal with his art.

FIVE

Lost in Translation
Kannada after Boosa

When the raingod's diamond
axed me at dawn,
glancing off a broken bottle
in the slum window

with half a broken wall,
it unbound the waters
throttled in my year of fever,
released a dynasty
in my throat.

—A.K. Ramanujan, *Soma: Sunstroke*

I

18 November 1973. Seventeen days after the state of Mysore was renamed Karnataka.

Under the aegis of an Ambedkarite organisation, the Hosa Alegalu (New Waves) conference is underway in the centenary hall of Maharaja's College, Mysore. A lawyer by the name of Sanjeevayya begins a speech in English, upon which some in the audience shout their desire that he speak in Kannada instead. Sanjeevayya continues to speak in English, undaunted. The blistering dalit politician B. Basavalingappa (popularly called BB) is also on the stage; he defends

Sanjeevayya's choice and makes a long statement expressing his personal thoughts on the subject. The following report appears in the Kannada newspaper *Prajavani* a few days later.[1]

Reading Kannada books will not boost your intellect or patriotism

> Minister Shri Basavalingappa is of the firm opinion that reading Kannada books will not improve anyone's critical thinking, courage or service-mindedness. There must be Kannada pride; we must speak in Kannada; Kannada must grow, said Shri Basavalingappa, who has worked as the secretary of the Karnataka Unification Committee. However, he added that reading in English could also impart critical thinking skills, an independent sensibility and love for one's country. Comparing Kannada books to boosa [cow fodder], the minister urged students and youth to disregard anyone who, under a veil of Kannada pride, asked them not to read English. Shri Basavalingappa, who spoke at length about New Waves, said that nobody in the orthodoxy whom he is protesting against has come forward to debate with him. If they can show with evidence and reason that I am wrong, I will become their follower, and if I show them otherwise, they should become mine, he said.

Notice the clickbait nature of the headline, and the selective positioning of Basavalingappa's combative personality. The article could have chosen to highlight his bilingual stance, but it instead finds the most negative element in the mix to twist out of shape. Basavalingappa had no clue how momentous his speech would turn out to be. His original intentions became irrelevant, as the media and public began to create their own interpretations of his words, and one word in particular: boosa.

Boosa became the magic word that suddenly opened up long-standing fissures in Kannada society. Writers, politicians, students and activists began to voice their responses, creating a polarised arena, where English was pitted against Kannada, dalits and upper castes mobilised against each other, and the world of letters was suddenly forced into critical reflection. Violence erupted across the Mysore–

Bangalore region. Buses were burnt, donkeys were paraded on the streets, schools were shut down, effigies were burnt in front of the Vidhana Soudha, and police resorted to lathicharge to subdue angry mobs of mobilised students. BB's statement had sent shockwaves across the state, setting the tone and tenor of social discourse for the tumultuous decade that the seventies will be.

Basavalingappa suspected that some of his own political colleagues had orchestrated his media trial. The matter reached such a fever pitch that Devaraj Urs ended up dropping him from his cabinet. Basavalingappa felt betrayed by his own comrades—but such is the nature of power politics. The controversy went on to make national headlines, and the ever blunt Khushwant Singh even wrote an editorial where he affirmed that boosa pervaded all regional literatures in the country, not just Kannada.

Basavalingappa later clarified his stance to journalists, saying;

> We have become caught up in a fabricated controversy. Resolving this controversy itself will be a New Wave. Regarding this subject, what I wish to say is that literature should become richer. The textbooks we currently have do not possess the substance to make our students more courageous, patriotic and socially aware. They are still founded on conservatism, exploitation and are essentially dry material. Our students must read revolutionary books in other languages and enrich the Kannada world. Any literature without this is boosa—this is what I had said in that situation.[2]

BB's gesture was widely commended and appreciated by many, including writers like U.R. Ananthamurthy. In his autobiography, Ananthamurthy remembers the deeply anti-brahmin atmosphere during those years, when he too faced exclusion from some literary meetings. He viewed this prevailing temperament as a historical necessity, and tried not to take it personally. Ananthamurthy points to the cyclical nature of history, and the creative necessity of ensuring the unhindered turning of the wheel of time, which in this case meant a whole-hearted recognition of the dalit movement for dignity and respect. 'With no movement, there is no vitality, and life is not creative.' Ananthamurthy sees hypocrisy in the way society accepts rebellion as an abstract concept, but fails to tolerate actual rebellious ripples in the sociopolitical sphere. He asks his readers to inquire into why Basavalingappa would utter such words, and what reflections this throws up about society at large.

On the other side of the coin, dalits began to face increased oppression for their support of BB's comments. The poet Siddalingaiah, who was yet to gain fame as a writer, was then a student at Maharaja's College. He remembers how dalit students were picked out and beaten black and blue by angry upper-caste peers. Some principled reactionaries went so far as to accost teachers and students and smear vibhuti on their foreheads forcibly—the controversy had taken a religious tinge, another example of how caste and religion are well-nigh inseparable. Many dalits skipped town and returned to their villages to avoid the onslaught. Siddalingaiah and his comrades courted arrest through protest and landed up in jail, where, ironically enough, they were safer than their brothers-in-arms out on the streets.[3]

Siddalingaiah and his band of brothers (sisters were still few and far between) were the first generation of politically organised dalits in the state, and the boosa movement was their first war cry, like the cry of Vritra after enduring Indra's vajra in the Ramanujan poem that begins this chapter. Siddalingaiah, who had grown up peering through the 'slum windows' of Srirampura in Bangalore, helped organise literacy campaigns in these deprived landscapes. I met communist veterans (all upper-caste men) in Bangalore who were part of these endeavours, actively teaching dalit children during weekends. One of them spoke a little mournfully about how Siddalingaiah had forgotten him upon rising to fame.

The movement was also aided by the fact that Chief Minister Devaraj Urs had fashioned a new paradigm in Karnataka politics by foregrounding leaders from backward castes, breaking the domination of vokkaligas and lingayats. He had also set in motion land reforms, and introduced a landmark reservation bill for backward classes under the stewardship of L.G. Havanur. This bill would greatly influence the Mandal Commission a decade later. Thus, building on a larger political scaffolding, the dalit movement began organising a collective of artists and writers who sought to create an alternative world of letters, as well as a new media landscape, to confront the social elites who had cornered the narrative until then. With this, the individualised, psychoanalytic, libidinous, self-exploratory aesthetics of the Navya movement—in the ranks of which were those like U.R. Ananthamurthy and Gopalakrishna Adiga—began to transition into the sociopolitical protest movement known as dalit-bandaya. Communities that had been oppressed and excluded for centuries were finally entering the literary arena, and all the accumulated anger and rage spilt over into the fiery verses of poets like Siddalingaiah. One of the most famous poems from his first collection, *Holemaadigara Haadu* (Songs of the Holeya-Madigas), simply titled 'A Song', begins:

> Bash them, kick them,
> Skin those bastards alive!
> God is one, they claim,
> But build a different temple on each street!
>
> (translated by Maithreyi Karnoor)

These were verses designed to be sung in the public square, crafted to rankle the caste orthodoxy and plunge it into unbelief. The use of violent and vulgar language was a literary ploy, an outburst meant to challenge anybody who was socially coy. Siddalingaiah's initial verses were all of this raging variety, though his work softens over time. His autobiography is uncharacteristically jolly for a dalit memoir, and his later verses too become gentler, more culturally welcoming, as in this one from a collection titled *Hosa Kavitegalu* (New Poems), published in 2000:

> Let new vitality, new emotions,
> be ushered in by a fresh Ugadi.
> In the sunshine of love,
> May Mother Earth forget herself.[4]

Despite the desire for cosmopolitan English pedigree that boosa espoused, the dalit movement was decidedly down-to-earth and desi. This new literary environment brought with it entirely new forms and dialects of Kannada, and rich streams of metaphors and idioms which had once been confined to the alleyways of backward boondocks. Standardised in the nineteenth century by German missionaries and the arrival of the printing press, Kannada had remained a phenomenon of the literary elite throughout the early-twentieth-century renaissance. Now, the 'saviraaru nadigalu' (thousands of rivers—a phrase coined by Siddalingaiah) of regional expression were finally reaching the ocean of Kannada literature.

The writings of Devanura Mahadeva carried a dialect so uniquely rooted in the villages around Nanjanagud that it has been seriously asserted that his works must first be translated into Kannada so that they may become more widely readable. His late-eighties novel *Kusumabale* reaches back to the unique champu-desi hybridised flavour of fifteenth-century oral epics like *Male Mahadeshwara Kavya* and *Manteswamy Kavya*. These epics had very much been in dialogue with the sharanas of the twelfth century, as the similarities between Manteswamy and Allama Prabhu's hagiographies demonstrate. They portrayed the various historical stages of civilisation through elaborate metaphors and imagery. *Kusumabale* employed this prose-poetry style to create a miniature epic that captures the realities of caste society in the modern world, and many, including D.R. Nagaraj, saw it as a genuine breakthrough in the aesthetic imagination of the dalit movement. A.K. Ramanujan had apparently expressed great desire to translate this work, but he doesn't seem to have got around to it.

In the March of 1979, on the very day the annual Kannada Sahitya Sammelana was happening in the religious town of Dharmasthala, the rebel literary conference Bandaya Sahitya Sammelana was symbolically held in Bangalore. The two conferences symbolised two sides of the same coin of idealism—one being a conservative-mindedness that sought to preserve a comfortably prestigious past, and the latter a revolutionary consciousness in the process of imagining a radical new future. When the poet Chennanna Walikar and his associates had asked Hampa Nagarajaiah, then president of the Kannada Sahitya Parishad, to allocate a special section of the conference for dalit writing, Nagarajaiah had sallied that there was no such thing as 'dalita, balita, kalita'. Gopalakrishna Adiga, who had in the spring of his youth rejected the likes of Kuvempu and Masti and the old guard, was now, as head speaker at the conference in Dharmasthala, subjected to a similar rejection by the succeeding generation—definitely a Rama Bhima Soma moment, if ever there was one. The rebels made clear to the establishment that this was not a protest against an individual or an organisation, but a much larger one, against an entire system of values.[5]

The first bandaya conference seems to have kicked off to a spirited, if somewhat delirious, start. The poet Sri Sri, as Prasanna recalled, had arrived drunk and announced that he was a prostitute

Proceedings of the first Bandaya Literary Conference underway.

because he had started writing for films to support himself—rank heresy for a revolutionary. Such raw honesty seems to have been integral to that historical moment. This was not a place for pretensions and false promises, but for (paradoxically) sober reflections on the social realities of the time: mass violence against dalits and workers, lack of employment opportunities, entrenched patriarchy, the rise of people's movements across the state, and so on. Among other speakers at bandaya were writers Devanura Mahadeva, Besagarahalli Ramanna, Chandrashekhar Patil, B. Krishnappa, D.R. Nagaraj and filmmaker M.S. Sathyu. The veteran Kannada novelist Niranjana, long cured of communism but ever one to stand by the disenfranchised and the underprivileged, was there too, a rare flash of seniority in a congregation of blazing youth. Though dominated by men, the bandaya movement sought to actively include women (and religious minorities) within its umbrella too, trying to articulate a broad subaltern solidarity. Ultimately, the uniqueness of the dalit identity, which had discomfited Hampa Nagarajaiah, also miffed the shudra writers of the bandaya group, who too refused to give it its due. The scholar and writer Aravind Malagatti explained this to me at length (a matter we will return to). He had quit the movement over the issue, which was also the reason for the emergence of the popular title 'dalit-bandaya'—a symbolic compromise. When I met Devanura Mahadeva, he only gingerly acknowledged the inaugural bandaya event, saying, 'Yeah, they called me, and I went, that's all.' He didn't seem very eager to be associated with the whole thing.

Of course, these are retrospective realisations, and back in the day, bandaya was a historical necessity that challenged the elite echelons of Kannada culture. Apart from dalits, it was women, in particular, who were being offered writerly encouragement they had never known before.

Picture the neglected attic of a Malnad homestead transformed into a drama school, sometime in pre-Independence India. Bedsheets and quilts of the house improvised into scenic props. Old silk garments from trunks excavated and employed in the service of theatre. Children with painted faces entertaining an audience of yet more children. A young boy fashions a percussion instrument out of a handy utensil, bringing forth an angry mother with no thoughts of sparing the rod. 'Without any care for that, he leapt around like Hanuman and strode like Hiranyakashipu. We had by-hearted all the songs of the plays. We played the harmonium, and yelled our hearts out without paying any heed to the adults,'[6] reminisces the Kannada novelist M.K. Indira about her younger brother's antics.

Born in 1917 in Thirthahalli, Indira's own journey towards becoming a writer resembled the liberatory spirit couched within the tale of Hanuman. Having been forced to abandon schooling at the primary level, she grew up in a prohibitive atmosphere, stealing out to swim in rivers, surreptitiously learning to play the flute in the woods and revelling in rebellious theatre activities. Her grandmother Phaniyamma was a veritable storehouse of tales, ranging from Vikram-Betaal and Arabian Nights to the Puranas, all of which Indira absorbed like a sponge. She was married off at the age of twelve, despite her feeble protestations. Her husband Krishna Rao was a progressive man, averse to superstition and ostentation, and Indira settled into a life of domestic satisfaction, interrupted cruelly by the deaths of four of her eight children. During a brief stay (1946–48) in Mandya, she met Triveni (Anasuya Shankar), the first famous female Kannada novelist, eleven years her junior. At a Rashtrabhasha exam (Hindi education was part of the nationalist spur) in Mandya that brought together six women applicants to condense Premchand's novel *Nirmala* into a six-page Kannada summary, M.K. Indira's version was deemed the finest, trumping the entries of others (including Triveni) who held proper bachelor's degrees. Triveni urged Indira to begin writing, but she shrugged it off on the pretext of having no formal literary education.

Indira began writing only in her early forties, after much prodding from well-wishers like Triveni, by then a celebrated novelist. She hesitantly pens her first novel, *Tungabhadra*, in the late 1950s, drawing on her childhood memories of Malnad, and sends the manuscript to the publishing house Manohara Grantha Mala in Dharwad. The famous Kannada critic Kirtinath Kurtokoti loses the manuscript (along with a thousand rupees) in a crowded Mumbai train, and she is apprised of it only two years later. She rewrites the whole novel in another two weeks, describing it as tapas[7] (religious penance), and resends it. It is finally published and instantly gains popular acclaim. She forwards the novel to Triveni, who never gets to read it. After two miscarriages, Triveni had died following a sketchy delivery. M.K. Indira went on to write tens of novels, becoming one of the most popular Kannada writers of her time, fetching her enough finances to keep living by her pen after the death of her husband.

Indira and Triveni were pioneers of a genre known as the 'social novel', and in the ambers of these novels, the fossilised remains of a home-bred feminist realism may be discovered. The films of Puttanna Kanagal, one of Kannada's most influential moviemakers, also championed women's freedoms through wildly popular adaptations of works by Triveni and M.K. Indira.

It is painfully ironic that the Kannada language has been repeatedly celebrated as a feminine entity (Kannadaambe is nothing if not a regional avatar of Bharat Mata), even as women have battled all odds to enter the literary sphere. After a flourish of emancipated women singing and composing vachanas during the twelfth century sharana movement, including Akkamahadevi, women are conspicuously absent until roughly the seventeenth century, when we meet Sanchi Honnamma, a courtesan at Chikka Devaraja Wodeyar's palace, writing a book detailing a wife's duties to her husband. Other women whose names have survived are widows who retreated to a life of isolation, where devotional poetry was the only salvation allowed in their lives. For instance, Galagali Avva (1670–1760 CE) was twelve when she was married off to a ninety-five-year-old man. Her life after marriage lasted for eight days. Widowed on the ninth day, she had to tonsure her head and observe societal seclusion. She would learn to read and write from her five grown-up stepsons, and become a composer of devotional songs later in life. Cut to the early twentieth century, and not much had changed. The poetess and Haridasi (Krishna-bhakt) Ambabai faced similar rejection after widowhood, only to be saved somewhat by a guru who discovered and fostered her talents. Nanjangud Thirumalamba, married at the age of ten and widowed at fourteen, learnt to read and write Kannada, Telugu and Tamil all by herself. She started a journal in 1916 and published several books of stories over the next couple of decades. One of her stories, where a woman reforms her philandering husband, who then apologises to her, was critiqued by Masti Venkatesha Iyengar, who objected to the idea of a husband apologising to his wife.[8] His attitude reminds one of the conservative backlash that Kamaladevi Chattopadhyay had faced—from no less a person than Sarojini Naidu, her domineering sister-in-law—over her divorce of her serially philandering husband. In any case, Thirumalamba was rediscovered in the late seventies, and an annual prize was instated in her honour. The plight of widows would remain an undying literary theme till the second half of the twentieth century—its apogee is M.K. Indira's *Phaniyamma*, a tale inspired by her own grandmother, which the director Prema Karanth (possibly the first woman filmmaker in Kannada cinema) turned into a famous film in the seventies.

Through the eighties and nineties, if there was one phenomenon that really captured the progressive zeitgeist of those pre-internet times in Karnataka, it was a man called Lankesh,[9] and his eponymous magazine *Lankesh Patrike*. Lankesh encouraged shy, upcoming writers (especially women) to write for his weekly, and this opened up whole new worlds. For instance, Sara Aboobacker's novel *Chandragiri Teeradalli*, a sharp critique of Muslim patriarchy and triple talaq, was serialised in the early eighties through his express efforts. He would even publish advertisements for wares like chutney powder, pickles and home-made products to encourage women to participate vigorously in the market. Devanura Mahadeva told me that Lankesh's editorials were a key node of political conversations that transpired during those years. Publishers of bandaya literature often lamented that their readership and book sales were subpar.

Literacy was only just being extended to the vast majority of the state, and it was tabloids and magazines that really garnered a steady audience.

Staying true to his given name, Lankesh (literally, emperor of Lanka) was an adversarial character, a radical contrarian who thrived in transgression. Just like the blasphemous anti-hero Naranappa in Ananthamurthy's novel *Samskara*, whose filmy avatar was essayed by none other than Lankesh himself—a stroke of casting genius. Lankesh's conception of a creative life straddled many realms. He wrote brilliant plays and short stories, directed award-winning films, was a muckraking journalist, but was also a man of the streets who found great pleasure in evenings spent betting on horse-racing, card games and similarly distinguished pursuits. I heard, across my interviews, of how his readers would hungrily wait each week for the next issue of *Patrike*. It was here that corrupt politicians were called out with biting headlines, translations of Western writers were brought into the world of Kannada letters, and social movements were highlighted and critiqued with equal concern.

The punch and vitriol of *Lankesh Patrike* often blurred the line between sensationalism and reasoned critique, but the overall thrust of the weekly favoured justice seekers, presented progressive social stances and broke important stories of corruption scandals. For a while at least, it seemed like politicians would have to think twice about their misdemeanours for fear of these being spreadeagled across the *Patrike*'s front page. When Lankesh died in 2000, a special edition of *Lankesh Patrike* was brought out in tribute, bearing letters from literati and close friends across the Kannada sphere. Ananthamurthy, who had become a bitter rival for various reasons, penned a piece that said that he would miss Lankesh, but also included a detached critique of his work. Conceding somewhat hastily that 'he was necessary for society—because when disaster strikes, he held the magical stick to save society', Ananthamurthy added:

> I have often been astonished by the extraordinary lengths to which Lankesh would go to carve out his own moral analysis, often to the point of mad bitterness, just to avoid reconciling himself

> with hypocrites. He was like a porcupine—the quills were all for self-preservation, perhaps for the protection of all the truths he guarded within himself. The times were such that if one had to be civil, there were only two alternatives, to shut one's mouth, or to remain absurdly naïve in one's understanding. Lankesh established himself as a man with a biting tongue and became independent of all these modes. Later, this became the leading contributor to Lankesh's fame, and also to his coffers. The contradiction here is that this slowly made Lankesh insensitive to truth itself. The desire to be impactful, the perceived necessity to influence people, I never liked his columns that often read like the diary entries of a teenage girl.[10]

Lankesh had wrecked his health through excessive drinking and smoking, and his death at the age of sixty-five always reminds me of the life and times of Christopher Hitchens—they were both men who railed against god and divinity, and consumed their life with fierce polemics. Profanity, however important to a writer, cannot always guarantee profundity. They were lovers of life and its pleasures, but a bohemian lifestyle can be your best friend and worst enemy at the same time, as Hitchens himself once put it.

Lankesh Patrike petered out slowly after Lankesh's death. His daughter Gauri Lankesh tried to resuscitate it and took over the editorship, painstakingly learning to write decent Kannada during the process. I found a well-curated special edition from 2005 commemorating twenty-five years of the magazine that contained, amongst others, an essay on Gandhi by Ashish Nandy, a piece on Dara Shikoh by Banu Mushtaq, a meditation on the critical insiders of Hinduism by Ananthamurthy, a report on Karnataka cricket by Ramachandra Guha, a translation of an essay by Salman Rushdie on religious fundamentalism, cultural commentary by Jayant Kaikini, bookended by photographs of glamourous cine-stars to give it a glossy, tabloid appeal.

Soon, political differences with her brother Indrajit Lankesh forced a split within the magazine's ranks, and Gauri started a fresh magazine with her own name. An unbridled critic of Hindutva politics, she was also equally critical of the Congress regime and Muslim fundamentalists—in this sense, following in the footsteps of her iconoclastic father, while also inheriting his feminist instincts. Though she had critiqued the regressive politics of S.L. Bhyrappa's novels *Aavarana* and *Kavalu*, she had applauded his subsequent novel *Uttara Kanda*, which was a humane retelling of the Ramayana from Sita's perspective. When Islamic patriarchs had threatened to boycott Banu Mushtaq for advocating women's right to pray in mosques, Gauri wrote to the noted scholar Rahamath Tarikere for a quick comment, and when Tarikere asked for some time to gather more details, she hastily condemned him as a fundamentalist in her piece. Tarikere observes, in a balanced tribute piece written after her assassination, titled 'A Wild Flower',[11] that Gauri was, by nature, a confrontational character, and that he sometimes 'did not like the way she criticised the Hindu faith when she criticised Hindutva politics'. He writes of how he observed her transformation as a journalist and activist, of how he 'saw from up close her simplicity, humaneness and commitment to social causes, alongside her blunt, rash and obstinate nature'. He opines that Lankesh had been somewhat wiser than his daughter when it came to linguistic finesse. Lankesh had also been a celebrated playwright and creative writer much before he jumped into journalism.

Gauri's public persona was also a product of the unprecedented immunity granted to increasingly bad actors on the political stage. The atmosphere had turned for the worse since the 2000s, and the strengthening of brute State power led to many BJP leaders filing defamation cases against her. Of course, her father—an inveterate polemicist who believed that conflict was the mother of all discourse—had faced flak too, but as Gauri herself wrote in 2017:

> It was not just Lankesh and his publication that were attacked by legislators. Even eminent journalists like TJS George were targets of abuse from the floor of the house. Over the years since, editors of prominent dailies and weeklies—including this writer—have been regularly summoned before the Privileges Committee.

> The committee seems to be of the firm opinion that referring to legislators in the singular, criticising their actions outside the house, or exposing their abuse of power is beyond the purview of journalists merely because they happen to be 'elected representatives' and hence more equal than others. Most complaints are settled with a reprimand or publication of an apology (however insincere), but the creeping trend of bullying the press is unmistakable.[12]

After Gauri was shot dead by right-wing fanatics in 2017, police investigations revealed that a 2012 video of Gauri condemning the actions of the Hindu Jagarana Vedike—a group that had brutally attacked young boys and girls vacationing at a homestay in Mangalore, in the name of 'defending' Hindu dharma—had been circulated across the country and used to brainwash her would-be assassins. Of course, the context of her speech had been completely stripped away. Even the official BJP Facebook page had shared the video, warning that a befitting reply would soon be given to her.[13] Encapsulated in the killing of Gauri Lankesh is the fall of adversarial Kannada journalism and the rise of malevolent vigilante groups that make little effort to even cloak their daggers.

One of my favourite Kannada movies is Shankar Nag's *Accident* (1984), the protagonist of which is a courageous journalist (played superbly by Nag himself) who sets out to hold a politician's son guilty for driving over homeless people during a night-time drug escapade. Many of his films spoke of a deep sympathy for the working class, and I've seen many auto-rickshaw stands named after him in Mysore and Bangalore, a nod to his popular 1980 film *Auto Raja*. Shankar Nag tragically perished in a road accident in 1990, and one can only wonder how much Kannada cinema would have been revolutionised had he lived on.

Today, Kannada media, especially television, remains largely cringeworthy, sold over to political naivety so much that one marvels at how *Lankesh Patrike* even managed to hold its own for decades. During the nineties, publications like Ravi Belagere's *Hai Bengaluru* went on to establish a precedent for bawdy cine-gossip and underworld stories that overrode the genuine political and social concerns that had found meaningful coverage earlier. I would encounter tens of such tabloids during my boyhood barbershop visits in the late 2000s. Though islands of good journalism, like *Deccan Herald* and its sister publications, soldier on, well-crafted political commentary remains conspicuously absent in the mainstream media space today.

Of course, English and Kannada were not the only ones jostling for attention back in those decades. A multilingual society gives rise to multidimensional linguistic anxieties. Tamil, in particular, has been a key bone of contention in Bangalore ever since the sixties, when theatres showcasing Tamil movies were attacked ferociously by Kannada activists. Writers like A.N. Krishna Rao had actively participated in establishing these fissures. The apogee of Kannada–Tamil tensions was reached in December 1991. Twenty-one people were killed in Bangalore, amidst ethnic violence and police firing, and the state witnessed an unprecedented exodus of Tamils. In her excellent study of Bangalore, *The Promise of the Metropolis*, historian Janaki Nair captures this milieu in great detail, and she argues that questions of land and water were what really framed this historical juncture. Seeing how these riots (and a future one against Muslims in 1994) were restricted to the western parts of the city, where land rights were most precarious and illegal constructions abounded, she argues that 'it was a time when the right to land within the city and beyond had become more uncertain and yet more critical as a resource in an informal economy'.[14]

Urdu and Sanskrit were politically linked to elite interests and daubed with communal colours too. Pro-Kannada crusaders had been railing against the inclusion of Urdu in radio broadcasts for some years, but the matter reached a head in 1994, when the local Doordarshan station introduced a daily ten-minute news bulletin in Urdu on the occasion of Gandhi Jayanti. It was perceived as an 'appeasement' ploy by the ruling Congress, and of course, those were years when Hindutva ideology was on the ascendant. What followed was one of the most violent riots in Bangalore's history. On 7 October, 'Kannadiga processions intentionally marched towards the southern part of the city, where the majority of Muslims live, shouting slogans in front of mosques. Uncontrollable elements attacked Muslim autorickshaw drivers and threw stones at *madrasas*, setting buildings on fire on their way. One week of uninterrupted violence followed, in spite of the announcement by the Chief Minister Veerappa Moily that the news bulletin had been stopped. There were no less than 30 dead and 343 wounded, and goods worth several million rupees were destroyed.'[15]

While a ten-minute bulletin was all that it had taken to rise up against Urdu, Sanskrit had thrived for decades as a 'scoring subject' in the crucial tenth-standard board exams. Until the eighties, Sanskrit was accorded first-language status, along with Kannada, English, Tamil, Telugu, Malayalam and Marathi, in high schools across the state. Even if Sanskrit was not taught in primary school, a student could opt for Sanskrit as the first language in high school, and begin learning from scratch—not very difficult, since it only involved rote memorisation, which is a national tradition in its own right. Evaluators exercised divine leniency, so if you chose Sanskrit as a first language in the tenth standard, you could score high marks and crush students who had chosen other languages. Moreover, students could answer Sanskrit exams in Kannada or English, and were not even required to write in Sanskrit. We are a competitive country, especially when it comes to exams, and the number of students choosing Sanskrit over Kannada skyrocketed. The inequity of giving first-language status to a subject only taught for three years—unlike, say, Kannada, which was taught throughout schooling—did not go unnoticed.

Public intellectuals wrote to the government to remove Sanskrit's status as a first language because it was unscientific on many grounds. How could a language that was not spoken at all be given the same status as the state language? In 1979, the Karnataka government led by Devaraj Urs gave an order to the effect that Sanskrit could only be studied as a third language. In 1980, when Gundu Rao became chief minister, he immediately yielded to pro-Sanskrit voices (Hindu orthodoxy) and restored its first-language status. Again, Kannada activists were up in arms, and the government was forced to name a committee in 1980, headed by the litterateur V.K. Gokak, to study the matter and provide a reasoned report.

Gokak, a diligent old man with a religious work ethic, travelled around the state for three months, conducting field work, and in many places, braving boycotts that cried *Gokak, Go Back!* The perception amongst many was that the committee was full of pro-Sanskritists, and that they would deliver an unfavourable verdict. Gokak eventually submitted a report that suggested Kannada as a first language with an exam carrying 150 marks, with a second language for hundred marks and a third for fifty. Until then, a third-language exam was not compulsory, but Gokak's report made it so. It also said that Kannada must be made compulsory from the third grade onwards, as preparation for high-school intensity. Now, activists carried out protests to *bring* Gokak's report into action, but things stagnated. Young bandaya apparatchiks also played an active part in these protests, courting arrest and challenging the police.

Gundu Rao announced that the report would be duly implemented, but another row soon erupted. Linguistic minority leaders protested against mandatory Kannada in primary schools, arguing that it would diminish their own mother tongues. The government grew silent again, prompting yet more protests. The story goes that Dr Vijayamma, one of the first notable female Kannada journalists, urged Dr Rajkumar to lend his persona to the Kannada movement and secure the report's implementation. Rajkumar didn't think twice about it—Kannada was after all his greatest muse—and plunged into a statewide mobilisation involving literati and the entire film industry. Rajkumar, along with other famous actors like Vishnuvardhan, Lokesh, Anant Nag and Shankar Nag, toured villages, towns and cities, clamouring for the government to immediately implement the Gokak Committee Report. The mobilisation drew lakhs of people across the state, and police struggled to control the burgeoning crowds. In some places, they even resorted to golibaar and a total of seven people died across the state during these protests. The government ruled that Kannada would be given sole first-language status.

Educational institutions run by linguistic minorities (backed also by upwardly mobile families who wanted to educate their children in English) challenged the constitutional validity of the state's diktat, and the High Court upheld these contentions in 1989. Sanskrit, too, found its way back into curricula as a first-language option. At the Kendriya Vidyalaya where I did most of my schooling, I did not formally study Kannada, though it was a language most of us spoke. We had to choose between Hindi and Sanskrit in high school, and I remember a lot of question paper swapping and other modes of surreptitious copying during Sanskrit exams. Like so many of my generation, I found myself embroiled in competitive exam fever for the next two years, after which I slunk into a local engineering college like a sheep herded into a pen. In the first year of the gauntlet that followed, a token Kannada course was made mandatory, where we only had to learn the alphabet to pass. To be honest though, I remember the Kannada and English communication electives more fondly than every engineering course I took.

II

I read of Raman's death
On a morning that had brought a bitter chill
To Shivamogga; the news made me restless, filled
Me with existential dread; unable to bear it any longer,
I decided to go for a walk.
The streets and fields were unchanged,
There was no hushed talk—I grieved
That no one was grieving.

—K.S. Nissar Ahmed, 'The News of (Sir CV) Raman's Death' (translated by Roopa Pai)

NASA says 'Om' is the sound of the sun.

—*viral WhatsApp forward*

The existence of a text known as the *Vymanika Shastra* was first noted in Mysore by a man named G.R. Joyser, founder of the International Academy of Sanskrit Research, in the year 1952. He affirmed that it was an ancient text, attributed to the sage Bharadwaja and passed on orally for centuries, that contained detailed instructions for the construction of 'various types of aircraft for civil aviation and for warfare'. In reality, it had been composed by a man named Subbaraya Sastry in the early twentieth century, riding on some remarkable flights of fantasy and imagination, written in a Sanskrit that was modern rather than Vedic in its metre and language.[16] The story goes that Sastry had taken to wandering the countryside after an attack of smallpox rendered him a cripple. At some point in this period, he met an unnamed guru who healed him through mystic powers and bestowed upon him this ancient text, which had been sitting in the guru's head fully memorised, awaiting the ideal disciple. By the 1950s, Sastry had died, although the exact year is unclear. But Joyser set about on his mission to get the text vetted, and even translated it into English in the hope of attracting Western attention. In the seventies, scientists concluded that the text 'shows a complete lack of understanding of the dynamics of the flight of heavier-than-air craft', that it violated Newton's laws and that 'the geometries are unimaginably horrendous from thc point of view of flying'.

Seen through the anti-colonial prism of the first half of the twentieth century, Sastry's inventive efforts seem oddly endearing. It was to correct this tendency that scientific temper was enshrined in the Constitution at the dawn of that midnight hour—an ideal that does not seem to have permeated into society at large, even after several decades of independence. In 1995, rumors that an idol of Lord Ganesh was slurping milk in a Delhi temple proved to be an ecstatic matter that unified millions of Indians, both in the country and abroad, who began to test the hypothesis on local idols. Published in the same year was Vivek Shanbhag's short story 'Kantu'[17] (meaning both compassion and a set date for a certain event), where we find a sympathetic portrait of the anxiety and excitement brought by science and globalisation into a South

Indian village. A stellar solar eclipse is set to occur, which brings foreign scientists and travellers rushing into the village, even as the local science teacher and the traditional astrologer debate with each other on how an eclipse even happens, although neither can explain himself well enough. The village experiences pride in their unique geographical position, where the eclipse shall be most vividly seen, but they are unable to accept that this unprecedented glory is unlikely to ever visit them again. Simultaneously, a dam project is all set to submerge the village, which pushes one of the villagers to expedite his efforts to unearth a lost treasure in the local temple, the exact location of which has been eluding him forever. As the villagers try to make the best of their fifteen days of fame, they begin selling off all the old items in their household to the moneyed guests, eventually culminating in an episode where a woman (with a propensity for hysterical outbursts) grows fearful, climbs up into an attic and sits shivering there believing that the pralaya, *flood*, is all set to consume them. Past, present and future are jammed together into a frenzy of apocalyptic anxiety.

Science in India remains a blend of reverential acceptance and wishy-washy excitement. A.P.J. Abdul Kalam, arguably the most popular scientific voice in modern India, once said that one must first dream before any dreams can possibly come true, and whatever else may be said about Prathap N.M.—a young 'scientist' from Mandya district, near Mysore—it cannot be said that he did not dream. For over two years, until the pandemic hit, Prathap toured the state's schools and colleges as a sought-after motivational speaker, where young children swarmed around him for a much-coveted autograph. Watching Prathap spin yarn after yarn, parents began reprimanding their own children for not achieving great things as he had. Prathap's usual routine involved peddling grand tales about his scientific genius, emotionally recounting his various trials and tribulations, and vaingloriously celebrating his international achievements in the field of drone-making. From saving the life of a Sudanese tribal bitten by a deadly Black Mamba to delivering swift relief during the Karnataka floods of 2019, Prathap's drones traced an endless journey of selfless altruism. In 2020, numerous media platforms thoroughly debunked every tall claim he had ever made, and many troll videos have popped up since then, ridiculing the whole affair.

Yet, the inventiveness and theatrics that Prathap employed to keep up this remarkable charade continues to amaze and entertain. One assumed that his antics would quickly be relegated to the amnesia of history, that his fifteen minutes of fame had firmly ended, but there were some intriguing developments to prove otherwise. Recently, he was inducted into the Kannada version of the reality show *Bigg Boss*, where he enjoyed popular support and snaked his way up to the last round of the competition. He then posted a video where he donates some of his winnings to school girls in need of money for their fees, trying to attract some good karma and social media brownie points in the process. He has thousands of followers on his social media profiles, replete with photographs clicked alongside unsuspecting personalities like Rahul Gandhi, and he has also created a few blogs that repeat the exact story he had once fabricated from ground-up. While one may simply see him as an innocuous straggler trying to carve out an aspirational space for himself, it is also important to recognise him as symptomatic of a larger disconnect with the world of science—a living example of how aspiration struggles to find real inspiration. Just as rare syndromes of the brain help in understanding the organ's functioning better, a closer look at Drone Prathap promises to throw up sobering insights regarding the place of science in the average Indian mind.

Drone Prathap's drone-like rise to fame followed an appearance on the TV show *Comedy Khilaadigalu* hosted by popular Kannada actor Jaggesh. The story, as Jaggesh narrates it, is both moving and hilarious. Jaggesh had been travelling in the US, where a random old man came up to him bearing an elusive packet of Pan Parag, which brought the two of them together. The old man let loose a sob story about his grandson—a gifted scientist from rural Mandya—who was full of promise, but was lacking institutional support. Jaggesh promptly agreed to feature him on his show, and even forwarded the young man's file to Union Minister Rajnath Singh. Catapulted into the limelight as a peerless wunderkind, Drone Prathap went on to sustain an extraordinary mass hoodwink for over two years. After his story went viral across platforms in 2018, multiple awards were bestowed upon him by magnanimous organisations, a biopic about him was being seriously planned by a Kannada film director, and Prathap grew confident enough to announce that he had turned down a lucrative job offer from Narendra Modi himself. At this point the bubble burst. The press caught on to this obvious lie, and a long litany of falsehoods came to light. Jaggesh soon received a reprimand letter from the Union government. The awards at international drone-making competitions that Prathap claimed to have won were shown to be non-existent, and the drones he claimed to have designed (all made from e-waste, no less) were, in fact, made by more accomplished individuals. Jaggesh has since tendered an apology, and voiced his embarrassment at having been taken in by the boy. However, even he cannot deny Prathap's unique penchant for yarn-spinning.

It doesn't take a hardworking journalist to uncover how the JSS College of Arts, Commerce and Science, an institution in Mysore recognised by the UGC as a 'College with Potential for Excellence', celebrated and promoted this young fraud, and posted this wonderfully eloquent all-caps release on their website, which deserves to be quoted in full:

> MR. M.N. PRATHAP HAS ACHIEVED AS GOOD RESEARCHER IN THE FIELD OF ‘BORDER SECURITY TELEGRAPHY, CRYPTOGRAPHY IN DRONE NETWORKING SYSTEM, DRONE IN TRAFFIC MANAGEMENT AND NATIONAL SOCIO DEFENSE

I think the Prathap story unveils a rather disquieting realisation, which is that few know, or care, what really constitutes scientific excellence. Does it mean working for hours in a lab, spilling chemicals and tweaking circuit boards, until a grand, rather unlikely, eureka moment presents itself? Does it mean getting a PhD, becoming a passionless professor, pushing half-baked papers at conferences and perpetuating the scheme of things that created you? Or does it mean working for the 'national socio defense' of the country, and winning laurels for your beloved nation on the world stage?

Reading the comments on his recent uploads, it is obvious that Drone Prathap is seen as a kind of teddy bear character, exuding simple-minded rural innocence, and people cheer him on with good-natured kindness. Here are some indicative samples:

> I respect your confidence bro
> This is real hiro God bless you bro
> Am glad for you Prathap. Do well. Dont bother about stupid people.

Among us live extremely kind souls who love rooting for underdogs. Even Jaggesh had not minded the fake antics as much as the fact that Prathap never even thanked him for the public boost he had been gifted. In a system where engineering is not presented as the single transcendental goal of higher education, where Drone Prathap would have been encouraged instead to explore his talent as an actor, perhaps he might have turned out to be a more authentic personality—he does speak well, and displays a certain proclivity for public life. Or maybe we should just be glad he has not turned to politics yet.

Scientific temper is tragically underappreciated in India today. Abdul Kalam's remarkable appeal cut across communities, age groups and political parties even, but his universal appeal was also a double-edged sword in many ways. I grew up reading all his famous titles as a young boy, but the only things that stayed with me were fleeting images of Kalam selling newspapers at a railway station and of him learning to play the veena. While Kalam had a natural propensity for simple speech, and his humility was commendable, he tended to speak mostly on a rather poetic, abstract level—of success, failure, hardships and so on—without getting into the nitty-gritty of developing a scientific spirit. In the average cultural consciousness, he was the 'people's president', a 'missile man', a charming leader who exhorted children to dream big and aim for the skies, who spoke of life and science in a transcendent, empowering tenor. It is only upon closely scrutinising the various books that he authored that one begins to discern the nuances of his grand vision of how science and governance may be dovetailed. If one were to expand on Kalam's utopian view of a developed India, there would be healthcare for all, the country's food crisis would be solved, and technological innovation would be decentralised and democratised. Had Kalam lived to see his prophesied year of revolution—2020—the collapsing healthcare system and the vast suffering of the countryside would have destroyed him.

Around the same time as Drone Prathap was droning on, the film adaptation of Manu Joseph's novel *Serious Men* was released, and this too caught on to the same phenomenon. In the movie, we see Ayyan Mani (Nawazuddin Siddiqui), working as a personal assistant to Dr Arvind Acharya (Nassar) at a research institute. Acharya is on a quest to find signs of extraterrestrial life, which seems like a pointless endeavour to Mani. Acharya's dismissive and supercilious attitude towards Mani aggravates the latter's desire for retribution. While Acharya refers to Mani by various epithets—moron, imbecile, knobhead—Mani too has a term for the grave and intense-looking physicists he sees at the institute—Serious Men—whose lives he views only in jest. Mani takes revenge against this world he hates by focusing all his energies on training his son Adi.

By filling Adi's head with an assorted collection of scientific jargon, by stealing school question papers for him and by constructing an elaborate myth of the child as a genius, Mani manages to make the kid famous, delivering a punch-in-the-face to the institute where he suffers insults every day. However, young Adi suffers a major mental breakdown because of all the stress, and the family is forced to move to a nondescript town to build their lives from scratch again. As a sociological cursor, *Serious Men* (like Drone Prathap) points towards a peculiar aspect of the Indian psyche: an ill-defined obsession with the idea of 'scientific genius', and an unfailing tendency to accept dubious claims of excellence. The tendency is always to invite miracles, and to then disregard all evidence to the contrary. Drone Prathap, aka Drone-acharya, teaches us precisely the same lesson—that scientific temper has become a veritable joke, and that television media has become a pedestrian TRP machine.

The Drone Prathap story exemplifies the stagnation of an education system that was never designed to provoke deep scientific inquiry. One may travel back to Nehruvian times to arrive at the root cause, where IITs and IIMs were given much fillip but primary education remained a black hole. In addition to this, it is also true that the cosmopolitan world of science has barely found its way into the Kannada world of letters—most of it is still boosa in this regard. Science journalism has remained restricted to newspaper or magazine essays and titbits of trivia. Writers who did attempt forays into the field, like Poornachandra Tejaswi, were satisfied with mildly interesting tales of animals and birds and so on. Of course, there have been dedicated science writers like Nagesh Hegde, who has been writing for decades on science and the environment, with many small books to his name. If you hunt for more meaty books, you might arrive at outliers like B.G.L. Swamy's *Hasiru Honnu*, a lovely travelogue-cum-botany lesson. There are numerous translations of English non-fiction books of course, but most people who tune in to *Bigg Boss* are unlikely to have such niche interests.

Still stagnating in superficially sentimental territory, Kannada media—especially television shows and news platforms—are predominantly dull and dumbed down. The vast creative potential opened up by the internet is yet to spawn the pièce de résistance of neo-Kannada culture. Slow changes are at present operating in the shadows, reshaping the creative economy. The novelist and short-story writer Vasudhendra, who has been doubling up as a publisher for many years now, recently spoke about how decentralised Kannada publishing has become, especially when it comes to translations. He finds a silver lining amidst all the pessimism while speaking of a recent translation from his one-man publication house Chanda Prakashana:

> We published a book whose writer is a ballet dancer from China. Someone from Australia translated it into English and published

> it. A woman from Singapore told me it would be nice if it were translated into Kannada. The cover of the book was supplied by a French citizen, while the back-cover photo was taken by an Englishman. Searching for a DTP expert, I found a Rajasthani-origin woman in Gulbarga, and the manuscript was proofread by someone in Manipal. It was finally printed in Pune. Now, if a reader in America wants to read the book, it will be digitally printed overnight and shipped by Amazon—this is done by a company in Delhi. Kannada publishing moves across the world, and whenever technology allows for seamless translation between languages, you should be able to read anything, anywhere, in any language.[18]

This is hearteningly optimistic, but Kannada books are not exactly selling like hot cakes. All said and done, I become a pessimist again whenever I think of the disciplinary penitentiary that is our primary schooling system. When I watch the prime minister give tips to young school children on 'managing exam stress', I fume and wonder how on earth we have not risen up against the truly depressing culture of exams and mugging and irrelevant knowledge. It is an incredibly partial system that selects those who are already good at a certain kind of 'problem-solving', alienating others who might be infinitely talented in other ways. What is lost in this whole charade is the push for truth, intellectual satisfaction and practical know-how. The more I think along these lines, the more I begin to empathise with Drone Prathap and his zest for fame.

III

With his wild Einstein hair, excited mannerisms and passionate gesticulations, K.P. Rao hardly evokes the calm resignation you might expect in an octogenarian who's had a long, eventful career. Anytime you go to meet him, he's sitting in front of his computer, taking some new course or exploring some cutting-edge research on YouTube. Famous as the man who introduced computers to the Kannada language, Rao is a curious cat with an enormous bag of interests—linguistics, typography, cultural history, nuclear physics and much more. Something like a Noam Chomsky of Karnataka, sans the political vociferousness.

Born in a village near Mangalore boasting of a syncretic culture, he is proud of how he learnt Sufi music, Catholic gospels and temple bhajans with equal facility during his childhood. It was also a multilingual upbringing, which set him up for a multifaceted career. He studied Chemistry and landed up at the Bhabha Atomic Research Centre in Bombay during the sixties, where the historian and mathematician D.D. Kosambi (who was at Tata Institute of Fundamental Research which, like BARC, comes under the Indian government's Department of Atomic Energy) became a good friend. In time, he was specifically called upon by Tata Press, in view of his special talents, to create a layout and font to enable the printing of the Indus Valley Script. In the eighties, Rao devised the first phonetic keyboard driver for Indian languages, allowing one to input Kannada (and Telugu) through a traditional QWERTY keyboard. He never patented any of his work, and his layout was accepted by the Karnataka government as the standard one. Later, software and applications like Nudi were rolled out, which were essentially built on K.P. Rao's original model. Soon, numerous other languages across the country built upon the foundation he had laid.

Though he has long since retired, Rao spends almost every day in an air-conditioned server room at the Manipal Institute of Communications, which has been converted into an office for him. We talked much about his life in Bombay, where he spent many formative years.

> KPR: In that Tata Press building, one floor had been given out to Tata Consulting Engineers. Now, engineers are not really good with English, and they wanted someone with good English to take care of their internal reports and so on. Shankar Mokashi Punekar was badly in need of a job, and he came there. That's when I met him. It was me who introduced him to the Indus Valley Script, which he used for his novel *Avadheshwari*! We were meeting every day at lunch.

Me: Ah! It is one of my favourite Kannada novels. But the introduction to the novel, when he talks about continental drift and his interpretations of Indus Valley Seals, it seems to be full of crazy leaps of faith.

KPR: Yes, yes, he was a dreamer! But I like it that way! He became really interested in them. He would show me a seal and say, *see, the mother is going to fetch milk for her child.* There was neither a mother nor a child there! It was like looking at clouds and making something out of it. Most of it is wrong, perhaps all of it is wrong only!

Me: But his other non-fiction writings are definitely thought-provoking, like that book *Harijan Contribution to Medieval Indian Thought…*

KPR: Yes, the Harijan bit is secondary, but yes, it highlighted the contributions of non-priestly classes. Quite often, I think that the Shramana system, which ran parallel to the Sanatanis, was also equally important. There was not much of a distinction as far as caste goes, but they were serious about trade and business. After my wife died six years ago, I wanted to become a shramana, take sanyas! They were not very different from the initial Sufi systems of thought—they lived by begging, whatever comes your way, enjoy your life! Happiness lies in you, and not in something external…

After an unsuccessful venture into manufacturing silicon-controlled rectifiers back in the sixties, K.P. Rao began delving into typography with great seriousness.

KPR: In 1983, WIPRO had received a call from Gita Press in Gorakhpur, saying they need an input system in Devanagari. I told them how we had done it for Kannada, and how it can be done through the English keyboard, logically. So, I designed 286 glyphs—characters—and gave it to them. Gita Press wanted to give me some money. How can I take money? We grew up reading their *Kalyana*, Mahabharata, Ramayana and all. First thing they printed was Bhagavad Gita, including the Vishnu Sahasranama also. Using my letters! It is now running into its eighty-fifth edition.

Rao loves languages for their own sake, and dislikes getting into political arguments. Bring up Panini, and his eyes light up. He loves going back to the Vedas and Upanishads in his conversations, which he sees as the country's first folk literature, as opposed to the divine voice of the gods.

> Me: Kalburgi makes this really questionable argument that the Battle of Talikota (which ended the Vijayanagara empire) was essentially a linguistic one—between the Telugu-favouring court and a Kannada-conscious public.
>
> KPR: Yeah, all questionable arguments only. Let me take you back a little! In Brihadaranyaka Upanishad, the dialogue between Gargi and Yajnavalkya is a very important bit. She asks him, where did this world come from? He says, it came from Agni. She keeps asking, where did that emerge from? And this keeps happening many times, until he says, *stop talking, or else your head will explode!* This was the method of education they had. On the other hand, in Milinda Panha, they don't fight with each other, they agree with each other, they respect each other. This is because when it came to Buddhists and Jains, they wanted to talk in local languages [Pali or Magadhi], and they also wanted to simplify matters. So, that kind of dialect simplification exists in non-Sanskrit texts of that time. On the other hand, until Sanskrit was standardised by Panini, they did not commit even Ramayana and Mahabharata to writing—so the common language required for intellectual agreement was not there at all. Panini's sutras were learnt by heart. They are formulae—like a+b whole squared…
>
> Me: It is a very curious inversion of the Marga–Desi conception …
>
> KPR: Yes, yes, that is exactly what I am trying to tell you! It is the local languages that really developed [intellectually]. They wanted people to understand, rather than just get mesmerised. They were actually telling people what it is. The Buddhists went with a begging bowl, there were no big sacrifices, no big debates…
>
> Me: But the Buddhists also debated extensively, right? It is not like they were passive recipients…

KPR: Yes, but they learnt Sanskrit only to compete with the brahmins and learned people. Vasubandhu and Assanga learnt Sanskrit only for that sake! A language needs to be standardised if it has to survive, otherwise it will just keep dividing into many, many dialects. That is why Sanskrit spread across the subcontinent.

K.P. Rao has written about these interesting observations at length in his 2021 linguistics novel *Varnaka*. Indeed, as Wittgenstein famously remarked, the limits of my language are the limits of my world. Today, English has become intimately enjoined with modern science, and it does seem like present-day English is no different from what Sanskrit had once been for the Buddhist philosopher Vasubandhu—a dialogic necessity, a mode of intellectual survival. English's level of standardisation is light years ahead of regional languages like Kannada, especially when it comes to scientific traditions. I was curious to hear about K.P. Rao's schooling, and the foundations of his own multilingual intellect.

Me: Your syncretic upbringing seems quite unique. What was schooling like in your childhood?

KPR: See, we never thought otherwise. Someone had established an Urdu school as early as 1904, and in 1908, they had started a Kannada school also, which is where I studied. But we had a very interesting situation. The Kannada school stopped at eighth standard and the Urdu school at fifth. So, they would come to our school and one of us would be assigned to each of them to bring them up to speed. That's how I became friends with Mohammad Hussan Baji, and I learnt Urdu from him as an exchange. He later became a right-hand man of George Fernandes in the Bombay Taximen's Union. George always used to address me as Baji's friend!

Me: What are your thoughts on the recent Kannada-language protests in Bangalore?

KPR: Waste of an effort, I'd say. See, you need a common language. There is nothing wrong with English. I was born in British India, hahaha, in 1940. So, I don't have any worries. If not for anything else, English is the best language for Artificial Intelligence, because other languages are not rich enough, as far as available literature on the Internet goes.

Me: And Kannada is already fusing with English…

KPR: Yes, does anybody use a Kannada word for bus, car or train? Why bother about it? Now, about this sixty–forty rule [that 60 per cent of the space on signboards should be occupied by Kannada type]. See, I'm a typographer. Now, as far as the ascender and descender is concerned, the main body of a Kannada character occupies 40 per cent of space, and the various horns and maatras take up the remainder. This 40 per cent is equivalent to 60 per cent of the main body of an English character [i.e. the body of an English character comprises 60 per cent, while ascenders and descenders occupy the remaining 40 per cent]. Now, if they do as they are really proposing—60 per cent in Kannada and 40 per cent in English…

Me: They will basically be the same size…

KPR: Yes, it will be fifty-fifty, really, haha.

Me: Do you think there will be a time when accurate Kannada–English translation will be made possible by AI?

KPR: I don't believe all that. I don't think it is necessary also. It is more important to develop Kannada better, and make good writings available to people.

Around the same time, I'd come across a rather unique ninth-century text called Siri Bhoovalaya, which had been written by a Jain monk named Kumudendu, employing only Kannada numerals. The claims were that it had coded innumerable texts in many languages into its compact numerical structure, but the essence of the text's literary value had eluded me. I sought clarification from K.P. Rao—of course he knew all about it.

Me: Have you come across this Siri Bhoovalaya?

KPR: Yes, yes, of course. Much about it is exaggeration, really. Karlamangalam Srikantaiah is supposed to have revived it. His uncle was the principal of Vivekananda College in Puttur, and they had published a booklet about Siri Bhoovalaya. I have read a copy of the text.

Me: Does it actually contain coded texts in many languages and all?

KPR: No, no. The text I saw had Kannada numbers. Just to say that each letter of the alphabet can be described by three qualities—hrasva, deergha and pluta[19]—is not enough to tell us much about the text. If three is enough, two is enough and one is also enough. Why Siri Bhoovalaya is not coded more efficiently, we don't know. I was not very impressed with the deciphered content also, to be honest.

I thought this was a bit harsh, and that Kumudendu's esoteric personality could at least be compared to other eccentrics of the medieval world, like the thirteenth-century Christian theologian and philosopher Ramon Llull, who once wrote: 'We have employed an alphabet in this Art so that it can be used to make figures, as well as mix principles and rules for the purposes of investigating the truth. For, as a result of one letter having many meanings, the intellect becomes more general in its reception of the things signified, as well as in acquiring knowledge.'

During another of my meetings with Rao, we were joined by his good friend, Thirumaleshwar Bhat, who translates between English and Kannada, and is a retired teacher of German.

KPR: He is translating Pampa Bharata (the tenth-century Kannada version of the Mahabharata) into English on his own!

TB: I'm translating a commentary of the text. I can't understand old Kannada, okay!

KPR: Quite a few of the things are not worth translating also. They might become controversial.

Me: What do you mean?

TB: See, in the text, in Sri Krishna's city of Mathura, Arjuna has been missing his wife Subhadra (who is Krishna's sister), who has gone away, and in a moment of angst he decides to go to the courtesans' street one evening! My daughter was irate when she heard of this!

Me: But mustn't we historicise literature and situate it within its times?

TB: Yes, [but] even if it is history, this particular practice [prostitution] must be condemned, no? And because I am translating it for an English audience, shouldn't we bear in mind how they might misunderstand our culture? Why should we remember things that are no longer there? Do you preserve dry leaves?

KPR: Language resides in the receiver. It need not be what the sender intended. If someone has deemed it unnecessary, why can't we respect the interpreter's choice?

Me (insincerely): Hmmm. Fair enough.

TB: But I did meet another person who was thrilled by this episode, and he wrote an article on it for *Sudha* magazine!

Me (overcompensating way too abstractly): Well, if you look at the present political moment, what you see is a big resentment over earlier historians glossing over certain aspects of history, and it has suddenly become a big war cry. If we continue along the thought process you are suggesting, wouldn't that be inadvertently making way for another political angle in the future, which will try to capitalise on perceived vacuums? It might come back like a boomerang and create even more misunderstanding.

TB: Not everything is significant enough to consider it that seriously also. For instance, in one of the scenes, they use a magnet to remove a bone from an injured soldier's head. How can they do that? It is just a mistake. I changed it from a bone to a piece of metal. If there is a mistake in the original, do you keep it?

I realised that their opinions were strong, and I turned the conversation towards the recent past. Circa 1970, Thirumaleshwar Bhat had been 'drafted' into a German study programme because there was a dire need for good teachers of foreign languages. He travelled to Germany for higher studies later too, and taught German to students in Manipal for many decades, but 'they are all beginners, and will remain beginners', he mourns. 'I did not succeed in making anyone a scholar.' These days, he is more involved in translation and reinterpretation of old Kannada texts. Both KPR and TB firmly affirm that science and Kannada have never come together actively in their lifetimes, and that they probably never will.

TB: We have to accept history—that modern science did not grow on this land, and in its languages. The wisest thing would be to stop trying to translate it into our languages. Indeed, it was stipulated that one should not learn the language of the yavanas, the foreigners!

Me: Similar to the rule that one must not cross the sea.

TB: Madi [purity]!

Returning to the German theme, we spoke about the famous Basel Mission Press (also known as the German Mission Press) in Mangalore, which was the first printing press to publish texts in Kannada back in the nineteenth century. I had never visited the place, and K.P. Rao told me quite scathingly that 'if you have not gone there, you have not gone anywhere'.

The taunt hit home, and I decided to pay a visit post-haste. The press still exists, though its name has changed, and the establishment now doubles up as an institute of printing technology plus theological college. When I arrived there early in the day, I witnessed morning mass happening in a church, and a few students, including burqa-clad women, assembling for classes. You can procure a Bachelor of Divinity degree here—it was the first time I was hearing of such a course. A timetable on the board announced classes bearing titles such as Introduction to Christian Theology, Feminist Theology, Discerning the Signs of Times, Modern Religious and Secular Movements in India and Pastoral Psychology. The library was largely dedicated to theology and religious history, and I began to feel that K.P. Rao's exhortation was uncharacteristically exaggerated, until I realised that he had meant it in a symbolic way. I could see why he held the place in such reverence. From a purely linguistic perspective, this was the exact geographical site where the Kannada language had been standardised two centuries ago, where the Lutheran priest Ferdinand Kittel had compiled the first Kannada dictionary and published scholarly studies of the language. Even today, the Mangalore dialect remains the standard 'textbook' version of the language, disseminated at Kannada departments everywhere.

The library was not wholly uninteresting to me though, and I spent some time browsing through the shelves. I flipped through a book on Pandita Ramabai—the esteemed Sanskrit scholar and cosmopolitan social reformer born in Mangalore in 1858—who had converted to Christianity because she found her native faith to be deeply oppressive to women and lower castes, whom she sought to uplift throughout her life. I saw a biography of Abhishiktananda, a French-born monk who renounced his Christian faith and became a devoted disciple of Ramana Maharshi, who is remembered today as a pioneer of Hindu–Christian dialogue. All in all, I got a rich glimpse of religious dialogue that blurred all boundaries, showcasing a history of cultural exchange and spiritual bonhomie that challenges the essentialised identities which the crusaders of the Hindu Right now propagate. I wondered if this might be a subject of serious discussion at any of the courses offered at the theological institute.

The next chapter trains its eye on precisely this phenomenon, of how modern anxieties are whipping up hate about religious pasts that are far too complex to be pigeonholed into simplistic ideologies, and how this has been overturning any progress made over the past two centuries. It is precisely this sense of uninformed history-making that has made K.P. Rao so averse to talking about current Indian politics. From time to time, the same sentiment rises up in me too, and I feel the ardent desire to get lost in a universe of literature and learning and languages, where unholy politics can never rear its distorted head.

SIX

On Conversions, Controversies and Communalism

There are different languages;
But there is one emotional appeal,
Be he a Brahmin [Hindu] or a Turk [Muslim].
He is only fortunate on whom
The Goddess of learning [Saraswathi] smiles.
O Ibrahim, the world only seeks knowledge—
Serve and meditate upon with steadfast heart
The power of words.[1]

—Ibrahim Adil Shah II, circa 1600

I

Riding up to Baba Budan Giri, I see a board that announces 'Land of Coffee—Chikmagalur', ironically in the foreground of a large areca-nut plantation. Areca is an interloper, a younger sibling to dominating Lady Coffea, but quickly gaining in popularity. Because its consumption is linked to cancer, attempts have been made to ban it—unsuccessfully. Areca continues to be a rising cash crop across Karnataka, especially in South Canara and Malnad.

I am bound for the Inam Dattatreya Peetha (as Google Maps calls it). The shrine is so unremarkable that I mistake the site for a mere police outpost and ride a further three kilometres up to a scenic waterfall. I backtrack to the shrine, park my bike, deposit my phone with the footwear guard (no phones are allowed inside), and travel down a claustrophobic cage-like staircase cluttered with CCTV cameras into the cool cave below. A visiting group of teenage girls hush each other and quit chatting briefly as we come into the view of two bearded men who solemnly man the entrance. The central sanctum has been barred by a grill, and another camera surveys us with its blinking eye just to be sure we touch nothing. There is no iconography—just a pair of sandals installed on the cave stone, acknowledged by garlands and other ceremonial offerings.

On a weekday in the middle of February, the crowd is thin, and the policeman sitting at the outpost is yawning into his phone. Just a couple of months earlier, in December 2023, during the annual three-day Datta Jayanti celebration, the police had been biting their nails nervously, as the place was overrun by bike-riding, saffron-clad young men. They had shouted slogans invoking Datta (and Rama), also yelling provocatively obscene rhyming couplets that made female visitors and devotees grow deeply fearful—all of which a police officer is reported to have found 'highly deplorable'.[2] Earlier in the day, one group had allegedly attempted to defile a nearby dargah on their way, where police filed a suo motu case against them. Nearly 13,000 visitors from across Chikmagalur had thronged to the hill during the three days, including former legislators and seers.

Datta Jayanti is a recent phenomenon, a little more than three decades old, and a direct result of the Sangh's push to convert the hill into another Ayodhya-like situation. The skirmish, interestingly, had begun in the 1960s, not as a tussle between Hindus and Muslims, but between the Karnataka Waqf Board and the Muzrai[3] Department, which are in charge of Muslim and Hindu endowments respectively. The custodians of the dargah had actually supported the Muzrai Department's stand, and argued that this was a syncretic shrine where both Hindus and Muslims prayed. The sajjada nashin (the Sufi caretaker of the shrine) had feared that the Waqf Board takeover would sharply reduce his own privileges.[4] It was only in the late eighteenth century, under the orders of Tipu

Sultan, interestingly enough, that religious institutions (mathas, chattrams, dargahs, mosques) began becoming bureaucratised. Slowly, systematised State supervisions oversaw land and money grants, and the Muzrai Department had become a powerful entity by the end of the nineteenth century.[5] The Inam Dattatreya Peetha is presently under the purview of the Muzrai Department, though it is being challenged by both the present sajjada nashin, whose family wishes to regain its erstwhile powers, and the Sangh, which wants to convert it into a purely Hindu site.

Before getting into details of the shrine's recent politicisation, it is instructive to first visit the history of the region, the attendant myths and legends, and the complex environment of communal relations across Karnataka over the ages.

Dattatreya is a puranic deity—a synthesis of Brahma, Vishnu and Shiva—who exemplifies the accommodative capacity of Hindu polytheism. Over centuries, Dattatreya has evolved into numerous regional avatars; in the Deccan, he represents a fusion of Shaivism, Vaishnavism and Sufism. Shankar Mokashi Punekar writes in his introduction to the Nathist text *Avadhoota Gita*:

> Two significant and seemingly contradictory accounts of Dattatreya's personality and role are to be met with in the *Markandeya Purana* and *Brahma Purana* respectively. They define the two concepts of the Datttatreya image held dear by two wide-spread Hindu devotional cults of a later period, both alive up to the present day, viz., (a) the Natha cult of Northern India, (b) the Dattatreya cult of Western India which created saints and sages including the translator [of the *Avadhoota Gita*] Sri Purohit Swami. The Natha cult extolled renunciation and asceticism leading to occult powers and mastery over nature; and the Datta cult was predominantly devotional, ritualistic, attempting to promote a social order under the promise of salvation through a hieratic duty-centredness, but enjoining on the Brahmins stricter social responsibility through Vedic ritualism.

The text's translator Sri Purohit Swami had been a good friend of W.B. Yeats in the latter's final years, resulting in some collaborative publications.

The Natha sect had very much been in conversation with the Veerashaiva movement of the twelfth century, famously encapsulated in the hagiographical encounter between Allama Prabhu and Gorakhnath, wherein the latter runs a sword through Allama's body and finds that it simply sweeps through without doing harm. Over time, these philosophical encounters spawned a whole host of desi sects that were all-embracing, enormously humanising and opposed to the rigid orthodoxies of their times. Veerashaiva and Sufi orders in North Karnataka have also interacted and fused with a rare syncretic spirit.[6] As Swami Vivekananda, a sensible surveyor of history, had once emphasised, 'it would be madness to think it [Muslim rule] was all sword and fire'. And, quite contrary to the present head priest of the Gorakhnath temple (Yogi Adityanath), the original 'Gorakhnath accepted both Hindus and Mohammedans as his disciples. Baba Ratan Haji was probably a Mohammedan follower of Gorakhnath and is said to have converted a number of Mohammedans to the Yogi's creed. In Kabul, they are known as faqirs of Ratan Haji.'[7]

In his excellent book on the gurupanthas (local guru–shishya traditions that stand outside of organised religious orders), scholar Rahamath Tarikere writes:

> The gurupanthas recognised that caste, untouchability, gender inequality and social concerns were the key hindrances to spiritual achievement. They realised soon, in the medieval ages, that religious differences between Hindus and Muslims were also becoming a real problem. Hence, they began reacting to it by expanding their ambit. Soon, the various gurupantha streams were engaging with Sufism. This paved the way for a supra-religious guru-shishya tradition to flourish. Politically, it was also helped in this endeavour by the lenience and tolerance espoused by Akbar in the north, and Ibrahim Adil Shah II in Bijapur. The gurupanthas sought to create a supra-religious darshana that could find strong roots in ordinary people. Hence, all religions became their enemies in equal measure. The temple-centred, caste-ridden dwija orthodoxy combined with the forces of the Muslim priestly orthodoxy in this regard.[8]

Ibrahim Adil Shah II certainly seems to have been of a rare kingly breed—a lover of arts and knowledge who even tried to change Vijayanagara's name to Vidyanagara (City of Learning), which didn't really stick, just like Abkar's humanist religion Din-i-Ilahi. Adil Shah's desire to rise above communal cankers is visible in lines from his *Kitab-i-Nauras*, which this chapter began with.

A rebellious syncretic milieu had thus been inaugurated in the Deccan. Among the several Muslim saints of the Deccan who have been worshipped by Hindus as Dattatreya are Shah Fakir, Chand Bhole (the Sufi preceptor of the brahmin Janardhana Swami) and, of course, Sai Baba of Shirdi. (It was his fascination and belief in the Dattatreya cult that made Shankar Mokashi Punekar a devoted bhakta of Sai Baba.) In all likelihood, the hair preserved at the Hazratbal mosque in Srinagar, the disappearance of which in 1963 provoked a massive Kashmiri outcry, belonged to Kodekallu Basava—the fifteenth-century mystic saint from Vijayapura who had been hailed as an incarnation of the Prophet in the Deccan.[9] Similarly, the myth of Baba Budan Giri goes that Dattatreya is none other than Dada Hayat Qalandar, a companion of the Prophet who came to India as a wandering dervish, according to the Dada's hagiographers. And from around the seventeenth century, we hear the tale of the Sufi monk Baba Budan, who brings seven coffee beans hidden in his beard from the port of Mocha on the way back from Mecca, shaping the hopes and slopes of what is now Chikmagalur.

Around a century ago, the Kannada novelist Masti Venkatesha Iyengar had encountered a barren emptiness during his travels to the hills of Chikmagalur, similar to what I experienced myself. Several years later, he wrote a marvellous work of historical fiction (Walter Scott was a big inspiration) titled *Chennabasava Nayaka*, which was first published in 1949. The very first page of the novel carries this devotional depiction of Baba Budan Giri:

> This is the Chandradrona Range, made famous by its place in Sri Rama's blessed history. The Sanjeevana herb, which roused the mortally imperilled Lakshmana and raised Rama from distress

> was born here. It is said that the Pandavas roamed around here in exile, and that Bhima created the pond at the head of the hill with a drive of his mace. Hence, people have named this village after Bhima's father [Vayu] and dubbed it Gaalikere [Wind-lake]. At a jump's length, there stands the Dattatreya Mahamuni's siddhi shrine … Today, an Arabic preacher—a maulvi who owes allegiance to Prophet Muhammad—sings of Dattatreya as his guru, and has been taking care of this shrine. Perhaps in no other place can we see one great religion celebrating another great religion in this manner. The hill is now known as Baba Budan Giri.

While serving in Shimoga as a civil servant a couple of decades earlier, Masti had collected many oral myths. About the emptiness of the region, the novel notes:

> The heart-rending barrenness of this region is less than a hundred years old. Just two hundred years earlier, this land was under the rulership of the Bidanur Nayakas. Back then, the villages here had been full of life. These fields were bountiful with crops. These very forests were once lit up by the joy of people living here … Bearing the motherly love of belonging to their own land, the pride of working in one's own home, the swaggering jeetagaras [landlords who owned slaves], the Heggades, made fortunes in these fields.

Though he subverts this utopian strain in some measure later in the novel, it is interesting to note that here Masti records bonded labour—jeeta—while being partial to the swaggering landlords who reaped its fortunes. He brushes over the feudal history like a boy skipping over a small stream and celebrates the time of kings and feudatories as a joyful time when 'those people, like toddlers in a mother's comforting lap, lived peacefully, without fear'. This is characteristic of all historical fiction in early twentieth-century Karnataka. How else could Masti, a strong proponent of unified Kannada statehood, of the Kannada motherland, present an alternative to colonial realities?

The oversight is telling when you contrast Masti's account with another tale of the land. According to Sufi myth, Dada Hayat

Qalandar was dispatched to this place by Muhammad himself, for very specific reasons:

> The Dada's hagiographers believe that he was especially commissioned by the Prophet to travel to Chandradrona hill, as Dada ka Pahad was then known, to put an end to the oppression of the poor by the local *palegar* landlords. The palegars, write Abdul Wasi Asri and Abdul Jabbar in their *Tazkira-e-Hazrat Dada Hayat Mir Qalanda*, 'had turned this natural heaven into a veritable hell with their oppression and cruelty', 'playing holi with the blood of innocents every day', sacrificing them to appease blood-thirsty goddesses. Moved to pity by the plight of the people, Muhammad had dispatched the Dada to rescue them.[10]

Masti, on the other hand, sees bonded labourers as sharing a symbiotic relationship with their masters. A running crisis in the novel traces the tale of a woman bonded to one master who seeks to marry her lover who is bonded to another, and the many challenges she must face to achieve this union. A truly gifted storyteller who is always able to home in on human frailties, Masti subverts his initial utopian presentation in numerous other subtle ways too. He recognises that the system of taxation employed by the Keladi Nayakas (which was called 'shistu', and remains a popular Kannada word that connotes efficiency) was ruthlessly sharp and often corrupt. He also shows how garadis, or wrestling arenas, were key nodes of power relations, and how kings as well as feudatories sponsored public wrestling matches where bonded men could demonstrate their strength, and by extension, their lords' strength. Indeed, the political history of the Keladi Nayakas is replete with extraordinary tales that have wrestlers at their heart.

If the eighteenth-century poet and chronicler Linganna is to be believed,[11] the first contact between the Keladi Nayakas and the Mughals takes place around 1556–70 CE, when a fighter named Dodda Sankanna Nayaka travels to Delhi as a pilgrim and subdues a wrestler named Amkusha Khan in Akbar's presence.[12] As a reward, Akbar confers lands and gifts on Sankanna, and grants him permission to build Jangama Mathas at Prayag, Kashi, Gaya and Delhi. A Portuguese record from 1640 notes that Keladi Virabhadra Nayaka, who was under pressure from Adilshahi invasions in the Deccan, had written to the Mughal emperor (Shahjahan, if the date is accurate) for help, and had offered tribute in return, but we do not know what the response was. However, two epigraphs from 1655, found at Kapila Thirtha in Uttar Pradesh, proclaim Keladi Shivappa and Venkatappa to be loyal servants of the emperor, which points towards continuing friendliness. By 1689, the Mughals and the Nayakas were definitely at war. This seems to have been a byproduct of the feud between the Marathas and the Mughals under Aurangzeb—back in Malnad, Queen Chennammaji had offered refuge to Shivaji's second son Rajaram and effectively joined the Maratha resistance.

By the next century, the rise of Haider Ali in Mysore would send the Keladi Nayakas into their final years of rulership. Indeed, it is this moment that Masti's novel captures so well. He treats Haider with remarkable historical caution, and portrays him as a warrior with a deep moral compass and a complex past, a 'namak halal' who always respects his Wodeyar lord who had allowed him to rise up militarily. The supposedly conservative Masti emerges now, suddenly, as a breath of fresh air, a man whose heart was not muddied by divisive political ideologies, for whom literature was indeed the first love. In its character creation, the novel is imaginative, subtle and humanist at its core. Yet, there was a controversy circa 1950 when it was to be taken up for translation into other languages. Lingayat protestors argued that the portrayal of the queen Veerammaji, who is shown to have engaged in an extramarital affair with a court worthy, was a deliberate insult to the lingayat community. There were other contributing factors too. For one, back in the early 1940s, Masti had edited and published a book on King Bijjala II, written by one Dharani Pandita, which had taken the liberty of portraying Basavanna as a schemer who employs poison to kill the king. What's more, the Kannada committee that had recommended the *Chennabasava Nayaka* translation consisted entirely of brahmins—

A.N. Murty Rao, Shivaram Karanth and V.K. Gokak.[13] Critics felt that if the novel was translated into other languages, Veerammaji's character would be smeared in the public eye irreparably. Implicit in this assumption is the notion that readers would not be able to tell the difference between fiction and non-fiction, which on balance is a fair assumption, then and now.

Across the twentieth century, Basavanna remained a controversial subject for writers to broach, though this never stopped them. Controversies abounded, and always depended on the prevailing political atmosphere. H.S. Shivaprakash's play *Mahachaitra*, a portrait of Kalyana after Basavanna is forced into exile from it because he has attempted to solemnise a pratiloma marriage between a brahmin woman and madiga man, was written and performed in the eighties by Samudaya (directed by C.G. Krishnamurthy) to great acclaim. It even fetched Shivaprakash the Karnataka Sahitya Akademi Award. In the mid-nineties, though, when the text was prescribed in Gulbarga University, a huge controversy broke out and the book was ultimately removed from the curriculum.

In late 2023, I attended a talk by H.S. Shivaprakash in Manipal, where he spoke about his poetry, and his renewed admiration for the love poet K.S. Narasimhaswamy. It seemed to me he had found sanctuary in the classical Navodaya period, as he also spoke passionately on Kuvempu's continuing relevance:

> I remember K.S. Narasimhaswamy telling me, *All your modern writers, like Ananthamurthy and Lankesh, require me to buy into their ideology before I can immerse myself in their work.* The earlier poets were far more universal, more all-embracing.

I understood the sentiment, but literature has always been intimately connected with the politics of its own times. It is easy to generalise, but far more important to historicise. Shivaprakash himself had taken bold political positions through his art, responding to the debates of his times, without ever diminishing its aesthetic sensibility. In *Mahachaitra*, Basavanna's character never appears on stage. Its showcasing of the lives of Kalyana folk responding to

Basavanna's exile has a ring of subaltern studies framing its concerns. One detail that stood out for me was that of a man in the play who muses, 'Basavanna told us compassion is the root of dharma, and made us stop animal sacrifices. And we did leave all that. Maybe that's why we are now in this situation'. It becomes, at once, immediate political commentary, and a kind of psychological meditation on the persistence of superstitions in the rationalised world of today, even after the finest of teachers have tried to dispel them.

The *Mahachaitra* controversy formed the loose inspiration for Githa Hariharan's novel *In Times of Siege*, where she captures the heart of the crisis quite wonderfully:

> Is there a single image, a simple one that will hold this knowledge of Basava? Shiv imagines a hospitable tree, the kind that attracts all sorts of vines and creepers. It is impossible to look at this tree, visualise it in all its wealth of detail, if the vines and creepers are cut out of the picture. But what happens when the parasites grow too thick and lush, when they rob the tree of nourishment? The tree sickens; it dies a lingering death. The hagiographies—the creepers—are an inevitable part of any reconstruction, historical or literary, of Basava's life ... But they [fundamentalists] use the creepers to prettify the picture; whitewash it; or even better, use them like brushes dipped in magic paint. It's safer that way.

Just like a vast, sprawling tree, there was no doubt a certain air about that talk I attended—the grand old man of Kannada theatre reminiscing about other older (and therefore grander) men. I was listening to a dynamically creative mind with decades of heterodox ideas having accrued in his brain's smithy. I was also sympathetic because Shivaprakash, like Shankar Mokashi Punekar, straddles a special line across common conceptions of political wings—there is a Marxist in him, but also a desi spiritualist who mourns the desacralisation and ethical erosion brought about by Western modernity and is willing to take the plunge into spiritual belief systems.

There was a similar duality within the worldview of the historian and scholar M.M. Kalburgi. He was a practising lingayat, but also a man of science who believed that religion should reorganise itself around the insights of modernity, however inconvenient it might be.

He would end up paying for his convictions with his life.

II

> Stalwarts of the Democratic Party concluded that the White House lawn was suitable for the protest. They carried out a march from the Washington Monument all the way to the White House. They submitted that the atrocities of Indian monkeys were directly aimed at America itself. However, members of the Labour Party argued that the monkeys of developing countries do not get riled up for no reason, and that they must be viewed with sympathy. The International Association for Fundamental Rights of Dumb Animals defended the violent actions of the Indian monkeys. Foreign communist parties congratulated the Indian monkeys. Islamic terror organisations celebrated them. Pakistan-affiliated terror groups announced an indefinite pause of their operations playing out in Jammu and Kashmir.
>
> —Kum Veerabhadrappa, *Jai Bajrang Bali*

In 1989, even as the *Satanic Verses* controversy was taking hold of the global literary firmament, lingayat orthodoxy in Karnataka had found its own little bone to pick. A Dharwad-based scholar, a practising lingayat proud of his religion, was found to be irreverently messing with their hagiographies, humanising their seers (the sharanas of the twelfth-century) and speculating on the actualities of their historical lives. Having made Basavanna a saint-god, they couldn't digest the suggestion that he was like any of us—searching for love, dying a natural death, prone to human flaws. M.M. Kalburgi's scholarship was meant to enrich our knowledge of vachana literature, and to rescue the egalitarian ideals of the movement which history had coated with so many layers of white paint. He was a walking encyclopaedia of medieval Karnataka, especially of lingayat history, and his very existence seems to have posed a threat. The orthodoxy roused large masses of their followers into fomenting hatred against Kalburgi, and what should have been a matter of civil, scholarly discussion was turned into a public trial by a fierce mob out for Kalburgi's blood. Kalburgi was shaken and—like Galileo—ostensibly recanted his work to save himself from persecution. The act would always haunt his conscience. Naturally, his curiosity never died and he kept up his research, coming up with more and more insights from the treasure trove that is vachana sahitya, a collection of around 20,000 verses.

In the manner of death, though, he differed from the Italian renaissance man, even if both died at the age of seventy-seven. Kalburgi was shot dead at his home in Dharwad in August 2015 by members of the right-wing extremist group known as Sanatan Sanstha.[14] Kalburgi himself was acutely aware of the threat to his life, and even wrote about making his peace with the idea of death by religious retribution. Every essay he wrote after the terror of 1989 carries an imprint of courage and foreboding in equal measure.

Very recently, the Congress party published a hagiographical full-page advertisement titled 'Iron Man of Bidar: Sri Bheemanna Khandre' in *The Hindu*. After speaking of his contributions to uplifting the Kalyana-Karnataka region, in creating farmers' cooperatives, in helping Bidar district become unified with Karnataka, it announced quite casually that he was a deeply religious lingayat, and that 'Sri Khandre [a Congress minister] held agitations both inside and outside the State Legislature demanding the government to ban and confiscate few books—[H.S. Shivaparakash's] *Mahachaitra*, [P.V. Narayana's] *Dharmakarana*, and [Banjagere Jayaprakash's] *Anudeva Horaganavanu* as the authors had not only insulted the Sharanas but also twisted history.' In 1996, after *Dharmakarana* had been selected by the Karnataka Sahitya Akademi as the best novel of the year, Bheemanna Khandre had indeed burnt a copy of the book in the state assembly—an act that should concern anyone who values free speech and liberty of expression.

What was the controversy all about? Just like *Chennabasava Nayaka*, the ferment around *Dharmakarana* too involved female sexuality. In contrast to India's exponentially radical neighbour—where Nawaz Sharif had made the death penalty mandatory for blasphemy in 1992, and extended it to names of the Prophet's family in 1993—attacking a book might seem innocuous indeed, but the similarities are troubling. *Dharmakarana* had fictionalised Basavanna's elder sister Akkanagamma, and taken the creative liberty of portraying her as a single mother who had brought up her son Chennabasaveshwara on her own without knowing who his father had been. The lingayat orthodoxy had found this blasphemous, and what's more interesting is that the Supreme Court had concurred with them. With regards to the plot, where Basavanna and Akkanagamma leave their town because of the public odium following the latter's out-of-wedlock pregnancy, 'the Court finally found that the explanation tendered by the author for the change of residence was the subject matter of a raging debate amongst historians and religious functionaries and [the claim that] he had merely adopted this story for the Novel was unacceptable and without any foundation'.[15]

In other words, the court was judging fiction by mapping it to history and hagiography, neither of which are entirely reliable anyway. Basavanna's life and legend were recorded and written about several years after he died. In this sense, nobody can possibly know the truth of those times. In fact, the entirety of *Dharmakarana* holds Basavanna in the greatest of lights, and celebrates his legacy as a social reformer. P.V. Narayana reconstructs a patriarchal society where men often exploit women (there's much evidence from history for this, certainly), and shows Basavanna as a bold voice who rejects such a system in its entirety. The key node of concern seems to have been regarding Akkanagamma's *caste*, which the author has, loosely and metaphorically, compared to that of Jabala, a courtesan from the Upanishads whose son Satyakaama famously employs only his mother's name to secure discipleship with his guru. The petitioners quoted Kalburgi's research that had shown that Chennabasavanna's father was unknown, and argued that the novel simply uses this uncertainty to underpin its fictional rendering. What the lingayat orthodoxy was also railing against was the very suggestion that women were once exploited by unscrupulous men. Unsurprisingly, all the objections came from men, including the Supreme Court judge. In essence, they were continuing the exact lineage of patriarchal rigidity that P.V. Narayana had tried to challenge, establishing his point even more forcefully than the book could have managed.

It was caste again that made Banjagere Jayaprakash's *Anudeva Horaganavanu* a controversial scholarly work: he suggested that Basavanna might not have been a brahmin as hagiographies maintain, and might instead have emerged from a subaltern background. It was banned in 2007. In 2012, the head of the vigilante group Shri Ram Sene—Pramod Muthalik, who cannot even remotely be considered a scholarly authority—got Yogesh Master's novel *Dhundi* banned within ten days of its publication and the writer was even arrested by the police. The novel interpreted the tale of Ganesha as a tribal deity who had entered the Sanskritic universe from the folk lands of adivasi imagination. It was no less creative than the mythological fiction created by Amish Tripathi, whose Shiva trilogy I'd enjoyed reading in my teens. In other words, whenever Hinduism (or Veerashaivism) was expanded to include the many castes and tribes of the land, local reactionary elements in Karnataka would rise up to challenge such interpretations, and the state would meekly buckle down to accommodate them.

It was caste too, ostensibly, that thrust H. Nagaveni's 1990s novel *Gandhi Banda* (Gandhi Has Arrived) into controversy. Built on a deep ethnographical study of South Canara, the novel travels back to the 1920s and '30s, presenting the various competing shards of a shattered feudal landscape reaching out to a more hopeful future, socially and politically. The story revolves around a young widow named Draupadi, who rejects traditional sequestering and marries a spirited Muslim youth named Adrama. This young man joins Gandhi in the freedom struggle and is martyred in the movement. Objections emerged regarding 'vulgarity' in the way certain castes speak in the novel, but the explosive suggestion of Hindu–Muslim bonhomie (in the freedom movement, no less!) also riled the

Rashtriya Swayamsevak Sangh—whose censorious efforts were met with a powerful defense from progressive Kannada forces.

Nowhere is vulgarity more visible than in S.L. Bhyrappa's novel *Grihabhanga*—also set in pre-independence India—largely inspired by his experiences of a poverty-stricken rural hellscape in a South Karnataka milieu. It is women here who mouth the foulest profanities, leading the reader to brood over how oppressed a society must be if it has reduced its women to such a depraved state. Drawing on his own childhood angst, it is Bhyrappa's bleakest and most raw novel. The overwhelming gloom reminds me of V.S. Naipaul visiting Iran in the wake of the 1979 revolution—in his travelogue *Among the Believers*—where he sees paintings of weeping women, whose 'big gelatinous tears, lovingly rendered, ran half-way down the cheeks'. His guide Behzad remarks that Persian poetry is full of sadness, to which Naipaul avers, *but tears for the sake of tears, Behzad*. And then, in another one of those piercing Naipaulian moments of clarity, comes Behzad's response:

> Firmly, like a man who wasn't going to discuss the obvious, and wasn't going to listen to any artistic nonsense, he said, 'Those tears are *beautiful*.'

I glimpsed the sequel to this book, *Beyond Belief*, in the bibliographical credits of Bhyrappa's novel *Aavarana* (*The Veil*). The rest of the list is dominated by explicitly Hindutva-nationalist writers who formed the bulk of his parochial reading list: Sita Ram Goel, Koenraad Elst, David Frawley, Ram Swarup, Sriram Sathe, Navaratna S. Rajaram and so on, whose scholarly credentials are questionable, to say the least. In this list is K.S. Narayanacharya, whose book about Kautilya's present relevance Bhyrappa had referred to. Narayanacharya was a revered Vedic scholar and preacher whose grasp of history was decidedly conspiratorial. He even wrote a book titled *Who Really Killed Gandhi?*, which seems to riff on the 'second shooter' theory associated with JFK's killing, and begins with the premise that the bullet from Godse's gun had never been fired, that someone else had fired the gun from somewhere else and that there lies a bigger 'truth' behind the whole event. The book is still available online—the author had deemed it important to translate the book into English himself. In 2014, his book *Valmiki Yaaru?* (Who Is Valmiki?), which claimed that Valmiki had been a brahmin, was banned tenuously; a year later, the ban was rescinded, and the book is now available online.

Historical bias might still have been alright if the creative writer in Bhyrappa was able to overcome it in the crafting of his characters. In *Aavarana* though, all the characters are caricatures being orchestrated by an authorial voice that does not even feign detachment. The protagonist Amir is a crude synthesis of everything Bhyrappa abhors—he is a Marxist, Muslim filmmaker who becomes a strawman against whom to pile ideological rebuttals through thinly veiled sarcasm, a cheap trick that a talented novelist should have avoided. It was in the wake of *Aavarana* that Ananthamurthy called Bhyrappa a debater rather than a novelist, as he is concerned not with exploring the complexities of human nature, but instead to use fiction as a means of ideological battle. In 2023, the BJP government conferred upon Bhyrappa the Padma Bhushan, a long-due recognition of one of its oldest (and perhaps the most gifted) literary sympathisers. Through the prism of their ideology, *Aavarana* might well be considered Bhyrappa's magnum opus—an agile demonstration of a political sentiment carefully nurtured for almost a century now. In her excellent intellectual biography of Savarkar, Janaki Bakhle submits, after showcasing Savarkar's wild diatribes against Gandhi, that 'if we wonder why the Hindu right constantly retorts to sarcasm, mockery, insult, invective, and fiction against their critics, or to Muslim baiting, we can find the roots here, in this style of writing.'[16]

In recent Kannada literature, Vasudhendra's 2019 novel *Tejo Tungabhadra* is a fine example of how to approach historical fiction without the baggage of political prejudice. He spins a lovely tale set in the Vijayanagara empire, situating the lives of ordinary people amidst the war-mongering tendencies of emperors and empires, against the backdrop of a global circuit of trade and migration extending to Portugal. Amongst the old guard, Niranjana had written some dispassionate historical fiction, settings including ancient Egypt and colonial Coorg, richly imagined and researched. Bhyrappa himself had penned *Saartha*, a novel set in the 8th century, exploring the competing threads of Buddhism, tantrism, and, brahminism, which was more picturesque than polemical. The primary subject of *Aavarana*, on the other hand, is love jihad gone wonky. A woman renamed Razia has converted to Islam to marry Amir, but she soon realises that she's married into a rigid patriarchy that is doomed to consume her individuality. Predictable narratives follow. It's historical references (the fall of Vijayanagara, the rapacity of Aurangzeb) are meant to suggestively provoke the reader rather than evoke any historical nuance. The novel does offer us a glimpse into Bhyrappa's literary ideology in uncanny ways. When Razia converts to Islam to marry Amir, her father utters the following telling statements:

> Your marriage with Amir doesn't concern just you or what you are doing now. Your child, or the child or children of your child, or someone in some future generation that you both will give birth to, will someday destroy our temples. It's best you understand right now that you will be directly accountable for that sin.
>
> The Mughal badshahs, Jahangir and Shahjahan, were both sons of Hindu queens. Yet, both of them destroyed Hindu temples when they ascended the throne. But we can't really blame them because their religion ordains them to destroy temples and idols—Jahangir and Shahjahan were merely adhering to its tenets, which remain unchanged till date. But you're in love. Your love and the excitement of youth blind you to this, you won't understand this now.[17]

It is precisely this sense of blurring the past, present and future that gives totalitarian ideologies their jagged edge—whether it is communism, fascism, Islamic fundamentalism or Hindu supremacism, the stage is expanded to a cosmic scale to facilitate emotional outbursts from its adherents. *Tears are beautiful.* Time is annihilated in this historical worldview, and in this past-present-future continuum of unchanging morality, the ideologue firmly upholds his own conviction regarding the truth of his teary vision. Any and all inconsistencies in this worldview are swept under the carpet by emotional peddling of historical half-truths completely removed from their contexts. In one essay from a collection of newspaper pieces,[18] Bhyrappa coolly equates Lenin with Genghis Khan and then proceeds to berate Nehru for once admiring Lenin (and therefore by extension Genghis Khan), leaving out some vital context in the process. The source of these reflections are Nehru's writings on Russia after a visit in 1928,[19] out of which choice statements are often plucked out by Hindutva ideologues to paint Nehru as a hardline communist. It is another matter that in the book you will find Nehru quipping that 'the orthodox Church is at a discount in Russia but the cult of Lenin is everywhere in evidence.' He had also grasped the horrors of the Bolsheviks' Red Terror because he had read Maxim Gorky closely, and concluded that the communist's blind conviction 'can only be compared with the faith and zeal of a religious enthusiast'. The glimmer of fascination with Lenin as a man of action was symbolic in those times of effervescent political struggle, exemplified by Bhagat Singh's reading of Lenin's biography during his final days in prison, just two years after Nehru's trip to Russia.

Bhyrappa's history-making is a virtual xerox copy of the Sangh Parivar's worldview, plunging into anti-Islamic, anti-communist rhetoric with fervour, lacking an understanding of how their own ideological gurus had imbibed many ideas from their intimate enemies. I discovered this in vivid detail during my conversation with Shrikant Shetty, a rising VHP ideologue from Karkala in South Canara. I had encountered his name in an unlikely place—as the writer and creator of an excellent documentary on the early twentieth-century philanthropist and banker Haji Abdullah (whom we will return to), who founded Corporation Bank in 1905. I saw that Shetty was also a talented singer, and enjoyed one of his bhajan concerts on YouTube. He is genuinely passionate about Tuluva culture, and has spent time documenting and speaking about local traditions. Coexisting with all this is an incendiary political persona that has become infamous for hate speech against Muslims, leading to more than ten police cases filed against him.

At a 2022 event dubbed Durga Daud, which took place in Udupi, 10,000 people had gathered in an explicitly Hindutva-themed roadshow, complete with the brandishing of swords and shouting of slogans for a Hindu Rashtra. It was not a coincidence that this event had been organised on a very particular date: 2 October. Just a few hours earlier on the same day, a small group of Udupi-based harmony activists had celebrated Gandhi's true legacy on his birth anniversary, urging for communal peace. The numbers attending this event were hardly a sliver of the crowd that would gather later in the day. Durga Daud saw Shrikant Shetty and Kajal Hindustani, a hardline Hindutva crusader from Gujarat, booked for hate speech by the police. Shetty had asserted that 'at the next Ayudh Puja, all Hindus should bear weapons at their homes', to prepare for a war with imagined marauders, presumably.

I met Shetty at a coffee shop in Udupi in early 2024. He was kind enough to offer an instant audience, and I was upfront about my strong reservations regarding his ideological location. Our conversation was not as confrontational as I had imagined it would be, and we traded disagreements civilly.

Me: I'm curious about your childhood.

SS: I was born in Ajekal, a small village near Karkala. I studied till the seventh standard, and then moved to Bombay, and did a diploma in Computer Hardware and Networking. Then I came back home, and I was working at a repair shop—phones, televisions and all that. I got into the habit of reading. There was a Sahitya Kendra there set up by the Sangh [RSS]. The Sangh's literature was very close to us, and that's when I started reading …

Me: Writers like?

SS: Babu Krishnamurthy,[20] Tejaswi, Kedambadi Jattappa Rai, Kuvempu, Adiga, Bhyrappa. But RSS literature is what we read the most, and my speeches are also more oriented towards that only. Right now, I'm very active in the Hindu Jagarana Vedike. I wrote a book on Pejawara Swamy [the pontiff of the famous Krishna Matha in Udupi], looking at him not as a saint but as a social reformer. For instance, take the Naxal movement. Most of us just opposed them blindly, but we wouldn't get to the root of the issue. Pejawara Swamy connected us with issues of water problems, unemployment and poverty, which is why the Naxals didn't get a base here. I also recently wrote a book about Jews, called *Yahoodi*—

Me: Yes, I listened to the talk you gave at the release of the book.

SS (grinning slightly): You probably oppose it?

Me: Well, I have some questions, definitely. You say that India should follow Israel's path. Now, as far as I can see, Israel has known little peace. I've met Israelis in the Himalayas, in Hampi, who've just come running away from a lifetime of war and suffering. Some are youngsters who defy the conscription and then come here. They can't even go back to their home for fear of the State. Now, even within Israel, there is a strong opposition to the Netanyahu regime, a rejection of Zionism, an extremely racist and divisive ideology. I see only bloodshed and terror in this history. How is this, in any way, admirable?

SS: So, Zionism's founders—David Ben Gurion, Golda Meir, Theodore Herzel, all of them came from the Left. Some were industrialists and businessmen, but most Jews were working as labourers back then. Now, if you look at Indian history, until 1526, just before Babur arrives, there is this huge struggle between civilisations, between '*bharatiya existence*' and foreign invasion ...

He shifts the subject seamlessly, and I have now forgotten my original question.

Me: What do you mean? You are talking about a tussle for power in North India. How does that encompass all of Bharat?

SS: No, no. In South India, Warangal has fallen. Devagiri has fallen. The Madurai Sultans kill the last Hoysala king Veeraballala III quite

> viciously. Then Bukka Raya comes back, and the War of Liberation begins. His son Veerakamparaya defeats the Madurai Sultans, and his wife Gangambika celebrates the victory through an epic poem, which she writes on the battlefield …

Titbits and trivia such as these are kept handy on his smartphone, which he sometimes fishes out to buttress his argument. It is points like these that he peppers his political speeches with. The profound contradictions implicit in his history are evident in every one of these propositions. Journalist G. Vishnu, who is the son of the noted critic and activist G. Rajshekar, both staunch champions of communal harmony in South Canara, phrased it perfectly when he told me, 'Hindus are the perpetual victims, but they are also eternally the most powerful. Shetty takes this ridiculous contradiction and turns it into a rallying cry.' There's nothing original about this, of course. It is Savarkar 101 for any aspiring Sangh leader. Shetty's theory of 'bharatiya existence' comes from the same faulty source. The postulation of essentialised Hindu/Muslim identities in medieval pasts is immediately confronted with problems that every historian must deal with, problems that ideologues can conveniently ignore. Even from just those times Shetty is referring to, what we see—from Bengal to Kashmir to the Deccan—is that Muslims and Hindus pervaded armies and administrative structures and cultural spheres across kingdoms, regardless of the religious identity of the king, and the fifteenth century saw a remarkable flourishing of indigenous cultural expression, across languages.[21] For Shetty, the value of these anecdotes lies in how they help create a flood of snowballs designed to provoke an avalanche of anxiety—that the danger of Muslim invaders destroying a civilisation was, is and will remain the greatest danger of all. When I brought this up with Shetty, he conceded that I had some valid points, but continued to hold fast to his rhetoric regardless. In medieval India, war was the order of the times, but to continually inhabit those battlefields and bring that sense of medieval warmongering into present-day politics is a worrying tendency.

In 1989, the VHP had organised the first three-day Datta Jayanti celebrations amidst tight police security. In the coming decade, it slowly built up the membership of its satellite organisations, including the Bajrang Dal. In December 1998 (they seem to love Decembers), a Rath Yatra was organised to Baba Budan Giri, and the police clamped prohibitionary orders around the dargah. The stormtroopers found enough blood support to swell their numbers and defy the orders. Ananth Kumar Hegde, a BJP MP from Karwar, had announced that he would send 'suicide squads' to see the mission through. A big fan of pilgrimages, he had personally participated in tearing down the Babri Masjid in Ayodhya in 1992—his first conquest.[22] In April of 1993, he was part of a riotous mob that erupted into violence because someone (nobody knows who) allegedly threw stones instead of bananas at a rath during a Ram Navami yatra in Bhatkal. The town, which had seen no violence even in the aftermath of the Babri destruction, struggled under curfews and violent vandalism for several months. Ten Muslims and nine Hindus died in those months, and religious ghettoisation was intensified. These years stoked the embers of Muslim fundamentalism in the region, and the town would later become infamously linked with terror after the arrest of the Bhatkal Brothers, co-founders of the Indian Mujahideen, which carried out a slew of terror attacks across the country in 2008.[23] In the aftermath of the 1993 riots, the BJP came to power in Bhatkal, and a doctor named U. Chittaranjan became the local MLA. He is said to have been something of a moderate character. Two years later, he was shot dead at his home while watching TV, which ended up creating a wave of sympathy for the BJP. We don't know who killed him, and the investigation reports pertaining to the murder have never been tabled.

What we do know is that, a month later, Ananth Kumar Hegde was elected MP from North Canara. A couple of years later, the man was fully active in the 1998 Baba Budan Giri siege, where he enjoyed much support. A swami of the little-known Ajjampura Matha announced that 'the shrine will be liberated or bloodbath is certain'.[24] The 'liberators' overwhelmed the police, tore down the green flags, threatened to cut off the arms of anyone undoing their actions and placed an idol of the three-headed Dattatreya within the shrine for the first time ever. Now, every December, an attempt to convert the dargah into a wholesale Hindu shrine continues.

The public support required for this movement was realised through some surreptitious deceit, according to revelations from the former Bajrang Dal leader Mahendra Kumar. In 1997, Mahendra Kumar had been anointed the local district head of the Bajrang Dal, and garnering support for the Dattapeetha cause was his prime purpose. Later in life, he would lead mob assaults on churches in Mangalore and count bars in jail, all of which he repented in due course. He has, along with many other RSS dropouts like A.K. Subbaiah, recorded many YouTube interviews detailing these ruminations. He was in the process of writing a tell-all autobiography, as a message to his brethren not to fall for the Sangh's dangerous ideology, when interrupted by an untimely death. His memoirs were taken up by the journalist Naveen Soorinje and published in a book recently, after corroborating facts with other Sangh veterans. Mahendra Kumar speaks of how they hired a carpenter in 1997 to craft the holy sandals of Dattatreya in order to parade them in a rath yatra and hoodwink the masses:

> Apart from the six of us, nobody knew the secret behind the Datta-sandals. The entire Hindu community naively believed that these were sandals worn by Dattatreya himself. We became strong. People's support and cash were now behind us. The government and local administration were not with us. They could not do anything apart from filing cases against us and throwing us into jail … In this interim, the carpenter who crafted the sandals—Murthy—came to us asking for compensation for his labours. Our boys beat the heck out of him and sent him off. Today, the whole government worships those sandals. The entire Hindu community prostrates before them. Thanks to those sandals, many became legislators and ministers. IAS officers are directed to stand guard over those sandals today.[25]

It is also important to not be swayed by dreamy conceptions of syncretism while looking at religious orders today, which bear the burden of centuries of power-hungry structures, and the dulling of once-original spiritual quests by other concerns. After showcasing instances from various religious sects that have basically become seats of power, Tarikere writes soberly:

> The inheritors of feudal economic structures carry very little cultural memory. It is safe to say that communities that deify Sufi saints have lost all creativity. The sajjada nashins seem more akin to traders who conduct festivals and collect donations.[26]

It was therefore a space of vacuous cultural memory, rendered uncreative and unresponsive by time and modernity, that the Bajrang Dal came to occupy in an act of premeditated malevolence. The subject came up in my conversation with Shrikant Shetty, who saw it for what it was—political malintent.

> Me: Do you support the 'liberation' movement in Baba Budan Giri?
>
> SS: Now that has become part of a land mafia struggle. If it was like earlier [before 1960s], we would have no opposition. The Wodeyars would go there to pray for children, and that's why they started adding 'datta' to their names. It was a repository of Natha traditions. Seven hundred acres—Inam Datta Peetha—it is called Inam because it was given as a gift by the king. Earlier festivals used to be conducted in harmony, but Muslims started avoiding Hindus. That's when a Datta Pooja Samiti was formed by a man named Vittal Rai—to allow an opportunity to worship Datta. So, when they tried to grab the whole place for themselves, the Hindus reacted, and then of course, C.T. Ravi and Sunil Kumar used it for their own political gains, which is true. Now, new archakas have been named. They can come and conduct worship. So, let this happen, no?

I was not surprised to hear him speak of politicians usurping power and sidelining party workers. Shetty had downplayed Modi's relevance as well, reflecting the RSS's fatigue with his cult of personality that the country would see play out in the 2024 general elections just a few months after this meeting. But more than politics, I was gripped by Shrikant Shetty's sense of history, and the morbid importance he drew from it. I waxed eloquent about the complexities of cultural and historical study, and of how what we now understand as Hinduism and Islam had themselves been internally fragmented landscapes. I tell him about the embracing attitudes of many Muslim kings, including Ibrahim Adil Shahi II, and he nods, telling me that he's read Manu S. Pillai's *Rebel Sultans*.

> SS: But right now, we are all one, right? At the RSS, we believe that the Lingayat, Shaiva, Shakta, Ganapatya, Hirangarbhavadis, Brahmakapalas, Ajivikas—are all branches of the same tree. Jains and Hindus go to the same temples now.
>
> Me: Such syncretism is there with respect to Sufism also, no?
>
> SS: But they are leaving that now, right? What else is the Salafi movement? Now, if you want to talk about Shishunala Sharifa or Haji Abdullah, I will be the first person to join you. We are only against fundamentalist Islam that says they won't rest until the whole world is conquered. If you go to the RSS office, you won't find a single photo of a godhead. The coast has become affected by this fundamentalism ever since the Gulf migration started. There, they encountered puritans, and picked up the habits of the Sheikhs—they started doing namaaz five times a day, stopped going to mazaars. *Pure* Islam, you know? Their own families got split generationally. The current generation's parents—Bharatiya Muslims—used to go to mazaars, to Urs, but the youngsters are not interested in that [syncretism].

The irreligiosity of the RSS aside, there is much to be unpacked in this stream-of-consciousness generalisation, but there is another context to be absorbed first. In 2022, the movement to ban hijabs in pre-university colleges in Udupi was spearheaded by the Hindu Jagarana Vedike, and Shrikant Shetty was intimately involved with the whole affair. Quite contrary to the reconciliatory strains he adopted in our conversation, that reactionary movement had aimed to try and particularise Muslims through the move against hijabs to add more fuel to a long-running campaign with a flagrantly divisive agenda. Destructive ideas have always prevailed over constructive suggestions—of which there are quite a few. In fact, the Kannada writer Bolwar Mahammad Kunhi, the only person to win a Kendra Sahitya Akademi award twice,[27] who also hails from South Canara, wrote a thousand-page novel that seemingly contains much fodder on communal brotherhood. Kunhi loves to point towards it as a mystical book of solutions, whose pages you can dip into for all sorts of sociological insights. As a student of (and believer in?) literature, what more could I ask for?

III

> A fresh, new dharma had to be written,
> since too many religious texts existed.

So writes Bolwar Mahammad Kunhi on the first page of his magnum opus *Swatantrayada Ota* (The Run for Freedom), a novel published in 2012. Bearing a distinctive black-and-gold aesthetic, with the title font stylised to look like Urdu, the tome resembles a hallowed, unapproachable religious text only in appearance. 'When I started writing four decades ago, I had in front of me several texts that sang of the supernatural world. Hence, I had to write for myself a book about this world, and I created this fictional town named Muttupady,' he clarifies in the page that follows. When I took up the book, I couldn't remember the last time I had read a thousand-page novel, let alone one in Kannada. But just a week later, I had breezed through half the book, even scribbling detailed notes along the way.

Shrikant Shetty's comments about Muslims reminded me of something Kunhi had said a few years ago while speaking about this novel: 'Today, in India, if a Muslim doesn't do namaaz five times a day, there is no place in heaven for him. The fun fact is that if anybody named Mahammad Kunhi or Ismail or Ibrahim doesn't proclaim five times a day that his allegiance is to India, and not to Pakistan, there is no place for him in the country either. This has become the reality.' Trapped between a rock and a hard place—between Pakistan and India, literally, and on a larger, historical level. Between fundamentalisms on both sides.

Swatantrayada Ota revolves around a man named Chand Ali, who arrives in Delhi from Lahore while helping a couple of Sikh women cross over during the Partition, and is unable to return to his home town. He witnesses Gandhi's assassination, acquires a Sufi preceptor and settles down in a fictional South Canara town named Muttupady. At various levels, Chand Ali's story mirrors how Islam first arrived in the subcontinent—not through sword-wielding invaders, but in the form of ordinary traders and travellers who came in search of livelihood, often by chance, often feckless and gullible. The individual seekers of Sufi mystic thought remain enigmatic travellers on the fringes of mainstream Islamic society, shaping it through mysterious acts of wisdom every now and then. I found the novel incredibly helpful in understanding the trajectory of the Muslim community in the unique melting pot that is South Canara.

Bolwar Mahammad's prose has a levity to it, a touch of light humour is always around the corner. He loves using the word 'motte' (egg), and there are little idea-eggs exploding across the novel, driving the characters' lives, prompting the reader's attention to the ways in which a new society is always hatching, every single moment, both on the pages and in our heads. Chand Ali is a decent, good-looking man—innocently conservative in his own way—who arrives in Muttupady and is accepted unreservedly by the local Muslim society. In the first few hundred pages, we see the domination of the local Jamaat and its patriarchs, even as women silently plead from the margins, articulating a fierce opinion here and there, yet cowering at home under pain of death soon enough. Chand Ali is too marginal to contest this domination in radical ways, so he remains a bystander, like R.K. Laxman's common man, wrestling with his liberating Sufi teacher's silent influence, while also making sure to navigate local norms without giving offence. He marries an intelligent wife and has three children, yet never sends his two daughters to school, which he comes to regret. Slowly, in the course of the story, young boys are weaned off madrasas and are beginning to enter secular government schools. Education and empowerment of women are compelling themes in the novel—what could be more important?

Towards the close of the first long section, a startling little story sears the terrifying force of this patriarchy into the reader's brain. We meet Khadar, who has come to Muttupady as a new teacher at the school, and soon begins interacting with everyone on his census missions. On one such jaunt, he meets the young and shy Zeenat, who falls for his lazy charm. Khadar himself is not really interested; he fancies Rukhiya, a slightly older woman, who is widowed, and is even more beguiling. Rukhiya and Zeenat are good friends, and Rukhiya brings them all together in her own home, surreptitiously of course, where they get to know each other—a mental menagerie of platonic affection, tinged with the delicious intrigue of a love triangle waiting to be resolved. Well, it so happens that Zeenat's father is Berkley Usman Sahib, who is famed for his strongarm orthodoxy, and rumours begin to go round that someone has tattled on the troika and betrayed their secret to the Sahib. Rukhiya panics, and confesses all to Zeenat's mother Paatumma, who panics even more, and organises a secret meeting at Rukhiya's home, where she intends to solemnise and finalise Zeenat and Khadar's marriage to avoid disgrace. Even as this meeting is taking shape, Berkley Sahib arrives at Rukhiya's door with Chand Ali, and calls out for the door to be opened. Paatumma and Zeenat go pale with terror, and slip out of the back door in the blink of an eye. Berkley bashes the door in and, even as Chand Ali watches helplessly, swears at the despondent Rukhiya, and physically assaults her, breaking her shoulder bones. At this moment, Khadar, still present in the home, comes out and challenges Berkley, armed with all the courage of his modern education. Now, Berkley's worst fear is confirmed—that the widow Rukhiya has been consorting with Khadar in private. The very next day, the Jamaat rules that Rukhiya must marry Khadar, else they will be excommunicated. In a crushingly ironic resolution to their romantic dilemma, they end up marrying.

Kunhi himself has a cameo in the novel. We see him as in real life, a precocious boy in a poor family of beedi-makers. His father, well versed in the Quran, dreams of a better life on the one hand, and on the other withdraws his daughter from secular schooling after five years, fearing for her unsuitability as a future innocent bride. The young boy Mahammad Kunhi studies hard, works part-time jobs to send money home, and everything still looks bleak until a scholarship is announced in Mangalore to uplift just one poor Muslim boy-child and send him to college. Like Naipaul winning the scholarship to travel to Britian and escape Trinidad, Mahammad Kunhi is uplifted from Muttupady and sent to Mangalore, where he aces his course and finds a bank job, and goes on to become a writer with a pen as capable of jolly humour as of dark realism. When we spoke on the phone, he told me that he had ensured the completion of his sister's education when he grew up, as he did for his wife. Indeed, now his entire extended family boasts of educated women, many of whom are gainfully employed in diverse professional streams. He told me that this is a trend that pervades Udupi—Muslim women are increasingly determined to secure for themselves an education, come what may.

As for the hijab controversy, Bolwar Mahammad affirms that these girls are braving the established patriarchy to come to colleges, and that they must be encouraged instead of being subjected to a gruelling trial by social media. Hotte-uri aagatte, *I feel a pang of loss*, he told me, fretting about the issue. Thousands of Muslim girls discontinued their studies due to the controversy—no doubt the atmosphere would have been tense for them on both school and home fronts. The growing enrolment of young Muslim women in Udupi over the years signifies that they are emerging from their cocoons despite the last few decades of intense communalisation and particularisation. They have also been doing very well academically.

An even more disturbing incident was when three bantering teenage girls who loved pranking each other somehow got caught up in a Twitter-led campaign that claimed that Muslim girls were out to 'shame' Hindu girls in Udupi colleges[28] by taking pictures of them in the bathroom. The extent to which this kind of hysteria has been normalised is mind-boggling. I was disturbed when a relative of mine said, on seeing some women in hijabs walking by her car, 'They only wear this to jeer at us indirectly!' Anybody could now be offended anywhere, for any reason or none, and register a protest.

While women in Iran and Afghanistan battle terrifyingly oppressive regimes that could murder them for not wearing a veil, how does one respond to young girls in Udupi fighting to attend school wearing a hijab? The increasing Wahhabisation of Sunni Islam, a process originating in Saudi Arabia—a theocracy with an abysmal human rights record—is certainly a matter of concern, having spawned debates around the world. The infiltration of this puritanical Islam into Kerala, in the form of the Popular Front of India, is an inarguable reality. Much of this comes from the influence wielded by petro-dollars amassed by the greasy Gulf. That such a fundamentalism is incompatible with democracy and individual freedom, leave alone feminism, is an argument that needs little elaboration.

Having spent my adolescent years listening to Christopher Hitchens and his scathing critique of Abrahamic religions, I found little to differentiate Shetty's formulations from them, except that they were located within the Savarkarite universe and couched in the idiom of Hindu nationalism. Unfortunately, Hitchens had endorsed the military invasion of Iraq, and I have grown up abhorring the mindless machismo that worships raw State power and holds it capable of utopian deliverances.

There is another anecdote from Bolwar Mahammad Kunhi's tongue-in-cheek autobiography *Monu Smriti* (Monu being a nickname for Mahammad) that deftly captures how the average Indian Muslim is presently caught between a rock and a hard place. In November 1981, under the aegis of the Pejawara Swamy, the Vishwa Hindu Parishad hosted a function in Belthangady celebrating its recent achievements. The head of the Jain/Hindu temple at Dharmasthala, Veerendra Heggade, was also present. They were ushering in the ascent of Hindutva and welcoming the latest entrants into its institutional fold—lower castes could now enter temples, and religious minorities could now convert back to Hinduism. A newspaper article that covered the event also printed another detail in bold letters:

> Amongst the brethren who have returned to the fold is Sri Ummar from Puttur, who is now named Umesh. It is said that he is the brother of well-known writer Bolwar Mahammad Kunhi!

Ummar, disenchanted with Muslim orthodoxy, had converted to Hinduism and changed his name to Umesh Kumar. Bolwar Mahammad castigates himself for alienating his young brother, for treating him unfairly when he decided to quit school after failing, and for repeatedly beating and berating him for his lack of scholastic aptitude. He told me that his own critique of orthodox Islamic society had been emulated by Ummar, which had unwittingly led the young man to another extreme. Umesh went on to become part of a gang of 'semi-RSS drunkards', and became a notorious name in local circles, often arrested by police for causing public nuisance. In those decades too, South Canara suffered a lack of substantial employment opportunities. Much is said about how the Congress government, despite the boom of the nineties, had failed to generate genuine employment opportunities in the region, which pushed youth into the arms of the burgeoning Hindutva Right.

The two Kunhi brothers drew the ire of Muslim orthodoxy in different ways. While the older brother did so through his liberal, rational criticism of orthodoxy, the younger one converted to Hinduism and married a Hindu woman. The tragedy is that Umesh's alcoholism overpowered his life, and ultimately led to his death at a young age. At his funeral, where his body was cremated by some of his RSS friends, a close friend who regretted that he had been unable to smuggle even a drop of alcohol to his ailing friend at the hospital, ran out to procure some and proceeded to pour it on the burning pyre.

In my conversation with Shrikant Shetty, I tried to point out the dangers of such polarisation, its potential to end up fomenting similarly tragic flames, naively believing that he did not understand the gravity of it. His responses were underwritten by brash bravado, which demonstrated how the Sangh is only interested in exploiting the situation for its own ends: until 'they' are forced *to live in peace with us but dreading us*,[29] as Savarkar had put it in one of his more lenient moments.

> Me: Look at what is happening in Uttarakhand now—the destruction of mazaars, en masse eviction of Muslims. Lynchings around the country, economic boycotts, systematic dehumanisation …

> SS: Those who wield power will do what they wish to do, isn't that how it has always been? Just how rajas used to do what they wanted with their armies, we are seeing an exercise of power.

It is the most blatant of his pronouncements yet, and I sense that the careful veneer of abiding by the law of the land, which he has tried to maintain throughout our conversation, has now been thrown to the wind.

> Me: How is that a justification? This is not an era of kings.

He laughs, almost derisively, as though the whole thing is a big joke.

> SS: When Indira Gandhi added the word 'secular' to the constitution, how was that democracy? There will be democracy only as long as Hindus are a majority. If 'they' take over, all that will be gone.

My own laughter has been overtaken by anger—anger at how he is able to maintain his own sense of victimhood at a time when Hindu majoritarianism has been shamelessly subverting democratic institutions. Of course, it is not just Muslims who are the 'other' in the Sangh's eyes; Christians and leftists are equal enemies in their ideology.

SS: See, our people have worked with great integrity. You should see Shivaji's letters. Even Govind Pansare, a big leftist, has written about Shivaji!

Me: Since you brought up Pansare, let me also bring up Dabholkar, Kalburgi, Gauri Lankesh …

SS: Yes, yes, Kalburgi's contribution is also great. It was wrong to kill Pansare. Gauri Lankesh was not a good woman, I don't feel that Dabholkar was a good man either …

During moments like these, when the accumulated essence of Sangh ethics surfaces in his words, when that casual black-and-white demagoguery rears its head, a chilling shiver travels up my spine, leaving me with a bitter taste in mind and mouth. He seems to like Kalburgi and Pansare simply because they studied aspects of history and religion that are important to the Sangh's ideology—they have scholarly credentials that the RSS can only dream about. The selfish morality of his words shocks me.

Me: It doesn't matter who you think is good or bad! Nobody should be attacked for expressing their opinions. Why hasn't the Sangh condemned these murders publicly and distanced itself from the murderers?

SS: It was the Yediyurappa government that rejected the bail plea of Gauri's murderers, no? Of course, all these people are criminals, no doubt. If you are writing a book, I should respond only through a book. It is not a purushartha to kill somebody for expressing something.

I realise that he is course-correcting because he has no better answer. At its core, the RSS and its more extremist satellites are vigilantes who think moral judgement is part of their contribution to society. In such a view, democratic rights are secondary to religious retribution and the Sangh's moral 'feelings'. When Bhyrappa was once asked about Kalburgi's killing, he had pithily condemned it and remarked that it had happened when a Congress government was in power, absolving the actual criminals and the attendant ideology of any complicity.

After a couple of hours of conversation, Shrikant Shetty says he's getting late and prepares to leave, but his closing remarks are full with the trademark contradictions that I have come to associate with him:

> SS: When it comes to rich and poor, I am with the poor. That is the leftist in me. But when it comes to being with those who are holding power, I am with the Right. When it comes to attack on our culture, I am with the Right. Muslims are now particularising themselves into a separate category—this is not good. Against such people, it is right to take up arms.
>
> Me (fuming): But this is also happening because the ruling establishment is actively enabling it. You are co-creating each other (like Netanyahu and Hamas).
>
> SS: No, no, we are trying to bring everyone together. If another Khilafat movement should not happen, another Calcutta massacre should not happen, they should move towards us. In a few decades, they will orchestrate a secession—we are already seeing this in Kerala, in South Canara, along the Malabar coast, where they are strategically increasing their population. You can't speak about all this in those areas this openly, you know?

He was swirling in Savarkar-land again, taken with the fanatical dilemmas of a man from a century ago, working himself into a dim ideological corner where reality and constructive action are both obscured by impending war. The truth remains that the present-day Islamic world is riven by its own internal contradictions. Much of it is split by heart-rending civil war—from Afghanistan to Yemen—and the threat of Islamic radicalism in certain pockets of North Kerala can hardly be extrapolated to South Canara. As for the population-increase bogey, it has been debunked by statistics that show steadily decreasing fertility rates for Muslim women (and women in general) in India.[30]

It is worthwhile to contrast Shetty's political imagination with more constructive ones from South Canara. For instance, the respectable and secular politician B.A. Mohideen, who served in the Ramakrishna Hedge cabinet during the eighties, did some commendable work to uplift the Bearys, an ethnic Muslim community concentrated along the coast, by facilitating better education infrastructure. Mohideen writes in his autobiography:[31]

> It was my sisters and relatives who gave me the impetus to work towards improving education. They were all illiterate. In those days, mullahs from Kerala would assert that education for women was against tradition. When I was young, women would go only to madrasas. Clerics would say that knowledge of the Quran was enough for them, and the innocent people had believed it.

When Sara Aboobacker's novel *Chandragiri Teeradalli* (On the Banks of Chandragiri) was translated into Malayalam in the mid-1980s, the final scene of the tale (where the protagonist Nadira rejects the pernicious practice of triple talaq and nikah halala, and kills herself by jumping into the pond of a mosque) was tweaked to her jumping into a river instead. Knowing well the impositions of an orthodoxy that did not take well to even symbolic rebellions, Mohideen began modestly by starting a nursery school within the madrasa in his native town of Bajpe, where they were not strapped by clerical domination. Later, he invested much of his time in setting up English-medium government schools, and began speaking vociferously for educational reforms in his speeches at festive gatherings. During the seventies and eighties, the Beary community set about establishing engineering and medical colleges in the region, and Mohideen pioneered scholarships and funding to build new institutions, often helped by progressive philanthropists from the Gulf. This led to the formation of the Muslim Educational Institutions Federation, and in the internal dialogues of this organisation, Mohideen began making a case for completely secular institutions:

> If schools are named Al-Badriya, or Islamiya, there is no chance that Hindus would attend them. Schools must be built outside of

mosques and madrasas, and must not be identified by religious names. Now, the Ideal School in Edapadavu, Chaitanya School in Krishnapura, Bertrand Russell School are all run by Muslims. Because they lie outside of mosques, children from all castes and religions are enrolled here. I have spoken about it many times in MEIF meetings ... There is also the allegation that educational establishments within mosques and madrasas do not permit song, dance, theatre and other cultural activities in their annual day programmes. This is wrong. Enriching children through cultural development is our responsibility. It is a necessity for our times. Children's talents will bloom and blossom, and lay the foundation for harmonious coexistence.

Many communal organisations here have been trying to particularise Muslims. Forget Muslim and Hindu students mingling with each other, they even rail against them talking to each other. By filling untruths like 'mixing with Bearys will lead to downfall', they brainwash innocent Hindu women and try to separate us from society in the most insidious ways. We must be extremely wary of divisive attempts to make islands out of the Muslim community.

Indeed, the bogey of love jihad is the most flagrant of these attempts. Shrikant Shetty had made some rather bold statements, similar to the above pronouncements, which had induced some hope in me. Sadly, his individual impulses are firmly held in check by the Sangh's larger ideological bandwidth.

SS: Madrasa education starts from the age of six. For so many years, if their heads are filled with the same stuff, what is the outcome? What happens in Vedic schools in the Krishna Matha is not different—they start blindly ranting against Shankaracharya. Both are equally 'communal'. All sects are devoid of conscience. We are not in favour of sects at all. We want a cultural revival, not a sectarian one.

Satyakaama [Anantha Krishna Shahapur] writes that there is no need for a god when you are meditating. Kuvempu says aagu nee aniketana [become unbound]—it is the search for a light, right? Nothing stays the same, all our spiritual quests are open-ended. Mansur-Al-Hallaj [the ninth century Sufi mystic] also belongs to this group. Why don't they [Muslim orthodoxy] celebrate Shishunala Sharifa instead of Tipu Sultan? If they take one step in that direction, we'll take two. There should be space for atheism in religious discourse too.

Me: Why don't you do that yourself? It can be a powerful gesture.

SS: We can, but people within the Sangh itself will begin to see us in a different way. Now, even when it comes to Bhagat Singh, many say he was a Marxist, atheist and therefore not one of us. Whatever that may be, he gave his life for the country. If he had lived, if Lala Lajpat Rai had lived, then Partition would not have happened.

This is the heart of the Sangh's reformist crisis. Even if there are individuals like Shrikant Shetty who might privately entertain humanist ideals, they are forced to cohabit with violent schemes (lynching of cattle transporters and attacks on churches are still fresh memories in South Canara) that they cannot distance themselves from. In fact, they choose to perpetuate them because that's the only way to stay in vogue, to scale the political ladder, to keep the party hardliners on their side. A similar paradox presents itself when it comes to caste.

SS: It says in the Manusmriti that molten liquids must be poured into dalits' ears if they hear the Vedas. Does anybody follow that now?

Me: I see lynchings and killings of dalits every other day in the news. Children have been killed for entering a temple or touching a well. Of course that stream of thinking is still there.

SS: But who does it? Not brahmins. Landed elites do it—vokkaligas, bunts in South Canara, thakurs …

Me: Yes, class relations are crucial factors, but the remnants of religious prestige have not been erased, no?

SS: This argument should apply to Periyar as well, right? Didn't he say that all brahmins are worse than snakes?

Me: No doubt Periyar's politics was a crude product of simplified history. I am a critic of Dravidian caste politics too—I find it counter-productive. But you can't say that the ideals of the Manusmriti have been left behind. They have taken other avatars, but they are still here.

SS: We have been working, as part of the Sangh, against untouchability. Savarkar also spoke out against untouchability. Shivaji did too. After Netaji Palkar converted to Islam, fought for Aurangzeb and returned to Shivaji, he was allowed to convert back to Hinduism and was not killed for his treachery. I don't see how the Left can create a big revolution when it comes to caste—we have done much stronger work.

Me: More than Periyar [or Savarkar], we should perhaps look towards Narayana Guru—

SS (interrupting me excitedly): Narayana Guru is god!

Of all the things I heard from Shrikant Shetty, his anti-caste reformist sentiment felt the most honest and heartfelt. This, in spite of the fact that his preceptor Savarkar had often employed anti-caste politics as a mode of deflection, 'marshalling a righteous outrage as an alibi against having to answer questions about his anti-Muslim prejudice', as scholar Janaki Bakhle argues.[32] Savarkar's anti-caste rhetoric was genuine (though patronising), but was always in service of the larger deity—the nation—a space that could never be occupied by religious minorities. It is this larger ideological project of the Sangh, its undeniable connection to preserving a form of socio-religious nationalism, that stymies individual tendencies to subvert it.

Interestingly, I had heard a take that slightly overlapped Shetty's from the dalit activist and writer Arvind Malagatti, who lived in South Canara for many years. What surprised me most was that Malagatti, just like Shetty, deemed the Pejawara Swamy a radical social reformer, commending many of his symbolic gestures—like inviting Muslims to break their Ramzaan fast within the Udupi matha in 2017. He had even invited Malagatti to critique the matha within its own premises around the turn of the century.

IV

A bust of the Buddha on the table to his left offers smiling commentary from the background as Aravind Malagatti speaks in rich, idiomatic Kannada with a booming baritone that is an interviewer's delight. I have come to his home in Mysore to hear more about his long, eventful life as a Kannada scholar, writer and dalit rights activist.

Malagatti's family was full of feisty individuals. Sometime during the mid-seventies, one of his elder brothers started a wing of Dalit Panthers in Dharwad, which was very active in local mobilisation and awareness programmes. Another brother once sent a letter to their father requesting money for hospital expenses, and when young Aravind went there to deliver the money, he witnessed his healthy brother busy rehearsing for Samudaya's play *Belchi*, which is what the money had actually been summoned for. Aravind too ended up playing a small role in *Belchi*, and the exciting milieu cemented his desire to move to Dharwad. When he arrived there in the late seventies, the Dalit Panthers were no longer an entity, and an organisation called DS4 would soon spring up in its place. During the Gokak agitations, writers like Chandrashekhar Patil and Patil Puttappa were Malagatti's heroes, and in his youthful passion had picked a fight with his thesis guide, who did not endorse young graduate students roving about participating in street protests. Malagatti got himself arrested during these demonstrations, and was packed off to Hindalga jail. In the years to come, he participated in numerous social agitations with equal energy.

> AM: During the Kudri Moti incident, me, Narendra Nayak [a famous rationalist from South Canara], Sara Aboobacker [the Kannada novelist], Ramachandra Uchil [CPI(M) and Samudaya member], Purushottam Bilimale [a prominent scholar]—we formed a team. Fakir Mohammad Katpady had written a play named *Dushasana*.
>
> Me: What is the Kudri Moti incident? I haven't heard of this.

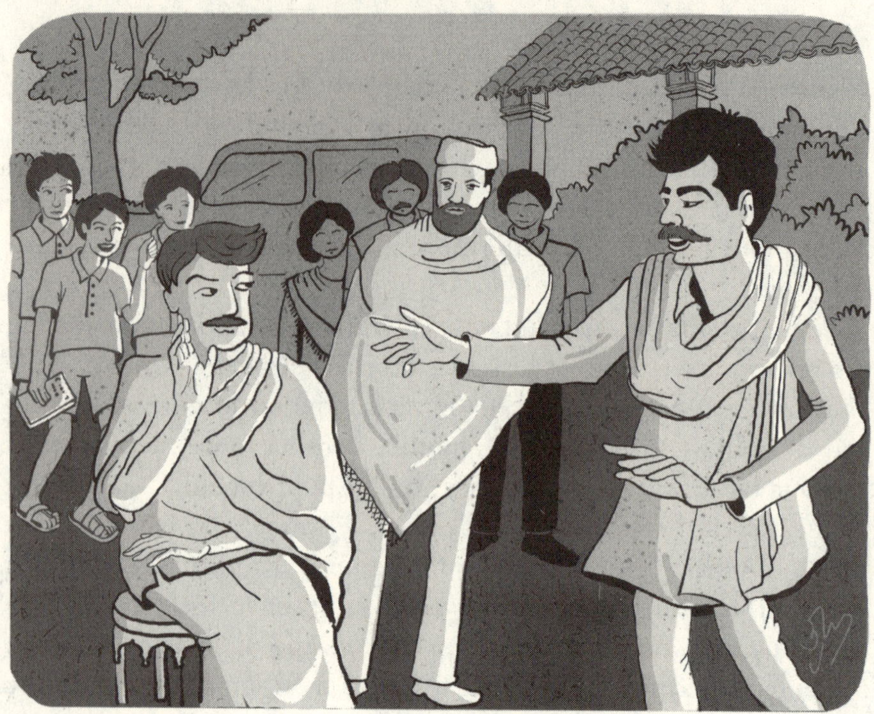

A scene from *Dushasana* being acted out in the streets of Mangalore. My favourite detail is the children watching attentively at the back—they've probably arrived here after bunking a boring schoolday. (Thanks to Aravind Malagatti for the photograph of which this sketch is a loose recreation.)

> AM: Kudri Moti is a locality near Mangalore. It happened during the eighties. A Swamiji had molested a poor woman, and we staged *Dushasana* as a street play, along with the devadasis, in protest—it was pretty big.[33] There were so many protests during those days. Once, the Congress politician Janardhan Poojary pronounced that Ambedkar never wrote the Constitution; we took out a huge rally in response. The CBI had been monitoring my home all night the previous day, trying to gauge who would be at the rally, what they would be speaking and so on.

Those tense and effervescent years were fertile ground for reactionary responses.

> AM: Chandrashekar Aithal, whom I have respect for, wrote a book called *Brahamana Bandaya* [Brahmin Rebellion]. It carried references to Ananthamurthy, to Basavalingappa, and even termed the latter as born-to-a-brahmin, because he was a little fair. He'd said stuff like, *Holeyas and Madigas are not fit to be teachers.* There were some other unsavoury bits there too. We got quite angry, and took out a protest to ban the book. We said, he is free to express his opinion, but peddling random speculations about someone else's birth and taking potshots at dalits is deplorable. It became a police case, and dragged on for a while. That book could have been a proper response to the dalit movement from a brahmin perspective. When Siddalingaiah was singing *Ikrla, Odirla* (Bash them, kick them), how must it have felt as a brahmin? This book could have become a genuine response to *The Songs of the Holeya-Madigas*, but it instead became a case of vulgarity-meets-vulgarity, and two negatives don't make a right.

He is quick to point out that Siddalingaiah and the dalit movement were vitriolic in words, but never so in actual life. I had read in Kum Veerabhadrappa's autobiography that his circle of friends used to call Siddalingaiah 'Bruce Lee', but when they actually invited him to poetry readings, the smiling, diminutive writer looked like an imposter to many. The dalit poetry of the seventies amplifies the angst of a long-overdue voice rising from centuries of oppression, and no one could expect it to be gentle and measured in tone. On the other hand, the brahmin response did not have much cause to be vulgar. Aravind Malagatti holds deep respect for Ananthamurthy in this regard—he always viewed the dalit movement with sympathy. Much later, around the turn of the century, Malagatti and Ananthamurthy clashed at a reservation debate in Mysore University:

> Ananthamurthy was arguing in favour of slowly removing reservations, and improving vocational training. He wanted to build strong walls instead of mud walls, which is what reservation is. I told him his thesis was fine, like the inside of Duryodhana's wax palace. But in actuality, it was a waiting fire pit. I said, first build a strong wall and see if it is working before breaking down the flimsy mud walls. I was most impressed by Ananthamurthy's

> patience—he really wanted a dialogue, to listen to the other side. Never interrupted me even once. Later, he came and put his arms around me, and we exchanged many long letters with each other after that. We need someone like an Ananthamurthy in today's environment more than ever.

Halfway into our conversation, his wife returns home from work, and we are introduced. Aravind and Dharanidevi Malagatti form, in modern parlance, a power couple. She is an IPS officer, recently appointed as director of the Kannada and Culture Department, who also writes scholarly non-fiction and has translated Malagatti's autobiography *Government Brahmana*[34] into English. Aravind Malagatti recently retired as director of the Kuvempu Institute of Kannada Studies, which is a part of Mysore University. They had married towards the close of 1992 and moved to Ullal, a coastal town near Mangalore. Malagatti's voice drops to a whispery tone:

> When the Babri Masjid was destroyed, I had been married for three days, perhaps. We had just moved to a new home in Ullal, and there were no supplies at home. All hotels were closed. Hindus had razed Muslim shops, Muslims had razed Hindu shops—Ullal was burning. The RSS's influence had become really terrifying, life-threatening. There are some parts in Ullal where Muslims live in higher numbers. We went to the police, but they said Home Guards will protect you, and we were returning home when the scooter got punctured. We started pushing it, and it was uphill, so we were really swamped. After a while, a Muslim man approached us and reproached us for dilly-dallying over there. Around a hundred homes in that neighbourhood were Muslim. We showed him the scooter, told him about our food crisis, and he understood. He took us with him, and fixed the puncture on the scooter. He invited us inside, but his wife questioned him on this. Now, we were also not really in a state of mind to go inside, so we just sat down outside. Finally, he gave us two eggs, a kilo of rice, after confirming if we ate non-veg. Then, he said, *See, in this situation, no Rama will come to save you.* I told him, *You are both Rama and Allah to me right now. I will never forget this humanitarian gesture. But please, let us all keep out of these violent activities.*

The communalisation of the South Canara region during the nineties was certainly an unprecedented phenomenon. It is also important to see these flare-ups in the context of the reorganisation of the local caste networks after Devaraj Urs's land reforms. In 1998, a major riot near Surathkal ended up killing sixteen people. Here, 'the riots were also used as a means to solve personal problems of individual eviction such as tenants' non-payment of dues, or business rivalry. Most of the deaths occurred either due to police firing or stabbing. Most interesting are the categories involved in the communal riots. The majority of rioters came from backward castes, partly from dominant castes and an ethnic Muslim group called Bearys or Mopillas.'[35] The Bearys had entered the larger economy, courtesy of the Gulf boom in the seventies and the proliferation of new industries in its wake. A steady stream of income began coming in to boost their industries, even as other backward communities struggled in small-scale industries and tiny markets. Involvement in finance and trade has also been a factor in Muslims breaking away from orthodox ranks, as Bolwar Mahammad's novel also captures.

Bolwar Mahammad's work had, of course, drawn intense scrutiny from Muslim fundamentalists. When his satirical debut novel *Jihad* (dedicated to 'The School-Going Girl') was serialised in *Taranga* magazine during the early eighties, orthodox pushback somehow got him embroiled in a fake murder case, forcing him to go incognito and stop working for eight months. However, his post-2000 works have been well received. In 2015, he published the first historical fiction in Kannada that portrays the life and times of the Prophet Mohammad—titled *Odiri* (meaning Read)—on Gandhi Jayanti that year; it has seen four reprints since. Featuring two chess pieces on its cover to adhere to Islamic taboo over anthropomorphic representation (incidentally, chess pieces got their abstract forms because chess travelled to Europe from the subcontinent through the Middle East, where visual representation of living beings was forbidden), the novel was written with the motive of introducing Kannada readers to the historical details surrounding the founding of Islam. Bolwar Mahammad writes with pride of his knowledge of Hindu myths and Sanskrit idioms, and with melancholy of the general lack of such general knowledge (amongst most of us) regarding Islamic history. In fact, even Muslim readers thanked him for rescuing the Prophet's tale from complex theology and presenting it accessibly. He followed this up with *Umma*, a fictional rendering of the Prophet's wife Ayesha, which too attracted popular readership, especially Muslim women. I asked him how *Swatantrayada Ota* had been received, and he laughed, 'They have to read thousand pages first, no? Who reads these days? In twelve years, that book has sold two thousand copies. Just because it is a winner of the Sahitya Akademi Award doesn't mean people read the book!'

Even as *Jihad* had been attracting the ire of Muslim fundamentalists, their Hindu counterparts were engaged in establishing deep roots in Karnataka, especially South Canara. In Mangalore, which was a hub for organised crime syndicates (the Bangalore don Mutthappa Rai hailed from Puttur), the RSS found violent dens to match the ferocity of their ideology. As Greeshma Kuthar writes in a comprehensive essay chronicling its rise: 'In the 1980s, as RSS influence grew in the district, many of the gangs transformed into Hindu-nationalist outfits. In 1989, the Hindu Yuva Sene, led by Gunakar Shetty, emerged as one of the strongest outfits on the ground, its cadre mostly former gangsters. In 1991, Shetty was killed by a rival Hindu gangster, following which there was a widespread crackdown on organised crime in the city.'[36] By the nineties, the most deplorable elements of the RSS's worldviews had fused together—the religious prejudices of Savarkar and Golwalkar blended with the lumpenism of local thuggees. It was also a dog-eat-dog world now, with the benefits of globalisation steadily accruing to the cosmopolitan classes, while the trickle-down was barely visible.

Towards the end of that decade, Aravind Malagatti moved to Mysore to teach at the university. But his links to South Canara had already been firmly established, and his stature as a scholar was well known.

> AM: I'd moved to Mysore from Mangalore. Pejawara Swamy called me up, and requested me to come to Paryaya [a ritual ceremony

that takes place every alternate year] in Udupi. I said, I don't go to mathas, I can't stand them. He said, please think for a while, you will have complete freedom, you can critique me also, you have absolute freedom. Nobody will ask you anything. You must please come.

I thought for a while. If I don't go, would that be right? The next day, I told him I'll come. The DSS was up in arms because they didn't want me to go, and they said they'll kick up a protest. They said only traditionalists will be there, they will not listen to you anyway. I began to feel that that is the exact reason why we must speak there, of all places! Even if one person in that crowd is touched by my words, that is progress, I told them. I asked them not to protest and all.

I am thrilled by how proud he is of his individuality—of sticking to his conviction regardless of the opinion of his peers. He accepted the invitation, and spoke at the Udupi matha with his usual vim and vigour.

AM: I was amazed by Pejawara Swamy's calm. My statement was direct. I told the Swamy that the reason you have invited me to talk here is not because of my professional or academic achievements, but because you want to present yourself as a tolerant leader. Even if you get a hundred people like me to talk, it doesn't make up for the fact that Kanakadasa[37] still stands outside the matha. So, by doing this please do not think that you can sanitise the matha's tainted history. There is cultural and physical evidence that untouchability was practised in the matha. Anyway, if you really want to make it right somehow, install Kanaka beside Krishna—give him space inside. This action would mean to the world that Kanaka, who always stood outside, now belongs inside. That would be a suitable metaphor to actually reflect your stance against casteism. Then, it would have some real meaning. He replied, 'We have even kept Garuda outside!'

Me: That was the exact response?

AM (annoyed at being interrupted): He was reluctant to continue the discussion on that stage. He requested that we take the matter to a private setting, where only scholars and pundits would be present.

I demanded an answer on stage, but eventually we went inside to another room. My point was simple: like Rama has Hanuman, like Gommateshwara has his Gullekayi Ajji, Krishna must be united with his great devotee Kanaka, because that's how they complete each other. Because that is the story local to this region. If making Kanaka stand on the right side of Krishna seems inappropriate to you, make him stand on the left, or even better, make him bow down, like how Hanuman sits in front of Rama. It will become a real form of bhakti. This change would revolutionise how religion is seen. A strong discussion ensued. The Swamy, after having listened intently to all this, admitted a fascination for my thoughts about the matha and conservative society as a whole, and he promised to look further into the matter. He said he would do everything within his power within the traditional framework.

As it happened, a year from then, Kanakadasa's statue was moved into the temple compound, if not the inner sanctum itself, and a hall named Kanaka Mantapa was constructed.

AM: After I spoke in the matha, there was some tangible change. Of course, I have faced some people who gave me the stink eye, grumbling in Tulu, wondering who I am to critique the matha. But that reaction from the masses was expected. They were hurt. However, my main point here is that those were times when society was trying to open itself up in some ways, and there *was* a genuine attempt at inclusivism. There was no struggle, unlike in every other religious struggle, which often resembles two rams slamming into each other. There were democratic opportunities for free and open dialogue. People listened with patience, and they were willing a take a few steps back to heal wounds, while dalits could come forward, and all this inspired other movements also—be it women or farmers or environmentalists. We were all part of a big community, everyone tried to understand each other and correct each other's mistakes.

His point is crystal-clear—the massive polarisation of our own times has given rise only to social media trolls and impatient dismissals. There used to be some space earlier where people could be *converted* or would least *consider* different perspectives, but now, one sticks by one's views like a pinned tweet. Back then, there were loud protests on the streets, which meant that communities were more aware of each other's genuine concerns. Now, everybody rages on their phones, but few are interested in trying to understand the nuances of our collective predicament.

In the same vein, Aravind Malagatti commended the Pejawara Swamy's gesture from 2017, when more than a hundred Muslims broke their Ramzaan fast within the premises of the Udupi matha. After facing some flak from hide-bound organisations like Sri Ram Sene (and from some Left activists, who said it was just a political gimmick), Pejawara Swamy responded, saying:

> This programme gives a clear picture that the Hindu community wants to live together in peace. Namaaz was not done in the temple; it was done in the dining hall. It's their custom to have snacks after namaaz and the hall was given for it. They are not the only people who consume beef, many Hindus do too. The Muslim community has stood with Sri Krishna Matha. They have expressed their solidarity with us during the Udupi Chalo movement and their cooperation during the Paryaya celebrations is commendable. In 1904, a seer was accompanied to the house of Haji Abdullah. There are instances of good relationships with Muslims.

Not just that, the Swamy had also gone and preached in mosques, and inaugurated mosques in Bhatkal, Udupi, Kasargod, Mangalore and other places. Malagatti too follows in the footsteps of reformers like Narayana Guru and Gandhi. He believes that radical ripples can also come from symbolic change within the establishment—Indian history is replete with examples of it. *You need two hands to clap, change can come only when communities come together*, he asserts. And yet, there is no denying that the Pejawara Swamy was at the forefront of the movement to reclaim the Babri Masjid in the eighties. Perhaps there had been in him, like in Gandhi, some moral evolution over the last decades of his life.

A similar handshake also took place *within* the Hindu socio-literary order back in the seventies, and this was no less surprising. As Aravind Malagatti recounted:

Before the dalit identity emerged, there was only 'shudra' consciousness. When the boosa incident happened, it was shudras who mainly supported it, people like Tejaswi, K. Ramdas. Now, the relationship between the dalits and the bandaya progressives was akin to a unique friendship between a tiger and an elephant. These two were willing to go to such lengths to accommodate each other that the tiger was willing to go vegetarian for the elephant's sake and the elephant was willing to take up eating meat. But when suspicions began to emerge that some were using these platforms for political gain, there arose a situation where nobody knew when the elephant would use its trunk and attack the tiger or when the tiger would field its claws. The argument was that women, dalits, religious minorities and progressives all came under bandaya—but I reparteed that the dalit identity is a whole in itself, that it is not the organ of some other larger body. If you do this, you are basically employing the same ploy that was used in history to enslave dalits. They thought I was merely lashing out against the progressives.

I said, the problem is that until now it has only been upper castes who have theorised who dalits are, but very few dalits themselves have done so. Some said only dalits can write dalit literature, but I countered that if Kuvempu writes about dalits, that is also dalit literature. I think Shivaram Karanth's *Chomana Dudi* is exceptional dalit literature. When that man is watching a dalit drowning in the river, shaking in his own conscience about whether he can go rescue him, it is a shattering image. If you impose your present moralities on a novel from the 1930s, and argue that Choma should have got a piece of land, then you're completely missing the point. Because, otherwise, you are simply recreating the sectarian thinking that we have been collectively enslaved by. That would be a grave mistake. Anyway, they later kicked me out of the organisation, in the nineties sometime, I think. Yet, bandaya was really important for the dalit movement to shape up.

I agreed with Aravind Malagatti strongly. When I'd met dalit activist Kotiganahalli Ramaiah, he'd leant towards the idea that dalit literature was undeniably the preserve of those who have actually experienced untouchability. It was a political argument more than a cultural one, I'd felt.

Unlike dalits, Muslims cannot claim a sympathetic ancestry across Kannada literature. They have largely been typecast in petty roles. Even in Kuvempu's fiction, we see them as small-time thieves and shady characters skulking in the background. In Ananthamurthy's *Samskara*, it is ultimately a few Muslim workers who faithfully cremate Naranappa's rotting corpse, after the brahmin community has spent days splitting hairs over how to deal with a fellow who had defied every one of their commandments, but had somehow remained a defiant brahmin even in death.

Bolwar Mahammad Kunhi told me there are few strong Muslim characters in Kannada fiction because most writers have simply feared broaching the subject. Poornachandra Tejaswi's short story 'Daredevil Musthafa', a story about a courageous young boy who does his best to fit in in a school where he is the only Muslim, was turned into a film recently that evoked *Malgudi Days* in its nostalgic appeal. But for the most part, Muslims were neglected by other writers, until *Aavarana* came around and broke Bolwar Mahammad's heart. 'I had such respect for Bhyrappa, I'd read everything he'd written. It pains me that he too fell for this. I critiqued it publicly too, but the media never covers these things in detail.' He also told me that the erstwhile Pejawara Swamy had continued to face flak from orthodox society over his attempts at communal harmony until his death in 2019. The ideological leanings of the present Pejawara Swamy—his successor—fall squarely within Sangh-land. He promptly began his tenure by rallying for the conversion of other mosques in North India into temples.

In December 2000, a group of progressive thinkers and activists decided to stage a communal harmony function in Chikmagalur, coinciding with the Sangh's Datta Jayanti plans, despite the state government's explicit orders prohibiting such a function.[38] Girish Karnad was stopped en route in Hassan, and Professor Rajendra Chenni placed under house arrest in Shimoga. Nevertheless, hundreds of activists did make their way to the designated field, where a few people playing cricket suddenly whipped out posters hidden in their clothes, kicking off a flash rally attended by hundreds of civilians.

Even as they were erupting into songs and slogans, the police arrived and began rounding them up into buses that headed to a freshly constructed prison nearby. Since most of them had come prepared for such a contingency, the atmosphere in the cells remained one of resolute fervour, almost like a festival of non-violent activism. The colourful diversity of the imprisoned crowd of hundreds is best captured by scholar Rahamath Tarikere, who too was a part of this motley crew:

> As evening fell, the chill of the ghats began to envelop us. Many had not thought about this, and had come unprepared. Since Chikmagalur lies high above sea level, the cold was biting. Those from places like Bellary and Raichur were shivering. Peer Basha had caught a cold . . . On one side were Bangalore's Ramdas Rao, Koppal's Allamaprabhu Bettaduru, Mundaragi's A.B. Hiremath, Bangalore's Shivaramayya, Shridhar of Vijaya College—a bevy of professors; on another side were Agni Shridhar, Basavaraj Urs, Gauri Lankesh, Bilidaale Eesha—a team of journalists. In another corner, sitting away from everyone, like a woman just out of labour, accepting the entreaties of younger comrades, was the senior CPI leader Ananth Subbarao. Elsewhere sat Swati Sundaresh, Siddanagowda Patil and other comrades. As though staying away from these senior leaders, some youngsters were sitting in a far corner, having started a small fire with some stray wood, laughing earnestly. In yet another group, a few women had wrapped themselves in rugs and were sleeping soundly, looking like rolled jute sacks.

What is remarkable is that it was a troop of progressive activists from *across the state* that had taken up this resistance movement—it was not staged by a political opposition or local minority groups. Later in his essay, Tarikere observes a distinction peculiar to Karnataka: 'Apart from S.L. Bhyrappa, Chidananda Murthy and Sumateendra Nadig, the Sangh Parivar has failed to attract Kannada literati to its ideology. In this sense, Kannada literature is also political literature. There is a strong tradition of humanist politics, from Pampa to Basavanna to Kuvempu to Devanura Mahadeva. In their own times, these writers have opposed the various forms of priestly orthodoxy prevailing in their times. Could it not be that today's writers are challenging yet another avatar of that force?'

I discovered another strain of this humanist literary tradition in the form of the comedian-novelist Goruru Ramaswamy Iyengar. Sometime early into this book project, I had purchased a copy of his 1930s comedy novel *Namma Oorina Rasikaru* (The Rasikas, or Aesthetes, of Our Town). Seeing this, my grandmother expressed an ardent desire to read the book—which she had heard much about—but she bore a sullen face when returning it to me a few days later. She had been looking forward to a very particular scene in the novel, where a brahmin shraddha ceremony, lunch-in-progress, is blasphemously invaded in the form of a shudra interloper who looks in through the window and urges them to not get distracted from their feast on his count. As it turns out, the scene has been summarily censored from current editions, presumably to satisfy concerns of controversy, and I could not find a single copy of the text that carried it. I was therefore glad to see Goruru's satirical takedown of caste divides take the stage in a theatre adaption of the novel performed in Mysore in 2023. It had, of course, now also taken on new flavours, blended with the political concerns of the present. The play featured a brilliant bayalata performance, a comedic episode set within the Ramayana, that drew enormous applause from the crowd. It told me, again, that creative critiques from *inside* cultures hold the greatest potential to become long-lasting, ever-innovating traditions in their own right.

SEVEN

Spirits of the Past
Lineages of Debt

> A new age does not begin all of a sudden.
> My grandfather was already living in the new age.
> My grandson will probably still be living in the old one.
>
> —Bertolt Brecht

I

Nargund Babasaheb was one amongst the numerous victims of Dalhousie's Doctrine of Lapse. His son had died in infancy, and the East India Company had rejected his request to adopt an heir. Inam Commissioner Jacob Manson sends an attachment notice to seize the king's properties and armoury in Nargund. The enraged Babasaheb gets in touch with Peshwa Nana Saheb, who finds himself at the forefront of the 1857 rebellion. Babasaheb's forces meet Manson's army at the village of Sureban in March 1858, where Manson is quelled, and his severed head is displayed as a trophy on the gates of Nargund fort. Babasaheb is eventually betrayed by his own courtier, and is captured. Brutal reprisals follow, and Babasaheb is hanged publicly by the British. His wife and mother soon embrace their fate, drowning themselves in the Malaprabha river.

It is the morning of 21 July 1980. A large group of angry farmers have laid siege to the tehsildar's office in the small town of Nargund in Dharwad district. In a bid to prevent the tehsildar from entering the building, they lie down on the ground, surrounding the entrance like a forbidding moat. Burdened by his own orders to resume work at any cost, the tehsildar decides to walk across this human obstacle course. It so happens that he belongs to a scheduled caste, and this blasphemous act of stepping on superior-caste members infuriates the already simmering mob. Stone-pelting begins, and as a protestor tries to burn a police jeep, a sub-inspector shoots at him, killing him on the spot. Meanwhile, the tehsildar has been brutally beaten up, and two reserve policemen who have exhausted their ammunition frantically shooting into the air have been killed by the mob. The sub-inspector is also tracked down soon enough to a nearby hospital where he has been hiding and is thrashed to death. Around the same time, a similar scene unfolds in the town of Navalgund, just twenty kilometres away. A protesting mob ransacks the irrigation department building and burns all bureaucratic records. There too, a police firing takes place, and one farmer dies. These gruesome events are a culmination of several months of protests by neglected and mistreated farmers' groups in north Karnataka. Little do the agitators realise that things are going to go from bad to worse in the tumultuous months to come.

In December 2021, I got a chance to meet the veteran Congress politician B.R. Yavagal at his office in Dharwad. A midnight's child, Yavagal was in his mid-seventies when I met him. He had started his political career with the Janata Party in 1983, becoming the first non-Congress MLA from the constituency of Nargund. Then he jumped to the Janata Dal, and after its dissolution joined the Congress in 1999, where he has remained for the last two decades. I wished to meet him to hear of the particular event that went on to shape both his own career and the history of the farmers' movement in Karnataka—the protests and police firings at Nargund and Navalgund in 1980. On the phone, I was struck by his keenness to grant me an immediate audience: 'proper documentation is lacking, people should know all the terrible things that once happened ...'

1980. A meteor of a year. The immensely popular Devaraj Urs had split from Indira Gandhi's Congress, and gathered his supporters into a party dubbed Kranti Ranga. But his vast support base in rural Karnataka had not clearly registered the splinter. They voted him out, half in ignorance, and Gundu Rao—who had carefully cultivated Sanjay Gandhi's favour—was installed as chief minister. A glorified chamcha vested with much power is how he was seen in those days by the media and commentators. On the day of the Gundu Rao government's swearing in, a group of Urs's supporters gathered nearby to register a peaceful protest. They were thrashed black-and-blue by Congress goons wielding clubs and razors, while the police looked the other way.

The chickens were coming home to roost. Devaraj Urs, a pragmatic man above all, had fostered the rise of rowdy elements within the party, employing the Emergency to his advantage, steamrolling his ambitious reforms while keeping his adversaries at bay, and unlike other Congress chief ministers, actually working hard to implement Indira Gandhi's twenty-point programme meant to help the poor. He had been crafty enough to keep his acolytes fat and well fed, and to even pull wool over the eyes of superiors at the Centre. He'd sent false sterilisation statistics and other assorted fictions, even as Gundu Rao, the Gandhis' inept spy, had failed to notice the treachery. Devaraj Urs was a merciless authoritarian where it suited him, and during the Emergency, RSS workers were thrashed in prisons,[1] and newspapers were censored accordingly. The actor, activist and Lohiaite Snehalata Reddy was imprisoned for eight months in the infamous Baroda Dynamite Case, suffering torture and inhumane treatment in Bangalore Central Jail. She would die five days after her release because of her deteriorated health. While Devaraj Urs relied on close connections with businessmen—like the liquor baron Ramachandra Khoday—to buttress his rule, his right-hand man was son-in-law M.D. Nataraj, who would go on to champion one of Bangalore's biggest dons, Jayaraj, and secure Urs a strongarm legacy.

When Urs handed Gundu Rao the presidency of the state's Youth Congress in the late seventies, the organisation was full of brash youngsters willing to do anything to quell their foes. After the latter jumped ship to the Gandhis' camp and procured the crown for himself, his band of followers got drunk on power like never before. The anointing of Gundu Rao as chief minister drove the final stake into the Congress's reign—in three years he would be booted out. But in the intervening period, protesting farmers would be gunned down in shocking numbers, illicit hooch would create the deadliest alcohol poisoning episode in recorded history and his thugs would trash newspaper offices for refusing to toe their line. Eventually, in 1983, the Janata Party led by Ramakrishna Hegde would form the first non-Congress government in Karnataka.

But even before that, things had hardly been rosy. Yavagal remembers those years as well as he might a gunshot wound. The former district of Dharwad (now sub-divided into Gadag and Haveri) is predominantly drained by the Malaprabha river, a tributary of the Krishna. In 1972, an irrigation project was commissioned in the region, but a serious drought struck before all the canals were dug completely. Devaraj Urs ordered water to be released into this half-formed system in 1973 to avert a crisis. The canals were sparsely used by some farmers during this period. By 1975–76, however, they had been constructed to a fair degree, enabling farmers to begin growing cotton. As this was virgin soil where cotton had never been grown before, the first harvests were bountiful, and yields were good across the Malaprabha area. However, in the succeeding years, the farmers' luck turned. Bollworm attacks devastated the cotton crops, and expensive pesticides failed to contain them. Meanwhile, the state decided to impose a betterment levy on the region that had received the benefits of the Malaprabha project—to be calculated with retrospective effect from 1973. How could farmers cough up such sums of tax money when they had barely enough for food? 'Arrears in the payment of the betterment levy had piled up over the years as successive governments had been deliberately lax in collecting dues, lest they alienate farmers. Gundu Rao, however, decided that the arrears should be collected aggressively, and all at once, to demonstrate that his government meant business. He ordered that debts should be collected by force, and that moveable property should be seized where cash payments were not forthcoming.'[2] The tehsildar's men would barge into houses and take away even utensils if there was no money to be found. Banks hired their own goondas to carry out these extractions.

The local farmers' leadership in Dharwad, which included Yavagal, unanimously decided to raise the matter with the government, and proceeded to meet the tehsildar, the assistant commissioner and the district commissioner, or DC, from whom no response was forthcoming. Since all revenue matters were handled by an officer designated as special DC, they went to see him, only to be received in cold silence. The special DC did not bother to read their petition, or even ask them to sit down, preferring instead to doodle on a notebook as they spoke. Flustered by this complete apathy on the part of the bureaucracy, Yavagal and co. decided to embark upon a peaceful satyagraha in Nargund, Navalgund and neighbouring areas. Between April and July, farmers and their families took turns to sit in protest every day, even as the local leaders deliberated on future courses of action. Sit-ins and Gandhian marches were conducted even in rainy weather, and some athletic protestors even demonstrated their dissent by standing on just one leg. Seeing no redressal in sight, the farmers' leaders finally decided to declare a bandh on 21 July, since the legislative assembly was meeting at the Vidhana Soudha in Bangalore on that day, and this would surely catch their attention. After the gory happenings on that fateful day, the protesting crowd dispersed quickly in Nargund and Navalgund, in deep fear for their lives—sobriety tends to strike hard after mob fury subsides. No police reinforcements had arrived immediately as the mob had cut off communications with administrative headquarters. Yavagal hastily retreated to Hubli to hide at a friend's place. As he recounts:

> When the mob entered the tehsildar's office, they unfortunately encountered a lot of arrack and alcohol. They drank that, I'm afraid, and started ransacking the place. You see, the excise department had run out of space in their building, and they had utilised a room in this office. These fellows stumbled on it …

There is profound irony in that image, for the alcohol industry has always found a second home within Karnataka's political corridors, even as farmers have suffered in debt for meagre sums of money (the average farmer's due during the 1980 protest was around Rs 300, says Yavagal). At the end of a long day of drudgery and continuing debt-bondage, many drink themselves to numbness, but thousands of farmers have also downed chemical fertilisers to end their misery more quickly.[3] When Vijay Mallya's United Breweries acquired Mangalore Chemicals and Fertilisers in the early 1990s, the irony was only magnified. Indeed, a key talking point of the farmers' movement in the wake of July 1980 was that the State was infinitely more lenient towards industrial loans and treated farmers with very little respect. When you are lending money to good friends, generosity comes naturally. When you are dealing with people you consider beneath yourself, the lathi comes down hard and fast. The Raj never really ended.

Inevitably, the days following 21 July were filled with brutal reprisals, and suspects were rounded up and seriously roughed up. Whatever else had transpired during those murderous hours, the mob had certainly achieved one of their goals—they had caught the assembly's attention. The matter was discussed at the Vidhana Soudha post-haste. Yavagal stressed on the fact that several sympathetic voices tried hard to save them from the wrath of the government. Meanwhile, farmers' organisations across Karnataka banded together in solidarity. In every one of Karnataka's 175 taluks, there was rebellion, says Yavagal, and the police repression was at its most brutal, with over 130 protestors shot dead.

The Gundu Rao regime was marked by constant disorder and chaos. His government has been termed a 'civil servant raj' and an 'extended holiday', as the chief minister left most of the governance to bureaucrats, remaining oblivious to communications from legislators on policy issues that affected their constituencies. At one point, thousands of files had piled up in his office pending signature, which Gundu Rao solved by simply shifting them to another room and claiming completion. His acolyte F.M. Khan, who held no official post, but was virtually as powerful as Gundu Rao himself, had become a cultivator of influential (and often glamorous) contacts in the worlds of industry and showbiz. 'While the civil servants found the diminished power of the legislators advantageous, such a situation severely undermined democratic principles and produced one of the least responsive and most insensitive state governments ever seen in India.'[4]

Even Gundu Rao could not afford to ignore the killings of July 1980, and he did meet with Yavagal and others for discussion in the months that followed.[5] It seemed remarkable to me that Yavagal still referred to him with respect, suffixing his name with *ji* every time he mentioned Rao, and even credited him with being sympathetic to them and entertaining their loan-waiver demands. I wondered if this was a symptom of Yavagal's loyalty to the Congress, or simply his genial temperament that seeks to capture the inherent goodness in everybody around him. His meeting with Gundu Rao would also prove to be a point of personal departure with the newly coalescing Karnataka Rajya Raitha Sangha, which Yavagal would later chalk off as an anarchist organisation that merely disrupted society. He would never become a part of it because Yavagal has never believed in purely apolitical organisations (he was always drawn to power), and he had met Gundu Rao to definitively seal a deal. This irked KRRS leader M.D. Nanjundaswamy, who wanted the organisation to remain an apolitical pressure group, as it did for many years. When Yavagal rendezvoused with Gundu Rao, the prickly, resolute 'Professor' Nanjundaswamy felt spurned. During the state elections of 1983—when several farmers' leaders, including the present chief minister, Siddaramaiah, had gathered to discuss the KRRS's political strategies—Nanjundaswamy asserted that the party was non-political, and that those who wanted to contest elections could leave to parley with another party. Many did so, and won in large numbers, which prompted KRRS leaders to reflect that it had been a golden opportunity frittered away.

Yavagal spoke candidly of the 1980 meeting:

> We were hard-pressed. There were innocents still in prison, and no bail had been granted to them. The entire farming sector was at a standstill. People were scared. Police force was everywhere. The tax recovery proceedings had to be stopped immediately. We needed to have a dialogue with the state. We wanted some immediate solution to all this. So, we went and met the CM independently. It was a very cordial meeting. It was a good session. He stopped the loan recovery for the time being. Bail was allowed. They gave us some soft loans. All this happened.

Thus, the Dharwad farmers under Yavagal kept out of the pan-state federation, while keeping in touch with the who's who of the political elite. With support from Devaraj Urs, they decided to embark on an ambitious foot march from Nargund to Bangalore, nearly five hundred kilometres. Urs, though plagued by ill health, flagged off the march and walked with them for a short distance in January 1981. He would die the following year. By the time the farmers reached Bangalore on 5 February, vast numbers of sympathetic civil society groups, including workers' unions and lawyers, had joined the protest, swelling the march to huge numbers. This was also around the time of the Gokak agitations, and a mood of public demonstration had gripped the city. The group marched straight to the assembly, deposited the 'farmers' flame' at the entrance, and submitted their memorandum to the assembly. Gundu Rao seems to have made a flippant comment at this time, calling the marching crowd 'Baadige Raitharu', or farmers on rent, and infuriated by this, the group marched into the premises of the Vidhana Soudha, shouting their hearts out. Even at this point, Yavagal refrained from taking potshots at Gundu Rao.

Later, as I reflected on my meeting with Yavagal, I felt his reverence for Gundu Rao spoke of an unspoken debt. I had gone in expecting him to lambast Rao and his goon squads, but instead encountered a serene man who faulted only the system, and not the individuals who greased its machinery. There was something endearing about his good-naturedness, but I felt it was unwise to take it at face value. My thoughts flew to the established template of most political speeches these days, where the hagiographies of erstwhile leaders occupy a good section of the speech. Could there be democracy within political parties? If not, shouldn't there at least be fresher imaginations of more accountable and self-critical organisations?

I extended this question to Aiyshwarya Mahadev, the present spokesperson of the Congress in Karnataka, in early 2024. She remarked somewhat obliquely that 'armchair social media people create kings out of clowns', and that 'some older Congress politicians are open to listening, but many from the current generation, who have got used to excesses, are so full of hubris that they can never listen to criticism'. Aiyshwarya is a fourth-generation politician from Mandya—an agricultural hub famed for sugarcane. She comes from a family of tobacco farmers. Her grandfather had once been the head of the local tobacco growers' association that had controversially challenged the World Health Organisation on its anti-cancer stipulations, arguing that many dangerous chemicals accrued to a cigarette outside of raw tobacco and that farmers should be afforded lenience. Her father, Manchanahalli Mahadev, was a widely respected MLA who switched from JD(S) to Congress late in his life. Aiyshwarya grew up in a 'hyper-public' household, where it was rare to wake up in the morning without some kind of hustle already in progress.

> My father passed away when I was nineteen, in 2011. At that point, I thought perhaps no more politics for me, and I can live my life for myself, because we've had such public lives. But what happens is, when an entire ecosystem—thousands of people—are dependent

on your family, or are used to having you around constantly, at some point or the other, that sudden vacuum creates a lot of torment for them. So, we started doing social work, the taluk did not let me go, my mum was trying to get a ticket, because of which you get sucked back into it. I don't think of myself as a full-time politician as much as I am a social worker. You'll never see me put on a stage programme, put up a banner—I think all that is a waste.

I do have the political and social capital which will get the tehsildar to listen to me. I can have a direct impact on people. Sometimes I think this is just some sadistic self-satisfaction, but it has really been fulfilling so far because of the sense of responsibility that comes with it. Not everyone gets power the way I have.

I think the system is too broken to fix. Electoral politics has become a money-and-caste game. I think it is extremely disgusting. Caste awareness, caste mobilisation and the backward caste politics started by Devaraj Urs was commendable, though Devaraj Urs, I genuinely believe, did it for his own political capital—he was a micro-minority OBC.

The sort of money you need to mobilise is ridiculous. We're farmers, and god has been kind, my mother is a banker, good with finances, and we have been doing well. My father, honestly, gave us debt, and when he left, we had nothing. And corruption doesn't come to us—I wouldn't even know where to begin. So, to mobilise crores and crores is something I don't want to be a part of. I don't want to be beholden to any industrialist that gives me money, and then have to listen to him dictate terms.

Aiyshwarya Mahadev had just finished harvesting her paddy fields, but the real challenge had been the transplanting a few months earlier. Labour is difficult to find, because her 'grandfather ensured the education of his labourers' children', and now most labourers travel to Coorg to pick coffee because it is far more lucrative. She is planning to invest in a coconut farm, which will take some time, but will help replenish the soil. A few years down the line, she dreams of a large community farm, where a cooperative coir industry can come up and secure local women reliable employment. Aiyshwarya feels that cooperative agri-businesses have great potential in combating unemployment. The work can be immensely dignified too. During the pandemic, she procured cloth for women in the villages around Periyapatna to stitch thousands of masks, which were then distributed to the Mysore Police, amongst others. Other interventions she is proud of include distributing plates, glasses and schoolbags to the poor children of local schools in the villages surrounding her hometown.

I've always known Mandya as the forty-five-minute landmark on the highway from Mysore to Bangalore. Now, it takes less than half an hour. But so far as I can tell, Mandya still remains an agricultural hub, and is unlikely to suddenly transform into, say, a university town. It was the first recipient of the KRS dam's irrigation rewards in the 1930s, and has prospered since. Ragi, paddy, sugarcane and pulses are some of the major crops grown in the district today. When I asked Aiyshwarya about the water-intensive sugarcane industry in Mandya, its connection with the liquor lobby and its perceived connection to the Kaveri-sharing crisis, she responded that the 'Kaveri dispute is more political than environmental'.

> There are strong arguments that the run-off in Tamil Nadu is so much that, if they had better storage facilities, Karnataka would have to give much less. As for sugarcane, when you have created a demand for sugarcane, when you have set up a factory and you have put farmers into the habit of growing it for you, the cost of trying to get them to shift is very high. Sugarcane is also an unprofitable crop if you don't have a processing unit close enough. Within the first few hours of harvest, if you don't make it to a crusher, you've lost most of your money. They shifted the processing unit from Mandya to Pandavapura, ruined the farmers, and allowed middlemen to step in. Now, they restarted it, but the cycle was broken. The efficiency of sugarcane in North Karnataka is massive. The processing units are right next to the farms, and the farmers benefit from this. For example, Murugesh Nirani, Lakshmi Hebbalkar and others run the entire sugarcane lobby, right? The only one that is not political is Nandi Sugar, which is run by a cooperative. But to get into the cooperative scene is also a political exercise. And because so many

> farmers are dependent on it, because so many votes come from it, it is a far more efficient model. The Jarkiholis are sugarcane barons today, but they started off being arrack runners, right? Everybody knows this. And today, the majority of their money does not come directly from sugarcane. It comes from the ethanol. It comes from the molasses. It comes from the run-off.

In 2007, the JD(S)–BJP government banned arrack in Karnataka. Some had argued that this only pushed the poor into drinking costly liquor and deepened their poverty, rather than curing them of alcoholism. However, the ban had emerged out of years, nay decades, of unignorable hooch tragedies. In 1981, a deadly bootlegging mishap had claimed more than 300 lives in Bangalore, crowding Bowring and Victoria Hospitals with blinded, writhing, incurable bodies. 'Previously, excise contractors had policed their own turf, wiping out moonshiners, but by now both the state and the arrack empires were too compromised to check them. Hooch poisonings recurred every few years, morbid reminders of arrack's fallen state,' journalist Raghu Karnad writes in an excellent essay on Bangalore's alcohol industry.[6] Gundu Rao had paid the victims of the tragedy a paltry Rs 1,000 each. In 1986, Ramakrishna Hegde had to resign (for three days) after the court held the Janata Party's act of awarding arrack-bottling contracts illegal, kicking up a major scandal—*Lankesh Patrike* had broadcasted the story with vigour.

Hegde submitted his resignation for good in 1988, after allegations emerged of phone taps on politicians and businessmen. A chief instigator in this regard was Subramanian Swamy, against whom Hegde would soon file defamation cases. Veerendra Patil led the Congress's return to power with a powerful majority in 1989. He was resolute in his desire to curb the 'seconds regime', which was a wily system of kickbacks that the IMFL, or Indian-Made Foreign Liquor, lobby had created to evade excise duties, diverting nearly half of the taxes back into their own pockets. 'His [Patil's] government raised the state export levy from Rs 2 to Rs 20 per litre, and passed a law requiring manufacturers to sell their liquor only to a government distributor, the Mysore Sales International Ltd (MSIL), nixing their ability to move excise-evaded liquor straight to the shop. He also banned the sale of traditional toddy, a generous favour to the arrack lobby,' Karnad writes. However, when Patil fell sick in 1990, the IMFL lobby quickly played their moves and curried collective favour with Rajiv Gandhi, who proceeded to instal S. Bangarappa as chief minister. Bangarappa promptly lowered export duties, cut taxes on beer and re-legalised toddy. It would take the political wherewithal displayed by S.M. Krishna at the turn of the century to end the seconds regime.

Yet, perhaps because liquor has continued to remain a dominant state subject from the time of Kautilya's Arthashastra, Krishna too was quite indebted to the revenue being brought in by IMFL. Between 1999 and 2001, a pest attacking coconut trees had spread to sixteen districts of the state, causing enormous losses to farmers. To address this, farmers had taken to toddy-tapping in large numbers, and when toddy sales began to shoot up, it began to significantly affect the coffers of the excise department and the foreign liquor posse. The state buckled down, and farmers protested again; in October 2001, two farmers were shot dead in a golibaar incident in Channapatna.[7] Three decades, marked by many political turns where the throttle was really in the hands of the bottle-men. Not exactly the most inspiring tale of democratic evolution, I'd say.

Today, innumerable beer gardens and pubs flourish in Bangalore as the watering holes of the swelling, swilling IT crowd. From a picturesque colonial cantonment town, Bangalore was adopted, post-independence, by the heirs of the liquor gods. In Raghu Karnad's memorable words, 'Alcohol printed the city's newspapers, produced its movies, put down hospitals and schools and sports teams—and ruled the men who ruled its people.' Vijay Mallya was elected to the Rajya Sabha from Karnataka twice in the 2000s, where he forged the connections that would enable his rise and fall. The city's beloved IPL cricket team is named after a lager, but just like the fortunes of the Mallya dynasty, the Royal Challengers (the men's team, at least) have yet to find their cup of unimpeachable glory. Deemed a wilful defaulter by Indian banks, who had allowed him to borrow money way beyond prudential limits, Vijay Mallya decamped to London where he lives today, despite many extradition attempts. Throughout his life, we see in him something akin to the medieval king's honour—like Yudhisthira in the Mahabharata—of being willing to play a game in which everything is staked, where grandeur and masculinity are directly linked with how far one can fall. I think it also explains why he captured the Indian imagination. Yet, when he loses it all, there is no need for an exile in the jungle; the British Isles will do just fine. The gamble is not really a gamble if the system ensures that you will be vouched for. The communism of the rich, they call it. How different is this from the rape-accused Nithyananda jumping ship and founding his own nation to escape to?

Vijay Mallya's son Siddharth has spent the last few years speaking about quitting alcohol, about how alcoholism can wreck mental health. In commendably candid interviews, he reflects on the instability of his childhood, equalled in intensity by the instability of his father's lifestyle and finances, which have always been precariously tipsy. Back on the ground, you have Alcohol Lovers' Associations across Karnataka, who actually put out press releases and hand out colourful demands to the government—lowering alcohol taxes, education assurances for the children of alcoholics who cannot study in peace because their fathers arrive drunk and rowdy in the evenings, celebration of 31 December as Drunkards' Day, rest houses next to taverns where people can pass out peacefully, and so on.

The lineages of debt are truly manifold.

II

The helavas (from the Kannada word 'helu', *to tell*) are a peripatetic community with a peculiar claim to fame. Their vocation, and purpose, is the narration of family lineages, although the gazetteer records grimly that 'begging has been their characteristic profession'. In many regions of North Karnataka, they still perform the task of carrying around large ledgers with intricate family trees, dating all the way back to the twelfth century, with details of when/where the forebears of the current generation lived, suffered, procreated and died. Modern education has been slowly enveloping the community, and the helava elders speak with both sobriety and melancholy when they say that their own children laugh at their profession now.

As the helavas narrate it, the story goes that Basavanna was assigning tasks to his followers, and only one man remained at the end of the exercise who had nothing to do. He was lame, and keeping his handicap in mind, Basavanna pronounced that he should ride upon a bullock and go around remembering and narrating people's lineages. Then, he should find himself a woman, get married and continue his own line. It is testament to Basavanna's power as a seer that his words were followed to the dot, and an entire community of people devoted to the task evolved, and have survived to this day. Today, those engaged in the tradition ride motorcycles rather than bullocks, use pens instead of quills, but it would be patronising to suggest that their practices are not anachronisms in the age of Wikipedia.

Why would Basavanna even feel the need for this task, one might ask. Today, of course, we'd consider the preservation of caste lineages an imprudent endeavour. But to place oneself ten centuries ago is to travel into a completely different moral landscape, with wildly different concerns. It is an important exercise, though, because much of modern political discourse (both Left and Right) tends to moralise about the past without an ounce of nuance. Historian Manu Devadevan answers the question well in his book, *A Prehistory of Hinduism*. This was a period when hereditary access to land, and to a genealogy of pride, had finally been expanded out of the realm of the king and his courtly orthodoxy. It was a momentous change, with enormous ramifications for how society would come to be organised in the centuries to follow. He writes:

> The rank and file of landholders had already swollen by the twelfth century, making individual landholders a force to reckon with. Holding land on a hereditary basis also made the family a deeply entrenched institution. Inscriptions begin to enumerate family

> lines with much greater frequency. Genealogy had until this time remained the preserve of kings and saints ... After the twelfth century, inscriptions carrying genealogies of the families concerned increased in number by leaps and bounds ... Hereditary access to land had begun to find a number of reified expressions, among them religious genealogies, castes, and entrenched familial legacies. Understandably enough, the past, upon which stories of succession are based, was also gaining in importance.

It was hereditary access to land—the onset of private property—that made the remembrance of genealogies so vital. The period between the eleventh and thirteenth centuries was one where peasant proprietors grew exponentially in number, matched only by the mushrooming of temples in the agrarian landscape. The lives of the helavas, as with other lower castes, came to be intimately embroidered with that of the farmers. As one helava man puts it, 'If the farmers don't give us anything, we have nothing.' They never really learnt farming, since it was never their job. And now, when some go in search of work, they can only do cheap, unskilled labour that pays a pittance. They lived as if in complete debt to the rural agrarian society around them, and it is heartening to see some youth now get educated and find other professional paths. There can be no farming without labour, which was inevitably borne by the lower castes. The holeya caste literally referred to an agrestic labourer or slave who worked in the field: hola. The holeyas, like the helavas, depended entirely on the patronage of the landlords. It was inevitable in a feudal society where caste, class and profession were inextricably enmeshed, spun into a totalitarian fabric.

It is because of this complex web of land and caste connections that the Karnataka Rajya Raitha Sangha never quite shook hands with the Dalita Sangharsha Samiti. Some, who straddled both realms, like Devanura Mahadeva, attempted symbolic overtures, but nothing substantial ever emerged. The CPI(M) leader Siddanagowda Patil, now editor of *Hosatu* magazine, told me that they too had tried to join hands with the Raitha Sangha, but had been snubbed. He also told me that Nanjundaswamy had regretted this much later in life. In 1987, Lankesh wrote an editorial urging a recognition of the fact that the Raitha Sangha was dominated by the landholding class. 'We have seen that the inherent dualities and internal structure of the Raitha Sangha are what have rendered its programmes unconstructive and uninformed by a strong political ideology ... It is necessary that people with the tenacity to change political, cultural, caste structures, by keeping villages as their base unit, should come to power. There is a need for a social and economic atmosphere that does not require loans. An arrangement is required by means of which money from cities may begin flowing to villages.'[8]

The problem, of course, was exactly that deep-set sense of hierarchy. The vast mass of the Raitha Sangha's membership was caste-proud, and they weren't about to allow the reorganisation of rural society, despite a progressive, Lohia-inspired leader in the form of M.D. Nanjundaswamy.[9] Local territorial battles turned out to be more pressing than the broader cause. The proliferation of caste politics, too, put paid to any ideas of agrarian unity. This also explains why Nanjundaswamy would have preferred that the KRRS stay out of electoral politics—its ideals could quickly become muddied by caste politics and money. But such risks would have to be tackled either way. In some alternative reality, the KRRS could have become a bastion of idealistic socialism, embracing the rural hinterlands as their core field of concern, serving as a foil to politics wholly dictated by money and industry. Perhaps the next time history serves up such powerful moments, we might learn from the past something of the art of negotiating power, of charting a vision for *longue durée* political goals.

H.R. Basavarajappa, who assumed the leadership of the Karnataka Rajya Raitha Sangha in 2022 after a corruption scandal rocked its earlier president Kodihalli Chandrashekar out of office, has also emerged as a comprehensive chronicler of the farmers' movement in Karnataka.[10] At the very beginning of his autobiography, Basavarajappa devotes a couple of pages to fleshing out his family tree. After briefly delineating the current professional and marital status of all his assorted siblings and their children, he writes:

'However, there is another family in my life, another family that has lodged itself in my heart. That is the Karnataka Rajya Raitha Sangha, its leaders, its workers, well-wishers, and all the moments we have spent together in the struggle.' He even goes on to say, in what is either a glorious demonstration of his loyalty to the KRRS or a subtle snub to his blood family, that 'it is this other family that has added colour to my life. Hence, without giving much attention to my personal life, I have endeavoured to restrict myself to the story of the farmers' struggle.' Later in his life, he would reject lucrative invitations from political parties and continue to work within the Raitha Sangha.

Basavarajappa remembers his father—a progressive man who stood his own ground against casteism and feudal authoritarianism in their village in Shimoga—to be his first teacher in the art of rebellion. He also brings up a curious story that the helavas narrate about his forebears:

> Apparently, our ancestors lived in the Bijapur region around the year 1600. They were zamindars who owned a significant amount of land. They would extract tax from the local peasants and convey it to their Muslim overlords. Once, when a Muslim official came on a horse and asked why tax was still overdue, our ancestor said that drought was wreaking havoc on the countryside, so where would money come from? At the same time, a young woman bearing a pot was walking towards them, and the official started harassing her. Livid at this, our ancestor chopped off the man's head, crossed the river Bhima and arrived at Arasanaghatta, before finally settling down Hanumantapura. This is not documented history or an event that I can affirm with certainty. Neither can I model myself on this ancestor. I have only brought it up here because it seemed to rhyme with the bold and rebellious streaks shared by me and my father.

Basavarajappa recalls an incident from the seventies, when his father had been visited by the tehsildar and his associates out to recover the mandatory produce that was to be submitted to the state. Farmers were in dire straits then and only had enough grain to feed themselves. Despite this, the tehsildar had asked his strongmen to barge into the house and forcibly relieve them of their stores. The moment deeply impacted Basavarajappa and pushed him towards the struggle. Later, the Raitha Sangha would make a spirited attempt to get rid of the levy system, which is being phased out now in many states of the country. Only in times of surplus harvests, and with a steady minimum support price, or MSP, guaranteed, can the levy system be acceptable to farmers.

Initially, Basavarajappa was an RSS supporter, because they had offered a sense of community bonding. But he soon became disenchanted with the increasing communalism, and found himself an ideological home in the Raitha Sangha, where non-violent Gandhian anarchism tapped into the raw force of sincere struggle. Its protest repertoire included methods like blocking roads, courting arrest and filling jails (in huge numbers, completely overwhelming the capacity of the state prisons), picketing and gheraos and hunger strikes. In spite of tens of casualties of police brutalities over the years, for which no police official faced any imprisonment, the movement has been steadfast in its idealism. On one occasion, more than 30,000 farmers were jailed en masse across the state. In his autobiography, Basavarajappa records a moving anecdote that captures the Gandhian soul of the movement. Once, many farmers were rounded up during a rasta roko protest, and packed off to the Central Jail in Hindalaga, Belgaum. Among this crowd was a veteran freedom fighter and Gandhian named Singanamane Siddalingappa. Many of those who had been imprisoned were farmers from small villages who had never seen indoor toilets, and could not bring themselves to use the closed toilets in the prison. They started relieving themselves in the cells, stinking up the whole environment. Seeing this, Siddalingappa decided to wake up every morning and calmly clean all of it himself, stunning the perpetrators into shame. Needless to say, they began using the prison bathroom.

In the early eighties, Basavarajappa was part of a rasta roko where a policeman had fired without provocation, killing a farmer as well as another civilian who was simply passing through. Raging with fury,

Basavarajappa followed the police jeep on his bike, like a trueborn South Indian movie star, all eager to kick up a storm in the police station and demand reparation. The police locked him up, thrashed him along with the lot of arrested farmers and crushed them under their boots. Across my readings, I encountered no dearth of police atrocities meted out to activists during the seventies and eighties. For instance, a professor of English at Bangalore University named Nagari Babaiah was tortured for three months in Bangalore for alleged Naxalite activities. As he endured the abuse, the terrified man remembered T.S. Eliot's play *Murder in the Cathedral*, where four knights surround an archbishop and kill him.[11] In his recollection of those ghastly days, Babaiah writes that the prison still remains a parallel state that is a law unto itself, where complete impunity reigns. In fact, Jayaprakash Narayan started the People's Union for Civil Liberties in the wake of the Emergency to fight against obscene police oppression. At Bangalore University, the PUCL found some very spirited human rights' activists, and was immensely active through the eighties and nineties—Babaiah too was a part of many fact-finding missions.

What the hard statistics convey is that a majority of those languishing in prisons belong to lower socio-economic backgrounds, often innocent or guilty of petty crimes, who don't have the resources to fight legal battles. Caste society reproduces itself within Indian prisons too,[12] as does communalism. The journalist Naveen Soorinje noticed, while imprisoned in Mangalore Central Jail on false allegations, that the jail was actually divided into Hindu and Muslim quarters. Very few people speak of reforming and humanising prisons today—certainly no political party has taken up the cause vigorously in the recent past. The realisation that police torture fundamentally deprives society of the justice it deserves has yet to impress itself fully on our conscience. On the other hand, Karnataka has proven quite restorative when it comes to dons and gang leaders; they have contested elections, summoned choice alcohol and biryani dispatches to prison cells, and turned to filmmaking and other fulfilling professions in life.

III

> These lands were in the region of Mempi, whose slopes were covered with teak and other forests, and at whose feet stretched acres and acres of maize fields, with stalks standing over a man's height. Margayya was carried away by visions of this paradise of blue mountains, forest, and green fields. It was wealth at the very source and not second-hand after it had travelled up to town. The more he listened, the more he felt that here was raw wealth inviting him to take a hand and help himself.
>
> —R.K. Narayan, *The Financial Expert*

In the 2017 novel by Shridhar Banavasi (pen name 'Fakeera'), titled *Beru* (Roots), we enter the brooding universe of a charitable health centre, long emptied of its founders' humanist ideals, and run mostly by men who live to exploit. We are thrust into the travails of a few misfortunate souls—a young girl paralysed from the waist down thanks to endolsulfan (a pesticide now banned worldwide) poisoning while she was in her mother's womb, a middle-aged farmer with brain damage sustained during a police lathicharge and a young man ailing from blood cancer. The story chooses to dwell more on the predicaments of their loved ones, who would go to any pillar or post to secure an end to their family's collective suffering. These are tales so often lost to the cold touch of the statistical welfare state—uprooted families navigating debt, depression and deprivation while craving a route back to normalcy and to the rhythms of rooted rural livelihood.

It is through these deep roots in the soil of lived reality that the countryside has always proven itself to be a conservative constituency, which is one of the reasons that the Left has always had a tenuous relationship with farmers' movements. The fury of indebted farmers surfaces across history, holding within it the revolutionary potential so envied by the Left, and yet also carrying the bedrock of rural feudalism that has always flummoxed it. At its heart, the farmers' cause strikes a universal gong of concern, but the paradox—of being conservative and radically revolutionary at the same time—has yet to be properly understood by a steady political ally. It is the reason why the farmers' movement in present-day India continues to be divided sharply along political lines. I sought to explore the many shades of puritanism that springs out of a deeply felt relationship with one's land.

I spent one chatty afternoon in early 2024 with Madhu Iyengar, an organic farmer in HD Kote (an hour away from Mysore), gazing upon a few modestly bountiful acres while lazing on the wide veranda of his farmhouse. Madhu was kind enough to let me borrow a couple of books from his heaving shelf, one of which was a collection of essays by the novelist and farmer Wendell Berry, who belongs to that fine American tradition of nature-lovers, passionate critics of the fast life, which began with Thoreau and Emerson in the nineteenth century. Berry wrote prolifically throughout the last few decades of the twentieth century, and what animates the bulk of his literary universe is the responsibility a writer owes to his native soil, a moral debt that expressed itself in action through Berry's environmental activism as well. Madhu had highlighted a few notable sections from an essay titled 'The Pleasures of Eating'.[13]

> The industrial eater is one who does not know that eating is an agricultural act, who no longer knows or imagines the connections between eating and the land, and who is therefore necessarily passive and uncritical—in short, a victim.
>
> Our kitchens and other eating places more and more resemble filling stations, as our homes more and more resemble motels.

Later in the essay, Berry does not flinch from connecting his distaste for the American industrial complex to the most inhuman manifestations of modern 'rationality':

> I like to eat vegetables and fruits that I know have lived happily and healthily in good soil, not the products of the huge, bechemicaled factory-fields that I have seen, for example, in the Central Valley of California. The industrial farm is said to have been patterned on the factory production line. In practice, it looks more like a concentration camp.

The dominant argument at present seems to be that science learns from its own excesses, *true* science that is, and the very idea of simplistically drawing a natural/chemical boundary is often counterproductive. Which chemical in what context and in what proportion is the crucial question. Arguably, it is a similar anxiety over external intrusions that propels the anti-vaccination movement, for instance, which is quite prevalent in America. In 2015, the politician Robert F. Kennedy (also an environmental activist) proceeded to link vaccines to autism in children (proven to be untrue) and proclaimed: 'They get the shot, that night they have a fever of a hundred and three, they go to sleep, and three months later their brain is gone. This is a holocaust, what this is doing to our country.'

The graceful traditionalism of Berry and his generation has been superseded by unruly conservatism propelled by the mushroom cloud of disinformation that has enveloped modern society. Here too, in India, political discourse has been stultified by the emergence of a brawl culture that seeks, above all, to diss and dismiss.

An hour into my conversation with Madhu, both of us sensed that a battle was brewing. His perspective was clearly that of provocative conservatism, in lockstep with the present zeitgeist. He spoke to me appreciatively of the Modi government's attempted 2020 farm reforms. Farmers around the country would have benefited from the chance to sell their wares to private players, he said. The conversation inevitably expanded into a politico-religious one, and he conceded that the present spokespersons of the Hindu Right were mostly of the impetuous and reactionary variety. He told me how Sadhguru's Isha Foundation had contacted him in order to take credit for the trees growing on his farm as part of their misguided project to rejuvenate the Kaveri. Kalla kalla ne, *A crook is a crook*, he averred. However, he maintained that this entire political environment was a necessary corrective to decades of Left domination: 'At least now we are starting to think that there was something valuable in our past.'

A brief primer on the present moment in the farmers' movement in India would be instructive at this point. The movement assumed its grandest proportions during the pandemic, when kisans from Punjab sieged Delhi for a year—the largest popular mobilisation in recorded history. The BJP's farm reforms were meant to enhance corporatisation of the agri-business industry, and streamline *contract farming*. The Union government had broken precedent by legislating authoritatively on agriculture, which is a *state* subject, and had flagrantly bulldozed three bills through the Rajya Sabha, without brooking any debate or allowing the opposition to air its views. The movement against the bills was instinctively wary of being exposed to the whims of corporations, which they predicted would quickly begin dictating terms and monopolise the agricultural sector. The failures of privatised agri-business (as witnessed in Bihar after the abolition of the mandi system, for instance[14]) in many parts of the country, where market prices had become increasingly unpredictable, also contributed to this unrest and lack of trust. Just like the dreams of Banker Margayya, which this section began with, the corporate caste has been yearning for a whiff of wealth at its purest source. At a time when market competition—and this is what capitalism was supposed to be a champion of—has largely devolved into the dominance of a few oligarchs who believe in buying up all their competitors, it is safe to say that the farmers' worries are not misplaced. Farmers from across South India, though not with the same intensity, also staged numerous protests; some even travelled to Delhi to express solidarity.[15] In 2024, kisans from Punjab again marched to Delhi demanding the implementation of a Minimum Support Price as recommended by the M.S. Swaminathan Report, and were again met with brutal State repression.

Another theme that comes out strongly in Wendel Berry's essays is his desire to restore a lost sense of community caused by mass exodus from the countryside. Something similar has been happening in India over the last few decades. As I sat speaking to Madhu Iyengar, his ten-year-old daughter tended to a calf, ran around energetically fetching stuff and swung merrily on a knotted rope hanging from a tree. For the last two years, they have been living in Mysore, close to Madhu's aged mother, and the farm has become more of a weekend retreat:

> Evenings are difficult for her [his daughter]. It becomes lonely. She prefers the city these days, because she has now got used to friends, you know? But this upbringing will stay with her, I think. Someday, in the future, all this will come back to her, in some way.

Wendel Berry's tradition of environmentalists had celebrated the beauty (and necessity) of common lands while still enjoying the earthly pleasure of mastering oneself and one's craft in one's own corner of the world. Perhaps these common landscapes that are vital for sustaining communities can make for interesting experiments when linked with agriculture as it stands today. Imagine a community-owned farm, where everybody owns a bit of everything, and the burden of landowning has been shared. Private ownership of homes combined with a trusteeship, or equal share-holding, of common lands. Diverse crops are grown by the community, and a human economy of local trade is allowed to flourish. These communities would be more secure and thus more productive. Tubers could be exchanged for gossipy rumours, cucumbers for a bottle of summer burns cream, and perhaps one part of the land doubles up as a cricket field for the young ones. Local markets would be linked to the global sphere, but only the surplus would be shipped for profit, the essentials distributed within the community itself, where fine schools and hospitals could allow both the young and the elderly to live without deprivation. Such endeavours would need subsidies and incentives from the State to begin with, but they would slowly outleap the necessity of such intervention. Meaningful community-building in the rural landscape, which requires less money but more spirit, could potentially fetch a party both moral and electoral victories. Sadly, extrapolation from the present situation predicts only further land degradation and food insecurity—yields per hectare have been decreasing across the country, parallelly with rapidly depleting groundwater levels. The expert consensus is that the shift away from sprawling monocultures must be ushered in immediately.[16]

The necessary foundations for polycultural changes are already being laid. 'Wake up before dawn, walk around in your farm all day, eat healthy produce only from your farm and you will live a long, fulfilling life,' submits Thammayya, a septuagenarian farmer and landscape regenerator who has gone viral on YouTube for being a walking horticultural encyclopaedia. Those of Thammayya's disposition will maintain that all your latest technological solutions will be useful only in the service of an intuitive understanding of land and its mysteries. A good servant, but a bad master. He is not taken by the high-flying acrobatics of drone technology.

Thammayya is today much sought after for taking up one-acre plots of barren land and repopulating them with rich, multilayered, time-tested ecosystems of plants and trees. His father was a 'chemical fertiliser man' until 1983, after which Thammayya has only followed organic farming. The word 'thota' (which means farm, but is closer to a self-sustaining forest of various species than a piece of mono-cropped land that must be tilled regularly) is his favourite word, which he pronounces most pleasurably with a porcine, nasal emphasis on the *tho*:

> There is a gaade [proverb] that my mother always brought up. If you want to be happy for a moment, have a good meal. If you want to be happy for one day, get married. If you want to be happy all your life, you need to create a thota.

These days, many city dwellers have been seeking out his expertise to transform lands they own in the countryside into fertile, therapeutic thotas. Thammayya lends his services pro bono, because he wants to usher in a new revolution in organic farming. A cultural shift unbound by connections to State or market. Demonstrating how he transformed an empty plot belonging to one of his 'clients' into a veritable forest farm in less than a year, he muses:

> See, in the future, you might be able to get employment, money and all that, but good health will be difficult to find. For that, you need healthy food and healthy land. Nowadays we are seeing how even ten-year-olds are getting BP, sugar, liver disease and all that you

> know? So many diseases. So, people are getting attracted towards the idea of having a small thota that they can come and spend time in. I don't charge any money for my consultations. If I see that someone is serious, I support them fully, because so many educated people from cities are coming to agriculture now. Our traditional farmers have become fed up—they are rejecting it and going to settle down in Mysore or Bangalore. But when you see these people coming from cities, it can serve as an example, no? Another tendency these days is to say agriculture itself is loss-making, and to sit down with resignation. Forty years ago, when organic farming arrived, they used to call us fools. Nowadays also, I tell people not to mention my name, because they will take them also to be a fool by association, eh, haha. So, everyone should come towards the countryside. When they come, there are simple paths that can be followed. It is not very difficult. But this land [referring to the client's one-acre plot] has a punya—it will never have to drink poison. Because they are indebted to this land, they have helped me help them transform this land.[17]

He proudly showcases how he has planted one row of *Gliricidia* (an exotic tree species), one row of agase (flawseed), one row of drumstick—1,500 of each in a one-acre farm, which will, over the course of the next few years, provide a natural source for oxygen, nitrogen, phosphorus and potash, replenishing the atmosphere and the soil. By then, the hundreds of other plants he has planted will also begin to flourish, and the land will be able to live on its own, without any need of pesticides and other intrusions. Here and there, there are patches of marigolds, which will attract and keep insects busy.

> There are many people who have gone on to do MSc and all, with chemical farming as their foundation. They cannot talk about anything else. This is a shame, but what to do? There are also a lot of scamsters who go around promising people that they will grow their farm on the same basis. My request is please don't pump poison into your soil. All your agricultural courses will teach you to put urea, sulphur, potash, but this kills the land. We need to

> start combating decades of soil pollution by slowly regenerating the landscape, replenishing its carbon …

Thammayya does not take well to State prescriptions, and prefers to be master of his own domain. Food security and financial concerns need not be antithetical to each other, he argues, as do many other farmers around the state who are opting out of monocropping and instead investing in small multilayer farms that are designed to keep yielding harvests throughout the year:

> Now, your companies, your government, ask you to grow capsicum. If you do that, who profits? The seeds are theirs, you have to spray the fertiliser they give you, and you have to sell it to them only. Only they profit. And if you eat this, you often get diseases. Why don't they promote horsegram? Because we have our own seeds. No diseases accrue to it. It is quite healthy.

In another video, he takes a tour around his own private farm, demonstrating how dry husks and assorted branches and leaves can become valuable fertiliser. Thammayya also makes natural pesticide himself, which he distributes to others in his circles. Opening a large blue can swirling with brown liquid, he says: 'This is Gokrupa Amrutham. We also call it [bacterial] culture. In it: 1 litre culture, 2 kg jaggery, 1 litre buttermilk sourced from a desi cow. The culture comes from Kaneri matha in Maharashtra. We spray this onto the leaves. There are no side effects, only side benefits.' Organic fertiliser formulations known as Jeevamrutha and Gokrupa Amrutham are made from this culture, and they contribute to restoring micro-flora in the farm environment. It takes time, effort and skill to get a farm to become organically self-sufficient, and oftentimes this might put off a farmer keen on immediate returns.

In a documentary book published in 2019,[18] I encountered tens of tales showcasing how ingenious farmers in Karnataka have adopted the natural farming methods of the agriculturist Subhas Palekar to overcome water challenges, pressures of impending loans and rising land degradation. Indeed, many are determined to keep at it, because the lifestyle *can* be sustainable and rewarding. Books and role models on YouTube abound, and information is always just a click or a phone call away.

Abhishek, a farmer in Parkala, the village where I live, has been farming organically for many years now. A couple of years ago, he had taken on lease a fifty-acre farmland in a much more remote village a few miles away, which housed a massive lake within its perimeter. Areca, coconut and chikoo trees grew bountifully there, and held promise of reliable harvests every year. He started growing other vegetables too, but the finances never worked out; he has now shifted to a smaller group of farms. There were other problems as well: 'My neighbour was using chemical fertilisers, and this eventually seeped into the lake, and into my farm as well. So, the organic movement can never be started individually. It has to be a collective, community shift, otherwise it will never work.' He too, like Madhu Iyengar, defended the 2020 farm laws, and the attendant political climate which had created it.

In fact, as I debated with him, questions of imminent corporate domination and the capture of the agri-market by wildly fluctuating market prices were quickly replaced by heated discussions on Hindutva politics, which had his firm stamp of approval. He told me that he had been attracted to the Left in his youth, but he was now convinced that such labels were foreign interventions that made no sense in India, which has always been a culturally centrist land. He casually dismissed the whole mass of protesting farmers in Delhi as 'foreign-funded' 'non-farmers' peddling larger geopolitical concerns rather than real issues of the land. It was another avatar of the anxiety of foreign infiltration, which seems to be the flavour of the globe at the moment. After a few exchanges, he conceded that if corporate domination did end up monopolising agriculture, it would be a sorry result. He maintained confidently, though, that this kind of monopolisation was impossible in a country with as diverse a crop base as India, and as accommodating a spiritual ethos as espoused by its religio-political overlords.

IV

The man in front of me was snoring loudly. A woman next to me was chatting away on her phone. I didn't feel like disturbing either of them. A play—titled *Direct Action*—was unfolding on the big stage in Kalamandira, Mysore, meant as a tribute to M.D. Nanjundaswamy, a champion of direct democracy. For the most part, it involved a juvenile screenplay and repetitive sloganeering, reminding me of annual-day plays we'd put up in high school on that very stage years ago. Still, it was nostalgic enough for the crowd—tens of farmers, all wearing green shawls—to erupt into laughs and cheers every now and then. I wasn't able to summon laughter, and the play, being largely hagiographical, wasn't very thought-provoking either. It ended up conveying a few broad imports of what the farmers' movement under Nanjundaswamy had done: fighting against the raw power of the police state and its loan-extracting apparatus, demonstrating against the rapacity of multinational companies out to capture the seed markets of indigenous farmers across the world. Once, Nanjundaswamy had gathered thousands of protestors outside the state secretariat to laugh in unison in a bid to shame their overlords. He had led his followers in an attack on the KFC building in Bangalore during the nineties, and for a brief moment, it had seemed like they were part of a coordinated global movement against debt-inducing foreign interventions in local agriculture. Nanjundaswamy himself comes off as a singularly goal-oriented leader. When a reporter character in the play questions Nanjundaswamy on his authoritarian streak, his character responds, 'Well if it was really so, would there be independent-thinking people critiquing me?'

The whole production seemed symbolic of the low ebb that farmers' mobilisation had reached in Karnataka. The play toured Karnataka in January of 2024, performing in many other cities, with the fine intention of rejuvenating a fallen farmers' movement. But it did seem like the makers of the play had jumped directly into action without appropriate direction. It was around the same time that I asked Aiyshwarya Mahadev about how much clout farmers' organisations today really hold.

> Back in the day, they had a large social responsibility. In some villages. Raitha Sangha was so strong, they would have their own prohibition, and you couldn't bring alcohol into this village unless the elders of the village affirmed the decision. The Raitha Sangha today is pretty much non-existent. They are basically like Stree Shakti Sanghas, they are pressure groups, when it comes to vote banks. That's it. They're an *ideal*, at best. I don't see how they are helping anybody at the end of it. They had far more bargaining power, but now they don't. But that's also because that sort of dependence on the Sangha came down. Lack of education used to be one of those big things before. But now, as you see, everybody has a rudimentary education. And the minute the leaders degrade, *and these are undoubtedly leader-based movements*, things change. Some of the older leaders—Nanjundaswamy, Rudrappa, Puttannaiah—the way they would speak, the way they would rally, they could bring governments to the ground. And politics of that day, for example, whether it is Ramakrishna Hegde, Devaraj Urs, J.H. Patel or Veerendra Patil, all of them were politicians conscious of pressure groups, they were very conscious of doing right by farmers. And that's because voters were also more conscious, the opposition would keep the pressure going. All that is eroded today. And the loser at the end of the day is the poor farmer, right?

The comparison to Stree Shakti Sanghas is interesting, because the farmers' movements of post-1970s India, rebelling against the West-driven agendas of the Green Revolution, had also been influenced by a new flavour of ecofeminism (exemplified by Vandana Shiva) that pushed back against modern science by seeing traditional farming (bereft of masculine Western influence) as an organic, feminine, desi alternative.[19] Yet, such blanket critiques masked the realities of patriarchy embedded in rural India, and the cultural disempowerment that women have been enduring for centuries.

It is not hard to see a strong strain of this male domination within the farmers' movement itself. Female leaders have been too few and far between. Nanjundaswamy has been strongly critiqued for assuming too much authority within the Raitha Sangha, and for doing precious little to foster leadership at the local level. Many were kicked out of the organisation and his good books for fomenting debate and voicing concerns. Leaders can make *and* break movements; one always wonders how history would have shaped up had someone else taken on the mantle. As I was watching *Direct Action*, I pondered (out of boredom, more than anything) what it would look like if the protagonist of the play had been the farmers' leader Kadidal Shamanna instead. It sure would have been jollier.

He was a multifaceted man: a talented photographer, a passionate musician who had once apprenticed under the sarod maestro Ustad Ali Akbar Khan, a gifted comedian, a connoisseur of antique motorcycles and a spirited social activist with that rare quality of indiscriminate compassion. Born in the small town of Kadidalu in Shimoga district, Shamanna spent his youth in the hilly, picturesque regions of Malnad, growing up in an environment of boyish mischief and adventure. His early friendship with Poornachandra Tejaswi prompted him to move to Mysore to pursue his studies, and the rest, as they say, is *geography*. Mysore's unique intellectual climate and cultural topology went on to define the formative years of Shamanna's life. In the early sixties, as he was studying in Maharaja's College along with Tejaswi, he found himself sitting in on coffee house poetry sessions chaired by the likes of Gopalakrishna Adiga and U.R. Ananthamurthy, partaking of the city's rich music scene and slowly internalising the progressive worldviews of the new generation of thinkers he was an integral part of. By the second half of the sixties, his transformation into a committed social worker was complete, and Shamanna moved to Shimoga to teach in a school. He had plans of cultivating a farm alongside his day job, but the idealistic Gopala Gowda Shantaveri dissuaded him from doing so by pointing out that holding two professions would mean that he was depriving someone else of an honest job. Thus, by the early seventies, Shamanna had moved to a small Malnad village along with his wife, where he began living as a full-time farmer. Around this time, he became active in the socialist politics of Shimoga, where the roots of the farmers' movement may be discovered.

Shamanna exemplified the figure of the austere socialist. His investment in the farmers' movement stemmed largely from his own personal struggles as a man tilling his own land. For a few years of his adult life, he lived in a humble hut on his farm in Bhagavatikere, his frugality astounding even his closest friends. There is a story that, one night, when Tejaswi and Lankesh were visiting Shamanna, Tejaswi's hand got stuck in a large rathole in the ground where he was sleeping. After extricating it with great difficulty, Tejaswi calmed down. But Lankesh, who had been stirred into stressful wakefulness, refused to sleep in what he perceived as conditions of poverty-stricken squalor. He went on to spend the night outside in Tejaswi's jeep. This integrity and strength of character in the face of adversity is what made Shamanna an immensely beloved figure across circles.

Kadidal Shamanna never really picked up the pen with much gusto. He wrote a few articles for *Lankesh Patrike* during the eighties, and his memoirs were narrated by him orally, which seems fitting, given his reputation as a captivating raconteur. When I began writing this book, I had hoped earnestly to meet and interview him, for I had come to admire his unique, zen-like persona, and the grandfatherly wisdom that animated his memoirs. However, he was an octogenarian by this point, and his brother informed me that Shamanna's memory was not what it used to be, and that meeting him would be a futile endeavour.

In the late eighties, Shamanna had once made a candid statement regarding the KRRS's electoral strategies, and urged them to consider merging with the DSS and other progressive forces to buttress their strength. He'd also used the word 'authoritarian' in a cautiously roundabout way. Nanjundaswamy had found this to be rank insubordination, and expelled Shamanna from the organisation. In response to this, an irate Tejaswi had written, in defence of his best friend:

> A genial temperament, never brooking a quarrel with anyone, and yet possessing a critical quality that made poets tremble with

> fear—these are the characteristics of this great man named Kadidal Shamanna. The reason for Shamanna's terrific reputation is his humour and lovability. It is for this reason that he was thrown out of the Raitha Sangha recently with a unanimous mandate. Any organisation that cannot tolerate Shamanna must necessarily thrive on ideological blindness, emotional fury and fundamentalism of some kind, I submit. If a sense of humour is destroyed in any person or organisation, only braggards emerge.[20]

We arrive at a rather sobering conclusion—that perhaps these mobilising spaces took themselves far too seriously, stripping them of democracy. Centralised authority can hold its own for a brief while, but only by diversifying, democratising and expanding debate can an organisation hope to keep growing. Certainly, the KRRS achieved great feats of mobilisation, bequeathed the legacy of the green shawl and raised the self-respect of farmers by showing them the broader community they could be a part of. It also contributed to the intellectual space that would help take the anti-corporation, socialist, pro-farmer ideology to the national and global levels. In his earthy monotone, H.D. Deve Gowda had delivered well-researched speeches in the parliament during the nineties, raging against Manmohan Singh for being blind to rural realities, quoting the economist Wilhem Steinitz to demonstrate the ill effects of globalisation on the farm sector, and arguing for the same talking points that the KRRS also stood for.[21] Punjabis had even named a paddy variety 'Dev Gowda', showing deep affection for his farmer-friendly rhetoric that had fetched them an attractive MSP for rice. Meanwhile, at the grassroots level, Nanjundaswamy's academic acumen, his knowledge of international law and his powerful speeches had been important in jumpstarting nuanced dialogues. Seen this way, Karnataka's contribution to the debates on agriculture look second to none. It all seemed to hold such potential. Why then has the raw bargaining power of rural Karnataka, and rural India by extension, been unable to generate a truly pan-Indian political presence?

A key problem seems to be that the politics around the farming sector is today shorn of all nuance. Its eyeball-to-eyeball battles of mobilisation lead to naive political allegiances as well. Aiyshwarya Mahadev had some interesting observations regarding the optics around farmers' movements and why the political sensationalism might actually be corroding their true potential.

> AM: The biggest problem is that agriculture and farmers are the holy cow [for politicians] in this country. You can't touch them. Look at Maharashtra. From Vidarbha to Satara to everywhere, the farmers are poor though they hold the capital to everything—from your cooperative politics to the farmers' unions. They are all still poor because their lands are basically beyond redemption, but nobody's going to touch the issue because they are too scared. It is the same with us too. If you go tell people not to grow something because its water-intensive, who's going to vote for you?
>
> Me: Hmmm. Political optics might be one half of the reason. What about the executive and bureaucracy? Would you say that the executive has become more strapped by the legislature?
>
> AM: Perhaps. But the executive is also a big gatekeeper. They don't care what dispensation there is. They are also looking for what they can walk out with. Today, it is not just IAS officers, if a class-one contractor or an executive engineer can be caught with 40 crores, are you saying the system is clean at any point? The sort of money these people make out of everything! I don't think the government or legislature has enough control over the executive. The politicians are just the fall guys at the end for it. If the politicians do not keep a close watch, the executive will throw you under the bus, and make more than a buck for it. I am seeing this right in front of my eyes. Corruption has become thoroughly legitimised—it's like a convenience fee or something.

I agreed with her that the bureaucratic arm is rarely strung up by the media for its failures. Aiyshwarya then went on to explain how cooperative banks perpetuate the indebtedness of farmers, and how crores are spent to ensure that one manages to win internal elections to become presidents of these banks, and their satellite credit associations.

What of the institutions that are supposed to keep a check on these exorbitant expenses? She thinks they are doing okay, but also laughs and brings up a recent incident where the Lokayukta (Ombudsman) went to raid a tehsildar's office in Yelahanka, Bangalore, but failed to meet the man because he was busy playing cricket in the backyard. She sees everything eventually reaching a boiling point, when change will be as inevitable as a summer bath:

> I think the will to change entrenched, parochial systems is the least when it comes to the political sphere. It is an old boys' club, it is patriarchy through and through. Politics is the last when it comes to adapting to change. There is a lot of inertia. I don't see change coming from politics anymore. I see it coming from society. For example, there are villagers that boycott leaders. They don't allow them to come in. Things like that create social pressure and also a pressure on the esteem and privilege of a politician. Sometimes, this pressure works. This will happen in the villages rather than the cities, where they just live within their four walls. *Whatever revolution will come will be silent, and it will come from the villages.*

V

> In being born, every being is born as debt owed to the gods, the saints, the fathers and to men. If one makes a sacrifice, it is because of a debt owing to the gods from birth … If one recites a sacred text, it is because of a debt owing to the saints … If one wishes for offspring, it is because of a debt due to the fathers from birth … And if one gives hospitality, it is because it is a debt owing to men.
>
> —*Shatapatha Brahmana* (circa 1000 BCE)

> Free your mind of the idea of deserving, of the idea of earning, and you will begin to be able to think.
>
> —Ursula K. Le Guin, *The Dispossessed*

In Besagarahalli Ramanna's 1965 short story 'Suggi' (Harvest), we enter a homestead busy harvesting rice during the winter. Work is hard enough without the sword of Damocles hanging over everyone's heads—the younger brother is determined to split the property into two and grab his rightful share. The older brother's pregnant wife, who has been made the scapegoat of this dispute, begs her husband to stop this, or else she will forever be known as a home-breaker. The poor woman is pushed violently in this heated altercation, and she falls on the bricks readied for building a wall to divide the compound. The story ends rather melodramatically with the two brothers reconciling, and the woman delivering a healthy male baby. The effect in the end is to collapse the harvest and the baby into the same category: fertility is what keeps agriculture and family going. Yet, despite the centrality of women's labour (in many senses) to the whole culture, she remains a secondary character who can be pushed around and dominated—until a male child is born and redeems her existence.

There have been some powerful studies that demonstrate how the burden of feudal oppression and caste society has always come down the hardest on women. Their sequestration has been linked to a changing sense of 'honour' on the part of men, represented well by the squabbling brothers in 'Suggi'. It is a fundamental unit of sociology—the organisation of the *family* in what we may call the Ordinary Social Life—that reflects the fate of society at large as well. The anthropologist David Graeber, in his magnum opus *Debt: The First Five Thousand Years*, captures the many dimensions—historical, economic, social—of this oppression, thus:

> In India, the caste system allowed what were otherwise differences between rich and poor to be made formal and explicit. Brahmins and other members of the upper castes jealously sequestered their daughters, and married them off with lavish dowries,[22] while the lower castes practiced brideprice, allowing members of the higher castes to scoff at them for selling their daughters. The twice-born were likewise largely protected from falling into debt bondage, while for much of the rural poor, debt dependency was institutionalised,

> with the daughters of poor debtors, predictably, often dispatched to brothels or to the kitchens or laundries of the rich. In either case, between the push of commoditization, which fell disproportionately on daughters, and the pull of those trying to reassert patriarchal rights to 'protect' women from any suggestion that they might be commoditized, women's formal and practical freedoms appear to have been gradually but increasingly restricted and effaced. As a result, notions of honor changed too, becoming a kind of protest against the implications of the market, even as at the same time (like the world religions) they came to echo that market logic in endless subtle ways.

It must be recognised that there were several matrilineal societies in South India, but this is rarely the equivalent of a 'matriarchy'.[23] There are also examples of brahmins practising bride price and bucking the trend. In the Konkan, they continued the practice until the Peshwas forbade them from doing so because it was not mandated by the shastras.

The overwhelming scholarly consensus is that economic disenfranchisement of women was inextricably tied up with caste and endogamy. Wendy Doniger writes about how the same theme may be understood culturally:

> For example, if we take a folktale originally told, in Telugu, by a caste of traders and merchants who were 'left hand' (unclean, lower caste), and compare it with the same tale retold, in a Sanskrit Purana, by the same caste when it has moved to the status of Vaishyas, some things change: In the folk version, the woman protagonist makes decisions for herself as well as for the caste, which in the Sanskrit version, the Brahmin priest makes all the decisions ... Sometimes the value system survives the journey, like a wine that travels well, and sometimes it does not.[24]

This corrosive patriarchal hierarchy penetrated the entire caste order, and the entire subcontinent. More devastatingly, it persuaded women themselves to abide by its diktats, establishing a cultural hegemony that kept reinforcing itself. It encourages the assertion that the contested word brahminism can actually be substituted with 'patriarchy' in many contexts without much loss of meaning, and can simplify social-justice arguments in political environments where nuance is difficult to incorporate. What I am trying to suggest is that a new political ideology (maybe a new party?) with feminism as its primary mascot can make a radically compelling case in its manifesto, backed by historical veracity, breaking across religious and caste boundaries.[25]

Change has only just begun to arrive. A study conducted in 2017 estimated that there are over 100,000 women sex workers in Karnataka, concentrated primarily in Bangalore and North Karnataka. More than half the women were married before the age of eighteen, and their husbands had either died, left them or were actively complicit in pushing them into prostitution. A majority of them were from lower castes, and a shocking finding was also that unmarried women formed only 6 per cent of the whole, which must force us to reconsider the repercussions of mandatory marriage. Half of these women had been sold for prices ranging from Rs 5,000 to 15,000, and around 60 per cent of the sex workers only managed to earn up to Rs 5,000 a month.[26] Many of the workers who migrate to Bangalore do so from rural hinterlands of North Karnataka, where drought is frequent and rain is proving ever more unreliable.

In much of contemporary Kannada theatre, especially Company Natakas that perform in North Karnataka dialects, I noticed the prevalence of a very specific character—a strong, independent woman who keeps berating her hapless husband, and is vocal in her yearning for active romance, often outside her flailing marriage.[27] You can see such a character in Jevargi Rajanna's viral play *Kunta Kona Mooka Jaana* (The lame one is crooked, the dumb one is wise), many versions of which are available on YouTube. The trope was popularised first by Umashree, a versatile Kannada film actor of enormous talent who became famous mostly for her comedy acts. Humour is a subtle, yet powerful, reservoir of social undercurrents. The popularity of this particular trope suggests that there is an underreported crisis of masculinity that is finding other vacuums to disappear into. The family as a social unit grew stronger and stronger for many centuries, until the nuclear age arrived and split the scene into its most basic unit. Burdens once divided were now to be shouldered single-handedly. Is it any wonder that the search for a larger family gripped Basavarajappa's life and continues to? Is it surprising that some seek a still greater sense of family at the pulpit of cultural nationalism?

As always, we must turn to history for the contexts that may illuminate this phenomenon. David Graeber's study of the history of the debt devotes a considerable number of pages to ancient India. After reflecting on the idea of debt in the Shatapatha Brahmana (the excerpt that begins this section), Graeber acknowledges that we know almost nothing of the society in which they were crafted, and he takes the liberty of arguing that 'the authors of the Brahmanas are offering a quite sophisticated reflection on a moral question that no one has really ever been able to answer any better before or since'. By recognising that there can be no real way to pay off one's debt to society, 'perhaps what the authors of the Brahmanas were really demonstrating was that, in the final analysis, our relation with the cosmos is ultimately nothing like a commercial transaction'. Is it possible then to have a Hindu Right that dissociates from hulking corporations exacerbating debt bondage and seeks refuge in the financial humanism of its oldest elders? Seems unlikely.

The centuries that succeeded the Shatapatha Brahmana also saw the creation of the Upanishads and the birth of the Buddha, whose contemporaries included Confucius in China and Pythagoras in Greece. This unprecedented cultural renaissance was accompanied by the birth of coinage, the first purpose of which was to sustain armies. Then came the rise of the Mauryan Empire that assimilated the small republics of the Gangetic plains and created a massive kingdom built on expansionism and armed power. The collapse of the Mauryan empire gave way to a succession of weaker and mostly smaller states, even as Buddhism took root and began to spread to the rest of South Asia. The decline of massive armies eventually led to the near disappearance of coinage, but also to a 'veritable efflorescence of increasingly sophisticated forms of credit'. Credit, of course, is the oldest form of money, and this was merely its latest renewal.

As coinage began to go out of circulation in medieval India, metal stayed put, awaiting deployment. A vast majority of it ended up in religious establishments, monasteries and temples; above all it was shaped into images of gods. This is also one reason why religious establishments were generally on top of the to-do list of invaders and marauders. In other words, when coinage began running out, credit systems centred in religious establishments began to emerge as major power centres. When Vijay Mallya donated gold doors worth Rs 80 lakh to the Kukke Subrahmanya temple in 2012, even as he was drowning in debt, he was being wishful, yes, but was also unconsciously and cosmically rhyming with the history of the land. So too seems to have been the practice of made snana—lower-caste devotees rolling over the leftovers of brahmin-meals to cure skin diseases and infertility—which had continued in that temple, even though the state government had banned the practice in 2010. Equally natural, though more surprising, is the fact that activists from adivasi castes protested against the ban, arguing that the practice was sacred for them, and requested the state to allow it to continue. It was the same argument that Ananthamurthy had held up when he had defended the practice of nude worship in Chandragutti (involving women mostly) during the 1980s, saying it was a voluntary religious practice. He had backtracked on this later. I was surprised to hear the dalit activist H. Govindaiah tell me that he agreed with Ananthamurthy's original statement. In fact, he argued that dalits were more 'spiritual' than any other community, and that this was his thesis for why they were historically sidelined—their raw belief in religious rituals threatened to overcome the belief hegemony of the prevailing orthodoxy. This Gandhian utopianism (encapsulated in the term 'Harijan') is not quite borne out by history.

When the Dharma Shastras, Hindu law codes, were being fashioned between 200 BCE and 400 CE, they were historically quite remarkable, and Graeber observes that 'Hindu law of that time was far more humane than almost anything found in the ancient world. Debtors were not, generally speaking, reduced to slavery, and there is no widespread evidence of the selling of women and children.' Over the next thousand years, much changed. The debt to the cosmos and the gods would be conveniently replaced by a debt to men, very particular men.[28] While earlier codes had imposed conditions on castes (such as the rule that brahmins could never lend money), it was slowly eroded away by succeeding elites, who began consolidating their moneyed positions. As castes began to try and inch upwards, which was often in the aftermath of war, famine or extreme events that violently displaced people from one context into another, they began securing for themselves the next best seat at the table, and prestige and honour was always at the expense of those left behind. While the castes in the middle battled on ambiguous terrain, the extremities of caste hierarchy were defined through direct opposition and contrast.

In R.K. Narayan's 1958 novel, *The Financial Expert*, we meet Banker Margayya, a small-time aspirant trying to make it as a middleman navigating loans for Malgudi's peasants. The endeavour fails after his naughty son throws his accounts book into the drain, following which Margayya grudgingly conducts an elaborate propitiation ceremony as prescribed by a temple priest. Soon, as if by divine providence, he meets a journalist who gifts him a book on the science of sex, which Margayya publishes at his own expense, making him a wealthy fellow. Later, we learn that Margayya hailed from a caste of cremators, who had slowly become agriculturists over the course of two upwardly mobile generations. He is anxious to prevent this fact from surfacing and haunting his son's marital prospects. But more than anything, he is steadfast in his own desire for wealth, which Narayan describes most interestingly:

> A rich man, according to his view, was just one caste below the man of wealth. Riches any hardworking fool could attain by some watchfulness, while acquiring wealth was an extraordinarily

> specialised job. It came to persons who had on them the grace of the Goddess fully and who could use their wits. He was a specialist in money and his mind always ran on lines of scientific inquiry whenever money came in question. He differentiated with great subtlety between money, riches, wealth, and fortune. It was most important people should not mistake one for the other.

When his son struggles with schoolwork, Margayya tells the boy to become devoted to Goddess Saraswathi, explaining how devotion and belief had helped him in his own business interests. His son immediately erupts: 'I know it is a different goddess you worshipped. It is that Goddess Lakshmi. I know all that from mother.'

That divisive note reminded me of D.R. Nagaraj's reflections on Lakshmi's symbolic significance in medieval Karnataka, which he reads in many of Allama Prabhu's vachanas. Allama Prabhu harbours open resentment against the 'elders' of tradition, who are 'gatekeepers of Lakshmi', whereas the general tendency within Indian philosophy is to lovingly critique one's forebears, if at all. The salutations to Goddess Lakshmi appear across courtly Kannada literature—from Pampa to Ranna—and Nagaraj sums all this up by concluding: 'Contemporary anthropological research into the nature of kingship provides support to my argument that Lakshmi is a metaphor for power. The gist of the argument is that royal power creates and enhances its charisma through charity and gift-giving. Charisma is the basis of power, and rulers in medieval India relied on donatives, land endowments, baksheesh and all sorts of gifts. Thus, the charisma of any material or worldly power in medieval Karnataka rested on its charitable endowments. In particular, charity to religious institutions was the basis of worldly affairs. There are several inscriptions[29] in Belligavi[30] from Allama Prabhu's time which support this argument.'[31]

This reverence for charity—a kind of medieval socialism—continues to influence present-day politics too, though it holds diminishing returns. When I questioned Aiyshwarya Mahadev on the rationale behind the five Congress guarantees that won them the 2023 assembly elections, she told me that free bus rides for women was her personal favourite scheme, as she sees everyday instances of how this had really empowered rural women to head out of their homes. She felt that, while loan waivers for farmers are a humanitarian necessity in times of natural peril, they are more akin to a band-aid rather than a genuinely healing force during other times. On the other hand, free electricity and women's empowerment programmes are more universal and carry broader appeal, she argued. I had imagined the guarantees to be mostly election gimmicks, but they turned out to be much less arbitrary. What is also true is that the BJP regime at the Centre, by neglecting education and health, has thrived on a paternalistic labharthi model that seeks to grant social securities, though it has vastly exaggerated its own achievements.[32]

Jumping to the beginning to the twentieth century, we meet Haji Abdullah, who founded Corporation Bank in Udupi in 1906, and is remembered even today as one of the city's greatest pioneers, famed for his charity. Presently, the Udupi matha is enriched by bountiful donations from around the world, but it had very few sources of revenue back then. Haji Abdullah had contributed to renovating and restructuring the establishment from his own coffers. Once, he had ensured that oil, wicks and lamps were promptly supplied from his own stores to the Udupi matha for its deepotsava celebrations after a rainstorm wrecked all their preparations.

Back then, there were not many Muslims living in Udupi, and even Abdullah's family originally hailed from Junagadh in Gujarat. Inheritor of over 700 acres of land, Abdullah was a trader who exported perfumed oil, dry fish and rice. When the British snatched away rice supplies from the farmers of Udupi during the First World War, Haji Abdullah imported rice from Burma at his own expense, and donated it to the starving masses. On his way back from Haj in the 1910s, he stopped in Mauritius and grew impressed by their sugarcane farming. He went on to introduce Mauritius sugarcane varieties to Udupi, which gave the local economy a colourful boost.

Abdullah was a dedicated follower of Kemal Ataturk, and his own social vision was secular, progressive and all-embracing. When Gandhi visited Udupi in 1934 as part of his campaign against untouchability, he did not visit the Udupi matha because it did not allow dalits entry. Instead, he broke bread with Haji Abdullah, who was the head of his welcome party, and who many years earlier had started a school for dalits in Udupi on his own lands. It had created a big flutter in town.

By this time, Haji Abdullah had been facing serious bankruptcy issues owing to the fact that three of his trading vessels had perished in the Indian Ocean on the way to Sri Lanka. His own brainchild, Corporation Bank, tightened the screws on loans he had taken, and the once regal man was forced to sell off his assets one by one, falling into grave debt. One morning in 1935, he was found dead in his manor. Some allege that the stress and angst of being betrayed by his own brethren, his own bank, had led to his death. The one documentary on Haji Abdullah available on YouTube[33] is appropriately celebratory, and claims that, 'It might not be an exaggeration to say that Haji Abdullah was another Shibi Chakravarty[34] sent down by God to uplift Udupi. He dedicated his entire life to it.' The litterateur Haridasa Bhat once called him 'Akbar of Udupi'. It would seem that some legacies can never be forgotten, they are too powerful. It is also telling that the Muslim orthodoxy in Udupi itself has spent little effort to remember and celebrate the memory of Haji Abdullah, whom they likely see as a betrayer of their faith. Perhaps some intrepid historian can try and track down the history of these many 'betrayals', and help create a fuller picture of twentieth-century South Canara.

In January 2024, saffron flags suffused Udupi, as lamps and diyas commemorated the consecration of the Ram Mandir in Ayodhya; it was a second Diwali of sorts. The craftsman of the Ram Lalla idol—a fifth-generation sculptor named Arun Yogiraj—happens to hail from Mysore, and I tried reaching out to him for an interview. But he was far too busy to entertain yet another nosy journalist. On Twitter, he'd posted a picture of his grandfather presenting an apsara idol to Nehru, and suddenly, I could see Yogiraj's tradition, his craft, his professional ethos, his claim to fame, distilled into a clear line of succession—at once a gift and burden of his past. Around the same time, my grandmother had pressed into my hands a WhatsApp forward she had received, a digital animation of the Ram Lalla idol smiling and moving its eyes. She was terribly excited, and wondered aloud how this was even possible. I tried to explain to her all the modern leaps of technology, but I am not sure if I managed to convey just how dramatically the world around us had mutated.

EIGHT

On Caste, Cultural Activism and Children

> Art is dangerous. It is dangerous, first, because all powerful things can be dangerous; and it is dangerous also because while we tend to venerate art as one great and good thing, its various uses are most often antagonistic: art can dignify and exalt the civilisation that gives it birth and also weaken and destroy it. Art can serve the Revolution or can detach an individual from the struggles of his age, making loyal citizenship appear to him as futile and perverse as revolutionary action.
>
> —Jacques Barzun, *The Use and Abuse of Art*

I

Murali Uncle had unfortunately chosen the wrong time—just a few months before the COVID-19 pandemic hit—to invest a huge sum of money in a sprawling homestay in Coorg. Business was stagnant for the first few months, and it only moderately improved after that. His main clientele was the IT crowd from Bangalore, who arrived here on weekends to relax in his languorous, breathtaking corner of the Western Ghats. A Kannada cine star was also on the list, as were families looking for a no-nonsense, no-party vacation. He would ensure that the ambience was just what each group wanted. I'd visited the place once with my friends in December 2020.

A year and a half later, in the summer of 2022, I rode up to his establishment from Mysore, on the gorgeous green trail through the ghats that R.K. Narayan had once dubbed the Emerald Route in an uncharacteristically dull travelogue of the same name. Snaking my way along dirt paths that had recently witnessed unseasonal showers, I finally arrived at Murali Uncle's retreat. I remembered the portrait of Osho on the security outhouse near the gate from my previous visit. This time though, I was here in working capacity, in search of stories.

C.S. Muralidhara originally hails from the village of Vemgal in Kolar district, and he has lived in Mysore for many years. In his youthful prime, Murali had actively participated in several social movements of the eighties and nineties, building a wide network of friends and fellow travellers. The breadth of his participation is not bound by ideology.

As we sit on the porch, a warm cup of chai in hand, he gazes deep into the distance and reminisces: 'I have seen it all. I used to be with the RSS for a while … you know there were some Hindu–Muslim clashes in Kolar during the eighties? I was with Nanjundaswamy when we threw stones at the KFC building in Bangalore during the early nineties. The dalit leaders in Kolar are very close to me—I used to be a part of their movement also. I had participated in the Appiko [local variant of Chipko] movement in Uttara Kannada as well. The communists spoke of things with such certainty, it put me off. Now, I'm all alone, here.'

As if to demonstrate his credentials, in case I consider him a mere braggart, he starts pulling out phone numbers. He calls up Nanjundaswamy's son, and speaks to him for a brief while. He tries reaching out to Devanura Mahadeva, but only manages to reach his assistant, who promises to pass on the word. Then, he calls up Padmalaya Nagaraj—a senior Dalita Sangharsha Samiti leader from Kolar—with whom he has a long, rambling conversation on speaker, winking at me every now and then.

The conversation begins with memories of a protest march in 1980, which was a response to the brutal killing of a tenant named Sheshagiriyappa. These were times when Devaraj Urs's land reforms were drastically transforming social relations across the rural landscape. In Malur taluk near Kolar, an extremely powerful landlord named Krishnegowda had murdered his tenant, Sheshagiriyappa, for claiming land that was rightfully his. The landlord had also been accused of raping Sheshagiriyappa's daughter Anasuyamma, who became the face of the historical protest that followed. The march exceeded all expectations, rousing righteous anger across Karnataka, and set the pace of the dalit movement in the state for years to come.

Nagaraj: Yes, yes, in every taluk, there are such hard-working people who left their personal lives and built the movement. It was in Malur taluk that it had begun, with the Anasuyamma incident …

Murali: Yes, I remember the song. 'Nanna Tangi Anasuya' [My Little Sister Anasuya].

Nagaraj: Yes, the one written by Kotiganahalli Ramaiah. There must have been at least a thousand people in that march singing it.

Murali: How can I forget? Even we children sang it loudly and came with all of you!

(It struck me that Murali must have been roughly ten years old at the time.)

Murali: I feel that the entire dalit movement in Kolar district revolves around the figure of Kotiganahalli …

Nagaraj: Well, yes, because he was a journalist, he was at the heart of the DSS there—writing songs, writing pamphlets and so on. But you can't single him out and say everything revolved around him. Because there are so many others who have worked just as hard, or even harder, than him.

Murali: But for some reason, their names haven't survived …

Nagaraj: Many have died in obscurity. Some made a name for themselves, some made some money at least. Ernagnalli [audio unclear] Ramachandra has nothing to his name now. He lost his job also.

Murali: What times they were. I remember they used to take me to write graffiti slogans on the walls because I had good handwriting. One of the slogans was: dalitaru endare ella jaatiya badavaru [*dalits are the poor of all castes*]. I'd written that all over Vemgal!

Murali veered the conversation towards nostalgic terrain. For a while, they lived in the eighties again, when people took to the streets for truth and justice, when it had seemed like whole communities were uniting and fighting for a better life. The DSS had seemed so powerful then, and exercised such pressure on the government. But Padmalaya Nagaraj was more concerned with the present predicament:

> Now, everyone is in their own bubble. That feeling of samudaya [community] is gone. Earlier, people would fret if something terrible happened to someone. Now, they rejoice. We would throng jails back then in such numbers. Now, if someone even sees the inside of a cell, he is already seen as a criminal by everyone, his life is over, boom!

Nagaraj went on to explain, with great angst, what his disappointments with the current generation were. In his eyes, they have all disappeared into their smartphones, content to spend their days aimlessly, sheltered under the savings of their parents' generation. They are not interested in the knowledge traditions of their predecessors. *They do not know hunger,* he says. *If only they knew.*

Meanwhile, I was still trying to understand the real significance of the past which Murali and Nagaraj had so indelibly evoked.

> Me: In your personal observation, what are the changes in rural society that the DSS ushered in?

Nagaraj takes a small pause, before launching into this recollection:

> Before the chaluvali started, dalits were living in a state of absolute desolation, where they felt that there was nobody who could resolve their miseries. Suddenly, courage and hope were in the air—we began to feel that there were others who could come to our aid. Most importantly, those like Baragur Ramchandrappa, Siddalingaiah and Devanura Mahadeva impressed upon us the importance of

> education and literacy. If there are so many dalits in government positions today, or those who went on to become lecturers, lawyers, policemen, it is because of the DSS's exhortations. Even in the seventies–eighties, in most villages, dalits were not allowed to wear slippers or dhotis within the village. If they had to travel somewhere, they were supposed to pack them in a bag, go out of the village, and only then wear them. They were not supposed to wear towels on their heads. If there was even a small robbery, they would be tied to a tree and beaten all night. It was the DSS that travelled to every village, and protested against all this. Then, there was bonded labour—that pernicious practice. My father was bonded to a landlord for thirty-two years for the salary of seven rupees a year. I know men of that generation who were bonded for even less—two, three rupees a year. It was unimaginable. Now, we can wear the same clothes as them, like shirts and jeans pants, and we can build our own houses, these are not ordinary developments. Thirty years ago, this would have been impossible. Caste consciousness may have become more marked and fragmented now, but these changes are monumental.
>
> The landlords were never the ones who bred oxen or tilled the land ever. It was the bonded labourers who did all the work. Even if all the rice in their house was grown by the backbreaking labour of the dalits, they would never give any of that rice to them—it was only ragi balls that the dalits received. How cruel that was. And they never gave them milk or curd either. Only saambaar.

After this speech, a deep and yawning pause pushed Murali Uncle to segue into some private jokes and personal gupshup. As the evening sun fully sunk in, a large campfire was kindled, and Murali decided to shift the scene there, casually informing me that he was going to burn a lot of old newspapers and stuff that had been accumulating inside. Half of the lot had already been consigned to the flames. I was aghast. *How old are these papers?* When I heard that they were at least two decades old, I told him I would browse through them once to see if there was something there of value to me. I ended up finding many copies of *Lankesh Patrike* from as far back as the eighties and nineties, and cutouts and snippets from newspapers and

Picchalli Srinivas, a noted singer from Kolar, with a troupe of dalit activists

magazines that Murali had once deemed interesting—all of which felt like a treasure trove to the total Kannada-nut I had become by that point. I also found some excellent samples of Murali's much-coveted calligraphy skills.

Murali spoke of a small school nearby, where he was trying to establish a library for children. 'I want to get children to start enjoying the pleasures of reading.' My thoughts went to the well-curated shelf of books I had seen at the entrance of his room. Later that night, Murali casually informed me that he had some recordings on his laptop that might be useful to me. They were video recordings of an enclave held in Kolar at an institution named Aadima, held under the banner of a Buddhist tradition known as the Achala Guru Parampara, where several dalit writers and intellectuals had delivered speeches. I learnt that it was Kotiganahalli Ramaiah—one of a few individuals Murali deeply respects—who had founded Aadima, marking the beginning of many an important conversation in Kolar's cultural sphere. Thanking him for the loot, and dutifully making a small donation to the nearby school where Murali Uncle was helping set up a library, I set off on my way the next day.

The very next month, I travelled to Kolar to try and meet Kotiganahalli Ramaiah. I would hear many moons later that Murali Uncle had sold the homestay, moved back to Mysore and started a non-profit called Naari Trust, which seeks to empower tribal women and children through health and education initiatives. He sent me a smiling photo of himself surrounded by a whole bunch of grinning kids. It looked like he had found himself a new home.

II

> The day after Diwali it was,
> The worst day of your life,
> In that sweltering afternoon sun,
> You sat guarding the guava plantation,
> My little sister Anasuya.
>
> —Kotiganahalli Ramaiah, 'Nanna Tangi Anasuya'

As Ramaiah narrates the tale, when Ambedkar visited Kolar Gold Fields in 1954, he had arrived in ebullient spirits, eager to meet the labouring masses. When he stepped out to meet them, however, his heart sank. The workers looked upon him as a veritable god, and fell upon him with one request after another. Someone wanted him to name their child, others wanted him to walk over them so as to bless them, and so on. Repulsed by this display of obsequiousness, Ambedkar walked away with sadness, not even delivering the speech that he had planned for the day. He had been expecting a crowd where rationality, sensibility and strength could be found, and was faced instead with the bitter realities of illiterate India.

In April 2022, as I rode into Kolar, the entity most associated with its name, KGF, or the Kolar Gold Fields, had been shuttered for over two decades. Based on impressions formed by pop culture and passing trivia linked to the gold fields, I must admit that I expected to be visiting a landscape ruled by gangs, greed and gold. It was, therefore, with surprise that I noticed the signboard calling it *The City of Silk and Milk*. I also realised that KGF lay some distance from Kolar town, and that the KGF township had its own distinctive history of migrations and settlements.

Riding in from the strictly policed precincts of Bangalore, Kolar seemed to me a freer town. Nobody bothered to wear helmets on the road, and traffic violations were reassuringly plentiful. It was the peak of summer though, and I was grateful for the meagre shelter provided by my helmet as I rode up a medium-sized hillock, dominated by a rocky landscape that brought Hampi to mind. Suddenly, the character of Rocky in the blockbuster movie *KGF* began to seem less incongruous. Atop one of these hills, amidst a cluster of boulders, sits Aadima, the cultural institution founded by Kotiganahalli Ramaiah and a few others. Its manifesto declares that its primary motivation is 'radical experimentation in children's theatre, education, caste consciousness and research into cultural politics and history'. Set up in 2005, it emerged from the ruins of Karnataka's faltering dalit movement—the result of a disillusionment with 'lumpenism' and factionalism within it. Ramaiah, like Ambedkar, had witnessed a blind irrationality in the movement that required a deeper cultural response through education. Some twenty brothers-in-arms had saved a rupee a day for many years in order to secure the capital required to start Aadima.

I had been informed that a weekend shibira, or camp, was taking place at Aadima as part of Ambedkar Jayanti observations. As I walked in, lunch was proceeding apace. I gratefully dug in, and chatted with the cohort assembled there. They were law students from Bangalore, all from marginalised communities, here to spend the weekend and learn more about Babasaheb's legacy. Soon, everyone decamped to a small hall, where some singers and percussionists had begun a medley of local folk tunes and other creative additions, such as Abraham Lincoln's famous letter to his son's teacher turned into a Kannada song. This went on for about half an hour, after which a speaker took to the stage for an introductory lecture on Ambedkar's writings. Afterwards, as everyone streamed out for chai, I introduced myself to the speaker, and told him of my project. To this, he made an immediate rebuff:

Why do you want to know about the dalit chaluvali in Karnataka? Just study Ambedkar, he had already predicted everything.

It was a strain of hero worship that I had not encountered yet, and I called his bluff. I reparteed, with a measure of restraint, that the dalit movement had traced different trajectories across different regions, and each history was unique, and in that sense outside of Ambedkar's prophetic ambit.

This created a minor flutter amongst the group of local DSS leaders there. Someone hushed the whole matter and drew the speaker away for snacks. Confrontations were undesirable in the bonhomie of that weekend's spirit. One of the leaders, H.M. Ramachandra, was sympathetic to my project, and advised me to go meet Ramaiah soon, else I might miss him. Someone else nodded in agreement, and explained the route up to Ramaiah's home.

Ramaiah lives higher up on the hill, half a mile from Aadima. It is situated in the centre of a patch of farmland, right opposite a dargah. Even from a distance, one can sense the bohemian atmosphere surrounding his home—there are large Warli-esque paintings adorning the exterior, and the architecture itself stands out in comparison with the ordinariness of other houses in the neighbourhood.

As I introduced myself and spoke about my project, he seemed initially reluctant to open up. He was bored and tired of interviewers. But he warmed up soon enough, perhaps sympathising with the effort it had taken me to ride up the hill under that sun. I tried to get as serious as I could, right at the outset.

> Me*:* I've been trying to understand why the dalit movement found such powerful roots in Kolar. How did it begin? I have heard about Sheshagiriyappa's murder ...

KR: No no, the movement started much before that. Sheshagiriyappa's killing was in 1980. The dalit chaluvali had started in '74, '75 itself.

Me: From what I gather, the proportion of dalits in Kolar is quite large, compared to other Indian towns. Probably because KGF had gathered so many dalit families into one large township.

KR: Yes, that might be one of the reasons too. But more than that, you have to look at education. There is a hostel called Nachiketa Nilaya in Kolar. A certain kind of consciousness is inculcated in the students who study and live there. When atrocities happen, this consciousness flares up instantly. Once, a student named Munivenkatappa was killed. This boy had scored higher marks than everyone else in the class, and his feudal-caste classmates could not tolerate it. One day, on the pretence of taking him to a 'second show cinema', he was killed by one of them, and his body was dumped into a lake. When the body floated up and was identified, the hostel students staged an agitation. That was the first seed of the movement in Kolar. Soon after this, I and a few other friends started a study group called Chandala Balaga [Circle of Outcastes]. This is all before the DSS was started. This group slowly started to read, socialise and learn about society. Then, the boosa controversy stirred us up, and we all connected at the Dalekayusam [Dalita Lekhakaru Mattu Kalavidara Yuva Sanghatane, the Dalit Writers and Artists Youth Organisation] conference in Bhadravati. That was the real trigger point, the womb from which the dalit chaluvali was birthed.

Me: How did literature shape and guide this movement?

KR: There would have been no chaluvali without literature. The Dalekayusam conference in Bhadravati was flagged off by Basavalingappa himself. The writers and artists who had assembled there realised that merely writing was not going to cut it, and that there were social issues to be tackled. The primary motive of the organisation became one of fighting for justice, and therefore, writers became activists in a very profound sense.

The hostel known as Nachiketa Nilaya has a rich history. In the early twentieth century, the social reformer Golpalaswamy Iyer (who is incidentally the grand-uncle of historian Ramachandra Guha) pioneered primary education for dalits in the Old Mysore region, having set up several hostels and schools. At one particular school in Chikkaballapur (once a part of Kolar district), he had become an outcaste because he would rub oil on dozens of young dalit boys out in the open and bathe them by the well. For years after his death, both the well and the school remained unused by the town, and was eventually demolished. One of Iyer's students at this school was a man named T. Chennaiah, who became the first SC/ST student from Mysore State to bag a BSc degree. He went on to become a member of the Constituent Assembly, and later a minister in Kengal Hanumanthaiah's state cabinet as well. Emulating his eminent guru, Chennaiah went on to set up two dalit hostels—Nachiketa Nilaya in Kolar and Siddhartha Nilaya in Mysore.[1] These would become founts of the dalit movement in profound ways.

Ramaiah himself seems to have been somewhat immune to the charms of formal schooling, though he was quite a precocious lad. One of the anecdotes I heard about him from others was that a fifteen-year-old Ramaiah had once been his schoolteacher's primary vessel of hope for securing a first-class result in the tenth board exams. On the day of the exams, Ramaiah skived off in favour of a new Rajkumar movie. The teacher had to rush to the theatre and drag him back to school to write the paper. Ramaiah's present views on education are quite non-conformist as well. He believes that we need to start thinking of alternative education models that completely step away from the system we currently have, which he knows (as well as any of us) to be alienating and oppressive. This perspective extends to his conception of the dalit movement as well—he thinks that all previous modes of thinking must be discarded for fresher ones. He has one eye on the past and one on the future. Even while he recognises the importance of staying close to one's cultural roots (Aadima roughly translates to *primal*), the search for a new medium is always part of the journey.

The heart of Aadima's cultural experiment was a monthly event called Hunnime Haadu (Full-Moon Songs), during which villagers from Kolar and nearby regions would gather for a night of song and theatre. Ramaiah himself would write and adapt plays for the children to enact. Film screenings were also organised—in 2012, for instance, Girish Kasaravalli inaugurated a Kurosawa festival, which saw hundreds of people from Bangalore and Kolar throng to Aadima. A few intermittent breaks aside, Hunnime Haadu clocked its 200th instance in 2024.

Ramaiah sees himself primarily as a communicator and educator, and in this role, performative arts occupy the highest rung of meaning. He has great regard for the Tamil filmmaker Pa. Ranjith, and once spoke approvingly of his latest film *Natchathiram Nagargiradhu*. Ramaiah himself has written scripts for several films and documentaries, the latest being *Kanneri*, a story of a tribal community violently uprooted from their forests and sent to a rehabilitation camp where they attempt to put their lives back together again. When I met him, he said he was working on a film with a rather interesting premise: 'Society makes Buddha kill. That's it. That's the theme of the movie.' I do not know what became of this idea.

'When did you start writing,' I ask, sitting on the parapet of his spacious veranda, sipping chai.

> I had started writing before high school only. I used to read a lot. In PUC, I started writing poetry. There was a magazine edited by the great professor and art critic M.S. Krishnaiah. He published a couple of my pieces. After that, I wrote very little. The dalit movement began, we would be making speeches, and I was completely absorbed in it. Then, we realised that one song was better than a hundred speeches, and so I started writing songs. I came to see the importance of performance. That's why I only began to write songs, plays and, later, films. We would be travelling from village to village, and sometimes the songs would have travelled faster than we did, and would greet us as we came. It was quite remarkable. Only thirty years later, I came back to poetry. [This last, laughing.]

We track back to the 1980 march, and I ask him how it became such a widespread movement, with such massive mobilisation. Did the media play a big part? His response to this was instantaneous and free-flowing, filled with verve and emotion. It is what prompted me to write this chapter in the first place—I have translated it word for word, without any editing whatsoever, with the hope of allowing his thought process to speak for itself:

> No. It was because of the songs. They held such power. That is the strength that we writers wielded. I mentioned how important writers were, right? I still remember one of the slogans I coined. We were sitting in Cubbon Park, trying to come up with slogans to write on the walls. I came up with this: Krishnegowda kedi, haki avnge bedi. [*Krishnegowda is a rascal, put on him a manacle.*]
>
> I wrote a song called 'Nanna Tangi Anasuya'.[2] It spread everywhere, and created a spirit of companionship, brotherhood and concern. Of course, the organisers were also exceptional. It was no joke, rising up against such a strong feudal force. Krishnegowda, who was the Taluk Board president, had openly committed heinous murder and rape. He had a notorious caste network under his wing. The victims were poor Kumbaras, potters. Just raising a demand for land had got the poor man killed. It was probably the only atrocity case that was fully successful. Krishnegowda was arrested, but he soon died off. He was in Gundu Rao's kitchen cabinet—he was that powerful. That's why Gundu Rao lathicharged the procession near Vidhana Soudha. It was a brutal assault. [Anasuya herself had walked the ninety kilometres leading the march, only to be assaulted by the police and arrested.] We can't even imagine that such protests happened in the state once upon a time. Inch by inch, it touched each and every village—where organised religion hadn't touched them, government hadn't touched them, no modern idea had reached these boondocks at all. After Gandhi, it was only the DSS that made every village simultaneously conscious.
>
> What greater power is there, I ask you? In a backward abyss where there had been no scope of fomenting consciousness, there

> was a sudden prajna-sphota [explosion of consciousness], which later spread to other parts of the state. And this, in turn, influenced culture, literature and politics. It brought so many beautiful things to the fore. That is how you must gauge the DSS movement. If you use any other yardstick, you are missing the point. You have to search for it in the memories of the common man.
>
> Wah! What a beauty it was. It was like poetry. The movement itself was flowing like a mahakavya [epic poem]. I still remember, I was once walking with Ramdev Rakhe, an editor of *Panchama* magazine, one night, around eleven. We happened upon a man drunk beyond his senses, and he was shouting, Eh Krishnegowda, en ankondidiyo nam sangha na, baaroo [*Eh Krishnegowda, what do you think of our Sangha, I dare you to come here*]. That's how folklore should become. Even in a drunkard, in that inebriated state, the consciousness had cemented itself. That really sums up what those times were like.

This sense of justice and retribution that invigorated the entire dalit community was what made the DSS such a powerful force. Even in Padmalaya Nagaraj's eyes, it was the writers and literati who gave the movement its crucial edge. Ramaiah's mahakavya comment hints at this too: that it was a special moment in history when art organically became political, like a rumble of thunder jolting a society, and then quickly subsided, awaiting the next charge. I was also struck by his emphasis on the etymology of his birth-village's name—koti + gaana + halli—which stands for 'village of innumerable songs'. Talk about living up to your name.

In the Venn diagram where art and activism intersect, there are certainly spaces where the two come together in profound ways. During the 1980 Vidhana Soudha march from Kolar, the CPI(M), its trade union cadres and their cultural wing had taken active part and supported the DSS. But more often than not, the artist and the revolutionary have scoffed at each other, refusing to budge from their respective places in the world.

III

Mr Mathematics is a big scholar,
ever calculating,
a modern Samkhya yogi.

No mental constructs,
save for numbers.
Soul thrills only,
to exponentials and infinity.

Even so,
when everybody else is asleep,
they know to seek out,
only the most melodious music.[3]

—Lakshmipathy Kolar, *Mathematics and Music*

Well before I happened to meet Kotiganahalli Ramaiah, I had already met V.S.S. Shastry, who was my first guide to Kolar and its intelligentsia. Like Ramaiah's home, the exteriors of Shastry's too boasted of vibrant wall art, always a welcoming sign. I met him numerous times, and our conversations were colourful and various. A passionate raconteur, Shastry enjoys long, meandering discussions, and loves to hold forth on everything under the sun, from politics to art history, even if old age has dulled his memory a little.

Now retired, Shastry used to work as a clerk in Canara Bank,[4] and became a part of leftist circles through his involvement with the bank's labour union. These days, he is an origami expert, an inventor of intricate designs and strategies, and a patient mentor who enjoys teaching children all the skills he has acquired. He has written several brief treatises on these subjects, and has travelled across the country to instil in school children an appreciation of the wonders of mathematics. These travels have also fuelled other hobbies he finds stimulating—like collecting fossils in Kashmir, or curating niche political observations, such as the fact that 'many RSS leaders across India are from Karnataka, and all of them are Brahmacharis'.

Once, I met Shastry in his second home in Bangalore, which became a necessity after his cancer diagnosis that required him to make repeated trips to the city for treatment. Inventive origami shapes were showcased on his shelves, as were a wide range of books. A man of science through and through, Shastry once told me that an understanding of abstract mathematics is of utmost importance if Marxism is to be thoroughly grasped. He seems to have a soft corner for the Bengali politician Shibdas Ghosh, whose denunciation of Gandhi he finds appealing. Shastry is well respected in the DSS circles of Kolar. But he is also a deeply critical man, with strong opinions regarding social movements, and in him, the dalit movement also finds its fiercest critic.

In his acclaimed book *Flaming Feet and Other Essays*, D.R. Nagaraj observed that the dalit movement in India has historically held one of two things as its primary goal—land and value. While Marxists treated the dalit question purely as a problem of agrarian relations and land redistribution, Gandhi and Ambedkar represented the idea of value, though in different ways. While Gandhi had sought to articulate a new value system within Hinduism, Ambedkar had rejected such an idea outright. Shivaram Karanth, in *Chomana Dudi*, had intuitively taken the Marxist line, highlighting Choma's deep desire for a plot of land. Reflecting on the history of these ideas, Nagaraj wrote:

> The land and value schools had stayed separate. Neither realized the tragic implications of such bifurcation. The concrete and the abstract were kept separate in an artificial way. The Marxists should have been able to fuse the two but they did not.[5]

Until I met Shastry, I had figured Nagaraj's analysis to be a theoretical one, to be understood broadly and generally. When Shastry, as an avowed communist, kept reiterating the land question and critiquing the dalit movement in Kolar for its inability to address it, I began to see the import of Nagaraj's insight. Shastry's argument was that, while the movement did initially take up several land struggles, they lost sight of the main goal after a while, and began focusing on trivial issues like promotions in administrative offices. It was yet another avatar of an old debate that has raged between Ambedkarites and communists in India—of rights versus redistribution, of identity politics versus the politics of economic policy. Ambedkar did carry a strong streak of anti-communism throughout his life, though he also realised the importance of land reforms later in his life. In 1956, his last year, he attempted to salvage what little he had found of value in Marx (changing the world is more important than metaphysical inquiries, the evil of private property) by reading the same points in the Buddha's teachings and arguing that the latter's modus operandi upheld the emancipation of the individual rather than the collective, and that this was more peaceable and sustainable and democratic. Having been appropriated by literally every political outfit, Ambedkar's original universalism has since become fragmented into mere shadows.

Shastry also spoke a lot about Kotiganahalli Ramaiah and the Aadima experiment. He extolled the man's talent for oration, pointing out that many a young child has been inspired and motivated by Ramaiah's mentorship. In another breath, he critiqued the man harshly and chalked off their cultural experiment as a trivial one: 'How can you imagine a social movement that is not at all going towards the people? That does not address the land question? Then these guys went and started Aadima, saying they want to do cultural rejuvenation. Where will this rejuvenation come from? Will it fall from the sky?'

To be sure, the dalit movement in Kolar, and in Karnataka at large, took up a host of land issues. The most prominent of these happened in the mid-eighties, when there was a sustained struggle to rehabilitate over a hundred newly freed bonded labourers near the town of Nagasandra, close to Bangalore. For close to two years, protests had tried to get the state to acknowledge their demands. Eventually, a 300-acre plot was forcibly occupied, and over seventy houses were built to accommodate the newly liberated families. The community was dubbed Shambuka Nagara, after the character of Shambuka interpolated into the Ramayana.[6] One of those who led that movement, H.M. Ramachandra, told me that Shambuka Nagara is in dire need of sociological study, because most of the residents have reverted to bonded labour (of a new avatar) and do not seem to have undergone the kind of upliftment that they ideally should have. Only a couple of youngsters from the newer generation have gone on to pursue higher education. Mere acquisition of land can get you only so far, the story suggests. Cultural rejuvenation is precisely what is required, one might argue here, to afford the younger generation a chance to aspire to real social mobility. The unexamined life can never be truly liberating.

There are other reasons why the dalit movement petered out as well. In Ramaiah's analysis, the mushrooming of identity politics in the nineties also served to dilute the movement.

> Me: Do you think that revolutionary dalit consciousness is completely depleted now?
>
> KR: Not that it has gone away. Instead of expanding, it has inverted itself.
>
> Me: What do you mean?
>
> KR: It is all because of identity politics. It has to do with who we are in this land, and what our questions are. Who were we? We were dalits—our smaller identities did not matter to us then. We used to be living in a stratified society, but then the dalit umbrella came to shelter us. Then, for many reasons, including representation, this unified identity kept breaking up and turned on itself. It became fragmented. That is the problem. We built Aadima to combat this very disintegration and lumpenisation. But the thesis itself became the antithesis, and I lost hope. That's why I said I did not want to talk about it.

It must be mentioned here that when Aadima was set up, the first president of the organisation's trust had been none other than V.S.S. Shastry. But he does not associate with Aadima now, and critiques it at every opportunity. This was a curious affair. Even Ramaiah refrained from elaborating on what exactly he meant by the 'thesis' becoming the 'antithesis'. Luckily, he had put me in touch with a scholar named Mohit Kaycee, who had lived with Ramaiah for many years and had been a part of Aadima during its heyday. When I posed this question to him, he felt that I was placing far too much emphasis on Ramaiah's dissociation from Aadima:

> Personally, I think Ramaiah is someone who is constantly searching for something. If there is something that constrains or stagnates that search, then it becomes imperative that he moves on. He's done a lot of things. He's been in very different places. At one point, *Lankesh Patrike* became very claustrophobic for him, and he left that. If you see how Ramaiah's plays progressed, from 2005 to 2013, which was when he left, you can see the evolution of his ideas—there is more self-criticism and his themes become darker. And that evolution of creativity may not always fit in with certain ideas of collectivities, you see? You have to also acknowledge how the times changed during that particular period. The emergence of social media, a certain kind of networking amongst dalit activists—what then becomes the position of a space like Aadima?

In other words, Aadima had come up at a time when it was most in need. And in the zeitgeist of the present world, buzzing through optical fibres under oceans, culture and education would also have to adapt and evolve. From other close associates of Ramaiah, I also heard opinions of how his plays, which began as refreshing reworkings of folk tales and tropes, tended to get more and more overtly political in recent times, and hence didn't lend themselves easily to working with children.

How did the Marxists perceive these developments, I wondered. In Mysore, I sought clarification about Shastry and Ramaiah's divergence from Aadima through Diwakar Narayan Rao—a columnist and translator with deep roots in Kolar. He is perhaps Shastry's closest friend as well, and is the liveliest Marxist I have met yet. His tone is light even as he speaks of things that he considers entirely serious. His response took a parallel path to Mohit's.

DNR: You see, Aadima was started as a cultural movement. Both Shastry and I believe that we need to give right-wing politics a cultural response. Shastry was very active in that, and Ramaiah was also very active. Later, some people say that Ramaiah started being autocratic and all that. Ramaiah is the kind of person who will not stick to one stance. He keeps shifting his stances.

Me: They keep evolving?

DNR: Not evolving. Shifting. Today he may say something, and a year later, he will completely change it. Once upon a time, he was praising Devanura Mahadeva like anything, and turned him into some kind of demigod. Now, he dislikes him. He thinks Devanura is trying to become some kind of a Gandhian saint. [Ramaiah] is not clear about his stance. Earlier, he was a Marxist. Later, he started disliking that, and he renounced it completely. Now, again he is talking about it, saying we need that vocabulary. There is no consistency. This, I think, is exactly what Shastry dislikes.

What Shastry and Narayan Rao expect from Ramaiah is unwavering ideological consistency, a fully coherent worldview. What they perhaps fail to see is that a creative, artistic journey is often incompatible with the moral certainties of political ideologies. This is not to say that conviction is undesirable, but only that an artistic search invariably traces meandering and contradictory paths, and oftentimes they may not be as clear-cut as an origami algorithm. Of course, such meandering paths might well hit dead ends too.

In any case, Marx is now abhorred within dalit activist circles. In the words of H. Govindaiah, a veteran DSS activist from Mysore, Marxism infused a 'black-and-white' thinking within the dalit chaluvali, and diverted it from a more complex (he uses the word 'sankeernate') understanding of life and the world. However, this rejection of Marx has not given way to a rich, complex political philosophy, but only seems to have been replaced by a rather tenuous Ambedkarism. To quote Narayan Rao:

> Even now, Aadima is unwilling to accommodate Marxists. In July end, there was a camp there. One boy, who was doing research at the Classical Language Institute in Bangarpet—a boy who was very close to me—he told me that he would invite me for the camp, for a talk about Marxism. I said okay, but it never transpired. There is this 'madivantike' [an interesting choice of word, for it connotes a brahminical sense of purity] amongst that group, amongst all extreme Ambedkarites.[7]

Narayan Rao told me that there exist no less than twenty-five dalit groups in Kolar now that have splintered off the original movement. Going variously by names such as Dalit Sene, Dalit Ravan Sene or Ambedkar Sene, each of these organisations possesses its own letterhead and publishes its own pamphlets. The way he says it, I am almost led to imagine that each of these is as powerless as that famous fictional band of brothers in Karnataka, the Huccha Venkat Sene.[8] However, Narayan Rao is quick to add that despite their outward disparity, the groups often come together on important issues and pool their resources for crucial struggles.

There is a more hopeful stance on this phenomenon. K.B. Siddaiah, one of the most original poets in the movement, was fond of arguing that this splintering should be seen with an eye on the future, where the various factions could come together strongly if the right historical conditions present themselves. In this sense, it is a latent force of potential energy, and not a dissipated and depleted one. The splintering can also be seen as a sign that the dalit movement has not remained stagnant, and has instead tried to explore alternative paths of building a different chaluvali. However, the sheer number of splinters point less towards ideological differences and more towards individualised power grabs.

Yet another perspective that emerged in my conversations with dalit activists was that the movement crumbled because of a lack of ideological strength. The class struggle had Marxism to hold it together, but the caste struggle could only boast of a diluted Ambedkarism, which never truly animated the discourse of the movement, in their eyes. When I brought this up with Ramaiah, he scoffed at it.

> Me: Some activists I spoke to in Mysore told me that the dalit chaluvali became fragmented and factionalised in the eighties because there was no strong ideological commitment holding it together.
>
> KR: These are all very subjective perceptions. What ideological commitment is required for social rebellion anyway?
>
> Me: Not for rebellion itself, but to strengthen and hold the organisation together is what they meant, I think.
>
> KR: They mean regimentation, I suppose. But once you regimentalise, the movement is finished. It is good that we did not do that. It meant that the movement spread organically, like wildfire. If we had tried to regimentalise, like the communists espouse, it would have taken a century for the movement to build strength. The people you spoke to are probably Marxists, no? Okay, forget about that. The movement managed to achieve what a regimented party has never done in Karnataka. How do you explain that? It was a very instinctive movement, you see. The historical conditions at the time facilitated it. The reasons for factionalism are numerous, and can't be boiled down to one or two. If there was no ideological commitment, how did it thrive for so many years? In all of India, such massive dalit mobilisations for land and dignity have not been staged. You can check the facts. How many land struggles, how many thousands of acres of land were distributed—you will be astonished that this level of struggle happened at the grassroots level. Even in Maharashtra, the Dalit Panthers did not penetrate into the community as much as the chaluvali in Karnataka did. I'm not saying there were no other successful movements—great things happened elsewhere too, like in Bihar for instance. But all of them were vanguard-led movements. Here, it came up right from below, completely self-sustained and self-led.

I was later reminded of this comment while reading Suketu Mehta's interview with Bal Thackeray in *Maximum City*. Responding to the communist leader S.A. Dange's comment that the Shiv Sena would not survive because it does not have a theory, Thackeray (a man 'comfortable with images and action, but not with ideas') had dismissed the remark as one of arrogance, and retorted, 'Then how has our organisation survived for the last eighteen years? And how is it that, despite a theory, your organisation is finished?' In the 1970s, the Dalit Panthers had emerged as a foil to the Shiv Sena. The Panthers had fused Marx with Ambedkar and Phule, creating a new variant of class struggle, but they were also reacting to the violent precedents already set by the Shiv Sena.[9] The DSS drew inspiration from the Dalit Panthers, though it was avowedly more non-violent than other dalit organisations of its time.[10] The DSS embraced a democratic mode of protest, and their definition of 'dalit' encompassed all oppressed communities. The DSS's primary audience lived in villages, those dens of ignorance and sinks of localism that Ambedkar had once emerged from and instinctively abhorred. Between the ideologies of Balasaheb and Babasaheb, a world of difference existed, which may be easily summed up in one word: education.

Me: I suppose all manner of ideologies were found enmeshed in the movement. There were those who called themselves Lohiaties and Marxists in the DSS as well, right?

KR: Yeah, well, all of these were just subjects to speak about in seminars and stuff. These ideologies did not reflect their way of life in any way, I'm afraid. What dictated our lives was material reality—a killing, rape or some form of immediate oppression. There was never really a question of choosing to see it through a Marxist lens, or a socialist lens, or such things. It was an instinctive, organic response.

Me: Hmmm. In a similar vein, I've been trying to understand D.R. Nagaraj's influence on the dalit movement.

KR: He was with Siddalingaiah during the boosa movement. Then, he was part of the dalit chaluvali for a while, and he wrote *The Flaming Feet*. After that, we would see him at academic conferences

> and all, but he was never really part of the movement as such. He wrote some extraordinary scholarly works on Allama Prabhu and Navodaya poetry. He was more connected with the bandaya literary scene, but never really with the dalit chaluvali at its grassroots. D.R. Nagaraj could have entered the heart of the movement. Why did the chaluvali pick up three individuals—B. Krishnappa, Siddalingaiah, Devanura Mahadeva—as its torchbearers? That's how the popular narrative goes, right? It is because they were all untouchables. Without experiencing untouchability, you can never really speak about it fully. Someone like Karanth can come close to it, perhaps. But even he could never hope to truly capture the misery of untouchability. Kuvempu also approached it from afar. Now, Nagaraj had all the rights to be a part of that trinity. But he stayed aloof—probably because he was more at home within the academic setting.

It is an interesting pronouncement, because D.R. Nagaraj was born in the weaver caste, though he was closely associated with the dalit movement and counted dalits as intimate friends. Ramaiah, of course, is sheltering Nagaraj under the broad-minded brotherhood of the dalit identity. But perhaps Nagaraj was not accepted as fully as the trinity because he had not experienced the brunt of untouchability?

Ramaiah moved on to the subject of oral myths and folklore and the reception of these ideas in the academic world. These are subjects that Ramaiah holds close to his heart, and that have been part of Aadima's deepest engagements as well.

> KR: In the eighties, when H.S. Shivaprakash wrote his plays *Manteswamy Kathaprasanga*, *Madari Madayya* and *Mahachaitra*, they were incredibly revolutionary. Very important recreations of long neglected cultural traditions. Until Shivaprakash came along, nobody had really taken the responsibility to convert these oral traditions into other forms. After that, studies began, and a serious collection of oral narratives started. I think these oral mythologians did a better job than modern historians. They built it in essence, through metaphors, while modern historians do it with theory and

language. To move forward, I think we should look to seek fuel from these myths.[11]

Me: What kind of metaphors? Can you give me an example?

KR: There are so many. What kind of metaphors do you want?

Me: I don't know ... Something to do with tilling one's own land? About forests?

KR: It is not so straightforward. For example, the myth that the universe was created from an egg—this simply alludes to how the earth is round.[12] Or for instance, a lamp burns wherever you place it, on a garbage dump, in a house where someone has died, or where a marriage has taken place. What does it mean? This is a principle of democracy, in modern parlance. How poetically they have communicated these principles, in those mahakavyas.

I should have brought up Ambedkar's sceptical observation that 'democracy is only a top dressing on an Indian soil which is essentially undemocratic', because I was not wholly convinced by what he was driving at, but the lamp had reminded me of the jotammas—talking lamp spirits—that animate Devanura Mahadeva's novel *Kusumabale* and give it a magical touch.

Me: Hmm. This cultural idiom has also surfaced in the writings of Devanura Mahadeva, no?

KR: His writing is beautiful, with some very evocative scenes. If you read *Male Mahadeswara Kavya*, *Kusumabale* will seem quite similar in the effect it produces. To take a work that is a classic in people's minds, to build a new language around it, and to make it come alive again—hats off to him for doing it. *Kusumabale* is a remarkable work. We must just feel proud about it, there's nothing else to say.

The importance of Shivaprakash's and Mahadeva's adaptations lies in the fact that these traditions were historically obscured from general knowledge, though they were once widely prevalent. In his study of the prehistory of Hinduism in Karnataka, historian Manu Devadevan identifies two broad sets of sainthood traditions (which are still further divided into a wide range of traditions internally): the Dasa and the Siddha ethics. The dasas—like Kanakadasa and Purandaradasa—comprised saints who followed Vedantic traditions like Dvaita or Vishishtadvaita. The siddhas—like Manteswamy or Kodekallu Basava—consisted of veerashaivas, aarudhas, avadhutas, nathas, dattas and adherents of other diverse non-brahmin schools. Before the nineteenth century, the dasas had no commemorative shrines or installations to their name, and their songs and legends only circulated amongst monastic communities. Yet, they are better known today for a specific historical reason, tied to the interests of an educated elite, as Devadevan writes:

> In a striking reversal of fortune in the late nineteenth century, the Sindhi- and Marathi-inspired professional theatre troupes in Kannada, and the emerging academic discipline of Kannada literature, began to foreground the dasas, to the disadvantage of the siddhas. Plays on the dasas were written and performed. Songs were composed in their honour. Their literary works were published in cheap chapbook form as well as in the form of carefully researched critical editions. Their songs were taught in schools, and school textbooks carried chapters about their life and work. In consequence, the Anglophone academia and much of the literate population in today's Karnataka have some familiarity with the names of Kanakadasa and Purandaradasa, if not a reasonable historical understanding, but they know scarcely anything about Kodekallu Basava, Kalaburagi Saranabasava, Tinthini Monappa, Sirahatti Fakirappa, or Savalagi Sivalinga.[13]

This goes to show how crucial theatre and the academy can be in shaping the knowledge of succeeding generations, and how it can foreground certain traditions while completely neglecting others. What also intrigued me was that Ramaiah had critiqued Ananthamurthy for being too liberal, arguing that the liberal 'cult' of cultural insiders created by those like Ananthamurthy had unwittingly played into the hands of the Hindu Right.[14] However, I could see a similar shade of cultural conservatism in Ramaiah's championing of fifteenth-century religious epics, *and* an equal distaste for Hindu supremacism. The recovery of the siddha traditions (through plays and literature, just like a century earlier) in the 1980s would thus prove to be a monumental act of reclaiming cultural memory. These traditions also provide oppressed-caste communities with rich spiritual histories to align with—histories that are not the prescriptions of a political party or a social elite. We are already seeing how these traditions are slowly being absorbed into popular culture and into the Kannada film industry. The first time I came to hear about the Manteswamy legend was actually through a wildly popular song from the retro detective film *Bell Bottom*, which remains one of my all-time favourite Kannada movies.

Back in 1957, a year after Ambedkar's conversion to Buddhism, the celebrated Gandhian and poet D.V. Gundappa (who too hailed from Kolar district) had written a small piece titled 'Harijanoddhara' (Harijan Upliftment) for a Kannada magazine on the occasion of Gandhi Jayanti:

> I beseech Vedic scholars and Shastra experts to take two important issues into consideration—the first is the belief in Hinduism that has travelled down since time immemorial and resided in the Harijan, and the second is Hinduism's need for numerical strength. Even if our varna-believing ancestors kept them away from knowledge, even after they abandoned them, they have held on to a simple belief in Hinduism, and have been worshipping the gods of the Savarnas. They believe that Hinduism is their greatest hope. To turn away those who come seeking shelter is not the quality of Hindu dharma; in fact it is no dharma at all.[15]

He goes on to add that dalits should swell the ranks of the Hindus in order for Hinduism to flourish—a numerical angle important for Gundappa, at least in this beseeching tone directed at the orthodoxy. Remarkably, there is no reference to Ambedkar or Buddhism in the piece at all. It is instructive to now turn to the scholar Chinnaswamy Sosale, editor of a comprehensive dalit history of Karnataka, who draws on Ambedkar to make a distinction between 'social untouchability' and 'religious untouchability'. While the former (physical segregation) was sanctioned and upheld by upper castes, the latter constituted a wilful embrace of religious traditions (nude worship, rolling on the leftovers of upper-caste meals, the devadasi system) by dalits themselves.[16] To deny the latter's agency would be to succumb to a smug elitism. He also points out that the twelfth-century philosopher Ramanuja had undertaken revolutionary efforts to combat untouchability and welcome dalits into the religious fold, though it is arguable to what extent these rebellious ripples survived after his time. Ambedkar had fashioned through Buddhism (and the Constitution) a rational and modern alternative which could break away from the hierarchical caste order completely and serve as a foil to centuries of accumulated untouchability—both social and religious. The dalit chaluvali in Karnataka did begin, during the seventies, with a hyper-rationalist tenor, as was inevitable in a landscape of oppressive superstitions. However, cultural excavations soon showed that what Gundappa had chalked off as 'simple belief' had really been much more than that—it had its own aesthetic and religious vitality, embedded deeply in the folk imagination. I caught a vivid slice of this aesthetic watching the play *Daklakatha Devikavya* in Rangashankara. It was a difficult-to-pull-off adaptation of the poems of K.B. Siddaiah, led ably by the young and talented director K.P. Lakshmana, who is also incidentally an Aadima product. This desire to carve out a unique aesthetic ethos for the dalit chaluvali traces its origin back to the seventies, where the search for a holistic identity begins to be articulated.

> KR: I still remember the speech Mahadeva gave at the Dalekayusam conference in Bhadravati. It greatly inspired me. He said, 'What I have written amounts to merely a couple of fingers or a hand. Now, imagine how it would be if the whole body of that hand began to speak for itself?' What must we do for the whole to express itself? That really got me thinking.

Ramaiah believes that the best is yet to come. Both Kannada literature and social movements are currently in a state of abeyance, waiting for a renewal of spirit.

Me: Why do you think there are fewer writers writing in Kannada today?

KR: There are actually many writers—but they are writing on Facebook, that's all. It is true. But they keep having to react to localised issues, and they are unable to maintain an integral whole. They all have the potential freedom to write, which was not there during our times. We had to be published by a magazine or something. Now, there is no question of rejection. So, a lot of kitsch turns up, but some of it can be really good too. The challenge is to move beyond their individual subjectivities, and see something larger than their own selfies. I think the future is bright. Our country has divided into two—Peshwe Bharat and Prabuddha Bharat. The former is currently in supreme power, with great resources at its disposal. Prabuddha Bharat does not have this, but it possesses one important element, what we may call a conscience or a cultural compound. To combat the former, we need a new form of cultural nationalism, a new idea of citizenship. This Peshwe Bharat is founded on two unethical doctrines: capitalism and brahminism. It cannot survive forever—it will die its own death, by its own internal contradictions. What remains to be seen is how we play our role at this juncture in history.

Much later, when I met up with Devanura Mahadeva, we ended up speaking about Aadima and Ramaiah. He summed up all his intimate insights into Ramaiah's dynamic mind in one sentence: 'Ramaiah will not accept anybody else's opinions. In the end, he will not accept his own too.'

IV

Leftist politics has always been accompanied by a cultural denominator, primarily out of necessity. The only way to take the revolutionary message to the masses, to those deprived (of both art and justice), is through song. Even serious and humourless Marxists, steeped in abstract realities, could see its importance. Following the momentum of Naxalbari during the late sixties, radical cultural activists in Andhra went on to set up the Revolutionary Writer's Association (Virasam) and the Jana Natya Mandali.

Safdar Hashmi, the leader of the CPI(M)-led Jana Natya Manch,[17] had once observed that, despite the fact that some of the songs in their plays were sung poorly, and that much could be done to raise the artistic merit of their performances to match the standards of proscenium theatre, the labouring masses still gathered in huge numbers to witness Janam's street acts simply because of the lack of art in their hectic, oppressed lives. In the middle of a desert, a glass of water can make a world of difference. And a glass of poison might also be just as easy to gulp down.

This grasping towards artistic fulfilment is something that is characteristic of the dalit movement in Karnataka as well. The birth of Aadima was an attempt to rise above ideological pigeonholes and to take art to its most vital beneficiaries—children. The intervention of a cultural space in the formative years of one's childhood is an extraordinarily meaningful event that is often underestimated. In today's era of competitive exams and online education, these important years are needlessly given over to kitschy content on a screen or uninspiring coaching classes where all curiosity is murdered. It was with the idea of kindling children's imagination that Ramaiah envisioned Aadima. For more than two decades, the institute has thrived and flourished, witnessing thousands of young children from all over the state participate in fests and fall in love with theatre. Ramaiah boasts:

> I can say with great pride that there is no other Kannada writer who has consistently written so many children's plays and helped them perform these. I don't like to pat myself on the back, but nobody is saying this, and so I have to say it myself. Writing children's plays is my political priority right now.

Quite apart from his labours of love, children's theatre is indeed a rising phenomenon across Karnataka, with talented troupes touring the state and putting on incredible performances. Ramaiah tells me how the DSS is presently deliberating the creation of a new manifesto:

When we studied the manifestos of every party, including the communists, we realised that there has never been any space afforded to this most vital of activities—giving children the freedom to imagine. We are building a new Cultural Liberation theory which revolves around a new definition of wealth. We say that each child, regardless of caste or creed or religion, is an asset, whom we must nurture and celebrate. We also condemn violence on women, and consider their emancipation as being of utmost importance.

I wholeheartedly agree with him, and towards the end of our conversation, sufficiently impressed by his eloquence, I naturally decide to throw in all my existential doubts.

Me: So, I have been thinking a lot about what I am going to foreground in my book. What would you expect from a new book about Karnataka, about the dalit movement, about that period, that would be useful and insightful from today's point of view?

KR (half-interrupting me): How can we imagine a futuristic Dalita Sangharsha Samiti? Your personal stance on it. Go by your feelings, don't go to your head. As a 'felt' emotion, how would you hope the dalit chaluvali shapes up? That would be very insightful.

Me: Well, from everything I have heard so far, I do feel that there needs to be more emphasis on the arts and cultural upliftment. I'm sure that's why you started Aadima as well. I do think we need more of that.

KR: Beautiful. Why don't you write that then?

Like the German writer Friedrich Schiller argued in his *Letters on the Aesthetic Education of Man*, published in the aftermath of the terrible excesses of the French Revolution, I do believe that art and nature improve human character, and beauty can supply the sense of morality that may check baser greed. This is why the neuroscientist V.S. Ramachandran argues for the inclusion of poetry, instead of grammar, in primary pedagogy. One picks up grammar on the fly, but learning to understand poetry and metaphor is a skill that requires a teacher worth their salt.

This is not to say that one must lose oneself in a life of aesthetic delights. Rather, it is to say that any social movement that recognises the importance of primary education and the cultivation of a generation of independent minds would be foolish to ignore the profound effects of visual arts, literature, music, cinema, theatre and other performing arts. Such an education would be founded on harmony and empathy, where one may learn to appreciate different worldviews, and not fall down insular rabbit holes dug by ideologues. At a time when a phenomenon dubbed as Hindutva-pop,[18] a home-bred cottage industry openly propagating Islamophobia and sinister exclusionary designs, is ruling the North Indian soundscape, in cahoots with innumerable other dangers masquerading as art, such a task seems all too important.

To answer Ramaiah's prompt, I instinctively imagine a futuristic DSS as one that is involved in setting up more libraries, schools, cultural spaces, art galleries, desi artisanal collectives, and encourages the formation of more bands, theatre troupes, filmmakers and everything alive and real that can combat the stultifying, depressing effects of social media and the attention gap at its heart. It would be a DSS that is able to shame the present schooling system into reforming itself, into abolishing rote exams and the psychologically demeaning practice of retaining 'failed' students in the same grade. The real critique of capitalism is not that it has deepened economic inequality—which it undoubtedly has—but that it has also failed to divert the gains it has made towards meaningful social progress. The proliferation of education scams like Byju's is a case in point. What capitalism has produced instead is a sense of false complacency and a desire for mindless consumption. Even as it has democratised education, it has also allowed the most crassly opportunistic to corner competition and carve out their own spaces of influence.

It would also be a DSS that recognises the importance of cultivating an early love for the natural environment, from which we are getting more distanced with every passing day. Aadima had taken on, at one point, the task of documenting and preserving local knowledge traditions that have accumulated over centuries of close life with nature. Padmalaya Nagaraj also prides himself on being a horticultural expert, and can hold forth on the colourful variety of herbs and medicinal plants that are endemic to this richly diverse land. He bemoans the fact that the current generations are so alienated from their natural heritage that they struggle to even identify common varieties of spinach and leafy greens. In other words, we must strive to achieve a balance between radical social change and deep, meaningful conservatism. We must hold on to the past where it is the richest, and unhesitatingly shed the painful baggage.

V

Around the time Murali Uncle was grappling with the lockdown of 2020, a remarkably resourceful IAS officer named Uma Mahadevan Dasgupta was engaged in the task of rejuvenating rural libraries across Karnataka, with an emphasis on getting all children free membership. Through a remarkable campaign, aided by numerous NGOs, over a million books were collected from the public over two years and distributed to renovated, refurbished and newly built libraries across rural Karnataka. Upwards of three million children have been enrolled into these libraries so far. Everyone is allotted a library card, and children can take books home—some of them being the first-generation readers in their family. Close to 4,000 libraries are equipped with computers, and 'bridging the digital divide' is a key part of Uma Mahadevan's vision. During the pandemic, these libraries helped close the gap between urban and rural children. They stayed open till late at night, allowing children to browse the web and study. Equipped with iPads and Alexas, these libraries also make for a great, and safe, space for children with learning disabilities. In 2024, 6,000 new libraries were inaugurated, with the promise of reaching millions of children.

'Libraries are now becoming a space for inclusive community-life,' she says.[19] 'Now we have chess boards and carrom boards at the libraries as well, and people of all age groups come there to spend time. There are beanbags, stools, tables and chairs; people can come and quietly engage with each other.'

All these advances have been achieved by encouraging the autonomy of village panchayats and only helping them make their own choices. Now, the libraries have taken on a life of their own. Launching into a brief history of libraries in India, she expands:

> The growth of village libraries was associated with the freedom movement. In the 1930s and 1940s, many little libraries sprung up. There were these boat libraries in Andhra, where books travelled on boats to a newly reading public. The Maharaja of Baroda, at the turn of the twentieth century, was so impressed by public libraries in England, that he had started a whole library network in Baroda state. This included not just a library for the literate, but also a visual library for people who can't read. Very radical stuff. Libraries have always been associated with being progressive and radical.

The first two public libraries in Karnataka came up in the 1910s, one in Mysore and one in Bangalore. Later, a man named S.R. Ranganathan, widely acclaimed as the father of library science in India, travelled to England, saw the limitations of the Dewey Decimal classification, and came up with an alternative he called the Colon System. Essentially, he argued for a sophisticated categorisation of books that would take multiple tags and labels, separated by colons.

In 1931, Ranganathan published what are known as the Five Laws of Library Science (I'm not joking), which are now widely accepted as sound philosophy by libraries across the world, including the famed Bodleian library at Oxford. The laws, deceptively simple in their structure, are as follows:

1. Books are for use.
2. Every person his or her book.
3. Every book its reader.
4. Save the time of the reader.
5. A library is a growing organism

Ranganathan's pioneering efforts opened up the public library network in India. Still, its reach was limited to certain urban pockets, and villages remained semi-literate for many decades. R.K. Narayan had once mocked the 'library movement', writing: 'Library science seems all concerned with systems of classification, shelves, furniture, locks, keys, registers, vouchers, and statistics, everything except reading. The most noticeable deficiency in any library today seems to be a lack of propaganda for books themselves.'[20] Things are certainly better today, but speaking from my experience, I think there is much scope for improvement. In the village where I live, the government library has been shut for months, and I've been unable to return a book I checked out more than a year ago. Readers are few, and the library itself is far too small and books are scattered in dusty bookshelves where poor lighting makes locating them that much more difficult.

During the 1970s, the dalit movement in Karnataka inaugurated a literary universe that sought to cultivate a newly lettered generation of writers and artists, amongst whose radical ranks Kotiganahalli Ramaiah had once been baptised through fire. Those were times when little magazines, newspapers and periodicals held sway over the public imagination. Journalists and writers had begun to give free rein to their literary impulses and to their social aspirations. They were radical progressives, and they too created their own spaces for an inclusive community life, where books, politics and social change were discussed by hot-blooded youth.

One such space that entered my research-vision was a library in Mysore, started in the early 1970s by a group of progressives, rationalists and scientists. It was closely connected to the dalit movement in Mysore, exemplifying the radical progressiveness which Uma Mahadevan Dasgupta sees as a library's core potential. In a dalit-dominated neighbourhood named Kukkarahalli, a Marxist Library had sprung up, riding on the wave of Left sympathy that the seventies witnessed across India. Fifty years ago, this was a neighbourhood that boasted of very little literacy, and the library would send ripples of revolution across a landscape clamouring for education. The next chapter is the story of these ripples. Set in motion at a precarious point in history, when the social conscience of a society was being stirred in such unprecedented fashion, they were accompanied by the best of intentions, and yet, the rudder of the ship was swinging wildly every which way.

NINE

The Marxist Library of Mysore

> Let heaven exist, though my own place be in hell. Let me be tortured and battered and annihilated, but let there be one instant, one creature, wherein thy enormous Library may find its justification.
>
> —Jorge Luis Borges

I

Perhaps the most enduring cultural reference to Kukkarahalli Lake in Mysore is the song 'Koorak Kukkarahallikere' from a forgettable 2005 romantic drama film. Essentially, the song points out the eminent suitability of the lake for amorous pursuits. Sung by the immensely popular S.P. Balasubramaniam, it is the kind of song that young boys and girls would bring up enthusiastically in a game of singing, anthakshari, always guaranteeing titters and chuckles from the crowd. Besides, the beauty of the lake has been extolled by the city's most celebrated writers, in both verse and prose—Kuvempu and R.K. Narayan immediately come to mind.

Quite apart from the mise en scène it provides for young love, Kukkarahalli Lake has stood witness to the cultural and intellectual history of Mysore in a way no other geographical marker has. Over the twentieth century, its position as the heart of Mysore was cemented further. When the University of Mysore, Karnataka's first, was established in 1916, the royals picked the idyllic lakeside,

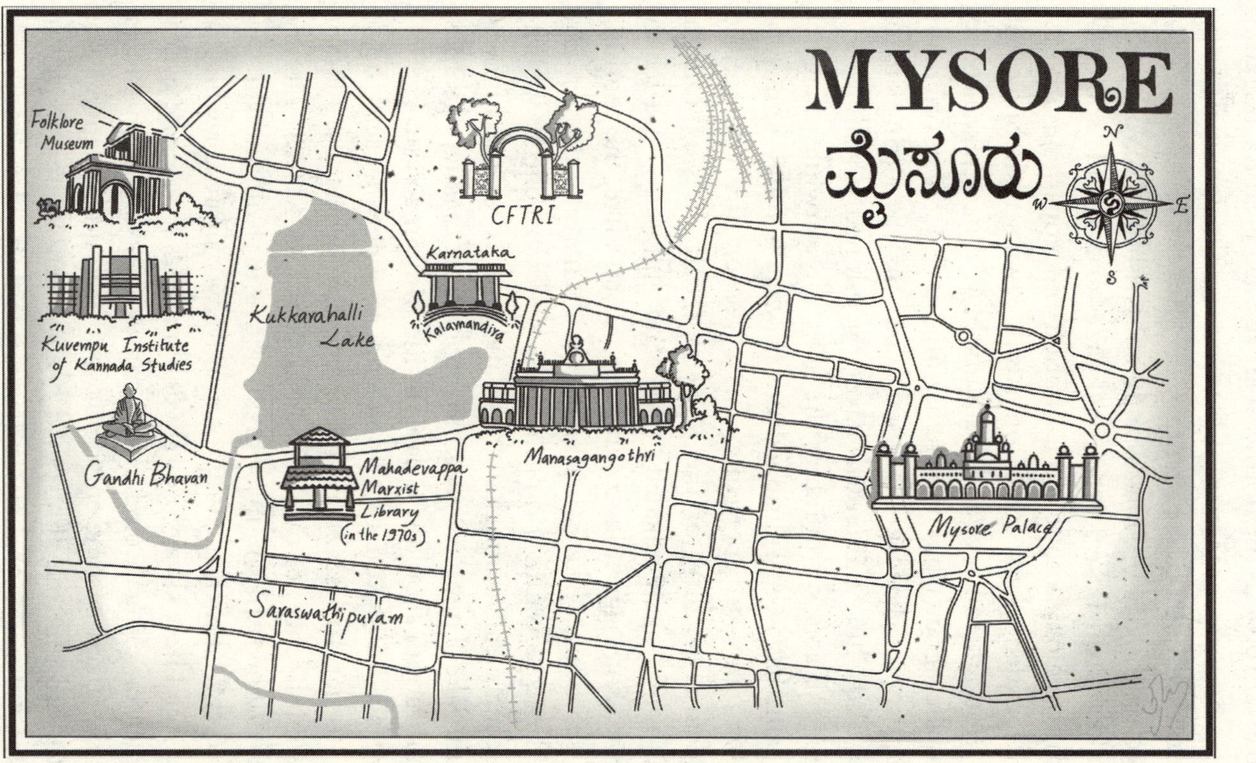

Long held in the popular imagination as a quaint cultural city, Mysore is best known for its centuries-long association with the royal house of the Wodeyars. Its clean bill of health often brings it into national attention, but Mysore has been changing rapidly over the last few years. In 2017, Mysore's population crossed one million, and it was officially characterised a metropolitan city with metropolitan problems in the making. Mysore University retains very little of its original intellectual glory today.

and so the gorgeous Manasagangothri campus lies sprawled on its western banks. Towards the northeast are the hallowed Kalamandira auditorium and the precincts of Rangayana, the famous theatre organisation set up by B.V. Karanth.

Created by the Mysore king Mummadi Krishnaraja Wodeyar in 1864, Kukkarahalli Lake served for decades as a reliable source of water for the region, both for consumption and irrigation purposes. After Independence, its condition steadily worsened. Since the eighties, efforts to conserve and clean up the lake have taken shape, buoyed by a few grants, but its water is unfit for either of its originally intended purposes. The lake also used to be a major roosting site for migratory birds, but their crowds have now thinned as well.

Most of the area surrounding the lake, the erstwhile village of Kukkarahalli, has been subsumed under what is today known as Saraswathipuram—an apt name, for it was originally conceived as a residential locality for the university staff. It is a beautiful neighbourhood, with shaded trees and pleasant, old-school architecture. For joggers, lovers and timepassers alike, the soothing effect of the nearby lake is a precious gift. The only danger, as I discovered every evening riding back home from college, was the omnipresence of all manner of bugs and insects on the highway hugging the lake. They have the annoying habit of making a goalpost out of your mouth should you dare to ride without a visor.

As I was working on this book and interviewing activists in Mysore, I began to hear floating references to a 'Marxist Library' in their reminiscences of the 1970s. Mahadevappa Marxist Library, as it was dubbed, began in a small house in Kukkarahalli that overlooked the lake, in memory of a university professor who had died of cancer. I have always thought of libraries as spaces where ideas commingle, travelling through the unconscious realm of the readers' mind-space, effecting some enigmatic, but profound, change. I was amazed to find that the library had been of central importance to everybody who spoke of their association with it. Here, some had met their future partners, some their gurus and all had imbibed the ideals that would go on to drive their actions in life. The library bequeathed a legacy of leftist intellectualism to the city, bringing together several individuals who might otherwise have never met. It seems to have manifested a very material reality, unfamiliar to my conception of the nebulous reverberations that books and libraries can create in you.

'That library began at my home,' says Dr S. Tukaram, speaking in rich Kannada with an attractive timbre, stroking his salt-and-pepper beard. He has lots of calls to attend to, and I get the impression this is an ordinary day in his life. Tukaram is currently one of the senior leaders within the ranks of the fragmented Dalita Sangharsha Samiti in Mysore. (It is generally referred to as an okkoota, or union, now, since there are many divisions.) Being something of an ajatashatru, one with no enemies, all the factions call him to deliver speeches, he tells me, proudly yet wistfully.

In the early 1970s, Tukaram's father constructed his first ever pukka house in the village of Kukkarahalli. Because a sizeable loan was taken out for it, he rented it out in the initial years to a motley crew of rationalists and Marxists—food-scientist Narendra Singh, Botany professor A.R. Ramalingam and a doctor named Laxminarayan, amongst others—who converted the house into the Mahadevappa Marxist Library in memory of their late friend.

Dr Laxminarayan passed away in 2024, but I was added to a WhatsApp group he used to oversee. It had started organising weekly talks over Zoom ever since the pandemic, featuring journalists, activists and writers speaking on a variety of subjects. I was struck by the fact that caste was the single most prominent theme that dominated these discussions. Sometimes, I would see them and their fellow travellers in the news, as part of small protests in Mysore against the ruling regime's communal politics—after a while, I began to feel that I was hearing the same things over and over again.

Back in the day though, their Marxism-inspired conversations would have been a radical novelty. Tukaram spent the formative years of his life in the company of the library, and he believes it changed his life: 'When I was studying for my Pre-University Course, I would keep visiting the library. My Kannada used to be excellent but my English was poor. I would only hear conversations about Marx, Lenin, Maoism, Maxim Gorky—these became my introduction to the world of discourse. I started reading Kannada novels also around this time. The first one I remember reading was Rao Bahadur's *Gramayana*.'

It was at the library that Tukaram met the two brothers T.S. Ramaswamy and T.S. Venugopal. I had heard much about them, especially the elder brother, affectionately called Ramu by his friends and well-wishers, of which there are many. 'You must try and meet Ramu at all costs,' the theatre director Prasanna Heggodu had told me. 'Theirs is an extraordinary family. That's all I can say.'

As it turned out, Tukaram was Ramu's brother-in-law, and they had been living together for decades now. He is heartfelt in his appreciation of Ramu's presence in his life: 'If Ramu and Venu weren't there, me and Kukkarahalli Basavaraju [a Kannada writer of Tukaram's generation] wouldn't have even finished our MA. We got food here, at this house. More importantly, we got a solid orientation.' It is to the same home that I have now come, a quaint one-storey building in quiet Saraswathipuram, with many little rooms tucked away economically inside, out the backdoor and upstairs. It has all the charm of a large joint family living together—chai and plates of murukku are flowing, jolly-hearted conversations are happening in various corners of the house, cosy bundles of washed clothes sit unfolded on a sofa, and I am almost expecting to hear the sound of coins swishing across a carrom board in that leisurely evening ambience.

The atmosphere at the Marxist Library, whose old premises lie roughly a kilometre away from Tukaram's present home, would have been starkly different. It had been transformed into the hub of a rising students' movement in Mysore, with the university being a crucial centre of political consciousness. The seventies were a time when the nature of the Indian state was in flux, and the Left was caught up in trying to understand this catalytic reaction and its volatile tendencies. Leftists across the spectrum gathered in the library to engage in dialectic and debate. The socialist and freedom fighter Asoka Mehta, a companion of Jayaprakash Narayan, was once invited to Mysore to deliver a talk. During the Emergency, things became tense and heavy, and the underground environment gave them a sense of revolutionary purpose that they had, until then, only encountered in history books.

Tukaram delineates his diverse intellectual upbringing meticulously, with the student politics of the Marxist Library only forming one facet of it. His formative years as a student in Mysore evolved through a three-pronged system of influence, as he himself categorises it. The first was a Gandhian idealism, which he attributes to two men named B.R. Pranesh Rao and K. Srinivasan (he gestures to me, keen that I include these now forgotten names) who were responsible for the upkeep of the primary school in Kukkarahalli, and went around to every street in the village urging parents to start sending their children to school instead of putting them to work. 'There was also a teacher named Chennabasavaiah—I owe him so much. Without ever seeking any personal gain like promotions, he stayed at the school until it expanded to high-school level, and really nurtured it.' Within this idealism, Tukaram recognises a moral agency that is rarer to find these days. He remarks that many radical thinkers who succeeded Gandhi failed to absorb his most relevant ideas, and so ended up rejecting him outright.

The second intellectual prong, courtesy of the library, was Marxism, tied up with a strain of staunch idealism emergent from the temper and tenor of the seventies. The Naxalbari movement was the beginning of a violent people's movement in the late sixties, which began in the titular West Bengal village after police opened fire on villagers (killing nine adults and two children) who were demanding their right to crops that they had sowed and harvested. The following decade saw these fires ignite in Andhra, where feudal relations and centuries of historical oppression were being challenged through the curve of a sickle and the barrel of a gun.

One of the founders of the library, the botanist A.R. Ramalingam, was born into a rich zamindar's family in Visakhapatnam district, and had moved to Mysore during the late sixties to take up his professorial position. Ramalingam was a serious Marxist of the radical Left variety, who went on to set up a small publishing house that translated revolutionary Telugu literature into Kannada. By all accounts, he lived a life of supreme austerity, and died in a rented house, with nothing to his name. Towards the end of his life, he rallied for the conservation of heritage trees, lectured on widespread water pollution and methods to combat them, and even unearthed a tea adulteration scandal in Mysore in 2008, which forced authorities to raid shops and confiscate adulterated tea powder.

This staunch idealism also brought with it a radical atheism, which almost threatened to alienate Tukaram from his community: 'We had become so arrogant that we had stopped worshipping our gods in our homes. At first, we believed that our own village elders were our foremost enemies. We thought, how can they still sacrifice animals at temples and so on? I think my parents began to resent me in some sense too. It took me twenty years to realise that that is not the way to critique superstition. It must be done with grace and composure, not with angst and anger.'

Thus, perhaps the Marxist legacy of the library was the most chequered of Tukaram's intellectual lineages. It was a Marxism that had arrived through sheer force of necessity, but had remained rigid and mechanical in its perceptions of Indian society. Having failed to recognise the essentially spiritual heart of the country, which Gandhi had so deftly understood, it spoke in abstractions that smacked of cocksureness and tended to overlook the social realities of caste society: 'The Marxist Library introduced us to the ideas of class struggle, but not so much about caste realities in India. This is also probably because our village, Kukkarahalli, was entirely populated by dalits, and nobody else. We would notice casteism only when the vokkaliga landlords from neighbouring villages would come to scold our sisters or mothers for not coming to work on their farms and things like that.'

The final sphere of influence was the DSS, which came together in the mid-seventies. Kolar and Bhadravati had developed as strong centres of mobilisation, and Mysore too was becoming an important fulcrum of the dalit movement in Karnataka. Inseparable from the movement was the unique literary and intellectual environment around which everyone coalesced: 'Once, Devanura Mahadeva came to the library. We knew him, because he was a famous literary figure by then, and it was through him that we came to know about the existence of the Dalita Sangharsha Samiti, and I began going there as well.'

The DSS was a bolt of lightning that sprung from the terrifying clouds of caste atrocities hanging over post-Independence India—the reactionary spasms of a society unable to come to terms with the upsurgence of long oppressed communities. As part of the DSS's cultural wing, young activists like Tukaram would take out rallies, perform street plays and bicycle around the countryside with songs of emancipation on their lips: 'From '77, to '85, every May Day we would go to factories in Mysore and perform outside them, talk to the workers and so on. We would go on cycles to villages around Mysore, and do jathas. These would all be stories about deceit, exploitation and emancipation. Ashokpuram, Gandhinagar—thickly SC-populated areas—we would do street plays there. You see, all these places in Mysore back then were hungering for rationality. People would marvel at our stories and be so interested. We also had a cultural team at the library. The idea for this had been given by Dr Ramalingam, and another CFTRI scientist named Ramakrishna. They would take the Telugu writings of poets like Varavara Rao and Gaddar, translate them into Kannada, and adapt them into street plays that we would enact.'

All in all, this was a deeply interconnected world of progressive people's movements, each an idealism unto itself. Yet, while all these disparate ideological threads seem to have found a common home in Tukaram's heart, they would each go on to develop a life of their own, often at odds with each other. Politics is, at its heart, a deeply divisive affair.

II

I heard it was you
Talking 'bout a world where all is free
It just couldn't be
And only a fool would say that.

—Steely Dan, 1972

As I turned my phone recorder on he assumed a stiff tone that was endearing in its sincerity. It was the tone of a storyteller who knew the value of a proper introduction: 'My name is Basavaraju. During the seventies, there was a fashion amongst writers to prefix their birthplace to their names. So, when I started writing, I began calling myself Kukkarahalli Basavaraju.'

Kukkarahalli Basavaraju was a poet, short-story writer, theatre artist, librarian and agricultural entrepreneur, all rolled into one. I write in the past tense, because he passed away, in his mid-sixties, less than two months after I met him during the summer of 2022. We sat outside his organic produce shop in Saraswathipuram on a breezy day. Listening to the recordings later, I felt that the constant rise and fall of the wind in the background was well complemented by Basaravaju's mercurial narrative style, jumping from one subject to another with great glee.

He grew up in the seventies, a contemporary of Tukaram's. They had both been regulars at the library, and the bond was cemented at Venu and Ramu's home, where they were always welcome. Basavaraju paints a colourful picture of how small a world Mysore was in those years. When lions roared in Mysore Zoo, they could be heard miles away. If a murder happened in the city, the news and gossip about it would spread at the speed of light.

Basavaraju and Tukaram both grew up in times when higher education still bore a distinct aura of emancipation. 'Those were times when even a BA degree was enough to ascend to the post of a District Commissioner,' Basavaraju informed me, his eyes wide with astonishment. They both procured their bachelor's degree at Mysore University, which also stirred their political awakenings:

> Gangotri Canteen, Gandhi Adhyayana Kendra, a large banyan tree—these were the main places where me met and organised. Those were times when people were militant about their protests. The State hadn't really become so powerful as to make us think twice about protesting. *Andolana* newspaper [started by Rajashekar Koti] gave a great fillip to these democratic protests.

These protests usually culminated in a gathering at Ramaswamy Circle or the Town Hall, and because Mysore was such a small town, all the chaluvaligars, activists, got to know each other quickly. The anti-caste movement inaugurated by Kuvempu had also brought with it the phenomenon of simple weddings that were not officiated by priests. Awareness campaigns out to debunk superstitions and phony godmen were the flavour of the season, spearheaded by rationalists like Hosur Narasimhaiah and Narendra Nayak. Basavaraju recalled the thrill of living in such times.

Having earned a post-graduate degree in Library Science, Basavaraju secured the post of librarian at Marimallappa's College in the late seventies, and worked there for thirty-six years, before finally retiring in 2015. Meanwhile, he had started the Nisarga Trust, which seeks to encourage organic farming and cut out greedy middlemen in the process. There are many kinks to be ironed out, however:

> What is happening today is that there is a lot of scepticism about organic produce. Farmers have realised that it fetches a lot of money, and they simply call all their yields 'organic'. It is becoming hard to tell what is organic and what isn't, and customers are beginning to lose faith. Organic food failed to stand up to malls. The vegetables you get at those big supermarkets are shiny, and look so appealing. They are chock full of chemicals, so no worm can even go near. Whereas, organic produce looks raw and misshapen, even if it is really healthy.

But he is quick to add, modestly and honestly, 'I am not a farmer, I'm not a peasant, I am just an employee in this shop.'

I was about to ask about the Marxist Library, when he seemed to realise exactly what I was thinking, and jumped into that story:

> KB: The Marxist Library came to Kukkarahalli sometime in the mid-seventies. Who was Marx, who was Ambedkar? We had no idea. We couldn't believe Ambedkar was one of our own. We had not a clue what he had written, what he had done.

> Me: How big was this library? How many books were there?

(I felt I would receive an accurate answer from a professional librarian.)

> KB: It was a 30x40 site. It was a library only in name [he chortles]. There might have been some 300 books there, perhaps.

What fascinated the young Basavaraju was the fact that, apart from teachers and professors, well-dressed individuals of high standing and educated upper-caste men and women came to this library that was situated in a predominantly dalit neighbourhood like Kukkarahalli. For his parents, it was blasphemy, anathema, almost revolting:

> When these library fellows came to our home requesting water, my parents would recoil in fear. They thought it would invite bad karma. They thought perhaps these upright people did not really know we were dalits, and that we should tell these ignorant people to stay away from us.

The library provided Basavaraju his first substantial education. Here, he first heard of Darwin's theory of evolution, the difference between modern medicine and prayers. He admits to being rather stunned by it all at first. 'We were not sure if we could believe all this. I mean, superstitions were our way of life before.'

Basavaraju was the star singer of the cultural team at the library, and he led the troupe during street protests. Tukaram was usually one of the supporting actors. Even if they were travelling on a bus, the singing would continue, and people would always look and listen. These days of reading, writing, acting and singing became very dear to Basavaraju indeed—this was when he discovered that he had a knack for writing. When other Kannada writers began recognising his work, it meant the world to him: 'In an environment where people where not allowing us to cross their thresholds, someone like Lankesh was encouraging us to write, and appreciating what we wrote. So many writers and singers were created. You cannot imagine how liberating that felt. It was almost unimaginable. The library gave us that upbringing.'

Of all the people at the library, Basavaraju looked up to Ramalingam the most. As he spoke about his foremost mentor, there was a reverence in his eyes and words that moved me: 'You will not find a man like Ramalingam any more. Pure, 100 per cent. He did not own a house till the day he died. He rejected his pension. Why? He believed that if he was not working, he did not deserve money. Where is this honesty today? You ask anybody—the Raitha Sangha, Marxists, DSS—there is nobody with that kind of pure idealism. People usually rail against him, saying he didn't take care of his family properly because of his stupidity. But, you see, these are the principles the man believed in, and he stood by them. He was a great man. Ambedkar might never have walked into my home, but Ramalingam once did.'

In due time, the activities of the library spread to Bangalore, and activists from there often travelled to Mysore to request Basavaraju to sing for their rallies and protests too. Most of these street acts revolved around local issues of misgovernance and injustice, of which stories abounded. While Basavaraju was turning into a rebel, his father mourned the loss of his only son's religious roots: 'He thought I was turning against him, because I protested against practices like sacrificing chickens at temples, worshipping walls, and so on. Yeah!'

Late into the seventies, the DSS had begun organising in Mysore, and young leaders often came to Kukkarahalli, and met up with the local activists being trained under the library's watch: 'Workers' struggle, language movement, dalit chaluvali, you name it, all of these struggles against the establishment were being talked about in Kukkarahalli. It became the hub of these discussions.' In this sense, there is a direct relationship, a passing on of the baton, that connects the Marxist Library to the slowly mushrooming DSS, though different ideologies operated within their respective ranks. For a moment, it seemed like there was a universal outpouring of sympathy for all the wretched of the earth, a single voice of concern. But of course, such notions of unity would quickly be dispelled.

> Me: Why do you think the DSS broke up within a decade of its zenith?
>
> KB: I have only a subjective opinion. I think it is because Ambedkarism never really developed as a strong ideology for the DSS. Dalits, by birth, as a people, are driven by immediate life-and-death concerns. They cannot stand by any of these political ideologies. They will say anything for the smallest improvement in their lives. Perhaps, if we had some stronger glue holding us together, history might have shaped up differently. What is the way forward for the emancipation of dalits? We still need a solid ism, a siddhanta, to guide us.

He then went on describe how the Mandal politics of the nineties diluted dalit political identity, absorbing their votes, even as the topmost leaders in every party carried on with their casteism.

> Me: Yeah, Siddalingaiah went on to sympathise with the BJP. I have heard he even presided over the book release of a revamped Manusmriti. It seems a little opportunistic …
>
> KB: See, when someone who has never seen jaggery in his life, who has always known it as something sweet to be savoured, finally sees it, how will he feel? He will feel that even theft is permissible, if only one small lick of it may be had.

I burst out laughing, wondering if this was a metaphor that Basavaraju had carefully curated and honed over years of personally knowing Siddalingaiah. However, having heard so much about

Siddalingaiah's all-embracing jocularity, I did not find it difficult to imagine him enjoying the formulation for its own sake. Basavaraju reiterated his admiration for Ramalingam in the same breath, moving on from the joke immediately:

> This is what makes someone like Ramalingam stand out. He had such unwavering principles to stand by. A casteless, classless, society was his goal. Everyone had to be grateful for just what was enough to live by. He would never have sold out like this.

The idealism which Basavaraju admired in Ramalingam is one that approximates religion in its scope. One's principal beliefs are set firmly in stone, and the moral conundrum has been unflinchingly solved. It brooks no deviation, will be party to no contestation. Later, as I sat listening to the interview, I couldn't help thinking of another Botany professor named Golwalkar, who too had subscribed to an ideology of collectives, to the grand dream of which an individual's entire life would have to be yoked. The two modern ideologies they represented—communism and fascism—were enshrined together at the altar of twentieth-century totalitarianism, where politics was synonymous with enmity. That said, these ideologies had taken on new avatars in Indian soil, and while they could be abstractly compared, Ramalingam and Golwalkar were ultimately nothing like each other.

These philosophical conundrums had become pressing questions by the early 2000s, when the extreme-Left in India was in its final throes and the Sangh was gaining in power. In a talk titled *Himseya Eda-Bala* (The Left and Right of Violence), U.R. Ananthamurthy tried to think these things through at a symposium held in 2004 at Ninasam, Heggodu. He starts his exposition with an abstract blueprint of how the Right inflicts violence on innocent people by citing religious wrongs perpetrated in some long-gone past, while the Left resorts to violence in the name of a utopian future. He moves on to more interesting specifics drawn from his own life. During the Emergency, Ananthamurthy had received a letter from George Fernandes, proposing that they meet up at a shady location in Bangalore, where Fernandes sat swaddled in layers of coats. Fernandes was considering lobbing a weak bomb at an administrative building during the night, when few people would be around, to signal to the citizens that resistance was underway. But the prospect of the inevitable death of innocents, however few, was too much for Fernandes to bear. Ananthamurthy goes on to bemoan the dispiriting political trajectory of his good friend George Fernandes—once a man who would've thought twice about the smallest act of violence, he went on to become a mouthpiece for the BJP and its open call for religious violence against innocent multitudes. When the Christian missionary Graham Staines (and his two young sons) were burnt alive by Bajrang Dal goons in 1999, Ananthamurthy had expected that Fernandes might at least express horror over a fellow Christian family's tragedy, but he had glibly delivered a statement to the effect that the killing was not done by Indians at all, but by foreign elements.

Despite the abstracted similarities in his intellectual ruminations, Anathamurthy's lived experiences as a deeply political man intervened to dictate his conviction that the phenomenon of violence on the Left and Right carry important distinctions. He writes of Lenin and Mao, for instance, as men who started out with noble intentions, 'but then lost their mental freedoms and became monsters'. He concedes that he could never deem them as purely evil men in the same way that he could pronounce the same judgement upon Savarkar, who had once endorsed the rape of Muslim women as appropriate political strategy for Hindus—a dictum that been widely deployed just two years before Ananthamurthy's speech, during the Gujarat pogroms. Comparing Left extremism to cancer and Right extremism to rabies, he argues that a tumour in an unequal society emerges out of its own body, from the grassroots of disenfranchisement, while the bite of a mad dog is an external intrusion that has little to do with the internal constitution of a victim. It is at least possible to spark arguments within the Left, he continues, a fact evidenced by the repeated fragmentation of communist parties in India. On the other hand, their counterparts on the Right were united in their unrepentant embrace of unabashedly violent streaks. K.V. Subbanna called the bluff on Ananthamurthy's cancer-rabies thesis, and pointed out that this was a skewed metaphor informed by Ananthamurthy's own political preferences, a point which Ananthamurthy conceded in his speech. He concluded by harking back to Gandhi, who remains *the* idealistic refuge for all those who abhor political violence of any sort.

Ananthamurthy's vulnerable (and flawed) ruminations mark a time when idealism had seemingly vanished from Indian political (and personal) life, and a desperate search for it had to be organised. This is also what pushed the Tamil writer Jeyamohan to write his collection of stories *Aram* (translated as *Stories of the True*). In twelve short stories, each profiling an extraordinary individual he has met, each with their own brand of civic idealism, Jeyamohan summons into imagination new avatars of moral activism somehow thriving even in the modern world of fragmented moralities. One amongst these is a selfless hotel owner who serves free food to everyone and only takes willingly offered donations. After Jeyamohan put the story out, he says he received tens of emails telling him about the existence of such eateries in whichever corner of the country they were from. I myself know a septuagenarian couple in the village of Parkala, where I live, who serve wholesome, unlimited Konkani meals for all of Rs 60. What Jeyamohan drives home in his stories is that when one's idealism becomes community focused, espouses love over violence, and is distanced from the entrapments of fame and glory, it can make for a powerful, extraordinarily meaningful ways of life.

Kukkarahalli Basavaraju had critiqued Siddalingaiah's deviation from his once-Marxist path and deployed it as a narrative motif to spell out an overall trajectory of betrayal, of losing one's way, of forgetting one's principles. Implicit in it was the accusation that the poet had ended up prizing personal enrichment over larger political ideals. He saw it as a metaphor for the dalit movement as a whole. It also reflected a sense of moral failure that had gripped Basavaraju towards the end of his own life: 'When parents find food somewhere, they pack it in a cloth and bring it home for the kids. They know that there are people at home who are waiting. They share what they have with others. They have an inner conscience and parental love. I'm sorry to say that the movement lost this basic courtesy which they owed to those who were still uneducated and impoverished.'

Tukaram, on the other hand, spoke more gently of the political and ideological trajectories of the dalit intelligentsia, trying to accommodate their trajectory in a sympathetic light. Humanising the individual was more important than the romanticisation of a collective ideal. When I asked him about Siddalingaiah, whom he knew very well, he said: 'Yes, most people keep saying that Siddalingaiah was pally with Amit Shah, and met him privately once. I remember asking him about it the same day. And he told us that he couldn't have denied meeting a big political figure. And that even during that conversation, he had only spoken about SC/ST scholarships that hadn't been disbursed yet. I think it is easy to point to someone's flaws. We should try to understand him positively—he was the poet who stirred the movement at its very origins.'

I did catch a glimpse of Basavaraju's cynicism through another veteran activist in Mysore, H. Govindaiah, whom I was put on to by Basavaraju himself. By the time I managed to secure an interview with Govindaiah, Basavaraju had passed on. It was heartening to hear Govindaiah present his own understanding of the dalit movement through ample references to Basavaraju's latest writings and words. Through his endorsements, Kukkarahalli Basavaraju had taken on a second life of sorts. However, what I found most intriguing was that Govindaiah had now transformed into the staunchest critic of someone who had once been his closest friend, and someone widely accepted as one of the finest creative voices in modern Kannada literature—Devanura Mahadeva.

III

November 2023, Kuvempunagar, Mysore

Turning onto Navilu Raste (Peacock Street), I look for the honge (Indian beech) tree that has been indicated to me as a landmark.

Devanura Mahadeva's secretary-assistant-bodyguard stands vigil outside, and ushers me into his home. I have been waiting a long time to meet him—his health had not been great over the last several months, and besides, he has always cultivated the intrigue of a mysterious personality.

As I wait in the small hall, where sits a small television screen, I see peacock feathers propped up at multiple spots on the wall. A bust of the Buddha, a cobalt-blue portrait of a beatific Hindu goddess, a few books and magazines on a table, an ashtray and a pack of Milds. I had heard through the grapevine that Mahadeva had long been a beedi-smoker, but septuagenarian health concerns have now rendered the filtered tip of a cigarette a necessity. His home is exactly how I had imagined it would be—quaint, spartan and inviting.

As Mahadeva walks in, he points to a book he's been reading about J.C. Kumarappa, the Gandhian economist. 'See, we are all people of an older generation—Gandhi is still in our lives.' I nod fervently, Tukaram's words flashing through my mind. Pleasantries are quickly dispensed with, and I open up the many questions bubbling inside of me. He accepts questions with a quirky *Vokay*, signs off punchy sentences with the same and quickly cuts me off when I'm overextending my questions.

> Me: Since the peacock theme has been suggesting itself to me all this way, let's start with that. So, in *Odalaala*, the little girl Puttagouri is sketching a peacock on the hut wall. Why peacock? And also—
>
> DM: One question at a time, please? Haha. Vokay. If you come to my farm near Bogadi, you can see a lot of peacocks there. Well, it is a rural motif. It is omnipresent in villages. Very simple. What is more interesting is that she sketches it starting from its legs, and not the head. The legs point earthwards, and so do her thoughts. She is illiterate, and her imagination begins from the ground up. Obviously, this is not what I was thinking when I wrote it. I just happened to realise it later. I myself might misinterpret what I have written, you see? So, I don't talk about my own writing much.

Mahadeva's novella *Odalaala* (literally, depths of hunger) was published in 1978, and is a miniature portrait of the travails of an old woman named Sakavva and her extended family, their poverty thrown into sharp relief by motifs such as Puttagouri's peacock sketch. It is interesting to note that some prehistoric boulder art recently discovered at Arsikere, achieved through red line strokes, were identified as representing peacocks—a primal image, indeed.

At the heart of *Odalaala* is a scene that has been compared to Van Gogh's 'Potato Eaters' in its evocative imagery: the entire family is huddled over a heap of stolen groundnuts in the evening light of a fireplace when a hungry visitor comes begging for some food. It is a scene of domestic solidarity. The family disregards their squabbles and gathers in unity over the heap of nuts. When one of them picks up a handful of groundnuts to give the visitor, Sakavva reaches into that handful, pulls back some more for themselves, and allows a little to be given to the guest. Mahadeva told me that later reflection has led him to believe that the scene was likely a legacy of reading Premchand.

It was this little detail that H. Govindaiah had brought up many months earlier, after which I had doubled back and re-read the story a few times. In this episode, which has always been seen as a 'trial of hunger', Govindaiah argued that there lies a literary, as well as philosophical, mistake:

'This valorisation of theft, of that grabbing mentality, is not dalit philosophy. There must be a more wholesome sharing attitude. The groundnuts are, after all, stolen goods. The hunger of *Odalaala* is an inextinguishable hunger, and could never act as the spirit of a community.'

He brings up a poem called 'Avva Barale Illa' (Mother Never Came), written by Kukkarahalli Basavaraju, where there is a similar scene but a different response: 'In Basavaraju's poem, there is again a household suffering from abject poverty and hunger. When a hungry visitor knocks on the door, the woman of the house, who herself is hungry, takes the last of whatever food they have and puts it into the hands of the visitor, saying "this will turn into mud, regardless of who eats it, anyway".' Now, that is a philosophy we must adopt—of sharing and compassion.'

Odalaala begins with Sakavva waking up one unfortunate day to realise that one of her hens is missing. The absent hen aggravates her anxieties, and she begins fighting with everybody in her extended family of three huts. It is only when one of her sons arrives with the bag of stolen peanuts, and the entire family unites over the spoils, that everyone begins sharing stories. It is a scene filled with a moving sense of solidarity, above all else. Later in the story, the police find out about the stolen peanuts and attempt to recover them, only to find that there are no peanuts left in Sakavva's house. They were so hungry that they had eaten them all. In the final turn of the story, Sakavva confides to one of the policemen about her missing hen, and tells him that it looked just like another hen that is still with her. The cunning policeman tells her that he will take the other hen with him, so as to help him identify the missing hen, and proceeds to do so. By the time Sakavva realises that she has been tricked, the policemen have made away with her last remaining hen. *Odalaala* is thus a story of exploitation, and rural innocence, and the small, brief consolations in a life of deprivation and tragedy, narrated with a descriptive restraint and sympathy that brings to mind the stories of Chekhov.

I came to know that sharp personal differences had erupted between Mahadeva and Govindaiah, and heard from the poet and journalist T.S. 'Ramu' Ramaswamy that the cause for it was some kind of legal dispute at the centre of which was a lake and a fishing venture on the outskirts of Mysore. Mahadeva spelt out all the details for me patiently, and it suffices here to say that it was not a matter that should have caused a difference between two friends who respect each other. At the heart of it lay a greater sense of injustice. I must also admit that, even in the space of a short conversation with Mahadeva, I did discern a distinct sense of his ego, which is also an inadvertent cause of personal fissures.

After the DSS was formed in the mid-1970s, Devanura Mahadeva and B. Krishnappa, two of its senior figures, emerged as prominent leaders. Mahadeva's life during these years involved running between pillar and post, and the DSS activism took up much of his time. He gave me a copy of his wife Sumitra Bai's autobiography[1]—a witty and moving memoir—saying that it held answers to many of my questions. Candid to the letter, the book speaks of the frustration Sumitra Bai experienced with Mahadeva's repeated absences on account of his activist work, and also offers clarifications regarding the numerous mudslinging campaigns that have been launched against him in the course of the rise and fall of this heated political space. When Mahadeva was writing his famous novel *Kusumabale* in the early eighties, a DSS activist and writer named Mulluru Nagaraj had visited their home and perused some initial drafts of the novel. Later, he wrote a letter to Mahadeva saying he was writing a novel too, inspired by Mahadeva's style. Sumitra Bai writes: 'I was glad to read that letter. But then, I was dumbstruck when he began saying that he had written his novel first, and that Mahadeva had copied the style from him. He then wrote a critique of *Kusumabale*, claiming that it was an anti-dalit work. Mahadeva did not respond to this at all.'

I did end up stumbling upon a reviewer's gloss of Mulluru Nagaraj's novel[2] that contrasted it with Mahadeva's writing, and found the former to be lacking in 'subtlety and suggestiveness'. I found Mulluru Nagaraj's critique of *Kusumabale* as well, which took crude umbrage at the fact that *Kusumubale*'s protagonist was an upper-caste woman, and concluded that the novel did not espouse the emancipation of dalits. What *I* concluded was that a certain measure of sledging and resentment over prestige had broken into the DSS ranks even in those years. All sorts of rumours float around even today.[3]

I first read *Kusumabale* in its English translation, which is not the greatest substitute for the Kannada original. More than the story itself, I was taken by the references to contemporary society that kept surfacing in the novel.

> Me: At the end of *Kusumabale*, there is a scene—a procession being carried out by many dalit activists from Kolar. I remember the

names of Ramaiah, Muniyappa—what was the significance you saw in this scene? It felt like you were trying to show the richly diverse set of individuals who made up the movement …

DM: Yes yes, I wanted to make it a janapada [folk] rendition of sorts. I wanted to make those characters come alive in a folk idiom. I did try to handle the scene in a realistic fashion, but my intellect began to intrude, and I don't like it when that happens. Then I lose the handle, you see?

Me: Did you ever keep these categories in mind—janapada, shastriya, marga, desi—while writing?

DM: I follow a very simple sutra: is this writer named Devanura Mahadeva directing the characters, or were they born organically out of the content? That is the testing point. One is artificial, and the other is creative. In *Kusumabale*, there are Sanskrit words, English words—I don't know whether that qualifies for being desi, or not. In any case, it is not important. What matters is that the core of the work has come out of this land. Pampa calls his language Puligereya[4] thiruluganmada [Puligere's Kannada marrow]. Why did he not simply call it Puligere Kannada? He was referring to the core of the language, not to the way people were actually speaking. It is, instead, the essence of the language, retrieved from the writer's mind, after a period of intense churning and healthy digestion.

In deriving inspiration from the grand lineage of Kannada poets, Devanura Mahadeva was essentially transporting the desi (the bard-style imagination of oral epics like Manteswamy Kavya) into the prestigious canon of the marga (the linguistic churn of high art). The novel is as much a story set in rural India as it is a literary *artefact.* This is what prompted the critic G. Rajashekhar to pronounce that *Kusumabale* was a novel written in 'bad faith', where he invoked Sartre to argue that the work was written with the 'pre-existing conviction of a certain kind of literary audience', and that it had a whiff of *artifice* to it. He argued that the jump to magical realism while the possibilities of realist literature in Kannada were still to reach its pinnacle might have been premature. D.R. Nagaraj, when asked about the cultural imagination opened up by the novel, said: 'In *Kusumabale*, there is a remarkable aesthetic device at play. However, I don't feel that Mahadeva is writing with a genuine belief in the faith that created these aesthetic devices.'[5]

Art and artifice are two sides of the same coin though, and the richness of a thirulugannada and its evocative qualities lies in its ability to, at the very least, suggest an imagination of centuries past, while still being situated within the rural realities of today. To read the novel is also to embody a cultural imagination that has persevered for centuries—it is an engagement with a community, and an oral tradition that it has kept alive and well. Even if the writer may not have faith in its liberatory powers, his creative endeavour might still carry enough resonances through its linguistic *gesture*. *Kusumabale*'s experimental style also reminded me of G.V. Desani's famous novel *All About H Hatterr*, which had created a similar potpourri of Indian English, a subcontinental *thiruluIndianEnglish*, if you will. It had attracted critical acclaim from numerous prominent English writers, but was summarily dismissed by George Orwell as profligate excess.

Consider this hilarious extract from its first pages:

> *Indian middle-man* (to Author): Sir, if you do not identify your composition a novel, how then do we itemise it? Sir, the rank and file is entitled to know.
>
> *Author* (to Indian middle-man): Sir, I identify it a *gesture*. Sir, the rank and file is entitled to know.
>
> *Indian middle-man* (to Author): Sir, there is no immediate demand for *gestures*. There is immediate demand for novels. Sir, we are literary agents not free agents.
>
> *Author* (to Indian middle-man): Sir, I identify it a novel. Sir, itemise it accordingly.

Essentially, *Kusumabale* does to Kannada what *Hatterr* did for Indian English at the cosmopolitan level—creating a linguistic *gesture* that goes straight to the heart of a people's imagination. The reverberatory effect it had on Mulluru Nagaraj is not so different from the effect that *Hatterr* had on a generation of Indian English writers, Rushdie being the most prominent. Yet, wonderful as gestures are at the outset of a literary tradition, they become unoriginal when repeated without innovation, as Nagaraj's failed literary endeavour and some of Rushdie's excessive linguistic high jinks testify. It is in light of this that Mahadeva's refusal to write any novel after *Kusumable* seems to me a decision of wise restraint. Desani too never wrote another novel. They are also united in the perfectionist modus operandi that governed their writing. Desani kept tinkering and tailoring with his drafts throughout the Second World War. They are both literary heroes whose talents culminated in one definitive work that continues to stagger readers. Both works were the first of their kind, and will also be the last of their kind.

Having spoken to Mahadeva about his writing for much of our conversation, I turn the conversation towards his politics. Only last year, a small book(let) critiquing the RSS created a record run of multiple editions, prompting Mahadeva to share the ebook for free, making it wildly popular. My grand-uncle sitting in the village of Talakad had read it, and endorsed it too. I was curious to know what young Mahadeva's political upbringing was like.

> DM: I was doing my MA when the attack on Ramalingam happened …
>
> Me: Attack? A physical attack?
>
> DM: Yes, yes. I came out in his support. A skirmish had erupted between Ramalingam and the head of the Botany department. Two opposing groups had formed, that's all. Ramalingam was the kind of man who minced no words. He was also a supporter of the Naxalite movement. All these things were there …

Mahadeva's political allegiances had been towards the socialist left, and reading an article written by Lohia (published in the aftermath of his death in 1967) had converted the young Mahadeva into a fan. He understands all his political influences through their essence: Gandhi, Ambedkar, Lohia and the Buddha would become similar influences of non-violence, compassion, harmony and desi philosophy, for instance. He'd briefly joined the RSS when young, but when he witnessed another young member expressing a fervent desire to take at least one Muslim life, he knew he had had enough. Later, the boosa movement directed his life towards an arena where his political ideals could be turned into action:

> Boosa effect is evident on the formation of the DSS, vokay? The message it sent out was that we wouldn't be able to survive if we kept silent. Many dalit organisations existed then, but then they came together after boosa …

Sumitra Bai intervenes at this moment, telling me that long conversations are taxing for him, and that I should try and wrap up quickly. He consoles both of us, saying he's fine, and requests some chai as a relaxant.

> Yes, so, most of those organisations were like-minded. After boosa, we all came together—there was a desire for state-wide unity. A meeting was called in Chikmagalur, and they had to decide on a common name. At that time, Visveswarayya Paper Mills at Bhadravati had a labour union—Dalita Sangharsha Samiti—which was conceived to fight untouchability. The same name was used. And so, the DSS became a medium that stopped so many caste atrocities, nipped it right in the bud. All in all, it became a strong corrective force that arrested murderous instincts … DSS supported the Bahujan Samaj Party when it emerged. There was a split in the eighties when Venkataswamy defected—it was a money thing, corruption had set in by then. When Mayawati began supporting the BJP in the nineties, a split happened, which I myself endorsed. It was an ideological split, no doubt.

During the eighties, the DSS and the Karnataka Rajya Raitha Sangha were trying to blend into a common platform where farmers and labourers could unite as a force. It was a botched endeavour. After the split within the DSS on account of BSP's alignment with the BJP during the nineties, Mahadeva attempted a fresh start.

In Karnataka, dalits are largely labourers. And farmers are mostly the landed class. They are communities who harbour intolerance for each other. Through the eighties, the DSS grew, and so did the Raitha Sangha. But they were different in the way they understood society. Since Nanjundaswamy's time, many of us tried to fuse the two. But it didn't happen. In Puttanaiah's time, this attempt continued. A few of the DSS factions, and the most significant part of the KRRS joined to become Sarvodaya Karnataka. In the beginning, I became the president, and Puttanaiah became the chief secretary. It started off as a statement [*another gesture?*]—we wanted to prove that this unity was possible. But we did not have the structure to follow this up and sustain it. The truth is that it will never become a proper party if only DSS and Raitha Sangha people are manning it. Other demographics need to come in as well. I tried to push for this too, but it didn't happen. Now, it seems like this fact is slowly being understood. The reach of Sarvodaya Karnataka extends only to zilla panchayat, gram panchayat, taluk panchayat elections—we begin there. Then it must grow …

By this time, the chai had come and gone, and I knew that my time was up. Pocketing some wonderful new books Mahadeva gave me, I took my leave. Later, perusing Sumitra Bai's autobiography, I would discover colourful anecdotes page after page:

In the thirty-three years of my service, I have not seen DM's writing progress speedily even once. Only if the structure, embellishments, tone and diction are all perfect, it progresses. Else, it stagnates wherever it is …

Hadupadu Ramu, also known as a walking encyclopaedia, once said: *If DM was Brahma, people's fates would fail to get written on time, and many humans would be born with truly empty slates …* This seems to be quite truthful. To this DM had responded: *How nice that would be, if everyone could write their own destinies …*

When conversing with DM, even if my thinking is along the same lines, his thought process resembles a long jump or a high jump event. Even when mingling equally with everyone else, his mind leaps at the speed of light. I cannot compete with him in these jumping events. Even if I cannot catch his ponytail, I try to catch

> at least his shirt (because I am a Kho-Kho player) and keep trailing behind him!

Mahadeva was deeply distraught when his close friend, the novelist Alanahalli Krishna, passed away at an unexpectedly young age, and the loss of several other close friends over the succeeding decades had reinforced a feeling of desolation. 'These days, DM is forgetting his sense of being abandoned in the company of Ramu Kaka [T.S. Ramaswamy aka Hadupadu Ramu],' Sumitra Bai writes. Her book was published in 2018.

Apart from his wife's tell-all autobiography, Mahadeva also recommended that I read a couple of promising Kannada books by young fiction writers that he had enjoyed recently—Gangappa Talwar's novel *Dhaavati* as well as a collection of short stories titled *Foo Mattu Itara Kathegalu* by Manjunayak Challur. I was struck by the fact that the dominant theme pervading these stories was the suffocation of the lives of women in rural hinterlands.[6] He also spoke highly of Kodagina Gowramma, one of the first women short story writers of the early twentieth century, and N.K. Hanumanthaiah, a gifted poet of the late twentieth century who tragically died at a young age.

I later discovered Hanumanthaiah's striking poetic imagery, and moving life story, in a personal essay he had written for the book *Talaparige*.[7] He narrates, in a laconic style typical of dalit memoirs, how he braved extraordinary childhood trauma (ghastly home environment, abject poverty, his father's suicide) to become a writer and poet of repute. I was taken with some other details too. For instance, he had published his first poem in *Lankesh Patrike* by masquerading as H. Govindaiah, who was amused to hear of this later. Hanumanthaiah had also faced a vengeful society hell-bent on finishing him off when they got word of his plans to marry a woman of the lingayat caste, and the couple had arrived in desperate straits at Mysore, where many, including Mahadeva and Govindaiah, had solemnised their simple wedding. One terrific image, culled from a love poem Hanumanthaiah had written when he was in college, stayed with me:

Look at me,
I have brought the clouds.
Into those parched eyes,
I will wring them out.

IV

T.S. Ramaswamy (Ramu) passed away in the wee hours of 13 June 2023. He had been in and out of hospital for many months as diabetes weakened his body, but it was a heart attack in the middle of the night that finally ended things. The next day, local newspapers carried loving obituaries, and many writers, journalists and even political figures whose lives he had touched came together to remember him. Through some stroke of sheer dumb luck, I happened to meet him the previous evening, only a few hours before he breathed his last, and we spoke for nearly an hour: a long overdue interview conducted in subdued haste. It had been a year since my last opportunity to speak with him, and I was worried that his failing health might prevent him from responding with the sharpness he was known for.

His voice was frail, his tone punctuated by painstaking wheezing sounds, and he once held his stomach and flinched in mild agony. (I was reminded of the last days of my own grandfather, who too had been a Ramaswamy, Ramu in his close circles.) But despite his poor health, all my questions were met with sharp responses, full of wit and insight. He spoke in a highly self-reflective and critical tenor, especially when talking about the Marxist Library and the culture it had spawned. Reminiscing about its conception with an expression that was half-laughter, half-pain, he remembered the university professor Mahadevappa's death, which had birthed the library.

We needed a martyr. So we made him a martyr.

This martyrdom had paved the way to a practical experiment in, let's call it, library 'science'. '[Marxism] was neither a true science, nor a true religion,' Octavio Paz, that staunch critic of Marxisms and pseudo-Marxisms, had once pronounced. This half-science, half-religion came alive during the weekends, when the members of the library met to debate and pontificate. At the Marxist Library, a good deal of verbal dialectics was directed towards the theorisation of what the 'State' was. Was it semi-feudal and semi-colonial, as those of the extremist CPI(Marxist-Leninist) argued? Wouldn't that mean that a war had to be waged on the feudal and colonial elements? Or was it a capitalist state, with remnants of feudalism, as those of the CPI(M) argued? These were very serious men indeed, poring over the theory, mapping out the contours of their ideological grasp of world affairs. It would take the dissipation of the Cold War and the globalisation of the economy in the nineties for the sun to fully set on those last gasps of twentieth-century Marxisms. Even before, though, there were many within its most fervent ranks who had already grown disenchanted with the lack of colour in that discourse. Gita Ramaswamy (yet another Ramaswamy!) writes of this in her extraordinarily candid autobiography *Land, Guns, Caste, Woman*. Growing up as a radical feminist in the Naxal heartlands of Andhra country, she had found the atmosphere of debate and reflection stifling. That incongruous vocabulary and the creeping voice of cocksure authoritarianism combined to form a picture so distasteful that Ramaswamy cut off all her party affiliations, and set about working independently, as a publisher of books, as a lawyer and as a human rights' activist.

Ramu too dismissed the whole gamut of these Marxism-inspired discussions as an exercise in futility. In his youth, he too had been an idealistic fellow traveller alongside the radical Left. In retrospect, though, he had only the sharp edge of a knife with which to deliver his verdicts:

> No real democracy came out of it. No intellectual came out of it.
>
> The state machinery was different than it was in the fifties and sixties. It is not so easy to define the state. We did not realise this then. We must revisit the Emergency, and study its impact again.
>
> The rationalist project also missed the point. We railed against superstition and religion. But these so-called superstitions often served as a psychological solace for the common man. We

> understood this only later. I often wonder if we were just anti-people back then?
>
> The dalit literati would celebrate oral epics like Male Mahadeshwara and Manteswamy Kavya, which are essentially religious epics, but when it came to villagers praying at a temple, they thought it was regressive.
>
> Then, there were the M-L groups that advocated taking up arms. One couldn't question these things also. They were mostly populated by upper castes, who were good at filling people with guilt.

I read this as a strong disillusionment with these ideological experiments, and said as much to Ramu, who responded with further nuance:

> Not quite. When I say that it was a students' movement which tried to contact the village people, and failed, it is not disillusionment. This is what had to happen. There is just not much to boast of with pride. The important thing is that this must also reflect a change in our own mind. This is important in the case of the dalits also. If one became even an IAS officer, they became corrupt there. Or, they would just be happy getting embroiled in love, romance and those kinds of cheshtes [mischiefs]. Why did this corruption set in? Why were women so secondary to all these movements? These are the questions that I would like to find answers to.

It would seem that Ramu, who never married, did not see much revolutionary potential in just the mere acts of secular romance that transpired on the grassy environs of Kukkarahalli Lake. 'The educated dalits might have married brahmin women, but this distanced them from the less uplifted dalits. A change should have reflected in their morality, but it did not really happen. They became content with moving away from the lives of their brethren.'

It is a curious corollary of this very point that Ramu employed in his critique of dalit literature of the eighties. Having moved away from illiterate society, dalit writers nevertheless carried a sense of guilt, and this surfaces in the characters that dominate their stories. Ramu argued that the creamy layer of dalits who went on to become writers always had as their subject a weak, meek and impoverished dalit—a monotype of a character that begins to seem increasingly dated after the seventies:

> The problems of educated dalits never made it into dalit-bandaya literature. A gulf came up between educated and uneducated dalits. Their issues were completely different. Dalit literature was only creating monotypes at this point. In other words, the writers never reflected on their own selves in their books. They had as their subject someone else altogether, who might or might not really exist in society. Literature became 'unreal' in that sense. [Devanura] Mahadeva is probably the most creative voice that came out of here.

Around halfway into my conversation, it became painfully obvious to me that talking was becoming difficult for him. I had to wind up swiftly. Tukaram intervened with a cup of chai and a veg puff, and I was supremely glad to break my line of inquiry and indulge in the snacks. I tried to remember what Ramu had said in my first ten-minute conversation with him over a year earlier. He had spoken about the lack of a powerful metaphor in any of these social movements. Literature could have been a source of such symbols, but that too did not happen, he had said.

> Me: What did you have in mind when you spoke of powerful metaphors?
>
> R: You have to look at Gandhi. The charkha was such a powerful symbol because it involved both the self and the other. You weave cloth for yourself, and for others too. Same with the Dandi March. Unless you have hypertension, salt is important for you. So, the symbol becomes universal, you see.
>
> Me: Hmmm. But how does that connect to literature? Was not the dudi in Shivaram Karanth's *Chomana Dudi* a great metaphor for the emancipatory power of art?

(I felt like my hurriedly worded question was a little inane, though Ramu salvages it with some interesting, if slightly disconnected, comments.)

> Well, the dudi was made just for the novel, not as a representation of Scheduled Castes. It has little place in a social movement. *Chomana Dudi* is a classic work of art, but even there, it is Karanth looking at a dalit from the outside. Even Ambedkar had his metaphor. The way Gandhi shed his clothes, Ambedkar donned his suit. Both serve the same purpose. Both of them are naked.

My final interaction with Ramu was to probe his thoughts on the unfortunate animosity between Govindaiah and Devanura Mahadeva. He seemed amused and melancholic in equal measure:

> Eh, it is some personal grouse between them that has expanded into this. I believe it is something to do with purchasing some water body, where they can fish, where Mahadeva apparently favoured his younger brother more than Govindaiah, or some such trivial affair. And one more thing also—Govindaiah is a madiga, while Devanur Mahadeva is a holeya. This too added fuel to the fire, I think.

Was it this self-knowledge that had also prompted Govindaiah's statement about the lack of unity amongst the Holeya-Madigas (immortalised in Siddalingaiah's first collection of poems *The Songs of the Holeya-Madigas*) becoming an internal contradiction that broke the DSS from within? In his articulation though, the divide had sprung up between Mahadeva and B. Krishnappa. It was a thought that kept presenting itself in many of my readings. Dalits in South India are divided into left and right castes,[8] and they are further split into subcastes who are yet lower in the pecking order. Govindaiah had even supported Gandhi's Poona fast, which had put paid to Ambedkar's idea of separate electorates for dalits, arguing that the latter idea would have only led to infighting between dalit castes. In its amoeba-like differentiation, Indian society ultimately collides with itself, and skirmishes emerge between those who share a largely common fate. This has always been the country's greatest weakness. After the Supreme Court approved internal reservations for dalit sub-categories in August 2024, Devanura Mahadeva gave an interview to *Ambedkarvaada* magazine welcoming the judgement, hoping that it might heal the bitter wounds of the last few decades.

When asked if this was only furthering division amongst dalits, he responded that it would be left to the people to transform this into a positive message: 'It is not that somebody else made dalits political untouchables—they brought it upon themselves. Unity was broken. Having tired of this, relationships are now sprouting once again.'

It was at this point that Ramu stood up to go to the washroom, wincing in pain, and Tukaram nodded to me that the interview was over. I felt grateful for the little window of time I had been afforded. When I heard the next morning that Ramu had passed away, I was shaken, and fell to brooding about my intrusive presence on his last day. Did it fit somewhere within the teleology of Ramu's view of the past? *This is what had to happen.* The obituaries in the newspapers told me that Ramu had worked as a journalist with *Andolana* magazine, where he is remembered as launching a new segment called 'haadu paadu', which I can only guess to be a cultural review supplement. At one point, *Andolana* had been associated with the literary elite, at the forefront of a vibrant intellectual discourse. Now, its sheen has dulled, and it has become more of a political relic.

The first time I met Ramu, in May 2022, I was working on a longform article profiling Saketh Rajan, a Maoist revolutionary from Mysore who had been shot dead by the State in 2005. I had learnt that Venugopal and Ramaswamy were his distant relatives, and I was there to speak to them largely in that context. It was then that I first met Tukaram as well, who told me that Ramu was unwell, but that I could just go say hi. During the few minutes I had spoken to Ramu, I brought up this subject, and Ramu dismissed Saketh with a single wave of hand, saying: 'Saketh Rajan. He did not even care about his own mother. What use is there?'

Indeed, Saketh's tragic life has invited many such brutal comments during the course of my research. I discovered in him that blinding singularity of purpose which is incapable of acknowledging contestation. His historiography was driven less by curiosity than by the desire to grasp history by its scruff and fit it onto a preordained map. It lacked sympathy for the past, and could not hope to understand what has been called, in an anthropological and philosophical sense, 'the genius of a people'. It was no coincidence that, during my final meeting with Ramu, he recommended to me multiple times the work of the academic S.N. Balagangadhara, who is a professor of religious studies, and has produced a body of work that attempts to emphasise the importance of native conceptions of history towards an 'Indian way of life'. Balagangadhara is also a vehement critic of identity politics as it took shape in India, and even suggests that the similarly charged movements that are now taking the stage in the West should learn from the pitfalls that their precursors in India generated. Fragmentation of identities could ring a death knell for humanitarianism in the unified sense. As I began reading Balagangadhara, the conservative shift in Ramu's own life became clearer to me. *We have not understood anything properly*, Ramu had said. What he meant was that the Left had failed to understand the complexity of India's cultural pasts, and that this was its grossest fault line. This, of course, is quite true.

I did, however, become quite exasperated by Balagangadhara's extended diatribe[9] that seeks to demolish the last 200 years of academic Indology—he loves throwing around words like 'nonsense' and 'bullshit' and 'bakwaas', but doesn't move beyond this superficial level. In the process, he seems to have only created a reactionary critique bordering on contempt for all Western scholars, which is also what has hindered the creation of original modern interpretations of religion and culture amongst the conservative right. Much of this kind of diatribe, underwritten by political prejudices, is lost in a forest of essentialist concerns. Seeking to bypass entire centuries of what it deems to be foreign invasions (Islamic and British),[10] it has landed up at some fork in the woods where all paths look unfamiliar. I have still to come across an Indic scholar who can surpass the curiosity and genuine love for Hinduism's cultural diversity that is displayed in the breathtaking scholarship of Wendy Doniger, say.

The following chapter turns to the misplaced idealism that Ramu came to vehemently reject, encapsulated in the myth of Saketh Rajan. The political history of Kudremukh (a spectacular region of the Western Ghats), and the tragedy of Saketh Rajan, through some intriguing connections, trace their way back to Mysore, to the idealism of the Marxist Library and its mysterious legacy on the shores of Kukkarahalli Lake, to the radicalism of young students in the seventies across the world, to a 'guilt' created in the minds of the socially fortunate, and to a way of thinking that (if one were to align with Ramu's deterministic view of the world) was only destined to falter and fail.

I later came to know that Ramu was quite an accomplished poet, and that the modesty he had feigned was deceptive. A collection of his verses, titled *Vishnukranti and Other Poems*, has been published under his penname Ramu Mysuru, and as I began thumbing it, I discovered an original lyrical voice that is deserving of close study. The titular poem 'Vishnukranti' is a moving elegy to Ramu's sister, who died at a young age, while another poem 'Bibinaachi', is a philosophical exploration of a myth involving the daughter of a Muslim king who is said to have become Ramanjunacharya's disciple, and dissolved into her beloved Cheluva Narayana idol which is worshipped in Melukote even today.[11] Imagined from the perspective of Ramanujacharya paternally reminiscing about the young woman during his last days, it carries a deep understanding of the intense intimacy of Indian devotionalism and its language of divine love. However, it is beyond me, and this chapter, to embark on a discussion of these elaborately imagined, many-paged poems written in a language that brings Bendre and Kuvempu to mind. I'll satisfy myself with a translation of one striking mini-poem titled 'Boulder' that keeps coming back to me:

> From that boulder's womb,
> A baahubali could have emerged.
> That sculptor,
> Oh, he put an end to it.

TEN

Two Rivers Diverged in a Wood

The Story of Kudremukh

To give away the thing that is difficult to part with,
Is the best offering amongst the alms.
Let this impure and sinful body,
Turn into something like a diamond.

—Tsan-Ning, a Buddhist monk from China,
circa 1000 CE

After all, is it not with blood and tears, the sacrifice of what is most precious—life—that history enriches posterity?

—Saketh Rajan, *Making History*, circa 2000 CE

I

6 February 2005. A band of five Naxalites weaves its way through dense forestland near Menasinahadya in the Western Ghats, landing up in a vulnerably bald patch of grass. Leading the troop is Saketh Rajan, and close by is his bodyguard, a twenty-two-year-old young man from Raichur named Shivlingu. Sensing the possibility of an ambush, Saketh dispatches the others to survey the surrounding areas. Having now emerged from forested cover, he and his bodyguard are sitting ducks when Karnataka State Police squads appear right in front of them. Shivlingu dies on the spot after taking a bullet

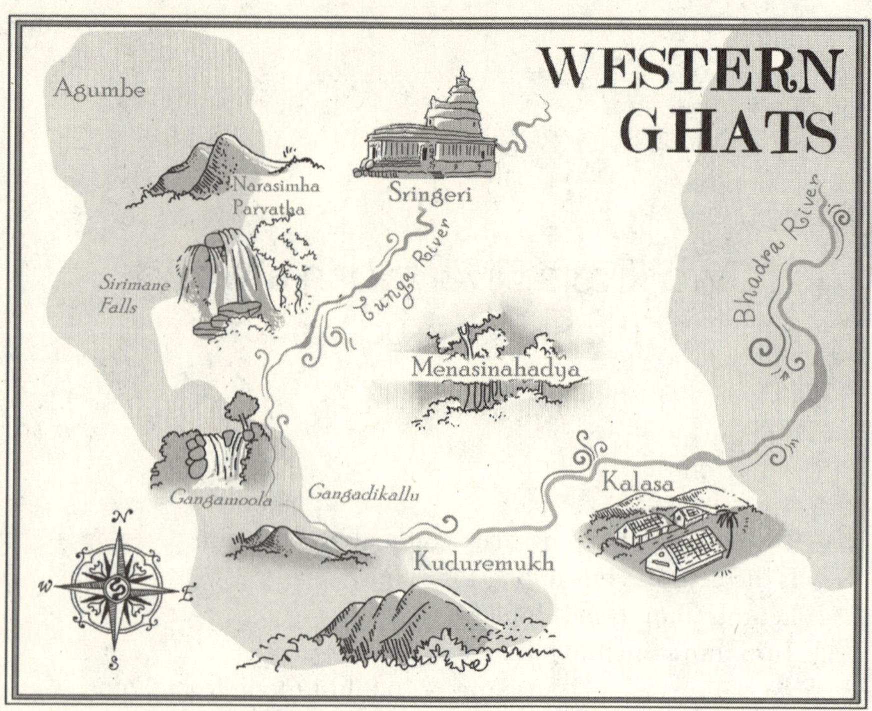

to his gut, while Saketh retreats behind a rock, where he urges the remaining three, on his walkie-talkie, to escape to safety. Saketh is later finished off by the police with a close shot to the head—there is an unnerving photograph of his half-blown-off head on the internet, but its veracity remains suspect.

It must have been a fairly sunny February morning, with little chance of rain. The cadres had arrived in Menasinahadya the previous day to threaten a police informant, but had committed the mistake of staying the night in the same region. Saketh was a well-built man, his ex-comrades tell me, who practised karate regularly and ate like a beast. He liked eating ants as well, for purely nutritional purposes. He had never taken to alcohol or tobacco and was always a picture of healthy energy. He might have recovered from the gunfight wounds if the police had arrested him alive; the two dead bodies had then been surreptitiously disposed of, never presented to the public.

One of the policemen involved in the encounter, N. Srinidhi, would suffer severe bullet injuries, be airlifted to a hospital in Bangalore and confined to the ICU for a month. Inspector Srinidhi would soon be conferred a gallantry medal by the President. He would briefly make the news again in 2007, for being sentenced to six months in jail on charges of assaulting his wife.[1]

Saketh Rajan was the leader of a Naxalite faction that had been attempting to stage a starry-eyed revolution in Karnataka for almost two decades. His death delivered the coup de grâce to the movement in the state, for there was no successor of his stature to receive the mantle. I don't know of too many Naxalites in the country who spent their days underground writing thick, valiantly researched tomes on the history of their birth-state. Indeed, Saketh's two volumes of *Making History*, which are available online, are possibly the most ambitious accounts of the history of Karnataka. Their scope ranges from the geological formation of the subcontinent millions of years ago, all the way till the nineteenth century. Notes had been made for a third volume, which would fill up the gap all the way till 1947, his ex-comrades tell me. But all of Saketh's large personal library and written material were confiscated upon his death and presumably destroyed.

If writing had been his sole passion, Saketh could certainly have fashioned a thriving academic career for himself. Or even as a journalist, for that is what he had started out doing, graduating from the Indian Institute of Mass Communication with four gold medals. But he saw himself as a man of political action, and in his conception of it, organising the people's revolution from below was the goal of all goals. It was in recognition of this tragic trajectory that chief minister Dharam Singh had mourned, during a speech in the state assembly, the death of 'such a brilliant man'.

The last few years of Saketh's life were spent in the bosom of the Western Ghats, amidst the Kudremukh range of hills, wellspring of the Tungabhadra river. *Ganga Snana, Tunga Paana*, goes the popular Kannada saying, meaning that a dip in the Ganga is every bit as revered as a sip from the Tunga. General knowledge has it that the

Tunga and the Bhadra originate at a point called Gangamoola in the Western Ghats, and then twist eastwards down the wooded slopes until they come together on the Maidan at Kudli village in Shimoga district to become the mighty Tungabhadra, along the banks of which the glorious Vijayanagar empire had once flourished. The local version that I heard is that the Tunga originates separately at a place called Gangadikallu, a hill that stands opposite to Gangamoola. In this understanding, the Tunga and the Bhadra are not the conjoined twins they are generally thought to be, but close-born sisters, between whose crisscrossing trails the Kudremukh cluster comes to life. This range gets its name from the fact that its tallest peak is shaped like a horse's (kudre) face (mukha).

During the nineties, when iron-ore mining operations happening at Kudremukh threatened to expand into Gangadikallu, environmentalists grew alarmed. Pollution along the Tungabhadra had been steadily increasing in the previous decades, and a mining venture at the roots of the river would only spell total disaster. Thus, the democratic Tunga Moola Ulisi (Save the Tunga's Source) movement was birthed in the Malnad regions of Sringeri and Thirthahalli, which successfully ended the operations of the Kudremukh Iron Ore Corporation in 2005.

Proceedings to establish a national park at Kudremukh had also been in the works for several years, which solidified after the year 2000. The adivasis (or the girijan, as they are locally called) living on the frontiers were to be displaced. The distraught adivasis' cause was taken up by several civil society organisations, and Gandhian protests such as rallies and picketing were held along the troubled margins. Meanwhile, Saketh and his troop of Naxalites had also sounded their support. These are the two divergent paths that the title of this chapter alludes to—slow, non-violent protest versus the dangerously romanticised way of the guerrilla.

At the turn of the century, when the Naxals gathered to fight for the adivasi cause, the Tungabhadra movement had already gathered much momentum and the national park project was at the cusp of implementation. To understand how Saketh landed up in this particular corner of the universe, where a host of ideologies had gathered in competition to support multiple causes, we need to travel back to the seventies—his formative years. It was a period of worldwide ferment, from the civil rights movement in the US, to students' agitations in Western Europe, Naxalbari in Bengal, the Cultural Revolution in China, anti-colonial self-determination movements across the Third World. The winds of change were afoot and the radically conscientious Saketh was determined to be on the right side of history.

Little is known of Saketh's upbringing and his early childhood. He was born circa 1960 into a prosperous Tamil Iyengar family in Mysore. Despite the silver spoons that were his for the taking, the young Saketh seems to have been a picture of diligent austerity. His father, a polished army man named Sounder Rajan, often reprimanded Saketh for his lack of refinement. Rajan Senior owned a petrol bunk near Ramaswamy Circle, and used the proceeds of the thriving business to fund his globetrotting, as well as his eclectic tastes in food and wine. (Interestingly, the circle is named after a teenage youth named Ramaswamy who died by gunshot there during a protest in 1947 for a responsible, democratic government.) Now, it would not be difficult to connect Saketh's disapproval of his father's lifestyle with his passionate hatred of the bourgeois life. But Saketh's life and trajectory is too peculiar and unique to be easily dismissed with a Freudian diagnosis.

He is said to have been a player of the mandolin, according to his hostel roommate. The seventies (in Bangalore, at least) was a time of rock, blues, psychedelic fusion, witnessing the arrival of original guitarists like Konarak Reddy. The mandolin maestro U. Srinivas was yet to popularise the instrument in South India by deftly adapting it to the Carnatic idiom, converting it from the multi-stringed original version into a five-stringed one. Saketh must have learnt to play the original-style mandolin, and for some reason, I just cannot picture him playing anything but an intense and sober tune on some minor scale. It seems like he abandoned his musical pursuits after a while, because none of the people from the later periods of his life associated him with it.

In 1977, Saketh enrolled in Maharaja's College for a BA in English and Journalism. As a smart and precocious young lad, he was considered a role model of sorts amongst family acquaintances, says T.S. Venugopal, who lives two streets from Saketh's old home in Saraswathipuram. Venugopal is a retired mathematics professor, who nurtures a deep love for Carnatic music. He has translated the vocalist T.M. Krishna's essays into Kannada, and also loves to hold forth on economics. He still writes about politics and economics for the Kannada magazine *Hosatu.* Back in the 1980s, Venugopal was active in the dalit movement, and had accompanied the DSS leader B. Krishnappa as a photographer when they demonstrated against the practice of nude worship in Chandragutti. Distantly connected to the Rajan family, he remembers Saketh from a very young age. Saketh had never been a visitor at the Marxist Library, although he looked up to Ramalingam, and would often visit his home. Like many others, Saketh had found in Ramalingam a role model whose austerities he could try and emulate. Venugopal fervidly disagreed with Saketh's radical solution of taking up arms and waging war against the State:

> I never thought it could solve any problems. I felt they were moving away from the people. What can you do while sitting incognito somewhere? I felt that contact with people was more important.
>
> He [Saketh] was very angry with me. He would say I'm thinking like a petit bourgeois, and point out that the State is not so powerful. It is not capitalist like you think, it is semi-feudal, you should read Che Guevara, Mao, he'd say.

This strain of Maoism and guerrilla warfare had a clear modus operandi: to destroy the brutal feudal structures in the villages by any means possible, to then encircle the cities and pave the way for the freedom of the oppressed communities. The result of an absolute lack of faith in parliamentary democracy, theirs was an unshakeable assertion that revolution was impossible without violence, that war was a justified mode of politics.

In 1980, the People's War Group was founded by Kondapalli Seetharamaiah, who was a veteran of the Telangana armed peasant struggle of the 1940s, and had been recognised early for his organisational abilities. Inspired by China's Cultural Revolution in the 1960s, he had begun organising students in Warangal, establishing a strong base in an engineering college.[2] Soon, these winds would begin to blow towards Karnataka as well, influencing young, hot-blooded souls like Saketh. However, the excesses and failures of the Cultural Revolution, the sheer horror of people turning on their own family members in the name of class warfare, all of this had been masked in the celebratory propaganda that arrived from China. As in China, radicalised youth decamped to villages to live with the agricultural proletariat, to understand their problems and to leave no stone unturned in the project of annihilating class enemies and dismantling feudalism.[3] Like all revolutions, this was also a point of moral turmoil—nothing of the old world order could be trusted.

By the early eighties, Saketh's turn towards the M-L ideology was complete. In the last two decades of the century, he would go on to reach the uppermost echelons of Naxalite leadership, dedicating his life to a quixotic quest the details of which he himself was yet to clearly sketch out. In parallel, he would go on to compose a thickly researched work of Marxist historiography called *Making History*. To know more about those decades, of how Naxalite ideology came to Karnataka and later to Kudremukh, and how Saketh managed to write those huge volumes while remaining incognito, it is imperative that we meet two of Saketh's comrades—Noor 'Shridhar' Zulfikar and Sirimane Nagaraj.

It's either the mind or the stomach that drives one towards the extreme-left, says Noor 'Shridhar' Zulfiqar who, after Saketh's death, was tipped to be the next leader of the CPI(M-L) in Karnataka. But Shridhar, as well as his comrade Sirimane Nagaraj, had long become disillusioned with the way the Naxals had operated in the state, and decided to bid adieu to underground life and return to civil society in 2006, the year following Saketh's death.

'It's either the power of ideology or the needs of poverty that draws you to revolutionary politics,' Shridhar tries to drive home the binary nature of the compulsion. All of them, including Saketh, had come to the movement from reasonably well-off backgrounds. Saketh famously carried around only two pairs of clothes. The journalist Chidanand Rajghatta remembers meeting him in a Bangalore University hostel room sometime in the early eighties, where he started making coffee without any milk or sugar 'in a beaker that was clearly purloined from the chemistry lab, with coffee powder retrieved from a balled-up newspaper'.[4] The house in Bangalore where Nagaraj stays at present, and where I have come to meet him and Shridhar, is similarly spartan, with basic furniture. Financially, it was a little difficult for them to emerge into mainstream society, they say, but their needs are modest and easily met. Chai and biscuits flow generously, as does the conversation, these are luxuries enough.

Noor Zulfikar was born into a liberal Sufi family in Chitradurga. His father had been a primary school teacher, whose motto was 'Dikhawa nahi, chalawa' (*Not mere showing off, but real action*), which he expected to be the dictum of the family as well. The young Zulfikar would hear tales of the revolution at school, where many of his classmates were from neighbouring Andhra. As the teenager slowly began to understand the cause, to reach for that irresistible dream of a fairer world, he grew convinced that *that* was the right chalawa for him. It is a filmy line, and certainly a practised one, but the gravitas and solemnity with which he says it help him pull it off. The thick Tom Selleck moustache helps too. 'The people did not even know what their rights were, and someone had to show them the way,' he says, distilling his drive for revolutionary politics into its most basic unit. His elder brother, however, maintained that one had to reach a certain height in society before being capable of giving back to it.

Zulfikar felt that such thinking was a cop-out because it did little to change the fundamentally lopsided nature of society. He felt social change was a cause requiring great devotion, passion and energy, beginning ground-up from the grassroots. The two brothers decided to follow their own paths, treat them as two different experiments, and respect each other's choice. While his brother joined the civil services and later became a municipal commissioner in Dharwad, Zulfikar devoted his life to social movements. He cherishes the close relationship with his older brother, who took care of their family after Zulfikar dropped out of engineering and plunged into the movement against the Kaiga nuclear plant in the late 1980s.

Sirimane Nagaraj, as it turns out, had lived in Mysore during the seventies, and was a regular during the early years of the Marxist Library, though he did not know Saketh back in those days. Later, he became fully involved in social upheavals. He helped run a newspaper called *Munjaavu* during the nineties, and was an active member of the Karnataka Vimochana Ranga, which played a part in the initial stages of the Tungabhadra movement. It is interesting that Nagaraj and Zulfikar entered the social fray through environmental movements. This streak of environmentalism is what separated the Naxalites from the communists, the latter being generally quite accepting of big developmental and industrial projects for the jobs they produced.

Saketh, too, had started his career as a journalist writing about environmental matters. In the early eighties, he reported strongly on the environmental hazards of the uranium enrichment plant now known as RMP on the outskirts of Mysore, about the deteriorating health of the Kukkarahalli Lake ecosystem, as well as the tribulations of tribals being displaced from the forests near Heggadedevana Kote because of the establishment of the Bandipur National Park. In 1984, he was part of a fact-finding team that travelled to Nagasandra to report on the prevalence of bonded labour in the region, and subsequently submitted a memorandum to the Rural Development Minister.[5] Those early years held the promise of a brilliant journalist in the making.

After studying at the prestigious Maharaja's College in the seventies (like so many other famous names, from Kuvempu to R.K. Narayan to A.K. Ramanujan), he went on to get a master's degree in Communications from Bangalore University, and then a post-graduate diploma from the Indian Institute of Mass Communications, Delhi, where he finished with as many as four gold medals. The story goes that, when the convocation ceremony at IIMC was taking place, Saketh refused to take the stage to receive his medals, because they were being handed away by Vidya Charan Shukla (a Congress politician who had served under Indira Gandhi during the Emergency), with whom Saketh presumably had profound political disagreement.[6]

The firebrand figure was his persona. A former friend remembers Saketh as 'the classic rebel who helped me deschool myself after introducing me to authors like Frantz Fanon and Paulo Freire'.[7] But the decisive shift in his life seems to have come during his stint in Delhi, where he came in touch with Cherukuri Rajkumar, the People's War Group leader from Andhra with a bounty of Rs 10 lakh on his head. By the mid-eighties, Saketh had joined the first band of Naxalites in Karnataka, which was forged in the north-east regions of Bidar and Raichur, close to the Andhra border. Naxal leadership in Karnataka was originally taken up by Cherukuri Rajkumar himself, after which it fell to a man named Manju (alias, Kuppaswamy), and in 1995, Saketh Rajan assumed control. Venugopal told me that he had attempted to persuade Saketh to return to civil society. However, he saw that after Saketh became a leader at the top level, it became less and less likely that he would ever retreat, as such an act would have reflected badly on the movement and the ideology that had taken over his life completely.

By this time, Zulfiqar and Nagaraj had also been inducted into the movement and the party. Throughout the nineties, attempts to orchestrate a people's war in Bidar and Raichur were on. This is because contact with the Naxals in Andhra was first established along the border near these regions. But the Naxals were unsuccessful in finding a foothold there. Again, Zulfikar refers to these efforts as 'experiments' that failed to yield any success; his repeated use of the word has led me to imagine him walking a garden of forked paths in his head, choosing one experimental way over another, not very much unlike the protagonist of the Netflix movie *Bandersnatch*. The reasons for the failure spawned further debate within their ranks, especially between Zulfikar and Saketh. Zulfikar broadly outlined their conflicting viewpoints thus:

> Zulfikar: Why has the Naxalite movement been failing in the country for well over three decades now? It is because we have failed to tune our ideology to the conditions that are specific to India. We cannot hope to transpose Maoism as it was practised in China to the subcontinent. This is also why we faced so many setbacks in Raichur and Bidar during the last decade in Karnataka.
>
> Saketh: No. We failed there because we did not attack the police forcefully enough. Had we fought strongly, we could have prevented them from entering the villages, and got for ourselves some space to mobilise.
>
> Zulfikar: We cannot hope to build a movement in the plains like they do in Dandakaranya. The State's apparatus is far better developed in these regions. Guerrilla tactics don't work here. As for the jungles in the Ghats, we still need more study to figure out the best course of action. We don't really know how the people here will receive us.
>
> Saketh: We need to redouble our efforts and build an army. We are still in the stage of forming small squads, whereas we should have been a larger force by now.

These debates had divided the Central Committee of the CPI(M-L) as well. In the year 2000, when the decision to shift the Naxals in Karnataka to Kudremukh was being considered, the vote at the committee had ended up in a tie. Eventually, the decision that prevailed was that the Naxal movement could not become restricted to Dandakaranya alone, and an insurrection was ordered in the Western Ghats. In any hierarchical top-down party system, especially one where the power flows from the barrel of a gun, there is no alternative but to submit to the demands of the decision-makers. Licking their wounds after their failures in Raichur and Bidar, the Naxals decamped to Kudremukh.

II

In the famous Kannada folksong 'Govina Haadu' (The Cow's Song), which is perhaps the oldest cultural legacy of the language, a cow named Punyakoti gets cornered by a tiger, manages to receive permission from it to feed her newly birthed calf, and returns willingly afterwards to offer herself to the tiger, following which the tiger magnanimously refuses to eat her and jumps off a cliff in a moment of self-sacrifice.

In Kalkulli Vittal Hegde's novel *Mangana Byaate* (The Hunt for the Monkey), neither predators nor humans care for such nuanced moral dialectic. A wandering cow with a penchant for misadventures is finished off by a leopard in the first few pages, and subsequently the narrative involves villagers hunting down pestilent monkeys. As Vittal Hedge points out, in certain regions of Malnad it used to be quite natural for monkeys to be hunted down mercilessly, as they were notorious for destroying crops, and therefore the ultimate farmers' bane. In fact, anybody who refused to join in the hunt was deemed a traitor by the village, and himself became a manga, a monkey. The practice died out in the twentieth century, but survives memorably in the novel, as do innumerable other rich details of tribal life in the hills. It is, essentially, an intimate account of life in the Ghats, showcasing all manner of wondrous local wisdoms, from locating rare mushrooms to tapping delicious flavours of honey that are found nowhere else, to catching elusive snake-fish and clambering up seemingly insurmountable trees.

Mangana Byaate is Hegde's only novel, and he is better known as an environmentalist and activist in the region. He was one of the prime movers of the Tungabhadra campaign in the nineties, and to hear of the decade-long movement in Kudremukh from the horse's mouth (if I may be pardoned the pun), I met him several times in Sringeri. His knowledge of the Malnad region, its abundant natural landscape, its history of activism and the lives of its local populace are second to none. When I visited him in early 2022, he had finished writing a PhD thesis on the biodiversity and natural environment of the Malnad region.

Sringeri. The hallowed temple town along the Tunga, where Adi Shankaracharya set up one of his four cardinal mathas many centuries ago, and which Tipu Sultan renovated and restored in the eighteenth century after it had been sacked by the Marathas. It has been Vittal Hegde's home all his life. I happened to unearth an interesting bit of historical trivia about his rather unique surname. 'Hegde' is a common surname in this region (from an old Kannada word meaning chieftain) but Vittal Hegde is a special surname historically linked with the town of Vittal near Mangalore. As it turns out, 'the Vittal Heggade was the representative of an old family of hereditary renters under the Bednore [modern-day Nagara in Shimoga district] government which was at first expelled by Hyder Ali, but restored when a number of the family pretended to become Mussalmans. They were again dispossessed, however, in 1768 for assisting the English, and the Heggade went to reside at Tellicherry [now Thalassery in Kerala] as a pensioner of the East India Company. Under the pretence of assisting the English, he made incursions into Canara during all the subsequent wars, and continued plundering the country after the fall of Tipu and the English occupation.'[8]

I asked Vittal Hegde if he was aware of this gory history, but he wasn't. That's fair enough, for he has absolutely nothing in common with his namesake from the eighteenth century. I was curious to hear how he had managed to source all the painstakingly detailed material for his novel, and to enter the world of the adivasis so naturally, unlike his plundering predecessor. His face assumes a boyish grin, and he says:

> I failed the twelfth standard. My childhood was spent in the wild, with the rest of the forest kids, doing all sorts of odd things in

the jungles around these parts. I never read anything during those days. It was only later that I came to reading and learning about the world outside.

It was during these days of reading and learning that Vittal Hegde became a part of various social movements that were taking shape in Karnataka during the eighties. He had been a member of the Democratic Youth Federation of India, and was later involved in setting up an independent farmers' association in Sringeri. He was also a participant in the anti-caste movement, and helped organise the first inter-caste marriage summit in Sringeri in 1987, inaugurated by the writer Poornachandra Tejaswi. It seems almost natural that the politically progressive Vittal Hegde went on to become an integral part of the environmental movements that were to follow at Kudremukh.

The presence of iron ore in Kudremukh had been known since the early twentieth century, though mining had only begun during the sixties. The Shah of Iran had invested US$ 630 million, and the venture opened up possibilities for capital growth in the region. The Union government set up the Kudremukh Iron Ore Company Limited, or KIOCL, in 1976. A new township came up in Kudremukh, a new port was established in Mangalore and sprawling state highways were built to facilitate the ensuing volley of trucks. In 1979, when the Shah's regime was overthrown, it was unsure if the company would survive, until Romania stepped in with capital to back it.[9] In the early nineties, as mining operations were all set to intrude into Gangadikallu, Vittal Hegde began leading a strong resistance. He and his associates embarked on a cycle jatha around the Tunga's path, spreading awareness. Other organisations, like the Raitha Sangha and Kannada movement collectives, also lent a hand during these protests. The agitation that followed forced the State to stop further mining expansion.

There is an amusing anecdote from the early days of the Tunga movement of how U.R. Ananthamurthy came to be a part of it. Sometime in the early nineties, Vittal Hegde had written a piece in *Lankesh Patrike* about the precarious situation in Gangadikallu. Having seen this, the acclaimed dramatist and writer K.V. Subbanna invited Hegde to the annual cultural symposium at Ninasam in the village of Heggodu. It was the first time a social cause was being discussed at the arts-dominated Ninasam. After two days, the stipulated time for discussion on social movements arrived, and a warm-blooded Hegde immediately set the pace for the discussion by asserting that, just like Nero had fiddled while Rome burnt, the intelligentsia of the state were fiddling around discussing Kumaravyasa and Kalidasa when capitalism and things like the GATT Agreement[10] were about to wreak havoc on the natural landscape. Caught off guard, Ananthamurthy had responded defensively, spawning a vociferous debate. At the end of the conference, he had put his hands around Hegde's young shoulders, and inquired into his education, background and so on, signalling the beginning of a friendship.

Ananthamurthy was initially unwilling to join the movement, as it was being organised primarily by the Karnataka Vimochana Ranga, which he thought harboured political extremists. He was right, in the sense that in its top ranks were the likes of Sirimane Nagaraj, who had politically aligned themselves with Maoism. Nagaraj told me that they had established the Karnataka Vimochana Ranga in 1991 as a pan-Karnataka forum for dalits, farmers and labourers. At the time, they were most keen on the task of articulating the concerns of nela, jala and bhaashe (land, water and language) within the Marxist vocabulary.

Vittal Hegde soon left the KVR (over political differences he refused to expand on) and a different collective was formed for the Tunga movement, in which Ananthamurthy participated enthusiastically. His presence certainly gave a huge fillip to the movement—it was perhaps *the* clinching factor. The fact that he shared a friendly relationship with former chief minister S.M. Krishna seems to have proved crucial in the early 2000s. The protests had now expanded from Sringeri to Thirthahalli to Shimoga and beyond, with several local organisations coming together to join the Tungabhadra campaign, forming a robust collective.

Initially, the collective decided to impose certain precautionary conditions and let the company continue their mining at the original location, since otherwise the lives of its workers and the existence of an entire township that had been built around it would be imperilled. However, when the company showed signs of extending their contract for another thirty years, and haughtily refused to enter into any negotiations over environmental concerns, the collective decided to demand its complete shutdown by July 1999, when its original thirty-year lease would expire.

This turned out to be wishful thinking. Environmental movements in India are long battles with long sieges. The Silent Valley movement in the seventies went on for a decade, and the Narmada Bachao Andolan persisted for several. Between the courts and the corporations and the countless activists, resolution and closure may sprout only after many storms have been weathered. Thus, it is no surprise that the KIOCL persisted illegally in its operations until 2005, when the political establishment finally found the wherewithal to end the mess. All through these years, sporadic protests, rallies and political negotiations continued.

Meanwhile, large swathes of the Kudremukh forest were being converted into a national park. Relocation notices had begun to arrive, and the adivasis knew that they would have to fight for their rights. Naxalite activity began in 2001, as Vittal Hegde recollects. Around that time, a district forest officer he remembers vaguely as Murthy was appointed to the region:

> Murthy organised several sabhas, and tried to convince the tribes that their land was being used for wildlife conservation, a noble cause for which they would have to sacrifice their lands. He began increasing restrictions on the normal life of the villagers by fencing the forests, refusing to let the animals graze by tying them up, jailing people for fishing or for even having matchboxes in their pockets, and so on.

It was harassment, pure and simple.

A frustrating cycle of negotiation, disappointment and re-negotiation is part of the reason why the Naxalites decided to reject any form of dialogue with the State. Some fence-sitters had initially joined the protests along with the local organisation Vittal Hegde had founded in Sringeri to oppose the creation of the national park. Hegde recalls that many of his own followers abandoned his methods and switched over to support the Naxals.

In the Naxal analysis, the whole system was semi-feudal and semi-colonial: 'semi-colonial because the Indian ruling classes are tied to imperialist interests, semi-feudal because the old feudal relations have not been smashed, only a certain amount of capitalist growth has been superimposed on them'.[11] Thus, the system was rotten and deemed ripe for complete takeover.

Consider the following snippet from one of Saketh's early academic publications, which offers us a clue as to how he might have viewed the tribal cause. In 1984, he published a paper in the *Journal of the Indian Anthropological Society* regarding the impact of commercialisation on the soliga tribes of BR Hills near Mysore. He concludes it thus:

> Commercialization has meant the ultimate destruction of Soliga life and culture. It has assimilated them as a laboring work force in the process of further commercialization, or it has made them agrestic slaves under feudal authority. The tribals are hopelessly led to partake in illegal felling, poaching and illicit cultivation, and sale of ganja. When commercialization intensifies and the contradiction ripens, they will be once and for all alienated from the forest and with one strong push will descend as free proletarians to the sprawling plains.[12]

His understanding of the situation in the Western Ghats would have traced a similar trajectory. The Naxals found in Kudremukh an ideal arena where everything they loved and everything they hated were clearly stacked against each other, crying out for battle—a multinational mining corporation that primarily exported iron to other countries at the expense of local ecology, and a Western model of wildlife conservation that threatened to alienate an indigenous population from their homes.

The split between the Naxalites and the Gandhian democratic protestors effectively spelt doom for the national park agitation. Research has shown that across the twentieth century, campaigns of non-violent resistance were twice as effective as their violent counterparts in achieving their stated goals.[13] The reasons are simply that the non-violent protests fare better at gaining higher participation, at garnering crucial public support and even at convincing the armed forces/police to stand down and support their cause. It promotes diversity of participation, and it becomes difficult for the State and corporations to pigeonhole the protestors into a particular category and dismiss them. With the strengthening of the modern Indian State, the efficacy of violent protests has drastically reduced. In fact, even in the case of brutal dictatorships, the research argues, non-violent protests stand a strategically greater chance of success.

In Kudremukh, the revolutionary consciousness that the Maoist ideology was designed to foment was nowhere to be found. When the Naxals urged the labourers to fight for better wages and collective rights, and to rise up against their landlords, there was a sense of hesitancy in taking up militancy. After all, this was around the turn of the century—land reforms, the rise of the dalit movement, liberalisation of the economy and the sobering effects of half a century of democracy had tempered feudal land relations to a certain extent. Economic exploitation was built into it, no doubt, but there was a nuanced edge to it all. The same applied to the adivasi cause as well, and as Sirimane Nagaraj himself told me:

> The atmosphere there was such that the people were hesitant to join us in arms. They supported us in principle, and had regard for us. Saketh was practically living in their homes, and had become one with their lifestyle. But you need more than admiration—what you really need is active participation.

Vittal Hegde's analysis is similar to this, perhaps more rooted in a genuine anthropological understanding than the Naxals'. He remembers Saketh, of course, but he knew him then as Pandu, his alias. Pandu was a charismatic figure who attracted the local youth through his knowledge of Marxism, and would often be found delivering talks on world history. But Hegde disagreed with his methods profoundly: 'Many youngsters were influenced by him. But it wasn't the right way to proceed. The locals here win through street smartness (upaayadinda gellovru), and adjust to life by slipping away from trouble. They do not hold a revolutionary mindset. The Naxals did not understand this at all.'

I wanted to know how violent the Naxal insurrection had really been. Vittal Hegde could not recall any killings as such. Just a few months before Saketh's killing, some Naxals had fatally assaulted a farmer who was thought to be a police informant. Nagaraj also mentioned the murder of an informant and landlord after they had left the movement. The sharpened optics were such that, once the Naxalites emerged onto the scene, it became very difficult for civil protestors like Vittal Hegde to catch the state's attention. As Hegde explained, 'The police started treating us as if we were Naxalites. We told them that we were democratic protestors. Talk to us, not the Naxals. But they never came into a dialogue with us. After the Naxalites went into the forest, everything became about them.'

The sudden arrival of a Marxist history, rooted in complicated dialectical analysis, would also have seemed discordant to the adivasis, whose understanding of the world was governed by myth and legend. This is brought out wonderfully in Na D'souza's novel *Dweepa* (Island), which was also adapted into an acclaimed film of the same name by Girish Kasaravalli in 2002. In the film, a newly built dam threatens to submerge a hill named Sita Parvata in the Malnad region. The inhabitants of the hill believe it to be the place where Rama and Sita had once lived, and refuse to budge from their ancestral homes, come what may. The puritanical idealism of someone like Saketh Rajan would also have been a far cry from the merry, year-long drinking cycle of the adivasis, where alcohol is known by a different name for every occasion it is part of. In *Mangana Byaate*, when news reaches a secluded tribal village that the government has banned them from making their own alcohol, an old man muses, 'Is something wrong with those people? Do you think our ancestors could have flattened this land, created this village, if they had nothing to drink?'

What kind of a life were the Naxals living in the forest at this time? It certainly wasn't anything comparable to Che Guevara's last days in the Bolivian forests, say, where Guevara and his band had to resort to eating horses and monkeys to sustain themselves. Still, it was an extremely risky existence, and they were always on the go. The police apparatus had been strengthened around the forested region, and the building of new roads had ensured that reinforcements could reach any point at short notice. The Naxals were essentially living and fighting thanks to the intimate relationship they shared with the girijan, the indigenous people of the hills, who supported them and supplied them with essentials. In spite of the fact that they were themselves reluctant to take up arms, the girijan had started to believe that this was the way forward, Hedge told me. The fact that the Naxals were taken so seriously by the State, as indeed anybody who is brandishing guns would be, made the adivasis inclined to ally with the Naxals more than with the civil protestors outside the forest.

What kept the movement alive was the romantic idealism that its leadership pumped into it. Zulfikar feels that this is what led to the downfall of the movement: *If you think you can wage war against the State from twenty backward villages, it is not a people's war, it becomes a romantic war. We had no plan of building a comprehensive and sustained struggle*. Whether this is merely a retrospective opinion, or an understanding that had already formed in Zulfikar's mind during those years is unclear. The fact that both Zulfikar and Nagaraj quit the party immediately after Saketh's death points towards an already uncertain mindset.

Yet, Zulfikar is quick to add that, despite their political disagreements, his personal relationship with Saketh was always cordial:

> He was really rarest amongst the rare. As far as intellect, commitment, and vision goes. Within the narrow perspective of Naxalite politics, his personality did not really grow to the potential one might have hoped for, but he was certainly an extraordinary man. Even though we had many political disagreements, it did not affect our personal relationship. I can't even begin to conceive of his stature as a political person. But then, he is also a good example for how a man from such a strong intellectual background could stumble in life. One may be able to think about a lot of grand things, but completely fumble the simpler ones.

What were these grand things that Saketh excelled at? For one, he possessed an unflinching dedication to the hard work of research and writing, which he did throughout his underground life. He had amassed a large personal library that housed many a rare book, and spent much of his life reading.[14]

Saketh's ideology found its sharpest articulations in his writings, which usually took the shape of crisp, cleaved and clear prose. If one tries to gauge his personality solely by the literary legacy he leaves behind, he comes off as a grave and solemn figure who was singularly smitten with Marxism and historical materialism—a humourless man with a capacity for magisterial thought.

III

> Love and politics are two poles linked by an arch: the person. The destiny of a person in a political society is reflected in a lovers' relationship, and vice versa. The story of Romeo and Juliet is unthinkable if we suppress the patrician quarrels in the Italian cities of the Renaissance and the same goes for Lara and Zhivago outside the context of the Bolshevik revolution and the civil war. Everything is linked.
>
> —Octavio Paz

The two volumes of *Making History* that Saketh composed while living incognito should astound us for a fundamental reason—that they were written at all. Composed while there was a bounty on his head, and constructed with painstakingly thick research, *Making History* shaped up over the eighties and nineties against all possible odds. It was his life's biggest project. It housed his grandest ambitions and fantasies, and framed them within more than a thousand pages of maps, diagrams, sketches, blueprints, statistics, and reams of quotations and expository prose. Beginning with the geological origins of Karnataka, Saki (his pen name) wishes to present a *total* history of the state, all the way till 1947. With remarkable confidence, he tackles subjects as varied as the development of medieval economic systems, prehistoric rock art, every peasant uprising in the known history of the region, the bhakti movement, numismatics, Kannada literary movements, the fall of Tipu Sultan and the taming of the Wodeyars. The sheer breadth of his undertaking is mind-boggling, and it is also perhaps what ultimately diminishes its veracity. He quotes extensive passages from a multitude of sources, showcasing a wide, if scattered, realm of interdisciplinary research. Reading it is like scaling an insurmountable mountain—one is always unsure where the path may turn treacherous, and where one may comfortably take a breather.

If *Making History* makes for difficult reading, reviewing it is harder still. Dr Vijay Thambanda, a professor of history at Hampi Kannada University, has closely studied Saki's writings through an academic lens. To put it bluntly, he does not think that Saki's work can be deemed History in the rigorous sense we now associate with the word. In a lecture delivered in Mangalore in 2019, he said:

> He had dreams of liberating Karnataka, which he threw into his writings, and called it history. Although it seems like he relies on D.D. Kosambi[15] a lot, Saki's real inspiration is Rajni Palme Dutt's *India Today*, which was heavily critiqued by Kosambi for being too mechanically Marxist.[16]

Dr Thambanda also argues that there are serious problems with some axiomatic generalisations that Saki makes:

> Saki argues that, linguistically, there exists a right to self-determination for three regions—Kodava (Coorg), Tulu (Tulunadu) and Kannada

> (Karnataka)—which must be recognised and fought for. When the movement for the secession of Coorg was taking place in the 1990s, the PWG [People's War Group] supported the movement, despite the fact that it was essentially a demand of the landed elite, the plantation owners, and which the labourers and lower castes completely opposed. These are contradictions and problems that cannot be overlooked so easily. There is a problem with the most basic assumptions and generalisations that Saki makes.

The movement for Coorg's statehood was essentially a product of modernised elite who began feeling unmoored from their cultural roots, not unlike the NRI nationalists of today. It ignored the distinction between Kodava and Kodagu, the former being just one landed community amongst a diverse religio-ethnic population. There was even a radical organisation called LIWAK—Liberation Warriors of Kodagu—that modelled itself after LTTE, drew from Maoist frameworks and portrayed the Karnataka state as a predatory entity. The people of Coorg soon distanced themselves from these attempts, and the movement petered out.

The M-L parties' political rhetoric appeared to have been cleanly picked up from other self-determination arguments happening around the world, as in Africa and the Middle East, and there was little effort to situate them within the subcontinent. It amazes me that Saki was able to mechanically transpose movements half a world away, from a diverse set of global contexts, into simplistic arguments for separatism in a federal, democratic country like India with its own unique predicaments. The right-wing is presently engaged in similar endeavours, a case in point being its fanatical support for Zionism. Even more striking is the fact that Saki was making this argument around the turn of the century, when even originally Marxist-Leninist parties like the Kurdistan Workers' Party, which was fighting for a Kurdish state, had realised that hierarchical, patriarchal party structures were antithetical to real democracy and change.[17]

After acknowledging the ambition of the work, its various problems, as well as the gruelling conditions under which it was fulfilled, Thambanda humbly submits: 'There is passion, certainly. Marxism itself had become a passion for Saki. But is that enough to write history? I don't know.'

The passionate Saki wrote passable poetry too, though only one of his poems has survived—a tribute to the Nigerian playwright, novelist and activist Ken Saro Wiwa, who was hanged by a ruthless Nigerian state in 1995 for his environmental activism against multinational oil companies ravaging Ogoniland. A small snippet from it:

> It was a lesson
> You learned too late.
> Your pen
> Playwright
> Should've been backed by the gun alright.

It is his recognition of the enormity of power vested in the powerful corporations that grew to control and exploit the global south that gives Saki his radical certainty. However, this strong conviction ended up masking other, equally important ones: such as the recognition of the unique khichdi that is India, and the trap of over-generalisation in a country of a million contexts. Maps and diagrams and abstracted class allegiances replace real life and lived social relations.

Even as we critique Saki's writings, it must be said that there is much to be learnt from reading *Making History*. One may not agree with its conclusions and declarations, but it calls for critical engagement all the same. As far as sheer documentation is concerned, it is an immensely helpful resource for scholars interested in Karnataka history, what with the large bibliography that it supplies, and the vast number of subjects that it touches upon.

Perhaps recognising this, Thambanda becomes more existential and compassionate towards the end of his talk, and says: 'Is this a problem of history? Is this a problem of history writers? Is it an inevitable consequence of the troubles of interpreting history in the first place? We are still caught between all these questions.'

Saki's interpretation of history is riven by his desire to employ it as an ideological tool to usher in a people's revolution. History is meaningless for him unless it helps us firmly situate our own political struggles *through* its lens. In his eyes, the mighty weight of history and all of its painful struggles must be redeemed by us, the posterity who often forget the brutal realities of the past, or else we shall have failed all those who have ever fought against oppression. For Saki, the failure to ally with the struggle of the wretched of the earth, which has been raging since time immemorial, would be tantamount to moral and ethical betrayal of the highest order. History becomes a living, breathing truth that must be hammered into the fabric of contemporary political struggle. In this sense, it is no different from the communal school of history writing, which seeks to harness the oppressions of centuries past into the deplorable act of turning modern communities against each other. As he writes in the introduction to the first volume:

> Whichever way one would choose to view it; feudalism before colonialism, or feudalism with colonialism, the unmistakeable truth of history lies in the fact that our society has, just as all others, rebelled against the rule of these classes. Popular struggle has been the motive force. Faced by oppression and with no room to turn, the masses will come of their own, and forging onward, they make their history. The purpose of this work will then be fulfilled. Cause would have met its culmination; historiography would have had its tryst with history.

This romantic tryst with history extended to Saketh's personal life as well. State Secretary Prem, as he was known, married a fellow revolutionary named Rajeshwari, with whom he lived underground throughout the nineties. Rajeshwari was a non-combatant journalist, also from Mysore, who helped edit and bring out the party magazine. Saketh is reputed to have been a college Romeo of sorts, having had many rumoured dalliances during those years, but it was Rajeshwari, with whom he shared an ideological bond of revolutionary purpose, who went on to become his life partner. Zulfikar tells me that the two were never really in love, and were just very good friends. The decision to get married had been largely motivated by a companionship based on their common drive and purpose—to be a part of the revolution, together. This is something that is common across revolutionary circles.[18] It is interesting to observe that even the renegade rebels of the Left haven't transcended the conservative institution of marriage, but in fact seek it out for its own sake. Most couples who dedicate themselves to the cause refrain from having children, though, for it diverts them from the revolution—Saketh and Rajeshwari made the same choice.

The second volume of *Making History* appropriately opens with Francisco Goya's famous painting 'The Third of May, 1808', which features Spanish rebels facing Napoleon's firing squad. It is followed by a photograph of a smiling Rajeshwari standing with an umbrella at Nagar fort, which was the site of a historical peasant revolt against the British in 1830. The volume itself is dedicated to her, for a moving reason—she was no longer alive when the volume was published in 2004.

In 2001, Rajeshwari was travelling to the vicinity of Visakhapatnam in Andhra Pradesh as a journalist. She was captured there by the police and put to death. In the introduction to the second volume, Saketh writes that she was captured by a twenty-member Special Task Force in the forest of Kothapalli, after which she was tortured for four hours, before being shot in the head. This, he writes, was witnessed by two children hiding behind a bush, who were so dumbfounded by the sight that they could not eat for three days. He pens a touching remembrance for her, while introducing her as an important contributor to the book itself:

> Raji had seen the past. She wanted to see the future. She chose to visit the villages of Andhra Pradesh where new democratic people's power was being forged. She wanted to study it, record it and broadcast its prowess among the masses of Karnataka. She interviewed scores of people. She recorded revolutionary songs.

> She made copious notes of what she had read and heard. She took photographs of the oppressed Adivasis and of their hope—the young guerrilla fighters in green … Her intellect was not insipid. She wanted to see and share the living popular experience of the proletarian democratic revolution.

It is difficult to imagine how Saketh must have felt upon hearing this news, and it is harder still to imagine him renouncing his cause after his wife was martyred. In the years that followed, the enmity between the Naxalites and the police intensified. It was at this tipping point, caught between imagined pasts and futures, between insipid intellects and courageous crusades, that Saketh's life would become irrevocably forfeit.

IV

About a year before Saketh's death, there was an attempt by the media to broker peace between the State and the Naxals. A team of journalists travelled to the forests in 2004 to hold a press meet with them, and one of them happened to be Gauri Lankesh. At this meet, she realised that the man whom they had known as State Secretary Prem was, in fact, Saketh Rajan, who had been her senior at Bangalore University, and later at IIMC as well. In her own words:

> The press meet shattered a few myths being spread by the police. For one, they were not Naxalites from Andhra Pradesh but were born and bred in Karnataka. Secondly, they were not some ragtag gang of misguided youth but a political party that had taken up the cause of tribals in the Kudremukh National Park. In their briefing, they said that they were ready for talks but would look forward to the government first meeting some Adivasi demands.[19]

Soon, Lankesh and others formed an organisation called Citizens' Initiative for Peace, CIP, which aimed to facilitate dialogue and reconciliation. No real progress was made on this front—the State continued its operations to flush out the Naxals, and the Naxals refused to lay down their arms.

When the encounter was announced to the public, Saketh's aged mother asked Chief Minister Dharam Singh to hand over his body to the CIP. Singh, however, had little control over the police force, and the two bodies of Rajan and Shivlingu (which were never properly identified) were stealthily disposed of. During this period, right-wing groups were attacking the CIP, despite the fact that they were the only group trying to sue for peace of some kind. Things deteriorated after Saketh's death. The Naxals retaliated, killing seven policemen and a civilian in an attack near Pavagada on the Andhra border.[20] The State redoubled its efforts to crush the movement after this attack. The resulting repression dealt a body blow to other Left movements in Karnataka as well. Environmentalist and anti-communal movements in the Malnad and Canara regions came to be typecast as Naxalite, and pushed to the periphery.

Staying true to Newton's maxim of equal and opposite reactions, the extreme Right has always had a rhyming relationship with the extreme Left. Muzaffar Assadi, an academic and scholar of social movements in Karnataka, wrote in 2004:

> Last year, the Hindutva brigade tried to disrupt the environment/ecology movement in the famous Sringeri area as it was supported and led by radicals. The Hindutva lobby is apprehensive about the radicalisation of social movements including Naxalites in Karnataka in recent times … Naxalite adventurism helps the Hindutva lobby to consolidate and expand its bases rather than the social movements and liberal space. Retrieving this space for both individuals and popular social movements therefore becomes all the more important.[21]

Assadi argues for an expansion of the space occupied by civil society activists such as Vittal Hegde. He writes of the Naxal insurrection as an anomaly that further marginalised social movements in Karnataka. Indeed, barring this instance, environmental movements in modern Karnataka have always based themselves on the Gandhian paradigm. The triumph of the long, arduous campaign to shutter the KIOCL is testament to the efficacy of civil, democratic protest, and the violent denouement of the Naxal movement must be read as a historical defeat for any form of militant misadventurism.

However, reality is not so symmetrically poetic either. The opposition to the Naxalites had not come from any meaningful debate or reasoned dialectic, but rather manufactured through a blind opposition to anything espoused by the Left. The former Bajrang Dal leader Mahendra Kumar admitted candidly:

> It must have been around 2002. A massive gathering had been organised by the committee formed to oppose to the national park, and the famous environmentalist Medha Patkar had been called to deliver a speech. They were also supposed to release a book about the Muslims who had suffered the onslaught of communal hatred. We had been made to believe that the entire environmentalist brigade was a Naxal organisation. The gathering was being led by the activist K.L. Ashok, professor Ramdas, freedom fighter H.S. Doreswamy, Kalkuli Vittal Hegde and Sirimane Nagaraj. In our eyes, they were all Naxals, and the Bajrang Dal was determined to attack that gathering.[22]

Prepared to bear any police assault that might come their way, the Bajrang Dal had thronged the gathering in the hundreds, but what awaited them took them completely by surprise. The Mahila Jagruti Vedike—a group full of spirited adivasi women—fell upon the goons of the Bajrang Dal with a ferocity they had never experienced before. Soon, they were given over to the police and packed off to prison. Mahendra Kumar had called for a Sringeri bandh from within prison, and attracted praise from RSS higher-ups.

In the years following Saketh's death, Naxal activity in the region waxed and waned. In June 2007, after the Kudremukh National Park was officially declared, five activists belonging to an NGO opposing the creation of the park were shot dead by the police who alleged that they were Naxalites. Over the next few years, skirmishes eventually dwindled. However, the shadow of Naxal activism continues to loom over the tribal people who live in villages situated on the frontiers of the protected area. It haunts others too, as I would find out, when a journalist passed me the number of an ex-Naxal named Neelaguli Padmanabha who lives in the region, adding that I should call him through a burner phone. 'I'm sure the police have surveillance on his phone.' Perhaps it was the weight of that warning, but I never did meet Padmanabha and hear his story.

This suspicion is everywhere. The malekudiya community, for instance, has long been protesting the lack of basic amenities like healthcare centres, tarred roads and teachers at the Ashram Schools set up especially for tribals. The State views them with suspicion and derision. In 2012, Vittal Malekudiya, the first ever journalist from the community, was arrested along with his father, both as suspected Naxalites. The charges were laughable, and the 'evidence' included the possession of books written by Bhagat Singh and Kuldip Nayar. They had to spend four harrowing months in prison, and it eventually took them nine years to get acquitted.[23]

In 2023, the intrepid Mangalore-based journalist Naveen Soorinje published a small book chronicling the entire ordeal, titled *Kutlur Kathana* (Kutlur Story). The reportage is classic Soorinje—built on years of close association and coverage. One marvels at how he is everywhere at once. In the pages of this book, and in his other writings, Soorinje confronts policemen, becomes the shoulder of support for those seeking justice, finds himself in courts and jails and in the offices of the powerful, and on one occasion, even manages to accompany the police on a Naxal combing operation, with a photographer from a rival TV channel for company. He becomes all the more important because most things passing for journalism in Kannada-language television are, and have been, of the sensational-illogical-predatorial variety.

Kutlur is a small village inside the forests near Belthangady taluk, home to the malekudiya community. It is a region that is teeming with forest produce: honey, cashew, cinnamon, nutmeg, ramapatre, mangoes and so on. Having recognised the potential for profit, some employees of the forest department contracted the job of extracting resources from Kutlur to two affluent condiment sellers named Saleem and Prabhakar. The two men divided Kutlur amongst themselves, circa 1995. Since it is impossible to navigate the treacherous jungle and collect the produce without local assistance, they enlisted the help of the adivasis, paying them a small wage, but usurping all of the produce and profit for themselves. This went on for a few years. Over time, they managed to groom a few locals in their stead, and when some others silently started collecting produce for themselves, these informants passed on the news to the forest officials. Some were arrested unlawfully, and released after warnings. In this way, greed and money served to set up a divide amongst the malekudiyas themselves. After this, the villagers assembled in unity, castigated the men who had betrayed them, and decided unanimously to stop working for Saleem and Prabhakar. As the calls for the demarcation of the national park grew stronger around the end of the millennium, this sentiment of rebellion grew stronger. As the State began making repeated attempts to evict the villagers of Kutlur, police raids and stories of torture surfaced. It was during these years that the Naxals reached Kutlur, and their ideology began to gain traction.

It was a few years after the death of Saketh Rajan that Naveen Soorinje began reporting on the trials of the malekudiyas, and he became good friends with Vittal Malekudiya. Inspired by the power he saw in bold journalists like Naveen, Vittal decided that he wanted to become a journalist too, and joined Mangalore University. On 3 March 2012, there was a police raid on his home in Kutlur, and Vittal received a call from their neighbour telling him that his father was being beaten up. When the young man rushed to Kutlur to find out what had happened, he too was arrested under the Unlawful Activities Prevention Act.

What happened next was a rare victory of civil society activism in the face of the draconian UAPA. Vittal Malekudiya's case was taken up pro bono by senior advocate Dinesh Hegde Ulepadi, who braved a predatory media trial, and secured bail for Vittal and his father. Since his case got reported nationwide, fetching names like Prakash and Brinda Karat to Mangalore, attracting street protests and vigilant journalistic attention, many writers, journalists and activists stood in solidarity with him. The local newspaper *Prajavani* lent great support to the struggle, and even offered him a job once he was released and completed his course. Vittal Malekudiya was eventually allowed to write his second-semester exams with his arms in chains and a police escort outside the examination hall—a haunting image.

Soorinje observes that it is the very fact that Vittal Malekudiya is a strong, courageous man who learnt to read and write that irked the police. As he puts it towards the end of the book:

> The adivasis living in the forest should not study. Their children should not go to the anganawadis. The local establishment has been stipulating systemic restrictions such as these in many places of this region. The reason is the presence of extraordinary amounts of natural resources in these forests. It is the adivasis who have safeguarded these until now. It is because of them that the resort, tourism business has been hitting dead-ends. The only solution is the eviction of adivasis. If they start studying, start talking about their rights, start writing, this eviction becomes difficult. Therefore, to keep the adivasis from education, away from rebellion, the government has spent crores and crores.

Now, the villagers of Kutlur have finally become free from police incursions, and in large part, this is thanks to the arrival of education and democratic dissent in the previously illiterate populace. In 2024, Kutlur was adjudged 'Best Tourism Village' by the Ministry of Tourism, in the 'adventure tourism category'.

Meanwhile, Kudremukh is now the undisputed dominion of forest officials and affluent tourists, Kalkuli Vittal Hegde notes. Evening parties take place at lodges and resorts, and there is even alleged hunting of game. Nobody else knows what is happening inside the forest. Basically—*who watches the watchmen*?

He also argues that the premise of a national park is itself dubious. It is ostensibly a tiger reserve, but the tigers do not live permanently on the steep slopes of the protected region, since there are no deer there. Instead, they prowl in the flatter territory, where the primary prey species live. 'There is a lot of international funding to save tigers, and thus these parks are formed without much relation to reality,' he says. He does not find the work of conservationist Ullas Karanth, who is the tiger expert under whose wings the Kudremukh National Park came to fruition, to be founded in reality: 'How much has wildlife increased in the two decades since the park was formed?' It must also be noted here that tiger-centric conservation diverts the focus from other, less glamourous species, like the wolf, which is facing a steep decline.

Ullas Karanth argues that there 'are powerful arguments ranging all the way from traditional tolerance of rights of other creatures to the twenty-first century needs of biotechnology for human welfare'. His contention is that the increasing density of local populations, who hunger for land, employment and forest products, cannot possibly coexist with wildlife.

To these exclusionary arguments, Vittal Hegde has some repartees to offer. In his eyes, the natural biodiversity of the Western Ghats is being usurped by large biotech corporations like Pfizer to make life-saving drugs to further their own profits. Overexploitation and over-reliance on these medicinal plants can deplete forest reserves if care is not taken.[24] Vittal Hegde remarks that:

> If the local people are doing something to exploit the forest, then restrict that. If they are hunting, or setting unnecessary fires, or encroaching upon land, treat that punitively. But what they suggest—to demarcate a boundary and expel the people from there—is not a tenable solution. Because it is ultimately the local tribes who take care of the forest too. Recently, 23,000 acres burnt down in Nagarhole. Why? Because there were no people there. All of them had been rehabilitated and expelled. If the adivasis were living there, would they have let the forests burn down? They would have controlled it, as they have always been doing.

This is a pertinent point. Wildfires have been proliferating across the globe, and in India, serial fires have been occurring in Uttarakhand, for instance, where it is the reserved forests (bereft of people) that have been incurring the most losses, compared to community-managed van panchayats.[25] These fires have accelerated in damage because a very small group of caretakers now attempt to control enormous swathes of depopulated lands. This is simply not feasible. New technologies involving helicopters and flamethrowers have emerged, but their efficacy remains suspect. The overall drift of Hegde's argument is that one cannot alienate the adivasis from their traditional homelands and attempt to control a mercurial landscape that has still not been fully understood by the conservationists. In other words, the current model of conservation is not conservative enough, as it forsakes communities and individuals that have developed cultures and norms over centuries.

The culmination of all these events, debates and many, many skirmishes is Kudremukh's present predicament—a testy peace brokered through steep sacrifice and hard-fought victories prevails, but the danger of ecological collapse looms large. The legacy of Saketh Rajan and the Naxal movement is one of shattered dreams and broken aspirations. Saketh's life and trajectory is cautionary, inspiring, moving and gripping in equal parts. As Zulfikar suggests, perhaps all of history is a series of experiments that yield unexpected results. Like a liquid in a titration tube, the colours keep shifting and changing, often baffling those donning the lab coats. What we seem to need is a new avatar of that century-old idea of experiments with truth, where science, humanities and activism may become healthy bedfellows, ushering in a more accommodative, and less polarising, discourse.

ELEVEN

Forests, Conservation and the Ecology of Change

> The tree which moves some to tears of joy is in the eyes of others only a green thing which stands in the way. Some see nature all ridicule and deformity, and by these I shall not regulate my proportions; and some scarce see nature at all. But to the eyes of the man of imagination, nature is imagination itself. As a man is, so he sees.
>
> —William Blake

I

5 August 2023. 7 a.m. I have just arrived in the city of Davanagere, and am already boarding another bus to the village of Kottur, sixty kilometres away. A garlanded photo of Ganesha adorns the centre of the windscreen ahead, most of which is blurred by the Tyndall effect of the thick incense of agarbatthis burning on the dashboard. I settle down on the very last seat—the only place where my long legs can find some reprieve. In front of me, a middle-aged man listens to a WhatsApp forward, which features a young local girl showcasing her prodigious memory. First, she reels off the names of all the prestigious kshetras, or temple towns, in Karnataka at astonishing speed, after which she belts out the names of the hundred and one Kauravas. Then a small bio follows: she loves to cook, and is especially proud of her vegetable pulao …

As the bus takes off, the incense and piety are replaced by a cool breeze and the loud blaring of popular Kannada songs. Schoolgoing children clamber on at the next few stops, and a man with a jetpack-sized pesticide spray comes in to sit beside me. Outside the window, I glimpse acres and acres of farms exclusively growing areca nut and paddy. I am travelling to Kottur to meet Kumbara Veerabhadrappa, or KumVee, as he is popularly called, which sounds like the name of a new model of that American military vehicle.

On further thought, there does seem something about the man—his extraordinary literary output, the bodybuilding days of his youth, his raw courage and adventurism—that makes a comparison to the six-foot tall, seven-foot-wide Humvee seem oddly appropriate. I have read a few of his novels, as well as his autobiography, and it will probably be a long while before I can make my way through the rest of his long bibliography. Munching on these kinds of thoughts, and awaiting solid food—KumVee has asked me to come home directly for breakfast—I peer out the window, and see that the bus has arrived at Harihara town. Wasn't this where that long-drawn-out environmental movement against the rayon-producing Harihara Polyfibres—which was injecting large quantities of effluents into the Tungabhadra—took place during the seventies and the eighties? The region was once an industrial hub, and Davanagere was once even known as the Manchester of India, because it was home to so many cotton mills. It was also from Harihara that the founder of the DSS, B. Krishnappa, hailed.

Mulling over these historical connections, I finally reach Kottur, which looks like any other small town of the country. It is centred around a crowded bus stand with people squatting on their haunches, garbage freely disposed of everywhere. The working class is out on the streets, hawking street food, selling goods schlepped from Davanagere to Kottur, and generally engaging in fervent activity. Its importance seemed to have declined over the centuries. Once a prominent economic hub, Kottur figures in the fourth-century conquest of South India by Samudragupta as well as the eleventh-century conquests of Rajendra Chola II. It remained a key religious centre during the heyday of the Vijayanagara Empire as well. As I stand observing my surroundings, KumVee's son arrives on a scooter to pick me up from the bus stand. I have been waiting a long time to meet his father, and my excitement is matched only by my hunger.

KumVee, in my humble opinion, is an under-celebrated master of the Kannada literary world. He does have a dedicated fan-following, whose ranks I had joined very early into this book project, but he remains largely unknown to the non-Kannada world. Though many of his works have been adapted into films, none has been translated into English yet.

In 1980, KumVee's close friend—the scholar and critic Mallepuram Venkatesh—sparked a bet with him that he couldn't write a full novel, as he had only been writing short stories until then. KumVee accepted the challenge, and produced a novel in eight days, written in the sooty light of a fireplace. Named after his soot-covered face in that frenetic week, *Kappu* (Black) won the Karnataka Sahitya Akademi award in 1981, and made him many enemies in the neighbourhood. The novel, written in appropriately raw language, revolves around the basavi (similar to devadasi) system and the oppressive patriarchy of feudal religiosity that enabled its sustained existence. It is a bleak story, but a certain page-turner. A beautiful young woman is picked out by a landlord, aided by the local priest, to become a basavi,[1] and a violent battle erupts with another landlord over the matter. Each is desirous of her, and eager to defend his own masculine honour. By the end, the landlords have killed each other off, like the Yadavas at the end of the Mahabharata, but the society that survives will not accept the woman's independence, being keen to push her into divinely sanctioned prostitution nevertheless. She ends up taking her own life.

KumVee won the award again for his novel *Shamanna*, a 600-page comic epic which explores the life of the titular protagonist who is brought up by an orthodox brahmin grandfather and a rationalist, rebellious father who dies after losing his leg in the 1962 war. This twin upbringing soon contends with the twin anxieties of Shamanna's over-solicitous, orthodox mother as well as the turbulent background of Indira Gandhi's rise to power. In 2007, KumVee bagged the Kendra Sahitya Akademi award for *Aramane*, his most ambitious work. *Aramane* took him fifteen years of meticulous research in the Rayalseema region, tracking down the legend of the British collector Thomas Munro, who lived a life of such incredible sympathy for the poor and the backward classes of the region that his legend and name survives on the lips of the locals even today. The novel is a tribute to Munro, and carries exceptionally researched accounts of the practices, dialects, myths and beliefs of the region where Munro still lives on. Besides these outstanding works, he has written tens of smaller novels, several biographies, including those of Charlie Chaplin and Krishnadeva Raya, hundreds of short stories and a few screenplays as well.

His autobiography *Gandhi Classu* was the first book I picked up, and I was hooked from the first sentence. There is a certain quality to his prose that I can only comparatively describe as Wodehousian. Wodehouse brought together jazz slang and sports slang and all sorts of references from history and literature, mashing them together to create his uniquely colourful language. KumVee, on the other hand, weaves in words and phrases from various other Indian languages (Hindi, Dakhni, Telugu, with a substantial recourse to Sanskrit), and constantly brings up references from the myths and epics. While Wodehouse frequently dipped into Tennyson, Shakespeare and other old masters for inspiration, KumVee celebrates the Kannada masters Pampa, Ranna and Kumaravyasa whose Sanskrit-infused Kannada created the golden age of Kannada literary renaissance after the tenth century. He is firmly rooted in the bard-style of meandering storytelling, but with a sophisticated, nuanced humour born out of linguistic extravagance, odd juxtapositions and extensive word-jamming. KumVee's distinct prose is in a league of its own, and he is certainly my favourite Kannada humourist.

We have a breakfast of oggarane (like poha, but with unflattened rice) and settle down at KumVee's garage-turned-library to talk. A police constable sits guard nearby. He has been assigned for KumVee's protection, because of death-threat letters that have been arriving from a certain radicalised clerk in Bangalore, who has been offended by KumVee's 'anti-Hinduism'. KumVee is certainly no fan of communal radicals, and in 2019, he wrote *Jai Bajrangbali*, a hilarious nonsense-fable, where a magically manifested monkey begins to be worshipped as a divine deity, and induces society into monkey-like behaviours in its wake. Baptised in the fiery crucible of the chaluvalis of the 1970s and '80s, he does not believe in holding back punches. In this sense, he is nothing like the apolitical Wodehouse, in all of whose collected works the word 'war' appears perhaps twice.

The terrain of feudal warfare pervades KumVee's fictional universe. He spent thirty-five years teaching at a primary school in rural, undivided Andhra, in the Kurnool, Anantapur region. This was a region rife with Naxalism, police violence and oppressive superstition. Across his eventful and adventurous life, he has broken bread with all manner of unsavoury characters, often making him wonder how he emerged unscathed. In the 1970s, he began admitting children from dalit and backward castes into the school, provoking a backlash from dominant-caste communities. That was when he received his first death threats:

> Dalit children did not even have names. They were called by whatever crude nicknames the upper castes referred to them by. I gave them names like Ramesh, Suresh, and admitted them to the school. It took a while before upper castes began sending their children to the same school. They had given one killer a supari of some 5,000 rupees to finish me off. I was a bodybuilder back then—very strong, not easy to touch me. I went to the fellow who had been given the supari, had a cup of chai with him, and I explained to him the reasons he was being given the supari, why it was important that everybody should be allowed into schools. I told him to kill me if he had the guts. Of course, he didn't. It is not so easy to kill someone. A killer has to train for many months, away from society, to prepare themselves. Which is why I am not so worried about these threats that I have been receiving now too …

I bring up Kalburgi's killing, and ask KumVee for his take on the explanations—internal factionalism within orthodox Veerashaivism, coupled with the right-wing fanaticism that took Gauri Lankesh, Narendra Dabholkar, Govind Pansare …

'All of these came together, no doubt,' he says, mindful of jumping to easy conclusions. 'I was in Bodh Gaya when I heard the news. As I see it, it was the media that killed him. There was that instance where Kalburgi brought up something Ananthamurthy had once written—that he had tried peeing on stone-idols when he was a child to test their sacrality—and TV9's Ranganath Bharadwaj pounced on this with vitriol on television news. It became such a huge thing. I see him as the prime culprit, if you ask me.'

This leads me to a question that I have been waiting to ask KumVee, regarding one of his most favoured terminologies, which he often uses to distinguish writers—upadravi (disruptive/disturbing) and nirupadravi (non-disruptive). Before I can finish, he nods vehemently and says:

> When you are riding a cycle, do you focus on the sitting part, or on the pedalling part? The former is a nirupadravi writer, and the latter is an upadravi writer, that's all. There are some writers who are okay with everyone, and don't trouble anyone. They write very well, no doubt, very beautifully. But they will never question those in power, or address questions of inequality in society. They create parks, gardens, where anybody can take a stroll, like some retired doctor or what have you, you know? Anybody can enter its world without worry. They are friendly with everyone. So many writers have got threat letters. Do they speak up about it? No. They like to be in the safest possible zone. A writer needs to have a social relevance, a social responsibility, right? This is a problem of our times today—even journalists and intellectuals are afraid to put their name next to a critical piece.

KumVee, on the other hand, specialises in the art of creating forests—dangerous, tense territory—where a reader may wander, explore and occasionally stumble too. The adventure is the reward. His autobiography, for instance, is a veritable maze of sub-plots, mini-tales, mega-deviations and micro-destinies. His smaller novels are a breeze to read, but his epic novels (matching the size of the book you hold) demand sustained attention, taking you into the heart of rural India and the myriad characters who populate it, which is where KumVee's heart also lies. As you take a big breath and begin reading, you quickly realise that he is always subverting ordinary expectations. The comic and the tragic coexist, the simplistic act of 'othering' a class or caste is never resorted to, and one marvels at his ability to holistically capture social ecosystems. In KumVee's novel-forests, the web of inextricable interconnection is paramount. In *Shamanna*, the rats and cats of the protagonists' homes are themselves detailed characters with complex histories of migration and domestic squabbles, who comment insightfully on the follies of their human peers.

Much of KumVee's combative sensibility comes from his intensely challenging youth: 'Much before the bandaya movement officially started, we already had it within us, so we did not really need that label. It is my poverty-stricken upbringing, filled with days of hunger and suffering that led me to seriously consider suicide numerous times, that has made me the writer I am today. During those years of my youth when I should have been dreaming, I was gripped only by nightmares. My children do not know of this kind of life. They do not know what hunger feels like.'

Nature is an integral character in his fiction, a sizeable chunk of which is set in the hardscrabble environment of the Karnataka-Andhra borderlands. In those dry landscapes populated by date palm, and partridges running from bush to bush, the rich teeming forests of the coastline and ghats would feel like a treasure indeed. He often employs the parched landscape to reflect the cold, brutal heart of the zamindari system that dominated these lands until not too long ago. He loves throwing in wildcats as metaphors reflecting the tamed brutality of caste society. Birds are important motifs too, and in one of his short stories titled 'Sootaka', a peacock desperate for rains becomes an arresting minor character. 'What does it matter how large the wings of a flightless bird are? Or how beautiful they are,' the narrator wonders, as the peacock groans at the agony of drought, and dances vainly under a cloud-free sky. In the same story, when the narrator is faced with the prospect of meeting an infamously brutal landlord, he gazes upon the forbidding landscape and grieves:

> The environment was rather dispiriting to one who was dreading the prospect of meeting Naidu at any moment. There was not a single coconut tree in the environs from which I could draw some moral support. Not one flower could be seen anywhere. A land deprived of water, a people distanced from normal life and a man who exemplifies this land—Naidu—must be exactly as I had heard he would be!

Yet, this Naidu turns out to be a veritable father figure, whom the narrator grows to admire with all his heart. Coexisting with all his revolutionary sentiments of social change, I glimpse in KumVee a conservative streak as well. English education, in his eyes, distances children from their parents, and drives them away to foreign pastures. He does not endorse the extroverted identity politics of sexual minorities, the turning of private, intimate moments into public outcries, though he is deeply sympathetic to their cause. He feels a pang of nostalgia for the primacy of emotions in rural society that is being overturned by the stoic sophistication of urban life. Throughout his life, he has always lived in villages, and has never been enamoured of cities. He often speaks of caste-dictated traditions—such as food habits—with respect, and sees them as authentic ways of life that are in danger of being bastardised. He understands the rigidity of orthodoxy, the psyche of those who subscribe to it, quite intimately.

Thus, when we are discussing Aurangzeb and his brother Dara Shikoh—the remarkably broad-minded prince who translated the Upanishads into Persian—he enters Aurangzeb's psyche with a nuanced historicising sensibility: 'You see, Aurangzeb was a staunch Muslim who believed in the Quran. He was not a womaniser, nor did he consume alcohol. He lived austerely, like a common man, without any ostentation. For such a man, Dara Shikoh was a heretic and an upstart, who deserved to be put to death.' Revisiting our conversation, and having devoured some portions of his massive literary oeuvre, I begin to discern a rare writerly quality within KumVee's worldview—the ability to put himself in someone else's shoes with genuine empathy. To condemn the crime, but not the criminal. It is a maxim that is easy to mouth, and easier to flout, but KumVee lives by his words. It is this very understanding that helped him bring the supari killer over to his side.

'How will you, who sees the oppressed man Duggupati Narayani and the zamindar Purushottam Reddy as equal participants in the game of chance, ever hope to understand their social relations and write a story,' the narrator in 'Sootaka' wonders. In his latest novel *Maakanaduku*, a similar first-person narrator (KumVee usually presents himself as a character; the device is rare in Kannada literature) walks into the home of a staunchly brahminical family, and observes their angst over a shudra entering their home: 'They too were unwitting inmates of the caste jailhouse, and I therefore did not make any comment.'

When the conversation turns towards Islamophobia and right-wing narratives, he speaks of S.L. Bhyrappa with similarly nuanced sympathy, 'I am an admirer of Bhyrappa's literature. I haven't read his later works like *Aavarana*, but I met him once during a stage function, and I remember him being very kind to me.' KumVee has also considered asking his present death-threat sender to lunch someday, and proceeds to sing to me one of Basavanna's vachanas that elucidates his point about treating one's adversaries with sympathy. His wife unfortunately vetoed the idea, he mourns, a slight snigger animating his face. I would soon discover in his writings elaborate fantasies of all manner of adventures embarked upon when the narrator's wife is away (gone back to her natal home to deliver a child, say), a devil-may-care kind of freedom having thus been sanctioned.

I ask him what he is working on these days, and it turns out that he has recently become fascinated by the life of Razia Sultana, whose dilapidated tomb he visited in Delhi, and whose tale he wants to channel into a novel. He adds, in a somewhat regretful tenor, that he is also mulling over a write-up about U.R. Ananthamurthy:

> I once critiqued Ananthamurthy—we had a few differences—and the newspapers really blew it up. I feel guilty about that, and want to rectify it. Ananthamurthy was a big intellectual, I respect him a lot. But there was a hypocrite in him. Once, Varavara Rao—who was urgently in need of some money—had taken me to Ananthamurthy's place. He did not even deign to see us. Now, Ananthamurthy has translated Varavara Rao's poems into Kannada, but he cannot bring himself to meet him, is it? He had an attitude of udaafe [callousness] towards rural writers, and only favoured university products, I'm afraid.

Ananthamurthy had once recalled, in a speech titled *Himseya Eda-Bala* (The Left and Right of Violence), how an unnamed Left radical had once woken him up in the middle of the night to go somewhere urgently, only to then tell him that he was only testing Ananthamurthy's loyalty to the cause. This had really irked Ananthamurthy, and made him averse to the friendship henceforth. I wondered if it was instances like these that led him to be circumspect about meeting activists. KumVee goes on to narrate a couple of instances where he felt Ananthamurthy had snubbed him too, and points to the establishment's rather excessive overtures to Ananthamurthy: 'They gave him the Basava Puraskara, which carries a purse of ten lakhs, because he needed money for dialysis during his final years. What has Ananthamurthy written or done with respect to Basavanna? If you are concerned about his health, give him as many crores as you want from your black money reserves, who is stopping you? Or give him a dialysis machine.'

I nodded sombrely in response. One of the common critiques I noticed amongst the writers of the post-Navya generation was their attempt to demolish the 'cult status' that seemed to have accrued to some of the big names of the prevailing establishment. The poet and playwright Chandrashekhar Patil had once expressed a similar grievance in a personal letter to Gopalakrishna Adiga all the way back in 1973:

> I'm proud of Girish Karnad. He's the one who has given an all-India glamour to Kannada. But does it mean that, because he has won many prizes and medals, he must be treated like a glorious exception and presented on each occasion as the brilliant young spark of the family? This is the psychology of snobbish parents … The theory that all 'criticism' stems from a feeling of 'envy' is rather cheap and narrow-minded. This is the theory one resorts to when one attains a particular stage of reputation and becomes touchy about contrary remarks about oneself by others. Most of our elderly writers have reached this stage now and they want to be accepted as they're made out to be. This is, I fear, the most disastrous aspect of the whole drama. I can't even breathe a word against writers like Adiga, Ananthamurthy, and now Karnad. If I do, the whole establishment is down on me![2]

It is not difficult to imagine how Ananthamurthy (with his extensive university training and Western education) becomes antithetical to the indigenous wilderness that KumVee emerges from. Interesting in this regard is M.M. Kalburgi's understanding of the marga–desi binary as reflecting a historical urban–rural divide, a sign of art becoming more alienated from nature as it has moved to cities, where the roots of political power have also lain. In KumVee too, as in Kalburgi, there is a deep conservative urge to preserve rural life and its dynamic janapada traditions where art is synonymous with life.

The young KumVee had revelled in telling stories, and he grew up absorbing the storytelling traditions of the North Karnataka region. His story 'Kathe Helo Kariajja' (Kariajja the Storyteller), which begins with the premise of a renowned village storyteller who has stopped telling stories, is an engrossing portrayal of the imaginative feats carried out by desi practitioners of an age-old artform, and the decline it has seen in modern times. Like all inheritors of vibrant oral-storytelling traditions (Garcia Marquez and Nikos Kazantzakis come to mind), KumVee tends to present a large cast of characters in his stories, all of them named, even if they play only a minor part in the plot. His knowledge of Indian myths and religious history enriches his raw storytelling talent with a deep sensibility of what lies at the heart of indigenous raconteurs.

As we sit talking, a bunch of young pre-university students from a neighbouring town arrive shyly, telling KumVee that their professor has sent them here as part of a project. He welcomes them, enquires into their lives, recognises that they are first-generation learners and offers some sober advice: 'See, you can find everything about me on Wikipedia, okay? All of you must read as much as you can. How much ever you read, it is less. Keep reading. Keep learning. I wish you the best …'

All the boys and girls nod sheepishly, satisfy themselves with a selfie and depart. Earlier that morning, a journalist had come to ask for KumVee's thoughts on Kannada in the education sphere. KumVee had firmly stated that those who studied in Kannada till the tenth grade must be given bonus marks, and that there must be reservations for Kannada-medium graduates in government jobs. A little while after that, the tehsildar of a nearby town also arrived to pay his respects—he received a garland and selfie in return. This seemed to be an ordinary day in the life of a man unassuming enough to claim that 'nobody in this town even knows me'.

'Those of my generation worked so hard, read so much to hone our skills. That discipline has to come to the present generation also,' he observes, as he waters the numerous potted plants in his garden. After lunch, we speak about films for a while, and I discover his taste in vintage Western cinema. He has watched almost no Kannada films for many years, but is a complete nut for English-language thrillers (*The Day of the Jackal*, *Mackenna's Gold*). Charlie Chaplin holds a special place in his heart for offering him solace during some hard times.

His novel *Kurmavatara* (The Tortoise Avatar) was turned into a film by Girish Kasaravalli, and is a meditation on Gandhi's contemporary relevance. An old man who knows nothing of Gandhi has been roped in to portray him in a television show because of his uncanny resemblance to the Mahatma. Soon, he becomes a Gandhian himself, creating ripples of change in his personal life. In striving after newly discovered ideals, he alienates his materially aspiring family by refusing to take bribes and kickbacks being offered to him, thanks to newfound television fame. A tortoise picked up from the streets becomes his only friend, and the effect is to compare the Gandhian vision of slow-but-sure change to the gait of the reptile. Each step of the way is hard-fought and steadfast (just like the act of successfully finishing this slow, enigmatic film)—the journey of discovering the right path matters more than the destination itself.

Humbled by the friendly and intimate reception offered by this celebrated writer, I took my leave with all the necessary ceremony. I vowed to read everything he has ever written, and hoped that we would meet again soon. I told him that I loved to trek, and the seventy-year-old man, still in great shape, thrilled me by saying that he would look me up if he ever happened to be near Udupi, and that we should take a hike up the forest trails of the Western Ghats together. Though this is unlikely to happen, the gesture moved me.

II

On the way back, I had a few hours to kill before catching my bus in Davanagere, and I had asked KumVee if there were any literary personalities whom I could briefly meet there. He put me in touch with the journalist and satirist B.N. Mallesh, whom I met in the printing press of the local Kannada daily *Nagaravani*, of which he was the editor. Mallesh had initially aspired to be a police officer, but an accident that broke his arm just prior to a crucial interview had crushed those dreams. Later, he chose to become a reporter instead, and now possesses an encyclopaedic knowledge of all things Davanagere.

I mention to Mallesh that I have heard about the strong working class movement in Davanagere during the sixties and seventies, and its eventual decline, but have been privy to very little detail. He nods solemnly at my prompt, takes a deep breath, and for the next forty-five minutes delivers a remarkable soliloquy on the rise and fall of the communists in Davanagere. The accuracy and speed with which he recollects everything reminds me of the girl with super-memory I had heard on the bus to Kottur just this morning. He tells me that his power of recall stems from the fact that he has written pieces about this history throughout his career. Almost everything he says corresponds well with material I will find on the subject later on.[3]

The tale begins in the 1940s, when groundnuts and cotton were the most prized produce in Davanagere. This has now been replaced by paddy, corn and areca, as I saw on the bus ride to Kottur. In 1936, the industrialist Rajanahalli Hanumanthappa set up the famed Davanagere Cotton Mills, and even before that, numerous ginning factories were alive and kicking. There were a number of factories manufacturing groundnut oil, employing thousands of workers. In subsequent decades, another industrialist named Gundi Mahadevappa entered the fray, and set up factories that produced cotton baniyans (vests). So luxurious and thick were these baniyans that they were exported to the West in record quantities, and Mallesh recalls how people queued up outside the factory to pick up slightly damaged and rejected, though still magnificent, pieces for as little as two rupees.

Not one to stand by and quietly watch his rival reap the spoils of the phenomenon that was the Davanagere baniyan, Hanumanthappa expanded his textile business. Soon, dyeing units came up, and pure cotton production diversified into hybrid terrycot. The latter replaced the former as a symbol of top-class sartorial style.

In the 1960s, trade unions representing the workers emerged in two avatars—affiliated to the CPI and the CPI(M). They managed to secure rightful wages for the workers, as well as payment for overtime. However, the antagonism between the two unions began to grow more and more violent. The CPI(M) was significantly smaller than the CPI, and was all the more combative for it. On the day the workers got their salaries, the union representatives would be waiting at the factory entrance to collect the monthly fee (a rupee or two) that was sent to the union funds. There would be skirmishes here, with each union trying to secure as many members as possible. Fights also emerged when the dominant union in a factory made a deal with the management. The owners gleefully used these internal clashes to their own advantage, sending in their own thugs to muddy the situation even further. In 1970, two CPI leaders named Suresh and Shekarappa were murdered at the All India Trade Union Congress office by goons wielding swords and cycle chains.

The next morning, as the CPI leader Pampapathi was sipping chai in a hotel, the thugs came for him too, dragging him out into the street, and bashing his head in with a stone. Through some blessed stroke of luck, the man survived, and recovered to become one of the most iconic leaders that Davanagere has seen. Support for the CPI rose sky-high after these attacks, and the party managed to make significant inroads in the city council elections. During this rise to power, there were also instances of a couple of managers being finished off by the workers' own goon squads. In 1983, Pampapathi managed to get elected to the legislative assembly, and was re-elected twice—such was the strength of the working class vote in Davanagere. 'During these years, the rule of the communists over Davanagere was absolute. The CPI party office was really a parallel government. Nobody went to police stations. Nobody could dare contest the communists' authority. That is how much power they ruled with,' Mallesh says, with thinly disguised fervour. He had grown up seeing Pampapathi from close quarters. The man had created many workers' colonies, distributed homes for cheap prices and planted innumerable trees in the city. His contribution, in Mallesh's view, was without par.

During those decades, roughly 9,000 workers were employed in the mills, and tens of thousands indirectly depended on them. One of the main fights waged by the unions was on the question of the yearly bonus, which would be put into the workers' hands on the eve of Deepavali. On that day, the entire city plunged into revelry and generous spending, a boon for the local economy. On May Day, or Martyrs' Day, the city became bedecked in red, as men and women wearing khadi pants and red shirts marched on the streets holding aloft sickle-and-hammer flags. It was a city that ran on the sweat and joy of its workers. I was reminded of this image when saffron flags fluttered all over Udupi in January 2024 to mark the consecration of the Ram Mandir in Ayodhya, and I wondered how a journalist four decades from now might remember the event.

During the eighties, Pampapathi had conducted strikes to win improved bonuses for the workers, and also secured the city's first local bus services to ferry them to the factories. Yet, it was a losing battle. The decline of the industry began during the eighties since the quality of textile production was simply falling south of market standards. The workers blamed the owners for failing to import the latest machinery, while the management blamed the trade unionists for fomenting agitation after agitation. As the economy became liberalised, the losses became impossible to sustain, and mills began closing down, resulting in mass unemployment. Laid-off workers desperately resorted to hawking egg fried rice and gobi manchurian on the streets, found temporary jobs as security guards, or, in the most tragic of cases, killed themselves or took to theft and murder.

The economy recovered slowly, with the mushrooming of educational institutions—medical, dental and engineering colleges. Students from across the country arrived in the wake of this development, bringing some wealth into the city. Now, engineering is flailing too, attracting less and less interest, but B.N. Mallesh says real estate seems to have boomed:

> Land is extremely expensive here now. Many farmers are selling their lands—the number of rice farmers is getting less and less. They are choosing to grow water-intensive areca—the water comes from the Bhadra canal.

I was curious to know of the afterlife of the many chaluvalis in Davanagere, but received a terse and disappointed response:

> BNM: Now, everything has fragmented. There are hundreds of Kannada Rakshana Vedikes. Tens of Raitha Sanghas. So many of them are vasooli veeraru [extortion experts]. Fifteen people holding a banner is what passes for a chaluvali these days. The CPI is

presently engaged in organising anganwadi workers, hotel workers, construction workers, getting them job cards, mid-day meals, basic stuff. A couple of cotton mills still exist, but of course there are no unions anymore. All work has been contractualised—they can access some schemes like ESI, PF, and all that …

Me: What has been the outcome of the many environmental movements in the region?

BNM: Mining has stopped in Bellary, and we are seeing some greenery now. Harihara Polyfibres (HPF) have made a small lake inside their own premises now. During the summer, they discharge their effluents there, and during rains, they slyly leave it in the Tungabhadra only. Who will know? The smell emanating from their eucalyptus process travels all the way here, twenty kilometres away, even today.

Eucalyptus wood is the primary raw material for rayon production. In 1984, a joint-sector company named Karnataka Pulpwood Limited was formed by the Karnataka government in collaboration with HPF. The plan was to capture 30,000 hectares of degraded forests as well as 'C' and 'D' class lands in Shimoga, Chitradurga and Dharwad districts for this express purpose. But the lands labelled as degraded in the eyes of the State were invaluable common lands of the rural populace, who depended on these for grazing their livestock, and for collecting fuelwood, herbs and handicraft materials. A strong grassroots environmentalist movement to arrest this phenomenon had triumphed. It had also successfully made the case that such farming should be conducted directly with individual farmers, similar to how coffee and tobacco farming works, so that they could be direct stakeholders in the business. This was a landmark moment in the expanding environmental consciousness that Karnataka was witnessing.

I hurriedly bid adieu to Mallesh, thanking him for his time and prodigious memory, and rushed out to catch my bus, while also trying to recollect what I knew about those days of spirited environmental movements. I wondered what difference it made whether the lake they were dumping effluents into was inside or outside their compound—didn't everything feed into underwater basins anyway? Could pollution really be abstracted into a private entity?

In December of 2021, I had heard all about the environmental struggles in the region from the very man who had championed both the agitations against Harihara Polyfibres and against the mining in Bellary. A veritable legend who has worked all his life to protect land, water and forests from crony industrialists and corrupt politicians; an unblinking force of non-violent activism named S.R. Hiremath.

III

> We cannot directly calculate what is right; but we jolly well know what is wrong!
>
> —E.F. Schumacher, *Small Is Beautiful*

December 2021. On a cold evening in sleepy Dharwad, passing the premises of the Dharwad Institute of Mental Health and Neurosciences, reflecting wryly on its droll abbreviation—DIMHANS—I turn onto D.R. Bendre Road, where the office of the Samaja Parivartan Samudaya (SPS) is located. It was founded in 1984 by S.R. Hiremath, amongst others.

Almost an octogenarian when I meet him, he is still active as an environmentalist and heading the SPS. Across his eventful life, Hiremath has led many a campaign against corruption and ecocide, pitting himself against dangerous political honchos and corporate bigwigs. Most recently, in 2011, he became widely known for helping lead a campaign against illegal iron-ore mining in Bellary, and in taking down the notoriously exploitative activities of the Reddy brothers. The kingpin Gali Janardan Reddy, who is a member of the BJP, had to cool his heels in jail for four years before being granted bail. Several administrative officers were sent behind bars as well, a historic moment by so many counts. Hiremath's other notable adversaries include the timber mafia in Bastar, no lightweights either.

As I enter the SPS building, Hiremath ushers me into the office enthusiastically, his energetic gait belying his years, as do his piercingly sharp eyes. For a good ten minutes, he proceeds to dissect my background and motives, taking copious notes. Having finally deemed me fit for conversation, he puts his pen down with a chuckle and begins to recount a long and well-remembered tale. Later, I read in his autobiography that he had always possessed a rather extraordinary memory, and that people always looked to him if they forgot something, because Hiremath made extensive notes of everything he found interesting! Even during our meeting, he mentioned a bevy of names—of the lawyers, doctors, scientists, activists, volunteers, administrators who came together in the eighties to challenge pro-industrial policies ravaging the environment—with such an intimate familiarity that I fretted about not being able to represent all their contributions in this condensed essay. As I began writing this, I felt as though I was compiling a meta-memory of memories, encapsulating the collective response of a community of Gandhian activists to the rapid destruction of our environmental heritage.

In March 1972, the Birla-owned company Harihara Polyfibres set up an industrial plant right on the banks of the Tungabhadra. By June that very year, it became obvious that the plant was releasing poisonous effluents into the river, and a warning was issued to the company from authorities in Dharwad, following complaints from the inhabitants of the nearby village of Airani. The Karnataka State Pollution Control Board (KPSCB) was set up in 1974, but it does not seem to have hindered the workings of the industry. A sister factory, the Gwalior Rayon Silk Company (better known to us as Grasim), was allowed to be set up in 1977 adjacent to the polyfibre plant, where it began to turn the rayon pulp into yarn. While villages in the interior were not too affected, the two villages of Airani and Nalavagalu were essentially dying. By 1981, the situation was so dire that health officials were considering the possibility of entirely evacuating Nalavagalu. The two units of HPF and Grasim collectively discharged 33,000 cubic metres of chemical effluents into the Tungabhadra daily, turning the river into a coffee-coloured monstrosity full of sodium hydroxide, sodium sulphate, carbon disulphate, mercury and zinc. It was only in December 1983, after over a decade of indiscriminate pollution, that work on an effluent-treatment plant commenced, though it is unclear if it was ever put to use sincerely.[4] A water-pollution study on behalf of the KPSCB concluded in 1986 that aquatic life had been obliterated, evidenced by thousands of fish flopping dead on the banks, and concluded that the poisonous vapours emanating from the tanks of the HPF unit caused 'skin eruptions, boils, a nagging cough and persistent stomach-ache'.

In 1979, Hiremath returned to India after having worked for almost a decade in the US. During the Emergency, he had taken part in agitations in Washington, establishing connections with fellow compatriots. Together, they had started India Development Services, a grassroots organisation dedicated to addressing the problems plaguing rural India. He was very much inspired by the socialist economist E.F. Schumacher and his book *Small Is Beautiful*. Carrying it as a manifesto of sorts, Hiremath moved back to India with his American wife—who happily converted to the lingayat faith in an officiated ceremony to satisfy her devout mother-in-law—with the primary motive of working to improve life in the hinterlands.

They chose a cluster of twenty-one villages in erstwhile Dharwad district to study and survey, eventually settling down in the village of Medleri. As it happened, nine of these villages were on the banks of the Tungabhadra, and the most immediate concerns they encountered were those of the fishermen, who were seeing a drastic drop in their catch rate. Shepherds noticed that their sheep were having more miscarriages than ever before, and groundnut crops were showing incredibly poor yields. The polluted water was affecting every mode of traditional life in the village, and Hiremath decided that radical action was the need of the hour.

Sometime in the early eighties, Hiremath met Shivaram Karanth at the annual gathering of a high school in Bijapur. After Karanth had given his speech, Hiremath spoke to him about the pollution along the Tungabhadra, and the need to begin resistance. The ever-vigilant Karanth immediately agreed to join the cause, and started writing articles in newspapers on the subject. His pen helped widen the ambit of the movement.

It was only in 1985 that the newly founded SPS filed a formal petition to the KSPCB against the two units. Fisherfolk whose livelihood was completely devastated by the death of almost every species of fish sued HPF for compensation. However, no matter what action the KSPCB took, the industries managed to obtain a stay order from the High Court. In December 1993, over a hundred satyagrahis chained themselves to the door of the KSPCB office, and on the fifth day of the satyagraha, the corrupt chairman of the board was sacked by the government. In 1994, astoundingly, HPF decided to claim that 'two helicopters had dropped poisonous fluids into the river for the sole purpose of maligning the HPF, and that the pesticides and fertilizers used by farmers on irrigated fields had polluted the river'. The case filed by the SPS and Karanth went all the way to the Supreme Court, which ultimately ruled against HPF.

A local watchdog committee was formed, involving all the stakeholders so that consensual and participatory solutions could be found for the region's water woes. The people's movement prevailed in the end, though it was a pyrrhic victory—the damage was already extensive. But it managed to prove one thing, that sustained activism backed by academic and legislative knowhow could bring the industrial–political nexus to submit to the public's demands, even if it required years of struggle to do so. It required shrewd political navigation too, and Hiremath never made enemies where it could be avoided.

When I opened the HPF website in 2021, it was suffused with shades of calming green. The promotional video on their front page was full of exasperating copywriting phrases such as 'unending pastures', 'the lap of untainted nature', 'old-school wisdom and new age values' and 'an endless river'. The overcompensation reeked of greenwashing.

Cynical perspectives on the legacy of the region's environmental agitations are aplenty. One such view was supplied to me by Vishnu Kamath, a scientist who took active part in the SPS and its work during these decades. Now retired, Vishnu Kamath was a professor of Chemistry at Bangalore University, and as a practising scientist in the eighties, he had written articles regarding the potential dangers of nuclear energy and other environmental concerns. These caught Hiremath's eye, who then recruited him into the SPS, and asked him to conduct studies on water pollution in the Tungabhadra.

Over some black tea and fruitcake at Koshy's in Bangalore, Kamath spoke to me about those days with a curious mixture of wry cynicism and jolly humour, not unlike the combination he'd ordered. When I asked him about the successful movement against HPF, he shrugged and maintained that no popular movement could completely unseat the widespread political corruption in Karnataka. 'People think of Bihar as a corrupt state. Somehow, Karnataka completely misses their radar, but it is just as bad here.' Minor victories are possible, but in the larger scheme of things, he feels that the system is too rigged. Still, he did agree that certain important boundaries had been breached by the movement—for instance, the addressal of local policing. Anybody drawing a salary from HPF, say even a watchman, could be highly antagonistic to the protesting environmentalists. The movement helped change this, Kamath said, as it forced the salaried employees to put themselves in the shoes of the those whose lives were being threatened by the company, and reconsider their loyalties. In other words, a modicum of empathy and social awareness was spread around, and the idea of a democratic environmental protest was normalised. Even if the protest against the Kaiga nuclear plant had not managed to stop its construction, it had held the scientific establishment accountable, and created a sense of healthy concern. For all his pessimism, even Kamath conceded that things have probably improved now, as far as industrial pollution levels are concerned. There have been developments in treatment technology, and the sheer prevalence of environmentalist concerns have forced industries to take measures, or at the very least, greenwash themselves.

When I tell Hiremath about my meeting with Vishnu Kamath, he guffaws heartily, knowing all too well the opinions of his old friend. He urges me to view the collective activities of the SPS over the decades as a whole, as a movement that pioneered environmental action in the state, learning and growing in its own way. The landmark court judgements that it generated, and the impact this had on other environmental movements across the country are not to be underestimated. He held that the National Forest Policy of 1988 came about directly as a result of the activities of the SPS, and sees it as a significant victory that overturned colonial forest policy and began empowering local communities in the protection of forests. One thing I noticed in my interviews is that environmentalists tend to see developments as stemming from their own efforts—for instance, the science-writer Nagesh Hegde spoke of his newspaper articles as being crucial catalysts. This is only natural and human. The bigger truth is that they were all equal participants in a vast ecosystem of academics, scientists, civilian demonstrators, forest officers, lawyers, administrators and activists that worked to create progressive and innovative forest management policies over years of sustained action, debate and dialogue.[5]

In my conversation with Vishnu Kamath, too, I had heard of figures within the movement who have been silhouetted by time and memory. He introduced me to the colourful life of one of them—Kusuma Sorab.

She died, aged just forty-four, in a hit-and-run accident in March 1998, struck down by a bus as she attempted to cross a road at midnight. Impaired vision in one of her eyes seems to have been what led to the tragedy. Her death was given short shrift by the press, and no political faction came out to mourn her as she deserved either. In the aftermath of the shocking incident, a tribute volume[6] was brought out by those close to her, and is the most accessible legacy of her life's work.

Kusuma Sorab grew up in picturesque North Canara, surrounded by the raw splendour of the Western Ghats and the cool sights of the Sharavati river. Born into a middle-class family that could afford to send only one child to college, a bristling Kusuma was forced to stay home for a few frustrating months while her brother went on to study further after high school. A stroke of luck enabled her to join a nursing course in Bijapur, and she moved to Bombay to pursue her dream of becoming a doctor. In the vein of Bombay stories, this too is one of hardship, struggle and immense fortitude. By 1974, Kusuma Sorab had earned her MS, and she returned to Karnataka to begin an extraordinarily committed social life.

In 1977, near the mouth of the river Sharavati along the western coast, after a whole deal of bureaucratic running around, she set up the Snehakunja Trust. When I visited its premises in December 2021, I saw a largely empty hospital where naturopathy and Ayurvedic treatment was offered to patients. As far as I could see, the place was populated by one doctor, one nurse and one elderly patient. It looked like the pandemic had thinned out the crowd. I also learnt that the trust has another branch of activity close by that works on conservation of coastal ecosystems and sensitive wetlands.

Kusuma Sorab's long list of concerns included the well-being of the marathi-halakki tribe native to North Canara, legal awareness programmes for young women, organic farming, cow-protection schemes, rehabilitation camps for those affected by floods along the tributaries of the Sharavati, awareness programmes in a few districts of Karnataka and Goa, a survey of the health of natural environments surrounding the Kaiga and Kakrapar nuclear plants, and agitations against liquor, hooch and the timber mafia. Like Aunt Sally adopting the wayward Huckleberry Finn, Kusumakka (as she was fondly called) also rescued many young girls from the clutches of poverty, 'civilising' them and training them in various vocations as best as she could.

Why is Kusuma Sorab's name still completely unknown, though? I extend this question to S.R. Hiremath. He knew her quite well, by virtue of the various movements they were part of together. It was Vishnu Kamath and the environmentalist science writer Nagesh Hegde who had introduced the two of them. He affirms her centrality and contribution to various movements in the state, especially the agitations against the Kaiga nuclear plant and the Sharavati Tailrace project,[7] but also adds:

> She was a good doctor, good volunteer and a very courageous lady, but I don't think she had understood the theory, methods and dynamics of social movements, like we had learnt from Martin Luther King Jr and Gandhi. There was no real, powerful satyagraha. To build pressure against the government, you need a different approach, you see, and this was absent in her.

From what I can surmise, it seems like the spirited Kusuma Sorab had taken up such a large number of issues that they failed to coalesce into one long, sustained endeavour. Sporadic protests achieve little; only sustained and organised pressure against the ruling elite may yield results. To be truly Gandhian in one's activism is to create a movement that is larger than life, that is utterly theatrical and dramatic in its conception, challenging the establishment by creating a broad opposition that is impossible to ignore. The SPS actually managed to create a movement of national proportions, involving activists and NGOs from across the country.

Towards the close of our conversation, Hiremath pulled out books carrying meticulous documentation of all their decades-long struggles, and I glimpsed in the grainy photographs many familiar faces—Chandi Prasad Bhatt, Shivaram Karanth, Ramachandra Guha. His nostalgia was undercut by the realisation that the present government had effectively put the kibosh on all their victories: 'With the advent of Modi, all this has gone haywire. All the forest policies have been upturned. We cannot fight them now. But once this regime goes, we will all unite.'

Through amendments to the Forest Conservation Act of 1980, the Modi regime opened up forests and 'degraded' lands—an old trick—to wanton industrial acquisition, by manipulating the definition of what a forest is.[8] Now, the environment ministry can pass orders to decide how forests will be leased out to corporations.[9] That the totalitarian power of the regime has forced even Hiremath—

once a spirited adversary of nothing less than the Emergency—to buckle, spoke both of his age and the unprecedented nature of the present regime's collusion with the forces of industrial capitalism. The KPSCB has fallen back into rampant corruption,[10] just another part of a huge money-making game.

As I came to find out, there exist legions of forest lovers and activists who have been fighting a silent battle in the shadows, waiting out a rapacious Central regime, training others in their stead, learning to regenerate and replenish what—after decades of chemical pollution—can now be seriously dubbed as degraded landscapes. And this seems to be true across the globe.

IV

'I can't function well in man-made environments. In the jungle, at every ten steps, there is a new tree, some new species of bird, some new insect—it felt like such a huge universe to me. Why should I go to school every day? Why should I go back to that small universe? There is no wonder. However, you can look at just one tree for hours.'

Such were urban forester and landscape regenerator Sheshadri Ramaswamy's thoughts during his schooling years. In January 2024, I met him at his friend's design studio in Malleshwaram, Bangalore, which is the default adda for his vibrant circle of artists, activists and kindred nature spirits. A graphic designer who recently resigned from a leading Kannada daily sat glumly next to us. 'There is too much casteism and elite domination within the organisation,' he fretted, adding mournfully that, once upon a time, the newspaper was a democratic space, famed for its egalitarian social stance.

Sheshadri Ramaswamy sports a faded earthy brown shirt, and speaks in a gentle whisper. His voice turns despondent as he says: 'I used to be a full-time environmental activist before 2014, but now there is no space for it at all. Systematically, all earlier forest laws have been amended. They are all human-centred now, very destructive for the environment.'

He currently works as part of an organisation named Forestry for All (FORA), which trains people in the craft of regenerating and rewilding barren lands. Sheshadri's forest journey began at the turn of the millennium, under the aegis of the famous Indian Forest Service (IFS) officer S.G. Neginhal, one of most passionate wildlife lovers you will ever read about.

In 1971, Neginhal attended the Forest Research Institute in Dehradun for a six-month certificate course in wildlife training, which set the tone for the rest of his life. He then travelled to various national parks across the country, learning to identify tigers by their individual pugmarks,[11] watching sarus cranes perform mating dances and absorbing the breadth of India's wildlife spectrum. The following year, he was posted to Mysore as a wildlife officer, where his purview included Bandipur, Nagarhole, BR Hills and Ranganathittu Bird Sanctuary. Work was hectic and took up all his time, and he writes that 'it may not be an exaggeration if I say that my wife used to show me to my younger children when I was asleep, with the help of a torch!'[12] As devoted as he was to work, Neginhal was also a deeply spiritual man—a devotee of the Mother in Auroville, Pondicherry—which may have been another contributing factor in his desire to dedicate his life to wildlife conservation.[13] He proposed and secured many wildlife sanctuaries, including India's first wolf sanctuary near Melkote. Rubbing shoulders with giants like Salim Ali and M. Krishnan, Neginhal became a walking-talking encyclopaedia who later authored the book *Forest Trees of South India* (Sheshadri helped edit it), which still remains the authoritative guide to the eclectic peninsular treescape that extends all the way to Orissa.[14]

SR: He was the DC [Deputy Conservator] of Bangalore between 1982 and '87, and that was when he planted and raised one and half million trees, with a success rate of 97 per cent. Throughout the year. Watering them once a week, manuring them …

Me: Wow. So basically, most of the trees we see in Bangalore today were planted by him?

SR: Yeah, it is all Neginhal's work—he had many trusty companions working with him too. Nowadays, all they do is greenwashing. Plant some things, take some selfies, it's just bookkeeping. They don't raise the saplings. Who's going to raise them?

Neginhal had not exactly volunteered to take up this challenge. He would have preferred to stay in Hubli with his family, but an impulsive decision taken by Chief Minister Gundu Rao, whose instincts were questionable on every other issue, had streamlined a long bureaucratic process that took many months into a quick, firm appointment letter that brought him to Bangalore. As usual, he fulfilled his assignment with extraordinary commitment.

SR: So, yeah, Neginhal passed away three years ago. I had been working with him for twenty years. Being with him in the forests, learning about forest ecology, especially about floristic structures. What kind of species are associated with what terrain, how they occur in dry lands, in ghats, on the slopes, riversides, sholas, etc. We also had a private company that used to plant trees on behalf of industries. Again, a lot of CSR goes into greenwashing these days. Slowly, we ran out of business because we don't do that kind of stuff.

Me: Do you see that kind of passion in administrative officers these days?

SR: No. Seems like it has vanished. Back then, the Executive was autonomous, and pressure from the Legislature was comparatively less. Even if there was pressure, they would fight it out. There was swabhimana [self-respect]—now that has all been sold out. Passion, knowledge, training, all are missing. You should see how RFOs [range forest officers] and ACFs [assistant conservator of forest] are appointed—they just get an appointment letter, a uniform, a weapon. That's it. It has become like just another government job. People see it as settling down. Inertia has set in.

It is safe to say that the bumbling passivity of Shikari Shambu (the cartoon character from *Tinkle*, and one of my childhood heroes) is not an ideal worth aspiring to. The seventies were certainly a time of unprecedented forest action. It was when the age-old tradition of maharajas doubling up as shikaris was finally relegated to history, the rapid dwindling of tiger numbers created Project Tiger and wildlife conservation was abuzz with energy. In 1973, the Rajkumar-starrer *Gandhada Gudi* (The Abode of Sandalwood Trees)—probably the first Indian film expressly promoting wildlife conservation—primed the Kannada public into respecting the state's efforts in the crackdown on smugglers and poachers. Rajkumar played the role of the courageous, incorruptible forest officer who would brave anything to catch the culprits. It is ironic that, three decades later, the brigand and sandalwood-smuggler Veerappan kidnapped Rajkumar, holding him hostage for hundred-odd days while Karnataka went into paroxysms of anxiety. In 2022, his son Puneeth Rajkumar posthumously starred[15] in a wildlife documentary, also titled *Gandhada Gudi*, where he is accompanied by filmmaker and wildlife photographer J.S. Amoghavarsha on trips across Karnataka's diverse natural landscape. While the older film carried the unmissable whiff of patriotic nationalism, the latter carries more universal concerns, no doubt being mindful of the unprecedented threat of rapid climate change. Every natural habitat, from forests to oceans to grasslands, is in dire need of care. The realisation of how enormous the challenge is carries with it a profound sense of helpless humility.

SR: It is humanly impossible to do ecological restoration. Flowering plants themselves are like 250 to 300 million years old. Humans are here from 200,000 years. And agriculture started around 12,000 years ago, I think. And only in the last hundred years, this industrial pollution has caused such extraordinary changes. So, we must understand our limitations.

Me: I am curious to know how you plan and implement regeneration projects in cities, and how it differs from larger restoration and re-wilding projects.

SR: In urban spaces, the treatment is different. Here, the emphasis is on aesthetics—flowering trees, bird-attracting trees and shrubs, butterfly-attracting species. People will be sane. It brings joy to life, and keeps you level-headed. There are some papers which suggest that violent crime increases where nature is not around, in highly concretised cities and all. Man loses it. Eco-restoration, re-wilding is very different. These are done on degraded lands as large as forty acres. You have to go to the surrounding forest, and see if it is undergoing progression or retrogression. You cannot alter that, of course. In your farm, because you have a borewell, you can change some things. But basically, you copy and paste from the forest next to you. You take the same indigenous species which are around you and plant them.

Me: What do you think of all these Save Soil, Save Kaveri, Sadhguru-type campaigns?

SR: None of that works. It is all greenwashing. No informed perspectives. You cannot suddenly go save a river like he proposes. In fact, it is counter-productive.[16] Sadhguru says they came out with a book at the end of it—I mean, come on yaar? So, there are people out there with money and resources, but they have no direction. Now, take the Modi government. Another cheetah died in Kuno yesterday, I think. Now, is that habitat conducive to the species? Was there a preliminary study done? No, it is proven, after so many deaths, that they are incompatible with this habitat.

Me: Yeah, the collars on their necks had also created wounds.

SR: Collars are a really bad idea. Earlier, they would have these huge collars with batteries. See, the female won't allow a male with a collar to mate. She'll say, *take that collar off.* When they make a kill, they can't bite properly, hunt properly, and when they're drinking water, the collar comes in the way.

Me: Animal conservation in Karnataka seems to have had a rich history …

SR: Animal conservation! I used to be very active twenty-five years back. It is going well. I feel the people of Karnataka are generally great lovers of wildlife and nature. I understand all the southern languages. I find that Karnataka has the maximum number of villages named after flora and fauna. Like Tavarekere, Alanahalli ['tavare' is lotus, and 'ala' is banyan]. You just take a list from the

> post office and see. In Tamil Nadu, names of people and kings are more prominent, like Periyanaayaganpatti, you know? Kerala also doesn't stand out in this matter like Karnataka does.

It was an interesting observation that also reminded me of Neginhal reminiscing about the village of Kokkrebelur ('kokkre' means stork) in his autobiography. Sometime during the seventies, he had followed some painted storks into a secluded village, and was stunned to find that the villagers were taking care of the storks that visited annually every March–April. The place had been known to birdwatchers for decades, but following Neginhal's serendipitous stumbling upon, it was declared a Community Reserve, officially recognising the villagers' conservation efforts.

Just a month prior to my meeting with Sheshadri Ramaswamy, the Kannada media was filled with heartbreaking news of the death of a beloved tusker named Arjuna, who had died in an elephant-monitoring exercise in the forestland near Hassan, where human–elephant conflicts have been on the rise. A team of eight elephants, including Arjuna, were taken on an exercise by the forest department, and the goal was to plant radio collars on wild elephants that were entering villages and devouring crops. However, the tranquiliser missed its mark, and because one of the enemy tuskers was in musth, it proceeded to attack Arjuna aggressively. Poor Arjuna, aged well over sixty, could hold his own only for twenty minutes, and succumbed to gore injuries soon after. Having carried the golden howdah during Mysore Dasara celebrations for a record eight times, the famous Arjuna was mourned by animal lovers across Karnataka, and a video of his handler bursting into uncontrollable sobs over Arjuna's corpse was heartrending.

Elephant–human conflicts in Hassan have become serious in the last decade, with eighty human deaths and fifty elephant fatalities.[17] While deforestation is a major cause of animals foraying out into human territory, the rise of invasive species like lantana, eupatorium and parthenium have also choked forests and their inhabitants. Lantana, in particular, has been estimated to occupy a whopping

40 per cent of forest cover in the country. Removing the bramble-filled plants and crushing them to use their biomass as fertiliser is one way of addressing the problem, while the production of lantana handicrafts has also been taken up by indigenous communities for almost two decades now, like the soliga community in MM Hills.[18]

SR: I don't like to use the word tribal. I say indigenous peoples. They use this word, 'moolavasigalu'. If they are the original inhabitants, what am I? I am an invasive species.

Me: Like lantana.

SR: Hahaha, yes. Our local floral species have become wiped out. Lantana is everywhere. They say we need 2,500 crores to eradicate lantana from forests in Karnataka. This is actually a small amount. It is how much they spend on road widening. The ecological security of our nation is not at all looked at. It is just as important as the security of our borders. Forests are really unhealthy in India. Ecological security also means fresh-water security. There are so many aspects to it. But how many of us are thinking about all this? Everyone is becoming part of the matrix. We've lost the ability to question. Maybe a few people like you and me are discussing these things.

Me: I feel like there is a small reverse-exodus back to rural India that is happening—some urbanites do want to go back, start organic farming and all.

SR: Yes, that should happen. But it is not so easy. I have seen so many people try to do this without understanding how difficult it is. You need to be physically fit, patient and have a lot of knowledge. Traditional ecological knowledge has to come down the generations. From your neighbours, your ancestors. From people working around you. It is practised knowledge. You can't open an Excel sheet one fine day and become a farmer, no? I've been seeing a lot of techies try to farm, and fail miserably.

Practised knowledge and the wisdom of indigenous lifestyles have not been truly harnessed into the service of forest management. The government's top-down plans have tended to prove counterproductive more often than not. When I wrote to the eminent environmentalist Madhav Gadgil to learn about his experiences with regards to the Western Ghats in Karnataka, he responded thus:

> Throughout my working life I have been involved in many ways in policy advice. The first of such assignments was as a member of the Karnataka State Board for Wildlife from 1976 to 1982. In that capacity I presented to the Wildlife Board a note on additional localities that merited protection as Wildlife Sanctuaries/National Parks in 1977. One of the localities suggested for such protection was Narasimha Parvatha, the tallest peak in the Agumbe Ghats in Udupi district of Karnataka, by including it in the Kudremukh National Park. I learnt later from my friends working in Sringeri College that this proposal was counterproductive. Till that time the local communities had been imposing quite moderate demands on the forest, primarily for fuelwood, but as soon as they learnt that they might no longer have access to the area they invaded the forest and cut down a large number of trees to create a stockpile of fuelwood in their homes.

Such experiences led Gadgil to espouse more democratic, ground-up solutions in succeeding years. He was an integral part of the Western Ghats Ecology Experts Panel (WGEEP) that released a report in 2011 which recommended decentralisation and active participation of local communities in conservation. Translation of the report into regional languages was urged so that villages could decide whether they wished to be classified as ecologically sensitive zones.[19] Yet, misinformation campaigns flourished in the wake of the report, and even serious journalists today find it to be 'radical' and 'extremist' in its recommendations, which were meant to be suggestive rather than imposing.[20] As Gadgil writes, 'the most effective weapon of the disinformation campaign has been the strong belief of the people that any attempt at conservation will be subverted by officialdom into a means of concentrating power in its hands to impose restrictions, which are then used as an excuse for extortion.'

The WGEEP was soon supplanted by the diluted and unscientific Kasturirangan Report, which was poised to facilitate greater commercial exploitation, especially mining and quarrying.[21] Neither the Congress nor the BJP governments in Karnataka paid heed to either of these two reports, choosing to perpetuate a standoff that has left the people living along the Ghats in a state of limbo.

Indigenous forest dwellers across India are united through their shared trauma of displacement and disenfranchisement. While the British employed them as bonded labourers in service of their love for timber, the Indian state post 1947 continued colonial policies vis-à-vis forests, deeming legitimate cultivators as encroachers, evicting villages en masse in the name of industrial projects and national parks. The 2006 Forest Rights Act was meant to arrest more than a century of sustained malintent. It recognised the rights of village communities to access and use forests and to own and sell minor forest produce, and most importantly, to manage forests under their own customary boundaries. It also laid down a democratic procedure for whether wildlife conservation in a particular region really necessitates the curbing of community rights. However, researchers have argued that the FRA has failed in its execution, marred by poor implementation and administrative incompetence:

> The biggest lacuna in FRA implementation is the extremely slow and incomplete recognition of community rights to access and manage forests [CFRs, or community forest rights]. The [still colonially structured] forest bureaucracy is vehemently opposed to these rights, as it stands to lose its zamindari: our estimates show that 70–90 per cent of the forests in central India should be under CFRs. The other departments and political representatives can only visualise forest dwellers as 'labharthis' [beneficiaries of State largesse], not as autonomous users and managers of their own forests.[22]

All of this has largely also arisen because political imagination, in general, has moved away from the rural countryside, and into cities, where infrastructure and industry and development are the only buzzwords. The increased power demands of rapidly burgeoning populations in cities, coupled with the perils of global warming, have created a deadlock difficult to break. The biggest concern, apart from land degradation, is of course water insecurity. When I spoke to environmentalist Leo Saldanha, who is part of the Environmental Support Group (ESG) in Bangalore, he affirmed ESG's interventions in water security as one of their most lasting legacies:

> One major challenge was how to imagine the water sector in an inclusive framework. Our work on lakes as water commons is important because we attacked the notion of privatisation successfully. We came up with a scheme for the rehabilitation of lakes that is ecologically wise and socially inclusive. It resulted in a law—Karnataka Tank Conservation and Development Authority Act 2014—which is a regulatory system created by the state, which indicates the seriousness of the problem. The judiciary has responded positively, by and large, which we are thankful for. Just imagine what it means when you have to protect around 45,000 tanks, thousands of ponds, all of which form this amazing water landscape. It is an acknowledgement of the traditional knowledge embedded everywhere, and is a critique of centralised water management. We can't depend on faraway water resources, and a kind of community-led decentralisation movement is picking up again. But saving water requires a lot of investment, unfortunately, which is not really forthcoming.

I had heard of groundwater recharging activities happening across Karnataka now and then, in the wake of the law. It seemed like the state had been pushed into action. However, Bangalore has already arrived at a crisis of grave water insecurity, and expensive tankers of water brought in from all over the region have now become a distressingly common sight in the city. Another startling fact shown by researchers recently is that nearly half the existing lakes in Bangalore are now being encroached upon, not by humans, but by invasive tree species like *Prosopis juliflora*, which were unscientifically planted too close to lake borders many decades ago. They now threaten to envelop and dry out many lakes in and around the city.[23]

Saldanha also spoke at length about ESG's efforts a few years back in highlighting the capture of Amrit Mahal Kavals[24] near Challakere in Chitradurga, where a massive 10,000-acre establishment—housing BARC, DRDO, ISRO and IISc[25]—was announced in 2010. Here, the state government had envisioned a 'Science City', where there would be astronauts training for space flight, air-to-ground weapons would be tested, research on renewable energies and water harvesting would transpire, and 'special material enrichment' (code for uranium enrichment) would be carried out. ESG contested the sheer scale of the land allocated for the project, and the impact it would have on local villagers (who would not be able to access the commons) and local wildlife, which includes the endangered Great Indian bustard. It was challenged in the National Green Tribunal, but the courts ruled in the state's favour, after imposing a few conditions on the establishment, such as not conducting ballistic tests.

Saldanha's anti-nuclear stance was forged in the late 1990s, during the peace movements emerging in the wake of the 1998 Pokhran tests, and it has never wavered since.

> LS: Those who were leaning towards the political right were clear that the nuclear bomb is different from nuclear energy. I thought this was schizophrenic. For me, India's nuclear energy is enmeshed with defence. In both forms, I think it is a really dangerous technology. We know enough to say it is not worth it. While I really took to James Lovelock's Gaia theory—seeing the Earth as one single organism—I was troubled by his endorsement of nuclear energy …
>
> Me: I believe Finland has been experimenting with deeply buried storage units where radioactive waste can be retired for long durations safely. Perhaps more such measures can be reassuring …
>
> LS: Have you ever been to a mine? I've seen mining in Kudremukh, in Bellary, in Orissa. It is appalling. One thing is for sure, even if uranium was not radioactive, mining it would be an ecologically devastating practice. It is found in extremely minuscule quantities—it is a rare earth metal. Modern electronics is also founded on rare earths. Ninety-nine per cent of uranium mining produces only

silt. These large solar plants are also being set in motion. They will completely wipe out grasslands while calling them wastelands. Very dangerous. I'm thinking on a long scale—500 years from now, what might still stand as relevant practices? We need to think on a larger time scale.

Sheshadri Ramaswamy too dismissed the idea of vast solar farms, speaking of how they would diminish grassland wildlife. He was more welcoming of nuclear energy, agreeing that it was relatively cleaner than coal, at least in the short run. In the longer run, reducing energy consumption, facilitating economic degrowth,[26] and moving towards a political environment that has come to be called eco-socialism might be the only way out of the climate and energy crisis. The contours of such a consensus will have to be global in nature, and cannot be spelt out in a set of bullet points. Ad such action will only be possible when power and resources are decentralised, legal recourse is decentralised and communities are given actual political responsibility to care for their environs. But it does seem like the powers that be will deign to take notice only after the milk has completely spilt over.

Before leaving, I picked up a few books that Sheshadri's friends at the studio had designed and published—like a Kannada translation of *The Last White Hunter*, which is the story of Donald Anderson, a forest aficionado who lived in Bangalore and hunted many a tiger in his life. I also saw that they had published a lot of dalit writing in translation.

The very next day, KumVee was releasing his latest book *Maakanaduku* in Bangalore, and I dutifully attended. He was surrounded by several of his close friends. Among them was a courageous police officer with an encyclopaedic knowledge of Stuartpuram, the town in Andhra named after the colonial administrator Stuart who started an experimental town to 'reform' the so-called 'criminal tribe' known as yerukulas, a wandering community with rich oral traditions deemed to be deviant in the colonial eye. Effectively binding them to this town, the British had used the community as cheap farm labour, benefits that the upper-caste communities reaped too.[27] It is now infamous for being a hotbed of crime, and has inspired multiple Telugu films. It turned out that *Maakanaduku* was a fictional rendering of the same environment, and it was exactly the kind of explosive subject, delving deep into the underbelly of suburban India, that I had come to expect from KumVee. 'There are people in villages who will commit murder just for a free biryani,' he began his speech. Hilariously premised, the novel follows the writer-protagonist who volunteers to go to the notorious town of Maakanaduku to take up the position of a school teacher, but really in search of stories and creative potential. The ghost of the ethnographer Verrier Elwin (who lived several decades among the adivasis) keeps intruding upon the narrator's mindspace, providing jovial inspiration to continue his journey, to live with the indigenous people of that elusive village with all the curiosity of an anthropologist. Arriving at Maakanaduku Cross in a rickety bus full of dopeheads and opium-smokers, he first meets a yerukula man who thinks of him as nothing less than god. The fellow refuses to even touch him, to engage with him on equal terms. And the narrator frets:

> This was not the first time I was interacting with those deprived of all civil infrastructure. As far as I am concerned, these deprived villages are bountiful mega cities and universities, and these people are inheritors of a rich culture. Their lives are, to me, nothing less than mahakavyas. Their trust is my safety armour! Oh, if only there could be bonhomie between the two of us!

In Poornachandra Tejaswi's debut novel *Kaadu Mattu Kraurya* (Forests and Cruelty), penned in the early sixties, a portrait of ecological destruction had co-existed with a critique of forest primitivism. The novel demonstrated how the Bhadra dam had inundated lands and snatched away homes in the Malnad, and also showed how the violence of the forest beasts fostered a similar cruelty among the lives of people living close to them. More than anything, the forest was an imposing barrier that dictated the horizons of those who dwelt within it, keeping them away from education and urban civilisation.

Sixty years later, in *Maakanaduku*, the critique of oppressive superstitions is still present, but ecological destruction has been subsumed into a much larger theme—the destruction of our very sense of bearing. So much so that one must journey back into the lives of the most deprived, into those brambled forests, into that complex ecosystem that we think we know so much about but actually haven't got the foggiest. At the very least, we may see how much of our world has remained distant from any sense of 'growth' or 'development'. It might lead us to better articulate what those hallowed words should really come to mean in the years to come, and to become better ancestors to future generations who are inheriting an already embittered present.

After a few minutes of prodding and pleading, the yerukula man gingerly accepts the narrator's friendship, expertly sunders some lantana and cactus that is blocking their path, and begins introducing him to the various species of animals and birds in the forest that he knows so well.

TWELVE

Cultures of Insecurity

Working for the Working Class

> A man is not worthy, in my judgment, to enlist in the services of the working class unless he has the moral stamina, if need be, to break asunder all personal relations to serve that class as he understands his duty to that class.
>
> —Eugene Debs

I

Eugene Debs was an American socialist, trade unionist and a stringent critic of the Wilson administration's decision to plunge the country into the First World War. This was a war that ran on the blood and sweat of the millions who greased its machinery and died on its frontlines. Those years saw the beginnings of a century-long tussle between socialism and capitalism, and ideals ran high. Generations of resolute and unflinching leaders emerged who devoted their lives to the cause of emancipating workers crushed by the capitalistic war machine. By the final years of the twentieth century, however, as the end of history was about to be triumphantly proclaimed, the global movement for solidarity of the working class around the world fell on its face. And so did its idealism. Private corporations gained a great deal of immunity, thanks to acceptance of the neoliberal paradigm in countries around the world, and workers' woes now became minor hiccups to be swallowed.

These were my vague, initial thoughts before I started working on this book. I knew that there had been spirited trade union leaders in Karnataka. However, even though the eminent Kannada publication house and bookshop Navakarnataka was started by the trade unionist B.V. Kakkilaya, scholarship and literature surrounding working class movements seemed scarce indeed. How had these movements changed the lived experience of the workers? Had they reflected on their failures? And how had they adapted to the monumental changes that the liberalisation of the economy had created? So much of the world has changed since the 1990s, and the global economic system has come to be increasingly called late capitalism, or more provocatively, techno-feudalism.[1] Yet, socialist workers' movements have begun to slowly reclaim lost terrain in countries like the US, fighting against the life-deadening atmosphere created by automation and cloud-based work regimes.[2]

Could it mean a resurgence of foregone ideals?

In December 2021, I paid a visit to the AITUC office in Bangalore to meet Ananth Subbarao, a legendary trade union leader in Karnataka. The union is associated with the Communist Party of India, and Subbarao, one of the grand old men of the labour movement in Karnataka, has spent the better part of his life representing the workers of the transportation sector. I have been led to him by another communist veteran who looks up to him as his guru. The same source had brought up in hushed tones some gossip about how Subbarao's ascent to leadership was resented by others in the movement. As a connoisseur of gossip, I found this only mildly interesting—for anyone to rise up through a hierarchy, others will have to be sidelined.

Though Subbarao is eighty years old when I meet him, he is perennially busy, and it has taken me over a month of persistent calling to finally secure an interview. He tells me, with a naughty grin that I will come to enjoy, that he has a stent in his heart, but is still able to work all day long. I am heartily welcomed into his office, but he has other matters to deal with first.

Opposite me sits a man with a puffed, sullen face. Chandrashekhar is a KSRTC employee, a workshop mechanic who has been transferred from Mysore to Ramanagara (which is close to Bangalore) with less than two years of service remaining. His voice trembles with every word. Chandrashekhar's wife is chronically diabetic, and she underwent a heart surgery recently; a cataract operation three months ago. She has lost a toe to gangrene and her foot is wrapped up in a cast. He cannot fathom the idea of a transfer. Who is going to take care of her? She is too weak to even administer insulin to herself. They are too old and infirm to shift from one city to another. Ananth Subbarao sympathises deeply, and vows to help him out. 'How did you allow gangrene to set in? Couldn't you have gotten her medical assistance from the beginning?' he castigates poor Chandrashekhar. Some phone calls are made, some strings are pulled. The wife comes hobbling over on one leg from the car outside to pay her respects to Subbarao, who finds these entreaties far too reverential and unnecessary.

After they leave, Ananth Subbarao shakes his head in disbelief.

> See, we had two divisions in Mysore—rural division and urban division. Because of this COVID, they want to economise, do some cost reduction. To reduce duplication of staff and all. What they should have done is made a list of senior workers and retained them. The buggers have collected money and retained the fellows who paid them off. These are all hard workers who have contributed the most to the industry. He probably could not cough up enough money, and now, at the fag end of his career, he is forced to come here and do this. Such a helpless situation.

When I spoke to the Kannada poet Mudnakudu Chinnaswamy, who retired as director and financial advisor of the Bengaluru Metropolitan Transport Corporation in 2014, he told me that the communists' confrontational tendency was one of the main reasons that KSRTC was split into four corporations (split geographically) in the late 1990s—the workers' union could organise pan-state strikes before and bring the entire transport sector to a standstill. Now, many unions had entered the fray, diluting their collective power. Chinnaswamy held that the division contributed to swifter administration, more streamlined operations and helped divert funds to regions of Karnataka where the transport sector not doing financially well. Subbarao's distaste for 'management' was echoed in Chinnaswamy's rhetoric of the 'communists who kept raising a hue and cry'. Yet, he spoke of Subbarao as a good friend, bearing only kind words.

Meanwhile, to return to Subbarao and Chandrashekhar's predicament:

> AS: I've noticed this psychology in KSRTC workers who ask for help. If someone asks them for money, be it 5,000 or 25,000, they will gladly part with it. Whereas if I tell them I will sort it out without such bribes, they don't believe me at all. [Laughs.]
>
> Me: How does one go about trying to mend this situation?
>
> AS: It is very difficult. The system is like this. In a factory, you have an HR department. Even if there are only two HR employees, they will do a good job. But here, it is neither a factory culture nor a purely government culture. These are all bureaucrats who are deputed by the government. So, they also try to adopt government standards and all that. In a vibrant industry like transport, you need a vibrant industrial relations policy. But what we have is a heartless bureaucracy.

The story of the hapless Chandrashekar's transfer is a smaller symptom of a larger network of administrative gangrene. The managerial class has always lived one notch above the actual workers themselves, holding the power to dislocate and disturb their lives, while also pocketing a bulk of the profits. It was to address this grave inequality that AITUC stepped into the picture in the first place.

AITUC entered the transport industry in the mid-seventies, a time when the existing unions were mere puppets of the State, quite happy to toe their line. The leaders of these union were all from supervisory positions, and drivers, conductors and mechanics had no say at all. AITUC wanted to democratise the situation, and decided to institute the secret ballot through which workers could choose their own leaders. This militant reform took over a decade to be implemented. Two hundred unionists, including Subbarao, were arrested and jailed in 1985. But the government had to agree to a secret ballot. It was a huge victory, and in 1987, AITUC got 53 per cent of the vote and was officially recognised. As Subbarao tells it:

> The officers and supervisory staff had fifteen days of casual leave per annum. Drivers, workers and mechanics, who formed 95 per cent of the workers, had only eight days. They were a neglected lot, and they never believed in strikes and all. When we got recognition, one of our demands was fifteen days for all staff. We were told that drivers and workers are very important, and cannot be afforded so much leave, whereas the supervisor position was unimportant. To this I responded that, if this was the case, then please pay the mechanic one rupee more than the divisional controller, a conductor two rupees more and the driver three rupees more. Shouldn't that be the case if their work is more important? We managed to get them an increase in casual leave.

Having begun the conversation this seriously, I try to enter more informal territory, and ask him about his childhood and youth. What was young Subbarao like? 'Communists are not bothered about their own selves,' he laughs.

This well-spoken octogenarian belonged to a generation of activists who were baptised by fire in the Left ideals of the 1960s. Gopala Gowda Shantaveri was his political guru. Subbarao had spent a great deal of time with him, and was by his side when he was on his death-bed. As it turns out, U.R. Ananthamurthy was Subbarao's English teacher at his first-grade college in Hassan, close to Subbarao's hometown Arkalgud:

> Everyone used to lovingly call him URA. Some mischievous boys would write URAFOOL on the board. He would smoke the very last puff of his cigarette and enter the classroom. Immediately, as the bell rang, he would go out and light up another. Such a chain-smoker he was. I once asked him why he smoked so much, since it seemed so expensive a habit and I was curious what he got out of it. He asked me to try one and find out for myself. I did. It became a habit, and I didn't quit until 1985. So, Ananthamurthy taught me both English as well as smoking! All these Lohiaite socialists, especially Lankesh, were extremists when it came to drinking and smoking. Us communists cannot drink so much. We have to be out on the streets with the chaluvali, you see? No time for drinking and all, hahaha.

I had never realised that degrees of vice could spell out the difference between a socialist and a communist. The communists thought that socialists like Ananthamurthy were fashionable men with expensive tastes. A true communist would eschew material comforts and live austerely. He would not believe in individualism, whereas Anathamurthy once said that he could have never been a writer had he not believed in the power of the individual. Communism, like religion, is a phenomenon of the masses, of class struggle conducted with belief and conviction. One's personal relations with the world had to be sacrificed for a larger puritanical ideal.

Ananth Subbarao had spent his youth out on the streets with the workers, in mind, body and spirit. He reminisces, with palpable nostalgia, about the militant energy of trade unionism in those decades. This was true of the movement across the country. George Fernandes, perhaps the most famous trade unionist in popular imagination, faced numerous jail sentences and police beatings. In 1970, Fernandes was beaten up so badly by the Delhi police while leading a demonstration of adivasis, that the injuries he sustained contributed to his Alzheimer's disease many years later.[3] Subbarao remembers an instance in the late sixties when he was lying supine on the ground in a protest in favour of bank nationalisation (Indira Gandhi soon implemented this), and two policemen just lifted him from two ends and threw him aside. In another protest in 1967, when there was a strike by employees of Kirloskar in Bangalore, the workers fell upon the police with a ferocity he had never seen. *The workers enjoyed it*, he says, his eyes sparkling with delight.

Subbarao belongs to the second generation of trade union leaders in Karnataka. The first grew out of the freedom movement itself, since organising the labour force was an integral part of the movement during the forties. From Subbarao's own town of Arkalgud, near Hassan, there had emerged at least two tall leaders of an earlier generation who would have inspired him—M.S. Krishnan and S. Suryanarayana Rao. Tiger Suri was the latter's sobriquet.

Bangalore seems to have been home to numerous Tigers back in the day, when its dark underbelly housed the dens of dons and pehelwans. The policeman Ashok Kumar had also acquired the nom de guerre Tiger, thanks to his daredevil acts of nabbing chain snatchers in exciting, perilous bike chases.[4] Once, Ashok Kumar fought on the streets with a chain-snatcher who cut his hands up with a knife, even as a crowd stood watching. When asked why they hadn't helped the brave fellow, people replied, 'We thought it was a film shoot.' In 1989, underworld don Jayaraj decided to contest a by-election with a tiger as his symbol—he even procured a live tiger from a circus to tour the streets with him as part of his election campaign. Cinematic times all around.

Tiger Suri was decidedly on the other side of the police–underworld nexus. He was instrumental in organising workers from various milieus in Bengaluru—MICO (now renamed Bosch), auto drivers, ITC—under the Centre of Indian Trade Unions (CITU) banner, which is affiliated to the CPI(M). In the nineties, just a few years before his death in 2002, he was rallying the employees of Vikrant Tyres in Mysore. Like numerous industries post globalisation, Vikrant Tyres was facing a financial and existential crisis. Privatisation of the company seemed inevitable, and Comrade Suri tried to ensure that certain labour standards—wages and overtime pay, for instance—were set in place as JK Tyres came to acquire a major stake in the factory.

In October 2022, I happened to meet a retired Vikrant Tyres employee named Srinivas, who originally hailed from Shimoga. He was admitted to Kasturba Medical College in Manipal, where a friend had summoned me to help translate his troubles into English. His left foot was in a cast, and I learnt that it was a case of cellulitis. I was immediately reminded of the gangrenous foot I had seen at Ananth Subbarao's office. Years of daily drinking had rendered Srinivas's immunity weak, although he had patronised a superior brand throughout his life—Black Dog whisky. I wondered if this might owe some thanks to Comrade Suri's efforts to secure increased wages.

My task was to get him to talk about his alcoholism, though the first thing he said was that it was the last thing he wanted to talk about. After a few pleasantries, I gently pushed the envelope, and he opened up.

'I only drink as much as necessary. One quarter every day. Not more than that,' he declared.

There was a rather silly question on the form that I was obliged to ask: 'Do you think you started drinking out of peer pressure?'

To this, he replied with a grin: 'Every evening, it was me who set the party and called my friends over.'

Srinivas was proud of one more thing: he had never smoked in his life, and he flashed a set of crystal white teeth to prove his point. He later admitted that the drinking had become a problem, and that he wanted to quit now. Srinivas spoke of his habit casually—it was a normal thing to partake of drinks after a long, hard day of work. What else was there to do?

He had been accompanied to the hospital by a young man. When I asked him how he was related to Srinivas, the fellow flashed a charming smile and said, kulabandhavaru, *clan brother*. He knew the older man by dint of their caste. He nodded a couple of times, as if to confirm that no other explanation was forthcoming. When push comes to shove, caste networks are the loyal support systems that ensure that you are taken care of in a distant city.

The mushrooming of Mandal politics and the sharpening of caste identities in the nineties also had a major effect on how trade unionism was organised. Caste unions came into existence, gaining precedence over the 'working class' identity that the labour movements had worked for decades to establish. Today, there are 'caste corporations' created by the Karnataka government, which receive State funds in the name of specific castes, and which they may use for facilitating credit and other developmental activities. These corporations are, in essence, middlemen who monitor the final link between the people and a corrupt state, therefore always prone to the whims of the ruling regime and its ongoing caste games. Ananth Subbarao drove at something similar too:

> The Lokayuta [Ombudsman] is like a rubber snake. It has no teeth to bite. The government is being increasingly dictated by caste equations, and there are too many unions in the mix. There is a gowda union, a lingayat union, a Muslim union—people are dividing, and dividing, and subdividing. It wasn't so bad in the seventies, at least we didn't have caste unions.

After my encounter with Srinivas, I also remembered Ananth Subbarao's comments on the workers' drinking proclivities. He had said that they had tried to combat alcoholism in KSRTC by conducting awareness campaigns and de-addiction programmes. 'The social and cultural life of the workers is also important. I know they think alcohol is like god, but imagine the plight of their households if they arrive drunk every night. Also, who will travel in these buses if they know the drivers are drinking? To a certain extent, our efforts were successful,' he shrugged.

On the economic front, AITUC managed to make several good settlements in the early nineties, but things then took a turn for the worse. The State stopped talking to them in good faith, and rendered them practically insignificant. AITUC's motto has always been to 'defend and expand'—to defend workers' rights and to expand the union's base. In this, it has been successful, Subbarao submits. Even if the union's strength has been curtailed in terms of actual influence on government policy, wage strikes in 2012 and 2016 did manage to secure better salaries. The base of the transport sector has also expanded significantly; there are now 24,000 buses across the state, and close to 1.15 lakh workers are employed in the sector.

Just a few weeks before I met Subbarao, LIC workers had called for a national bandh, and lakhs of employees had joined the protest. It was barely covered by the media, and the government had taken little to no interest in it.

> Me (somewhat bluntly): What are the present challenges of the labour movement? What does it seek to achieve?
>
> AS: Now, the task of the trade unions has shifted. It is not a fight between the unions and the managements any more. It is a fight between the working class and the government. Everything needs a policy change. Our demands are clear. We want a uniform wage structure across the country. Pension is at the mercy of the share markets. We want pension to be paid from a consolidated fund of India, as it was earlier. Most importantly, contract labour must be abolished. Until then, all contract labourers must be paid regular wages.

The shift in dynamics began many decades ago. By the eighties, trade unionism in India had moved away from its militant past. Careerist attitudes and corruption crept in, and leaders were increasingly less idealistic than they used to be. The protagonist of Vyasaraya Ballal's 1985 novel *Bandaya* is a charismatic union leader with seemingly boundless resolve and energy. The novel investigates the effect of politics *within* the trade union networks in Mumbai. Within the multiple unions jostling for supremacy, there are murders, shady deals and tenuous negotiations that rendered Indian trade unionism unproductive.

I first encountered these observations regarding trade union culture from an unlikely source—a photographer and artist in Mysore named Raja, whose father had been a labour leader at Kolar Gold Fields, back in the seventies.

II

I meet Raja Uncle at his photo studio in Mysore—a small, no-fuss establishment, where most of the space is occupied not by technical photography equipment, but by Raja's handcrafted cement sculptures. This includes a decorated water fountain and a pair of birds. 'Just one stork wouldn't be effective at all, you need two storks being together to evoke empathy and feeling,' he says, pointing towards a wonderfully sculpted artefact of a mother stork feeding a fish to its young one. Raja sits cross-legged behind his work desk, king of his small territory, master of his domain, a half-smile permanently set upon his lips. His face is weather-beaten and his eyes see deep, signs of a man who has lived a long, exhausting life.

Rajendra 'Raja' Kumar was born in KGF, and grew up there. His father, Maruthavanan, orphaned early in life, was adopted by a worker who migrated to KGF from near Thanjavur sometime in the 1930s. The KGF community was immense, housing well over 30,000 workers, and Raja gestures to me vigorously to note down the large list of facilities within the self-sufficient KGF precincts: a dairy, an electric plant, a fire brigade, a rescue team, multiple schools, hospitals, a tram and a ration office. Much like the character Tabara in Poornachandra Tejaswi's story *Tabarana Kathe*, who looks back upon colonial rule with fond nostalgia for its efficiency, Raja looks upon the British as magnanimous overlords who provided everything for the workers they were employing. To this day, he only watches BBC for news, quips Raja, who also loves The Beatles as well as Pink Floyd, and speaks excellent English inflected with local colloquialisms. Indeed, his father Maruthavanan also gained from the British schooling system, studying until the tenth grade, at which point his foster-father promptly got him married, and told him that he had done all that could be reasonably expected of a man. 'Fair enough, no,' Raja guffaws.

Maruthavanan studied further, accumulating degrees in sociology and law, and eventually became a labour leader at KGF during the seventies. Raja remembers that there were three main unions during those times—affiliated to the DMK, the Congress and the CPI—as well as other smaller ones. Maruthavanan was a member of the DMK union, Raja remembers vaguely, because Tamil affiliations still ran fairly strongly in his blood back then. I ask him about the unions, what they were fighting for and in what ways they helped the workers. He laughs, and says, 'If there was only one union, it might have been helpful in some way. But three unions? They just fought amongst themselves!'[5]

Raja inherited his father's street-smartness and resourcefulness. Arriving in Mysore from KGF during the nineties, he cut his teeth in the burgeoning field of advertising, mastered the technicalities of print publishing, and became one of the first web designers in town. Now, the industry has little need for creativity, especially in a city of small businesses like Mysore, and Raja states that he would prefer a humble photo shop making simple money rather than endure indignity in a market of white-collar pretentiousness. The pandemic was disastrous, and healthcare expenses within Raja's family have exacted a heavy toll. Yet, he owns his own time now. Raja has always been artistically oriented, and the two birds outside his studio are just the culmination of a vibrant creative journey. Perhaps it is this aesthetic sensibility that makes Raja look at KGF through a sympathetic, almost romantic lens. While other accounts of life in KGF highlight the squalor and misery of the workers (especially dalits), or the anxious families waiting outside the mines not knowing if their husband/father/son would make it back alive, Raja's anecdotes are more nostalgic. He tries to remember and sing an old Tamil song that captures the historical trajectory of the miners through the evolution of the lights they held as they went down the dreary tunnels—the carbide lamps of the early twentieth century, followed by Petromax lamps, finally to be replaced by the compact headlamp.[6]

To be sure, KGF was controlled through draconian colonial laws aimed at whipping up a docile workforce, and Janaki Nair reminds us that the Mysore Mining Rules of 1897, for instance, 'were not tinged by even the dimmest promise of protecting the rights of free-born citizens'.[7] From 1891 to 1940, an average of sixty men lost their lives annually, with hundreds of others permanently maimed. After the mines were nationalised in 1956, Indian elites took over the establishment and perpetuated the hierarchy of officers and workers which the British had so firmly instituted. Of course, Raja (or his father) had never gone down the mines and romance is easy to summon, but it did make me wonder about the value of distant opinions, which is what most of us can boast of. If nobody commemorates the risky life of the miners, would that amount to neglecting an important part of their culture and legacy? How is it that soldiers who perish at the border are celebrated as martyrs, but miners, construction workers, frontline healthcare staff or truck drivers, who routinely court mortal peril, are never remembered for their heroism? Is there a preordained hierarchy of causes worth dying for? When the civil servant M.A. Sreenivasan, who served in Karnataka before 1947, described the mines as an 'incredible, labyrinthine wonderland' where tragic casualties give a grim hint of the 'eerie, ceaseless adventure' going on underneath, was it a statement of casual ignorance or of well-deserved awe? There are no easy responses, and we must all persist in our own moral inquiries.

We arrive at the apotheosis of this mode of questioning when it comes to the most unglamorous work of society—sanitation. I'd heard a heartbreaking anecdote about sanitation workers in KGF from the columnist Diwakar Narayan Rao. He had once accompanied some leftist activists attempting to put an end to the practice of night-soil carrying a few years before the mines were shuttered in 2001. The aggrieved dalits tearily resisted them, simply because that would leave them with no job (and no identity) to lay claim to—neither the British nor the Indian State had bothered about their education and upliftment. It bears mention that the noted activist and Ramon Magsaysay awardee Bezwada Wilson—who is one of the biggest voices for the abolition of manual scavenging in India—was born in KGF in a cleaner's family in 1966.

Gandhi had tried to tackle the issue by completely upending the hierarchy. In an infamous 1936 essay, he wrote:

> The ideal Bhangi of my conception would be a Brahmin par-excellence, possibly even excel him. It is possible to envisage the existence of a Bhangi without a Brahmin. But without the former, the latter could not be. It is the Bhangi who enables society to live. A Bhangi does for her society what a mother does for her baby. A mother washes her baby of dirt and insures its health. Even so the Bhangi protects and safeguards the health of the entire community by maintaining sanitation for it. The Brahmin's duty is to look after the sanitation of the soul, the Bhangi's that of the body of society. But there is a difference in practice; the Brahmin generally does not live up to his duty, the Bhangi does willy-nilly no doubt. Society is sustained by several services. The Bhangi constitutes the foundation of all services.

It is a feat of extreme idealism, and his idea of the 'dutiful' work of the bhangis can invite only the strongest refutation. Like most things in our country, questions of value and morality are inextricably tied to caste. And the predicament of caste, of the politics of impurity, becomes the gravest when it comes to the question of who takes care of our waste. I wanted to find out how the sanitation workers of Karnataka have fared over the last few decades, and whether Gandhi's ideals were still in circulation.

III

> The night before the murder,
> they hid the sun and the moon,
> dug up the treasure-chest,
> stuffed the tricolour in her mouth,
> snatched her voice away.
>
> —Du Saraswati

A women's rights activist and storyteller, Du Saraswati is a distinct voice within the artist–activist milieu in Karnataka. She has lived most of her life in Bangalore, and continues to do so. Over the last couple of decades, she has become a well-recognised face in the city's theatre circles, not to mention the slowly mushrooming spaces of labour activism. In recent times, her identity has become fused with her alter ego, Santhimmi, a chatty grandmother character who speaks of all things under the sun in a humorous dialect of Kannada that is peculiar to the Tumkur region. Santhimmi is the dynamic, evolving persona that Du Saraswati assumes in her one-woman drama performances—a cumulative accumulation of several indomitable women Du Saraswati has met across her life. It originally started out as a two-character show, where another performer would throw all manner of questions at her, to which Santhimmi would improvise quirky and thought-provoking answers. Santhimmi soon came to represent Du Saraswati's inner conscience in a way that even she does not understand.

I first heard of Du Saraswati as I started delving into the history of sanitation workers' struggles in Karnataka. She has been working on behalf of the sanitation workers, known as pourakarmikas, since the turn of the millennium, and recently completed a PhD thesis on the subject. The word 'pourakarmika', literally 'civil worker' in Kannada, was coined in the 1970s by B. Basavalingappa as an alternative to the casteist slurs that were the only point of reference earlier. One of Basavalingappa's first achievements after being elected to the state assembly was to ban the pernicious practice of dalits made to carry shit. In 1976, a man named I.P.D. Salappa, a close associate of Basavalingappa, produced a pioneering report that laid down detailed recommendations to uplift the pourakarmikas. In a rare government document that critiqued the State itself, he advocated higher wages, promotion opportunities, provision of safety equipment as well as the construction of creches, nurseries and primary schools for the children of workers. The report also elaborated on measures that could relieve the stress and struggle of their labour. No government has heeded these recommendations yet.

When I asked Du Saraswati about her thoughts on Gandhi and his famous bhangi essay, she offered a nuanced, well-considered response:

> It is very tricky. I don't think Gandhi glorified the work, as much as approached it from a spiritual angle. He makes Jamnalal Bajaj

> clean the latrines at his ashram, and Kasturba too. That is a big deal. When Ramakrishna Paramhamsa was asked whether he would pick shit or gold if offered a choice, he opted for the former. Because from this shit something can grow. Nothing grows from gold. Now, I am being very careful here. I am not saying that this is great work, and they should continue doing it. What I am doing is deconstructing this idea of purity and impurity. Shit is just another form of food. It becomes great manure. I have friends who are using shit for organic farming. With the right treatment in open air, you can't even smell it, and it becomes fine enough for you to run your hands through it. Ultimately, everyone should learn to manage their own shit. In that process, to understand the thin line between purity and impurity, this angle becomes important, that's all. What Gandhi said is not meant for the pourakarmikas, but for everyone else. If one starts thinking of their shit as normal, they won't need someone else to manage it for them. Now, when do we normally do that? For children, or for the elderly. I have seen nuns taking care of terminally ill cancer patients. How much love they perform it with. There is not a single grimace on their face. I think that is the most extraordinary service one can provide someone. You have to see it from that angle.

Having said this, she immediately points out that the pourakarmikas have been pushed into this profession without any choice. They are a 'community under siege'. The onset of urbanisation foisted these jobs onto them, neglecting the various other talents that these oppressed castes possessed. Migrant madigas from Andhra Pradesh, who form the bulk of the sweepers in the state, used to be accomplished leather-workers. In the course of her research, she also found that amongst the pourakarmikas live exceptional dancers, body-builders and sportspersons. She submits that they have never been allowed to explore their cultural strengths, and have been condemned to work as cleaners, generation after generation.

Her words carry the imprint of years of travel across the state, speaking to workers and entering their lives with an urge to learn. I am curious to know how she forayed into activism, which has been part of her life from a young age.

> From the age of nineteen or twenty, I have been exposed to the women's movement. I joined the organisation Vimochana in 1982, and was with them till 1985. During this time, we were having an internal conversation about whether to accept funding for this work. Many of us, who wanted to keep this work self-funded, retreated from the space. It was purely voluntary work, you see. Songs, street plays, writing for periodicals—there were many volunteers for this, and this kept the fire going. Those of us who wanted to keep this purely democratic space alive decided to start a journal called *Manasa*. *Manasa* was active for almost twenty-five years, from 1985 to 2010. None of us had any professional training in journalism or communication. It was purely a labour of love, and we felt that there needed to be a forum where women's woes could be voiced. It was relentless activity—writing, awareness programmes, publishing pamphlets, conducting small discussions—and we did all this from our own pockets. We did not depend on this work for our livelihood.

Domestic violence against women was a criminally underreported phenomenon, in both domestic and media domains. In Bangalore, cases of suicide by women were rampant, a result of the combined oppression of patriarchy and illiteracy. In 1972, the custodial rape of a tribal girl named Mathura, in the Gadchiroli district of Maharashtra, led to the mobilisation of women's organisations. Throughout the next few decades, other such national rallying cries emerged, sewing together a patchwork of feminist organisations across the country. Until the end of the 1990s, Du Saraswati held down a day job for her livelihood. Activism was what she did in her spare time, contributing to the creation of a radically alert space that championed women's rights. She came to be involved with the pourakarmika struggle around the end of that chapter of her life, a turn she looks back at with candid self-reflection:

> It was in '99 that I was first introduced to the pourakarmikas. I left my bank job in 2000. We formed a group to represent them, and we got started on all the groundwork. Lobbying, publishing pamphlets, procuring the required documentation for them, forming a union (trade union leaders helped a lot)—that took nearly ten years. After

> all those years, a minimum wage for the pourakarmikas was finally declared. This was a big victory. Then, there was the big question of forming a leadership from their own ranks. That's when we understood our own limits. Until that point, the work we did was necessary. There needed to be a middle-class intervention in their lives. They wanted me to become general secretary, but I felt that the leadership should rest with them. At that point, I personally feel that we collectively failed to build another leadership. We failed because we were good at certain things only—writing, analysing, theorising, lobbying, and so on. We did that so quickly and efficiently. And this the pourkarmikas could never have done, because they are all mostly illiterate. We were running, and we made them run with us. They had to run behind us for lack of choice. They found it hard to carry on this work independently. And the union floundered for a bit.

It was also this realisation—the limitations of analysing and theorising—that led Du Saraswati to switch to cultural activism through theatre. *I am a storyteller*, she says proudly of her primary identity now. One of the major critiques of the Left-led union movements is that they focused purely on economic and material benefits, neglecting other spheres of emancipation. Yet, it is hard to imagine any intervention that would not have begun with those aims.

As we sit talking, Du Saraswati's helper and housekeeper brings us chai and snacks. I learn that she had worked for eight years in a garment factory before finally quitting it for good. A care job was immensely more satisfying and rewarding than labouring in a sweatshop that can just close shop overnight. The wages had been terrible, the working conditions oppressive. Most women only worked there for a few years, to save up money to marry off their daughters or other such things. Now, in many places across the state (and the country), like Bellary in North Karnataka, certain stages of production are outsourced from the factory into the homes of the poor. The eight-hour work week no longer exists.

> If you are working at a factory at a certain time, there is an identity as a worker, with some allegiance to the institution. But if you are

> working at home, then the identity becomes blurred. What these women go on to think is that there is some male member who is working full-time, and that her work is merely supplementary, even when she is working perhaps three jobs at once. The most monotonous and boring work is thrown at these women. If you go to a garment factory, you will see them hunched over a cloth, doing the same repetitive work. Only if you drone away like that will you reach the desired output by evening.

She has been working with the garment workers in Bengaluru for many years now, and her recent interventions have been largely in the cultural sphere. She conducts theatre sessions for them, and engages with them in Santhimmi's vocabulary, and not the academic feminist voice that makes up the left side of her brain:

> The activist language is sometimes so twisted that it goes over their heads. I have also undergone this—I've come back home to refer to the dictionary. One thing I realised is that if we want to work with the workers, we need to speak their tongue. Whether it is Marx, Engels or Babasaheb that you want to expound, it is important that you break it down and explain it to them in their own language. I changed my language for that. Santhimmi came from there. I have gone around to many movements, and I have been trying to connect this academic understanding of politics and power to the lives of the workers. It is an important task. Santhimmi can talk about anything. She talks about the Buddha, about love, she narrates stories from the Ramayana, about patriarchy and violence.

Through Santhimmi, she has essentially been creating a brand-new mythology. In one of her acts, called *Pakshi Purana*, Santhimmi imagines an alternative universe where men might search for the caged birds within themselves, birds that may preen and cavort and beautify themselves like a male peafowl or cuckoo, moving away from unnecessary displays of machismo. When the transgender community asked Du Saraswati to write about love, she retreated for inspiration into the Santhimmi zone, where her alter ego–conscience did not disappoint. Her act, *Love Purana*, came out of these reflections.

In general, queer and transgender voices have been sprouting strongly in Bangalore theatre, slowly making way for a broader empathy. Trans-rights activist Akkai Padmashali writes in her moving autobiography[8] of the patriarchy that used to dictate hijra culture in Bangalore, accompanied by the firm hand of the local jamaats. She writes of how she challenges this culture from *within*, because these milieus are also vital safe spaces in their own right and cannot be rejected outright, especially in a society that is defined by its scorn for whomever it considers outsiders. She affirms how much change *has* taken place over the last couple of decades—transpeople can now enter restrooms, malls, cinema halls and other public spaces more freely than earlier. When I was studying in Manipal, I met Trinetra Haldar Gummaraju, Karnataka's first transgender doctor, who was also a student there. The tales I heard were harrowing. In the medical community, transphobia runs high, and a lack of humanities education within the sciences exacerbates these prejudices. Trinetra has now jumped into acting full-time and she even made her OTT debut recently—the performing arts seem to be welcoming of progressive ideas, and might well be the most important way of engendering newer paradigms.

Apart from her work in theatre, Du Saraswati has written short stories and poems, and edited and curated anthologies of essays. Writing came to her as a necessity more than anything, and she sees it as an act of inducing empathy within herself. Buddhism has also intimately impacted her writing, and her activism:

> Thich Nhat Hanh is very dear to me. Discovering him felt like meeting my mother again. I lost my mother at a very young age. Buddhism is what made me reflect on my role as an activist with a critical eye. Otherwise, it is very easy to take power, become a leader. I think Buddhism helped me stay away from all that. I should not become a general secretary—this was a strong feeling I had—and I was adamant that I should resist. I share a very organic relationship with the pourakarmikas. There is very deep trust. I don't have any words for it. The deep trust they have in me is my reward.

I am struck by her active refusal of power. There is a Gandhian ring to it. She told me that the Buddha and Gandhi were important figures in her childhood: 'I always had bhakti in my heart, and I enjoyed doing pujas when I was young—lighting lamps, ornamentation. My mother used to love it too. I had a smooth and peaceful journey with god, he never troubled me, never held me in fear. When I came to these radical Left spaces, there was a 360-degree turn. I agreed with the urge to fight against oppression, but I felt something was missing here, you know? My spiritual, devotional side was left aside.'

She has since rediscovered that side. Vipassana has proven to be a blessing in recent years, and she also meditates regularly. She channels her empathy towards imagining a more humane justice system, towards restoration of the conscience, rather than incarceration. Speaking of the punishment due to the men accused of raping Bilkis Bano in Godhra, she says they must be dispatched to a maternity ward and made to wash the bloodied cloths of women in labour, day after day.

From there, our conversation turns towards more existential questions. We skirt the issues of climate change, the global pollution crisis, and she makes a lovely closing remark: *I think we should call the pourakarmikas Earth Workers. It is an environmentalist position. They are the real environmentalists, keeping the planet clean. Their worldview is cyclical.*

As I would soon learn, the divisions of caste and gender are not the only axes along which the working class is being challenged. There are equally grave predicaments, effected by religion and language, that labour activism is only beginning to grapple with.

IV

> Astonishingly, we are saved not by a special apparatus known as religion, but by the quality of our everyday relations with one another.
>
> —Terry Eagleton

As of January 2023, Akbar Ali has been living on the outskirts of Bangalore for over four years. He speaks a Hindi that is heavily touched by a lilting Bengali accent in a hushed tone of resignation. He has been unable to secure gainful employment, and has a severely disabled brother to take care of along with his family—his savings are fast depleting. The brother sits on a chair outside their shanty, half-muttering something, completely immobile. Ali's wife and mother stay with him, and they politely offer me a glass of sweet lassi and a bottle of Sprite. As I tackle this strangely appealing offering, struck by the hospitality, they narrate their woes, as though I am in some position to actually help them. The thought is immensely humbling and dispiriting.

When it rains heavily, the waters of the neighbouring sewer overflow right into their homes. Bangalore recorded its highest annual rainfall ever in 2022. Akbar Ali and his family live in a sea of shanties that spreads out across waves of undeveloped tracts on the north-eastern fringes of the city, where only a few apartment buildings and schools exist. It is predominantly occupied by a very specific group of people—Bengali-speaking Muslims who work as waste-pickers. A few miles south of the upmarket enclaves of Whitefield, much of the locality's garbage comes here to be aggregated and segregated in these shacks occupied by migrant labourers. They are mostly Muslims from the state of West Bengal, as well as a few who have crossed over from Bangladesh.

Whitefield, a locality named after an Englishman called White who envisioned an exclusive community for Eurasians and Anglo-Indians in the nineteenth century, is better known for what Bangalore has now become synonymous with: an IT hub. Offices of Dell, IBM and Cisco operate from here, as do those of local consulting giants like Infosys and Wipro. It is also a plush residential area, where fine wining, dining and shopping opportunities are aplenty. Much of Whitefield's garbage is packed off to this settlement of sheds, shanties and half-houses I have arrived at, where close to 40,000 Bengali Muslims are reported to live and work. Most of the area is owned by well-heeled, politically influential landlords, who rent out shacks to the workers for a few thousand rupees a month. One of the landlords, as one of the workers recounted, has a tendency to arrive drunk and spout abuses at them all, just to reinforce power over his dominion.

These migrant workers eke out an existence by bringing the garbage of the city into their very homes, to be cleaned and segregated by hand. The refuse of the metropolis travels to many of these settlements across the city's outskirts, on agonisingly pedalled cycle rickshaws, or in a fury of autos, vans, trucks and other assorted modes of transportation. This entire enterprise—a million-dollar industry involving corporations, politicians, NGOs, environmentalists, landlords—hinges on this lowermost yet absolutely vital workforce of manual waste-pickers for whom life is immeasurably tough. They are paid no fixed salary, and must subsist only on the money they make from turning over the junk, which is abysmally low: anywhere between Rs 3 and 10 per kilo of segregated waste.

Being strangers in a strange land, Ali and his neighbours are exploited by the ruling establishment and face social isolation too. Immigrants constitute half of the city's population, but some are treated more derisively than others. Only recently, a young Bengali man with a body-builder's physique was thrown out of a city bus, even while he was ready to purchase a ticket, because he was unable to speak in Kannada with the conductor. The locals who encountered the fallen man on the street advised him to take the matter no further, fearing that 'they' might just bulldoze all the shanties in the settlement, purely out of spite, to show these migrants their place.

All this I have come to learn from R. Kaleemullah, an activist working with the Swaraj India political party. He is the one who introduced me to Akbar Ali. He opens a rickety shack, right in the middle of the shanties, and ushers me into his makeshift office. A couple of small 7-Up bottles quickly find their way into our hands, courtesy of Kaleem's hospitality.

Kaleem has been working for the welfare of the Bengali Muslims for many years now, and his face bristles with weary concern. 'What kind of stories do you want,' he begins. 'You want stories of ragpickers? Bangladesh stories? Murder? Rape? Gang stories? Police?'—trying to impress upon me the enormity of the trauma that these shanties experience. He speaks of a divide even within these shanties, between the Bengali-speaking Indians and the immigrant Bangladeshis. Though their collective fate is largely similar, the latter are loosely linked to a powerful mafia, with connections to high political positions and the local police, Kaleem claims. He says he is 'on the side of the Bengalis'. Further, he alleges that the thugs belonging to this mafia are perpetrators of heinous crimes on Rohingya refugees from Myanmar (yet another 'other' in this subcontinental stew of Muslim refugees), and possess a fearful reputation. A more arresting allegation he makes is that: 'The Bangladeshi immigrants here have impeccable credentials—they have Aadhaar cards and Voter IDs. They form a significant vote bank, and have been surreptitiously sought out by the establishment. On the other hand, the Bengali

Indian migrants are largely devoid of any identity cards. They struggle against their anonymity …'

While Kaleem's rhetoric might imply an easy binary of internal opposition, the bigger truth remains that most of the immigrant labourers are brought here by exploitative traffickers, and are equal victims of dire circumstances. In late 2019, the BJP-led government in Karnataka announced that it would introduce the National Register of Citizens in the state, which was followed by the inevitable displays of local vigilantism and fear-mongering. Demolitions of shanties occupied by alleged Bangladeshi immigrants followed, and hundreds of workers fled the city in terror, fearing torture and imprisonment. The intrepid journalist Sudipto Mondal, who travelled with many of these immigrants on a train back to Bengal documenting the whole event, writes that 'the nexus between human traffickers, the Border Security Force (BSF) and the police is an open secret'.[9] The border-crossing is dangerous nonetheless, and there have been instances where guards on both sides have targeted migrants with equal impunity. Bangalore, for many, is a no-man's land where the smallest homes and hopes can go up in smoke at a moment's notice.

Kaleem takes me around the Whitefield-adjacent hovels on his motorbike, weaving through mud paths surrounded by mounds of assorted junk. I see flashes of local enterprise—tea shops, provision stores, eateries, hawkers selling vegetables at modest prices. Children play about in the muck, and men bathe by the roadside, where lines of large, blue water cans have been arranged specifically for this purpose.

Kaleem's presence has a noticeably reassuring effect on the shanty-dwellers. He is the man on whose shoulders all their worries fall. The workers pour out their grievances. Living quarters are ramshackle, every family has someone suffering from serious health conditions, and there is never any money to address anything beyond their immediate survival. They have no safety equipment, and must forage through dangerously unclean waste with naked hands. On top of it, their domestic lives are tumultuous. There is no security, of any sort. Kaleem offers consolation where he can, promises what he can afford to, and is constantly receiving calls seeking counsel on some or the other contingency.

'They were all peasants and farmers, basically,' Kaleem says, 'who had to leave because the profession is completely untenable there [in the Bengal/Bangladesh region]. What I have heard is that if the Bangladeshis pay Rs 10,000 at the border, they are allowed to cross over. Then they find work as wage labourers.' The rise of a new waste-picking class across India, from Delhi to Hyderabad to Lucknow, populated largely by Bengali-speaking Muslims has been well documented.[10] An intricate network of handlers enables this mass diffusion of itinerant labourers. All manner of extrajudicial atrocities transpire within these shanties, especially by the police. Kaleem flips out his phone and shows me a picture of a young boy, stark naked, hanging from a ceiling fan. 'Does anyone hang themselves without clothes? Can't we see the bruise marks on his body? Who do these people think they are kidding,' he cries, and I see his point. 'The police is bahut ganda [really bad] in Bengaluru, really corrupt.'

Someone calls him on the phone for help, and Kaleem asks me to come along. We ride to the shed of a family in panic. The son of a migrant Bangladeshi man has eloped to Goa with a Bengali woman, leaving his own wife and child in the lurch. The woman's family is threatening to call the police. Kaleem consoles the sobbing wife, and urges her to speak truthfully to the police—'you have not committed any mistake'. 'You speak to this young man here, he's a journalist. He will do stories on both Bangladeshi and Bengali people,' he tells them, pointing to me as though I am the universal conscience present there.

The man introduces himself as Shakir Ali, and when I offer a handshake, he gestures to the black grime on his hands and retracts them behind his back sheepishly. When I ask if he works for the BBMP, he shakes his head and says, 'No. Commercial. Commercial.' He is employed by multinational companies who need his efforts in recycling their plastic waste. Only, in their eyes, he is as disposable as the waste he is recycling for them. Wages are bleak, and no safety equipment has been provided for him—housing, education and healthcare are still light years away.

These migrant waste-pickers form the very last rung of the sanitation workers' hierarchy in Bangalore. Like Indian society in general, the sanitation workers of Bangalore are also further stratified into varying degrees of vulnerability. First come the sweepers, who scour the streets and collect garbage into large piles. Then there are the drivers, helpers and loaders, who move this to landfills and dumping spots. At the bottom of the pyramid are the invisible masses of waste-pickers who manually sort through this putrefying mass of unsegregated garbage, and perform the tasks that nobody else is willing to do.

The Bengali Muslims who seek refuge as waste-pickers in Bengaluru today are recent entrants. They started arriving in large numbers less than two decades ago. Prior to the 1990s, the BBMP employed local permanent workers for solid waste management. On grounds that 'operations were becoming prohibitively expensive (consuming 40-50% of the municipal budget), the BBMP decided to privatise the work of garbage clearance in 1995, and started outsourcing the task to private contractors, many of whom were from the Reddy community who hired their own contract labour in a majority of Health Wards in the city. 80% of these contract labourers were dalit women working under extremely exploitative conditions. They were paid a sum of Rs 500–600 per month from 1992 till 2000, and Rs 900–1000 till 2003.'[11] From the 2000s onwards, there emerged long-fought union struggles that bequeathed to the dalit women slight material benefits, and they now constitute most of the sweepers' positions. The proliferation of the contract system (and the sheer amount of waste generated by the city), created a new vacuum of cheap labour, though, which could now be filled by trafficked immigrants from across the country.

Of course, the insecurity is not just limited to Bangalore. In 2014, nearly five hundred pourakarmikas in Kalaburagi staged a protest against abrupt termination of their contracts, rallying under the leadership of S.K. Kantha, a trade unionist and former minister for labour. They knew no other profession, and were left out in the streets to fend for themselves. Even after a token reinstatement, they worked for almost a year without pay, whereupon they approached the labour court, which ruled in their favour. The State then attempted to sabotage their protests by burning their tents, lathicharging them, and some miscreants 'threw photos of Ambedkar and Gandhi into the gutter'. Over the next four years, many protestors were jailed for months on end, a few even died in the protest tents, and the workers were finally reinstated in 2017.[12]

One of IPD Salappa's main recommendations was to increase the pourakarmika/population ratio—this would decrease work burden and improve the quality of waste management dramatically. But even today, there are officially only around 40,000 pourakarmikas working across the state, not counting the tens of thousands of migrant labourers who work outside this formalised system. Of course, calling the system 'formalised' doesn't imply justice and fair pay. Many pourakarmikas are still subject to the whims of their contractors, who hire and fire them on a temporary basis, treat them with derision, and often extract cash from their already inadequate salaries. Sometimes, no salary is forthcoming for months on end, and there have been many reports of suicides.[13]

In July 2022, a historic four-day strike was organised in Karnataka, when pourakarmikas across the state stopped collecting garbage, demanding permanent jobs and regularisation of pay. It was a strike that had taken years to coordinate. This was the first time that sanitation workers across the state had simultaneously stopped work, and the government was forced to take note. After many months of backtracking and negotiations, the government finally agreed to make most of the jobs permanent. When the Congress came into power in 2023, it initiated a measure to secure free education for the children of pourakarmikas. It is not clear what has become of this initiative, and as of now, the transition to permanency has still not been completed, though the union considers the movement successful.

This victory owes credit to the All India Central Council of Trade Unions (AICCTU), which is affiliated to the CPI(M-L). Maitreyi, one of the lawyers working with the AICCTU, who prefers to discard her surname, spelt out the legalities to me. She surmised that, under the present ideological dispensation, the 'worker' has become a dispensable entity, and that courts have also begun to interpret workers' rights apathetically:

> The nature of the working class itself has really changed over the decades. There was a time when you had a thousand [workers'] cases in court. Today, you have maybe fifty. So, it is not the case that things are fine, or that managements have become more benevolent or something. Back in the seventies and eighties, the courts were more worker-friendly, and there was a socialist understanding of things. Since the nineties, there has been a dramatic shift in the way the courts have understood the position of the worker. There is this all-pervading neoliberal belief that everything must come with a temporary contract.

'Thekedaar', contractor, is a word you'll hear often in these workers' shanties. Local contractors hire and fire them with casual ease. Grotesque amounts of money have been siphoned off in the process over the last two decades. At the fag end of this system, the waste-pickers receive none of the huge sums of money exchanged between the corporate companies and NGOs and politicians and other satellites which govern this whole business of waste recycling.

Kaleemullah spoke of the AICCTU and its legal victories with fond admiration. He described them as the real heroes who were slowly transforming the lives of the pourakarmikas through democratic activism. 'The real change can come only from the courts,' he averred. However, even the AICCTU cannot hope to unionise the enormous numbers of waste-pickers who operate on the fringes of the system. The workers who fall under the ambit of the legal victories are highly mobilised, thanks to dalit politics. They are locals and live in designated slums, unlike the migrant populations. Kaleem claims that 1,50,000 Bengali migrants (of just one constituency, where this settlement is located) do not possess Voter ID cards, and he is out to ensure that this is addressed soon. If this happens, he is confident that an honest, educated, well-spoken MLA can be groomed from amongst them who would be capable of taking their case to the political arena. Maitreyi did tell me that some Bengali-speaking workers have been joining their union of late too.

For all this, progress is slow and the situation is dire. Despite the fact that the tech hub of the country is situated in their very backyard, Bangalore's waste-pickers do not even have access to such basic equipment as gloves, let alone machines to completely eradicate manual scavenging. The only technology to have arrived has to do with surveillance—biometric scanners that often malfunction—ending up in loss of a day's wages, which has also reduced the ambit of the payments to an arbitrary circle of pourakarmikas. What seemed like a progressive turn in political willpower during the 1970s has since faded into an apathetic and corrupt system that only feigns dreams of social change. The technocratic class has done little to influence the political (re)imagination of the city, and has only cosied up to the establishment. It is civil society that has been bringing concerns of waste management into the public sphere, what with organisations like Daily Dump pioneering zero-waste and composting solutions, and artists like Vasu Dixit writing songs about the pourakarmikas' daily challenges.

As we were saying our goodbyes, Kaleem requested me to definitely include one particular nugget. During the pandemic, when Bangalore was battling wave after wave of deaths, there was a serious lack of blood in hospitals. Kaleem himself organised blood donation camps to make up for this deficit, and it was the Bengali migrants who had gathered in the largest numbers to donate blood for the city's benefit. *Their blood courses through you too*, he wants to convey to the citizens of Bangalore.

Blood was always meant to be circulated.

V

> We are in great haste to construct* a magnetic telegraph from Maine to Texas; but Maine and Texas, it may be, have nothing important to communicate … We are eager to tunnel under the Atlantic and bring the old world some weeks nearer to the new; but perchance the first news that will leak through into the broad flapping American ear will be that Princess Adelaide has the whooping cough.
>
> —Henry David Thoreau, *Walden*

In December 2023, Union Minister Nitin Gadkari (who has made a name for himself as a veritable Construction Man) released a biography of the industrialist and institution-builder M.S. Ramaiah, best remembered for the technical colleges and hospitals he built in Bangalore over the last quarter of the twentieth century. In fact, one prevalent rumour on the grapevine is that Ramaiah fervently believed that his family would be visited by death if he stopped building even for a day. Therefore, he kept felling walls and reconstructing them just for the sake of building something all the time, the tale goes. Of course, what this probably reflects is financial expedience, whereby continuous reinvestment in infrastructure building might have helped reduce Ramaiah's tax burden.

Construction magnates like M.S. Ramaiah became increasingly prominent from the 1970s onwards, when they began purchasing agricultural lands and converting them into Revenue Layouts, as they were called, meant for housing the working classes of Bangalore, who mostly worked for public sector institutions then. 'If the public sector trade union leaders combined wage and housing struggles, what we see in the 1971–1991 period is a severing of these struggles, with informal developers (many of them with trade union origins) stepping in to respond to the housing needs of the flexible labour force.'[14] These decades were also slightly paradoxical in the sense that workers might have voted for trade unionists like M.S. Krishnan,

---

* *construct. noun.* From Latin con- 'together' + struere- 'build'.

but would have had to rely on land brokers like M.S. Ramaiah for pro-poor housing, a phenomenon which eventually helped the latter species consolidate large vote banks of their own. After Devaraj Urs established the Bangalore Development Authority in 1976, the city witnessed the emergence of a new land regime that worked in cahoots with the informal real estate sector. The BDA did not respond well to the housing needs of the working class, and by the eighties, trade unionists themselves became constructors of unauthorised Revenue Layouts. Many trade union leaders, like S.R. Viswanath, S. Muniraju and V. Somanna, emerged as wealthy land brokers with substantial political clout that carries over to this day. Because these Revenue Layouts were essentially converting agricultural land into 'illegal' residential areas without the official sanction of city planners, they were often built without following basic standards regarding road access and proper sewer lines—issues that compound Bengaluru's multi-pronged water crisis today.

After the reforms of 1991, the mushrooming of dedicated real estate politicians became widespread, reflecting a nationwide trend, and even a global one, exemplified by the rise of Donald Trump. Presently, having legalised and legitimised corruption, the land mafia is virtually indistinguishable from the political establishment, exerting powerful influence on the lives of immigrant workers like Akbar Ali. With skyrocketing costs of living, affordable and comfortable housing still remains a dream for all those whom Bangalore cannot digest.

Organising workers and challenging government policies in courts can become just as frustrating, and it is easy to devolve into merely reactionary posturing or even become a part of the establishment. Trade unionism in Karnataka has seen trenchant critiques too, and the present movements (which includes other milieus such as healthcare workers) are self-aware phoenixes rising from the ashes of triumphalism. In a piece titled 'Socialism's Final Fall', published in 1991, Poornachandra Tejaswi wrote a passionate epitaph, tying the demise of socialist ideals to political corruption and myopic labour activism:

> It is laughable to see labour leaders expecting social responsibility and patriotism that has been lacking in themselves for so long. Even a few years ago, on the outskirts of Mysore, it was a common sight in front of factories to see labour leaders raising red flags and fomenting hurrahs inside tents. Now, these factories have closed for good, and are rusting in peace. The vulgar cries against the management, graffitied on the walls, tell us the story of why this came to be. Java, Mahindra, Krishnarajendra—there are tens of them. Each of them was offering livelihood to thousands of people. Even now, if you ask them, these union leaders will maintain that they taught the industrialists a good lesson, and twirl their moustaches. When they say this, only the owners are on their minds, and not the labourer who has lost his job, or the nation that has been left in the lurch. The truth of the matter is only this: that concern for the nation must not be expected from others. It must be within us. When I see these labour leaders boasting boldly about fallen industries, I wonder if this class even understands what patriotism even means. I am amazed. If the workers had accepted that it was okay for the capitalists and industrialists to earn four times their salary, if only it allowed the industry to flourish, and created more jobs, then our country's history might have been very different. The way corrupt politicians have colluded with this class over the last forty years, the word socialism has completely changed meaning, and has now come to signify poverty, corruption, the net of government restrictions and the naked dance of inspectors. Our very ideals have become the noose around our necks … But is privatisation the solution to all ills? What are its advantages/disadvantages? It is important that we think seriously.[15]

Tejaswi's biting remarks must be seen as disillusionment with the adversarial tendencies of traditional trade unionism, where the managerial and industrial class were generally seen as staunch enemies of the working class, which fed conveniently into gang wars on political turfs. These ideals, the 'noose around our necks', seem to have come with a strong expiry date, when individual concerns of leaders like Ananth Subbarao became subsumed by a larger fog of ideological inertia. It is interesting to note that the RSS-linked trade union Bharatiya Mazdoor Sangh begins gaining popularity during the 1990s, riding on the workers' disaffection with other trade unions. A 1998 paper reported that 'the number of unions affiliated to BMS is far more than the unions affiliated to any other federation in centres like Mysore, Harihar–Davanagere and Hubli–Dharwad. Many personnel executives in these centres stated that the BMS affiliated unions are more positive, accommodative, reasonable, are interested in the survival of the organisations, do not make unreasonable demands, and are more democratic in internal functioning'.[16] Only a dire vacuum could have led the BMS, which proclaims in its prospectus that 'it doesn't believe in class concept and rejects the class theory propounded by Marx', to rise to represent workers' interests. It is therefore unsurprising that the BMS's present relevance has fallen flat after the rise of its political mothership.

Traditional Left trade unionism, unbound to real estate and establishment interests, has only slowly been shaping up. The casualisation of jobs since that momentous decade has paved the way towards yet another kind of ideological inertia, giving rise to a class of workers (not just in India, but globally) dubbed as the *precariat*, a precariously poised proletariat that is only expanding in size. While the precarity of what has been dubbed the gig economy—delivery workers, drivers and other service providers whom you can summon with a click—has slowly entered public discourse, what hasn't yet been fully acknowledged is the fact this isn't just a blue-collar problem but one that has enveloped an entire slice of the middle-class. For instance, in November 2023, thousands of guest lecturers working at degree colleges across Karnataka began boycotting classes, and staging protests for permanent jobs and regularisation of pay. These are well-educated men and women, with higher-education degrees and PhDs, who have been unable to settle down in their jobs because contracts are renewed every year and their posting could be changed to anywhere in the state. Around the same time, I was reading *Prophet Song*, the Booker Prize-winning novel revolving around a spirited organiser of teachers in Ireland who has been disappeared by the State for his trade union activities. It is a bleak and shattering projection of a future that seems eerily probable.

The moustache-twirling machismo that Tejaswi once abhorred in the trade union sphere has since found more worthy successors who embody more rooted, and more long-term goals. What I found intriguing about Du Saraswati's unique cultural project is how the individuality of modern theatre (one-woman shows are quite common in Bangalore today) is shaping fresher imaginations of workers' collectives, without dissolving either of these identities. The unionist who doubles up as your comedian-friend. This is also what has created the special bond with the pourakarmikas, garment workers and sex workers that she treasures so very much. *The so-called civilised world owes them dignified jobs,* she told me, *and we have many things to learn from them too.*

Coda

I

'This used to be a garbage dump here, ten feet high, like a mountain. There are around 50,000 households in this locality. All their waste would come here. People would cover their noses with a cloth while walking on this road. Somebody has to clean it right? Corporation does not do it. Municipality does not do it. I had 15,000 rupees with me. I decided to take matters into my own hands.'

In 2012, Syed Issaq accosted a truck driver and told him that he would give him Rs 200 for every load of garbage ferried away to a landfill. Issaq himself would do all the loading—the driver would just have to come park his vehicle there. Over the course of twenty-five days, Issaq single-handedly shovelled all the garbage out and cleaned up the entire five gunthas of that land, filling three truckloads full of garbage every single day. After this, he fenced the land with bamboo, and rebuilt his personal-public library from scratch.

Just a few months earlier, Issaq was running a hut-shack library housing over a hundred books at a different location. But when he relaxed his vigilance because he'd contracted dengue, some lumpen elements in the locality, whom he calls Kannada-virodhigalu (anti-Kannada elements), burnt down that library. Everything he had collected was incinerated, and the saplings he had planted on the road were pulled apart. He lost his mind, Issaq says, but it took him only a month to become determined to begin anew. That is when he found this new spot and began clearing up the garbage dump. Eight years later, in the summer of 2020, in the thick of the pandemic, after he had built up a collection of 11,000 books, the library was gobbled up by flames again, possibly by accident. This time, though, Syed Issaq was not alone. Social media amplified his cause and help poured in from Kannadigas across the country, and from overseas as well. They sent money, books and helped him reconstruct the library. Today, there are over 18,000 books in his collection, predominantly in Kannada. Daily newspapers alone cost him Rs 3,000 a month, and it takes Rs 15,000 every month to maintain the place. He sleeps there every night. Tens of visitors come every day and read—entries are marked in a register. A photograph of Kuvempu greets you at the entrance. Inside hang portraits of every major Indian general-knowledge figure, from Gandhi to Ambedkar to Lata Mangeshkar, with inspirational quotations displayed all around. At the centre is the largest frame, dwarfing everything around it, commanding Syed Isaaq's devotion like nobody else can—a garlanded portrait of Dr Rajkumar.

Located in Rajiv Nagar, a Muslim neighbourhood in Mysore, Issaq's library stands out like a red rose. A red-and-yellow rose, to be more precise. From the library décor to his visiting card to the little band around his wrist, the colours of the Kannada flag are everywhere. What once was a garbage dump is now a bright, accessible location on a wide, well-paved road.

Syed Issaq cannot read a single word; he attended school for all of fifteen days. Every now and then, someone comes and helps categorise the books. In January 2024, I spent a couple of afternoons in the library, helping Issaq organise some of the vast masses of Kannada books. I began dividing one big, inviting chunk into fiction and non-fiction. Beaming with delight, Issaq went off to fetch some coffee, while I dealt with the dust bunnies. Most of the books donated carried literary significance—there was no lack of taste in the donors' choice of titles. Vintage copies of old novels were plentiful. Having discovered a rare biography of T.P. Kailasam written by A.N. Krishna Rao, I was immersed in reading when one of Issaq's close friends arrived, looking for a chat with him. I will call him Abdul.

Abdul cremates unclaimed dead bodies in Mysore. During the pandemic, his work was geared into overdrive, and he still continues his social work. 'Abandoned bodies know neither religion nor caste. They just need to be shown respect. All the local politicians—yes, even BJP—know me. I don't take any money from any of them. People forget that they owe a debt to society. The best way to live is to be of some service to society, no?'

Suddenly becoming aware that he has been sitting for too long, he straightens his back and gets up to leave. 'See, as far as I am concerned, god made men and women, that's it. We are all humans. It is the politicians who drive poison into people's hearts, and make them act blindly.' He walks away with this taut closing comment. My eyes travel to the three books arranged on the top of the central mass behind him: a Quran, a Bible and a copy of Kuvempu's *Ramayana Darshanam*. I thought these kinds of spaces existed only in films. But hope survives.

To hear Syed Issaq speak of the syncretic environment he grew up in is to be transported into a world that seems almost unreal today:

> I was born in Srirangapatna taluk, Ganjam village, in the firewood choppers' street. Our house was separated from the Ram Mandir by a single wall. Common wall. When puja happened there, we would hear it. If the Quran was being read here, it would be heard there. This was a 200-year-old tradition. To the left of the Syed family, there lived lingayats, behind us were vokkaligas, nayaks—we all lived together. Seventy feet from there was the Maramma shrine. Two hundred feet from there was the Masjid. I grew up in this kind of an environment. When was I born? 1959. When I was a kid, all of them took care of me, fed me, brought me up.

When Syed Issaq was seven years old, he had already become a bonded labourer. A landlord had given him two rupees to purchase supplies. Somebody cheated the young boy out of the money, and fearing retribution from the landlord, he did the only thing he could think of—he left Srirangapatna, left his family, and fled as far as he could until he fainted for lack of food or water in a village near

Channapatna, many miles away. A man named Nagrajanna, 'the chairman's grandson', found him, gave him food to eat and employed him as a caretaker of cattle. There, as a young Issaq worked day after day, he would pick up lines of Kannada lessons being recited in the school nearby. Circa 1980, a flower wholesaler met him on a Mysore–Bangalore train, recognised him as the young boy whose family sold flowers near the Ram temple in Srirangapatna, and reunited them after so many years. His father had died by then, but his mother and siblings were alive and well, and they had not given up their search for the young wayward boy. The young man they met now was a resourceful youth living out his life through Rajkumar movies.

> Annavru [Rajkumar's sobriquet] is the biggest inspiration for me, and for this library. Lecturer, professor, father—he is all this to me. When I was a kid, I would only watch his films. More than one hundred and eighty films I must have seen. He can play any character. Perfect for any role. There is only one Rajkumar in this universe. Nobody else like that will ever live again. I needed money to watch his films. How to get? The landlord would give me two or three paise even after a day of grazing the cattle and taking care of the farm. He would throw brass paisa coins at me. *Throw?* With love only he would throw. What can I do with three paisa? I would go to the riverbank, where kids would be playing games like gilli-danda and all. I would not play with them. I would dig ditches, where I would collect all the cattle dung. It would get filled within a week. I would sell it for two-and-a-half rupees, or three rupees. A cinema ticket cost sixty-five paise—I would sit like a king and watch Rajkumar movies.

In a few years, he got married, and came to Mysore, to Rajiv Nagar, where he has lived for the past thirty-five years. Coming to a city after years spent labouring in rural Karnataka, Syed Issaq had to pick up new skills to survive. He started working as a mason, as a painter, as a handyman, and doing intermittent coolie labour. Yet, this was far from sufficient, and after he got married and moved to

Mysore, the burden of his family also pressed on his shoulders. He decided to start cleaning kakkas lines (shit sewers).

> Back then, chamber lines had not come up. There were only ditches. I would clean the ditch, go dig another ditch in a field, bury the waste, and then clean the original ditch. They would give me fifteen rupees for doing this. *Smell?* Haha, of course, it used to smell. Well, when people steal and murder and cheat and exploit others, doesn't that stink up the air too? This is hardly as bad. Waste must be cleaned—it can't be left alone, can it? I cleaned it.

When chamber lines were laid, Syed Isaaq began breaking jelly stones for a livelihood. One day, he was sitting at a chai shop when he spotted a discarded newspaper with Rajkumar's face on it. He asked one of his literate friends to read the article for him. It was interesting. So, he started buying Kannada newspapers—*Andolana*, *Mysooru Mithra*—and bringing them to the teashop to get other people to read, from which he would absorb as much as he could. That was the seed for his library idea. His project has flourished despite the nastiest assaults from petty arsonists, 'anti-Kannada' elements, who he wishes will be 'imparted some maturity by god soon enough'.

He speaks vibrant Kannada full with idioms and literary flourishes.

> This is a slum. Ninety-nine per cent of what is spoken here is Urdu. There is a dire need for Kannada in this place. Of all the places in Mysore, this place needs a library the most. There is no need for a library in places in Srirampura, Vijayanagara, Agrahara—there education has already reached. But here, oh, there are no good schools also. People didn't have any idea of what a library is. We need education. Young girls seem to be studying, at least till tenth standard. College dreams are far away. Boys, if they make it to sixth standard, it's a big deal. The politicians are interested only in maintaining things as they are. They don't want to let people get educated. Otherwise, who will vote them in? Till now, no political party has helped me monetarily at all. When my library burnt down in 2020, the local corporator called only after three days. By then, Siddaramaiah and U.T. Khader had called. They extended moral support.

These days, he picks up waste plastic and metal to make ends meet, and numerous felicitations and awards and recognitions have also pooled valuable cash towards the upkeep of the library. Many young girls come there to read, and local bookshops have also recognised him and offered support.

As I prepare to leave, after having made a small donation to his project, he slowly walks over to his desk. I stare at the large photograph of the library scientist S.R. Ranganathan plastered on the wall behind him. He opens up a locked drawer, pulling out a tiny notebook. Here, only the names and contact details of the people he likes most are allowed entry. He extends it to me.

I write out my name in the most beautiful handwriting I can summon.

II

- a plain and open field.
- the field or ground on which a battle is fought; a battlefield.
- any part of the earth's surface not covered by a body of water; land.
- a vast extent of level land not having vegetation, human habitation, etc.
- something that is useless, or the quality of being useless.
- a disclosing of a secret; a secret become disclosed; disclosure.
- cessation of one's life; death.
- that part of the land in a region that is cultivated.
- that which is clearly seen, known or understood.
- the sky.
- that which is outside or beyond one's control or hold.
- absence of form; formlessness (as of Shiva, in Veerashaiva philosophy).
- a becoming one with the formless Being.[1]

The word 'bayalu' is truly multidimensional, its meanings clashing with and contradicting one another. Across its history, it has opened up to fresh meanings at every juncture, showcasing the metaphorical richness of the Kannada language. In the twelfth century, the paradoxical mystic Allama Prabhu translated the Buddhist notion of shunyata, emptiness, into the image of bayalu, a barren field. It was a conceptual leap that transformed a philosophical abstraction into the immediate visual vocabulary of the workaday world. The word 'bayalaata' (folk theatre such as Yakshagana, for instance) literally means playing on the open field, and what sets apart indigenous theatre is the complete absence of elaborate props, and the imbuing of characters and actors with all the colour you could gather. There does seem to be something essentially desi about that burst of colour, like the screaming back of a truck on an empty highway, animating an otherwise barren land. Like the Chola bronzes on which the elaborate reliefs of the adornments highlight the smooth skin of the dancer-woman. The characters and their gestures speak for themselves—as in Syed Issaq's library, where the barren bayalu is transformed into a vibrant pulsating organism. On dreamy days, I tell myself that the empty bayalu, the void, the number zero, maya, were all invented in India through a kind of cultural necessity, to avoid being overwhelmed by its infinite diversity, to create a space where all of it could find order and meaning through sheer power of contrast.

In my readings, I kept encountering resonances of this remarkable word, and its weblike genealogy astounded me over and over with all its accumulated history. In Chandrashekhar Patil's poem 'Bandaya', which captures the futility of militant atheism, it comes up as a representation of the religious void which the radical rationalists of the seventies presented to their bewildered elders:

From the confines of my veranda, I sent flying,
All those trivial godheads.
Some vibhuti to rub on wounds?
I sent that ash flying too.
Walls now full with portraits of mere mortals,
Amavasya, Yugadi, and all those festivities

Mere dots on a flawless calendar.
Avva [mother], who came from the village,
Saw the vast, sprawling void [bataa bayalu]
And crawled back, worshipping
A linga in her concealed palm, whispering
To herself, that all this was her karma.

Then, detailing some more radical attempts on the narrator's part, the poem goes on to end with a silent reclamation of what had been lost:

One sudden day,
Creeping upon me surreptitiously,
Came a spiralling fragrance,
Upon whose back I rode,
To a shelf in the kitchen.
Fragrance, kumkuma, vibhuti,
A nameless flower,
An agarbatti,
A blinking wick of a lamp.
I turned to launch a question,
My wife—drowning in the din of utensils,
The little boy—grinning ear to ear,
And my daughter—sitting, smug with a smile.

I encountered the word again in K.V. Subbanna's Kannada translation of Ram Manohar Lohia's collection of essays *Interval Between Politics*: 'Now, the European value system is being used as a yardstick all across the world. It is extremely important that non-Europeans consider [these values] seriously with a critical eye. They must blow the gaff [bayalugolisabeku] on the illusion that this system of values is acceptable to the entire world, and must work towards the creation of an excellent system of fresh values …' Apart from this sense of bayalu as a verb that debunks illusions (in this case, colonial morality), it also came up as a reference to the 'historical void' in the desi imagination, pointing to the mythical sense of time which preceded the arrival of the modern sense of linear history. This recognition need not lead us to a 'neither can live while the other survives' type of prophecy, but instead to the realisation that history and literature can thrive alongside one another, co-creating a more lucid understanding of the worlds behind our worlds. The spanner in the works at the moment seems to be the Loudmouth School of historiography, whose utterances are unerringly fashioned into political barbs that continue to distract our collective historical understanding with all the inaccuracy of a blunt cleaver being swung by a drunken brawler.

The fact that Lohia has thrived in Kannada, with translations by literati as eminent as Subbanna, also owes something to his vision of decentralising knowledge through empowerment of regional languages. It was a similar vision that made Allama Prabhu—who managed to convert philosophical ideas into vivid metaphors—such a radical poet. Lohia embraced metaphors as an eminent way of understanding politics. His most famous one is the allusion to all politics as an exercise in care, as in cleaning up one's home. Things will get dirty, but it is up to us to ensure that we care enough about upkeep and maintenance. To ignore the elephant in the room, or the stinking mess in the backyard, is to be devoid of basic cleanliness. There is a circularity to Lohia's sense of history, spirituality *and* politics that helps accommodate dynamic challenges aimed at a stultifying world. It acknowledges the validity of other ways of being. It was bearing such an understanding that Ananthamurthy, so hugely influenced by Lohia, welcomed the boosa predicament with understanding, seeing it as an inevitable unfolding of the cycle of history. It is the same understanding that prompted him to see caste as a force of creativity, which spawned a controversy with Chandrashekhar Patil who could never associate the two words. In the open field where that primordial game of Rama Bhima Soma unfolds, the ball will eventually pass into the hands of one who has never held it—the inevitable instance of history fulfilling its promise. Yet, when the ball begins to become monopolised by a few crafty individuals, challenging them becomes the game's duty, and restoring balance becomes paramount.

In Gopalakrishna Adiga's satirical poem 'Become a Stone', I saw echoes of his profound disillusionment with our collective tendency to idolise and idealise, the root of all forms of oppressive hierarchy:

> Become a stone! Within life's whirlwind,
> Stand firm, O spirit!
> How long, this relentless struggle?
> Fecklessly trailing behind the mirage (bayaludore)[2]
> To what end?
> The good and beautiful life,
> Abandon those yearnings!
> No space for grass-life here!
> No brace for old flowery vines!
> Only for the stone, a face, someplace.

In the verses below by Pratibha Nandakumar, I glimpsed the historically barren landscape from which women have emerged with defiant honesty, in spite of centuries of accumulated suppression, if not systematic slavery:

> A poem's journey was always imperilled
> By the rise and fall of empires
> In the wake of betrayals and back-stabbings
> Amidst broken ruins and knick-knacks
> Under the thorny gaze of many eyes,
> A step must be taken, braving all birthmarks
> This is a land [bayalu] with no shade
> My poetry is no demure damsel
> So I ask,
> What is a secret?
> What is honour?
> What is shame?

In other words, the void is never only void, and the bayalu is never fully barren. It is also an open field for rediscovery and reevaluation, creation against all odds, meaningful preservation of nature and traditions, cultivation of playful bonhomie and fertile honesty. There is a profound sense of non-duality that pervades the word across its myriad deployments.

In the same way that a blank page requires absolute solitude to unearth its richest possibilities, the imagination of a future society seems to be in need of a searching quietude. It is akin to what John Keats once called 'negative capability', which is the ability to lie dormant, accepting mystery and befuddlement without grasping for an underlying rhyme or reason, and letting the ideas battle themselves out in one's head in that open field of fertile possibilities. Gopalakrishna Adiga, in another biting poem titled 'Do Something Brother', had realised that the age of action was leading to grave peril and fanaticism, and that the old adage of the devil's workshop had to be reformulated for the modern age:

> Do something brother
> Keep doing
> Something, anything
> You mustn't be idle
> Pull out this plant,
> Nip this little leaf,
> Crush that flower,
> There's grass,
> Run your brand through it.
> Burn it like Lanka.
>
> (Translated by A.K. Ramanujan)

The paradox is that the horses of the mind may only be tamed by refusing to place a girdle on them. To let them run free and fair—such is the ideal. The poem continues to mock the 'brother' who has set out to transform the world:

> Disasters are the test of your genius' galloping dance
> Something must crash every minute
> Brother, act, act at once, do something.

It is safe to say that the galloping dance of the developing world has now transformed into a whinnying cry for help. The disasters have begun their testing. We avoid heatsinks by slinking into well-cooled cars, men die in Africa when a cartoon is published in Europe, vast farms are filled with livestock to be fattened and gutted. In the meantime, debt and depression unites the world, insecurity haunts our workspaces and farmlands, and a global food crisis seems all but imminent. International politics, instead of trying to deal collectively with this crisis, has begun to morph into authoritarian islands where national identities and religious identities are being twisted into war cries. Radical identity politics have opened up our imaginations to the richness of the sexuality spectrum, unwittingly spawning more confusion rather than clarity, while medicine has begun exploring the void at the heart of depression and psychiatric disorders with a determinist fervour ... But there is no such thing as an exact science when it comes to these things yet, everything is being tested and contested. A spanking new political imagination that synthesises the best of everything we have learnt about ourselves, and that moves beyond the mere weaponisation of victimhood, is still in the works.

Zooming back into Karnataka, we may recall how the dawn of the twentieth century witnessed a cultural renaissance that dovetailed with a humanist aspiration for more enlightened politics. Through the figurehead of someone like Kuvempu, we see how culture tried to take over the transcendental capabilities that had once been the sole preserve of religion. Some began to believe that it could single-handedly usher in a brighter world. The notion was quickly challenged, but it was only by the 1970s that it become quite clear that culture had assumed too much for itself, and that it was essential to bring culture down from the clouds in order to accommodate the aspirational vocabulary of all those whom Nehruvian socialism had yet to touch.

Within the next few decades, this humbling of culture would segue into another watershed event—the wholesale arrival of consumerism. Culture could now (substantially if not in full measure) be repackaged as the upliftment of the striving individual, encapsulated in the possession of an automobile, television or smartphone. In this process, people also became more estranged from nature than ever before. In other words, the very act of economic participation (also an act of gratitude) implicitly became a subscription to the neoliberal paradigm. The gratitude extends to the present day, most noticeable in the form of social media platforms, where anybody can open an account and begin *influencing* culture. Even as culture's ambit expands, masking the exponential growth of global inequality in this process, it has also turned on itself by bringing out the most distasteful parts of humanity to public view, as even a cursory Twitter scroll sufficiently reveals. It is the re-awakening of the colosseum—one revels only at the expense of someone else's fall. The gladiatorial games of the Roman emperors produced only a revulsion for democracy in Europe for centuries, because they had demonstrated how vile ordinary citizens could become if left to their own ends. Today, the proliferation of fake news and the muddying of journalism may also be found in this arena of cyber-bullies—the modern-day like button is only a perverse inversion of the thumbs-up given to the gladiators about to be put to death in ancient Rome. Yet, these are still the teething moments of new media, and I am hopeful that a generation that has seen through its toxicity will spawn better avatars.

It was roughly around the dawn of this new millennium that many on the traditional Left (in Karnataka, and India at large) began realising that they had woefully neglected the importance of religion and transcendentalism of the old sort, while the Right began realising that the time was ripe to latch on to this void instrumentally, to acquire political power and wrest it from the former elite. The radical Left had already connected with a strain of modern fanaticism (the now moribund cult of Mao, say), which provided some firewood for their reactionary peers on the radical Right. Religious fundamentalism (of all stripes) fills the void of modernity with nothing less than a war cry—history becomes an eternal battle that can be rekindled at a moment's will. While I do find that the cognitive tendencies of the political Left and

Right sometimes resemble each other, I'd argue broadly that we find ourselves caught between a futurism that is trying to make meaningful sense of our cultural heritage, and a medievalism that is engaged in transplanting poorly grasped histories into political ideologies that simultaneously (dis)locate themselves in the past, present and future. The former demands patience, while the latter essentially thrives on impatience.

As far as political structures go, little evolution has taken place. I have with me a special 1990 edition of the famous *Shudra* magazine, titled 'Gandhian Philosophy and Decentralisation'. Several thinkers had reflected on the decentralisation efforts in

Shudra: Gandhian Philosophy and Decentralisation, 1991.

Karnataka—invigoration of the Panchayat Raj in Karnataka during the mid-eighties, courtesy of rural development ministers like Abdul Nazeersab—and their own conceptions of a future society. D.R. Nagaraj had argued that such a society would have to move past the idea of a paternalistic welfare state towards becoming a creative, self-dependent force that is able to find what it seeks without having to reach out to the State. Of course, this process can be best initiated by the State itself, by dispelling the stigma attached to budget deficits, increasing government spending on health and education, and discarding unproductive tax regimes that exacerbate middle-class debt. Nagaraj makes a distinction between representative democracy and participatory democracy, the former being a weak and passive form of administration, and the latter being a state of heightened awareness and vitality. For Nagaraj, the welfare state is only a banal caricature of the true potential of Panchayat Raj structures. The rigidity of the institution—and the complacency it induces—can only be arrested by genuine people's movements for decentralising power. Many of the other pieces held forth in a similar tenor, and homages to the recently deceased Nazeersab were pervasive. On the whole, everyone seemed to recognise that preparing a grassroots revolution would take far more education and awareness than actually existed. Three decades since that momentous year, the paternalistic welfare state continues to be the default model of Indian governance, and its desperate expansion serves as its own ringing critique. Addressing poverty and inequality remains like a game of whack-a-mole for the Indian state. Just like the chasm between the human development indices of India's northern and southern halves, Karnataka too possesses a barren bayalu in its arid northern regions, which has seen little investment towards substantial structural change.

From time to time, I *am* heartened by some developments taking shape in the background—when I see a man accused of shoplifting lingerie taken first to a psychiatrist rather than a magistrate, or popular Kannada grandmothers' magazines championing LGBTQ causes, and in general the permeation of the best of modernity (AI can potentially democratise knowledge) into a desi world that is still numb to its more deleterious impacts. My biggest grouse remains that the rhetoric of rapid urbanisation—of highways and high-rises and other high jinks—has been blindly accepted as a progress-marker. This should ideally be displaced by environmentalism, imaginative education and healthcare and public transport reforms, as well as cooperative building in the countryside. If a community feels that an expressway passing through its vicinity is pointless, it should be able to powerfully reject the proposal and demand a library or health centre or science club or recycling plant or affordable housing instead.

When Syed Issaq tells me he does not wish to go to any political party for help, but will do everything himself, by any and all means available to him, he becomes a political bird taking solitary flight. For the young boys and girls who come to read at his library, there will be some for whom it will feel no less liberating than a cultural revolution. By demonstrating how individuals can single-handedly empower their communities, he is shaming the non-power of the non-performing State. In this, he is by no means alone, as this book has tried to show. Just like the explosive potential of the word 'bayalu', the possibilities of civil society standing up for itself can induce much optimism in thinking minds. As Syed Issaq is fond of saying, *You don't need an appane (order) from anyone to begin doing something good.* Coming from a man who spent fifteen years (beginning from his childhood) as a bonded labourer, you can be sure that his realisation has traced a radical journey of self-discovery.

Notes

Prologue

1. James P. Carse's book *Finite and Infinite Games: A Vision of Life as Play and Possibility* is an enjoyable meditation on this theme.
2. B.M. Puttaiah, *MukhaMukhi: Samaja, Samskruti, Chaluvali.*

1. Marga, Desi and the Battle of Identities

1. See S. Settar, *Halagannada, Lipikara, Lipi Vyavasaya,* p. 54. Studying over two thousand medieval inscriptions and copper plates in Kannada (and Sanskrit), this exemplary work of scholarship challenges many prevailing norms in South Asian studies, especially concerning the near synonymous usage of 'Sanskritisation' and 'brahminism'.
2. See Sheldon Pollock's essay 'Creating a Regional World: The Case of Kannada' in *The Language of the Gods in the World of Men*.
3. Already, the blurring of the marga–desi binary can be discerned. D.R. Nagaraj sees an unmissable desiness in Pampa, while H.S. Shivaprakash decidedly calls him a marga poet. Nagaraj was forced to introduce another category he called the adhikruta-desi (official desi), which he saw as an attempt staged by the desi rebels to cement their place in the canon of the marga. However, these categories are vaporous entities, and they surface most illuminatingly only when they are in the process of rupture and change.
4. D.R. Nagaraj wrote a virtuosic, if difficult to read, essay on the various contestations and tensions within the history of Kannada literary culture, which has largely inspired this chapter. He passed

away even as he was about to complete this essay, leading one to wonder how he would have ended the story. See 'Critical Tensions in the History of Kannada Literary Culture' in *Literary Cultures in History: Reconstructions from South Asia*, edited by Sheldon Pollock.

5. While Veerashaivism is held as the theological abstraction that birthed Lingayatism, the latter is often used in particular reference to Basavanna's transformation of the tradition. In recent years, scholars like MM Kalburgi have sought to differentiate between the anti-caste inclinations of Lingayatism and the more brahminical associations of Veerashaivism. The word 'Veerashaiva' itself only begins to be used abundantly in non-vachana Kannada devotional literature some two hundred years after Basavanna's time. The scholar Gil Ben-Herut prefers to use Shiva-bhakta instead of either Lingayat/Veerashaiva to describe the twelfth-century milieu, because neither of the words appears even once in Harihara's hagiography-documentary *Ragalegalu*, written around half a century after Basavanna's time—the closest source describing the Sharana movement. See *Siva's Saints*.
6. One notable highlight of this period was the rise of small principalities ruled by kings from shudra backgrounds across South India. These rulers created a cultural zeitgeist that celebrated their caste origins and imbued it with religious prestige. See *Symbols of Substance, Court and State in Nayaka Period Tamilnadu, p. 75*
7. Sukantya Shantha, '"Interconnected": A Court's Words on 4 Rationalists' Murders Highlights What Probe Agencies Ignore', *The Wire*, 19 July 2024.
8. This is a genre of prophetic vachanas influenced by folk, Sufi, and Veerashaiva traditions in North Karnataka from the fifteenth century onwards. For instance, the *Ghattivalavyya Kalajnaana Vachana* describes the rise of 'petty Mahomedan principalities' after the fall of Vijayanagara and how they subdued some Beda leaders who had emerged to fill the vacuum. See Madhava, K. G. Vasanth. "Kannada Sources of the Adilshahis of Bijapur 1555-1686."
9. From an essay titled 'The Destruction of Temples', M.M. Kalburgi, *Marga*, Vol. 3.
10. See Richard Eaton, *Temple Desecration and Muslim States in Medieval India*.

11. According to the scholar Prithvi Datta Chandra Shobi, it was this particular historical moment that rearticulated and refashioned the vast corpus of vachana literature within the social and religious contexts that are commonly associated with it today.
12. Sheldon Pollock (ed.) *Literary Cultures in History: Reconstructions from South Asia*, p. 379. Also see Mark Wilks, *Historical Sketches of the South of India*, p. 205–8.
13. While the sixteenth century did give rise to an upwardly mobile class of Beda leaders, it was not wholly unprecedented. According to historian Duncan Derrett, the Hoysala dynasty—which ruled most of Karnataka between the tenth and fourteenth centuries—was founded by kings from Beda backgrounds. See J. Duncan M. Derrett, *The Hoysalas: A Medeival Indian Royal Family*
14. Caleb Simmons, *Devotional Sovereignty: Kingship and Religion in India*, p. 77 onwards. Simmons's book is an excellent study of how Tipu Sultan and Krishnaraja Wodeyar III navigated the changing political landscape of their times by turning to religious and mythical pasts to reinforce their sovereignty.
15. T.P. Kailasam, *The Purpose: A Playlet of Ekalavya*.
16. B.C. Mahabaleswarappa, 'Swadeshi Spirit Through National Schools In Hyderabad Karnataka'
17. Pandit Taranath, *Antinda Nantu*, p. 210.
18. A. Ramachandran & C. Heffernan, 'A Distinctly Indian Body? K.V. Iyer and Physical Culture in 1930s India' in *The International Journal of the History of Sport*.
19. Mark Singleton, *Yoga Body: The Origins of Modern Posture Practice*.
20. K.V. Iyer, *Physique and Figure*.
21. Mark Singleton *Yoga Body: The Origins of Modern Posture Practice*, Chapter 6.
22. *Dinakarana Chaupadigalu* is a nice collection of all his verses, available in print.
23. R.K. Narayan's views on the caste system were often flippant, and he does not seem to have recognised its insidious nature, even if he did espouse its eradication. It must also be said that Narayan was not as talented an essayist as he was a novelist. See 'Castes: Old and New' in *A Writer's Nightmare: Selected Essays, 1958-1988*.
24. M. Madhava Prasad's *Cine-Politics: Film Stars and Political Existence*

in South India is an excellent resource for understanding the larger-than-life personalities of cine stars in the south.

25. Mirza Ismail's *My Public Life* is an elegantly written memoir that is dedicated to the Maharaja of Mysore, Krishnaraja Wodeyar Bahadur.
26. Hermina Cielas Leão, 'Voices from the stone, figures on the stage: the development of Avadhāna and Avadhānī's identity' in Paola M. Rossi (ed.), *Liminal Spaces, and Identity Transformations in South Asian Literatures and Arts: Essays in Honour of Professor Alexander Dubyanskiy*.
27. See Caleb Simmons, *Devotional Sovereignty: Kingship and Religion in India*, p. 194 onwards.
28. Interview with D.R. Nagaraj (in Kannada): https://youtu.be/ZB2EWZOfF2M?si=0syRE5foSw12YDQP.
29. Attention is a philosophical concept with pan-civilisational resonances, close to wisdom because it is also close to empathy. Indeed, McGilchrist's characterisation of our present is that the quality of attention we pay to the world and people around us has drastically deteriorated. For a lucid account of attention as a philosophical category, with particular reference to Buddhist thought, see Jonardon Ganeri's *Attention, Not Self.*
30. Prateek Goyal, 'The anatomy of Dabholkar's murder and how its "mastermind" walked away scot-free', *Newslaundry*, 17 May 2024.
31. Ramachandra Guha's personal essay *Rooted Cosmopolitan: D.R. Nagaraj* is a lovely tribute to the man. It is part of the collection *An Anthropologist Among the Marxist and Other Essays.*
32. For instance, he saw how the non-Vedic Pancharatra Agamas found a home in the philosophical explorations of Yamunacharya, who fused them with Vedic sanction, and passed them on through his disciple Ramanuja, famed for his revolutionary drive to break caste barriers. See D.R. Nagaraj, *Allama Prabhu Mattu Shaiva Pratibhe*.
33. As Dr Sarjoo Katkar writes in his introduction to *Kambara Kavya Kaarana,* a study of Kambar's poetics.
34. For a deep history of Tantrism, see Shingo Einoo (ed.), *Genesis and Development of Tantrism*.
35. Tennant C. Wright, '"Left-Handed" Hindu Tantrism' in *Religious Studies*.
36. Wendy Doniger argues, employing Buddhist tetra-logic, that deviant

sex and drugs were both symbolic and literal, neither symbolic nor literal, sometimes symbolic but not literal, and sometimes literal but not symbolic. The evidence is thin. But given the fact that these practices have survived to this day, a reasonable assumption can be made that they were practised in whatever measure earlier too. Certainly, the erotic reliefs in Khajuraho point towards a definite celebration of sex as a way of reaching divinity. See her chapter 'Sects and Sex in the Tantric Puranas and the Tantras' in *The Hindus: An Alternative History.*

37. It is reflected in a divide between mobile groups (pastoralists, traders, artisans) who were dubbed 'left-hand' castes, and settled groups (peasant farmers and warriors) who were dubbed 'right-hand'. David Shulman describes this divide most curiously in *Tamil: A Biography*, p. 83: 'Each of these two large social configurations comes with its own moral universe: left-hand groups tend to gravitate toward universalistic, context-free values, including an ideal of self-sacrifice; right-hand groups, committed to a homeostatic order on the ground, are intimately tied to a sacrificial ideology with an inherent element of normative violence.'
38. 'Why I have never learnt Sanskrit language' https://www.youtube.com/watch?v=bvGVwdpc_II.
39. Chandan Gowda, 'Two writers—in 1928 and in 2016—wrote of the value of physical work, and its caste connotations', *Scroll.in*, 8 September 2023.
40. One such version may be viewed at: https://www.youtube.com/watch?v=lKnpO_fr8EE&t=23s.

2. Of Attics and Romantics

1. The interview is available here: https://www.youtube.com/watch?v=Ytjpg_d_Uqk&t=783s.
2. James Manor, *Political Change in an Indian State*, p. 32 onwards.
3. Chinnaswamy Sosale (ed.), *Karnatakada Samagra Dalita Charitre*, p. 82.
4. Titled *Annana Nenapu,* it is a nostalgic recollection of random flash-bulb anecdotes involving Kuvempu.
5. V.K. Gokak's *Bendre: Poet and Seer* is a lively introduction to Bendre and his association with the Geleyara Gumpu, although it tends to get hagiographical at times.

6. I'm thankful to Dr Rajendra Chenni for priming me on these pivotal historical times.
7. It is interesting to note that the attention paid to Urmila is also a feature of some Jain retellings of the Ramayana many centuries earlier.
8. Retrieved from Devaiah Harave, *Dalita Sahithya Mattu Itara Lekhanagalu*, p. 63.
9. The most accessible biography of Gopala Gowda is Nataraj Huliyar's *Shantaveri Gopala Gowda*. The book synthesises personal correspondence, interviews with close associates, tribute pieces and intimate personal diaries collected in a larger volume titled *Shantaveri Gopalagowda Nenapina Samputa.* I have drawn all of Gopala Gowda's biographical details from these two books.
10. Tripurdaman Singh's *Sixteen Stormy Days*: *The Story of the First Amendment to the Constitution of India* is a riveting account of the authoritarian manner in which the First Amendment—which regulated free speech and challenged the Constitution's liberal fundamentals in the name of zamindari abolition, nationalisation and reservations—was set in motion.
11. The history of the rebellion has been comprehensively written by G. Rajshekar in his book *Kagodu Satyagraha*, a fine work of journalism and fieldwork that is every bit as illuminating and piercing as that other classic written in the seventies (while also being set in newly independent India), M.N. Srinivas's *The Remembered Village.*
12. Nico Slate, *Kamaladevi Chattopadhyay, The Art of Freedom,* p. 75.
13. Though there seems to be a long history of such association, there is just one mention of 'untouchables' in Kannada hero stones, dating back to 997 A.D, where a madiga hero named Arivarma is commemorated by an upper-caste headman for laying his life down during a cattle-raid on their village. The sheer lack of such references highlights the marginality of dalits across history—their identity and allegiance had always been taken for granted. See *Kannada Sahityadalli Asprushyateya Parikalpane,* p.25
14. See Satish Patil's *Hebballi Bhoohorata*.
15. See Rahamath Tarikere's *Lokavirodhigala Joteyalli.*
16. *Shantaveri Gopala Gowda Nenapina Samputa*, p. 122.
17. All quotations have been taken from Narayan Hegde's English translation of *Avasthe.*

18. An interesting trivia shared by Neelagangayya Pujar in the aforementioned interview was: 'Devaraj Urs did not have a Lohiaite background. He had a son-in-law named Badrinarayan Iyengar. Brilliant fellow. Supreme court advocate. He had a *social perception*. He became Urs' guru. He was the one who impressed upon him the need to form a non-lingayat front, to form a coalition of backward classes. It was him too who gave the writer Chaduranga many sociological insights …'
19. This is from a collection of Adiga's essays titled *Kannadada Abhimana Mattu Itara Lekhanagalu,* which was published in 1972. A more comprehensive collection titled *Vaicharika Lekhana Vachike* was published recently. I have sourced all my quotations from these two collections.
20. Johanna Bockman's *Markets in the Name of Socialism: The Left-Wing Origins of Neoliberalism* is a thought-provoking work that navigates the complex interplay of socialist and neoclassical economics, the threads of which are inextricably dovetailed across the intellectual and political histories of the twentieth century.
21. Soutik Biswas, 'Electoral autocracy': The downgrading of India's democracy, BBC.com, 16 March 2021.
22. Another example of a flourishing genre of *narrated* biographies, *Kadatoreya Jaadu* is a delightful and endearing ramble of a jolly-hearted man who lived his life in people and stories.
23. 25 November 1998, p.6. The journalist who penned the piece goes by the one-worded name, Basavaraju.
24. While the vokkaliga title Gowda, connotative of a headman, is used in South Karnataka, there are lingayats from North Karnataka who bear variations such as Goud or Goudar. A few other communities like Kurubas and Kumbaras also affix Gowda to their names sometimes.

3. Art as Life

1. The English translation by H.Y. Sharada Prasad is a condensation of the much larger Kannada original, *Huchhu Manassina Hattu Mukhagalu.* I have sourced all of Karanth's autobiographical recollections from these two versions.

2. Serialised in the early 1980s, it was an award-winning novel that was soon translated into English as *Vasudeva's Family*.
3. Research has shown that languages that originate in warm, humid environments are more likely to have a wide range of tones because human vocal cords become more elastic in such environments. South Canara is most certainly hot and humid. Devrupa Rakshit, 'How the Climate Subtly Shapes the Way We Talk', *The Swaddle*, 9 September 2023.
4. Better known as the Devadasi tradition, this practice of dedicating women to temples was opposed by many prominent Kannada literati of those times, including the poet D.V. Gundappa. This opposition faced a pushback from Devadasis themselves, such as the famous performer Bangalore Nagarathnamma, who argued that such rhetoric would prove detrimental to their tradition and craft, and that allegations of prostitution were a crude caricature of their culture. The practice would ultimately be banned across India in 1988. For a good primer on the early twentieth-century debates, see V. Sriram, *The Devadasi and the Saint: The Life and Times of Bangalore Nagarathnamma*.
5. H.Y. Sharada Prasad's excellent translation is also complemented by a cover that features a stunning K.K. Hebbar painting of a woman playing a veena. Sadly, the book is out of print.
6. Meenakshi Kapoor & Mahabaleshwar Hegde, 'Displaced by the sea. Failed by the state', *Scroll.in*, 20 December 2024.
7. Divyashri Mudakavi, 'Tigers of Muharram and the Colours of Harmony', *Deccan Herald*, 29 August, 2020.
8. Naveen Soorinje's book of reportage *Netravatiyalli Nettaru* is a worm's-eye view of the political changes across the last few decades in South Canara. It is an especially important document that showcases the unholy nexus between the police establishment in the Mangalore region and the crass brand of vigilante activism set in motion by groups like the Sri Ram Sene and Bajrang Dal since the early 2000s.
9. The book is titled *Sanjeevana*, and is a product of numerous interview sessions conducted by writer Prithviraj Kavattaru, during which Sanjeev Suvarna candidly narrates his eventful life, which includes his lifelong tryst with Shivaram Karanth.

10. See interview with Sharanya Ramprakash here: https://www.youtube.com/watch?v=ccZ2-H9ZBys.
11. V.S. Acharya was the home minister when the infamous attack on the Milagres Church in Mangalore was carried out by the Bajrang Dal in 2008. The Bajrang Dal leader Mahendra Kumar would later allege that Acharya, along with other Sangh ideologues such as M.B. Puranik and Kalladka Prabhakar Bhat, had orchestrated church attacks across the state, motivated by alleged conversion activities. See Mahendra Kumar, *Nadu Baggisida Edeya Dani*, p. 117.
12. Mulk Raj Anand, *The Singing Line: Drawings by Hebbar*.
13. D.R. Nagaraj makes this point very well here: https://www.youtube.com/watch?v=yKcOXGkJGUs&t=3507s.
14. Written by GM Carstairs and RL Kapur [Kapur was Karanth's son-in-law], this 1976 book sought to study the psychiatric health of three Kota castes. Amongst other interesting conclusions, it showed that Bunts—a caste just lower than brahmins—faced more stress as far as men were concerned, because they were affected both by the dominance of the brahmins in jobs, and by the slow rise of the Mogaveeras up the socio-economic ladder. Women of the latter two castes, who had been following a matrilineal system of inheritance, were significantly more prone to psychiatric stress than brahmin women, and one of the reasons seems to have been a shift from the matrilineal to patrilineal system, which meant that they no longer split their time between their husband's home and mother's home, but stayed with their husbands full-time.

4. Saakshi

1. Dr Sumateendra Nadig (ed.), *Gopalakrishna Adigara Patragalu* (Collection of Letters of Sri Gopalakrishna Adiga).
2. In this context, one is reminded of A.K. Ramanujan's famous 'Notes on Mescaline', a prose-poem-essay in which he records the stream of his thought after ingesting the very drug that writers like Aldous Huxley had experimented with a couple of decades earlier.
3. In a letter to V.K. Gokak, Sadashiva Rao explains this choice: *Lorenzo the magnificent, lord of Florence, great statesman, poet, scientist, who liked his Florence to be gay.*

4. A.V. Navada, *The Collected Works of Pejavara Sadashiva Rao.*
5. Kusuma Shanbag, *Putagala Naduvina Navilugari*, p. 162.
6. Kodagina Gowramma (tr. Deepa Bhasthi), *Fate's Game and other Stories.*
7. Ananthamurthy, incidentally, was among those who pressed the Karnataka government to change the name of Bangalore to Bengaluru in the 2000s.
8. There is certainly a psychological phenomenon at play here, whereby the angst of a lost mother is rearticulated in the nationalist idiom of a mother-nation. In a poem about Shivaji, involving his mother Jijabai, Savarkar had once projected the language of 'abused motherhood', 'the mother as cow, the earth as mother, both defiled by strange men'. See Janaki Bakhle, *Savarkar and the Making of Hindutva,* p. 288. Bhyrappa's novel *Orphaned*, titled quite uncannily, transposes the lost mother into the image of a sacred cow that demands protection from foreign defilers.
9. In his book *Being Different,* Rajiv Malhotra argues that *both* universal and contextual poles co-existed like a bifocal (as opposed to bipolar) lens within the Indian imagination, and that 'the highly contextualised path ultimately seeks freedom from all contexts'. His argument has poetic appeal, certainly, and he engages with Ramanujan's essay reasonably well, but he errs in his tendency to resolve all contradictions by subsuming them under a utopian sense of the pre-modern past—in a 'higher principle of unity', as he calls it. Such utopianism cannot really reckon with why caste and hierarchy became so deeply entrenched in Hindu society, and indeed, why they continue to be so.
10. R.L. Kashyap translates *rta* as *truth-in-movement*, which is appropriate to this chapter's theme of relentless self-discovery. *Vritti* means profession, and *kula* refers to clan/caste.
11. His English works are surprisingly unavailable in India. I had to ask my uncle returning from the US to fetch his book of essays, *The Indo-Anglian Creed and Other Essays*, and a collection of poems, *The Pretender and Other Poems.*
12. See introduction to Shree Purohit Swami's English translation of *Avadhoota Gita*, 1979.
13. Punekar seems to have derived this from the fact that brahmanical

philosophical debates sometimes involved such questions as whether a caste universal such as 'Brahman-ness' was the same as other universals like 'cow-ness', and so on. A great deal of mental energy seems to have been expended on such trivialities. See Wright, S. (2015). History in the Abstract: "Brahman-ness" and the Discipline of Nyāya in Seventeenth-Century Vārānasī. *Journal of Indian Philosophy*, 44(5), 1041–1069.

14. See Nathan McGovern, *The Snake and the Mongoose: The Emergence of Identity in Early Indian Religion.*
15. Wendy Doniger, *The Hindus: An Alternative History*, p. 384.
16. R.N. Nandi, 'The Boyas—Transformation of a Tribe Into Caste'.
17. S. Settar, *Halagannada: Lipi, Lipikaara, Lipivyavasaaya,* p. xxi.
18. Until the eighteenth century, the Chitpavans (or Konkanastha, which is a geographical marker of the same community) were held in low esteem by the Deshastha, the older established Brahmin community of the Karnataka-Maharashtra region.
19. This is a complex phenomenon, and we don't have much evidence regarding the actual lived experiences of caste society a thousand years ago. However, some recent scholarship has been shedding light on how exactly this 'othering' was carried out over the last few centuries. See Divya Cherian's *Merchants of Virtue: Hindus, Muslims, and Untouchables in Eighteenth-Century South Asia* for a scholarly exposition of how 'Hindu' identity was formulated with explicit contrast to 'untouchables' in pre-modern Mewar.
20. Raghavanka (Vanamala Vishwanatha, tr.), *The Life of Harishchandra*, Murthy Classical Library of India, p. 327.
21. 'Jogyora Anjappana Kolikathe' in S. Diwakar (ed.), *Shatamanada Sanna Kathegalu.*
22. See Johannes Bronkhorst, *How the Brahmins Won: From Alexander to the Guptas.*
23. Janaki Nair, *Modernity and 'Publicness': The Career of the Mysore Matha, 1880-1940*, p.14–15.
24. Karnataka Hindu Religious Institutions and Charitable Endowments Act, 1997.
25. Centuries ago, 'Sanskrit' essentially meant a more sophisticated form of the raw, indigenous language, 'Prakrit'. Malayalam is pervaded by Sanskrit like no other South Indian language.

26. The story is titled 'Octopus'.
27. The title of the autobiography, *Anudinada Antaragange* (The Inner Ganges of the Workaday), is taken from the lines of a Ramanujan poem, to which Pratibha had responded with another. Basically, to the question Ramanujan raises, *One may cross the Amazon / But how to cross the inner Ganges of the workaday?,* Pratibha responds: *By sweating profusely before this fever drops, everything inside must be released ...*
28. Pratibha posits the origin of Mahisha in the ancient cattle species known as Aurochs, whose most recent remains from present-day southern India were found at Banahalli in Karnataka, with an age of about 4,200 YBP. There are much more recent archaeological references to Mahisha as well. There is plenty of evidence to show that present-day Mysore was known as Mahisha-Mandala during Mauryan times, and that the region was also referred to as *Erumainadu (Bull-Land)* by Tamil Sangam poets many centuries later. See S. Settar's *Sangam Tamilagam Mattu Kannada Naadu Nudi*, p. 138.
29. Pratibha Nandakumar's talk is available at https://www.youtube.com/watch?v=A5U1kNs6iVw&t=2263s.
30. Mysore gets its name from Mahishasura, and its most famous geographical landmark is Chamundi Hill, on which a hallowed temple to the Goddess Chamundi sits proudly. Of late, excessive developmental activities on the hill have made for road collapses, traffic issues and ecological degradation. There has even been talk of a ropeway that is supposed to come up, which has faced flak from environmentalists.
31. See the chapter 'Goddesses and Gods in the Early Puranas' in Wendy Doniger, *The Hindus: An Alternative History.*
32. Pratibha Nandakumar, 'Ramachandra Guha fully deserves Rajyotsava Award, critics wrong in questioning his facility with Kannada', *Firstpost*, 1 November 2017.
33. Not unlike the revolutionary poet Sri Sri at the bandaya conference, as Prasanna describes in Chapter 1.

5. Lost in Translation

1. Sourced from Rahamath Tarikere, *Kannada Sahitya Vaagvadagalu*

(2019), p. 140. This is the most comprehensive and well-researched monograph on the subject I have been able to find.

2. Ibid., p. 143.
3. I have sourced these details from an essay by Siddalingaiah titled 'Boosa Prakarana: Nanna Anubhava' (Boosa Incident: My Experience), published in 1974 in the magazine *Panchaali* that was edited by P. Lankesh.
4. All of Siddalingaiah's poems have been gathered in a recent collection titled *Meravanige*, bearing an excellent foreword by D.R. Nagaraj, which he wrote sometime before his untimely death in 1998. Nagaraj had known Siddalingaiah through close association for more than two decades.
5. I have sourced these details from Baraguru Ramchandrappa's autobiography, *Kaage Karunyada Kannu*. He was the first president of the bandaya movement, and continued to remain associated with it until its dissolution.
6. I have drawn from Mandakini Purohit's PhD study of M.K. Indira's life and work, accessible at https://archive.org/details/bmshri.mkindirasamagraa0000drma_q2j8/page/n7/mode/2up.
7. See this AIR interview with M.K. Indira: https://www.youtube.com/watch?v=WC2_6nZxHIg&t=1515s.
8. Suganthy Krishnamachari, 'Soaring high with bhakti', *The Hindu*, 18 August 2011.
9. A fair number of Kannada books have been written after Lankesh's death in 2000, carrying personal reminiscences of a man who seemed to have shared a special love-hate relationship with his closest ones. Of these, Nataraj Huliyar's *Inti Namaskaragalu* is the most sympathetic, while the journalist N.K. Mohanram's *The Capital: Lankesh Private Limited* is the most critical (and hilarious).
10. *Lankesh Patrike*, 9 February 2000.
11. Chandan Gowda (ed.), *The Way I See It: A Gauri Lankesh Reader*, p. 247.
12. Ibid., p. 236.
13. See this report: https://www.youtube.com/watch?v=8dFKOKT_NOM.
14. See chapter 6, 'Language and the Right to the City' in Janaki Nair, *The Promise of the Metropolis*.

15. Jackie Assayag, *At the Confluence of Two Rivers*, p. 234
16. See Siddhartha Deb's essay 'Impossible Machines' in *Twilight Prisoners: The Rise of the Hindu Right and the Decline of India.*
17. One of six short stories in his wonderful collection titled *Huli Savaari.*
18. Vasudhendra's speech, where he makes this point, is at https://www.youtube.com/watch?v=FJqhLAq67ZA&t=619s.
19. They represent short, long and prolated vowels, respectively.

6. On Conversions, Controversies and Communalism

1. Richard Eaton, *The Sufis of Bijapur, 1300–1700*, p. 99.
2. G.T. Sathish, 'Datta Jayanti: Some visitors raise insensitive, provocative slogans atop Bababudangiri in Chikkamagaluru', *The Hindu*, 27 December 2023.
3. The word Muzrai derives from the Persian word 'Mujra' that means allocations or endowments, and refers to grants for religious and charitable purposes.
4. See the chapter on Baba Budan Giri in Yoginder Sikand, *Sacred Spaces: Exploring Traditions of Shared Faith in India.*
5. J. Nair, 'Modernity and "publicness": The career of the Mysore matha, 1880–1940'.
6. Rahamath Tarikere, *Karnatakada Sufigalu.*
7. 'Introduction' in Shri Purohit Swami (tr.), Shankar Mokashi Punekar (ed.), *Avadhoota Gita*, p. 11.
8. Rahamath Tarikere, *Karnatakada Gurupantha*, p. 147.
9. Manu V. Devadevan, *A Prehistory of Hinduism*, p. 91.
10. Yoginder Sikand, *Sacred Spaces: Exploring Traditions of Shared Faith in India*, p. 60.
11. See Linganna Kavi, R. Shama Shastry (ed.), *Keladinripa Vijaya.*
12. K.G. Vasantha Madhava, 'The Mughal and the Keladi Nayakas'.
13. See Rahamath Tarikere, *Kannada Sahitya Vagvadagalu.*
14. PTI, 'Same group behind killings of Dabholkar, Kalburgi, Gauri Lankesh; members linked to Sanatan Sanstha: Police', *Hindustan Times*, 16 September 2018.
15. *Sri Baragur Ramachandrappa & Ors vs State Of Karnataka & Ors*, 2007 (5) SCC 11, available at https://indiankanoon.org/doc/1494506/.

16. Janaki Bakhle, *Savarkar and the Making of Hindutva*, p. 131.
17. S.L. Bhyrappa, Sandeep Balakrishna (tr.), *Aavarana.*
18. S.L. Bhyrappa, *Saakshi-Parva.*
19. Jawaharlal Nehru, *Soviet Russia: Some Random Sketches and Impressions.*
20. A Savarkar bhakt who has translated his works into Kannada, Babu Krishnamurthy said a few years back, 'I wonder if all those who critique Savarkar are fit to live in India. The first qualification for any citizen is surrender to his motherland, to be obedient to this motherland.' His speech is available here: https://www.youtube.com/watch?v=OZXkzsDIlSc.
21. Richard Eaton's *India in the Persianate Age* is an excellent work of scholarship that breaks free of religious sectarianism and delves richly into this historical period.
22. Yoginder Sikand, *Sacred Spaces: Exploring Traditions of Shared Faith in India*, p. 66.
23. Shishir Gupta's *Indian Mujahideen* is a well-researched primer on the motivations of the organisation and its irreligious perpetrators who were responding to real (and imagined) threats to the Muslim community in the wake of the religious polarisation of the 1990s onwards.
24. Yoginder Sikand, *Sacred Spaces: Exploring Traditions of Shared Faith in India*, p. 66.
25. See Naveen Soorinje, *Nadu Baggisida Edeya Dani*, p. 70.
26. Rahamath Tarikere, *Karnatakada Sufigalu*, p. 11.
27. His book *Paapu Gandhi Gandhi Baapu Aada Kathe*, an accessible biography of Gandhi, won him his first award in the Children's Literature category. It was turned into a highly popular play by director Shripad Bhat, which toured schools in Karnataka and put on over 1,500 performances in 2019. The official numbers indicate that it reached over seven lakh people, and garnered praise from all quarters, not least schoolchildren themselves.
28. See Naveen Soorinje's story (in Kannada): https://pratidhvani.com/behind-the-udupi-college-student-video-controversy-is-a-story-of-harmony/.
29. Janaki Bakhle, *Savarkar and the Making of Hindutva*, p. 126.
30. 'Hamare Baarah and the myth of India's Muslim population "explosion"', *The Indian Express*, 26 June 2024.

31. B.A. Mohideen (adapted by Mohammad Kulayi and B.A. Mohammad Ali), *Nannolagina Naanu*.
32. See chapter 'A Social Reformer' in Janaki Bakhle, *Savarkar and the Making of Hindutva*.
33. https://indiankanoon.org/doc/393646/
34. The phrase comes from Malagatti's youth, when the stamp of caste on government papers would lead others to dub dalits as 'Government Brahmins'.
35. Muzaffar Assadi, 'Communal Violence in Coastal Belt', pp. 446–48.
36. See Greeshma Kuthar's May 2023 *Caravan* cover story, *All Santhosh's Men*.
37. The story goes that Kanakadasa, the sixteenth-century bard and folk-singer, arrived at the Krishna temple in Udupi, but was not allowed inside because of his low-caste birth. In response, Lord Krishna's idol had turned on its axis to face his devotee through a back window and granted him divine audience.
38. I have used Rahamath Tarikere's engrossing and moving essay 'Jailina Eradu Dina' (Two Days in Jail) as the primary source for the details of this incident. See *Dharma Pareekshe*, p. 132 onwards.

7. Spirits of the Past

1. A work of non-fiction titled *Bhugilu,* edited by Gopalakrishna Adiga amongst others, is an excellent resource that documents the underground resistance to the Emergency in Karnataka, carrying testimonies from a wide range of observers and writers.
2. E. Raghavan and James Manor, *Broadening and Deepening Democracy,* p. 104.
3. According to a study conducted by the University of Mysore in 2019, about 11,000 farmers died by suicide since 1996, and one of the main reasons was exorbitantly high interest rates on loans. In 2023, Siddaramaiah argued that, at the district level, applications for compensation were being stymied by inactive district administrations. See '251 farmers end lives in Karnataka since this April', *The New Indian Express*, 13 September 2023.
4. E. Raghavan and James Manor, *Broadening and Deepening Democracy,* p. 103.

5. In his 1976 novella *Bara* (Drought), Ananthamurthy presciently portrayed an idealistic civil service officer who ends up resorting to brutal police violence out of sheer desperation. The officer's deep disconnect with the land (as his socialist idealism cannot reconcile with the rough-hewn nature of local politics) becomes the leading cause of the disaster in the story.
6. Raghu Karnad's 2012 essay 'City in a Bottle', published in *The Caravan*, is an exceptionally well-researched history of the alcohol industry in Bangalore and its enormous impact on the life and culture of the city itself. It remains one of my all-time favourite pieces of longform journalism.
7. H.R. Basavarajappa, *Hasiru Haadiya Kathana*, p. 269.
8. I am grateful to Ramesh Aroli for forwarding me notable excerpts from his PhD study of *Lankesh Patrike*.
9. For a detailed study of Nanjundaswamy's life and political philosophy, see Savita B.C., *Hasirushaalu Baarukolu*.
10. His autobiography, *Hasiru Haadiya Kathana* (The Story of the Green Path), published in 2022, is an intimate account of the rise and fall of the Raitha Sangha.
11. Nagari Babaiah, Nataraj Huliyar (tr.), *Kaggatthala Jagattalli Tombattu Dina* (Ninety Days in the Depths of Hell).
12. Sukanya Shantha, 'From Segregation to Labour, Manu's Caste Law Governs the Indian Prison System', *The Wire*, 10 December 2020.
13. Wendel Berry, *What are People For?*
14. C.K. Manoj, 'Bihar scrapped APMC Act, mandi system 14 years ago; here's what it did to farmers', *Down to Earth*, 7 December 2020.
15. 'Farmers' protests not limited to Delhi: South Indian farmers oppose Union govt claim', *The News Minute*, 12 January 2021.
16. Anitha Pailoor, 'Soil crisis: Yields, dreams turn to dust', *Deccan Herald*, 26 March, 2023.
17. See this video testimony (in Kannada): https://www.youtube.com/watch?v=9Jir2JKLlfk.
18. Chinnaswami Vaddagere, *Banagarada Manushyaru: Belakina Besayada Kathana* (Golden Men: Leading Lights of Farming).
19. See chapter ten in Meera Nanda's *Prophets Facing Backwards* for thought-provoking reflections on this theme.
20. Poornachandra Tejaswi. *Vimarsheya Vimarshe*. p. 35.

21. See Sugata Srinivasaraju, *Furrows in the Field.*
22. I caught a glimpse of this history of objectification within the genealogical nomenclature of my own family, encapsulated in the term *koti* + *kanya* + *daanam* (innumerable bride charities), which fell out of vogue only by the time of my generation. Google tells me there are twenty-six individuals still bearing this clan name today.
23. See the chapter 'The Evolution of Patriarchy' in Suvira Jaiswal, *The Making of Brahmanic Hegemony.*
24. See chapter 'Goddesses and Gods in the Early Puranas' in Wendy Doniger, *Hindus: An Alternative History.*
25. One may take inspiration from the tiny region of Rojava in Northern Syria, home to the Kurdish people's movement, where a grassroots revolution championing direct democracy, feminism and secular egalitarianism has been thriving even as it is staving off attacks from NATO-allied Turkey. It is the brave members of this very revolution who had also defeated an enemy as repugnant as ISIS, with America as its ally in the fight. Since then, the purportedly largest democracy has only been interested in shoring up oil-support and exacerbating civil war, and has completely ignored the revolution in Rojava, which is a unique and watershed event that is trying to uphold anti-capitalist ecological principles in the heart of the oil-world, championing feminism and democracy in a desert of dictators and patriarchs.
26. Devajana C. Nanjunda and Pulamaghatta N. Venugopal, 'Boundaries of Contagion: The Unheard Plight of Sex Workers in Karnataka'.
27. It is indeed similar to the trope of the wronged and harassed woman who features as a sympathy-figure in all the major oral Kannada folk epics - Male Madeshwara, Junjappa and Manteswamy in South Karnataka, Halumata Purana in the North. While women do get a voice in these traditions that is denied to them in more 'classical' ones, the institution of feudal patriarchy remains essentially unchallenged, if not reinforced.
28. It is with respect to this that M.M. Kalburgi's argument—that Veerashaivism had successfully transposed the idea of a debt to the divine into the idea of a debt to society (as opposed to men) during the twelfth century—becomes important.
29. These inscriptions were specifically associated with the Kaalamukha sect, and make for arresting reading. An inscription from the year

1124 narrates to great effect the story of a heroic philanthropist named Bommagavunda. We are given to understand that his desire to offer an endowment to the Brahmeshwara temple of Abbaluru was stronger than the desire to unite with his wife. He mounts his horse and declares that he will donate as much land as the galloping horse covers. Then, he offers worship to the holy feet of the Kaalamukha guru, Jnanashakti, and donates the land to him. Charity was also considered essential for purification of social stigma, and for spiritual renunciation too.

30. The birth place of Allama, now in Shikaripura taluka of Shimoga district in central Karnataka.
31. See chapter 6 in D.R. Nagaraj, *Allama Prabhu Mattu Shaiva Pratibhe*.
32. For an analysis of infrastructure building vs social protections, see Gaurav Mukherjee, 'How Hindutva is reshaping India's classrooms', *Scroll*, 1 May 2024.
33. Documentary available at https://www.youtube.com/watch?v=YgbzD0Oad1U&t=2244s.
34. A mythological king from the epics who is famed for his generosity.

8. On Caste, Cultural Activism and Children

1. Common critiques of caste-hostels include the one that argues that they should never have been limited by caste in the first place, and should have included everyone. The poet N.K. Hanumanthaiah writes of a no-caste hostel he lived in during his school years (sometime in the eighties), which truly carried a sense of emancipation and dissolved barriers. However, such a possibility seems to have been difficult to conceive in the early years of Indian independence, thanks to the sheer omniscience of caste-based segregation.
2. He sang one line of it for me. 'Koti koti baadhegalalli, lakshantara novugalalli, nee hutti belade, nanna tangi anasuya' (*Amidst a million adversities, and innumerable traumas, you grew up, my little sister Anasuya*).
3. Thankful to Dr A.R. Mitra for uploading a reading of this lovely poem with a wonderful commentary, online: https://www.youtube.com/watch?v=b-YpnegpE3s&t=315s.
4. Interestingly, the revolutionary Telugu balladeer Gaddar had also been

a clerk at Canara Bank in Kondapalli. Ramaiah, too, worked at Canara Bank for a brief period, before he quit and turned towards journalism.

5. D.R. Nagaraj, *Flaming Feet and Other Essays*, p.77.
6. In the 1940s, Kuvempu wrote a play titled *Shudra Tapaswi*, based on this incident from the Ramayana. The synopsis of the story is as follows. A brahmin's son dies. The brahmin believes that this is because a shudra has been performing penance, which he had no right to. He takes the matter to Rama. Rama quells this shudra—whose name is Shambuka—and this brings the brahmin's son back to life. In Kuvempu's play however, Rama's arrow refuses to hit Shambuka, and turns around to hit the brahmin. Rama is forced to recant his weapon.
7. In his recent biography of Ambedkar, scholar Anand Teltumbde traces this twin tendency to Ambedkar himself. After quoting some of Ambedkar's questionable statements from the 1950s, he makes a startling and provocative argument: 'This crude caricature of communists and socialists is not unsurprising from him. What is surprising is his silence on the Hindu fundamentalists—RSS and Hindu Mahasabha—who condemned it outright and who were a much bigger threat to the Constitution than the communists and socialists combined in those days. Such prejudiced comments coming from him have filled Dalits with hatred for the Left and eased their move to serve the Brahminic forces to bring about a Hindu Rashtra.' See Iconoclast, p. 453.
8. Huccha (Madman) Venkat is a film producer and actor who believes (modern medical diagnoses would deem it schizophrenia) he is the leader of a global army of fan-followers that he has dubbed the Huccha Venkat Sene. He has been magnanimously embraced by the Kannada showbiz landscape.
9. Already, in 1970, the Hindu-nationalist Shiv Sena had fomented religious riots in Bhiwandi, where 250 people (predominantly Muslims) perished.
10. In 1968, the radical Ambedkarite B. Shyam Sundar (who had rejected the non-violence of Buddhism) launched the Bhim Sena in the North Karnataka district of Kalaburagi, which sought to violently reshape feudal India. Within a decade it spread across the region, and was brutally crushed by the state for its radical streaks. Congress

leader Mallikarjun Kharge was a part of the Bhim Sena briefly in his youth, after which his Buddhist leanings pulled him out of the violent organisation and led him to join the Congress. See Sudipto Mondal, 'Mallikarjun Kharge's Ism: An Ambedkarite manifesto for the Modi years', *The News Minute*, 18 April 2024.

11. The separation of history and myth is usually performed on the fact-fiction axis, and some recent scholarship has argued that such a divorce is unhelpful in understanding early modern India, where history and literature become quite inseparable, where 'all is discourse, internal to language itself.' See *Textures of Time*, written by Velcheru Narayan Rao, David Shulman, and Sanjay Subrahmanyam.
12. The cosmic egg is a motif that is actually as old as the Vedas and the Upanishads. The complex interplay of Vedic and Non-Vedic traditions is one we are yet to understand fully. When the English translator of the Male Mahadeshwara epic, CN Ramachandran, was interviewing a prominent singer named Hebbani Madayya, he heard some matrimonial suggestions regarding the four types of men and women and how they must be paired suitably, first noted by Vatsyayana in the Kamasutra, which had somehow percolated into the unlettered balladeer's imagination too. The epic itself contains diverse references to cultural markers like the Ramayana, Lord Venkateshwara of Tirupati, the brahmins of Kashi, Allama Prabhu and the sharana movement, and so on. Oral epics like Male Mahadeshwara were collected, written down, and translated after the 1970s, and these texts seem like a palimpsest of cultural influences - in some, the British also feature as characters who are warded off by the epic's hero.
13. M.V. Devadevan, *A Prehistory of Hinduism*, p. 117–8.
14. Meera Nanda's 2002 book *Prophets Facing Backward* makes this same argument in dense detail, scrutinising the postmodernist relativism of scholars like Ashis Nandy and Partha Chatterjee, and comparing them with the rhetoric of decolonisation and Vedic science that has animated the Hindu right's intellectual oeuvre since then. Ananthamurthy's search for non-Western models of morality traces a similarly complex trajectory.
15. D.V. Gundappa, *Rajakeeya Prasangagalu—1,* p. 25.

16. Listen to Chinnaswamy Sosale here: https://www.youtube.com/watch?v=-3Fj9qZh988&t=965s.
17. Safdar Hashmi was brutally murdered by Congress goons in 1989.
18. Kunal Purohit's book *H-Pop* is a riveting and troubling account of this burgeoning mediascape.
19. You can view the interview with Uma Mahadevan Dasgupta here: https://www.youtube.com/watch?v=i81l1ONOwD0&t=1181s
20. R.K. Narayan, *A Writer's Nightmare*, p. 65.

9. The Marxist Library of Mysore

1. It is titled *Sooladi Bando Tirutirugi*.
2. Giraddi Govindaraj, 'The Kannada Scene: A Year of Big Projects'.
3. Another fabrication I heard many times was that Siddalingaiah had once dubbed the BJP politician B.S. Yeddiyurappa a modern 'Basavanna', while in fact it was someone else who had done so.
4. Puligere was Pampa's hometown.
5. Nataraj Huliyar's *Inti Namaskaragalu* is a warm recollection of the author's years spent with two of his foremost gurus—Lankesh and D.R. Nagaraj—full with interesting quotations as this one.
6. From S.L. Bhyrappa's *Grihabhanga* and Kum Veerabhadrappa's *Kappu*, to the young writers presently showcasing harrowing tales of how society collectively murders the dreams and aspirations of its women, Kannada literature has continued to reflect on a subject that has firmly refused to become a cliché.
7. An unusual and important document on untouchability in Karnataka, edited by Kotiganahalli Ramaiah.
8. For a historical explanation of the origins of left-right castes, see Chapter 1, note 37.
9. See *Cultures Differ Differently: Selected Essays of S.N. Balagangadhara*.
10. See J. Sai Deepak's *India, That Is Bharat.* Seeking some pure 'Indic' consciousness that predates the arrival of Islam and Christianity, the book flounders in its historical inquiry and fails to show us what it is really searching for. By defining this object of inquiry as the antithesis of everything it abhors, it falls into a self-imposed essentialist trap that is impossible to escape.
11. This story is interestingly preserved in reverse form in the Kannada

oral epic Junjappa, the last section of which has nothing to do with the titular hero Junjappa, but rather narrates an unrelated Vaishnava legend about the love of Venkatramana (a form of Vishnu) for a Muslim girl named Sel Boobi. The assimilation of this tale also signifies a moment in history when the Kaadu Golla (the cowherds of the forests) community, with whom the epic is primarily associated, embraced Vaishnavism, sometime after the twelfth century.

10. Two Rivers Diverged in a Wood

1. Award winning cop convicted for assaulting wife', Bangalore Mirror, 3 June 2011.
2. Bernard D'Mello, *India After Naxalbari*, p. 39.
3. Dilip Simeon's *Revolution Highway* is an excellent novelistic portrayal of a generation of youth driven by Maoist ideals, and of the fiery historical times that made it possible.
4. Chidanand Rajghatta, *Illiberal India*.
5. The report of the fact-finding team is available here: http://www.unipune.ac.in/snc/cssh/humanrights/06%20STATE%20INDUSTRY%20AND%20WORKERS/08.pdf.
6. In a curious twist of history, Shukla perished in a Naxal ambush in Chhattisgarh, in 2013.
7. Madhu Bhushan, 'Of mourning and memories: Reconnecting with Gauri', *The News Minute*, 8 September 2017.
8. John Sturrock, Harold A Stuart (eds.), 'South Canara', *Gazetteer of India*.
9. Muzaffar Assadi, "Kudremukh: Of Mining and Environment."
10. The renewed General Agreement on Tariffs and Trade, or GATT, signed by the Indian government in 1994, was aimed at further liberalising trade in goods through the reduction of tariffs and other trade barriers. It enabled multinational companies to entrench themselves in the country, and set up large industrial complexes.
11. As articulated by Cherukuri Rajkumar.
12. Saketh S. Rajan, 'Commercialisation of Forest and its Impact on the Soliga Tribes, Biligiri Rangan Hills'.
13. See Erica Chenoweth and Maria Stephan, *Why Civil Resistance Works: The Strategic Logic of Nonviolent Conflict*.

14. I heard from Murali Uncle (who features in chapter 8) that Saketh had stayed with him, in incognito mode, for a few weeks at his home near Bangalore. Murali came to know who he was only later, and remembers him as a quiet man who stuck to his books.
15. The polymath Marxist who wrote *An Introduction to the Study of Indian History*.
16. Dr Vijay Thambanda's lecture is available here (in Kannada): https://www.youtube.com/watch?v=fA-BHXxKlm8&t=385s.
17. See Abdullah Öcalan, *The Political Thought of Abdullah Öcalan*, Pluto Press.
18. For instance, the activist Gita Ramaswamy records in her memoirs that when she married her husband Cyril Reddy, it too was a marriage founded on ideological affinity rather than romantic desire.
19. Gauri Lankesh, 'In Death, A Star's Dawn' in *The Way I See It: A Gauri Lankesh Reader*.
20. Gauri Lankesh, *The Way I See It: A Gauri Lankesh Reader*. p. 175.
21. Muzaffar Assadi, 'Forest Encroachments, Left Adventurism and Hindutva'.
22. Mahendra Kumar, *Nadu Baggisida Edeya Dani*, p. 93–94.
23. The ordeal was the inspiration for the 2023 Kannada film *19.20.21*, directed by Manso Re. When I went to watch the film in a theatre in Mangalore, the showing was cancelled because there were less than five interested viewers. I ended up watching it a year later, when it released on Prime Video.
24. A 2011 paper reported: 'The Western Ghats is one of the major repositories of medicinal plants. It harbours around 4,000 species of higher plants, of which 450 species are threatened. Currently, the number of species added to the red list category in this region is increasing, and the valuable genetic resources are being lost at a rapid rate. Demand for medicinal plants is increasing, and this leads to unscrupulous collection from the wild and adulteration of supplies. Providing high-quality planting material for sustainable use and thereby saving the genetic diversity of plants in the wild is important.': Peringattulli Narayanan Krishnan & S.W. Decruse & R.K. Radha, *Conservation of medicinal plants of Western Ghats, India and its sustainable utilization through in vitro technology*.
25. Ishita Mishra, 'The burning hills of Uttarakhand', *The Hindu*, 18 May 2024.

11. Forests, Conservation and the Ecology of Change

1. A 1990 PhD study of the Basavi system in the Kurnool district concluded that: 'The latest dimension of Basavi system in Karnataka is the engulfing of commercial prostitution which facilitates the Basavis, especially those of Scheduled Caste to become prostitutes providing sexual intercourse for men, not necessarily of their own or upper castes. Consequently, they do not enjoy the same high social esteem that they once had in the closed circle of a village. Hence sporadic attempts have been made right from 1892 for the eradication of this social evil through legislative measures.' See J. Sujana Mallika's PhD thesis on Shodhganga, 'Basavi system in Andhra Pradesh with special reference to Kurnool district',
2. From Sumateendra Nadig (ed.), *Gopalakrishna Adigara Patragalu*.
3. Communist veteran B.V. Kakkilaya's autobiography *Bareyada Dinachari Mareyada Putagalu* is a good primer on the trajectory of working class movements in Karnataka.
4. Sadanand Kanwalli notes in his book *Quest for Justice* that though they had an effluent treatment plant worth Rs 2.3 crores, they never ran it as it cost Rs 37,000 every day to do so.
5. For a rich and detailed study of environmental movements of the 1970s and '80s, and their relationship with Indian society and politics, see Madhav Gadgil and Ramachandra Guha, *Ecology and Equity: The Use and Abuse of Nature in India*.
6. Some of the essays in the book *Shatamanada Kusuma*, especially one by K.V. Subbanna, seem highly hagiographical and exaggerated. However, they must be taken with a pinch of sympathy, as they stand as a heartfelt tribute to a woman who died much too soon, and showcase the immense respect and affection that this 'thin, slender woman of thirty kilos' had commanded during her storied life.
7. With seven dams over it, the Sharavati river contributes 40 per cent of the hydroelectric power in the state. In 1987, a group of 1,500 activists demonstrated against the Sharavati Tailrace project, which was proposed to tap the tailrace discharges from the Sharavati power station and the Mahatma Gandhi Hydro Electric Project through the construction of a fifty-eight–metre–long dam across the river. They argued that fixing inefficient power lines was enough to secure the small rise in power generation that the project would produce. There

was also fear that an infectious disease transmitted by monkeys, called the Kyasanoor Forest Disease, would appear again if forests were cut down. Legal petitions and stays from the High Court followed and in 1995, a Swamiji of a local matha was also roped in to amplify the cause. The State argued that hydroelectric power was comparatively cleaner, and that the forest loss was minimal. After almost a decade, the project was successfully completed.

8. In February 2024, the Supreme Court ordered the Centre to use the 'dictionary meaning' of forest, which would bring back 1.97 lakh square kms of forest land into purview.
9. Tapasya and Nitin Sethi, 'A hollow assurance: How Modi govt turned its back on forest conservation', Reporters' Collective, 19 September 2023.
10. Chiranjeevi Kulkarni, 'Days after complaining of scam, Karnataka State Pollution Control Board's member secretary ousted', *Deccan Herald*, 17 July 2023.
11. Decades later, conservationist Ullas Karanth employed remotely activated sensor-based cameras to conduct more accurate tiger censuses.
12. Neginhal's autobiography *Memoirs of an Ardent Wildlifer* belongs to that quaint genre of administrative memoirs which are simply written, but always spirited and humorous.
13. I was also reminded of how deeply the sense of the divine can become dovetailed with a love for nature while reading Pamela Gale Malhotra's book, *From the Heart of Nature*, which is an account of how she and her husband created a private wildlife sanctuary in Coorg by regenerating barren land and converting it, over two decades, into a lush 300-acre forest where tigers, elephants, and umpteen other species of animals and birds now live. Throughout the book, god, divinity and nature become synonymous with each other.
14. The book contains local names of trees in numerous South Indian languages, and so you can refer to the local name in the index and be directed to the scientific description in an instant.
15. Puneeth Rajkumar passed away in 2021 at the tragically young age of forty-six, and lakhs of fans thronged to his funeral to pay their respects to an actor who was much beloved.
16. Environmentalists have scathingly critiqued Sadhguru and Isha

Foundation's Cauvery Calling campaign, which sought to plant thousands of trees along the banks of the river. They argued that planting rows of trees is a simplistic solution that when overdone can have unintended, destructive consequences like drying up streams and other bodies of water, and disrupting wildlife habitats.

17. Abhilash Pavuluri, 'Elephants in the Room', *FiftyTwo*, 21 January 2023.
18. This study has been pioneered by the Ashoka Trust for Research in Ecology and the Environment, a conservation non-profit based out of Bangalore.
19. See Madhav Gadgil's paper "Western Ghats Ecology Expert Panel: A Play in Five Acts" for a detailed explanation of the committee's recommendations as well as the response that it garnered.
20. Nitin Sethi, 'Western Ghats reports have an ugly side', *The Reporter's Collective,* 16 August 2024.
21. Shobha Warrier, 'The Kasturirangan Report is a disaster for the Western Ghats', *Rediff*, 30 December 2013.
22. As articulated in *The Hindu*, December 18, 2023, by Sharachchandra Lele, a Distinguished Fellow at the Ashoka Trust for Research in Ecology and the Environment.
23. See this report on the impact of the *Prosopis juliflora*: https://www.youtube.com/watch?v=5MW8QRBke6w.
24. The Amrit Mahal is a South Indian cattle breed. They were used by Chikka Devaraya Wodeyar in the late seventeenth century, upon whose instructions a portion of land had been tasked with the express purpose of producing milk and butter for the royal house. Haider Ali and Tipu Sultan dedicated vast tracts of semi-arid grasslands, spread across the state, to rearing these cattle, which they used to carry weapons across long distances. At the time of independence, the state had nearly 400,000 acres of Amrit Mahal Kavals, which have dwindled to less than 30,000 acres presently, which are also in varied degrees of degradation.
25. Bhabha Atomic Research Centre, Defence Research and Development Organisation, Indian Space Research Organisation, Indian Institute of Science.
26. See Jason Hickel's *Less is More: How Degrowth Will Save the World* for a lucid delineation of the idea.

27. P. Samuel Jonathan, 'The Agony of Stuartpuram', *The Hindu*, 25 November 2017.

12. Cultures of Insecurity

1. The Greek economist Yanis Varoufakis's *Techno-feudalism* is a disturbingly lucid book that delineates his long-standing theory that capitalism has effectively been taken over by the techno-feudal, rent-extracting monopolies that are reorganising the global sphere through virtual cloud-capital.
2. The months-long strike by Hollywood screenwriters, and slowly mushrooming rebellion against the oppressive work regime in Amazon warehouses are a couple of notable examples.
3. Rahul Ramagundam, *The Life and Times of George Fernandes*, p. 161.
4. Jyoti Shelar's *The Bhais of Bengaluru* is a fun dive into the days of the Bangalore underworld. Also Agni Shreedhar's *My Days in the Underworld*.
5. This also corroborates Bridget White's observations in her book *Kolar Gold Mines: Down Memory Lane*, where she writes about the unions and how the end of KGF can at least partly be attributed to their internal rivalries, which the Indian government used to its advantage, playing one union against another.
6. M.A. Sreenivasan records in his autobiography, *Of the Raj, Maharajas and Me*, his experiences in engaging with workers at KGF, a dominant chunk of whom were Tamil migrants: 'Tamilians are, in general, good workers. They are also a canny, cheerful lot, with an incurable itch to invent epigrams, compose and sing instant ballads on every exciting topic.'
7. See Janaki Nair's painstakingly detailed study of KGF—*Miners and Millhands: Work, Culture and Politics in Princely Mysore*.
8. Akkai Padmashali, *A Small Step in a Long Journey: A Memoir*.
9. Sudipto Mondal, 'Bengaluru's Bangladeshi labourers should be proud; the shame is ours', *The Federal,* 12 November 2019.
10. Bhargabi Ghosh and Harshika Tripathi. 'A Journey from Barpeta to Lucknow: The Plight of Waste-Pickers in the City.' Policy and Development Advisory Group Blog, February 19, 2024.

11. This history has been comprehensively documented in Du Saraswati's PhD thesis titled 'Community Under Siege: Socio Cultural Study of Safai Karmacharis in Karnataka from a Feminist Perspective'. It is available on the Shodhganga website. I have sourced/corroborated all details of the pourakarmika movement in Karnataka from this text.
12. See chapter 6 in Du Saraswati's PhD thesis.
13. Prajwal Bhat, Theja Ram. "No pay for 6 months: Why Bengaluru's civic workers are being denied salaries." *The Newsminute.* 9 July, 2018.
14. Balakrishnan, Sai, and Narendar Pani, 'Real estate politicians in India'.
15. Published in *Lankesh Patrike*, 4 August 1991. Retrieved from *Hosa Vicharagalu,* pp. 3–4.
16. B.R. Patil, 'A Contemporary Industrial Relations Scenario in India: With Reference to Karnataka'.

Coda

1. From the excellent online dictionary *alar.ink*.
2. An interesting play on multiple meanings. 'Bayaludore' can mean either mirage (water in a barren field) or simply a landlord. These dynamics are characteristic of Adiga's multi-directional wordplays.

Select Bibliography

Aboobacker, Sara. *Chandragiri Teeradalli (Kannada).* Chandragiri Prakashana, 2023.

Adiga, Gopalakrishna. (ed. Jayarama Adiga) *Vaicharika Lekhana Vachike (Kannada).* Kannada Pustaka Pradhikara, 2021.

———. *Kannadada Abhimana Mattu Itara Lekhanagalu (Kannada).* Akshara Prakashana, 1972.

———. Seshadri, H.V. (eds.) *Bhugilu*. Rashtrotthana Sahitya, 1977.

Ananthamurthy, U.R. (tr. Narayan Hegde) *Avasthe*. HarperCollins, 2020.

———. (tr. Chandan Gowda) *Bara*. Oxford University Press, 2016.

———. (tr. Susheela Punitha) *Bharathipura.* Oxford University Press, 2010.

———. (tr. A.K. Ramanujan) *Samskara.* Oxford University Press, 2015.

———. *Bhava (Kannada).* Akshara Prakashana, 2014.

———. *Valmikiya Nevadalli (Kannada).* Abhinava, 2009.

———. *Divya (Kannada).* Akshara Prakashana, 2017.

———. (tr. S.R. Ramakrishna) *Suragi.* Oxford University Press, 2018.

———. *Prajne Mattu Parisara (Kannada).* Ankita Pustaka, 2011.

———. *Himseya Eda-Bala (Kannada).* Abhinava, 2007.

Aradhya, S.R. *Kayaka Jeevigala Kanmani: Comrade Suri (Kannada).* Kannada Pustaka Pradhikara, 2017.

Assadi, Muzaffar. 'Communal Violence in Coastal Belt'. *Economic and Political Weekly*, 34, No. 8, 1999.

———. 'Kudremukh: Of Mining and Environment'. *Economic and Political Weekly*, 37, No. 49, 2002.

Assayag, Jackie. *At the Confluence of Two Rivers: Muslims and Hindus in South India*. Manohar, 2004.

Awad, Eknath (tr. Jerry Pinto). *Strike a Blow to Change the World.* Speaking Tiger, 2018.

Babaiah, Nagari. *Kaggatala Jagattalli Tombattu Dina (Kannada).* Lankesh Prakashana, 2016.

Bai, K. Sumitra. *Soolaadi Bandoo Tirutirugi (Kannada).* Abhiruchi Prakashana, 2021.

Bakhle, Janaki. *Savarkar and the Making of Hindutva*. Princeton University Press, 2024.

Balagangadhara, S.N. *Cultures Differ Differently: Selected Essays of S.N. Balagangadhara*. Taylor & Francis, 2021.

Balakrishnan, S., Pani, N. 'Real estate politicians in India'. *Urban Studies*, 58(10), 2079–2094, 2021.

Ballal, Vyasaraya. *Bandaya (Kannada).* Kannada Sahitya Parishattu, 2015.

Banavasi, Shridhara 'Fakeera'. *Beru (Kannada).* Panchami Media, 2017.

Barzun, Jacques. *The Use and Abuse of Art*. Princeton University Press, 2020.

Basavarajappa, H.R. (ed. Girish Talikatte, K.L. Ashok). *Hasiru Haadiya Kathana (Kannada).* Gauri Media Trust, 2022.

Ben-Herut, Gil. *Śiva's Saints: The Origins of Devotion in Kannada according to Harihara's Ragaḷegaḷu*. Oxford University Press, 2018.

Berry, Wendell. *What Are People For?*. Catapult, 2010.

Bhardwaj, Ashutosh. *The Death Script: Dreams and Delusions in Naxal Country*. HarperCollins, 2020.

Bhyrappa, S.L. (tr. Sandeep Balakrishna) *Orphaned*. Rupa, 2019.

———. *Aavarana (Kannada).* Sahitya Bhandara Prakashana, 2007.

———. *Saartha (Kannada).* Sahitya Bhandara Prakashana, 2021.

———. *Sakshi-Parva (Kannada).* Sahitya Bhandara Prakashana, 2016.

———. (trs. S. Ramaswamy, L.V. Shanthakumari) *Bhitti.* Prism Books, 2021.

———. *Daatu (Kannada).* Sahitya Bhandara Prakashana, 2000.

———. (tr. L.V. Shanthakumari) *Grihabhanga.* Rupa, 2019.

———. (tr. Sushma Chandrashekhar) *Vamshavriksha.* Affiliated East-West Press, 1995.

Bilimate, Purushottama. *Bandaya-Dalita Chaluvali Mattu Sahitya (Kannada).* Abhinava, 2017.

Bockman, Johanna. *Markets in the Name of Socialism: The Left-Wing Origins of Neoliberalism*. Stanford University Press, 2011.

Branigan, Tania. *Red Memory: The Afterlives of China's Cultural Revolution*. W.W. Norton & Company, 2023.

Bronkhorst, Johannes. *How the Brahmins Won: From Alexander to the Guptas*. BRILL, 2016.

Nanjunda, D.C., and P.N. Venugopal. 'Boundaries of Contagion: The Unheard Plight of Sex Workers in Karnataka'. *Journal of the Anthropological Survey of India*, 69(1), 33–46. 2020.

Carse, James. *Finite and Infinite Games*. Simon and Schuster, 2011.

Carstairs, M.G., and R.L. Kapur. *The Great Universe of Kota: Stress, Change, and Mental Disorder in an Indian Village*. University of California Press, 1976.

Chandrika, P. (ed.) *Yaara Japtigoo Sigada Navilugalu (Kannada)*. Abhinava, 2022.

Chenni, Rajendra. *Samskrutika Rajakeeya: Indina Itihasa (Kannada)*. Abhiruchi Prakashana, 2023.

Chenoweth, Erica, and Maria J. Stephan. *Why Civil Resistance Works: The Strategic Logic of Nonviolent Conflict*. Columbia University Press, 2011.

Cherian, Divya. *Merchants of Virtue: Hindus, Muslims, and Untouchables in Eighteenth-Century South Asia*. University of California Press, 2022.

Chinnaswamy, Mudnakudu. *Dalit Cosmos: Understanding Caste, Marginalisation and Dalit Literature in India*. Routledge, 2023.

Chittal, Yashwant. (tr. Pratibha Nadiger) *Shikari: The Hunt*. Penguin, 2017.

Crasta, Richard. *The Revised Kamasutra*. Penguin, 1994.

Dalrymple, William. *The Golden Road: How Ancient India Transformed the World*. Bloomsbury, 2024.

Deb, Siddhartha. *Twilight Prisoners: The Rise of the Hindu Right and the Fall of India*. Westland, 2024.

Derla, Narendra Rai. *Advitiya: Sheena Shetty-Krishna Moolya Sevakathana*. Aakruti Aashaya Publications, 2022.

Derrett, J. Duncan M. *The Hoysalas: A Medieval Indian Royal Family*. Oxford University Press, 1957.

Desai, Dinkar. *Dinakarana Chaupadi (Kannada)*. Kannada Sahitya Parishattu, 2017.

Desai, Shantinath. *Mukti (Kannada)*. Sapna Book House, 2023.

Deepak, J. Sai. *India, That Is Bharat: Coloniality, Civilisation, Constitution*. Bloomsbury, 2021.

Deshpande, Sudhanva. *Halla Bol: The Death and Life of Safdar Hashmi*. LeftWord, 2020.

Devadevan, Manu V. *A Prehistory of Hinduism*. Walter de Gruyter, 2016.

Dharampal. *The Beautiful Tree: Indigenous Indian Education in the Eighteenth Century.* Other India Press, 2000.

Divakar, S. (ed.) *Shatamanada Sanna Kathegalu (Kannada)*. Prism Books, 1997.

D'Mello, Bernard. *India After Naxalbari*. Aakar Books, 2018.

Doniger, Wendy. *The Hindus: An Alternative History*. Penguin Press, 2009.

Durant, Will., Durant, Ariel. *The Lessons of History.* Simon & Schuster, 2012.

Eagleton, Terry. *Culture and the Death of God*. Yale University Press, 2014.

Eaton, Richard M. *India in the Persianate Age: 1000–1765*. Penguin, 2019.

———. *The Sufis of Bijapur, 1300-1700: Social Roles of Sufis in Medieval India*. Princeton University Press, 2015.

———. *Temple Desecration and Muslim States in Medieval India.* Hope India Publications, 2004.

Einoo, Shingo. *Genesis and Development of Tantrism*. Institute of Oriental Culture, University of Tokyo, 2008.

Gadgil, Madhav, and Ramachandra Guhar. *Ecology and Equity: The Use and Abuse of Nature in Contemporary India*. Routledge, 2013.

———. *This Fissured Land, An Ecological History of India.* Oxford University Press, 2021.

Gale-Malhotra, Pamela. *From the Heart of Nature*. Penguin, 2022.

Ganeri, Jonardon. *The Lost Age of Reason: Philosophy in Early Modern India 1450-1700*. Oxford University Press, 2011.

Ganesh, Shatavadhani R. (trs. Sandeep Balakrishna, Hari Ravikumar). *Ksattra: The Tradition of Valour in India.* Prekshaa Pratishtana, 2023.

Ganesh, Mogalli. *Kannimale: Kathegalu.* Ankita Pustaka, 2010.

Gidla, Sujatha. *Ants Among Elephants: An Untouchable Family and the Making of Modern India*. Macmillan, 2017.

Gokak, Vinayak Krishna. *Bendre: Poet and Seer*. Somaiya Publications, 1970.

Gouramma, Kodagina. (tr. Deepa Bhasthi) *Fate's Game and Other Stories.* Yoda Press, 2023.

Govindaraj, Giraddi. 'The Kannada Scene: A Year of Big Projects'. *Indian Literature*, Vol. 30, No. 6 (122), pp. 79–92. 1987.

Gowda, Chandan. *Another India: Events, Memories, People.* Simon & Schuster, 2023.

Graeber, David. *Debt: The First 5,000 Years*. Melville House, 2014.
Guevara, Ernesto Che. *The Bolivian Diary*. HarperCollins, 2009.
Guha, Ramachandra. *An Anthropologist Among the Marxists and Other Essays*. Permanent Black, 2001.
———. *India After Gandhi*. Pan Macmillan, 2008.
Gundappa, D.V. *Rajakeeya Prasangagalu – 1 (Kannada)*. Sahitya Prakashana, 2021.
———. (trs. Malathi Rangaswamy, Hari Ravikumar) *Foggy Fool's Farrago*. W.I.S.E. Words, 2016.
Gupta, Shishir. *Indian Mujahideen*. Hachette, 2012.
Harave, Devaiah. *Dalita Sahithya Mattu Itara Lekhanagalu (Kannada)*. Kannada Sahitya Parishattu, 2015.
Hardikar, Jaideep. *Ramrao: The Story of India's Farm Crisis*. HarperCollins, 2021.
Hariharan, Githa. *In Times of Siege*. Penguin, 2019.
Hasan, Roopa. *Mahasangrami: S.R. Hiremath Avara Rachanatmaka Prayogagala Balkathana (Kannada)*. Abhiruchi Prakashana, 2023.
Hebbar, K.K. *The Singing Line*. Abhinav Publications, 1982.
Hegde, Kalkulli Vittal. *Mangana Byaate (Kannada)*. Vilina Prakashana, 2012.
Hegde, Nagesh, and Sharada Gopal (eds.) *Shatamanada Kusuma: Dr Kusuma Soraba Avara Jeevana Darshana (Kannada)*. Akshara Prakashana, 1999.
Hickel, Jason. *Less Is More: How Degrowth Will Save the World*. Random House, 2020.
Hiremath, S.R. (ed.) *Forest Lands and Forest Produce as if People Mattered*. Samaja Parivartana Samudaya, 1997.
Huliyar, Nataraj. *Inti Namaskaragalu (Kannada)*. Pallava Prakashana, 2015.
———. *Shantaveri Gopalagowda (Kannada)*. National Book Trust, 2018.
———. (ed.) *Hasiru Senani (Kannada)*. Pallava Prakashana, 2017.
Ilaiah, Kancha. *God as Political Philosopher: Buddha's Challenge to Brahminism*. Popular Prakashan, 2001.
Ismail, Mirza. *My Public Life*. Unwin Brothers Limited, 1954.
Iyengar, Goruru Ramaswamy. *Namma Oorina Rasikaru*. IBH Prakashana, 2019.
Iyengar, Masti Venkatesha. *Chennabasavanayaka (Kannada)*. MVJK Trust, 2009.

Iyer, K.V. *Physique & Figure*. Bangalore Press, 1940.
———. *Shantala (Kannada)*. Vinay Prakashana, 2022.
Jaffrelot, Christophe, and Pratinav Anil. *India's First Dictatorship: The Emergency, 1975–1977*. Oxford University Press, 2021.
Jaiswal, Suvira. *The Making of Brahmanic Hegemony: Studies in Caste, Gender and Vaishnava Theology*. Tulika Books, 2018.
Jeyamohan, B (tr. Priyamvada). *Stories of the True*. Juggernaut, 2022.
Kailasam, T.P. *The Purpose: A Playlet of Ekalavya*. B.S. Rama Rao, 1966.
Kakkilaya, B.V. *Bareyada Dinachariya Mareyada Putagalu (Kannada)*. Navakarnataka Publishers, 2019.
Kalburgi, M. M. *Marga, Volumes 1-4 (Kannada)*. Sapna Book House, 2010.
Kambar, Chandrashekhar. *Shivana Dangura (Kannada)*. Ankita Pustaka, 2018.
———. (tr. Krishna Manavalli) *Karimayi*. Seagull, 2017.
———. *Deshiya Chintana (Kannada)*. Ankita Pustaka, 2020.
Kanwalli, Sadanand. *Quest for Justice*. Samaj Parivartan Samudaya, 1993.
Karanth, Shivaram. *Antida Aparanji (Kannada)*. SBS Publishers, 2021.
———. *Moga Padeda Mana (Kannada)*. Sapna Book House, 2020.
———. *Chomana Dudi (Kannada)*. Sapna Book House, 2018.
———. *Marali Mannige (Kannada)*. SBS Publishers, 2021.
———. *Hucchu Manassina Hattu Mukhagalu (Kannada)*. SBS Publishers, 2021.
———. *Tungabhadrege Rakshe (Kannada)*. Samaja Parivartana Samudaya, 1991.
Karanth, K. Ullas, Malavika Kapur and Kshama Rau. *Growing up Karanth*. Westland, 2021.
Karnad, Girish. *This Life at Play: Memoirs*. HarperCollins, 2021.
Karnad, Raghu. 'City in a Bottle'. *The Caravan*, July 2012.
Kashyap, R.L. *Rig Veda Samhita, Mandala – 9*. Sakshi Trust, 2009.
Katkar, Sarjoo. *Kambara Kavya Karana (Kannada)*. Yaji Prakashana, 2018.
Kavattaru, Prithviraja. *Sanjeevana: Yakshagana Guru Bannanje Sanjeeva Suvarnara Apoorna Atmakathana (Kannada)*. Abhinava, 2018.
Kosambi, Damodar Dharmanand. *An Introduction to the Study of Indian History*. Popular Prakashan, 2023.
Krishnamurthi, Kaidal (ed.) *Chandrashikari: Chaluvaliya Asali Kasubudara (Kannada)*. Viplava Prakashana, 2021.

Kumar, Mahendra (ed. Naveen Soorinje). *Nadu Baggisada Edeya Dani (Kannada).* Ladai Prakashana, 2024.

Kunhi, Bolwar Mahammad. *Monu Smriti (Kannada).* Navakarnataka Publications, 2022.

———. *Odiri (Kannada).* Muttupadi Pustaka, 2018.

———. *Swatantryada Ota (Kannada).* Muttupadi Pustaka, 2022.

Kurtukoti, Kirthinath. *Vimarsheya Vinaya (Kannada).* Manohara Granthamala, 1996.

Kuthar, Greeshma. 'All Santhosh's Men: The BJP's re-engineering of Karnataka'. *The Caravan*, May 2023.

Kuvempu (tr. Ramachandra Sharma, Padma Ramachandra Sharma). *The House of Kanooru.* Penguin, 1999.

———. *Nenapina Doniyalli (Kannada).* Udayaravi Prakashana, 2020.

———. *Aatmashreegaagi Nirankushamatigalaagi (Kannada).* Udayaravi Prakashana, 2020.

Lankesh, P. *Hulimavina Mara (Kannada).* Lankesh Prakashana, 2017.

———. (ed.) *Panchali, Deepavali Rajyotsava Sanchike.* Lankesh Prakashana, 1974.

Lingappa, Konandur (ed.) *Shaasanasabheyalli Shantaveri (Kannada).* Aharnishi Prakashana, 2023.

Lohia, Ram Manohar (tr. K.V. Subbanna). *Rajakeeyada Madhye Biduvu (Kannada).* Akshara Prakashana, 2021.

———. (trs. Nataraj Huliyar and S.R. Ramakrishna) *Kannedurina Prashnegalu – Volume 5 (Kannada).* Directorate of Kannada and Culture, 2000.

Lynch, Paul. *Prophet Song*. Simon and Schuster, 2023.

Madhava, K.G. Vasanth. *Kannada Sources of the Adilshahis of Bijapur 1555–1686.* Proceedings of the Indian History Congress, 39, pp. 378–84, 1978.

———. *The Mughals and the Keladi Nayakas.* Proceedings of the Indian History Congress, 37, pp. 259–62, 1976.

Mahabaleswarappa, B.C. *Swadeshi Spirit Through National Schools in Hyderabad Karnataka*. Proceedings of the Indian History Congress, 56, pp. 557–60, 1995.

Mahadeva, Devanura. *Edege Bidda Akshara (Kannada).* Abhinava, 2012.

———. *Kusumabale (Kannada).* Pustaka Prakashana, 2020.

———. *Dyavanuru Haagu Odalaala (Kannada).* Pustaka Prakashana, 2019.

Malhotra, Rajiv. *Being Different.* HarperCollins, 2018.

Malagatti, Aravinda. *Neevu Devaraagi (Kannada).* Ladai Prakashana, 2021.

Manjappa, Kadidal. *Panjaravalliya Panju (Kannada).* Department of Kannada and Culture, 2008.

Manor, James. *Political Change in an Indian State, Mysore: 1917–1955.* Manohar, 1977.

McGilchrist, Iain. *The Master and His Emissary: The Divided Brain and the Making of the Western World, Second Edition*. Yale University Press, 2019.

———. *The Matter with Things: Our Brains, Our Delusions, and the Unmaking of the World*. Perspectiva Press, 2021.

McGovern, Nathan. *The Snake and the Mongoose: The Emergence of Identity in Early Indian Religion*. Oxford University Press, 2018.

Mehta, Suketu. *Maximum City: Bombay Lost & Found*. Penguin Random House, 2017.

Mitta, Manoj. *Caste Pride: Battles for Equality in Hindu India*. Westland, 2023.

Mohanram, N.K. *The Capital: Lankesh Private Limited (Kannada).* IBH Prakashana, 2021.

Mohideen, B.A. *Nannolagina Naanu (Kannada).* Bharatha Prakashana, 2018.

Mokashi-Punekar, Shankar. (tr. Banjagere Jayaprakash) *Harijan Contribution to Medieval Indian Thought (Kannada)*. Charu Prakashana, 2023.

———. *The Indo-Anglian Creed and Allied Essays*. Writers Workshop, 1972.

———. (ed.) *Avadhuta Gita. With English Translation by Purohit Swami.* Munshiram Manoharlal, 1988.

———. *Avadheshwari (Kannada)*. Abhinava, 2021.

Muralidharan, Karthik. *Accelerating India's Development: A State-Led Roadmap for Effective Governance*. Penguin, 2024.

Nadig, Sumateendra. *Gopalakrishna Adigara Patragalu (Kannada).* Ravi Graphics, 2012.

Nagaraj, D.R. *Allama Prabhu Mattu Shaiva Pratibhe (Kannada).* Akshara Prakashana, 2021.

———. *Amrutha Mattu Garuda (Kannada)*. Akshara Prakashana, 2009.

———. (ed. M.S. Ashadevi) *Belebaaluva Barahagalu*. Vasantha Prakashana, 2015.

———. (ed. Prithvi Datta Chandra Shobhi) *The Flaming Feet and Other Essays*. Permanent Black, 2010.

———. (ed. Prithvi Datta Chandra Shobhi) *Listening to the Loom*. Seagull, 2014.

Nagavara, Kalegowda, and G.V. Ananda Murthy. *Shanthaveri Gopalagowda Nenapina Samputa*. Hampi: Prasaranga, Kannada University, 1997.

Nagaveni, H. *Gandhi Banda (Kannada)*. Aharnishi Prakashana, 2013.

Naipaul, V.S. *Among the Believers: An Islamic Journey*. Pan Macmillan, 2012.

Naik, Vishnu. *Dinkar Desai*. Sahitya Akademi, 2012

Nair, Janaki. *Miners and Millhands: Work, Culture and Politics in Princely Mysore*. SAGE Publications, 1998.

———. *The Promise of the Metropolis: Bangalore's Twentieth Century*. Oxford University Press, 2007.

———. 'Modernity and "publicness": The career of the Mysore matha, 1880–1940'. *The Indian Economic & Social History Review*, 2020.

Nanda, Meera. *Prophets Facing Backward*. Orient Blackswan, 2006.

Nandakumar, Pratibha. *Coffee House (Kannada)*. Ankita Pustaka, 2012.

———. *Anudinada Antaragange*. Aharnishi Prakashana, 2014.

———. *Avana Mukha Maretu Hogide*. Aharnishi Prakashana, 2022.

Nandi, R.N. *The Boyas—Transformation of a Tribe into Caste*. Proceedings of the Indian History Congress, 30, pp. 94-103, 1968.

Narayan, R.K. *Swami and Friends*. Knopf Doubleday, 2012.

———. *The Bachelor of Arts*. Indian Thought Publications, 1970.

———. *The Financial Expert*. Knopf Doubleday, 2012.

———. *Writer's Nightmare*. Penguin, 2000.

Neginhal, S.G. *Memoirs of an Ardent Wildlifer*. Notion Press, 2021.

Nehru, Jawaharlal. *Soviet Russia: Some Random Sketches and Impressions*. Chetana, 1949.

Öcalan, Abdullah. *The Political Thought of Abdullah Öcalan: Kurdistan, Women's Revolution and Democratic Confederalism*. Pluto Press, 2017.

Padmashali, Akkai. (ed. Gowri Vijayakumar) *A Small Step in a Long Journey*. Zubaan, 2022.

Patil, B.R. 'A Contemporary Industrial Relations Scenario in India: With Reference to Karnataka'. *Indian Journal of Industrial Relations*, Vol. 33, No. 3, 1998.

Patil, Chandrashekhar. *Champakaalam: A Collection of Editorial Columns in Sankramana Literary Magazine (Kannada)*. Sapna Book House, 2018.

Patil, Sateesh. *Hebballi Bhoohorata (Kannada)*. Prasaranga Hampi University, 2007.

Paz, Octavio. *Convergences: Essays on Art and Literature*. Harcourt Brace Jovanovich, 1991.

Pillai, Manu S. *Rebel Sultans: The Deccan from Khilji to Shivaji*. Juggernaut, 2018.

Pollock, Sheldon. *Literary Cultures in History: Reconstructions from South Asia*. University of California Press, 2003.

———. *The Language of the Gods in the World of Men*. Berkley and Los Angeles: University of California Press, 2006.

Prabhu, Allama, and Manu Devadevan. *God Is Dead, There Is No God: The Vachanas of Allama Prabhu*. Speaking Tiger Books, 2019.

Prakash, Gyan. *Emergency Chronicles: Indira Gandhi and Democracy's Turning Point*. Penguin, 2018.

Prasad, M. Madhava. *Cine-Politics: Film Stars and Political Existence in South India*. Orient Blackswan, 2014.

Prasanna, Heggodu. *Yantragalanna Kalachona Banni (Kannada)*. Ontidani Prakashana, 2009.

———. *Desi Jeevana Paddhati (Kannada)*. Ontidani Prakashana, 2014

Purandare, Vaibhav. *Shivaji: India's Great Warrior King*. Juggernaut, 2022.

Purohit, Kunal. *H-Pop: The Secretive World of Hindutva Pop Stars*. HarperCollins, 2023.

Purohitha, Mandakini. *M.K. Indira Samagra Adhyayana (Kannada)*. Hemantha Sahithya. Accessed July 26, 2024: http://archive.org/details/bmshri.mkindirasamagraa0000drma_q2j8.

Puttaiah, B.M. *Mukhaamukhi: Samaaja, Samskruthi, Chaluvali (Kannada)*. Siddhartha Prakashana, 2008.

Raghavan, E., and James Manor. *Broadening and Deepening Democracy: Political Innovation in Karnataka*. Routledge, 2012.

Raghavanka (tr. Vanamala Viswanatha). *The Life of Harishchandra*. Harvard University Press, 2017.

Rajan, Saketh. *Making History, Volume: 1*. Vimukthi Prakashana, 1998.

———. *Making History, Volume 2*. Vimukthi Prakashana, 2004.

Rajashekar, G. *Kagodu Satyagraha (Kannada)*. Akshara Prakashana, 2021.

Rajghatta, Chidanand. *Illiberal India: Gauri Lankesh and the Age of Unreason*. Westland, 2018.

Ramachandra, C.N., and L.N. Bhat (trs.) *Male Mahadeshwara: A Kannada Oral Epic, as sung by Hebbani Madayya and his troupe*. Sahitya Akademi, 2001.

Ramachandran, V.S. *The Emerging Mind*. Profile Books, 2003.

Ramachandrappa, Baragur. *Kaage Karunyada Kannu (Kannada)*. Ankita Pustaka, 2023.

———. (ed.) *Bandaya Kavya (Kannada)*. Directorate of Kannada and Culture, 1990.

———. (ed.) *Kannada Sahityadalli Asprushyateya Parikalpane (Kannada)*. Karnataka Sahitya Akademi, 1992.

———. *Kannada Prajne (Kannada)*. Kannada Sahitya Parishattu, 2013.

Ramaiah, Kotiganahalli. (ed.) *Talaparige: Jeevanadiya Jaadu Hididu Asprushyalokadallondu Payana (Kannada)*. Chowki Samskruthi Kendra, 2005.

Ramanna, Besagarahalli. *Samagra Kathegalu (Kannada)*. Kannada Sahitya Parishattu, 2015.

Ramanujan, A.K. *Journeys: A Poet's Diary*. Penguin, 2019.

———. *Soma: Poems by A.K. Ramanujan*. Penguin, 2023.

———. *The Collected Essays of A.K. Ramanujan*. Oxford University Press, 2004.

———. *Speaking of Siva*. Penguin, 2014.

Ramasheshan, N.K. *T.P Kailasam (Kannada)*. Prasaranga Mysore University, 2019.

Ramaswamy, Gita. *Land, Guns, Caste, Woman: The Memoir of a Lapsed Revolutionary*. Navayana, 2022.

Ramu, Mysuru. *Vishnu Kranti Mattu Itara Padyagalu (Kannada)*. Aharnishi Prakashana, 2022.

Rangarajan, Mahesh. *Environmental Issues in India: A Reader*. Pearson Education India, 2009.

Rao, K.P. *Varnaka (Kannada)*. Ankita Pustaka, 2018.

Rao, Mukunda. *Sky-Clad: The Extraordinary Life and Times of Akka Mahadevi.* Westland, 2018.

Rao, Raja. *The Meaning of India: Essays*. Penguin, 2020.

Rao, Pejawar Sadashiva (ed. A.V. Navada). *Samagra Barehagalu (Kannada).* Sahitya Akademi, 2015.

Rao, Velcheru Narayana, David Shulman, and Sanjay Subrahmanyam. *Symbols of Substance: Court and State in Nāyaka Period Tamilnadu.* Permanent Black, 2024.

———. *Textures of Time: Writing History in South India, 1600-1800.* Other Press, 2003.

Reddy, Srinivas. *Krishnadevaraya of Vijayanagara.* Juggernaut, 2020.

Rushdie, Salman. *Victory City.* Penguin, 2023.

Said, Edward W. *Covering Islam: How the Media and the Experts Determine How We See the Rest of the World.* Random House, 2008.

Saraswati, Du (ed.) *Neeradaari: Dalita Mahila Prajne Vibhinna Nelegalinda.* Kavi Prakashana, 2014.

———. *Community Under Siege: Socio Cultural Study of Safai Karmacharis in Karnataka from a Feminist Perspective*. PhD thesis completed under Karnataka State Women's University, 2019.

Satyanarayana, K., and Susie Tharu. *Steel Nibs Are Sprouting*. HarperCollins, 2013.

Satyanarayana, Viswanadha. (tr. Velcheru Narayana Rao) *Ha Ha Hu Hu: A Horse-Headed God in Trafalgar Square*. Penguin, 2018.

Savitha, B.C. *Hasirushaalu Baarukolu (Kannada).* Yaji Prakashana, 2017.

Schiller, Friedrich. *On the Aesthetic Education of Man*. Courier Corporation, 2012.

Schumacher, E.F. *Small Is Beautiful: A Study of Economics As If People Mattered*. Abacus, 1974.

Shah, Alpa. *Nightmarch: Among India's Revolutionary Guerrillas*. University of Chicago Press, 2019.

Shahabuddin, Ghazala. *Conservation at the Crossroads.* Permanent Black, 2010.

Shamanna, Kadidal (ed. Akshatha. K). *Kadatoreya Jaadu (Kannada).* Abhinava, 2011.

———. *Aa Dashaka: Articles and Letters of the Eighties (Kannada).* Aharnishi Prakashana, 2013.

Shanbag, Kusuma. *Putagala Naduvina Navilugari (Kannada).* Ankita Pustaka, 2013.

Shanbhag, Vivek. *Ghachar Ghochar (Kannada).* Akshara Prakashana, 2017.

———. *Huli Savaari (Kannada).* Akshara Prakashana, 2021.

Shelar, Jyoti. *Bhais of Bengaluru.* Penguin, 2017.

Shettar, S. *Halegannada: Lipi, Lipikara, Lipi Vyavasaya (Kannada).* Abhinava, 2017.

———. *Sangam Tamilagam Mattu Kannada Naadu Nudi (Kannada).* Abhinava, 2017.

Shivaprakash, H.S. *The Word in the World: Essays and Lectures on Indian Literature and Aesthetics.* Routledge, 2023.

Shulman, David. *Tamil: A Biography.* The Belknap Press of Harvard University, 2016.

Siddalingaiah (tr. S.R. Ramakrishna). *A Word with You, World: The Autobiography of a Poet.* Navayana, 2013.

———. *Meravanige: Holemaadigara Haadu, Saviraru Nadigalu, Kappukaadina Haadu Mattu Hosa Kavitegalu.* Ankita Pustaka, 2021.

Sikand, Yoginder. *Sacred Spaces: Exploring Traditions of Shared Faith in India.* Penguin, 2003.

Simeon, Dilip. *Revolution Highway.* Penguin, 2010.

Simmons, Caleb. *Devotional Sovereignty: Kingship and Religion in India.* Oxford University Press, 2020.

Singh, Tripurdaman. *Sixteen Stormy Days: The Story of the First Amendment to the Constitution of India.* Bloomsbury, 2024.

Singh, Upinder. *Political Violence in Ancient India.* Harvard University Press, 2017.

Singleton, Mark. *Yoga Body: The Origins of Modern Posture Practice.* Oxford University Press, 2010.

Slate, Nico. *Kamaladevi Chattopadhyay: The Art of Freedom.* HarperCollins, 2024.

Soorinje, Naveen. *Kutlur Kathana (Kannada).* Aharnishi Prakashana, 2022.

———. *Netravatiyalli Nettaru (Kannada).* Kriya Madhyama, 2022.

Sosale, Chinnaswamy. *Karnatakada Samagra Dalita Charitre (Kannada).* Navakarnataka Publications, 2023.

Sreenivasan, M.A. *Of the Raj, Maharajas and Me.* Ravi Dayal Publishers, 1991.

Sreedhar, Agni. *My Days in the Underworld.* Westland, 2013.

Srinivas, M.N. *The Remembered Village*. University of California Press, 1980.

Srinivasaraju, Sugata. *Furrows in a Field: The Unexplored Life of H.D. Deve Gowda*. Penguin, 2021.

Sriram, V. *The Devadasi and the Saint: The Life and Times of Bangalore Nagarathnamma*. East West Books, 2007.

Sturrock, John, and Harold A. Stuart (eds.) *South Canara: Gazeeteer of India*. Chief Editor, Karnataka Gazetteer Department, 1894.

Subbanna, K.V. *Kavirajamarga Mattu Kannada Jagattu (Kannada)*. Akshara Prakashana, 2016.

Subbarao, T.R. *Nrupatunga (Kannada)* Gourishankar Book Trust, 1955.

Subrahmanyam, Sanjay. *Connected History: Essays and Arguments*. Verso Books, 2022.

Subramaniam, Arundhati. *Sadhguru: More Than a Life*. Penguin, 2013.

Sundaram, R.V.S. *Kavirājamārgam*. Manohar, 2017.

Swamy, B.G.L. *Hasiru Honnu (Kannada)*. Vasantha Prakashana, 2018.

Talavar, Gangappa. *Dhaavati (Kannada)*. Tamate Publication, 2023.

Taranath, Pandit. (M. Dhruvanarayan, and Ki. Ram. Nagaraj, eds.) *Antida Nantu*. Abhinava, 2021.

Tarikere, Rahamath. *Karnataka Gurupantha (Kannada)*. Prasaranga, Kannada University, 2020.

———. *Kannada Sahitya Vagvadagalu (Kannada)*. Abhinava, 2022.

———. *Karnatakada Sufigalu (Kannada)*. Abhinava, 2021.

———. *Loka Virodhigala Joteyalli: 15 Vaartegalu (Kannada)*. Abhinava, 2011.

———. *Dharma Pareekshe (Kannada)*. Navakarnataka, 2018.

Tejaswi, K.P. *Hosa Vicharagalu (Kannada)*. Pustaka Prakashana, 2022.

———. (tr. Srinivasa Gowda) *The Story of My Environment*. Pustaka Prakashana, 2006.

———. *Kaadu Mattu Kraurya (Kannada)*. Pustaka Prakashana, 2020.

———. *Chidambara Rahasya (Kannada)*. Pustaka Prakashana, 2015.

———. *Annana Nenapu (Kannada)*. Pustaka Prakashana, 2021.

———. (tr. Padma Ramachandra Sharma) *Carvalho, Men of Mystery*. Penguin, 1990.

———. *Vimarsheya Vimarshe (Kannada)*. Pustaka Prakashana, 2017.

Teltumbde, Anand. *Iconoclast: A Reflective Biography of Dr Babasaheb Ambedkar*. Penguin, 2024.

Tenen, Dennis Yi. *Literary Theory for Robots: How Computers Learned to Write*. W.W. Norton & Company, 2024.

Upadhya, G.N. *Shankar Mokashi Punekar (Kannada).* Navakarnataka, 2023.

Vaidehi. *Asprushyaru (Kannada).* Bengaluru: Akshara Prakashana, 2022.

———. *Vaidehi Kathegalu, 1979-2016.* Akshara Prakashana, 2018.

Vaddagere, Chinnaswamy. *Bangarada Manushyaru: Belakina Besayada Kathanaka (Kannada).* Abhiruchi Prakashana, 2022.

Varagur, Krithika. *The Call: Inside the Global Saudi Religious Project.* Columbia Global Reports, 2020.

Varoufakis, Yanis. *Technofeudalism: What Killed Capitalism.* Random House, 2023.

Vasudhendra. *Tejo Tungabhadra (Kannada).* Chanda Pustaka, 2019.

Veerabhadrappa, Kum. *Shamanna (Kannada).* Bengaluru: Vasantha Prakashana, 2023.

———. *Gandhi Classu.* Sapna Book House, 2015.

———. *Maakanaduku (Kannada).* Vasanta Prakashana, 2023.

———. *Jai Bajrang Bali (Kannada).* Sapna Book House, 2019.

———. *Kumvee 70, Kathe 50 (Kannada).* Suvvi Publications, 2022.

Venkatarao, Alur. *Karnataka Gatavaibhava (Kannada).* Directorate of Kannada and Culture, 1983.

Vettese, Troy, and Drew Pendergrass. *Half-Earth Socialism: A Plan to Save the Future from Extinction, Climate Change and Pandemics.* Verso Books, 2024.

Wilks, Mark. *Historical Sketches of the South of India.* Asian Educational Services, 1996.

Wright, Tennant C. '"Left-Handed" Hindu Tantrism'. *Religious Studies,* Vol. 6, No. 4, pp. 345–57, 1970.

Acknowledgements

Firstly, I am indebted to everyone who agreed to be interviewed, either virtually or in person: Aiyshwarya Mahadev, Ananth Subbarao, Aravind and Dharanidevi Malagatti, Ashok Raj Kadbettu, Boluwar Mohammad Kunhi, B.R. Yavagal, Diwakar Narayan Rao, Devanur Mahadeva, Du Saraswati, H. Govindaiah, G. Rajashekar, G. Vishnu, Janaki Nair, Kukkarahalli Basavaraju, K.M. Srinivasa Gowda, K.P. Rao, Kotiganahalli Ramaiah, H.M. Ramachandra, Manu Devadevan, Manu Chakravarthy, Malini Mallya, K.S. Parthasarathy, Kum Veerabhadrappa, Kalkulli Vittal Hegde, Madhu Iyengar, Abhishek Gatti, Maitreyi, Nanda Halemane, N. Thirumaleshwara Bhat, P. Mallesh, Mudnakudu Chinnaswamy, Mohith Kaycee, C.S. Muralidhara, Madhav Gadgil, Leo Saldanha, Nagesh Hegde, Noor Zulfiqar, Sirimane Nagaraj, Padmalaya Nagaraj, K. Phaniraj, Purushottam Bilimale, Prasanna Heggodu, Pratibha Nandakumar, R. Kaleemullah, Akbar Ali, Rajeev Gowda, Rajendra Kumar, Rajendra Chenni, T.S. Venugopal, T.S. Ramaswamy, Sanjeev Suvarna, V.S.S. Shastry, Siddanagowda Patil, Shrikant Shetty, Shripad Bhat, Sheshadri Ramaswamy, T.N. Seetharam, S.R. Hiremath, S. Tukaram, Syed Issaq, Vishnu Kamath and Vivek Shanbhag. I hope I have done justice to your recollections and stories.

The New India Foundation, for transforming a doubtful twenty-something with no publication record into an eager beaver who began to believe that he could perhaps research and write a book after all. Rivka Israel, the first to read and refine all my drafts, had only kind words even when they were still rough-hewn. Ramachandra Guha, for his insightful comments on the first full draft of the manuscript, which helped weed out many immature elements of my writing, and for the numerous encouragement-boosts he offered throughout this project. Yauvanika Chopra, for always sharing books and cheers.

Translators, editors, publishers, commentators, YouTubers, and all those who champion the world of Kannada letters, often thanklessly.

Gayathri Prabhu, Purushottam Bilimale, Rajendra Chenni and Samvartha Sahil opened me up to the wide world of Kannada literature and scholarship at the beginning of the project, giving me a foothold to begin my own explorations.

I'm grateful to Anjum Hasan, Ramachandra Guha, Srinath Perur, Manu S. Pillai and Mudnakudu Chinnaswamy for their kind and evocative endorsements.

Indira Arunachal generously parted with her curated collection of newspaper clippings and books documenting the Tungabhadra environmental movement.

K.M. Chaitanya helped me out with numerous contacts.

Ramesh Aroli was kind enough to forward me important extracts from his PhD thesis on *Lankesh Patrike*.

Nikhil Govind, who needled me into writing my first MA term paper on U.R. Ananthamurthy instead of some other half-baked idea that had been brewing in me, and for offering thoughtful comments on this manuscript.

Neha Chatterjee, for inculcating in me a love for rigorous history.

Libgen, Sci-Hub and Archive.org—an armchair researcher's best friends.

Sudhamshu, for introducing me to Borges, Vargas Llosa, Paz, Fuentes and the Latin American boom, whose ideas I found to be a refreshing alternative to obscure literary criticism often held up by the academic establishment.

Faisal, whose encyclopaedic knowledge of South Canara culture was just as helpful as his photography skills.

Prajwal and Sudipto at *The News Minute* for their political insights, and for helping me with contacts for ground reportage.

Nikhil, the first to tell me about Saketh Rajan, which inadvertently kicked off this whole book. The umpteen conversations we've had over the years about politics, philosophy, and indeed, this book, have been just as stimulating.

Karthikeya and Akshata offered soberly helpful feedback on some of the early chapter drafts.

Apoorva broadcasted to me, exercising extreme prejudice, only the most interesting stories of patients that she encountered at Kasturba Medical College—a veritable microcosm of societal ills.

Shreyas helped me understand Kalburgi's scholarship and medieval Karnataka better.

Hari, for all the passionate discussions about mainstream economics' fraught relationship with the very idea of 'growth', and for his extended perorations on the liberatory potential of Modern Monetary Theory.

Harsha and Deepu transcribed some excruciatingly long interviews that proved quite invaluable in the final dash.

Pradhan designed the sleek and elegant website that is this book's online companion.

Trupthi sketched all the wonderful illustrations and the vivid cover, coolly finishing off in a few weeks what she'd been idling on for many months. I'm also grateful to Saurabh and the design team at Westland for converting this book into a lovely artefact.

Ajitha, for her thought-provoking and highly exhaustive editorial comments that added a fine layer of polish to the manuscript. The months-long editorial process itself was hugely enjoyable in its back-and-forth energy—almost as joyous as the unending days-evenings-nights of writing that went into this book. It was also on account of her astute suggestion that 'Rama Bhima Soma', originally just the heading of my introduction, transformed quite aptly into the book's title.

My parents, for fixing me up with whatever book I have desired since age six, and for all their support throughout the turbulent wanderings of my twenties. Lucky Pati, for helping me with Kannada translations at a moment's notice, and Raju Thata, for letting me raid his sizeable treasure of old Kannada magazines and books.

Index